Library of
Davidson College

LE CORBUSIER AT WORK
The Genesis of the Carpenter Center for the
Visual Arts

LE CORBUSIER AT WORK
The Genesis of the Carpenter Center for the Visual Arts

Eduard F. Sekler

William Curtis

with contributions by

Rudolph Arnheim

Barbara Norfleet

Le Corbusier at Harvard University, June 1960.

Harvard University Press

Cambridge, Massachusetts

London, England

1978

Published under the sponsorship of the Carpenter Center for the Visual Arts, Harvard University, and the Fondation Le Corbusier, Paris. Publication has been aided by a grant from the Graham Foundation for Advanced Studies in the Fine Arts.

Copyright © 1978 by the President and Fellows of Harvard College
All rights reserved
Printed in the United States of America

Book design by Roger Brandenberg-Horn
assisted by Amato Prudente

Library of Congress Cataloging in Publication Data

Sekler, Eduard Franz.
  Le Corbusier at work.

  Bibliography: p.
  Includes index.
    1. Jeanneret-Gris, Charles Édouard, 1887–1965.
  2. Harvard University. Carpenter Center for the
  Visual Arts. I. Curtis, William, 1948–   joint
  author. II. Title.
  Na1053.J4S44   727'.4'7   77-7315
  ISBN 0-674-52059-9

CONTENTS

Josep Lluis Sert	**Foreword**	**vii**
Eduard F. Sekler	**Introduction**	**1**
William Curtis	**Description of the Building**	**9**
William Curtis	**History of the Design**	**37**
	1. Outline of the Task	39
	2. Captain Giedion's American Problem	45
	3. Finding the Building's Form	57
	4. The Presentation	85
	5. A Conference at Sert's	101
	6. Conflicts in the Design	109
	7. The Day of Crisis: The Second Project	139
	8. Le Corbusier's Definition of Reinforced Concrete	157
	9. Transatlantic Details and the Modulor	171
	10. Construction	201
	11. The Image and Idea of the Building	221
	Interpretation and Evaluation	**227**
Eduard F. Sekler	The Carpenter Center in Le Corbusier's Oeuvre: An Assessment	229
Rudolf Arnheim	Notes on Creative Invention	261
Barbara Norfleet	The Hand and the Head at the Carpenter Center	267
	List of Correspondence and Documents	**275**
	Appendices	**279**
	Bibliography	**307**
	Notes	**309**
	Acknowledgments	**327**
	List of Illustrations	**329**
	Index	**335**
	Plans, Sections, and Elevations	**343**

FOREWORD

Le Corbusier came to the United States after the war full of great hopes that his hour had come—the time at long last to do great things in this big country. In Europe, reconstruction was still a vast promise: new cities would grow over old ones. Not just single buildings but whole new communities animated by a new spirit, "l'esprit des temps nouveaux," could become a reality.

The United Nations, replacing the former League of Nations in Geneva, was to establish its headquarters in the United States. Finally justice would be done and the unfair competition judgment of 1927 corrected. Le Corbusier felt he was the best prepared for the important new buildings for which America was the most fertile ground. With Claudius Petit (Minister of Reconstruction) and other French architects, as well as the engineer Bodiansky, he crossed the Atlantic in one of Kaiser's "liberty ships," a mass-produced war miracle. It being a long trip, on board he advanced the work on the Modulor book and study.

The discoverer in him makes him feel young again after all the long war years. The beauty of New York, the scale of things American: he comments on the skyscrapers' being "too small," a way of hiding his real feelings. New York fascinates him: "Cette ville a une lumière de diamant."

But the rejuvenated Corbu is soon to be disappointed. In his work as adviser for the selection of a site for the United Nations, he travels from east to west. The Presidio site in San Francisco impresses him most; he sees the U.N. buildings on "a magnificent site, an acropolis bathed by the bay and the ocean." Instead, a small but precious piece of real estate, seventeen acres on Manhattan, is chosen. The "fall of Icarus" lands his dreams in the East River! He goes back and forth to France. His dreams are systematically defeated in each trip. Icarus falls again and again. No real commission materializes. He finally returns to France. The United Nations goes up on the East River, but it is not his building: compromises and committee work rejected his plans and clipped Icarus' wings.

Years go by and one day in 1958 at Harvard University I am asked to advise President Pusey and McGeorge Bundy, Dean of Harvard College, on the selection of an architect to design the new center for the study of the visual arts. The building is to be rather small but could become a lively center for experiments and training of young people from every part of the world. Funds for this building had just been donated by the Carpenter family. This building, one of the last on a fund-raising list, was, to everyone's surprise, one of the first to be funded.

I knew Corbu was rightly disappointed about the country he expected would give him full recognition. With great reservation about the possibility of his accepting the commission, I recommended his name to the President and the Dean of the college. They were intrigued at the idea. I left them together to make a decision. Later that same day, a telephone call from Dean Bundy asked me to contact Le Corbusier and try to get his acceptance.

The "fall of Icarus" all over again, this time from the East River to the Harvard campus! His first commission for the design of a building in the United States materialized in 57,000 square feet of space on Quincy Street.

But after hearing a long description of the important role of such a building in the Harvard campus and the fact that it would be a "meeting place for the new generation of young people interested in experimenting with the visual media"—something very much needed in a university that boasts so many libraries—Corbu decided to undertake the commission. "A meeting place of head and hand," he baptized it.

He visualized how alive it could be. It would become his only building in the United States. After having conceived such grandiose plans for this continent and having influenced so much of the architectural work in the Americas as far south as Buenos Aires, the Carpenter Center, along with a small villa at La Plata near Buenos Aires, stands today as the only example in this hemisphere that has followed his design in every detail.

Le Corbusier came to Cambridge on November 12, 1959, to look at the site. Walking across the old Yard, he commented on "the green, the trees," his "ville radieuse" dream. He carried his dreams and ideals wherever he went in his travels around the world (his little notebooks document this). India—Chandigarh—was very much on his mind in those days. It was there and only there, strangely enough, that his larger dreams would materialize, in a poor developing country that, with Nehru, was willing to give him a chance. Wealth does not always help make big decisions; what he hoped America would give him he found in another hemisphere where he least expected it.

He got over his disappointments and bad feelings and, when he came a second and last time to Cambridge, in 1960, he brought with him his beautiful schematic plans and a modest, rough little scale model that could not compare in workmanship with some student exhibits. With these plans, which were presented in University Hall to the Harvard Corporation members—those around the table and those in gilded frames on the walls looking down on them—Corbu, with me acting as interpreter, explained his ideas with the conviction and faith he had in everything he did, big and small. Harvard politely smiled and accepted.

Some time later—when the structure of the building was completed—one winter day after a big snowfall, the telephone in my office rang, and I was asked by the administrative vice president to accompany the members of the Corporation who "had finished their meeting ahead of schedule" to visit the building. They climbed the slippery ramp, looked at the soaked, dirty, unfinished concrete. I expected difficult moments, but nothing happened. So much had been printed about the great man, that everybody was convinced Harvard was getting something unique, right on Quincy Street across from the President's house, between the Faculty Club and the Fogg Museum, in the sanctum sanctorum. Regardless of understanding and appreciation and in spite of criticisms and protests, Harvard had the courage that other patrons lacked.

The tremendous interest and response from the students soon drowned the protests and jokes of the more conservative members of the community. This 57,000 square foot building has created stimulation and established a record of photographic footage per square foot of construction unmatched in the world! Too bad the United Nations did not dare to do what Harvard had the courage to do. If Icarus had not fallen in the East River, New York could have had a unique monument.

Josep Lluis Sert

LE CORBUSIER AT WORK
The Genesis of the Carpenter Center for the Visual Arts

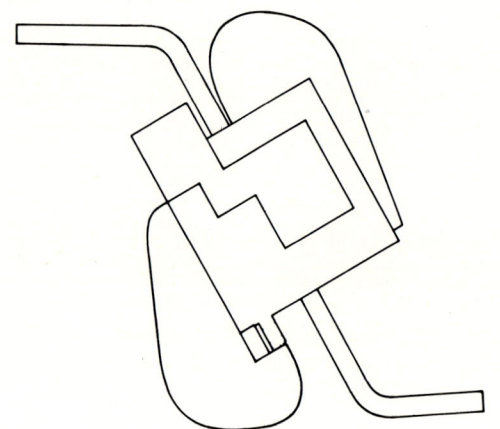

INTRODUCTION

Eduard F. Sekler

Publier les croquis de naissance d'une oeuvre architecturale peut être intéressant.

Le Corbusier, 1964

An act of artistic creation cannot be reenacted; we may make it less mysterious through study but not less mythical. It remains dependent on myth because every creator lives by a myth—public or private. When form motivated by myth is treated as something autonomous and is imitated in its external manifestation, it loses authenticity. The result is formalism, meaningless except perhaps as an interesting, even beguiling, historic phenomenon or symptom. But when form is studied with a view to understanding the conditions of its genesis, the results of such study, concerned with the structure of form and the form-giving process, will be meaningful beyond the limits of the individual case—unless one denies that there is a substratum of common structure to all human experience. Consequently the documentation of a form-giving process and its results may serve a double purpose: on the one hand it may yield clues to the nature of the underlying myth; on the other hand it may contribute to a better understanding of the way in which creative work is done.

In this sense it may indeed be said that "to publish the sketches of the birth of an architectural work can be interesting."[1] This was Le Corbusier's comment on a chronological selection of his sketches for the church of Firminy. Together with the way his sketches and notes were usually dated and carefully preserved, it indicates that he must have considered later study of his own design process worthwhile, an attitude which is also expressed in his stipulations for the Fondation Le Corbusier, the legal heir to his estate. The task of the Fondation was, in his own words, to "place the testimonies of my researches and works at the disposition of all those who would want to consult them."[2] One purpose of the present book is to do just this: it presents as completely as possible the studies and designs for one building, the Carpenter Center for the Visual Arts at Harvard University.

For a number of reasons, the Carpenter Center turns out to be an important building. To begin with, historic accident has placed it at the very end of Le Corbusier's total architectural oeuvre. The visual arts center, the sluice at Kembs-Niffer, and some work at Chandigarh and Firminy are the last constructions that were still carried to completion during the architect's lifetime, with his personal attention attested even in matters of last minute detailing. Other projects that had occupied his office between 1962 and 1965 remained on paper as designs in various states of elaboration or were only finished after his death.

Le Corbusier meant the building to be a special demonstration because of its location in the United States. It was to be what the *Oeuvre complète 1957–1965*, in its description of the center, called "une démonstration des théories de le Corbusier" ("a demonstration of the theories of Le Corbusier") where one could find "de nombreuses idées directrices qui lui sont propres" ("numerous direction-giving ideas which are typically his own"; p. 54). Le Corbusier's only building in North America had a deep meaning for him and was intended to illustrate all the elements of a highly personal architectural language which, however, made a more than personal, in fact a universal, claim. Evidence for this and for other aspects of the Carpenter Center design is unusually comprehensive; much that normally would have gone unrecorded had to be spelled out across the Atlantic.

The Carpenter Center was a building for whose program the architect could feel a special sympathy. Its educational goal corresponded—in the words of the *Oeuvre complète*—to "le voeu social le plus important de Le Corbusier" ("the most important social wish of Le Corbusier"). This enthusiasm for a program of visual studies because of its social significance becomes understandable when one relates it to Le Corbusier's own education and early activity as a teacher of design; after all, at La Chaux-de-Fonds he began his career in an atmosphere imbued with the Ruskinian ideals of the Arts and Crafts Movement.[3]

Although the position of the Carpenter Center as a work of maturity at the conclusion of Le Corbusier's oeuvre, his avowed intention to make it a special demonstration of principles, and his sympathy for its program account for the great historic significance of this building, nevertheless, thus far no publication has presented and discussed it adequately. At the time of the center's opening a number of illustrated articles appeared, but they did not deal with the history of the design and were mostly uncritical picture reports. Even an otherwise perceptive article in the *Architectural Review* of December 1963 was illustrated with plans that did not correspond to the actual building. They were the same plans that are given without indication of scale in the *Oeuvre complète 1957–1965*. In that publication, not only the plans are misleading. In addition, the drawings of sections and elevations represent an interim stage in the development of the design and not the final version, while photographs, though they are excellent, convey a one-sided impression: they mostly perpetuate the memory of forms in strong sunlight—a condition that does not always prevail in New England. Enshrined in this way in the mythopoeic pages of the *Oeuvre complète*, the Carpenter Center cannot be recreated with any accuracy in a reader's mind; the preconditions for thorough study, understanding, and reasoned evaluation remain lacking.

The lack of adequate data for and discussions of many buildings by Le Corbusier, even those of recognized historic importance, mirrors the fact that not much more than a decade has passed since his death. Comprehensive research became possible only as his vast legacy became increasingly accessible, whether at the Fondation Le Corbusier or elsewhere. Moreover, his activity still belongs in a zone of transition between "personal time" and "historical time" and calls forth the typical reactions of a generation that has to cope with the legacy of its immediate predecessors.

The term "personal time" in this context refers to the conscious personal life span of a historian. Events occurring during this period and perhaps involving people he knows personally will affect him differently from those in some distant past; he will be tempted more easily into the polemical stance of the critic without, however, always making his position explicit and thus acceptable. In contrast, "historical time" refers to the vast expanse of the past during which no personal contact was possible between the historian and the events he is writing about, a condition that alters the nature of his evidence though it may leave his polemical stance unchanged.

As far as the reaction of one generation to the work of its immediate predecessors is concerned, the interests of those in the vanguard of architecture frequently have shifted away from the interests of Le Corbusier and his immediate followers. It remains to be seen how far the appreciation of his oeuvre and impact will follow the usual pattern of an eclipse if not negation preceding rediscovery and renewed admiration, and all this at a quicker pace perhaps than in previous periods and less easy to perceive in the tangle of pluralistic complexity that characterizes today's architectural scene. Yet one thing seems certain: future evaluations—whether they are positive or negative—will be the more valid and meaningful, the more they are based on a comprehensive review of accurate information. This volume aims to provide such information.

Books on individual buildings have a long and honorable record in archaeology and the history of architecture, and while a sum of monographs will not add up to a reasoned account of a historical period, it is hard to imagine such an account without the groundwork of these studies. Yet when it comes to the architecture of the twentieth century there are many volumes on individual architects but few on individual buildings.[4] Partly this may be so because much of the historiography of architecture has been patterned on that of painting and sculpture, which has stressed, ever since Vasari, the importance of the individual artist and paid less attention to the role of client and social context. Yet the single most significant methodological change in architectural history and criticism of the recent past has been precisely the move toward seeing a building not only as an isolated aesthetic object to be analyzed and classified stylistically, but in a wider context as part of an ongoing manifold process, with interactions beginning long before the foundation stone is laid and continuing as long as the building conveys its message, both as an object and as a memory and influence.

Accordingly, this study begins with a very brief history of Harvard University's offerings in the practice of the visual arts, including the facts that led to the need for a new building. Their account is given in a subsequent section of this introduction. Later in the book I also try to assess the Carpenter Center in the context of Le Corbusier's total oeuvre. I was personally involved in some of the events recounted, and knowing Le Corbusier was a powerful personal experience. By contrast, the sections describing the building and offering a detailed history of its design and construction began as a dissertation at Harvard University by William Curtis, an architectural historian young enough to react to Le Corbusier as a historical phenomenon entirely outside the sphere of the personal past. When Le Corbusier, soon after his second visit to the site of the future Carpenter Center, suggested that the care of his material and spiritual legacy "must be left to the young and not to the people in place,"[5] he was referring to the generation to which William Curtis belongs.

Following the presentation and interpretation of the building and its history, an essay by Rudolf Arnheim, for several years a mainstay of the Carpenter Center's teaching program, discusses psychological aspects of the creative process in architecture on the basis of evidence provided by Le Corbusier's sketches. In the concluding chapter, Barbara Norfleet, a sociologist deeply interested in visual experience and also familiar with the building through extended personal contact, reports on her interviews with students and faculty about their emotional reactions to the building. A selection of pertinent documents has been assembled as an appendix; others have been collected in a separate, unpublished volume for deposit in the Harvard University Archives, where a complete catalogue of all pertinent drawings can also be found as part of William Curtis's thesis. The contributors to this volume hope that their attempt at a multidisciplinary approach to the history of a twentieth century building will pave the way for many others to follow.

The process that led eventually to the formulation of a building program for the Carpenter Center can be said to have started almost a century before there was any thought of an actual building. It was a process of interaction between an institution and a concept: Harvard College was facing the idea that the practice of the visual arts might have a valid educational function in the academic curriculum of a university. Over the years attitudes in this matter varied greatly, mirroring changes in societal values in the United States.

By the time Charles Eliot Norton began teaching the history of art at Harvard in 1874, many shared his conviction that art was the "expression of a nation's highest moral aspiration."[6] Following the precepts of John Ruskin, he wanted to improve his students' artistic understanding and taste through historical, theoretical, and practical instruction. For this program he found a congenial colleague in the landscape painter Charles Herbert Moore, whom he invited to teach Fine Arts I, a course on the principles of design in painting, sculpture, and architecture which included practical exercises in drawing and watercolor.[7]

Prominent among later artists with an interest in combining theory and practice who taught in the Department of Fine Arts were Denman Ross (1853–1935) and Arthur Pope (1880–1974). Both, through their teaching and publications,[8] exerted influence in the professional realm and in art education on all levels well beyond the confines of the university. Some of their students made a name for themselves as distinguished visual artists, such as Hyman Bloom and Jack Levine; others became prominent as poets, like T. S. Eliot and e e cummings, or architects, like Philip Johnson. Since there was also an interest in conveying to future art historians a practical knowledge of the most important artistic techniques used in the past, it is understandable that the studios and facilities for the practice of the visual arts were included in the building which in 1927 replaced Hunt Hall as the home of the Fogg Art Museum.

In 1929 the chairman of the Department of Fine Arts was willing to express the conviction that "the training of eye and hand is no less important than the training of memory," and he even added, "those who look forward to a graduate school of sculpture and painting may yet see their hopes realized."[9] However, such enthusiasm for instruction through practice, ultimately derived from the same spring of Ruskinian teaching that had nourished young Le Corbusier in the school for decorative arts at his native La Chaux-de-Fonds, did not last. By the middle of the century, under the impact of changes in art-historical methodology brought to this country by distinguished scholars from Europe, the emphasis at Harvard's Department of Fine Arts had changed. A high level of rigorous art-historical scholarship was attainable without training in the practice of visual arts, and therefore such isolated offerings in artistic practice as survived carried little weight in the curriculum.

On the other hand, the importance of practical art training as part of instruction in architecture and related disciplines was never in doubt. In 1941 when a separate undergraduate Department of Architectural Sciences was set up, it included courses in drawing and basic design among its offerings; their approach, however, was different from that of earlier art courses in Harvard College. They were less indebted to academic art teaching than to the Bauhaus experience, less directly related to Ruskinian precepts and more to the thought of, among others, Konrad Fiedler and John Dewey. The teaching of Josef Albers, Johannes Itten, Paul Klee, and Laszlo Moholy-Nagy provided sources of inspiration for courses in the Department of Architectural Sciences after it had been created on the initiative of Walter Gropius, founder of the Bauhaus, and Joseph Hudnut, the dean who in 1938 had invited Gropius to become chairman of Harvard's graduate department of architecture. Gropius understandably took a special interest in the way in which design and the visual arts were taught in Harvard College and this interest was shared by his successor to the chairmanship, José Luis Sert,[10] who became dean of Harvard's Graduate School of Design in 1953.

In the same year the presidency of the university passed into new hands, and with the new president, Nathan M. Pusey, came a search for new policies regarding the arts at Harvard. There were several reasons for this. In general, the early fifties were years of great enthusiasm about the role of the arts and of architecture in society and on university campuses—an enthusiasm that can best be compared to the enthusiasm and concern for environmental issues of the early seventies. In this spirit Harvard University invited Ben Shahn and Sir Herbert Read to give the prestigious Charles Eliot Norton lectures on different aspects of visual creation. Ben Shahn talked about "The Shape of Content" and Sir Herbert Read, under the title of "Icon and Idea," made an eloquent plea for recognition of the primacy of the visual over the conceptual realm in the history of human culture.[11]

Mr. Pusey himself as an undergraduate in Harvard College had been an eager student in Fine Arts I, which at that time still dealt with a combination of theory, history, and practice; when he returned to Harvard as president, such a course no longer existed. But a recent report existed in which a visiting committee of the overseers recommended "that a careful study be made to help determine the future course of the arts at Harvard." The president responded by speedily appointing a powerful committee of enquiry under the chairmanship of John Nicholas Brown, which in 1955–56 released its report.[12] The Brown Report recommended among other things the creation of a new department of design and the construction and endowment of a design center. This recommendation was implemented by the appointment of a standing committee on "the practice of the visual arts" and eventually by the creation of the Carpenter Center for the Visual Arts, designed to fit the program envisaged by this committee.[13]

The architect's brief for the new center that emerged in the end was kept quite loose and open. This was done deliberately, not only to profit as fully as possible from Le Corbusier's intuition and imagination but also because the committee members who, under the chairmanship of José Luis Sert, drew up the educational and eventually the building program represented a variety of divergent attitudes from different segments of the university, including those of the most directly concerned departments: Fine Arts and Architectural Sciences. These men were eager to arrive at positive results expeditiously and were in agreement that the pitfalls of dilettantism and academic art teaching should be avoided, an agreement that was also expressed in their eventual decision to adopt the inclusive title of "Visual Studies" for the new program. However, in the limited time at their disposal, and respecting each other's positions, they found it less easy to agree on an educational program sufficiently precise and concrete for the definition of specific building requirements. From every point of view it seemed better to leave things as widely open towards the future as was consistent with a realistic allocation of funds. Accordingly, only a general description and rough size of necessary spaces was given.

For certain areas of the program it was possible to assess needs in the light of experience with courses offered at the time by the Department of Architectural Sciences, where, after Richard Filipowski and Costantino Nivola, the Italian sculptor Mirko Basaldella was teaching two- and three-dimensional design and Eduard Sekler was offering "An Introduction to Design in the Visual Arts," slated to become a core course in the new program. Mirko brought a rich imagination and great pedagogical sensitivity to the task of inventing stimulating assignments for his students, and his ideas about the needs of studio facilities were based on extensive practical experience. There was no comparable experience at Harvard with courses in photography and film, except the work of Robert Gardner, who taught film-making to graduate students of anthropology. He had his headquarters in some basement rooms of the Peabody Museum, while studio courses in design were given in a former university maintenance building that faced the Charles River near Dunster House. That rough factory-like structure with open floors offered a welcome anonymity and, at times, beautiful views of sunsets reflected in the river. But otherwise it lacked essential amenities and was too small and too remote from the centers of college activity.

Thus, there was a real sense of urgency and exhilaration when in 1957–58 the Committee on the Practice of the Visual Arts outlined its program for a new building (see appendix 1) and thus set the stage for the events recounted in this study. Roughly five years after the committee's first meetings the building on Quincy Street was ready for occupation.

DESCRIPTION OF THE BUILDING

William Curtis

1. *Aerial view of Harvard Yard, early spring 1972, showing diagonal paths running between formally arranged buildings. Main buildings and streets are*

    A. University Hall
    B. Hunt Hall (since demolished)
    C. Memorial Church
    D. Widener Library
    E. Sever Hall
    F. Robinson Hall
    G. Emerson Hall
    H. Fogg Art Museum
    I. Carpenter Center for the Visual Arts
    J. Faculty Club
    1. Massachusetts Avenue
    2. Quincy Street
    3. Prescott Street

Le Corbusier designed one building in the United States, the Carpenter Center for the Visual Arts, to which he gave the code name VAC BOS, Visual Arts Center Boston. It lies about two miles to the west of Boston's city center, in the town of Cambridge, Massachusetts. Here the buildings of Harvard University are arranged in and around Harvard Yard, an enclosed precinct planted with trees and surrounded by railings and walls. This area, which approximates a parallelogram and measures about 330 × 345 yards, has a number of functions: it is simultaneously the university's central route, capitol, forum, and repository of memories. To the east side of it is a narrow strip of land between Quincy and Prescott Streets, about 73 yards wide and 270 yards long and well off to one side of the university. This contains four buildings that play an important role in the life of Harvard: the Freshman Union, the Faculty Club, the Fogg Museum, and the Carpenter Center for the Visual Arts (fig. 1).

Le Corbusier's building is far more easily understood from the air than it is from the ground, which is not surprising, since he discovered the re-

2. *Oblique view of Carpenter Center from Harvard Yard (Sever Quadrangle) in winter. A corner of the Fogg Museum shows to the left, the Faculty Club in the distance to the right.*

3. *View of the building from Quincy Street just outside the Yard.*

lationship of the major forms through aerial view drawings (plan 7). At the center is a square to which are abutted two smaller rectangles (vertical circulation towers) and two freehand curved forms of equal size and shape. The square is set strikingly at an angle to the grid of surrounding streets and buildings, and its sides align approximately with the compass points. The curves appear to pull away from the stable form at the center and to rotate it. But any suggested dynamism is held in check by an opposing diagonal symmetry, that of the S-ramp which anchors the building to the parallel streets it connects. Diagonally placed in its slim slot of space, the Carpenter Center is pinched by the rear corner of the Fogg Museum and the jutting north wing of the Faculty Club. Le Corbusier's building refuses to conform with the stability, rectangularity, and respect for the street lines that its neighbors show; it is vital, its curves reach out and interlock with surrounding space, and it is assertively independent of surrounding geometries.

Such are the simple schematic relationships, but they are never grasped so simply from the ground. Approach to the building might be by way of Harvard Yard, through a series of incidents in a pastoral setting, which need describing in some detail.

The Yard is divided into three main spaces. Its buildings are mostly rectangular (like the Carpenter Center's neighbors) and vary in style from Georgian to neoclassical, whether forty or two hundred years old. Blocklike, they are tidily marshaled along axes. Mostly they are red brick, but there are some fine granite exceptions, and in places there is white painted woodwork. The Yard is further textured by steps and railings, grass and foliage, and people who pass along a network of paths; some of them run with the grid, others pass diagonally under the trees through gaps between the corners of the main buildings.

Of the Yard's main spaces, the central one is most formal. Its focus is the white wooden steeple of Memorial Church. To the west stands Bulfinch's gray granite University Hall (1813); to the east, Richardson's Sever Hall (1878). The latter is swelling and massive and gives its name to the easternmost court of the Yard, Sever Quadrangle.

This quadrangle provided Le Corbusier with his only long view of the Carpenter Center. One sees it obliquely, framed by the edge of the Fogg Museum to the left and Emerson Hall to the right—buildings whose cornices and attics suggest the outline of a proscenium (fig. 2). Carpenter Center is sandy-colored concrete, while its neighbors are red brick, and its volumes are powerfully modeled, as one might have guessed from the air. It is five stories high (though at first sight the subdivision into floors is not as legible as in the surrounding buildings), and from reference to its neighbors one sees that the Carpenter Center is angled to the street. The tension observed in plan is exciting in volume: Le Corbusier's building is highly charged but still in repose.

From this approach, three primary forms impress themselves upon the viewer. In the background is a rectangular, towerlike mass (the larger of the circulation towers seen from the air) and projecting from its side at right angles is another rectangular shape (part of the square). This catches the light in its strongly articulated front and comes to a point in a jutting corner. Beneath this corner, and hovering out from the ninety-degree cleft between the primary rectangles, is a curved volume which pushes towards the Yard. It is an impressive beginning and a calculated first view. The building immediately holds one's attention as the point of greatest architectural intensity in sight. It captures the diagonals of the Yard, supplies its own genius loci, and from this angle makes its strong presence felt over a long distance. Carpenter Center's three major forms hold their stable relationship as one approaches a gateway out of the Yard, while a fourth form comes into view to the right: the curved ramp which runs into the building at the third level.

From just outside the gate, one sees the building from below in dramatic silhouette (fig. 2). A brief glimpse of a path which edges past the stair tower, and of a forest of pillars recessed in a dark flat-bottomed pit under the curved projection, is superseded by impressions from the center of attention: the curved strip of fenestration at second level, made up of chinks of glass and slender concrete struts irregularly spaced (ondulatoires) which accentuate the curve and ripple into motion if one changes position. The curve appears to float above the shadows beneath it and objects perceived through the glass make one realize that this is a studio area. Behind, in perspective, the rectangular concrete shapes of the higher levels with their diagonal sun-baffles (brise-soleil) are definitely subordinate in the performance, though the contrast is striking between the smooth, almost blank flank of the stair tower and the intricacy of the humanly scaled central portion. At the top of this portion, three freestanding concrete pillars (pilotis) support beams running back into the roof and form a row of crowning portals (fig. 3).

Inner force in the forms, compression and poise, expansion and equilibrium, are felt through empathy even as one stands still. But if one moves on along Quincy Street, the elements also shift across one another at different speeds and in different depths of parallax, so that parts of the building seem held tenuously in midair. Ramp curve and studio curve come into violent opposition. A point is reached where the energy of curves and diagonals is felt at a maximum; then onwards the building begins to unfold, eventually seeming to relax when faced frontally (fig. 4a,4b). This is also an excellent vantage point for examining the elements of Le Corbusier's architectural language and the way they are used in this building.

The ramp is cantilevered from a central spine: a curved concrete beam supported by a few pilotis except in one place, where a slab of concrete (which it intersects at right angles) supports and stiffens it all the way across. As the south side of the building becomes visible, the curved third level studio emerges in the background, to the right

4a. *Quincy Street facade.*
4b. *Quincy Street elevation. The principal elements of Le Corbusier's architectural language used in this building are:*
   A. *pilotis: cylindrical reinforced concrete columns*
   B. *pans-de-verre: panes of glass running from floor to ceiling*
   C. *ondulatoires: vertical struts of reinforced concrete placed at varying intervals on the curve*
   D. *brise-soleil: fins of concrete placed in the fenestration to guard against direct rays of the sun*
   E. *aérateurs: vertical pivoting wooden doors for ventilation*

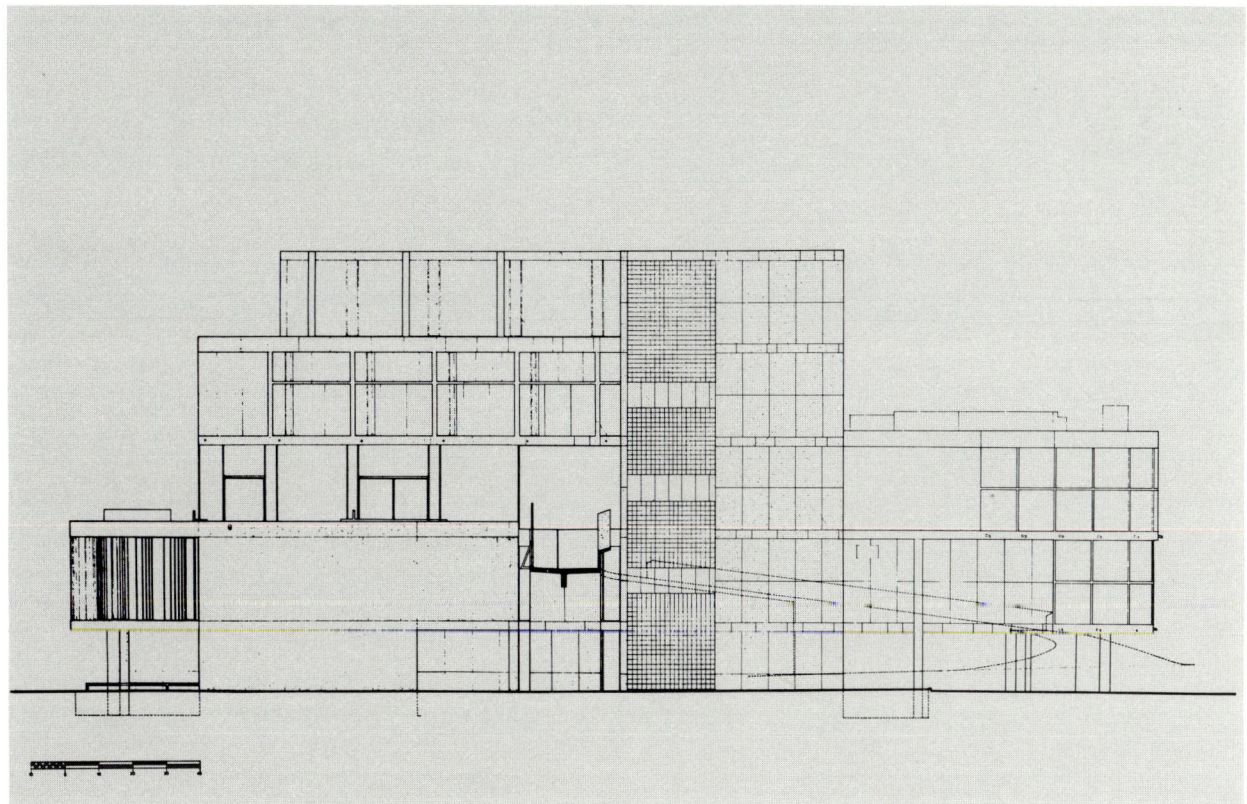

5. *Detail of northwest corner at fourth and fifth levels showing the extremely smooth concrete work typical of pilotis, brise-soleil, and flat walls. Formwork divisions are made by a slight V-shaped ridge of concrete.*

6. *Detail of Quincy Street curved studio wall after a rainstorm. The concrete is typical for curved parts of the building: slender, vertical formwork and deep grooved incisions above and below slab-ends.*

of the stair tower. Spread to maximum horizontality, the building contrasts with the compactness of our first view but it has lost nothing of its visual complexity.

In order to understand more clearly what has occurred it is helpful to pause briefly for a formal analysis of the means by which such effects have been achieved—variations in height, shape, and visual weight, in surface treatment, and in the scenographic disposition of different major building planes in depth.

The first, the foreground plane, is virtual, not actual: it is a line that is implied merely by the edge of the Quincy Street sidewalk just a few feet in front of the base of the ramp. From this plane the curves of studio and ramp depart, drawing close together, until they enter the building. The convergence of these curves creates a dynamic effect of speeding up towards the point where the ramp penetrates.

The other planes are parallel to one another and at approximately thirty degrees to the first. Plane number two corresponds to the vertical concrete fin that supports the ramp after its turn; a tangent to the curve of the wall under the second level studio would run just a little in front of it. Plane number three can be extended from the face of the stair tower and serves as the major depth reference. Plane four corresponds to the third and fourth level facade, appears also as a large window set back between stair tower and studio wing on ground level (some forty feet behind the concrete fin of plane two), and corresponds exactly to one side of the square that is so noticeable as the central figure in the airview (plan 7). Plane five is virtual again, suggested by the structural pillars on top of the building (fig. 4a), while plane six is defined by the recessed fifth level facade and, at the same time, by the line of the intersection between the third level (south) studio wing and the stair tower. Under this studio wing a seventh plane can be discerned eventually: the unbroken concrete wall of the second level workshop (fig. 7). The actual, not virtual, planes two, three, four, and five are arranged in a rhythm of acceleration, being spaced more closely as one moves from front to rear.

Carpenter Center is very sensitive to light and climate on its outer skin (figs. 3, 5, 6). The concrete reflects the early morning sun, forms and contains afternoon shadows. The sun cuts deep shadows into the brise-soleil, shimmers on the glazed bricks, and lays a sheen on plate glass; it also picks out the dividing lines in the smooth surfaces of the stair tower, or the slight vertical articulations left by the formwork on the curved studio walls. The concrete absorbs the heat and after rain breathes light clouds of mist. When twigs and leaves pattern their shadows on the building's skin, the tactile qualities of the finishes are enhanced: on the curved parts shuttering marks suggest the feel of timber, on flat sections, the rigor and ring of stone. And all this changes with the time of the day, with the seasons, or with the passing of a cloud.

In spring, cherry blossoms stand out pink against gray steel railings and against concrete lightly tinted ochre. Summer gives strong light to forms whose full vitality depends on it (figs. 5, 8), conveying that Mediterranean quality the architect loved. With the coming of autumn the greenery recedes, edges are left bare, and relative colors shift in value, with a peculiar clarity of forms and hues on certain windy days. In a rain storm the gutters shoot water onto terraces or directly onto the ground where pebbles have been laid in rough beds, and the water gurgles and overflows onto grass and clover. Rain streaks the concrete (fig. 6), which has weathered gray and brown in places like a piece of driftwood, and darkens the columns, so that one can feel the air around them when they are damp, as though they were glistening trunks of trees. In winter, the concrete looks gray—on the curves, like an elephant's hide—unless it is dappled orange by a few rays of the low evening sun. Crystals of snow bank against the glass panes of brise-soleil ledges blotting out the light, while icicles encrust the water spouts, which have been known to snap on occasion (fig. 7).

To come closer to this object which seems endowed with natural qualities, one finally crosses Quincy Street to the base of the ramp, where one is presented with a choice of pathways: either to descend to the entrance, recessed on the ground level of the building's south side (fig. 7), or to ascend the incline of the ramp (fig. 8). The path to the side entrance is steeply sloped and indicates that the site as a whole slopes down from Quincy to

7. *Winter view along the south side past the stair tower toward the Prescott Street studio and workshop wing. The ground level entrance is recessed to the left.*

8. *View up the ramp in summer on the Quincy Street side of the building: the beginning of Le Corbusier's precisely controlled "promenade architecturale." The ramp is bounded to the right by a sloped parapet for sitting. A groove for drainage runs down, off-center. The ramp floor is rough and scored in rectangles laid out according to Le Corbusier's proportional system, the Modulor.*

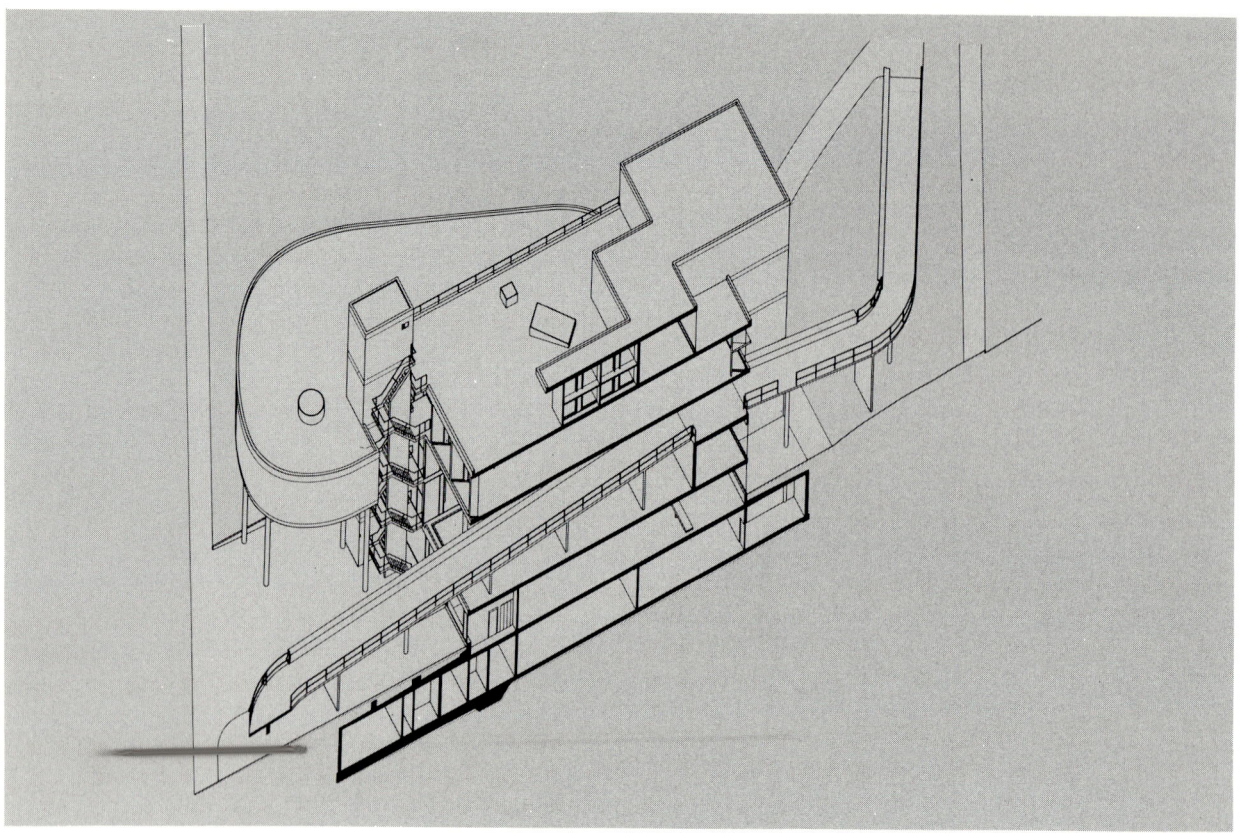

9. *Isometric section showing the way the ramp penetrates the building.*

10. *View into the heart of the building along the ramp toward Prescott Street. The stair tower is to the right.*

Prescott Street. The ramp dramatically advertises itself as a bridge with the outside world (figs. 9, 10). What constitutes the inside world—the other end—is still not apparent.

Although it actually rises only one story, the ramp is steep, and in winter the climb can be treacherous because of caked snow and ice. In sunshine its concrete floor sparkles slightly as it curves to enter the building at right angles. It is scored at proportional intervals and a groove runs its entire length (figs. 8, 10). To the left is a steel railing which allows visual penetration, to the right, a concrete parapet with a slightly inclined coping which also acts as a seat. The view back to the Yard is expansive, encompassing roof lines and steeples. In summer, greenery in the roof garden picks up the foliage of the trees. It is as if Quincy Street no longer exists; instead: space, light, and sky.

Having lured one up the ramp towards an obscure objective and disallowed any penetration beyond the frontal planes of the building, the architect suddenly allows the eye to pass into depth, into the realm of the interior (figs. 10, 11). And where does it go? Out the other side again to Prescott Street, whose apartment buildings define the end of a perspective. On each side of the rectangular tunnel ahead, plates of glass present reflecting surfaces because they are seen at an acute angle against a darker background. These mirrors come to a halt at the back plane of the building, where a rectangle forms a window to the Prescott Street world. In a blow, even before we have entered it, Le Corbusier has told us the depth of his building.

If one expects enclosure on entering the rectangle of shadows, this is not surprising given the liberation of the ascent, but glass turns the corner and ceases to be a reflecting material, dissolving instead into transparent layers. The plunge

through the gap and the building's fourth main plane is like breaking the surface of the sea, through which one passes into a world of grottoes, tall caverns, shifting shadows, and filtered light. Concrete experienced as dense mass a moment before now dematerializes into thin planes.

Directly ahead the ramp descends in a straight line beyond the Prescott Street end of the building to curve out of sight beyond more trees and shrubs. Space expands in all directions: ahead as far as the apartment houses on the other side of Prescott Street; below, into the two-story ramp gallery, two bays wide, with its three slim pilotis (fig. 12); sideways through transparent glass into studios, a workshop, and an exhibition space, regularly articulated by smooth pilotis rising clean through the slabs. Only the soffit above asserts its weight, giving downward pressure. The spine of the ramp which forms the building's axis runs straight ahead for more than a hundred feet and draws one into the gradual descent.

The landing at the top of the ramp is a still point; exterior curves halt here, the rise and fall of the walk stops. Glass doors, left and right, lead to exhibition space and studios; unfortunately they must be locked for security reasons, which makes nonsense of the ramp as means of entry (figs. 11, 13). Descent is gradual and has the quality of a ceremonial procession. The ramp is a way of inspection: simultaneous views of activities without interrupting them, framed views of the Faculty Club brickwork, with sprigs of ivy through brise-soleil.

The view into the building from the ramp resembles a picture whose foreground contains the structural frame. The picture plane is semitransparent and defined, in any case, by regularly spaced ventilating doors (aérateurs) out of line with the grid and by the first range of pilotis just

11. *View of the ramp gallery toward Prescott Street. The mirror effects of the side glazing dissolve into transparent layers if one moves on a few more feet.*
12. *View of the ramp gallery back in the direction of the third level landing with doors to the exhibition gallery (top right). The ramp gallery is a double-floor volume with three pilotis and is approximately two piloti-bays wide.*
13. *Ramp gallery at night.*

inside the membrane of glass. From the ramp one can read the building as it would appear in a section.

To each side of the ramp the curved studios fluctuate and have different fenestrations. The Prescott Street studio has brise-soleil that are placed perpendicular to the direction of the central portion of the ramp so that only their narrow ends are visible; plates of glass are set parallel to the ramp, back and forth between the concrete elements. The concrete fins are spaced at varying intervals, gap sizes diminishing rapidly towards the climax of increasing curvature.

The Quincy Street studio, on the other hand, has ondulatoires in its curved portion which do not encroach so deeply on the interior and are harder to examine from the ramp, being back, down, and to the left (fig. 14). The effect of an enclosing, taut membrane, or skin of glass and concrete, which was registered on the exterior (fig. 3), is magnified here. The ondulatoires interfere less with the experience of the curve of the plan than do the brise-soleil in the third floor studio.

As the eye probes its way from the ramp, past the light fixtures and ducts clamped to the underside of slabs, to the outside edges of enclosed territory, it finds its way through openings in places to pass a few feet or a few hundred yards to fragments of trees, brick walls, railings, steeples, or people, or to a continued exploration of the soffits cantilevered into the outside air. Of the expected rigidly defining cubic form, so clearly seen from the air and experienced on the ground, there is little sign. Set down among the curves, its sides are dissolved away by the careful handling of the fenestration.

When people, mechanical equipment, tables, and other objects are glimpsed through sheets of semireflecting glass (sometimes three at a time) that catch angles of light, houses, and other reflected matter, the analogy with the fragments of dismembered reality in Cubist painting is strongly

14. *Second level curved studio (northwest), viewed at night from the ramp.*
15. *View in the late afternoon from the ramp into the third level studio (southeast) and second level workshops.*
16. *View, with reflections from the third level studio, across the ramp gallery toward the exhibition room and Prescott Street.*

17. *View back toward the Prescott Street facade from approximately halfway up the ramp.*

18. *East and north facades viewed from Prescott Street, showing the convergence of the main forms on the elevator tower and the ramp gallery.*

felt (figs. 14, 15, 16). And to the observer moving on the ramp, the shift of red, green, and other colored aérateurs, of pilotis, and of fins across one another at different speeds has the intended rhythmical effect of music translated into visual terms.

The ramp is provided with a slightly inclined ledge, on which it is comfortable to stop and sit. On reflection, ambiguities about one's state of place emerge. Is this interior, or exterior? Is one inside or outside the building? Is it the public or private realm?

The vision of four different sets of people simultaneously and independently working behind plate glass gives the spectator the privacy and distance of a voyeur. But the ramp also resembles an interior public street, and the terrace at the base of the gallery suggests an elevated ground. The implication seems to be that one is still in public space. Reflecting on this, one passes the last of the three tall pilotis in the ramp gallery—the one clearly lit—and catches a glimpse to the left through diagonal brise-soleil of trees next to the Fogg Museum, to reemerge in the open air. Looking back along the straight line of the ramp, one realizes what an achievement of fantasy it is. At the top is the small rectangle of light (from the other side it was a rectangle of dark), perfectly framing the sky and the tops of trees—an abstracted rectangle of arcadia that tempts one to reascend towards it.

But the ramp is a fantasy of another order, involving the fulfillment of a primordial dream of the Modern Movement in painting and sculpture: projection of the spectator into the heart of the work of art to experience its facets, illusions, and ambiguities from within. This fantasy is the more alluring since it is on such a large scale and since devices developed earlier in the illusionistic world of the picture plane subtly reappear here as methods for the enclosure of real space.

Moving further down the ramp (figs. 17, 18) one is aware that the building is once again mass, not space: a cliff of unexpectedly monumental brise-soleil has shut off most of the transparency, defining the back plane (scarcely sensed when passed) of the cubical central volume.

But then if one walks back towards the building from the foot of the ramp, and along the facade to its north corner, the impression of massiveness disappears again (fig. 19); looking back from the corner towards the ramp, one faces the thin ends of the concrete fins which form the brise-soleil and the panes of glass between them. Transparency prevails, the facade dissolves away, and at the junction of east and north facades the feeling is of complete dematerialization, the more so because at ground level the corner is turned by two unframed panes of glass under a cantilevered concrete slab.

The north elevation is hard to see because it is so close to the Fogg Museum, but its very subtle treatment repays careful study (figs. 19, 20; plan 12). Here no sun was to be expected, so the architect composed mainly in two dimensions; he organized a visual treat of plate glass insertions into the concrete skin of the building. Each plate is set back just a little from the exterior plane to give the slightest sense of depth. In the daytime the glass reflects and becomes a dark surface to be looked at and not seen through; there are no visible frames and the glass is sealed in the concrete. Careful thought has been given to the coincidence or not of a window's edge and the scoring marks of the concrete: here, as elsewhere in this building, detailing and finish are integral with the overall forms and guiding ideas of the design.

On a larger scale this side is interesting for the way in which the flat side of the main body of the building is made to interact with the curved second level studio. As the curve comes from the Quincy Street side it flattens into a straight line that comes closer and closer to the side wall of the main volume. It never reaches it, though, because it is cut off some five feet behind the plane of the Prescott Street facade. Here a piece of flat wall at right angles to the side wall makes the link and creates a strong, unequivocal articulation (fig. 19; plan 3).

As the curve pulls further away from the rectangular north side, a glass area that began as a strip expands into a full floor-to-ceiling pan-de-verre ("pane of glass"; fig. 20). Then as speed in its curvature increases towards Quincy Street, the pan-de-verre breaks into the rhythm of the ondulatoires. In this entire transition along the north side of the building, it is as if a single piece of glass has been modulated by separate intrusions of concrete—or alternatively, as if a single surface of con-

19. *View from the north corner, along the Prescott Street facade.*

20. *View along the north side toward Quincy Street.*

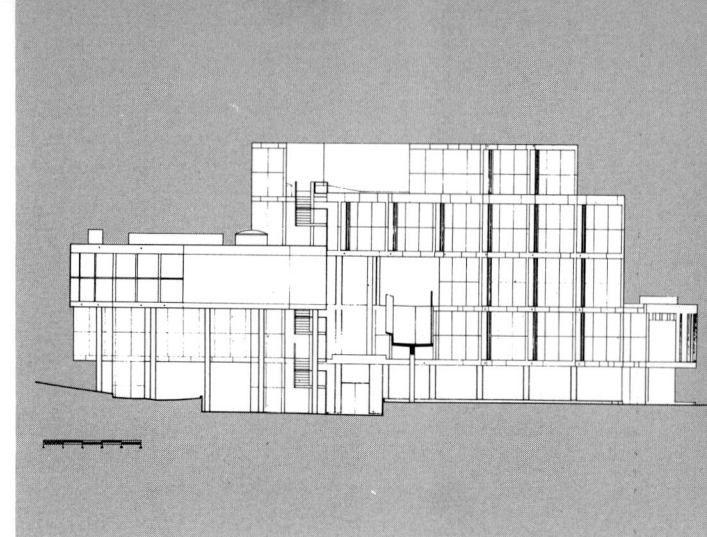

crete has been punctured and articulated by differently sized pieces of glass.

The Prescott Street elevation is less complex visually than its counterpart on Quincy Street and less complicated in meaning (figs. 18, 21a, 21b). Essentially it consists of three loosely joined elements: the curved volume of the third level studio in mid-air, the elevator tower, and the cubical main body of the building. Though the latter appears quite substantial, there is a vast amount of unenclosed space on the south side of the facade to the left under the studio which echoes laterally the big opening of the ramp gallery. To the right of the ramp, three ranges of brise-soleil regiment the eye towards the large space where the ramp passes into the central opening of the building. The top range of brise-soleil continues as a bridge over the ramp space to meet the elevator tower to which exposed fire escape stairs are abutted.

This tall, slender tower is a nodal element: it links the curved third level studio with the main body of the building. Clasped to its side, a free-standing vertical slab of concrete has flights of steps cantilevered from it that echo the obliquity of the brise-soleil in a different plane and introduce a brittle, almost restless quality (fig. 18). The curve of the studio, on the other hand, is so large and ample that it exudes tranquillity; it has run all the way from its point of origin at the flank of the main stair tower before coming to an end here where it meets and stabilizes the directional forces of the brise-soleil. Because the ramp is straight for some distance before entry, it is neutral in this drama, rushing straight ahead into the enclosed space, without diversion to either side, apparently projected of its own accord: the fins and pilotis supporting it are scarcely visible. Emphatically it is a discrete circulation element, emphatically the building's spine (figs. 17, 21a).

There are disturbing tectonic shocks in this facade: a heavy cliff of brise-soleil rests visually on plate glass and flimsy aérateurs at ground level; or, again, the bulk of the curved studio is supported by pilotis so slender it seems miraculous they do not crumble or topple. The necessary structural adjunct to these fine cylinders is a bastard pier, on the transversal axis of the building's grid. One may read this either as a wall (the missing second level is scored upon it), or else as the continuation of a brise-soleil out of bounds (fig. 22). The architect christened it "strange tree in the forest of firs which are the pilotis" (appendix 14).

The expressive quality of the curved volume on Prescott Street is unfortunately hard to examine because the street is so narrow (fig. 23). The brise-soleil are deeply carved into the shape and spaced closer and closer together as the curvature increases: another instance of an accelerating rhythm in the building. The effect is enhanced by tubular water spouts placed parallel to the fins (figs. 22, 23). As the facade curves from Prescott Street towards the Faculty Club to the south, the double row of brise-soleil, corresponding to one room height behind, is suddenly joined by an identical double row underneath it, because here the second floor workshop extends all the way out. The impression is of a boxlike element suspended from a large double shelf above.

Brise-soleil cover two stories here and stand out to form deep crates into which plates of semire-

21a. *Prescott Street facade from a raised point on the opposite side of the street in early morning light.*
21b. *Prescott Street elevation.*

22. *Detail of the Prescott Street curved wing showing brise-soleil, water spouts, formwork articulation, and the one brise-soleil in this building that descends to the ground as a pier.*
23. *View of the Prescott Street curved studio from southeast, in winter sunlight. Deep-cut brise-soleil make this curve appear heavier than its Quincy Street counterpart with its ondulatoire struts. Double-height pilotis here appear particularly slender.*

24. *Prescott Street facade at night.*

25. *Quincy Street curved studio at night, showing illuminated glass bricks on the stair tower and transparent cells of light in the depths of the building.*

flecting glass are set. In one place, a piloti cuts through the exterior in an expression of defiance: free facade and structural grid have here come to very special terms. Aérateurs are situated in each pane and vary the visual weight as they are opened or closed, according to the haphazard needs of the users. They allow a modicum of personal involvement with the facades: their colored doors are liable to be changed in angle day to day according to weather, the force of breezes, the clothing and whims of people inside.

At night, many of the visual relationships of the building reverse dramatically. The eye can penetrate the structure to warm volumes of elevated light that invite involvement and suggest communal activity (figs. 24, 25). The colors of the insides of brise-soleil fins fan the light out on the concrete soffits in pastel shades of red, yellow, and green. Restrained floodlighting bathes the concrete walls and on special occasions images may be projected on some of them. On Quincy Street the glass bricks filter the light slightly green, and obscure shapes shimmer behind the wrinkled surface as people pass up and down the stairs. But electric light most subtly transforms views from the ramp. The semi-reflecting qualities of the "picture plane" are lost; the eye penetrates deep into the interior, but stops suddenly at the jet black surface of the glazing on the opposite sides of the studios where, before, it had been possible to glimpse the surroundings. Night has fitted itself to the external contours of ondulatoires and pans-de-verre, and filled the intervals between the brise-soleil.

The south facade is dominated by the interaction of the curved third floor studio with the staircase tower and the central cubical volume of the building. As on the north facade, the intersection between the flat and curved surfaces could so easily have been a calamity, but again the architect managed perfectly (figs. 7, 26); he adeptly placed glass just beneath and above the curved volume. This dematerializes the flat wall by suggesting that the curved studio wall is weightless, an impression enhanced by the deep shadows undercutting the studio, by the single tall piloti that supports it, and by further undercutting of the main volume of the building into which, at this point, the entrance is set. Typically, though, the weightless feeling belies

the sense of substance given by the deeply cut brise-soleil.

The entrance, sitting in a side facade on ground level, can be reached from Prescott Street by walking on a path between the pilotis that hold up the third floor studio and the second floor workshop, or from Quincy Street, along the path that passes beneath the curved second level studio opposite the Yard (figs. 3, 7; plan 2). In the undercroft beneath the studio, shaded and a little damp, is a flat-bottomed plaza with benches set about in concrete. The plaza is sunk three feet, surrounded by a concrete rim, and cut off from the path by another bench. It is accessible only from the interior at ground level through a large, pivoting door ostensibly linking the plaza with the interior foyer. This door is rarely open because the foyer is air-conditioned and access to the interior is normally from the main entrance.

Once reached somewhat circuitously around the stair tower, the main entrance consists of two pairs of glass doors set in a concrete box in the entirely glazed south wall of the foyer. The concrete box

26. *Overall view of south side in winter; the entrance is set back under the overhang to the left.*

27. *Ground floor lobby with the main entrance door to the left and the staircase in the background. The thickness of pilotis at this level and scoring on the concrete floor are clearly visible.*

28. *Underside of the ramp seen from the lobby when looking out toward Quincy Street.*

protrudes equally outwards and inwards from the surface of the glass, and enough room is gained in this manner for a square area between the two sets of glass doors—a miniature lobby—to catch the wind. The height of the box is just sufficient for the doors. Accordingly one enters the foyer by way of a very small and comparatively low preparatory zone of transition, and the ensuing experience is one of liberating height and breadth.

One enters a room that is essentially one large rectangular body of space, but its many glazed surfaces, projections, and boundaries make it seem larger than it is (fig. 27). Straight ahead is the pivoting door with the sunken plaza beyond it; to the left, the underside of the ramp shoots overhead, not unlike a freeway (fig. 28); and all around, the cylinders of pilotis rise upwards from the irregular site. Thus exterior features are experienced as interior ones, and it even requires slight effort to concentrate on the room itself. The pilotis here are fat and smooth, and the floor is scored with lines in proportion. There are benches and two flights of stairs. The first is to the left behind doors with glazed surrounds that allow a glimpse of glass brick on the inside of the stair tower. The second is to the right just inside the entrance. There are also various doors to other rooms. The most conspicuous are to the far right, through a bright red-painted wall. A double door gives access to a service area (including a kitchenette, the receiving area next to the freight lift, and the rear door), while at the wall's other end, a single door opens into the administrative offices.

Opposite the glazed wall in which the entrance is set is a concrete parapet with a useful ledge, some three feet deep. The long horizontal opening above the parapet is glazed and allows one to look down at events in the auditorium below, though normally curtains behind the glass are drawn to ensure undisturbed privacy for this space. The right half of the foyer is often used for small exhibitions while the left half serves as a point of social contact and information exchange (bulletin boards, posters, and notices).

The stairway to the right of the main entrance may be taken down to the basement (plan 1), which extends far beyond the visible confines of the building and houses the center's Light and Com-

munication division. The main functions of this division are linked by a wide corridor that runs from front to back. Film, including animation, is at the east end by the freight lift, photography is at the west end by the main stairs, and the auditorium is in the middle. Activities in the basement are everywhere closed in by walls, lit by electric light, and surrounded by machines and their sounds: the click, hum, and burr of projectors, muffled voices of synchronized tapes, even the subdued breathing of the air-conditioning system whose bright green rectangular ducts snake in and out of closed rooms beneath the concrete slab. Walls are painted white, canary yellow, or bright reds and blues—typical Corbusian colors which one might also associate with new tractors and machinery.

The bustle of people and equipment in the basement is continual, especially since the auditorium is located here (fig. 29). In its front part this is a space two stories high, and the glazed partition at the rear of the high portion—when the curtains are drawn—permits a view down from the lobby, as we have just seen. Underneath this partition the auditorium continues one story high with a single piloti

29. *Auditorium seen from under the overhang at the rear, showing the zigzag side wall and facilities for cross-projection. Right wall is painted red; left is white, blue, and green. Beams are white and suspended acoustic screens are black and white. The ceiling between the last beam and the rear of the room is yellow.*

in the center helping to hold up the floor of the lobby above.

The same simple colors occur in the auditorium as in other parts of the basement; except for one red wall, they are reserved for its upper portions, the rest remaining white. The left wall is slightly zigzagged for acoustical reasons. Chairs are not fixed (the capacity is three hundred), so the space can be used as a multipurpose studio. For events like symposia the chairs are sometimes arranged in curves facing the left wall rather than in straight rows parallel to the end wall.

Parts of the basement and ground floor, together with the exhibition room on the third floor, constitute the truly public zone of the Carpenter Center. The core of studios and the workshop off the ramp are public only in the limited sense that they can be seen from the ramp. The most private areas are the studios and seminar rooms at the fourth level (in the top of the cubical main body) and the fifth level artist's studio, which is a world of its own. These are all reached, and linked, by the main stairs.

At each level, the stairs are separated from the areas served by glass fire partitions and doors, which, unfortunately, mute the rich variety of spatial experiences and views as one arrives at the top of each flight. This is not to suggest that the stair tower itself is a neutral zone. Its interior, a single shaft of space some seventy feet high, plunges to the basement and rises to the fifth level, where it serves the roof and the isolated studio at the top. Concrete flights of stairs are inserted into this elongated void (figs. 30, 31). Since they span between floor slabs and half landings, there is no need for them to touch the side walls; like the landing they are set back. The vertical continuum of space is enhanced by a paneling of oak plywood which sheathes the full height of one side (the inside of an outside wall). On the other side where a partition wall encloses the staircase, concrete is left bare. Lights are recessed into the sides of the stairs; in this manner glare is avoided and at night the column of space is also a column of light. During the day, the glass bricks ripple the light onto the interior concrete. Again the undersea image comes to mind: but this time one is in the depths looking up at a fairly turbulent surface from beneath. Even so,

30. *View down the stairway toward the glass brick wall. Metal railings of this type are used on all stairs and on the ramp.*

31. *View up, inside stair tower.*

32. *Second floor landing, with views into machine shop and ramp gallery and reflections from other portions of the building.*
33. *View toward the Yard through ondulatoires of the second level curved studio.*
34. *Interior of the third level curved studio shortly after completion, showing slender pilotis, scored floors, smooth ceilings, irregularly spaced brise-soleil, and round skylight.*

the ascent is slightly claustrophobic since views outward are impossible. It is a relief to pass horizontally into one of the studios whose clear glass allows expansion into the surrounding structure and trees beyond. The theme of free movement sideways through structure is then recaptured.

The most dramatic arrival point from the stairs is at the second floor landing (fig. 32; plan 3). This acts as a transversal connector between the curved sculpture studio and the machinery workshop, each lying on opposite sides of the ramp. As one emerges one can catch a glimpse of Quincy Street through plate glass and of people walking on the path underneath the ramp. But the real surprise is in the other direction because one comes face to face with the ramp gallery rising stunningly to the soffit of the fourth level (figs. 32, 12, 13). Its tall pilotis are clearly silhouetted against the light streaming in from Prescott Street, and the ramp descends past them. Ambiguities about the gallery space revive: is it not a large room?

Clearly this landing is a focal area: it lies directly beneath the static point of the ramp; it is a pulse where forces around can be felt. Quincy and Prescott Streets, interiors, and the ramp gallery are simultaneously visible. The dissolution of edges is nearly complete: one is in an "infinite" space into which the architect has set down minimum interruptions; glass and skeleton construction lend tremendous freedom.

From studio to studio one can see across the ambiguous ramp space. The main axis of the building—the ramp—is experienced kinesthetically. It slices diagonally through the section of the slabs and adds vitality to the interior. Personal relationships are reversed: the ramp becomes subject matter. The voyeur, walking next to the three columns, is also spied upon.

The curved studios are particularly rich (figs. 33, 34). The grid is less obviously insistent than it was from the ramp, whose direction encouraged perception of the grid's axes. Emphasis shifts to curvature. The second level curved studio, in particular, is felt as a whole on entering. The anatomy of the building has been beautifully revealed from the second level landing, where there is distinct identity of place. Each of the main studios is large enough to accommodate a number of zones (figs.

35. *Interior of the third level curved studio during a class.*

36. *Second level studio during a class.*

37. *Walter Gropius, member of the Visiting Committee, in the second level studio, 1965.*

35, 36, 37). Lighting, structure, and feelings of enclosure contribute to form episodes and highly charged areas—focal points, concentrations—that may be located at odd places: beneath a skylight (as at the third level) or between pilotis. The grid of the structure does not bully.

The pilotis are like trees with clearings among them where groups form around a drawing teacher, a piece of equipment, or a desk demonstration (figs. 35, 36). None of the furniture is fixed, so classes can concentrate anywhere: in front of blackboards, to the sides of rooms, in the small triangular areas formed by the brise-soleil, close to fenestration for all kinds of views, next to curved wooden paneling for a feeling of privacy. The denseness of walls and the openness of fenestration is felt in most places, yet the interiors are large and simple enough to turn into an almost anonymous background for concentration on one's own work:

standing somewhere in the middle of a wide space amidst a lucid geometry of planes and cylinders of concrete, one may well forget completely about the sculptural excitement of the architecture.

One such area exists in the rear of the third floor painting studio (plan 4). Here the ceiling slab breaks open dramatically to the sky, a pure circle of blue or passing clouds seen through a plastic bubble captured as through a camera lens (fig. 34). The circular skylight with its red-painted drum filters a slightly eerie light into the interior and attracts people to itself. A similarly powerful effect is achieved in two seminar rooms on the fourth floor (plan 5). One of them is painted black and has a small square skylight with green walls set into its ceiling. The other is painted white and has a rectangular skylight set diagonally (fig. 38). This has red sides and plunges down from the yellow ceiling so that the whole becomes a study in the torsional effects of different colored surfaces. Through the building color is used as one means for modulating and articulating space and form.

Electric lighting is of two kinds: direct spots and high intensity reflecting lights hung in troughs from the same rail. In places pipes are left bare. Black ones are interior drain pipes from terraces, green ones (the same shrill green as the ducts downstairs) are exhausts or feeds for the heating and ventilating system.

Only the basement and first floor are air-conditioned. The upper floors are served locally by heating and ventilating units, warm air being pushed through channels concealed in the slab. Sleeves and grills are at the edges of the rooms. Air at room temperature can be circulated by the machines in summer, but it is not filtered or cooled. The difference of temperature between exterior edges and the shaded ramp gallery encourages the flow of drafts through the aérateurs, but this is not enough to counter the clammy heat of Cambridge summer. Most of the heating and ventilating units are hidden away in soundproof cupboards. The studios are accompanied by a hum when the system is on—about the same intensity as would be experienced in cabins not far from the engine room of a ship.

Equipped in the same fashion as the curved studios for two- and three-dimensional work on the lower floors, the graphics studio on the fourth floor is square: it is one large room (corresponding to the square shown on the airview) into which the volume of three contiguous seminar rooms has been set on the south side (plan 5). On the north side the room is bounded by an unbroken wall, except for a pane of glass at the northeast corner, and on the east and west side it is enclosed by walls with brise-soleil. Temporary partitions of less than ceiling height have been set down into the large space since the building was taken into use. Here slender pilotis reassert the grid. The swaying curves below are temporarily forgotten.

Although the building is endowed with a compact monumentality on the exterior, most views from inside belie this impression completely, as if the edges were dissolved away. These views, and the sense of expansion and physical freedom one feels while in the building, are of course possible because of its skeleton construction; piloti and slab generate those other elements of the facades that control penetration from within of the building's perimeter: infill walls, pans-de-verre, ondulatoires, aérateurs, and brise-soleil. Position, height, type of fenestration, and prospect effect the quality of the view; in all cases the exterior world is carefully scaled.

The most extensive inclusion of the exterior is allowed by the plain pan-de-verre. A good example is in the arrangement of reflecting and transparent panes of the exhibition space, which offered such a crucial experience in the first approaches to the building. From the interior these panes are completely transparent, allowing a confusion of the bushes in the roof garden with the treetops of Harvard Yard beyond. Ondulatoires cut the view into verticals, as if a photograph had been sliced with scissors at varying intervals: people and cars moving outside are broken into separate episodes (fig. 33). Brise-soleil create small triangular work spaces at the room's edge, and minute terraces to the outside (fig. 39). They angle the view and allow isolation from the interior, so that one is in direct contact with street, ramp, or trees below.

The roof gardens give views in all directions and are open to the sky, the weather, the air (fig. 40). But only the third level garden in front of the exhi-

38. *One of the seminar rooms at level four, with a seminar of I. A. Richards' in progress beneath one of the diagonal skylights in the building, 1964.*

bition space is planted: elsewhere open-air extension of interior activities is seriously underutilized. One may glimpse the possibilities at an exhibition opening in the spring, when the glass doors to the front are slid open. The smell of bushes and the evening light infiltrate the rising noise of conversation and the cigarette smoke. One steps onto the terrace, glass in hand, and leaves the noise behind for breezes, peace, and fading sky.

The roof gardens also allow a middle distance scrutiny of the building's own qualities while level with rooftops or trees, they are semipublic spaces, with the possibility of contemplation, visual involvement with, or detachment from, the activities, passing people, or cars below. But in proportion as one rises in height, the roof gardens become a more private zone, offering experiences the normal building cannot, and ever greater lengths of view (figs. 40, 41). First it is the cornice

39. *View through brise-soleil in third level studio toward Prescott Street. The aérateur is closed; behind the glass, a piloti on the outside is visible.*

40. *View of the ramp and Quincy Street from the fifth level roof terrace. The third level terrace is visible in the foreground.*

levels, then the slates of roofs, then wooden skylights, Harvard domes and steeples, and open sky; below, the building becomes increasingly available for inspection: the ramp, the Quincy Street curve, the Prescott Street curve, the square top of the building.

The last earthbound point is the artist's studio at the fifth level (fig. 41; plan 6). This was seen in the first long view of the building, set back from the Quincy Street facade, prefaced by a peristyle of pilotis surmounted by beams. It is reached from the stairs through an enclosed seminar room and past an office. The studio's double doors open from a corridor that has long views over the Yard and originally formed part of the studio itself. One can see the route to the building past Widener Library, Sever, Robinson, and Emerson halls. There are the paths, the trees, the gateway onto Quincy Street, the granite and the brick.

To open these doors is to step into an element of Le Corbusier's dream: he might have designed this place for himself (fig. 41). Cylinders of the peristyle catch the light, structure opens to admit "espace ineffable" ("ineffable space") and clean-cut geometry recalls "l'Esprit Nouveau" and the twenties. A large roof terrace extends under the sky; below and to the west spread the trees of the Yard. Here detachment is complete. Below, the world flows in and out of the cube along the S-ramp. In the east, skyscrapers filled with glass lift their activities bodily into the sky and airplanes descend slowly behind them along the axis of the city.

41. *View from the fifth level studio and adjacent terrace toward the northwest, showing the roof of Richardson's Sever Hall and the spire of Memorial Church. The artist at work is Mirko Basaldella, 1964.*

HISTORY OF THE DESIGN

William Curtis

1. OUTLINE OF THE TASK

If garrets are desired, Harvard too can provide them.

The Brown Report, 1955

The Carpenter Center is a work of art and a virtuoso sculptural statement, but it would not have existed at all without the initiative and judgment of a client. It resulted from a marriage between the aspirations, stated needs, and values of an institution, and the architectural language, philosophy, and intentions of an architect. Moreover, Carpenter Center has to be understood as a cumulative solution to many problems. Most obviously it is a solution to the client's program, though the architect perceived this program in his own way; his solution evolved through a lengthy design process and many factors influenced the result. He set his own aims as well as listening to those of his client, and the finished building bears the imprint of priorities beyond the contours of the architectural problem as it was laid out in advance.

Even so, one must start with the parameters which confronted the architect when he began design if one is to understand how and why the building's forms, functions, and effects were eventually achieved. To begin with, there was the idea that a practical course of visual studies had a rightful place in Harvard University. In the mid 1950s, the idea flowered and became a policy, then an educational program. The Brown Report, prepared in 1955 by a committee under the chairmanship of John Nicholas Brown, laid out the bare bones of the arguments in favor of a new department of design and suggested that it be put in a new building. At the time activities relating to the arts at Harvard were scattered about in a number of edifices, none of which had extra room for the proposed department. It was common Harvard procedure to think of individual departments as synonymous with individual buildings, and the Committee for the Practice of the Visual Arts, appointed to implement the Brown Report, felt that their ideas were sufficiently new in the university context to merit symbolic expression. They therefore suggested that the new department be housed in a distinguished example of modern architecture to be designed by "a first rate American architect." Here again tradition was influential, for, since the nineteenth century, it had been customary at Harvard to employ the highest quality architects of each period, both to edify the university and to turn the campus into a sort of historicists' stage for the exemplary ideas of each epoch. The design center architect, whoever he might be, would find himself in the august company of representative works in many styles by architects such as Charles Bulfinch, Ware and Van Brunt, Henry Hobson Richardson, Richard Morris Hunt, McKim, Mead, and White, and Walter Gropius.[1]

Thinking of the area to the east side of the Yard as a possible "arts quarter" for the university (it already contained the art history[2] and architecture departments in the Fogg Museum and Robinson Hall respectively), the committee recommended that the design center stand on a site between Prescott and Quincy Streets. It also recommended that a center for the performing arts be integrated with the new design center so that "active humanities" would be united under a single roof.

The Design Center, built adjacent to the present Fogg Museum and the Theatre could extend along Prescott Street for approximately 160 feet. It could house, in three stories, workshop space for painting, drawing and the graphic arts (including printing); sculpture, wood and metalwork, and ceramics: photography, lighting and display, and the theatre design workshops . . . The entrance to the Design Center could be on Prescott Street and, since the building would also be near the present Fogg Library, access in the evening could be had to both areas without the necessity of entering the Museum proper.[3]

The Brown Report gave some thought to desirable functions for its design center: it outlined a sculpture garden in "an inner court," two studios for visiting artists and a profusion of well-lit and well-ventilated work spaces, "a flexible foyer-cum-exhibition space" (to provide a ready link with the Fogg Museum) and another exhibition space to accommodate student work. It emphasized that the department should be open to everyone in the university, and set a budgetary limit at 1.3 million dollars.

For two years after the publication of the Brown Report, debates took place over the role of the arts in the university, considering such questions as the integration of practice with the ideals of a liberal education, or the precise nature of studio activities; ultimately these debates had little effect on the final shape of the building or the process of its design. Whatever the spectrum of supporting arguments, the idea for the foundation of the new Visual Studies Program was carried. Supported wholeheartedly by President Pusey, it became incorporated with the Program for Harvard College, a fund-raising drive of the mid-fifties.

Response was rapid: in 1957 St. Vrain Carpenter, an alumnus of Harvard College (1905), pear farmer and businessman from Oregon, supplied 1.5 million dollars. As late as September of that year he had been intending his gift for another item on the list, a theater (Mrs. Carpenter was an active supporter of the Shakespearean Festival in Ashland, Oregon), but their son, Harlow, diverted their attention to the design center. He was a Harvard College alumnus, lived on the east coast, was in closer touch with developments at Harvard, and had been a student at the Graduate School of Design in its Gropius days when Harlow had even been assigned the problem of designing "a new Center for the Visual Arts at Harvard."

The gift acted as a catalyst, and in the new year of 1958 the Committee for the Practice of the Visual Arts turned its attention to the business of a building program, using the recommendations of the Brown Report as a point of departure. Thus nearly half the total space was alloted to studios and workshops, a quarter to exhibitions, and the remainder to a lobby-vestibule, a lecture hall, seminar rooms, offices, storage, and services. One hundred and twenty square feet was allowed per student in student areas and a budget figure was calculated at roughly twenty dollars per square foot. Since one million dollars was set as the upper limit for capital construction expenditure, an earlier suggestion for 750 students was rejected, 500 being suggested instead. The functions were then distributed in a three-story structure with a basement. Each floor contained 12,600 square feet (outlined in appendix 1).

The overall positioning and relationship of the main functions seem to have obeyed a vague logic. The two main ateliers (for two- and three-dimensional work) were placed on each of the two upper floors where they could be well lit and relatively quiet. The exhibition space was put at ground floor entrance level, where it could attract people from other parts of the university who might be passing by; and the auditorium was set in the basement from considerations of darkness and artificial lighting.

The committee's assumption of a three-story structure (which the Brown Report had also made) is of interest, since the finished building has five floors in all. No building program is ever innocent of certain preconceptions, and although a "modern architect" was being assumed, so was a somewhat traditional blocklike structure. The format was all too common at Harvard: rectangular or made up of rectangular elements, with fairly high ceilings, walls with windows punched through them, interior circulation by means of corridors and stairs, and—most important—the main entry at ground level.

The program evolved at this early stage was not precisely the one given to the architect; small changes were to occur. For example, the Light and Communication division, dealing with film and photography, was shifted from the second floor to the basement (a sensible move when one considers the amount of darkness required for such facilities), and the 1,600 square feet allocated for this area and a photo laboratory was later found to be an under-calculation and so was increased. Moreover, a degree of looseness in the program was deliberately encouraged so as not to restrict the architect.[4] When it came to it, though, the client showed himself surprisingly intolerant of some of the architect's imaginative rearrangements.[5]

Next it was necessary to decide where the building should stand. The Committee for the Practice of the Visual Arts rejected the Brown Report's suggested site (and the one where the building eventually stood) because they realized that the building as they proposed it would not fit: a structure 160 feet along Prescott Street could only have involved ripping down the Faculty Club—hardly the ideal way for a new department to begin its career. In the meantime a separate grant had been received for a performing arts center and the decision was made to build the theater on a different site at the opposite end of the university. Even with this reduction, the visual arts center seemed to require the demolition of the Faculty Club or, at the very best, the destruction of its parking area. In any event Farlow House, a little wooden nineteenth-century structure next to the Fogg Museum, would have to be demolished. On many counts the site seemed inappropriate, so attention was turned to five other sites compared by means of analytical site plans and considered from the same eight criteria (appendix 1).

Application of these criteria (and they included such features as parking, "position relative to the rest of the University," capacity for expansion, and so on) and consideration of prior claims from other departments of the university led to the eventual, unanimous choice of a site on Kirkland Street next to the new lecture hall, about 150 yards north (and a little east) of Harvard Yard. Interestingly, stylistic and visual restrictions were not listed among the criteria, and perhaps this too was another typical feature of Harvard (and many other American campuses) where new buildings tend to be thought of as freestanding entities, rather than as extensions of preexisting architecture.

In any case, these were not hard and fast decisions but mere recommendations. Moreover, the committee report gave no hint of which architect might be employed. Behind the scenes, though, this topic was being discussed. In a letter dated July 3, 1958—within a month of the report—Dean McGeorge Bundy wrote to José Luis Sert, Dean of the Graduate School of Design and chairman of the committee, "I doubt if we should pick an architect before we have a definite decision on the site, but as soon as that is settled, I hope we can go ahead, and my vote is with yours" (7-3-58).[6] Fortunately, Sert's "vote" is preserved in the earlier letter.

> I don't know how much in a hurry you are to decide about these matters and when you think it will be the right moment to consider an architect for this building, but I would like to repeat, as I once said to you and Nate, that I believe it would be wonderful for the building and for Harvard and also for the new centre itself, to ask Le Corbusier to design this building.
>
> There is no Corbusier building in this country which is as strange as if there were no Picasso paintings in our museums. I don't know how familiar you are with any of Corbusier's work and his great influence not only in architecture but in all the visual arts. At this moment when the studies on French culture in the University are being expanded it would be, I think nice to have the outstanding French architect design this building. Will you communicate with Nate on this subject? (6-26-58)

In part, of course, this was an appeal to Harvard chauvinism, and there are later examples of modern architectural competitiveness with, for example, Yale. Sert's comparison with a Picasso in a museum was apt, for American universities have tended to turn their campuses into museums of monuments by fashionable modern architects. The gentle tone of persuasion of Sert's letter was typical; without his diplomacy and patience Harvard would not have had their "Le Corbusier." Within a fortnight of his letter the decision on a site was nearer crystallization and the latest proposals were forwarded to Harlow Carpenter, who was living in Vermont and acting as his parents' "mouthpiece and seeing eye" (as St. Vrain Carpenter put it). The Carpenters were consulted on all major decisions.

> After considerable thought the President has asked the Committee to discard sites North of Kirkland Street and to concentrate on three areas: the area next to the Fogg Museum on Quincy Street, the space now occupied by Hunt Hall at the North end of the Yard, and a third site which I have marked X on your map, at the corner of Plympton and Mount Auburn Streets. Mr. Pusey's feeling is that while none of these three sites is quite as large as some of the others which have been considered, it is a matter of the highest importance to keep the Visual Arts Center near the heart of the College. (7-11-58)

Placement near the heart of the college was what the Brown Report had recommended and the three sites suggested were all quite close to that. In the same letter, Bundy spoke of the need to build the smaller of the two versions in the Committee for the Practice of the Visual Arts Report, "not simply for reasons of economics," but also "not [to] dwarf the students in it," adding, rather feebly, "it is clear that there is a rapidly growing demand for this kind of work, but we ought not to run too far ahead of it." But he must also have realized that the Quincy Street site quite literally disallowed "running ahead" at any future date because it was so small. It was cramped in all directions, not simply by the Fogg and Faculty Club to the northeast and southwest, but also by Quincy and Prescott Streets to the northwest and southeast. He might more truly have said "not to dwarf the Faculty Club," for it seems that President Pusey was determined to put the building where Farlow House then stood:[7] the size had to be kept down to fit onto a narrow site and not threaten neighbors, for it was still assumed that the building should be three stories high. (For dimensions of the site, see plan 7.)

Thus with regard to the future position of the building the committee's objections to the Quincy Street site were overlooked; the Brown Report criteria won. And if the choice of this site eventually led to a master stroke from the architect, it also hedged him in with problems that were perhaps never solved. Whatever one's views on this matter, a persistent theme was ordained at the outset: the building's size and its relationship to its neighbors. For even the smaller version of the committee's program required that 50,000 square feet somehow be accommodated on the constricted site. No wonder the architect immediately discarded the client's assumption of a three-story building; here as in many other ways, Le Corbusier was to show himself well suited to Harvard's problems.

It cannot be stressed enough that the nature of the program and its conceptual and functional lack of definition were among the most cogent arguments in favor of Le Corbusier's employment. If a detailed technical program had been necessary (as for a science center, for example), it is unlikely that he would have been considered for it. But in Le Corbusier they knew they had an architect who could supplement the committee's idealistic aspirations for the arts with firm beliefs (even if his view of the role of the arts was not exactly as theirs) and who could give stimulating character to a free space which the program itself did not inject with definite content. The corollary to this was that Le Corbusier was to be given almost total freedom as an artist to mold those spaces—an opportunity he exploited to the full.

Moreover, in retrospect, and with historical distance, the Le Corbusier suggestion comes as no surprise. Not only had Sert worked with him previously, but Harvard University and Cambridge, Massachusetts, had become one of the outposts of the Modern Movement in America. Through their presence in the area, such men as Walter Gropius and (at times) Sigfried Giedion had set the foundation unwittingly for a future alliance with this architect. It is even arguable that ideas of Modern Movement extraction had been partly responsible for getting the educational idea on its feet in the 1950s in the first place.

Be that as it may, Sert's proposal that Le Corbusier should be the architect was forwarded to the Carpenters. They accepted it enthusiastically and then gave *their* opinions on the ideal site.

We hope you will be able to obtain the service of Le Corbusier to do the architectural planning of the building. We think that the building should be on a large enough site to allow room for [sic] considerable area of trees, shrubs and flowers. Unfortunately the only section of Cambridge which has any senic [sic] value is that which borders the Charles and I understand from your report that no site on the banks of the River is satisfactory to President Pusey. It is my thought that the Visual Arts must have their foundation in mountains, hills, streams, forests and trees, shrubs and flowers, pastures and fields. And as these are not available in Cambridge, I suggest some room be provided for these in the site of the building. (7-21-58; appendix 2; see also appendix 9)

While writing, St. Vrain Carpenter could see out over the tops of the fruit trees of his farm Topsides towards the mountains, streams, and trees of the Oregon countryside. His pastoral vision of a setting for the arts was in accord with the university's requirement for open-air exhibition space, or the Brown Report's plea for peace and quiet for the artist. Le Corbusier may never have seen Carpenter's letter, but the effects desired by donor and client corresponded loosely with the aims of their architect. To provide features of the countryside with a building, on a narrow site, preserving parking at ground level, providing a profusion of well-lit, well-ventilated, and flexible work spaces, encouraging the passage of the various disciplines—this was to put the problem in terms the architect could regard as "correct."[8]

But before he could be made attentive to the constraints of the little site on Quincy Street, the legacy of his quarrels with the United States had to be overcome. At this point Sert, as friend and previous collaborator of Le Corbusier, became the key personality, and decisions affecting the future of the project shifted temporarily to Paris.

la spirale du toit du musée doit devenir une piste de jardin et zocarló derrière dans le paysage et formant paysage.

2. CAPTAIN GIEDION'S AMERICAN PROBLEM

I shall come back to America. America is a great country. Hopeless cities and cities of hope at the same time.

Le Corbusier

When Le Corbusier was first approached in October 1958, it was a private letter from Sert, not an official university letter, that extended the invitation to design the visual arts center. At the time Le Corbusier was weighed down with the last stages of Chandigarh, of La Tourette, and with the various Unités. In reply to the cursory details that Sert enclosed concerning the choice of a site, method of collaboration, and fees, he insisted that the site should not be bought before he saw it "because certain dimensions might be hostile to the project" (10-27-58; appendix 3).

The last time Le Corbusier had had dealings with America was over the United Nations building, when he had chosen the site and argued the virtues of a high-rise concept only to have the commission wrested from him and his concept imitated. It was not the first time he felt he had been cheated out of a major commission, and in this case it led to bitterness against a monolithic adversary: "American Officialdom." Moreover Le Corbusier's last years were clouded by ill health, the death of his wife, and the sheer pressure of overwork.[1] He showed initial interest in the Harvard project, but his attitude quickly soured. If José Luis Sert had not been one of Le Corbusier's closest friends, Harvard might have had its visual arts center from another hand, and the United States might not have had its Le Corbusier building at all.²

In April 1959, after delay concerning zoning, the university followed up Sert's letter with an official invitation. It stressed that Harvard was offering an opportunity to integrate the arts and society, to synthesize all the arts in a single building, and to design a building for international use—all Le Corbusier "soft spots," especially the last two, for the idea of a *Gesamtkunstwerk* ("a synthesis of the arts") preoccupied him in his last years, while the internationalism of the building might make it appear a vicarious United Nations opportunity.³ Addressing an architect who repeatedly used the phrase "l'Académie ou la Vie" ("the Academy or Life") and who was much concerned about siting, the invitation letter steered carefully clear of ivory tower connotations and details of the tiny site.

> We are happy to learn from Dean Sert that you are willing to accept the designing of the future Visual Arts Center for Harvard University.
>
> As a matter of fact, this project is of the utmost importance to us and will be an object of concern, not only to the University, but also to the general public.
>
> The importance of this building is due not so much to its dimensions—limited as you know by a budgetary framework of 1,200,000 dollars, but to its significance and to the function which it has been assigned.
>
> Students from all points of the globe will study there and your architecture will be a source of constant inspiration and encouragement for them. That is why we thought it fell to you to design it—we also thought that the creative possibilities involved could interest the architect, the painter, and the sculptor in you to an equal degree.
>
> Therefore it is on account of both its architectural importance and the determining influence that it will have on our important program of studies that we will be happy if you will be willing to undertake the creation of this building.⁴ (4-23-59; appendix 4; see also appendices 5 and 6)

The trump card, later in the letter, was that Sert was willing to take the scheme from preliminary plans to completion. Le Corbusier had insisted on an arrangement with an American firm beyond the preliminary plans that he would do himself and had adduced the successful experience with Mayekawa, Sakakura, and Taka on the Tokyo Museum, but if he expected the American architect would be Sert, he made no mention of it (10-27-58; appendix 3). The suggestion clearly delighted him. He had known Sert for many years and had first met him as the result of an earlier Sert invitation—on that occasion to lecture to architecture students in Barcelona. This event was recalled by Le Corbusier in a note scribbled along the bottom of a letter of 1959.

> Tu occupes une place privilégiée dans mon petit coeur depuis cette première rencontre, quai de la gare de Barcelone 1927 ou 28. Tu te dressais au milieu de ta troupe: tous au niveau < 1 m 56!
>
> You have occupied a privileged place in my little heart since that first meeting, the platform of Barcelona Station 1927 or 28. You stood there in the middle of your troop: all at a height <1 m 56!⁵ (11-5-59; appendix 8)

Even before he saw the site, Le Corbusier found something to complain about in the fees. Enclosed with the official letter was a copy of the standard American Institute of Architects (AIA) agreement stating that 9 percent of "total construction cost" was normally allotted for "complete architectural services," 25 percent of this percentage (in other words 2.25 percent of the total construction cost) for work up to preliminary plans. Although the university was making exceptions for him from the outset by offering him 30 percent (close to 3 percent of the total, or $32,400), he was not at all satisfied. Sert had even made the offer of reducing his own fee so that his friend could have more. Le Corbusier's feelings became obvious in a letter to Sert in the otherwise pleasant context of plans for the summer holidays.

Tu ne pourras me joindre qu'avant 8h 30 du matin sinon je suis à l'eau et, le reste de la journée, je suis dans des lieux indéterminés . . .

Il est bien temps qu'on se voie un peu après tant d'années de séparation! Le problème américain, dont le Capitaine Giedion m'a parlé hier matin, au téléphone, d'un ton cominatoire et dictatorial, est, paraît-il, dramatique! Qu'est-ce que tu veux que cela me foute de devenir le sauveur ou le sauveteur; il faudra que ceux qui m'emploient "payent". Mille regrets d'être aussi goujat, mais . . .

You will only be able to reach me before 8:30 in the morning, otherwise I am at the water and the rest of the day I am in indeterminate places . . .

It is high time that we saw each other a little after so many years of separation! The American problem, about which Captain Giedion spoke to me yesterday morning on the telephone, with a threatening and dictatorial tone, is, it seems, dramatic. What the hell do you think I care about becoming saviour or redeemer; it is necessary that those who employ me *pay*. A thousand regrets for being so vulgar, but . . .[6] (6-25-59; appendix 7)

A few weeks later Sigfried Giedion was writing in exasperation to Sert: "Corbu does not understand or does not want to understand the great importance that a building designed by him stands amidst Harvard. After all the gimcracks of Yale and M.I.T. It should be as exciting as Ronchamp. I hope you can persuade him to an understanding by 'more details'(!)" (7-9-59). While the matter of fees should not be minimized, and Le Corbusier might well not have designed the building without extra money, Giedion, who knew Le Corbusier well, was probably correct in pointing to psychological causes for the architect's obstinacy. Le Corbusier seemed to suffer from fear of rejection mingled with love of it. His American experience gave him no grounds for reassurance, but he had certainly given his bitterness scope.[7] He would not come clean until he could see Sert personally—a meeting whose importance the university had anticipated.

In July a dossier of such details as site, surroundings, and the committee's program was hurriedly assembled. Armed with his natural talent for diplomacy, Sert left for Europe at the end of July. Maeght had just asked him to design a museum in Provence, a valuable link with the job that he was determined Le Corbusier should do in that it involved the creation of an environment for the arts and such old "copains" of Paris days as Joan Miro and Fernand Léger. The two friends were reunited in Paris on July 23, where they discussed Captain Giedion's American problem, "a smile on the lips," "le verre de pastis à la main" (6-25-59; appendix 7).

"Such a small commission from such a large country" was Le Corbusier's initial reaction to the site when he confronted it for the first time.[8] The Chapel at Ronchamp addressed itself to the four horizons; Chandigarh, a city for half a million, stood at the base of the Himalayas; but Sert's photographs showed a site that was not only less than an acre, but also squashed in by neo-Georgian buildings. Sert countered with a tender representation of the university's arguments, but he only really won Le Corbusier over when he described what the building might be like with people in it, through it, and around it. They had had many discussions of this type before when anticipating the impact of urban complexes on human life at CIAM (Congrès Internationaux de l'Architecture Moderne) meetings or trekking the Mediterranean coastline together in search of what Sert called "the spontaneous architecture of the people."

Of the virtues of educating the hand and eye Le Corbusier needed no convincing. His own training and his career led him to believe that the education of hand and eye might deliver twentieth-century man from the chaotic results of industrialization. Le Corbusier felt the need was especially strong in America. He had always admired the country for its technical expertise (starting with its grain silos, which he illustrated in *Vers une architecture*), but he lamented the lack of personal integration and inner feeling. Time and again he returned to the evils of American materialism and the shallowness of American life.[9] Sert directed him away from his narrow anti-American bias by an appeal to CIAM ideals, for both architects shared an idealistic framework within which it was the business of the architect to dispense "the essential joys" regardless of national barriers, yet with due regard for regionalist culture, techniques, and beliefs.[10]

But Sert's stirrings went further than this. Le Corbusier had himself taught in an art school as a young man, had designed one before World War I, and had been preoccupied with ateliers and exhibition spaces all his life. At the eighth meeting of CIAM in the Palazzo Vecchio at Bergamo, less than ten years before, he had stated in a speech:

> I am hoping that a permanent center for the plastic arts may be inaugurated. This would be an experimental work which will be taken down and rebuilt each year. It would be a shell within which we could experiment with external and internal spaces in complete shadow, in full sunlight, and so forth; where one could develop examples of plastic art from the first drawings to their full scale expression in color and volume; a place where one could try out all that the plastic arts can do for architecture—whether by rendering homage to their walls or by destroying them, or by evoking symbols, and so on. This center would become a manifestation of human poetry—a manifestation of the sole justification for our existence: a center for which we must produce works that are noble and irrefutable witnesses of our age, and not works which are full of excuses for our failings.[11]

As in many other instances, Le Corbusier had the ideas long in advance, but had to await the opportunity to build.

Their meeting had only lasted a few hours, but it had been enough to convince Le Corbusier he would do the job. Sert left for Venice to meet Maeght and the following week Le Corbusier also went south to spend the summer in his cabin. The day before he left he jotted down one of those "comptes rendus" ("summings up") of the atelier's activities which he occasionally made: on one side of the page works recently completed, on the other, under "travaux" ("projects") he inserted in the list the single word "Boston" and linked it with the name of a member of his atelier, Jullian de la Fuente, who later became codesigner of the building.[12]

Le Corbusier had every reason to be satisfied. Along the bottom of the second sheet of the notes that he took at the meeting he wrote: *"L-C décide il reclame = 25m = 50,000"* ("L-C decides he requires = 25m = 50,000") just below some calculations from dollars into francs taking percentages of the total $1,200,000.[13] Either Sert had set more favorable conditions or Le Corbusier more unfavorable ones: whichever, $50,000 was the sum eventually paid, an increase of $18,000.

The other notes seem to be an item by item response to the Committee on the Practice of the Visual Arts' building program. He referred to a core of functions, those "flexible studio spaces" of the 1958 report: "The 'core' workshops mixed together (technique) = large workshops for students very flexible" and a "lobby space, not forseen" in contact with "the public exhibition room."

He spoke of "realizing contact between 'men' searching and searching for themselves," and there were references to external and internal spaces for exhibiting the work of students and artists, small individual workshops for visiting artists, and a laboratory workshop for useful tools. Some notes related to Le Corbusier's own general improvisations; thus his phrase "the contents should be very clearly seen from no matter where" was the verbal ancestor of a number of schemes stressing transparency, while the phrases "that will serve others equally who will look at it to inform themselves" and "public exhibition room (destined to be seen by the students of the entire university)" may have formed the embryo of the master circulation concept.

Or they may have just formed its egg. For one should beware of reading the forms of the building retrospectively into the loose contours of the problem he was mapping out for himself. These nebulous ideas served to direct his observation, but real insemination probably did not occur until he had observed the site firsthand. Before that could happen Le Corbusier had to agree to the terms of the contract, something he seemed unwilling to do. In reply to a letter of October 6, 1959, from the university confirming $50,000 as the fee, Le Corbusier returned the AIA agreement with his own modifications scribbled on it, half in English and half in French to make it completely clear he would be responsible only as far as the completion of preliminary studies (10-19-59). He agreed to "hold himself at the disposal of the client" at all stages, stated that he wished his first payment of $20,000 to be made the day of contract, and supplied his account number at the National Bank of Commerce and Industry. Sert was "to be responsible for all services except the completion of preliminary plans." Then, towards the end of the letter, he melted completely:

La rédaction des paragraphes contractuels que je vous propose ci-dessus découle des expériences vécues à l'occasion de travaux faits à l'étranger. Je vous serais obligé de bien vouloir les accepter.

Vous voudrez bien établir le contrat et dès que j'aurai ce contrat signé de vous, je vous retournerai l'exemplaire vous concernant et je réserverai ma place d'avion pour le voyage à Boston au cours du mois de novembre.

The wording of the contractual paragraphs which I propose above stems from experiences I have had in connection with works done abroad. I would be obliged if you would accept them.

You will be good enough to establish the contract and as soon as I have this contract signed by you I will return to you the copy which concerns you and will make an air reservation for the trip to Boston in the course of the month of November.

As usual, Sert was partly responsible for this softening attitude. On the same day at the university, he had written to Paris: "Once more I would like to tell you that you have real friends at Harvard who are very happy to have a Corbu building even if you royally don't care a damn about them, this continent, etc.!" (10-6-59).[14]

At Harvard this rather undecorous behavior on the part of their "great French architect"[15] must have been slightly humiliating. They were, to put it bluntly, being made to crawl, and out of atonement for previous events which they had nothing to do with. After a frantic array of telephone calls, Edward Reynolds sent off a letter agreeing to Le Corbusier's terms, excepting the escrow payment, and on October 30, 1959, the contract was signed. Swollen feelings were quickly forgotten in the excited arrangements for Le Corbusier's visit.

He arrived within a fortnight and stayed from the 12th to the 15th of November at Sert's home. On the first morning they crossed Harvard Yard together from Harvard Square to Quincy Street.[16] Le Corbusier was impressed by the enclosed space, its ordered layout, organized circulation, and geometrically arranged buildings, just as he had been twenty-five years before by the campuses at Princeton and Yale. Then he had eulogized the campuses in the quasi-Hellenic terms of "la mystique du corps" ("mystique of the body") as paradises of health populated by youthful athletes and bright-eyed amazons. The chapter on American universities in *When the Cathedrals Were White* was entitled "Everyone an Athlete"; Vassar he called "a joyous convent," Princeton, an Elysian field: "Colleges and universities, then, have a very particular character. Everything in the interest of comfort, everything for the sake of calm and serenity, everything to make solid bodies. Each college or university is an urban unit in itself, a small or large city. But a *green city*. Lawns, parks, stadiums, cloisters, dining halls, a whole complex of comfortable quarters."[17] "An urban unit in itself . . . a small or large city . . . a green city," it was the terminology of *La ville radieuse* that had been the subject of his lecture tour in the United States in 1935. These were also the terms, Sert recalls, that Le Corbusier used that morning in the Yard. He commented on the greenery, the open spaces, the protection from the racket of the traffic. The Yard was the purveyor of the "essential joys," light, space, and greenery, just as the radiant city was supposed to be.[18]

They turned into the main space of the Yard past University Hall which Le Corbusier noted was gray granite (fig. 42), then passed on through Sever Quadrangle, emerging on Quincy Street. There was a certain irony involved in this, one of the arch antiacademics crossing one of America's leading campuses to meet the senior officials. Possibly he recalled his own investiture at Cambridge University, six months before, which he had gleefully depicted in his notebook with a satirical sketch of chancellor and deans, himself and Henry Moore striding pompously to receive degrees, a student portrayed leaning out of a window above the procession, his arms flung wide, hollering "à bas l'académie" ("down with the academy")—so mouthing Le Corbusier's own true sentiments.[19]

In front of Farlow House members of the faculty were huddled together. Le Corbusier inspected the site with the president, some deans, and other officers of the university and expressed his disappointment giving, as Pusey has put it "a Gallic shrug of the shoulders as if to say 'well if it has to be here we'll do it!' "[20] He was immediately led to thinking of a diagonal route through because at that time there was still a wall in the Fogg Museum garden and there was the projecting wing of the Faculty Club. Slightly later, at a dinner party at Sert's, Agnes Mongan of the Fogg Museum pleaded with Le Corbusier that he save the Fogg garden. This he promised he would try to do. He also had strong feelings about linking the university with the society outside, and Pusey stressed the need to bring teachers and students from all the other departments in. They told him that the university anticipated eventual expansion beyond Prescott Street, that is, on the other side of the site from the Yard. Perhaps the idea of a path through the building originated then.

Le Corbusier carefully examined the surrounding buildings for their textures, colors, materials, and cornice heights. His grasp of the site was immediate. He told Sert he wanted to have people moving through the building and that he was thinking of its use at night as well as in the day. He stated that the side wall of the Fogg would be "his wall."

But perhaps Le Corbusier's concept of the building was most influenced by an accidental experience that occurred away from the site altogether. What most fascinated the architect about the Yard was the way the fixed rectangular buildings defined a grid through which the paths of circulation flowed. Once during his stay he was discussing the program with some members of the faculty in an office in Thayer Hall that overlooked the Yard. Outside the bells sounded on the hour signaling the end of a large number of lectures. Le Corbusier's attention was riveted to the sight of the Yard below him, one minute empty and still, the next, crossed by lines of people approaching one another under the trees along the paths. The others present realized they had lost his attention and fell silent. When he turned back to them he remarked on the beauty of what he had just seen.[21]

Two months later, on February 2, 1960, he wrote a "note to Jullian's attention"[22] (Jullian de la Fuente, codesigner of the building):

OBJET: Visual Arts Centre
Il faudra préparer une route de traversée du bâtiment par les étudiants entre les heures de cours.

Une route touristique peut être en spirale si nous faisons monter le batiment.

Des sonneries électroniques seront composées et réalisées pour 1, 2, 3, émissions par jour, à heures fixés, émission de nature formidable de douceur ou de puissance.

Ces émissions seront selon une route sonore, stéréophonique,
  –en spirale montante, descendante
  –en verticale montante, descendante
en mettant du sonore au sol et au ciel.

OBJECT: Visual Arts Center
It will be necessary to prepare a route across the building for the students between the times of courses.

A touristic route perhaps in a spiral if we make the building go up.

Electric ringing sounds will be composed and emitted once, twice, three times a day, at fixed times, emission of a formidable nature of softness and of power.

These emissions will be according to a sonorous, stereophonic route,
  –in a spiral, going up, coming down
  –in a vertical going up, coming down
placing the sound in the ground and the sky.

The poem was signed and dated, and at the bottom of the page was a reminder to his collaborator:

P.S. Demandez-moi ce matin d'extraire de mon sketch-book de Boston les notes prises à Boston

P.S. Ask me this morning to take out of my Boston sketchbook the notes taken in Boston

in which were found, jotted down at the time of his site visit (fig. 42),

le spirale du toit du musée doit devenir une piste de jardins et rocailles dense dans le paysage et formant paysage.

the spiral from the roof of the museum must become a track of gardens and dense rockeries in the landscape and forming landscape.

Thus it was circulation that captured his attention. The emissions of sound spreading out towards the sky and surrounding trees and the students passing through between classes seem to provide a poetic equivalent to the experience in the Thayer Hall office. If so, then we have here another case of Le Corbusier selecting the ordinary, the everyday, and transmuting it into a formalized resplendent idea.[23] The synthesis involved recent experiments: Le Corbusier, with Xenakis, had already designed the Phillips Pavilion, "le Poème Electronique" ("the Electronic Poem") which made extensive use of stereophonic sound.[24] Sound fascinated him in his late years, not simply as an added element to the building—he referred to the Chapel at Ronchamp as "la synthèse des arts majeurs" ("the synthesis of the major arts") and scheduled it for stereophony[25]—but also as the audible equivalent to the kinesthetic sensations transmitted by plastic architectural compositions, rhythmical, spatial, and formal. He thought of buildings as field forces of energy, emanating their effects into surrounding space and objects. Normally a paradigm of repose, even the Parthenon could achieve such highly charged and noisy levels:

ACTION OF THE WORK (architecture, statue, or picture) on its surroundings: vibrations, cries or shouts (such as originate from the Parthenon on the Acropolis at Athens), arrows darting away like rays, as if springing from an explosion: the near or distant site is shaken by them, touched, wounded, dominated or caressed . . . a true manifestation of plastic acoustics.[26]

This was "architecture acoustique" ("acoustic architecture") and Le Corbusier also referred to pieces of sculpture "qui émittent et écoutent" ("which emit and listen").[27]

The spiral to which he refers in his notebook was a theme of long life in Le Corbusier's work. As a student he sketched the shells of snails. The form occurred in the Museum of Unlimited Growth in the thirties and recurred in the ziggurat Museum of World Culture which he planned alongside the United Nations building.[28] The verbal slip "museum" in the notebook (instead of "arts center") is indicative of the strength a previous solution was capable of having over his mind when approaching a new problem, especially in the emotionally charged context of planning for the United States.[29]

There may have been several reasons why the spiral seemed specially appropriate. It was associated with his proportional system the Modu-

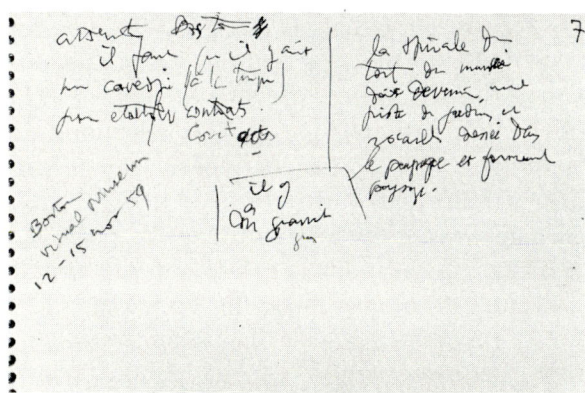

42. *Notes taken by Le Corbusier during his November 1959 trip to Cambridge at the time of his site visit (notebook P59, p. 7). He refers to gray granite in the Yard and to a spiral idea for his eventual building. Transcription: "Arts Centre Boston il faut qu'il y ait un cavedji à la turque pour etablir contacts. Boston Visual Museum 12-15 Nov 59. il y a du granit gris. Le spirale du toit du musee doit devenir une piste de jardins et rocailles dense[?] dans le paysage et formant paysage." ("Arts Center Boston there must be a Turkish coffeehouse to encourage social contacts. Boston Visual Museum 12-15 Nov 59. There is gray granite. The spiral from the roof of the museum must become a track of gardens and dense[?] rockeries in the landscape and forming landscape.")*

lor—one of his worldwide leitmotifs. It was also applicable as a symbol of ordered growth on a site which related to a campus he had understood would grow beyond Prescott Street, though admittedly this remained symbolism and little more: there was scarcely room on the Farlow House plot for the building itself to expand.

Le Corbusier also visited the old maintenance building on Memorial Drive that had housed the studio courses of Architectural Sciences, and there he examined student work, some of which led him to comment on the peculiarities of tetrahedral forms. He also spoke with the sculptor Mirko Basaldella and had his handprint made in plaster. The rest of his brief stay was spent discussing collaboration with Sert, meeting Sert's partners, whom he referred to as "dattiers," and relaxing in the Sert household.[30] Some of the partners he had met before. Joseph Zalewski, for example, had passed through the atelier after the war and worked on St. Dié.

The greater part of the pages in Le Corbusier's Boston notebook was taken up with sketches of the Boeing aircraft on which he crossed the Atlantic, or sketches of furniture, fixtures, and fittings at Sert's. He seems to have been especially interested in one of Sert's stools, a 1956 design by Sori Yanagi; he even drew a section of it, something he rarely did with buildings.[31] His inventions for buildings are all the more stunning through contrast with the odds and ends surrounding them in the notebooks. But it was precisely trivia of this kind that nourished his imaginative appetite continually, and the aluminum of the Boeing may have led to experimentation with that material in the visual arts center designs.

On the last day of his visit some students from the Graduate School of Design discovered the presence of the incognito visitor by accident. They instantly produced a party for him in the large central space of McKim, Mead, and White's Robinson Hall. He had specifically asked that nothing special should be arranged for him so that all the short time available could be devoted to the building, and the impromptu gesture may have caused the official organizers slight anxiety. But Le Corbusier entered into the spirit of the thing completely; he was very amiable, reminisced to Eduard Sekler about his contacts with Josef Hoffmann and Adolf Loos, and, to the amazement of more staid members of the faculty, climbed onto the imitation Palazzo Farnese balcony above the central space and delivered a speech in bad English and incoherent French, finishing up with a message for Americans (whom he had always called the "timid people"): "Il faut avoir du courage!" ("One must have courage!")[32] The students had improvised a mural of a Modulor man discovered and chased by Indians;[33] he replied in kind, plucking the beard of a student on the way out and saying "Farewell, Léger." The party was precisely what was needed to complete the thaw.

Le Corbusier did not come to America again until June 1960 when he presented the model and plans of his building. During this period of just less than seven months two parallel processes of clarification were in progress with only slight links between: at the atelier in Paris there commenced a long period of gestation, no designs being made until April; and at Harvard the Committee for the Practice of the Visual Arts and Arthur D. Trottenberg, the committee secretary, set about clarifying their program and needs.[34] He sought views from all over the United States, including Alfred Barr, James Johnson Sweeney, and staff members of major museums. Only a few modifications of the program resulted from this. Extra stress was laid on film (with important effects later on) and more thought was given to special media and their requirements. There were panics over the square footage and the budget, and one proposal reduced the total area twenty percent to 40,000 square feet, to save money for equipment. There were occasional addenda "for the architect's attention" suggesting such features as the preservation of parking, the provision of a route from Quincy to Prescott Street by the Faculty Club, the saving of the Fogg garden, and the provision of glass on the ground floor for views in and out. Yet, despite all these attempts at clarifying the problem for the architect, the architect seems to have been quite capable of continuing his own way. Thus as late as April 1960 the university was writing for his advice on their program, while he kept total, independent silence.

Of course one of the reasons the university had

employed Le Corbusier in the first place was his ability to give forms and an image to a program that was imprecise, and they realized that a tight functional brief with invariable logistic constraints might have tied his formal imagination. In this case Le Corbusier had almost carte blanche. Even such exact provisions as the auditorium and offices still left him more than fifty percent of the space—flexible workshops and exhibition space—with which to play as he liked. There might have been the danger that the program did not provide enough on which to bite, except that Le Corbusier supplied his own ideas of the problem and found inspiration in data beyond the program altogether, in the realm of circulation and topography, and in preexisting ideas of American association. He had chosen what to the faculty were everyday occurrences and transformed them into the stuff of his vision, features which became integrated with free sculptural expression over and above simple fulfillment of the client's stated needs. In mid-April 1960 some suggestions that might have directly affected the appearance of the building were forwarded to Paris, but the main lines of the building had already been achieved and did not require alteration: the architect had seen what he needed during the visit.

A discussion held at Harvard in March does deserve mention, however. John Coolidge, director of the Fogg Museum with experience of its management, spoke wisely when he criticized the program for its lack of private working spaces for teachers and storage space for exhibitions, as well as its failure to emphasize photography. He stressed again that the Fogg should be linked to the new center but advised caution against cramping future museum growth. His suggestions were forwarded with the aforementioned ones on April 14. At the end of his report he provided the first documented concern for the appearance of the building that was simultaneously taking form in Paris.

> Doubtless everybody has thought of one matter which I have never heard mentioned in the committee meetings. One virtue of Quincy Street at present is the fact that all the buildings along it are similar in scale, in material and color. I, for one, profoundly regret the tell-tale gray brick of Allston Burr. Doubtless we can trust Le Corbusier's urbanity both to make and to preserve the most of his site, but I confess there are moments when I shudder at the thought of a white whale stranded on stilts in our midst. If by some mischance this should happen, Le Corbusier might well reply, "If you did not want this sort of building, why did you send for me?" as Bernini remarked to Louis XIV. (3-60)

Over a century before there had been a furor at Harvard over a similar transgression of local taste when Bulfinch's gray granite University Hall departed from the customary red brick. History was amply repeating itself, for Le Corbusier had been impressed precisely by the granite of University Hall. He saw it as an element in the alternation of materials of the surrounding area, in the rhythm of red brick/gray stone in the Yard, and therefore as a precedent for his concrete building inserted among the red-brick ones of Quincy Street. He had also observed stone in balustrades and moldings of the structures immediately adjacent to the site.

Conveniently supplying the traditionalist point of view, the director of the Fogg regarded the uniformity of Quincy Street, formed by its rectangular, red-brick buildings, as sacrosanct. Le Corbusier took entirely the opposite view—that the rhythm of stone and brick, of form and scale, could be exploited, the curved gray forms of Allston Burr even enhanced, by the placement of a concrete building on the site.[35] To make and to preserve the most of his site were not compatible demands, and Le Corbusier came down strongly in favor of making the most of it. And making the most of it meant breaking through the old street face, linking his building with the Yard, and loading it with symbolism and meanings. The opinions of the quoted passage do more than illustrate a faction of local taste; they set a norm by which Le Corbusier's radicalism may be measured. And the surrounding buildings did more than pose an inconvenience; they supplied an architectural context that could give Le Corbusier's demonstration point. In linking the expectation of a certain kind of building, a Le Corbusier building, with a threat to the old Quincy Street, the Fogg director was more right than he knew. Above all else Le Corbusier was to produce a building embodying Corbusian devices of reinforced concrete in a didactic, almost sermonizing fashion. "Urbanity" was out of the question: he was intent on producing a manifesto.

1 avril 60   pour Boston
             visual Art.

I   pelote totems
II sculpture
III peinture
V   exposition

← route ascensionnelle

ondulatoires
partout

3. FINDING THE BUILDING'S FORM

He told me that the visual arts center was to be his only American building . . . and that he would therefore put all his architectural elements in it.

Jullian de la Fuente

During Le Corbusier's visit to Harvard, a member of the faculty asked him when he would produce the plans. The architect replied that he did not know, that it was up to "his little machine."[1] His "little machine" mingled his firsthand impressions with preexisting ideas to produce the spiral poem in February. Literary expression preceded drawn design.[2] No sketch appeared till April 1. The scheme then developed with astonishing rapidity, the architects finding their forms within a fortnight of the first sketch and a week of the second.

Sert sent a site plan, photographs of surrounding buildings, positions of trees, and a copy of the Committee for the Practice of the Visual Arts program to Paris in January. At the atelier they constructed a model of the site and surrounding areas and studied circulation with the help of colored cardboard cutouts.[3] Le Corbusier made no communications with Cambridge during this period—a silence interrupted only in mid-February by Sert inquiring what stage the plans had reached and telling him that the university wished to know when they should evacuate Farlow House to let demolition begin.

In the meantime Le Corbusier was turning the problem over in his mind.

Le silence est d'or (comme dit le proverbe). Je suis en train d'emmagasiner dans ma centrale téléphonique interne (ma cervelle) les données du problème. Je fais fabriquer une maquette du relevé des immeubles sur le terrain. Je sais par expérience que la conception d'une construction surgit au moment voulu et je pense que je ne pourrai pas donner les plans avant la fin juin.

Silence is golden (as the proverb says). I am at the moment in the midst of storing in my internal telephone exchange (my brain) the constraints of the problem. I am having a model made from the survey of the buildings around the site. I know by experience that the conception of a building surges when it is ready and I think that I will not be able to give the plans before the end of June. (2-15-60)

One such "experience" had been the design of the Chapel at Ronchamp where conception also surged "en une fois" ("all of a piece") after a long period "s'intégrant dans le site" ("absorbing oneself in the site").[4] There his site overlooking the Vosges Mountains had been a wish fulfillment of a vision from youth while climbing mountains with L'Eplattenier.[5] But no such involvement with the "genius loci" of Harvard was possible; the site was in every way contrasting; and the architect had a totally different set of attitudes towards the United States. These attitudes were mythical but well formed, the seed for most of them having been planted during his first trip to the country in 1935.

Essentially they were missionary in tone. They unfolded around questions of industrialization and urbanization. Le Corbusier felt that America was a land of hope because of her sheer technical adeptness but a hopeless land because of the manner in which these potentials were squandered and misdirected, particularly, in the organization of cities.[6]

Bearing in mind that Le Corbusier let it be known before he began design that this, his first American building, would also be his last, it would be odd if he did not regard this as an opportunity requiring special intentions, and odder still if he were to have ignored completely his earlier American obsessions. The evidence that Le Corbusier did think of this occasion in special terms is abundant.[7]

The occasion was felicitous if he had polemical aims in mind because he was being given freedom to do exactly as he liked by his client. The program could be regarded as a starting point for statements of a general architectural and urbanistic kind: Corbusian correctives for the machine age society that he could see going off the rails. For the joining of head and hand which Le Corbusier saw as the essential purpose of the visual arts center was closely bound up, in his own mind, with the reorganization of modern industrial society that his architecture and townplanning were ideally to achieve.

In the months preceding the first sketch Le Corbusier seems to have been grappling consciously and unconsciously with the problem on many levels from the practical to the mythical, blending earlier typologies with American associations, selecting from recent experience and the data of the program whatever might point to a solution. In his barrage of methods and attitudes there were clearly standards which might nicely handle program requirements, but the question was, which ones? in what form? and, in response to what intentions?

Here the Quincy Street site offered creative limitations. It was constricted and the only breathing space was across the road towards the Yard. Perhaps he would have preferred a site there among the trees and open air that recalled the "radiant city." He had warned that "certain dimensions might be hostile to the project" and asked that a site "not be bought" without his consultation (10-27-58). But the predetermined site held out a challenge to which he reacted with characteristic audacity. Unable to put his building in the Yard, he would do the other thing: put the Yard in it.[8]

The first drawn idea surged on April 1—a sketch that appeared on a page of its own in notebook P60 and was carefully dated (fig. 43). He seems initially to have envisaged a temple of light, glazed all around, lifted up off the ground on pi-

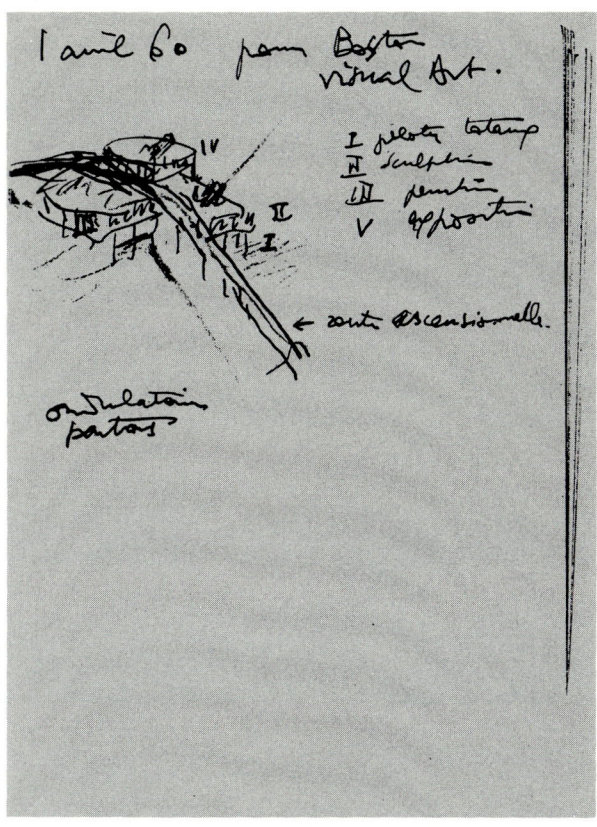

43. *The first drawn idea of the visual arts center, Le Corbusier, April 1, 1960 (notebook P60, p. 26). (No definite scale; 17.5 × 11 cm; drawn on plain paper.) This rapid pen and ink sketch with colored crayon additions captures the guiding idea of his building and most of its major laws. The inscription reads in full:*

"*1 avril 60 pour Boston Visual Art   ("1 April 60 for Boston Visual Arts*

I pilotis totaux	I pilotis all over
II sculpture	II sculpture
III peinture	III painting
V exposition	V exhibition
IV, II, I	IV, II, I
ondulatoires partout	ondulatoires everywhere
route ascensionelle."	ascending way.")

Interestingly Le Corbusier numbers the exhibition space incorrectly since there is as yet no fifth floor. The use of yellow to signify circulation (here shown on the ramp and under the pilotis) and green for verdure are Le Corbusier conventions.

lotis, buoyed up by the ramp that passed through the main jostling volumes. It was a sculptural, free-flowing conception, actively contrasting with the axiality of the surrounding structures. The ramp ran straight through from street to street at the third level where it abutted two curved studios, one at the third level, the other at the second, marked painting and sculpture respectively, each served by an adjacent terrace. The composition was topped, the ramp bridged, by a near circular structure for exhibitions. Profuse greenery was indicated by green crayon blobs on terraces and at the foot of the building. Circulation was shown in yellow crayon passing up the "route ascensionelle" ("ascending way") or tracking under the pilotis from the direction of the Yard. By running the ramp up through the heart of the main volumes, providing showcases of activities and architecture, his "route touristique" ("touristic route") became a "promenade architecturale" ("architectural promenade"). Fenestration was scheduled all around for ondulatoires—full length glazing with vertical concrete struts that appeared to set the facade in motion, undulating to the passing spectator. To treat a fully glazed curved surface in increments of plain glass held in by struts made eminent technical sense because it avoided the need for curved panes. But Le Corbusier exploited the effect by laying the struts in ratios, thus making "proportion, time and space . . . music."[9] The fine membrane edges of light drums poised on stilts would have accorded well with the emissions of real sound. Ondulatoires had the additional value of incorporating human scale and avoiding the monotony of the unarticulated pan-de-verre.

There was no sign of the spiral in this idea. Perhaps the spiral, his spontaneous initial concept and an ideal geometrical form, could not accommodate the real data of site, program, and even architect's own aims. To have descended to the ground floor from the apex while embracing the necessary functional volumes on the restricted site would have been impossible, given the small base area available, without an extremely steep ramp. And the spiral, being a centralized form, did not pass through the building from street to street as the architect desired. A reminiscence of the forms' characteristics combined with the last named

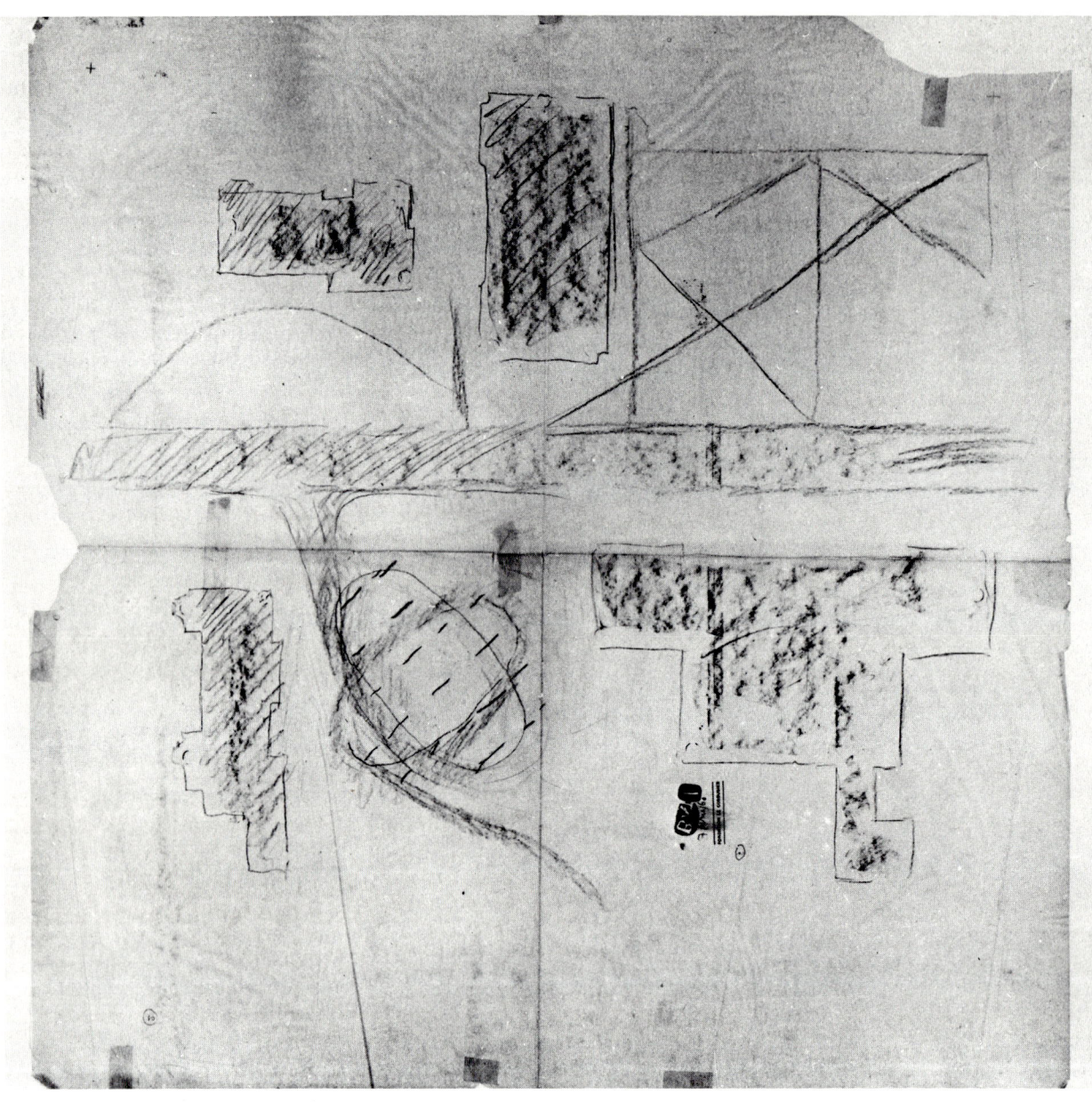

44. *Tentative plan of the whole building and its surroundings, Le Corbusier, April 7, 1960. (1:200; 91.5 × 92 cm; onion skin.) From the beginning Le Corbusier violently asserts the independence of his building from the grid of surrounding streets and architecture. Colored crayons are used to distinguish parts and to give depth to the drawing. The Fogg Museum and the Faculty Club are drawn in brown as are the President's House and Emerson Hall on the other side of Quincy Street. The pathways of Sever Quadrangle are drawn in yellow. The main curved forms of the building and the structure are red; the ramp is mauve. It encircles the building completely like a freeway interchange.*

intention of the architect did occur in a second sketch on April 7 (fig. 44). This was done on a large sheet of tracing paper: design had now begun in earnest.

The President's House, Faculty Club, Fogg Museum, and Emerson Hall were drawn in brown crayon; circulation, Quincy Street, and the light web of paths in the Yard were in yellow. From the sidewalk of Quincy Street he envisaged a curved ramp that rose, circled the building still ascending between levels two and three, crossed over itself, and then descended the long distance to Prescott Street. At face value, the building was formed by two red ovals, one on top of the other, their longer axes at ninety degrees, skewed askance from the definite Beaux Arts grid of surrounding streets and buildings. Within the ovals there was a grid of supports whose main lines were arranged parallel to the main axes of the curves. In turn, these aligned with the diagonal paths of the Yard and came close to the main compass directions. The "temple of light" metaphor applied to the first sketch seems all the more appropriate here since the curved forms were very like orbits. And the feature of planetary rhythms was to recur, referring—as in Le Corbusier's late tapestries, Indian enamels and reliefs—to the respect for the rhythms of day and night which the artist felt should be at the base of all urbanistic and architectural enterprises. Whether there is symbolism here or not, the orientation and shape provided a large area of ondulatoire glazing protected from the direct rays of the sun.

The ramp curving through greenery has associations with freeway intersections. These were a key to urban problems, as was the inclusion of countryside in a building. His idea for rockeries and greenery to either side of the ascending walk of the visual arts center in the Boston notebook—"dans le paysage et formant paysage" ("in the landscape and forming landscape"), "rocailles dense" ("dense rockeries")—seem to echo a panegyric he wrote on the subject of the Westchester Parkway, along which he traveled in 1935: "when the slums of New York have been left behind, you enter a Parkway, a recent American development which consists of automobile highways carried through attractive sites: the pavement, framed by borders, is perfect; intersections are at different levels . . . Pretexts are sought to pass over intersecting roads on picturesque bridges; curved junctions wind among rocks, fine shrubs, flowers and lawns. Parkways will cover the whole extent of the USA with a sinuous, charming, picturesque—and slightly arranged—network of roads."[10] However, having reflected on the parkway after his return to Europe, Le Corbusier decided that it was a basic principle of the well-planned modern city, being a means of introducing countryside and free traffic circulation simultaneously.[11] In *Manière de penser l'urbanisme* he even singled out and illustrated the Hudson Parkway at the side of Manhattan island as a portent of future urban harmony (fig. 47); New York, he argued, would be saved by the introduction of the parkway principle to the center of the city's built-up area, for when this happened the choking "rue corridor" ("corridor street") of the old city would disappear and the ideals of the "radiant city" would be achieved. His drawing also illustrates what the city would be like once this occurred.

The plan of April 7 was centralized (fig. 44). However, it would be incorrect to speak of this mode of representation simply as a plan or, for that matter, simply as an aerial view. The rapid sweep of the artist's hand gave a dynamic quality to the image—perhaps a graphic equivalent to Le Corbusier's idea of a building as a "field force" affecting its surroundings. Such a distinct sense of energy is captured in the thrusting sculptural forms of the final building. The architect's concern for the circulation from the Yard was shown by intensified diagonal hatching on Quincy Street. The circulation was thus absorbed into a vortex at war with the surrounding rigidity. It is what Sert might have characterized as one of Le Corbusier's "biological" plans.[12]

On a separate sheet the same day, Le Corbusier examined more closely the way in which the program requirements could be arranged (fig. 45). The separation of these processes deserves mention in itself. The swirling plan (fig. 44) seems to be his desired ideal, his symbolic equivalent to the original experience of movement through greenery, while the second plan done the same day (fig. 45) is a schematic study of the main relation-

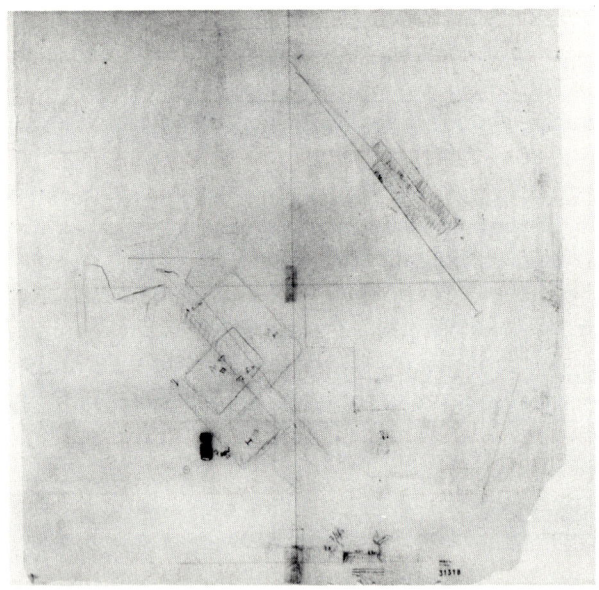 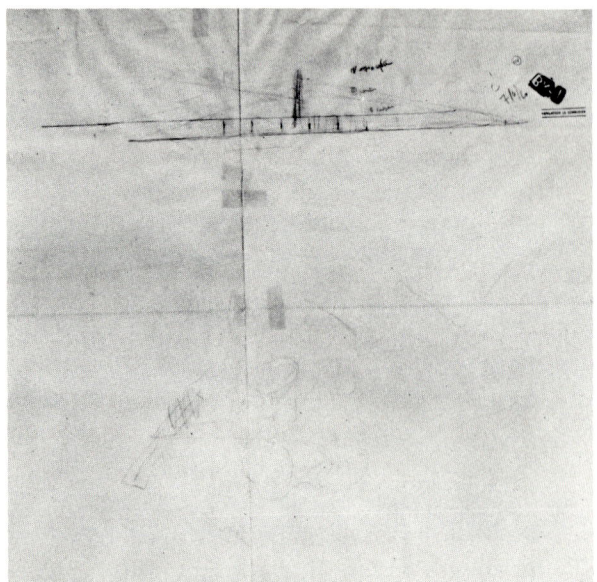

45. *Schematic plan and sections, Le Corbusier, April 7, 1960. (1:200; 91 × 95 cm; onion skin.) The rectangles of the plan were traced from cardboard cutouts equivalent to the studio areas demanded in the program. Deleted numbers show hesitation over relative floor levels of the main functions and entrances. The section to the top right assesses volumetric relationships and the ramp gradient. A smaller sketch section to the bottom right studies the ramp with people on it and includes the tree to the Quincy Street side of the site.*

46. *Section and sketch plan, Le Corbusier, April 7, 1960. (1:200; 80 × 91 cm; onion skin.) Here the architect experiments with ramps of different gradients running to different levels. He has discovered that the narrow site and the demands of a reasonable ramp slope conflict with his original idea for a ramp running to level three.*

47. *The Hudson Parkway, New York City, related to the "radiant city." Plate from Le Corbusier,* Manière de penser l'urbanisme, *1947. In this book Le Corbusier argues that the parkway is a new organism that will regenerate cities by freeing traffic circulation and by bringing countryside to the city center. The diagrams illustrate the architect's idea of New York (top) as a source of tools which, guided by the right ideals, may create the supposedly unalienated radiant city (bottom).*

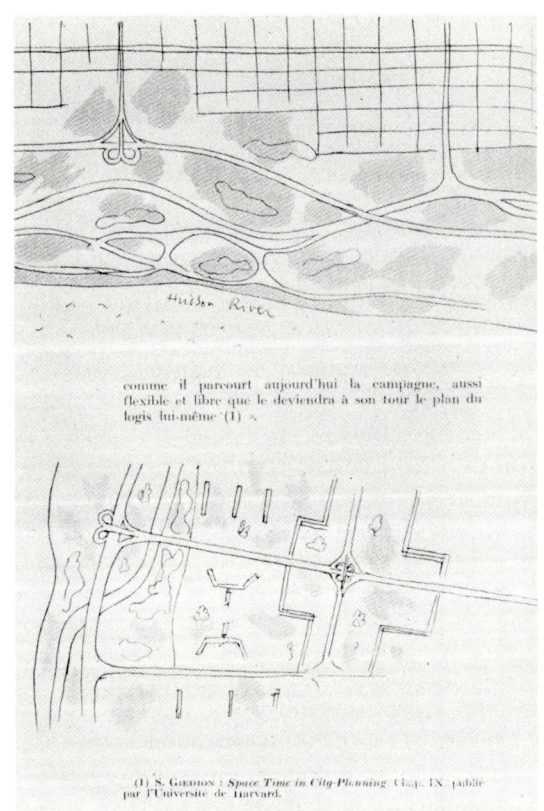

ship of the two large studios requested in the program and of the smaller studio space—the client's demands. He must have singled out these functional units as the most appropriate formal generators long before, during the period of gestation. In the beginning of April paper cutouts ("papiers découpés") were made of the area requirements, a piece for each major function defined in the program. This was the method always used in Le Corbusier's atelier.[13] The cutouts were shifted about over a site plan in experimental shapes and functional relationships until the architect was satisfied, and then he simply traced around the edge of the cutout and proceeded, as in this case, with his drawing.

As the April 1 notebook sketch hinted, he placed the studio spaces to each side of the ramp, one facing the Yard over Quincy Street, the other facing back towards Prescott Street (fig. 45). In the center he put the exhibition space but showed some hesitation about the relative levels by placing it first at ground level, where the program suggested, then on top of the building as in the first sketch. Clearly he was thinking that this, the most public space, would act as an enticement to the public to use the ramp. The studios also went through changes of level; the Quincy Street studio eventually was put on the third level (rather than the second) because the site was higher on that side. A section was drawn on the same sheet showing people ascending the ramp and approaching the building at second and third levels. To one side there were calculations of floor heights and slopes.

The curved ramp scheme (fig. 44) was a more sensational display of circulation than the first sketch scheme (fig. 43), which had the ramp running straight through, and in some ways was more sensible because it gave extra distance to climb the height—reasonable gradients. To the extent that it pushed the ramp ends off the site and took no account of the slope of the site away from Quincy Street, the April 1 sketch had been an idealistic visualization. On April 7, on another sheet, Le Corbusier did a number of studies of different ramps to investigate these constraints (fig. 46). Ramps were shown running from street to street, one even running directly to the fourth level. Interior auxiliary ones were also tried. Since it was the point in the building where the ramp touched that conditioned the slope, in turn tying in the floor heights, he drew in a set of small people in light pencil to investigate scale.

The section was marked "IV expo and Cafeteria, III peinture, II sculpture." Painting was thus lit from the north, as is customary, while the combination of cafeteria and exhibition space could be a magnetic source of attraction to the public and to visitors from the other departments of the university. In his November 1959 notebook (fig. 42) he wrote "une cavedji à la Turque pour établir contacts" ("a Turkish coffeehouse to encourage contacts")[14]—a remarkable recall of a feature observed some fifty years before in his "voyage d'Orient." There are frequent references to his early years in the late notebooks. And the visual arts center ramp was explicitly linked by the architect to another early travel experience in the Near East—the system of access ramps to the Suleymaniye Mosque, which he sketched while conferring in Cambridge at the time of his first project presentation, in June 1960 (fig. 91).

On the section, the elevator tower was drawn midway between the streets, and the first floor was shown with pilotis in it. The considerable variation of level between Quincy and Prescott Streets was clearly acknowledged. The slope ran down from Quincy to Prescott Street—the highest corner of the site was on Quincy Street next to the Faculty Club, the lowest corner was diagonally opposite behind the Fogg Museum—and adjoining buildings channeled the flow of space in the same diagonal direction. In the lightest pencil to the bottom of one of the sheets Le Corbusier delicately scribbled a sketch of a field of supports transversed by the ramp (fig. 46). Where the ramp came to the street, he turned it back on itself in an acute angle—supposedly to fix it on the site. Then he changed his mind, scribbled over the idea, and switched the tip of the ramp so that, on the Quincy Street side, it descended to meet the gently rising slope and made an obtuse angle with its own main spine. This cranked ramp form was to be refined later. It led to a confluence of circulation and the natural directional forces of the site, and on the Quincy Street side, it reduced the gradient problem.

Thus in one afternoon he outlined the theme of the building and some of its uncertainties. His rough drafts done on thin onion skin tracing paper now awaited transfer onto the paper of another member of the atelier. He drew the sections in colored crayons which he usually carried in his pocket wrapped in a rubber band.[15] Color gave distinct meanings to different lines, could be used to suggest depth on the page (plans veritably generating three-dimensional forms), and added considerable beauty to visualizations. Throughout the project one notes a simple joy on the part of the artist in playing with materials, whether soft lead pencil on hard tracing paper, thick crayon lines, or a variety of collage techniques and models. Occasionally media were combined: fragments of old prints, for example, would be used when functions were being reshuffled.

Usually Le Corbusier worked directly on plan and preferred to leave sections to collaborators. In this case, with a scheme concerned so much with circulation in its early stages, he preferred to work on the ramps himself. Only on April 10 did he hand the scheme on to the man he had decided should be the codesigner. Le Corbusier had earmarked this member of the atelier as early as the summer preceding his official acceptance of the job. Jullian de la Fuente, the youngest member of the atelier, had arrived not many months before. Though he was Chilean, he possessed what might be termed "l'esprit Méditerranéen" ("the Mediterranean spirit"), something that endeared him to Le Corbusier, and a strong bond eventually developed between them. He was a superb draftsman, able on occasion to clarify Le Corbusier's own ideas for him. And he was adept at turning poetic suggestions to practical use: the spiral poem had been addressed to him.[16]

Using Le Corbusier's three sheets as a guide, Jullian drew four plans (figs. 48, 49) and four sections (figs. 50, 51, 52) on April 10 to further investigate large-scale volumetric possibilities. He departed slightly from Le Corbusier's guideline in the elaboration of a structure four stories high with a free ground floor beneath the pilotis. Taking the program requirements and inserting them in the structure from the second floor up, he left room for the auditorium at the first level. He

48. *First exploration by Jullian of Le Corbusier's guiding ideas: ground level schematic plan and circulation study, April 10, 1960. (1:200; 47 × 32 cm; thick paper.) Although the plan is rectangular, there was never any intention of a noncurved building. Yellow crayon here seems to indicate different circulation paths. Jullian's style is heavier and bolder than Le Corbusier's. He uses chunkier crayons and presses harder. It was standard atelier practice to sign, date, and entitle all studio drawings in the manner shown here.*

49. *Second level schematic plan, Jullian, April 10, 1960. (1:200; 45 × 31 cm; thick paper.) Jullian continues to experiment with Le Corbusier's basic ideas. The roof garden is marked in green.*

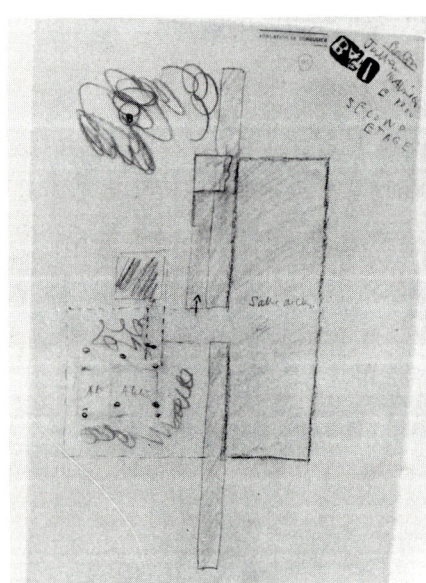

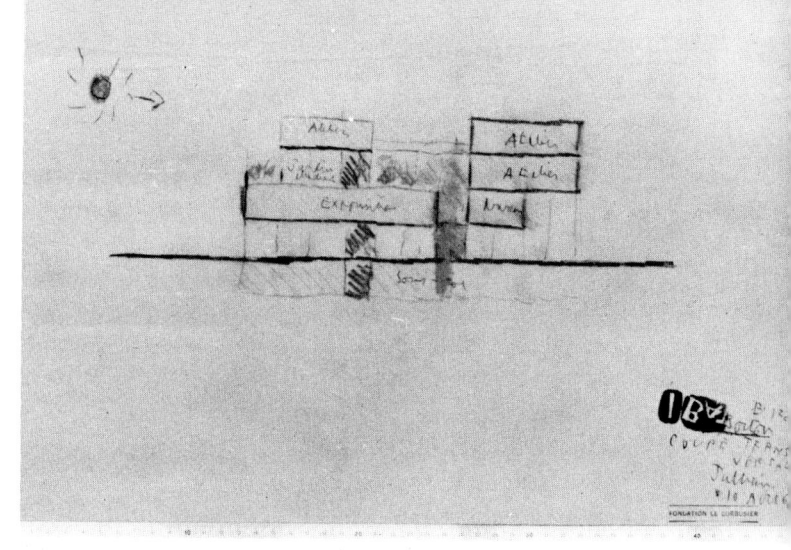

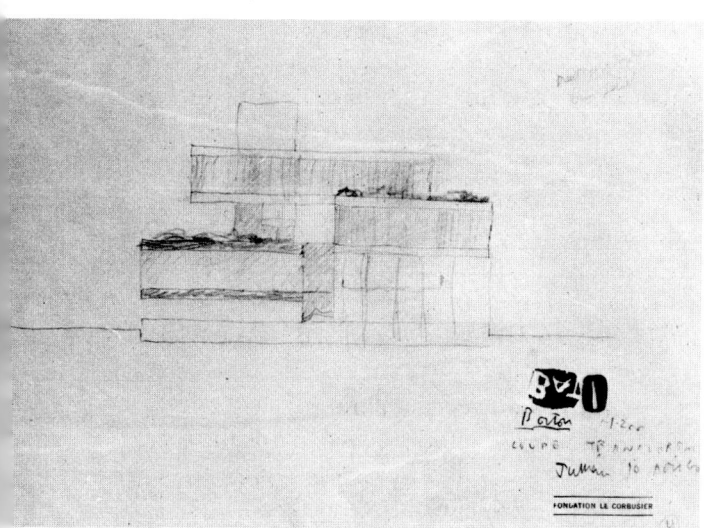

50. *Transversal section looking from Prescott Street, Jullian, April 10, 1960. (1:200; 33 × 46 cm; thick paper.) The inscriptions read (bottom to top) "Sous sol, Exposition, bureau, Jardin etudiants, Atelier, Atelier, Atelier" ("basement, exhibition, office, student garden, studio, studio, studio"). Black crayon is frequently used in the atelier to indicate structure in sections and for outlines in plans; green is used to indicate greenery, blue for glass. A drawn sun to demonstrate the south direction is another standard atelier device.*

51. *Combined elevation, transversal section, Jullian, April 10, 1960. (1:200; 32.5 × 50 cm; onion skin.) To the top right Jullian scrawls "nettoyage vitrage brise-soleil" ("cleaning of sun-baffle glazing").*

52. *Longitudinal section, Jullian, April 10, 1960. (1:200; 34 × 45 cm; thick paper.) This drawing captures the essential idea of an ascending walk through a semitransparent structure set about with greenery. Ondulatoires (irregularly spaced vertical fenestration struts) are shown. Here the main ramp runs to the second level only.*

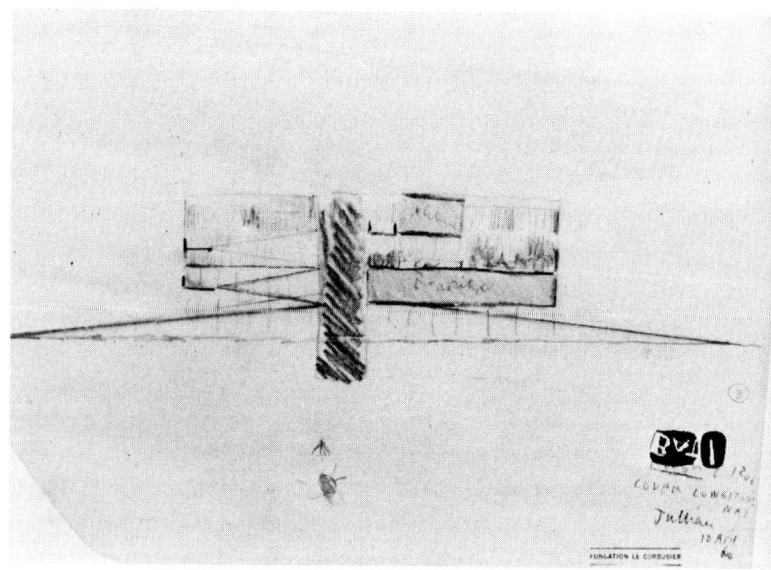

preserved the idea of a three-story building, only jacked it up a floor. And in the basement he put the storage.

Although the plans were rectangular, there was never any question of an alternative to a curved building. This "building" was simply schematic, and assembled (as Le Corbusier's of April 7) from cardboard cutouts whose outlines were traced. Although it could be entered from any side because of the free ground floor, he took pains to emphasize the circulation from the Yard with a bold yellow arrow. Following the lead of the first sketch, he used a straight ramp, which the restricted site allowed to rise one story only. The rest of the way up the building was dealt with by means of dramatically ascending interior ramps. They carried the visitor up and threaded him through the nearly transparent skeleton structure to the heart of the idea: a luscious roof garden.

The elevator tower was entered from the open air at its base and stood sentinel: the only stable element holding the forms together. Again it was set halfway between the streets. Otherwise the essence of Jullian's idea followed from Le Corbusier's—a formalized walk cutting through the levels of the building, criss-crossing it in section, providing views out over the Yard and into the various studios. The fenestration was reduced to a minimum light membrane of struts and glass— ondulatoires. Studios and other functions were so many glazed boxes poised lightly in space on pilotis. At any point in the ascent, the anatomy of the building was entirely clear.

At the third level, Jullian's scheme opened out to the sky as a roof garden partly screened by a double level bank of glazing belonging to adjacent studios. Such an elevated arcadia calls to mind the garden of the Villa Savoye at Poissy, but here the intention was for a wilder effect. It is not known if Le Corbusier knew of Carpenter's request that the arts be kept in contact with "hills, streams . . . trees, shrubs . . . pastures and fields" (7-21-58; appendix 2). He scarcely needed to, for his own idea of the "toit-jardin" ("roof garden") in later years was that it should be a veritable jungle, untended, grown accidentally from carried seeds, composed of hillocks—like Le Corbusier's own garden above his apartment in Paris, which prompted one of his previous assistants to say, "It is only weeds."[17]

To the south the garden opened to the sky and to the sun, which Jullian drew in his chunky hand emphasizing its rays streaming down warmth into the trees beneath (fig. 50). Lifted free on pilotis in the middle of the garden were the two ateliers for visiting artists, entirely freestanding, alone. Underneath they made a cave, a place for visitors to chat with resting students even in the rain. There was subtlety in the placement and isolation of these studios, something of a conceit, for the studios call to mind the Paris studio houses of the twenties. So read, the greenery at their base ceases to be a roof garden, becoming instead the ground. To a visitor passing through, the significance might be that he was reentering the Yard. As he continued along the ramps, up another floor, the visual link between the greenery to either side of him was easily made.

Much as it offered the "essential joys," this enchanting fantasy of glass and greenery did have its drawbacks. If the sun streamed down onto the trees it also poured into the studios through the glass and pushed the temperature up. The glass would also present other problems. Jullian reminded himself and Le Corbusier of such realities by writing "nettoyage vitrage brise soleil" ("cleaning of sun-baffle glazing") next to one drawing (fig. 51). Unprotected ondulatoires had been a fantasy of the first sketch too, but they did constitute, precisely, Le Corbusier's fantasy—what he wanted. His earliest idea had been for a structure whose activities could be "seen from no matter where," so the flickering edges that the ondulatoires engendered were best left uncluttered. But here he encountered a problem to which there would be no satisfactory solution: how to combine brise-soleil with ondulatoires? He might have stepped around it by dropping brise-soleil and using air-conditioning for the upper levels, but he had been told in March that the client did not require it (3-14-60). Besides, Le Corbusier disliked using air-conditioning on its own and probably wished to demonstrate his own devices for dealing with the sun: the brise-soleil and the aérateur.

On April 11 Le Corbusier drew four sketches at great speed in red and purple crayon and soft lead pencil (figs. 53, 54, 55, 56). The first was a circle in red that was placed in a position of tension between delineations of the Fogg and Faculty Club (fig. 53). This recalled the drum on top of the April 1 sketch, and the centralizing theme, and was obtained by pricking around the edge of a paper cutout approximately equivalent to one typical floor area as required by the program. The circle served the double function of guiding the building's zone to a correct spot on the site and ascertaining the approximate "center of gravity" of the project. Next, on thin sheets of paper through which it was possible to see the guiding circle, he rushed the building through amorphous transformations. At one moment he suggested a centralized scheme, at another, a scheme with strong directional qualities; but first he combined them in a single image. Thus, one sheet portrayed a swirling, amoebic confusion of curved studios abutted to the ramp in combinations of longitudinal and transversal positions (fig. 54). At the Prescott Street end of the building he also experimented with alternative positions for a stair and elevator tower.

Next he judiciously separated these confused studios onto two separate sheets. In one drawing (fig. 55) the sculpture studio was recorded in two stages of bifurcation at ninety degrees to one another, the ramp running into the angle between them (so incorporating the transversal qualities); and on another sheet (fig. 56) he distilled the longitudinal qualities of the swirling image in a manner recalling the configuration of the studios in the April 1 sketch (fig. 43), but with two notable additions: a rectangular crosspiece that showed the impact of the transversal experiment, and an S-shaped ramp that rose from the highest point of the site on Quincy Street, passed through the center of the building, and descended to the lowest point of the site on Prescott Street.

This ramp was considerably simpler to construct than the "freeway intersection" ramp; it simplified the contact between the ramp and the building as Jullian had done, it was curved, allowing the slope to the third level as Le Corbusier wished, and it had additional formal and symbolic qualities. Formally it was a counterpoint to the studio curves, symbolically it drew, like the spiral, on Le Corbu-

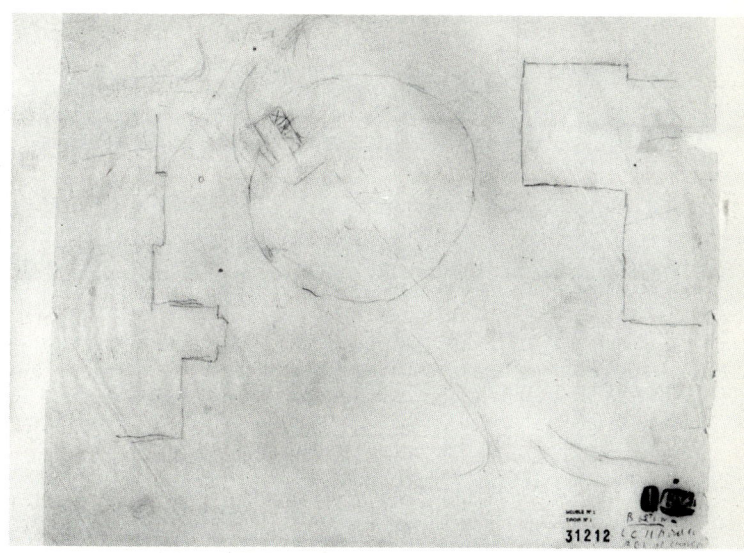

53. *Schematic plan examining position of building on site, Le Corbusier, April 11, 1960. (1:200; 45 × 52 cm; onion skin.) The Fogg Museum is to the right, the Faculty Club to the left. The circle in between is approximately equivalent to one average floor area and is a device to help fix the "center of gravity" of the building on the site. The ramp form is hinted at. This drawing was stuck together with figures 54, 55, 56—other onion skin sketches of this date—so that they could be examined together in overlay.*

54. *Sketch plan, Le Corbusier, April 11, 1960. (1:200; 46 × 61 cm; onion skin.) In rapid, swirling pencil and crayon curves, Le Corbusier examines the relative merits of different studio and stair tower positions and of schemes with either longitudinal or centralized qualities. The cranked ramp idea of April 7 is here smoothed into a curve. The forms in flux were centered over the circle of figure 53.*

67

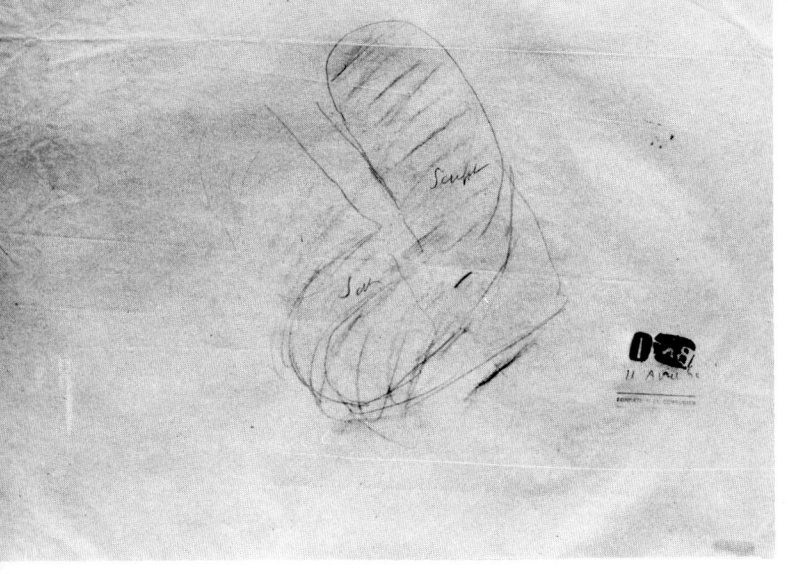

55. *Sketch plan examining alternative studio positions, Le Corbusier, April 11, 1960. (1:200; 46 × 58 cm; onion skin.) The curves are inscribed "scult" and "scul'lpt"—short for "sculpture." Here Le Corbusier's thinking is caught in action, but indecision remains as to the main directions of the building.*

56. *Sketch plan, Le Corbusier, April 11, 1960. (1:200; 46 × 62 cm; onion skin.) A moment of harmony and resolution: here, in its essentials, Le Corbusier finds most major features of the first plan for the visual arts center. Notice the S-ramp, the curved studios, the Quincy Street roof terrace, and the beginnings of a rectangle at the center. The drawing is faintly colored in mauve, gray, and green.*

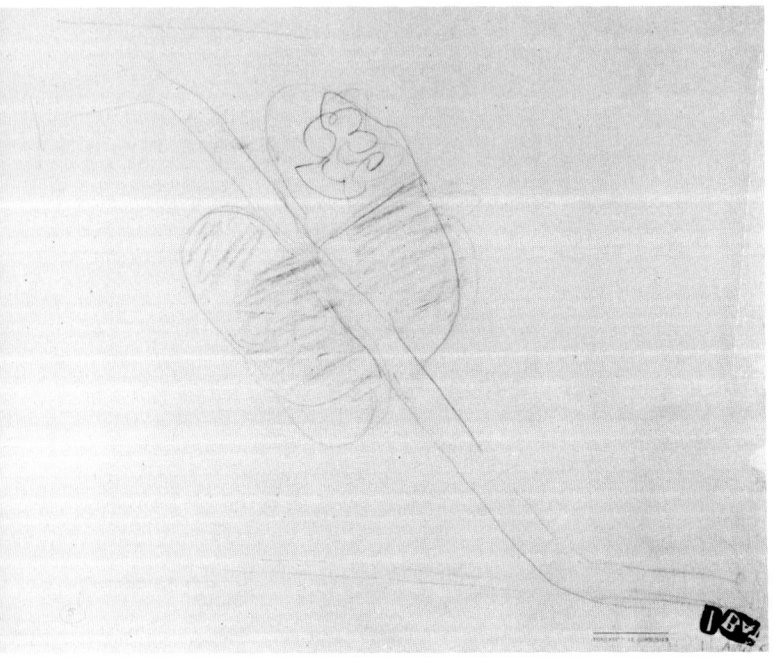

sier's fund of cosmic signs. The S-shape signified the rhythm of day and night, "the measure of our urban enterprises" (fig. 57)—appropriate to a building that was to be used in the night as well as the day, especially when the aesthetic effects of transparency could be viewed inside and outside, day and night, from the ramp. But like the inclusion of the countryside in the heart of the building, the freeway intersection, and the parkway, it denoted wider references in Le Corbusier's attitudes towards American urbanism. He felt that the organization of cities and work needed to recognize the fundamental cycles, if life was not to deteriorate. In 1947 in the introduction to the English edition of *Quand les cathédrales étaient blanches*, he dedicated the S to America: *"This is the measure of our urban enterprises. If, in the course of the mutation of machine civilisation, I have been able to contribute something, as a person with some rationality and intelligence, as a technician, as a thoughtful man, it will be this sign. If I can be useful in some way to the United States now, it is in commending this sign to the meditation of those whose mission it is to see clearly and lead."* [18]

On top of the building was a rectangular cross piece sketched in light mauve—the first sign that he was aiming at a central rectangular core. A section done the same day by Jullian examined the effect of a stable central mass with floors protruding into space at different levels, and sanctioned the most recent gradient of the ramp (fig. 58). This was the way forward, and on April 12 Jullian drew the ramp form in great detail (fig. 59), examining its position relative to the trees, the street lines, and the nearby buildings. It confirmed that it was all right to take the ramp to the third level, made one of his previous interior ramps superfluous, and so saved space.

On April 14, Le Corbusier drew an aerial sketch showing the Fogg and Faculty Club and including the tunnel that was supposed to link the history of art with its practice (fig. 60). The sweep of the second floor space back towards Prescott Street was drawn in red, the third in purple, the fourth blue. This last was almost square, thus fulfilling the rectangular promise of the drawing made April 11. It resulted in a form at the center of the building fairly close to a cube.

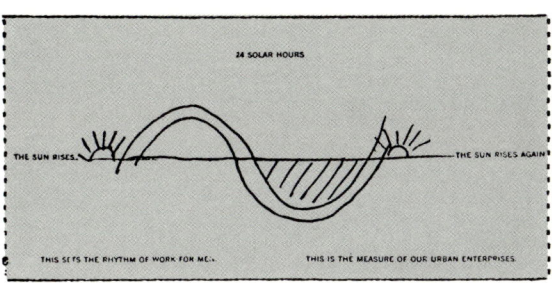

57. *Le Corbusier's S-shaped cosmogram signifying the rhythms of day and night—"the measure of all our urban enterprises"—from* When the Cathedrals Were White. *In the introduction to the American edition of the book, the architect solemnly offers the sign to the future leaders of the United States in the hope that they will implement the social, urbanistic, and architectural ideals to which it refers.*

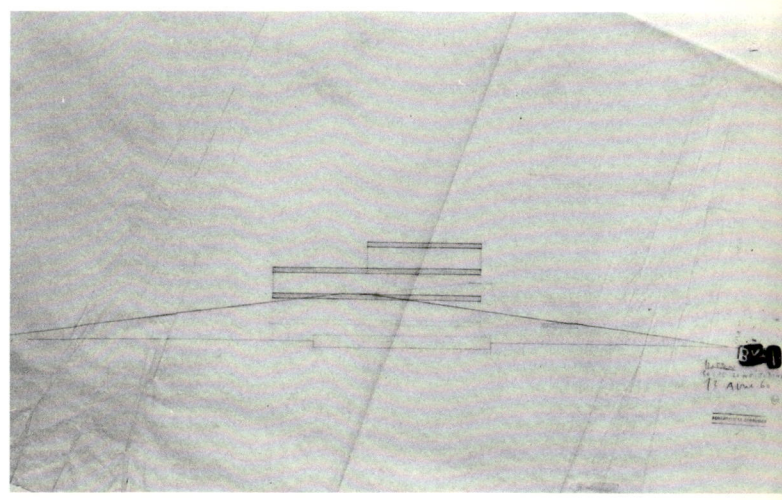

58. *Ruled longitudinal section along ramp, Jullian, April 12, 1960. (1:200; 60 × 89 cm; onion skin.) Jullian here tests Le Corbusier's intuitions of April 11 to see how the ramp, the streets, and the building volumes will relate.*

59. *Ruled plan of ramp, site, and trees, Jullian, April 12, 1960. (1:200; 66 × 49.5 cm; onion skin.) Jullian here examines the ramp form of Le Corbusier's most recent proposals. It can just be made to fit between Quincy and Prescott Streets but will involve the destruction of trees.*

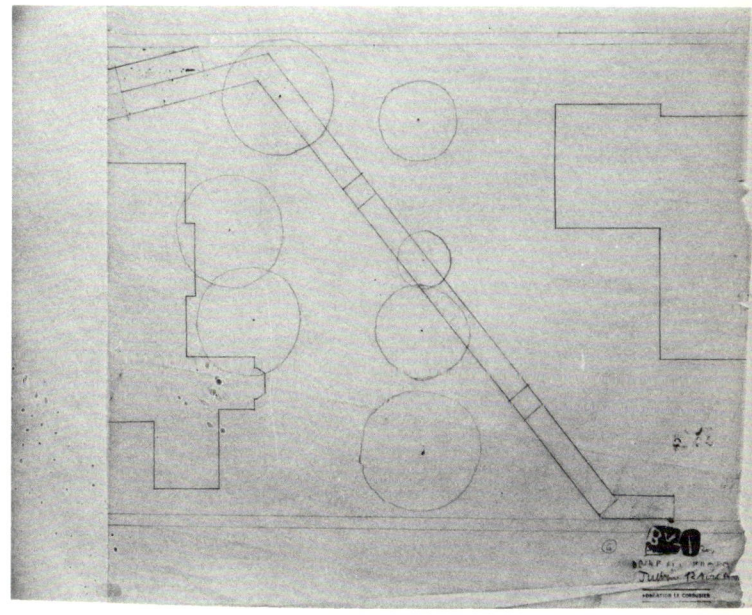

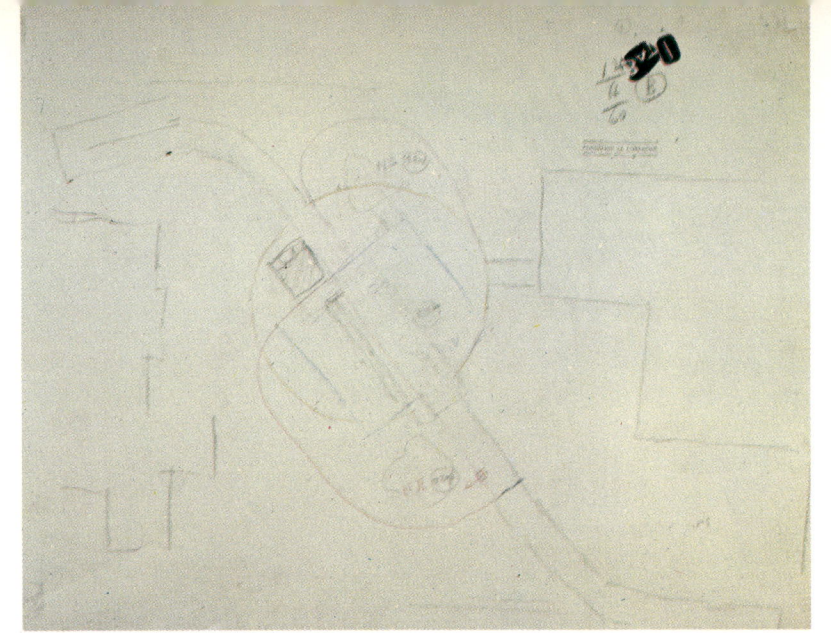

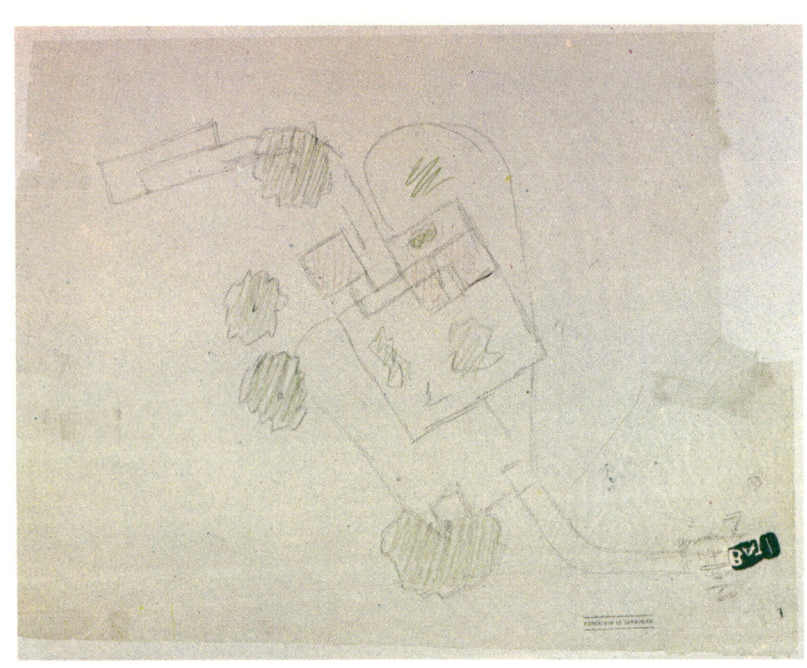

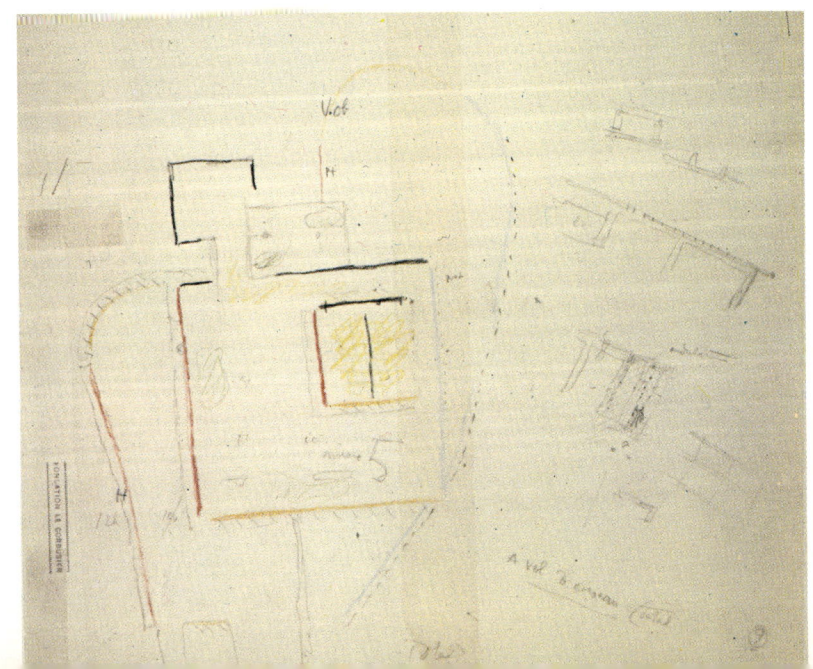

60. *Aerial view of the building, Le Corbusier, April 14, 1960. (1:200; 46 × 62.5 cm; onion skin.) With the aid of colored crayons (to distinguish the levels) and dimensioning (to give ceiling heights from the ground), Le Corbusier attempts to find a resolution for his building between the demands of area requirements, reasonable ramp gradients, and formal clarity. Here the earlier circle becomes a formal generator as well as a technical aid. The rectangle to the center and an interior ramp reinforcing the longitudinal spine have been clarified. The tunnel to the Fogg Museum is also shown. The building as a whole is still four stories high but the large curve to the rear will have only a short life: to the bottom left-hand corner of the sheet is a tiny sketch of a square with two small rectangles set to one side of it—Le Corbusier's hypothesis for the eventual fifth level.*

61. *Aerial view of the building, Le Corbusier and Andreini, April 14, 1960. (1:200; 46 × 62 cm; onion skin.) The Prescott Street curve has been cut back drastically, lending an even more directional quality to the whole. A notch has been cut to save the tree. The visiting artists' studios appear on the roof. A tiny query appears to the northeast corner: how to join rectangle and curve? Here, in a blow, the forms of the building are achieved.*

65. *Plan of level 5 (aerial view of the building) and small sketches of details, Le Corbusier, May 1, 1960. (1:200; 39 × 38 cm; onion skin.) The architect gives the drawing the title "A vol d'oiseau = Total" ("Bird's-eye view = Total"). Here is the plan that will generate the overall forms of the building. Brise-soleil fins are attached to south and east facades. To the right, sketched sections of the building's edge examine problems of brise-soleil junction with beams, slabs, and ondulatoires. For the moment these problems were left unsolved, but they reared their heads later. Typically, a small man is drawn for scale.*

It scarcely needs emphasizing that the square is a primary generator of the golden section and the Modulor, and that the cube was one of those Platonic forms singled out in *Vers une architecture*. But the cube seems to have had other possibilities of meaning for Le Corbusier. He used the phrase "le cube bâti" ("the built cube") in a somewhat personal sense to refer specifically to the built volume of cities.[19] In this precise sense, the metaphor of "le cube bâti" occurs in his book *Sur les quatres routes* where he discusses it in relation to the United States in the context of technical facilities necessary for achieving his ideal city, and refers to urbanism as "la science des cubes bâtis" ("the science of the built cubes"; p. 59). Le Corbusier's prescriptions for the correct placement and construction of "le cube bâti" are spelled out in detail in the same book: it is to climb to great height through the use of modern frame technique and is to be oriented to the compass points (like the visual arts center). It is to be served by the distinct formal element of circulation ("two completely distinct adventures—to live, to circulate"; p. 68, my translation) which bears traffic rapidly to and from country and city. The circulation is to be surrounded by greenery and free to follow the sinuous topography of the site. This modern city is to obey the daily rhythms of the sun. Greenery and circulation are to be combined with buildings according to the theoretical prescriptions of the radiant city.

I think it possible that the cube at the heart of the visual arts center is, like the S-ramp, one of Le Corbusier's urbanistic metaphors, representing in this case the built forms of the city. The freehand curves bearing greenery on their terraces seem to represent the other major element of the radiant city, nature brought into contact with circulation and with buildings at the city's heart. It is unlikely to me that, in his only American building, Le Corbusier would have suddenly abandoned a town planning polemic towards the United States that had been going on for over twenty years. The symbols of his remedy for the problems of American cities were first stated in writing (the cube in *Sur les quatres routes*, the S-shape in *When the Cathedrals Were White*), and they represent simply a plea for the harmoniously organized, high density, centralized city, as against haphazard and wasteful

71

suburban sprawl, which Le Corbusier understood to be fundamentally disruptive of communal life.

Formally the rectangular shape seemed to emphasize the stability of a central mass set about with radiating curves. The S-ramp ran through the middle and was turned back on itself at Quincy Street so that it would catch the circulation from the Yard and further decrease the gradient. On the same drawing the architect placed an interior ramp running from third to fourth floors parallel to the main ramp. All the levels were marked with numbers denoting ceiling heights—2.96 meters, 7.48 meters, and so on—and the ramp was shown touching at the second level, giving access to the red backward extension. Allowing 0.86 meters for the slab plus beam, it followed that the point of contact with the ramp had to be 3.82 meters above the base figure. In extending that far back, the red space required the destruction of a tree that the architect carefully marked and went to great pains to save. Apart from this backward extension the scheme possessed an elegant compactness. As a comparative cipher of his centralized scheme, he traced the circle from a sketch of April 11 onto his plan. This only served to emphasize the ungainliness of the red space. Moreover, the three-meter height that the ramp had to achieve from the sidewalk of Prescott Street (probably some way below the base level) made for an impossible gradient.

The circle, which was traced from the April 11 drawing, was more than simply a comparative cipher, however, and more than a zoning device for calculating the "center of gravity." It was what Jullian has since referred to as "a mechanism" in response to which Le Corbusier later put in "eventualities and virtualities"—a sort of master generator of the building's form, an initial statement at the start of a dialogue. And if the other forms resulted from a reaction to this primary form, they nonetheless remained linked to it: in this case the circle lies at the center of a Cubist continuous line, like the line in a Le Corbusier painting that becomes one form, then another, without the brush leaving the canvas: a general form comes first and is modified to suit particular conditions.[20]

Then Jullian added up his floor heights and checked his figures on an adding machine. These figures are of great interest because the constricted site and desire for ramp access meant that the site size and floor heights were in direct relationship. As his zero he took 70 centimeters below ground level, as it then was, in the center of the circle. He then computed a floor-to-ceiling height of 3.66 meters and a floor (slab plus beam) thickness of 0.86 meters.[21] His arrayed floor heights read as follows: N1, 3.82 meters; N2, 8.34 meters; N3, 12.86 meters; N4, 17.38 meters. But on the adding machine ticket there was another figure, 21.90, which suggests he was thinking of going up another story, and this is confirmed by a note scrawled on the ticket: "atelier d'artistes toit plus m" ("meters more for artist's roof studio"). To curtail the backward extension of the second level and to make room for the ramp to rise with reasonable gradients, it had been necessary to expand the structure upwards.

But on this difficult site—difficult in the vertical as well as the horizontal dimension—further measures were necessary, measures that tended to contradict the aesthetic and theoretical idea of the piloti liberating the ground by lifting the building's body into space. The slope of the site made it necessary to dig part of the building into the ground (the slope had also influenced the placement of the Quincy Street studio at the third level so that the pilotis would not seem jammed into it); to fit the functions and the ramps onto the site, it was also necessary to expand the structure downwards.

On the same date, April 14, Le Corbusier in another drawing cut back the extension, saved the tree, and put the lost area back on top of the building in the two studios for visiting artists that nestled together on the roof, just back from the edge, with their own miniature roof garden in front (fig. 61). The studios were entered from the top of the elevator tower by a covered corridor. The tower was placed forward to the southwest corner. The tree was only saved by a device like that used in a similar situation at the Maison La Roche of 1923: a small notch was cut out of the back end of the studio. This notch, the curve to the Faculty Club side (slightly concave giving a flue effect), the new placement of the elevator tower, and the spine of the ramp gave a longitudinal orientation. There was an inescapable sense of the Quincy Street side being the front, the Prescott one the back.

The soft, billowing curves mark this out as one of the most sensitively drawn plans of the entire design process, but in retrospect the plan is astonishing for the information it contains. In a blow the architects had captured the final forms of the building. The main forms were thus confidently achieved in the miraculously short time of two weeks from the first sketch—and before Reynolds' mid-April letter arrived with its networks, diagrams, and program refinements (4-11-60). Though these curves were sanctioned by Le Corbusier, they were first suggested in rough by another member of the atelier, Andreini. He recalls that Jullian did not want curves "dictated by architectural considerations" and asked him on the spur of the moment to suggest the outline.[22] Le Corbusier concurred in the desire for "free curves." Again they were made in thick paper cut to shape. A transference sketch was also made, but like some other working sketches of the project, this was thrown away the day it was done.

These were the final forms, but it should be emphasized that the core of the idea had been grasped in the first sketch. The long period of gestation had allowed a thorough synthesis; the born idea carried its own unity and configuration of rules by which the creator felt bound to play. An insight into the process, and into possible interference with it, is offered in the last essay Le Corbusier wrote, a month before his death.

> Yes, the general rule commanding life is play . . . When a client of mine stuffs my head with such and such little requirements, I accept, yes, I accept up to the point where I say no, impossible! For then the thing gets out of the rules of my game, of the game in question, the game of this given house, of this combination whose rules have emerged at the moment of creation, have developed, affirmed themselves, becoming commanding.[23]

And there was magnificent ease in the way this living thing, with its own determining laws, was left aside for nearly three weeks.

The building had been discovered as a "vue vol d'oiseau" ("bird's eye view"), a type of visualization of all the floors at once that Le Corbusier traced to his experiences of buildings and landscapes seen from airplane windows.[24] In color this mode of visualization had noticeable close affinities with the "simultaneous" views of fragmented elements, overlapping contours, transparent planes, and fused images of Cubist pictures.

On May 1, the architect made the layers into a series of plans (figs. 62, 63, 64, 65, 116) for closer examination. In some cases the floor immediately above or below was also included. At the fifth level, his visiting artists' studios were approached by a passageway from the elevator tower. The freight lift made its first appearance at the eastern end of the building. A strong axis between both towers was maintained by the interior ramp. The exhibition space at the fourth level was expanded to the north end to provide space for the access passageway above and to allow a little extra for the interior ramp. The purity of the central square was violated slightly by this. Loose partitions were set down in the space.

The third level (fig. 116) was studied in a detailed plan and in a view relating it and the second level to the surrounding buildings—as if two images had been recorded a few seconds apart from an aircraft slowly rising above the site. The third level was the heart of Le Corbusier's circulation conception, the life of the building on the interior; its exterior also emanated furthest into the surrounding space—the flow of space becomes clear from the longer view. It is as if the building were sensitized to its hard-edged neo-Georgian context and simultaneously, to the movements of its internal circulation—truly an organism. The curves to the south side, for example, were made slightly concave, withdrawing from the jutting form of the Faculty Club dining room; those to the north were made convex, swelling out towards the Yard. The building and ramp sat neatly in the diagonal slot of space between the two neighboring buildings, in a responsive state of flux to them.

The parallel ramps gave a strong backbone to the project, but the third level around the interior ramp was somewhat cramped. An arrow was shown squeezing its way around the edge of the ramp by the freight lift. To one side appeared a question mark. Elsewhere circulation was indicated by arrows. The painting studio and storage ap-

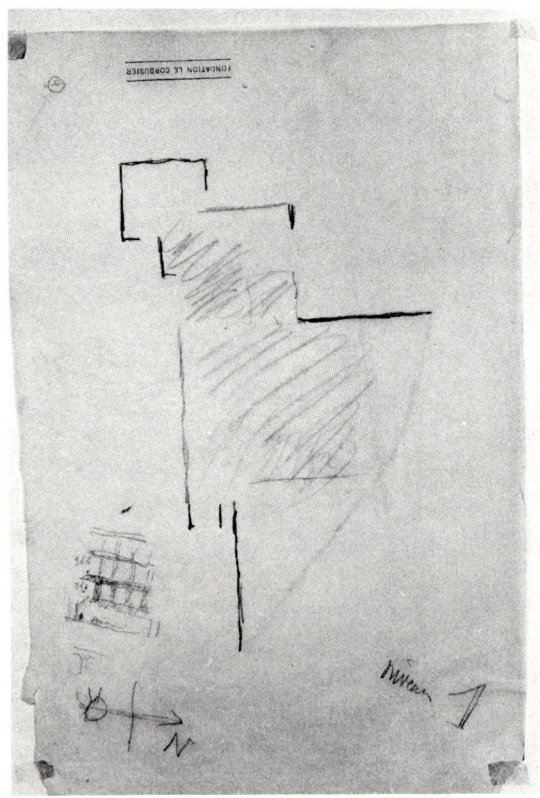 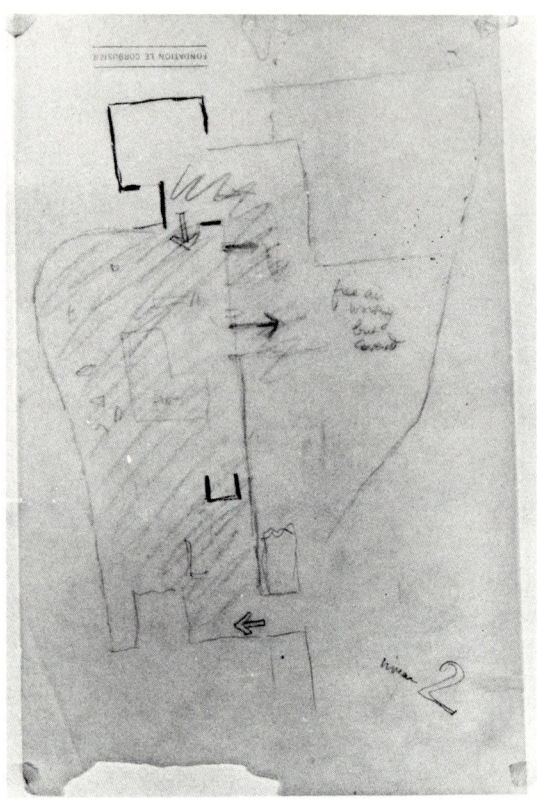

62. *Plan of level 1 (ground floor), Le Corbusier, May 1, 1960. (1:200; 37.5 × 25 cm; onion skin.) Entrance lobby and auditorium are situated here. The plan opens out into the surroundings to include views. Colored crayons are used on all drawings of this date to distinguish walls (black), fenestration (blue when protected from sun, orange when partly protected, red when fully exposed), main spaces (ochre), and greenery. At bottom left the architect sketches a structural section examining a lattice beam at level 2 (to bridge the auditorium) and a mushroom capital at a column head.*

63. *Plan of level 2, Le Corbusier, May 1, 1960. (1:200; 36.5 × 25 cm; onion skin.) Sculpture studio to the left, covered garden to the right. Over the latter the architect wrote in English: "free air working but covered."*

64. *Plan of level 4, Le Corbusier, May 1, 1960. (1 : 200; 38 × 23 cm; onion skin.) The exhibition space is entered from the interior ramp (which rises from level 3), from the passenger elevators to the west end, or from the freight lift at the east end. The spine-like quality of interior circulation is evident. Le Corbusier indicates his concern for the sun by color coding the fenestration and by drawing in pencil an "extra" sun to the southwest to examine whether or not sun protection should be provided on the Quincy Street facade.*

peared to the north, with partitions; director's studio and administrative offices were to the south, without them. The inclusion of storage areas was the only sign of reaction to the material sent by the Committee for the Practice of the Visual Arts during the second week of April—testimony to the way Cambridge requirements could be accommodated easily with a free plan without effect on the overall form or the integrating rules of the building.

If the third level was a sort of "piano nobile," the second was its base (fig. 63). Access was shown by means of arrows—from the main ramp at the back, from the elevators at the front, across the spine of the building midway underneath the main ramp. The sculpture studio lay to the south with a storage area provided. Opposite it was a garden, marked in English, "free air working, but covered"—a terrace in the air.

Finally, the first floor was drawn to contain the auditorium and entrance lobby, its lines invading the surrounding space like a Mies plan of the twenties (fig. 62). To one side appeared a small sketch of a section showing a lattice beam in orange to deal with the auditorium space.

As drawings, these were strikingly bold roughs of the building done with colored crayon stubs of blue and black, orange and green, yellow and red. The lines were strong and vibrant and gave energy to the biomorphic plan forms. Blue signified glass out of the range of the sun (the Quincy Street curve was safe for ondulatoires alone); red and orange signified glass to face the rays (red for intense sun—Sert's vital notes on the climate had just arrived and brise-soleil made their first appearance in frames tacked onto the windows); black signified ordinary concrete walls; green, the roof gardens; and ochre, the main functional spaces. The brise-soleil calculations were made by Jullian on the basis of Sert's data and for a room height of 3 m 66 (fig. 66).

The same day, May 1, 1960, Le Corbusier reconstituted the separate layers into a "vue vol d'oiseau ("birds'-eye view"; fig. 65) made by tracing directly over the "vue d'avion" ("aerial view") of April 14 (fig. 61). This May drawing also served as a study of the fifth level, showing the visiting artists' studios neatly in position. More clearly than its

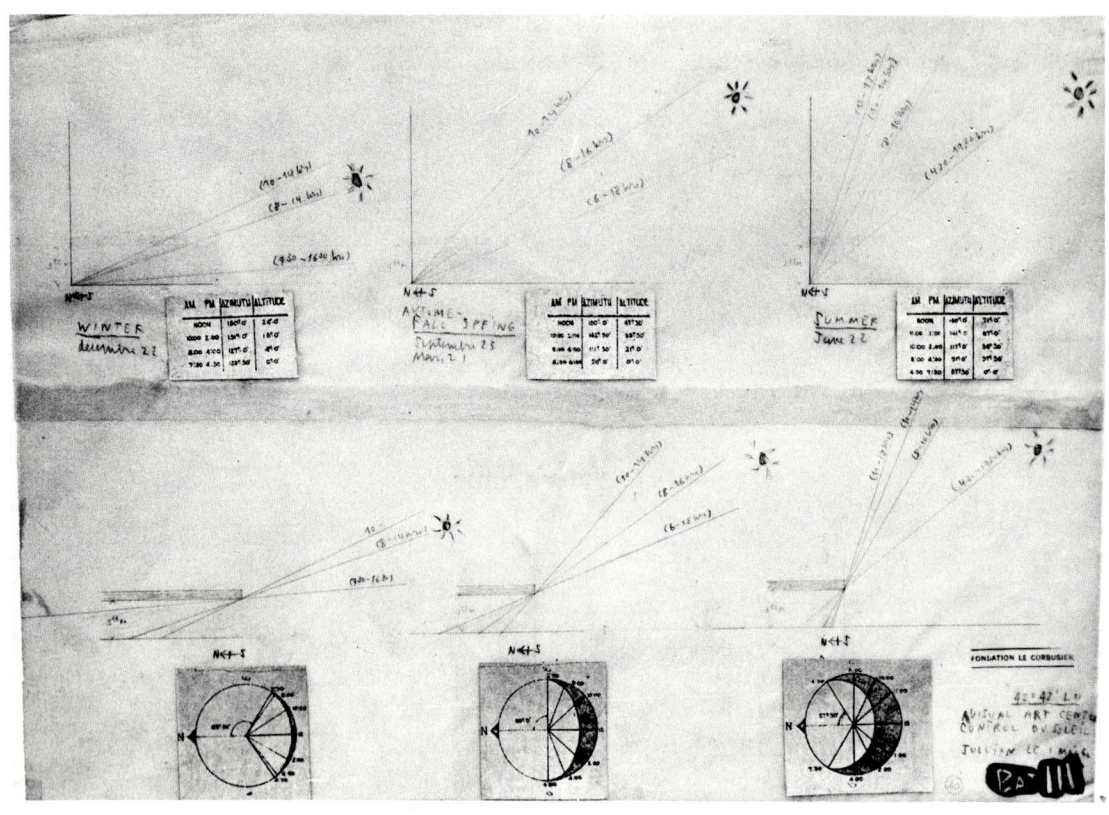

66. *Brise-soleil angle calculations, Jullian, May 1, 1960. (1:200; 40 × 55 cm; thick paper.) On the same day that Sert's climatic data arrives, Jullian calculates the main angles and spacings for the fins using 3.66 meters as his floor-to-ceiling height.*

predecessor, though, it demonstrated the formal qualities of the building as a whole. As well as giving information, color coding had the effect of suggesting pictorial depth and the spatial separation of the various levels. In purely formal terms one is struck by the visual repetition of rectangular elements (fifth level studios, stair tower, notch to the rear) and their subordination to and resonance with the larger master rectangle at the center. The counterpoint of the contrasting curves swaying and pulling away from the stable central mass is also most clear in this drawing. The whole is integral, fused, overlapping, dynamic rather than particular, additive, static, made exclusively from discrete parts. The whole has life; it is in tension. It would seem that to the architect the site was a neutral field like a bare canvas to be energized by the insertion of curved and rectangular forms. With a simplicity of means born from years of experiment in painting, the artist thus visualized and portrayed his finished building.

Attached with cellophane tape to the May 1 drawing was a sheet of structural studies consisting of a half dozen sketches done in light pencil, addressed to various problems (fig. 65). The main structure was envisaged as a pilotis and slab system with beams, in reinforced concrete, but there were difficulties in jointing such a structural skeleton to some other parts of the building. One such part was the lattice beam over the auditorium (which was christened "les portiques," "the porticoes," for the trellis-like effect it made in the roof garden above); another problematic joint was at the building edge, where beams and ondulatoires met with some difficulty. Even the fenestration seemed to cause some problems: Le Corbusier sketched brise-soleil and ondulatoires together, but still gave no indication of their fixing and precise interrelationship: this threw a shadow of doubt over the fenestration altogether. For the moment the architect pushed this problem aside: when the structure came to be drawn for the presentation, he simply dropped the beams without suggesting any other means of reinforcement at the column heads.

The next day Jullian traced out these results using a ruler and T-square to make careful scale drawings (fig. 67), taking care to round off the northeast corner, which before had clashed with a curve. The next day he set a grid of pilotis in place within the prescribed outlines (fig. 68). The contours were conceived first and the structure was put in place later, though of course a structure of this kind had been envisaged all along. There could be no clearer demonstration of that Corbusian "point of architecture," the independence of elevation and structure, than the *order* in which the visual arts center was designed: the assumed structural system had allowed Le Corbusier's and Andreini's formal instincts free rein.

Indeed, this sense of freedom may have been too much, bordering on a license that contained the seed of future conflicts between form, function, and structural means. The plans showed beams entering somewhat incongruously at various places (fig. 68) to deal with cantilevers, and spans made larger to accommodate circulation (for example, over the underpass on the Faculty Club side). A more noticeable and serious problem was the placement of pilotis just inside the glass between interior and exterior ramps: structure now blocked the gap from any use as a passageway

67. *Ruled plan of level 2, Jullian, May 2, 1960. (1:200; 45 × 23 cm; onion skin.) This is one of a series of ruled drawings done in early May to examine the project more closely, to analyze the eventual relationship of structure to plan shapes, and to begin preparing presentation drawings.*

68. *Ruled plan of level 1, Jullian, May 3, 1960. (1:200; 45.5 × 23 cm; onion skin.) Set square, ruler, and sharp pencil replace thick crayon as an attempt is made to coordinate the structural grid of pilotis with curved outlines. Here the grid is uneven in its spacing, and a mixture of transversal and longitudinal beams (signified by dotted lines) is used.*

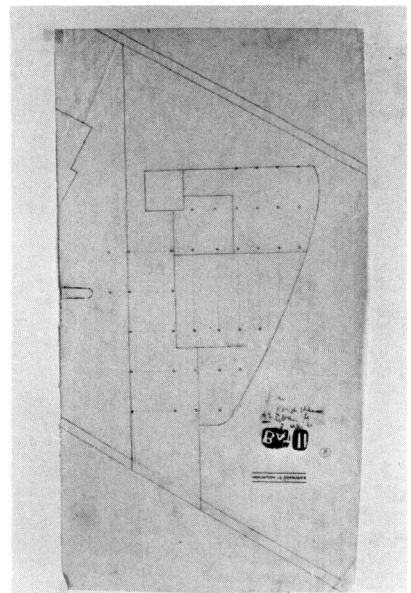

for objects from the freight lift to the painting studio; it would have been necessary to pass through the director's studio and by (if not through!) the administrative offices. The "architectural considerations" that Andreini had been asked to ignore had begun to assert themselves already.

In the next week the structure was studied for its relationship with the building's outlines in sections (fig. 69), and a model was made with pilotis in place (fig. 77). The "sections" were such convincing three-dimensional images that the term does not seem appropriate. Slabs were drawn in black without beams; spaces were shaded thin watery blue; ramp cuts, pilotis, and parapets pure white—hovering bands against the background. Jullian gave them titles like "petite rampe," "grande rampe," which cleverly focused attention on the subjects. In effect they were rough drafts of the presentation drawings. Fenestration was shown with ondulatoires but without brise-soleil: the latter did not appear again until June in the final presentation set.

The next step was to make tracings suitable for the production of prints (fig. 70). A number of sets of prints were made, some of which were cut up around the building's silhouettes then stuck onto plain paper backgrounds so that the architects could experiment with presentation colors and stencils. In sections the pink/brown color of the print strips was retained to indicate concrete, and blue crayon was used (as usual) to mean glass. In plan the print strips indicated functional spaces, and yellow crayon was employed to mean circulation. In addition, floor scorings "au Modulor" ("according to the Modulor") were incised in pen. Paper cutouts had their uses in the latest as well as the earliest stages of the project.

The plans were set aside for three weeks, while final presentation prints were being prepared from tracings; Le Corbusier and Jullian had completed their project with time to spare (fig. 73).

69. *Longitudinal section along main ramp with attached detail of stair tower, Jullian, May 10, 1960. (1:200; 44 × 65 cm; onion skin.) In the second week of May a series of studies was done on thick tracing paper and in pen and ink to analyze the relationship of structure and form. Pen lines and black and white hatching give a sense of space to the section, enabling the perception of three-dimensional relationships. The use of tape, transparent overlays, and odd bits of paper for effects is typical of the craft methods used in the atelier.*

70. *Longitudinal section BB, Jullian, May 12, 1960. (1:200; 43 × 70 cm; thick paper.) At the end of the second week in May, a master set of ruled pen-and-ink drawings was prepared with stenciled lettering, annotations, and so on. Transparent copies were made from these so that prints could be produced in the future. The main step to the presentation drawings lay in the choice of colors.*

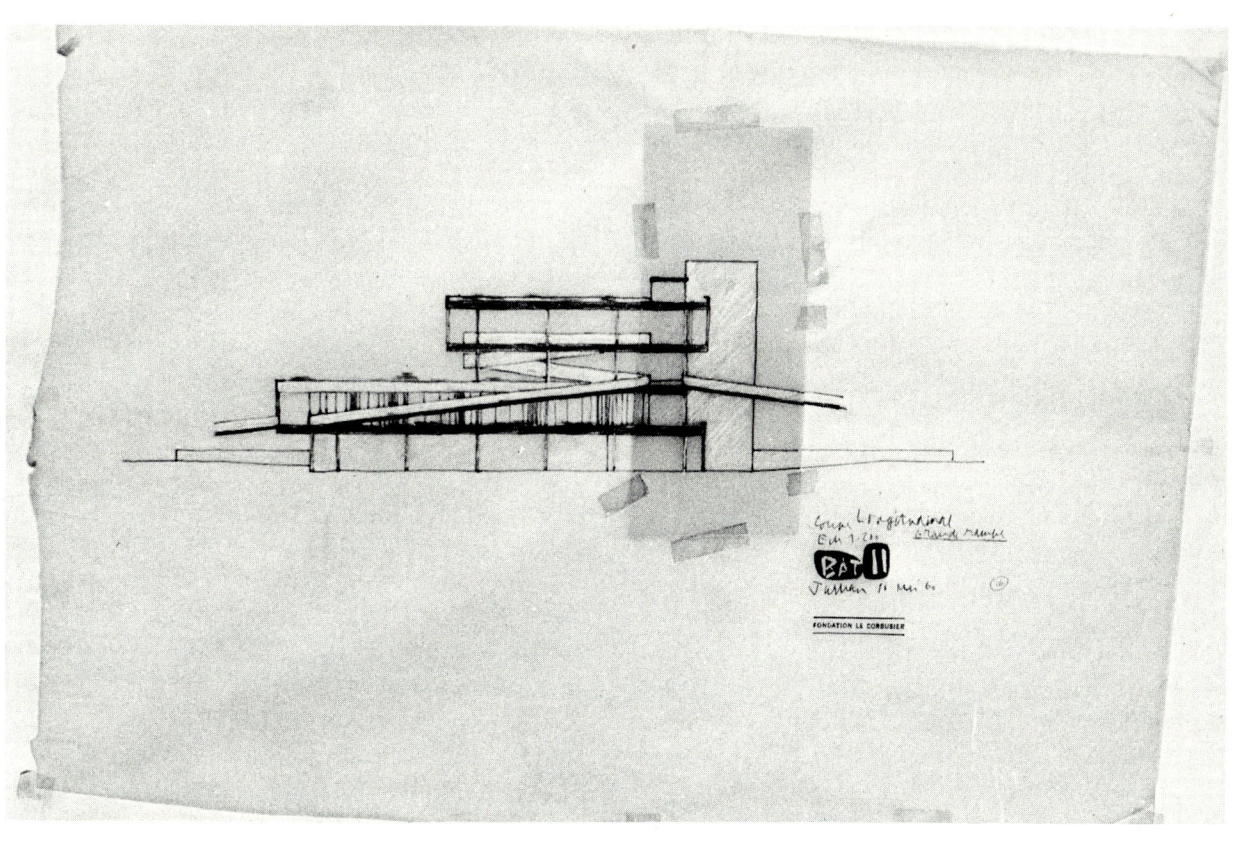
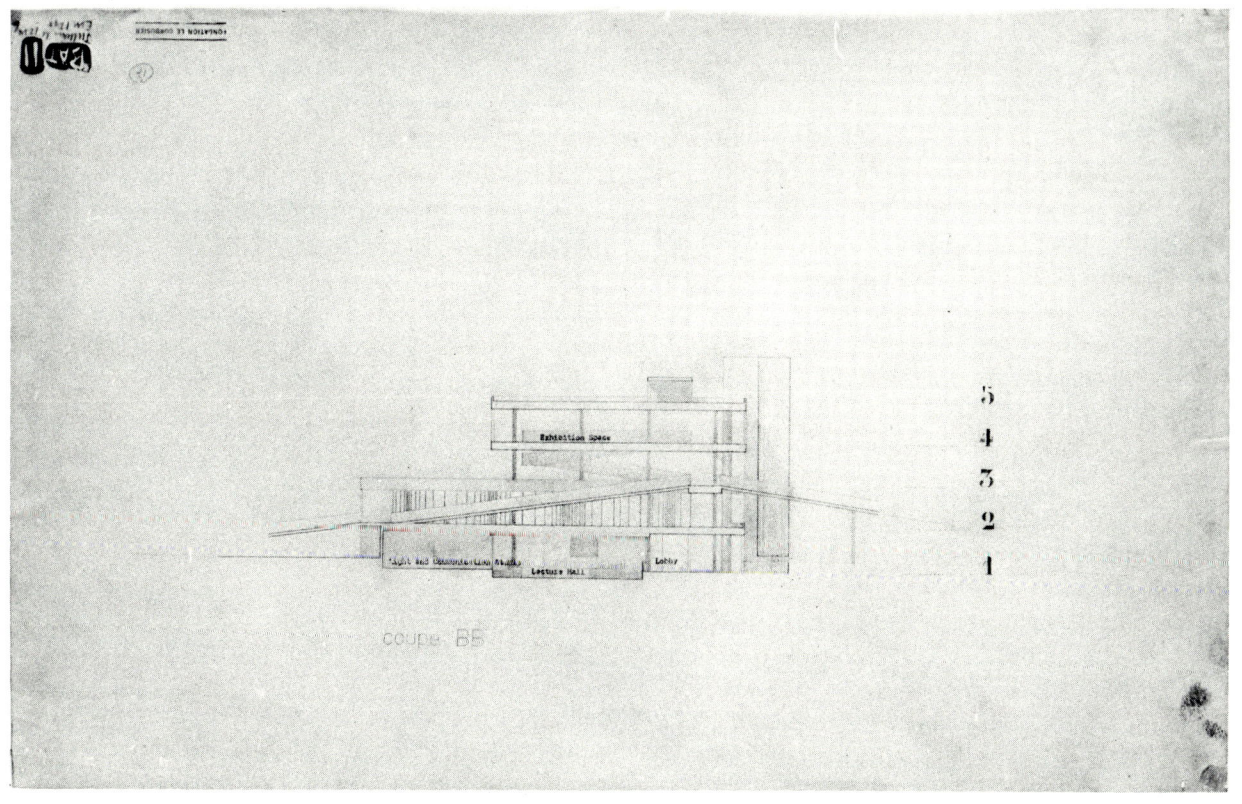

Before following the project back to Cambridge to be reviewed by the client, I would like to attempt some further interpretation of the building's forms as understood from these preparatory drawings. Of all the drawings of the visual arts center, those of May 1 provide perhaps the most stunning images, and invite comparison with Le Corbusier's late paintings and sculptures.

Amusingly, Jullian has described the way in which a mural at 35 rue de Sèvres was raided for its curves.[25] The anecdote serves only too literally to underline the fundamental formal correspondences between Le Corbusier's activities as an artist in whatever medium. It seems especially appropriate that he should have generated the image of a visual arts center from plans so closely related to his experiments in painting, sculpture, tapestry, and engraving.

The sculptures offer the closest formal similarity. These are executed in wood with rough chiseled edges and are frequently brightly colored like the plans. Their forms are usually anthropomorphic with strong references to actual objects in the outside world. But the same curve that might seem to represent a foot or an organism becomes, in a matter of inches, a simple abstract arabesque. One piece in particular comes to my mind to compare to the visual arts center plans: a "sculpture acoustique" ("acoustic sculpture") with silhouetted "ear" held up on a stalk (fig. 71). In the sculptures the meaning is partly overt, but there are deeper layers of content; in the late paintings deliberate ambiguity between detached arabesque and the curves of a woman or landscape implies a universe of forms with many levels of reference and suggests an ideographic method for portraying the artist's subconscious symbols.

The sculptures had deep personal meaning to Le Corbusier that would be difficult to fathom. There was an erotic ingredient, certainly, but also a humorous, Surrealist overlay. Thus, during World War II, when he was living in the Pyrenees, he invented some sculptures of bulbous humanoids which he christened his "Ubus." These primitivist creations look forward to the forms of the postwar buildings containing "hints of landscape, of lagoons, or beaches or other things" (the landscape being especially significant in this case), and he forecast an Ubu raised on posts.[26] Ubu was, of course, Alfred Jarry's monstrous and preposterous creation, and Le Corbusier, like Jarry, relied on the reversal of normal categories and expectations for effects of profound irony and wit. These twists and turns, tricks and contradictions permeate Le Corbusier's works and show that if Cubism influenced his architecture by opening the way to pure form, it was no less important to Le Corbusier as a source of puns, double-entendres, ambiguities, and a continual game on the borderlines between fact and artifice, the banal and the heroic, nature and art. The images under review—the May 1 drawings—seem themselves to shift between pure forms and recognizable objects, to be images with multiple levels of meaning.

The curved forms, for example, may be interpreted on the basis of a wide variety of possible associations. Le Corbusier himself referred to the curve jutting out over Quincy Street as the "coup de poing"—a term which might be intepreted either as a prehistoric implement or else literally as a "punch." Jullian referred casually to the curved forms as "mandolins" (thus recalling the influence from the Heroic period of Cubism), while at Harvard, references were made to grand pianos.[27] However, the architect's intentions, which were not necessarily fully conscious, seem to be along the organic, biological line, especially since the documentation suggests he was seeking images of flux, symbols of circulation, and antimechanistic associations.[28] It is perhaps to the pebbles, bean pods, shells, organisms, and other "objets à réaction poétique" ("objects with a poetic effect") dotted about the notebooks that one should turn for one set of visual sources of these designs.

Although the private visual universe of forms and associations to which the visual arts center plans belong is rich, complex, and partly obscure, it so happens that similar forms had a fairly precise and explicit meaning defined by the architect in previous architectural and urbanistic contexts. Two of these previous crystallizations seem particularly relevant to the visual arts center. The first is Le Corbusier's conventional representation of landscaping in his "radiant city" and "unité" plans, which employ free-form curves like those of the visual arts center to border water and earthworks, in firm contradistinction to built forms that are rectangular; the second is his metaphor of a pair of lungs to mean the provision of fresh air in the city through the planting of trees and the liberation of traffic circulation in the city's core (fig. 72). Employed with this sense, the metaphor is illustrated in several of Le Corbusier's major works on urbanism and has strong connotations of urban surgery[29]—the healing of the city's biology through correct town planning. The visual arts center's forms, with its curves on either side of a central tract of circulation, do indeed bear an uncanny resemblance to a pair of lungs.

Such associations as these would be profoundly consonant with the urbanistic symbolism of the S-ramp and "built cube." Thus, on one level the visual arts center's forms would seem to refer to a city correctly planned according to the principles of the radiant city—the principles Le Corbusier had tried to persuade Americans to accept during his 1935 visit and in numerous publications after the visit. The city, Le Corbusier's central American obsession, was, in his eyes, an indicator of social health. His view of the United States had been based disproportionately on New York—the miniature workhouse of the new era whose technical features fascinated and horrified him and whose principal shortcomings concerned the lack of space, light, and greenery between the tall buildings, the grid street pattern with traffic lights interrupting the flow of circulation, and the surrounding suburban sprawl. Indeed, Le Corbusier pinpointed the suburb as the central problem of the United States in an essay entitled (and one cannot stress the import of this title enough) "What Is the Problem of America?": "The suburb is the great problem of the USA . . . Manhattan is so antagonistic to the fundamental needs of the human heart that the one idea of everybody is to escape. To get out . . . to see the sky. To live where there are trees and look on grass. To escape forever from the noise and racket of the city. All that remains is the dream—the dream of being free . . . the hours spent daily in the metros, buses and pullmans [cause] the destruction of that communal life which is the marrow of a nation" But Le Corbusier also had an answer to this social disruption: not to retreat further into the country-

71. *"Ubu" sculpture, Le Corbusier, 1947, which displays affinities with the biological forms of the visual arts center.*

72. *A pair of lungs from Le Corbusier's book* Urbanisme *(1925). Here lungs have metaphorical significance as a model for the city whose air and traffic circulate freely, and whose greenery and open space allow it to "breathe."*

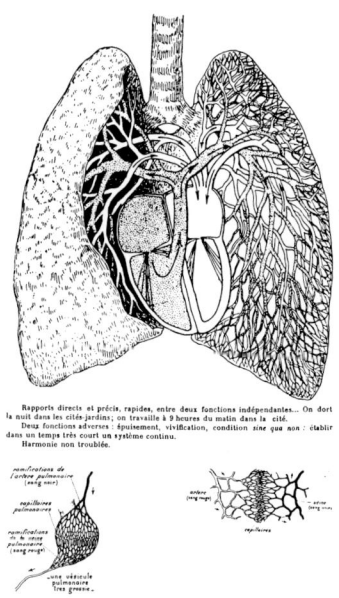

side and turn away completely from industrial life and the city, but to return to the city and replan it completely, using industrial technique: "You can have lots of trees, the whole expanse of the sky and immense open spaces free from cars if only you will return to the city and make it into a 'ville radieuse.'"[30]

And in the United States Le Corbusier found the raw technical tools at hand to achieve this dream of a vertical city with countryside at its heart; all they required, he thought, was the guidance of his own urbanistic prescriptions. A corollary of his belief in the disastrous effects of the unplanned modern city on the tenor of modern social life was an equally tenacious belief in the social ordering potential of the architect through his form giving capacities—as if harmony in matter (architecture) could be expected to bring a social and spiritual harmony with it.

My suggestion is, then, that the primary forms of the visual arts center should be understood on one level as the architect's metaphorical answer to what he had defined as the problem of America. While the preliminary drawings reveal Le Corbusier to have created Harvard's visual arts center in the image of an abstract sculpture, fusing formal devices from the Heroic period of Cubism and from his own earlier explorations as a painter, I believe that these forms have an even wider range of meaning, that we have to do here, as in Le Corbusier's architecture generally, with a synthetic and syncretistic imagery of great complexity. "To make a plan is to determine and fix ideas," writes the architect in *Vers une architecture*. "In a form so condensed that it seems as clear as a crystal and like a geometrical figure, [a plan] contains an enormous quantity of ideas and the impulse of an intention."[31] His intention here was to gather into a single statement those of his doctrines he had singled out as relevant for what he had decided would be his only building in the United States.

73. *View of the atelier at 35, rue de Sèvres, early June 1960. The presentation aerial view of the visual arts center lies complete and ready for Le Corbusier's departure to Cambridge for his second visit.*

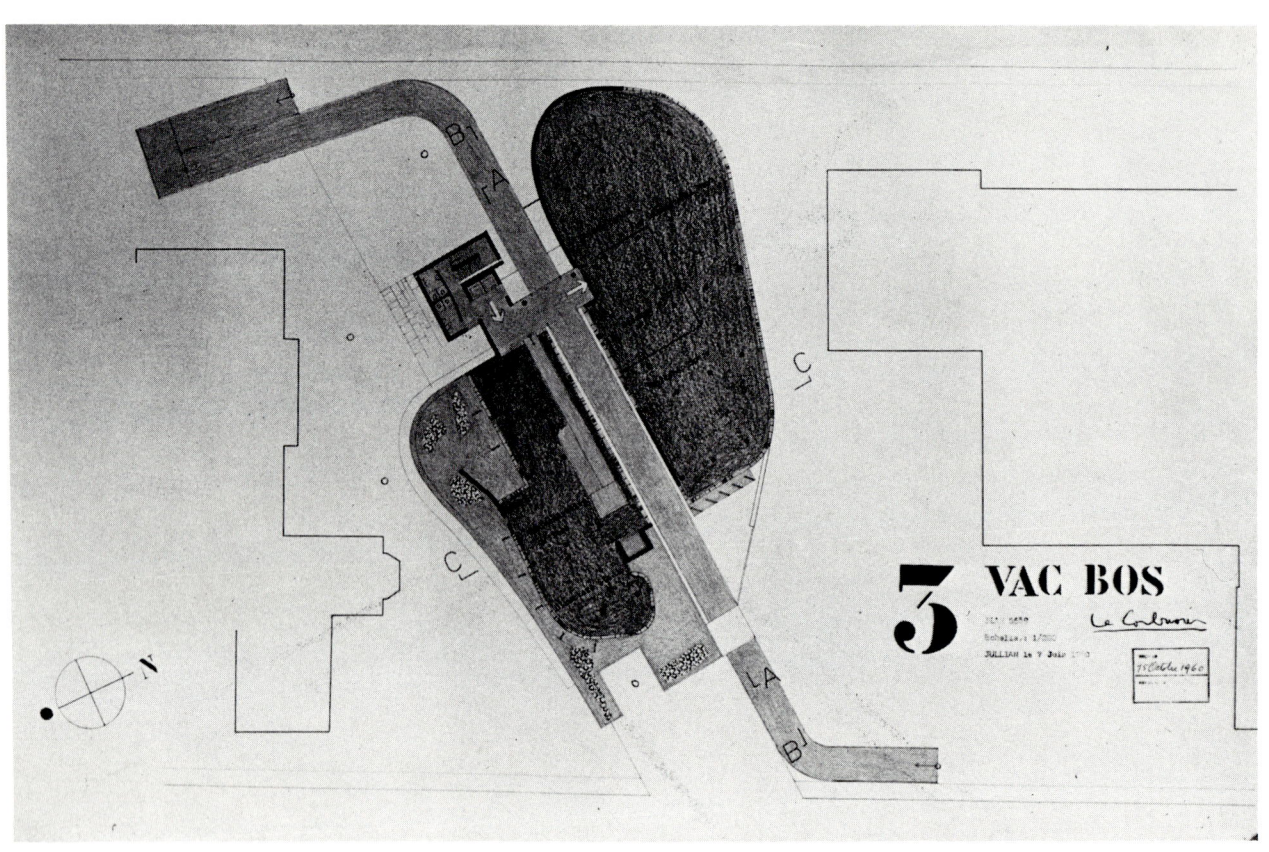

4. THE PRESENTATION

The "old man," however, has performed even better than we had all expected, and all of us here in Cambridge are in a state of euphoria.

A. D. Trottenberg

When Le Corbusier flew to America in June 1960 with his model of the visual arts center, he looked down from the window of his Boeing at the coast of the United States far below, fringed with white beaches and the shadows of clouds drifting slowly over the greenery of the hinterland. He took out his notebook, sketched the furrows of cloud beneath, and scrawled the phrase, "une fois, deux fois, répétition latéralement"; then looking through to the approaching land: "de Terre Neuve à Boston" (fig. 74).

The pressure of work had been enormous—not from Boston so much as from Chandigarh. The notebooks of the period give glimpses of his mind at work, frequently in airplanes. At the beginning of the year he was mulling over ideas on the "Poème Electronique" and an "institute of audio visual teaching and preservation" for Chandigarh—both schemes with a bearing on the visual arts center problem. His attention shifted from current plans to his own past—"L'Eplattenier 1907, Perret 1908," "UNESCO trois vetos" ("UNESCO three vetos")—to a magazine article for Jullian, to Mont Blanc, or the Red Sea, or the groves outside

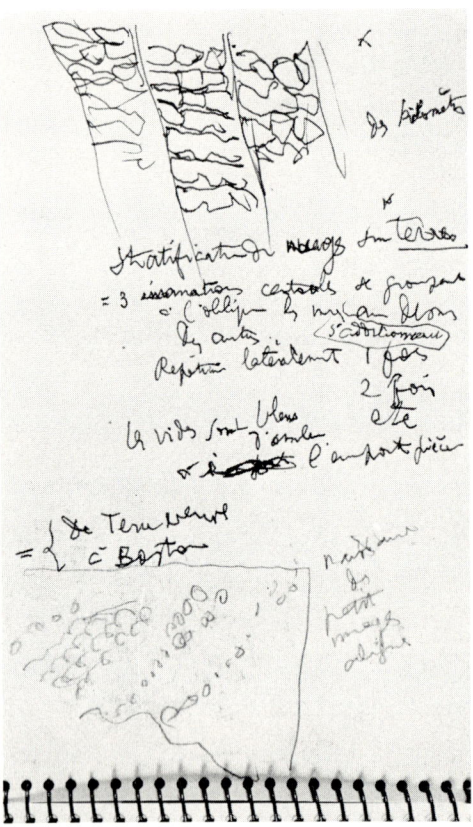

74. *Sketches of clouds from Le Corbusier's notebook P61 which he carried with him in the Boeing from Paris to Boston. Alongside one sketch he writes "de Terre Neuve à Boston."*

Baghdad beneath the airplane. There are occasional dogmatic remarks—"L-C considère . . ." ("L-C considers . . .")—a quote from Valéry, a sketch from Chandigarh, then a detailed sketch of accommodation on board the Boeing.[1]

Aircraft fascinated Le Corbusier in the twenties for their lightweight economic construction and their machine age associations, which he attempted to transpose into architecture. Later, when he was preoccupied with town plans, the airplane became his indispensable tool for observation, and also provided opportunities for a poetry of cosmic events: the sweep of mountain ranges, the shifting of weather in banks of clouds, geological formations, the rhythm of the sun. In shifting clouds of vapor and waterways ribboning the landscapes, he discovered images of flux and flow—as in the airfoil forms of airplanes. Air journeys offered him detachment—thought above the level of passing events—and distance from himself: there is an eerie sense in his autobiographical aircraft jottings of a man who looks back on his life as if it were a part of history already complete.[2]

The visual arts center crystallized in May, about a month earlier than anticipated. His drawn contributions were made in a month from April 1 to May 1; Jullian's part in the project had thus been considerable. In June prints were made of plans and sections which were then carefully prepared for presentation with colored washes and stenciled lettering. Outline tracings were included with the presentation set, to enable Sert to make further prints. The spring model was done up with white paint.[3] Reservations were made for a flight from Orly to Boston on June 11, returning the 14th. Special provision was made for a sixteen kilogram case containing the model. A note was dashed off at the last minute:

> Je vous réitère la même prière instante: pas de cérémonie, pas de banquets, pas de discours. Je suis crevé de surmenage. Je conserve le coeur tranquille; je ne suis pas devenu misanthrope mais tout cela m'enquiquine. J'aime mieux l'amitié pure et simple; la vôtre, si vous le voulez bien.
>
> I reiterate to you the same earnest prayer: no ceremony, no banquets, no speeches. I am dead

from overwork. I am keeping my heart calm; I have not become a misanthrope but all that irritates the hell out of me. I much prefer friendship pure and simple; yours if you would like it. (6-7-60)

Actually, Le Corbusier had been very gregarious during the first trip and had ended up leaving everyone else exhausted.[4] Sert had even reached the point where he exclaimed that for the sake of his own health he would be glad when his guest had left. Le Corbusier had been indefatigable and had never stopped talking. He had risen early, done business in the morning, taken a nap in the afternoon (when Sert had crept away to deal with his own affairs), and had been fully alive in the evening for cocktails or whatever else Sert had arranged. At seventy-two Le Corbusier had succeeded in running everyone else off his feet.

Le Corbusier's behavior in Cambridge had tended to contradict the rumor that he had become extremely reclusive in his late years. He may have been distant in Paris—bitterness was written into his features—but in Cambridge bitterness had been temporarily laid aside. "You have real friends at Harvard," Sert told him in one letter (10-6-59). This was true and it drew Le Corbusier out of himself. Many old acquaintances were in the area. As well as the student party with the Modulor mural, there had been a warm evening at Sert's in November when Sert's partners, their wives, and such old companions from CIAM as Jacqueline Tyrwhitt and "Captain" Giedion had been present. John Nickols, Sert's office manager, was also there. He jotted down the following description soon afterwards:

I looked over the old chap. He is a man of ordinary stature 5′8″ or 9″, bent slightly forward. Sert said he is now 72 years old. Zalewski said he is slightly deaf. His face is a little heavy, the great black spectacles rode low on his bulbous nose. The wrinkles that creased his forehead above two black heaps of eyebrows were perpetual. As he talked he gestured slowly with his two large hands, the fingers outstretched and his flat hands now together, now in a gesture of separation. From time to time he lifted the large glass from which he drank. He wore a dark flannel suit with wide pointed lapels, a bow tie, blue with red figures, flower like, an inch wide, and a pale blue shirt. A white handkerchief was tucked low in his breast pocket. He appeared to be a polite and proper man anxious to be friendly and kind. He was most polite.[5]

A genuine affection developed towards Le Corbusier so that when he returned in June, it was to an atmosphere that dispelled his prejudices. He recovered quickly from his flight and was curious about everything and everybody. Sert took him to libraries and (as if to make a point) showed him French periodicals and newspapers. They strolled together in the Yard (fig. 75) with Jackson and Zalewski and revisited the site, which he saw in ideal, sunny conditions. His photograph was taken in front of the trees of the old Fogg garden (fig. 76).

There were no banquets or speeches, just a quiet dinner party and a cocktail party at Sert's. When the guests arrived they found Le Corbusier standing among the early arrivals in the patio to the rear of Sert's house drinking Pernod. During the day he had spoken in English, but now he spoke in French. His conversation was serious—mostly on architectural matters. But it was interrupted by a squeal and peals of laughter from the end of the garden: a female guest had succeeded in getting stuck in the vertical pivoting aérateur Sert had installed in the patio wall to catch the summer breezes. Sert tried pushing her then pulling her, but in the end she disappeared except for a leg and an arm. Had the aérateur now become a door? Intense architectural debate of this question followed, while the excluded one found her way back to the front door. "Is it Modulor?" someone shouted. "Of course it is Modulor," said Sert. In a flash Le Corbusier stepped forward, applying his steel measure to the opening. He misread in inches, then read correctly in centimeters: it was Modulor.

"This was his forte, the measure of man, or more properly the measure of woman," commented Nickols. "We have changed the Modulor, you know, to six feet," said Le Corbusier. "Because of the English, because they are larger, we have changed it to six feet." A period of intensive mea-

75. *Le Corbusier and José Luis Sert in Harvard Yard, June 1960. In the background to the right is the gray granite Boylston Hall. The Yard here appears in perfect "radiant city" conditions.*

surement ensued. Ron Gourley volunteered himself as six feet tall; Nickols measured his foot with Le Corbusier's tape; Le Corbusier said he thought feet and inches were stupid, then corrected himself, "maybe not stupid, no good." Le Corbusier started measuring everything but got tired. "You are young," he said, "but I must sit down." Over half a dozen stools of the kind that had intrigued Le Corbusier in his first visit stood on the patio, and he began measuring them to decide which was appropriate. Nickols pointed to a wide one. "No, no, it is not so wide!" said Le Corbusier (referring to his rear end) and sat down on a smaller one. With his exceptionally large hands he resembled the Modulor man in the sitting position. Nickols describes the rest.

> Shortly after he was up again. In the middle of a conversation I glanced over the top of the garden wall. The slow, long sweep of a jet trail curved through the evening sky . . . from the east it rose over the high elms and arched across the heavens. I touched Corbu lightly on the shoulder to draw his attention. He backed across the terrace and onto the lawn to see more clearly. "It is beautiful," he said, "it is beautiful." He held his gaze aloft. Someone attempted to explain that it was not one plane but three. He did not understand. He stood entranced. In a moment another trail broke over the rooftop of the house, more to the northeast, a straight line steeply climbing into the heavens, spewing its slender cloud like a line engraved on the sky. Corbu appeared unable to turn his attention from the heavens until the vapour trail began to drift and fade from view. He lowered his head and walked slowly to the group.[6]

Even the serious business of the presentation was conducted in relaxed surroundings. There were two presentations in all: a small one to Sert and Trottenberg alone in Trottenberg's office (where Le Corbusier had looked down at the Yard), and the main one at Sert's home at a dinner party where Pusey, Trottenberg, and the Carpenters were the only other guests. The Carpenters had arranged to visit Cambridge in late May in any case, and were now meeting their architect for the first time.

The material of Le Corbusier's presentation comprised six plans (figs. 78–83), an aerial view (fig. 84), three sections (figs. 85, 86, 87), the model (fig. 77), and an accompanying note: "Construction of a Visual Arts Center." The drawings were colored yellow for circulation, red for the main functional spaces, gray for terraces and roof gardens, and blue for glass in sections. The note was written in two parts: a preamble on Le Corbusier's early experiences at La Chaux-de-Fonds, the disastrous effects of the rupture of head and hand, and so on; the second, a point-by-point breakdown of the building. The charming pidgin-English of the translation is preserved and the document quoted in its entirety.[7]

76. *Le Corbusier's "American photograph," June 1960. Asked by John Nickols, who took this picture, how he would like himself taken, he replied: "with verdure." Here he is seen alongside the site, by the greenery of the Fogg Museum garden.*

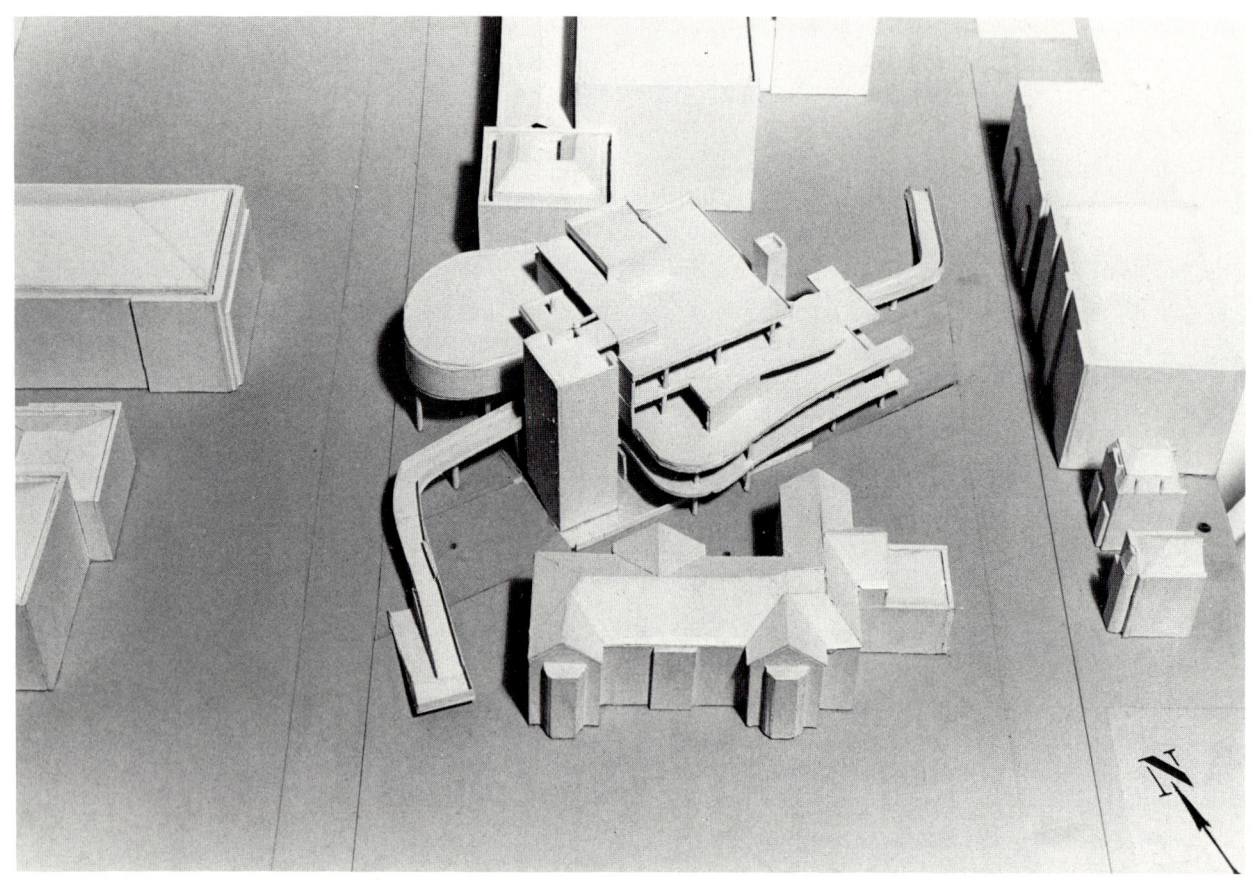

77. *The visual arts center presentation model, Le Corbusier and Jullian, May–June 1960. (1:200; 9 × 100 × 102 cm; wood, gray and white paint.) Here the building that might have been is seen from the south over the Faculty Club roof. The ramp and third level curve on the Quincy Street side (left) extend almost to the street, and the ramp end is cranked to gather circulation from the Yard.*

78. *Presentation plan of the basement, Le Corbusier and Jullian, June 7, 1960. (1:200; 43 × 70 cm; high quality thick paper.) The entire presentation set is carefully rendered in black ink and water color, with red for major functioning areas, yellow for circulation, and gray for ancillary and outside areas. In sections, light blue indicates glass.* VAC BOS, *the code name Le Corbusier gave to his project, stands for "visual arts center, Boston." The project was eventually discarded in favor of* VAC BOS II.

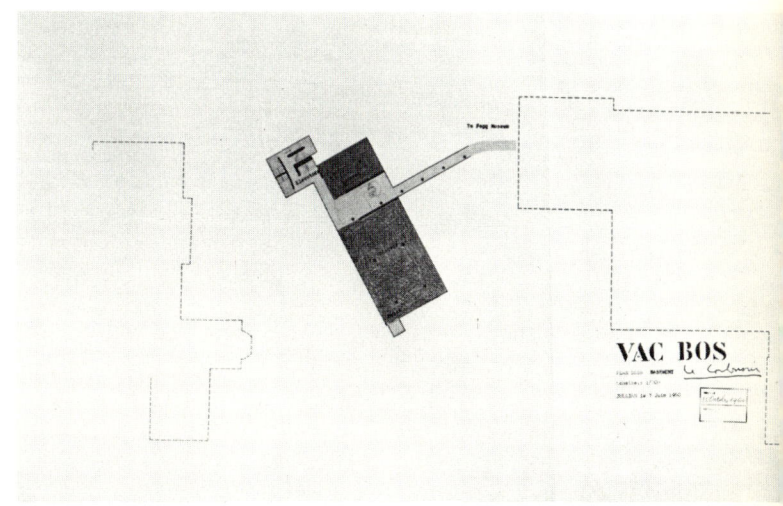

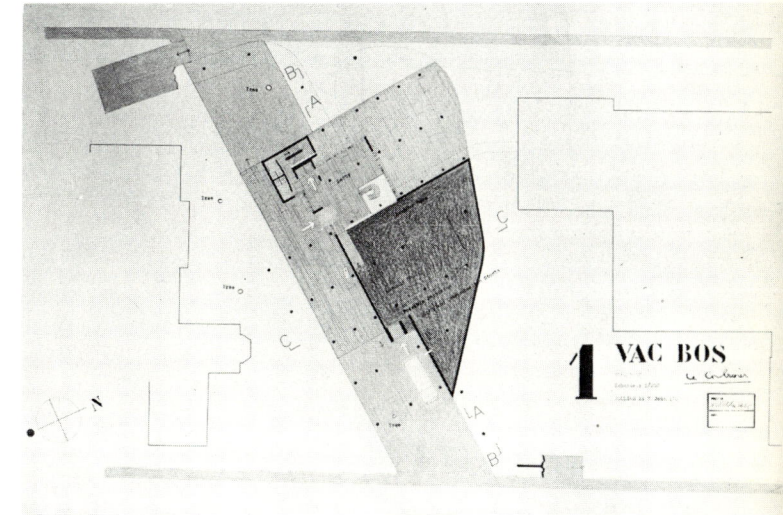

79. *Presentation plan of level 1, Le Corbusier and Jullian, June 7, 1960. (1:200; 43 × 70 cm; high quality thick paper.)*

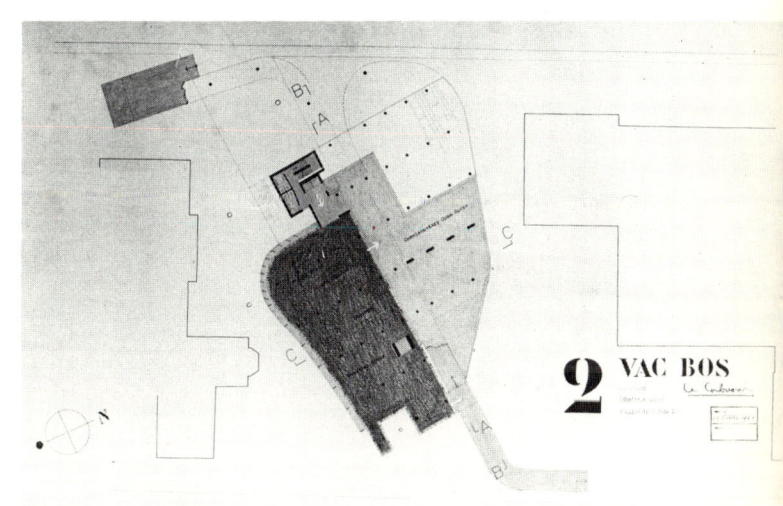

80. *Presentation plan of level 2, Le Corbusier and Jullian, June 7, 1960. (1:200; 43 × 70 cm; high quality thick paper.)*

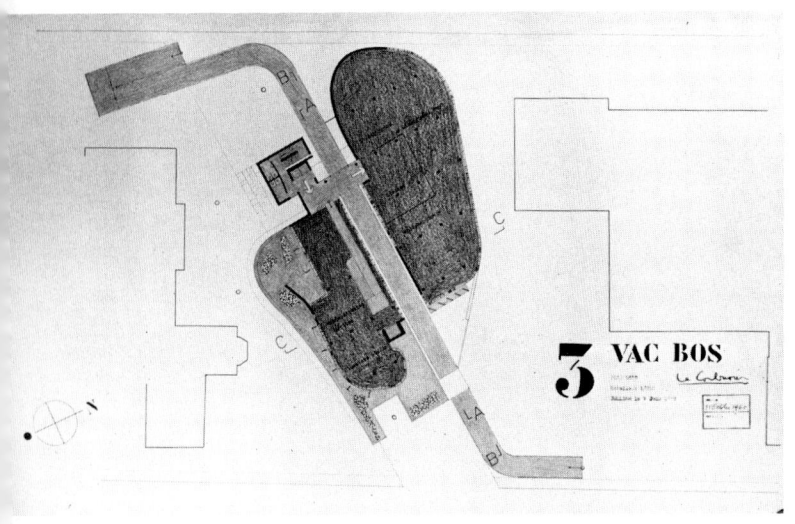

81. *Presentation plan of level 3, Le Corbusier and Jullian, June 7, 1960. (1:200; 43 × 70 cm; high quality thick paper.)*

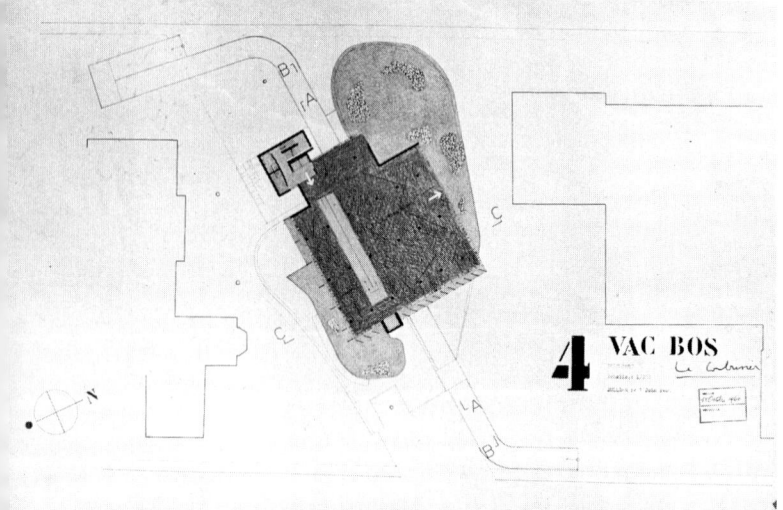

82. *Presentation plan of level 4, Le Corbusier and Jullian, June 7, 1960. (1:200; 43 × 70 cm; high quality thick paper.)*

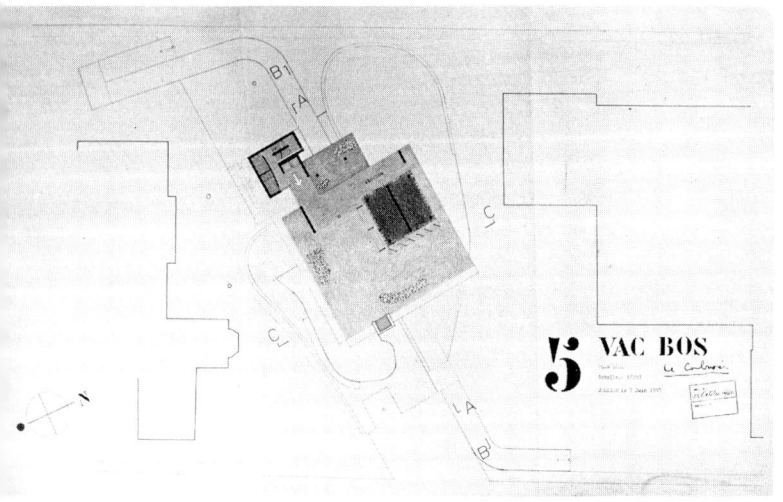

83. *Presentation plan of level 5, Le Corbusier and Jullian, June 7, 1960. (1:200; 43 × 70 cm; high quality thick paper.)*

84. *Presentation aerial view, Le Corbusier and Jullian, June 7, 1960. (1:200; 43 × 70 cm; high quality thick paper.)*

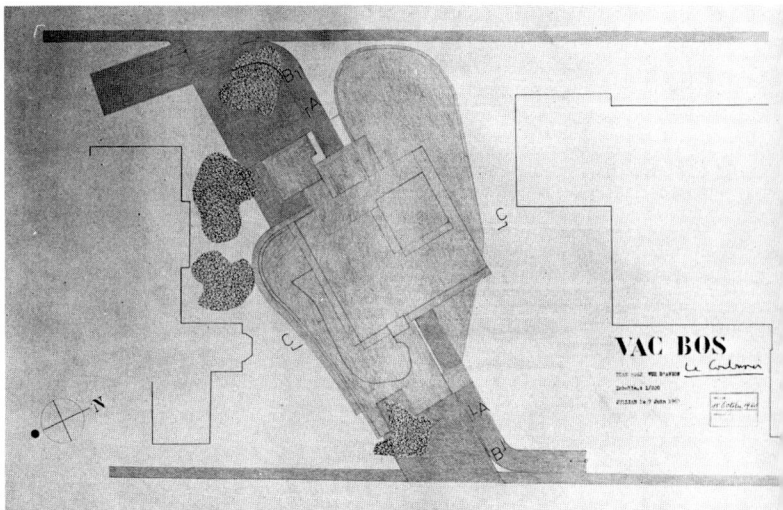

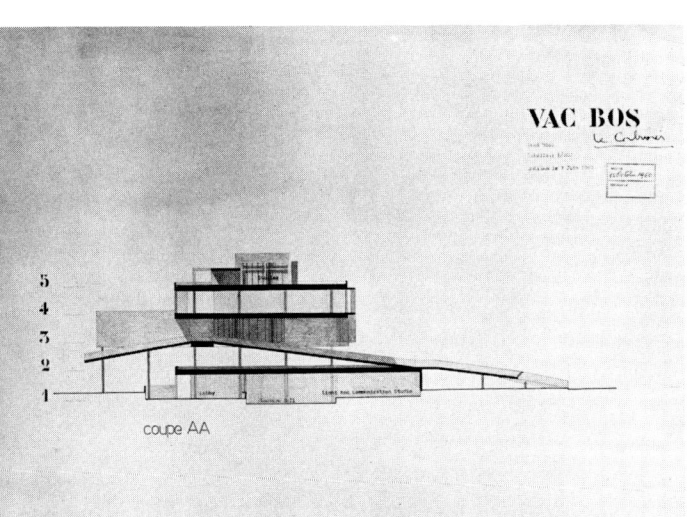

85. *Presentation longitudinal section AA, Le Corbusier and Jullian, June 7, 1960. (1:200; 43 × 70 cm; high quality thick paper.) As in the plans, the outlines are here ruled in black ink. Gray crayon indicates structure, blue indicates glass. Pale blue indicates interior space; there are gray shadows in places.*

86. *Presentation longitudinal section BB, Le Corbusier and Jullian, June 7, 1960. (1:200; 43 × 70 cm; high quality thick paper.)*

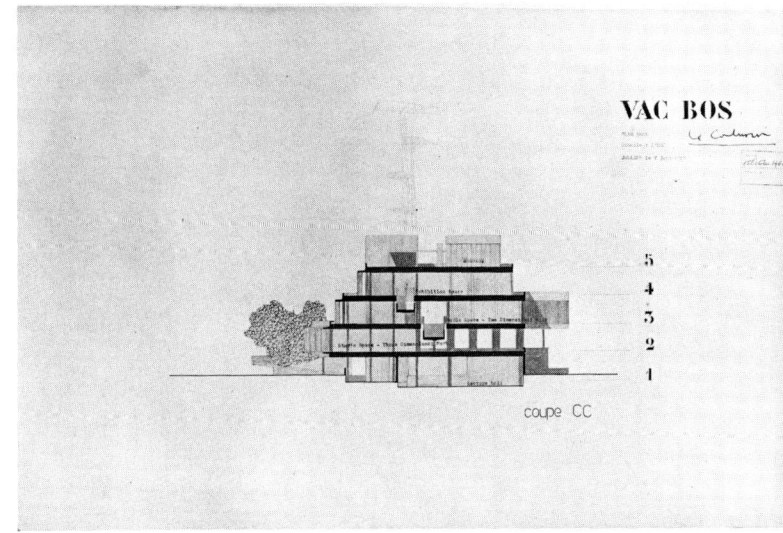

87. *Presentation transversal section CC, Le Corbusier and Jullian, June 7, 1960. (1:200; 43 × 70 cm; high quality thick paper.)*

CONSTRUCTION OF A VISUAL ARTS CENTER

Introduction

Between 1902 and 1917 Le Corbusier was, in his native country, closely involved in the birth and organisation of a special educational section for architectural evolution. Thanks to an exceptional teacher, young and full of initiatives (L'Eplattenier), an educational center limited to twenty students, men and women, existed during fifteen years exciting the interest and the hostility of people. In one single place were taught drawing or color, volume, modelling, etc. . . . , construction (furniture etc.), jewellery, embroidery, etc. etc. . . . Le Corbusier began with a burin in his hand and the goldsmith's hammer and chisel, realising, though very young, excellent works. He made his first house when he was seventeen and a half without ever having studied architecture. This house subjected to the influence of that time and of his teacher L'Eplattenier, gave an opening to architectural decorations: "scraffiti," mural painting, furniture, wrought iron, embossing, etc. . . . During the following year this school undertook building works (decorative, of course, since it was the fashion at that time): metal, stone, mosaic, stained glass window (concert-room, church, fragment of a public edifice, etc. . . .). One day everything collapsed before the rivalry and the hatred which had roused the old school against this New Section. The evolution of men, the manifestation of individualities, the divergences, finally overcame the enthusiasm.

And the whole concern collapsed!

From this first experience Le Corbusier has kept the instinct of the fatidical, indispensable, practical and beneficent relations *between the hand and the head*. The rupture of this collaboration of the hand and the head brought by the mechanism and the bureaucracy has fomented little by little a monstrous society which would be on the decline if no reaction interfered. The Harvard University's initiative has therefore found in Le Corbusier a ground which is naturally favorable to the implantation of the ideas which constitute the present programme of this University.

This must have given Pusey special pleasure, as he had supported the educational idea right from the start. It was followed by a section headed simply "The Building." In the architect's own tabulated explanations of the building's features special note should be taken of those parts dealing with fenestration, outdoor spaces, and the ramp, "a new road for walks or to pass through the campus."

1) The Building contains 3 essential Departments:
   a) Teaching of Two-Dimensional arts (level 3)
   b) Teaching of Three-Dimensional arts (level 2)
   c) Teaching of "Light and Communication" arts (level 1)

Must one subdivide by partitions each of these three departments or can one admit that each Department will only have one single premises [sic] where everybody works on different subjects under the control of the instructor whose explanations can alternatively be individual or general thus allowing each one to participate directly or indirectly in the practical or intellectual inventions of each of these disciplines.

2) The project therefore provides these three Departments. The work which takes place in the two first—which make use of the daylight and artificial light—can be observed from the outside by the people who take a walk or pass on the road of access.

3) The road of access is a new road for walks or to pass through the campus. It rises gradually above the ground to reach the level of the Three-Dimensional Department and afterwards to reach the Two-Dimensional Department. From there it descends and is connected with the extant paths of the campus.

The access of the third Department: "Light and Communication" different since it is a question here of obscure premises where one only makes use of artificial light.

4) This road for walking which goes up and down again through the new building is extended at its highest point (level 3) by an inner ramp placed in the Exhibition Room (level 4). The visitor can thus end his visit by examining the works which are exhibited.

5) The building is conceived on piles (pilotis), concrete walls and concrete columns, which are round or otherwise, leaving open all the facades of the edifice. These facades will probably be equipped with full glazings named "undulatory" (glazed at a 100%) and provided with the necessary "aerators" to ensure the *transaeration* of all the premises.

6) A "sun-control" will complete the installation of the "undulatoires." This sun-control changes according to the orientation of the different facades and their curvature. This sun-control can be realized either in aluminium or in concrete. It will comprise on the outside, an equipment for the easy cleaning of the glazings and inside, a screen or heavy curtains which can obturate, partly or completely, the sunlight according to the needs.

Each of the floors of the workshops assigned to the:

Three-Dimensional work
Two-Dimensional work

continues *on the same level* by outside terraces, covered garden or open skies, where outdoor work can be realized at the favorable moments of the year: sculpture, painting, etc. etc. . . . (as well as the outdoor control of the works realized in the workshops).

7) The Lecture Hall (Level 1) for seminaries etc. . . . cinema, is very important. It is placed under the piles (pilotis) at the level of the natural ground of the campus. This area is accessible by its entrance hall which is protected by the piles. It can also be connected, at the same level, with the "Light and Communication" premises.

8) At the top of the building (level 5) are two workshops for Visiting-artists which open on the roof-garden and which have the benefit of exceptionally favorable conditions.

9) Vertical and horizontal circulations:

The lifts for students or visitors start from the Entrance Hall; they serve the different levels 2, 3, 4, 5. A staircase completes these lifts. The toilets are located in this part of the building, at each storey.

A "monte-charge" at the other extremity allows the loading or unloading of the materials and of the works, avoiding the sheltered entrance and being connected directly with the lorries' access.

10) On the plan "level 1", two columns are suppressed in the middle of the room (Seminar Room Lecture Hall). The "Section CC" shows a bridge which is installed at level 2 at this place. This bridge forms a "lattice-beam", in concrete, capable of spanning the open space of 12 metres.

11) The road for lorries, pedestrians, cars, etc. . . . occupies a large way under the piles of the building. This diagonal way is connected with the two roads which limit the site of the Visual Arts building.

12) An underground passage is provided for the access to the Fogg Museum.

Paris, the 8th June, 1960
LE CORBUSIER

Obviously Le Corbusier had responded strongly to his client's intention of having the older university departments involve themselves with the new arrival. From the architect's explanation, it is clear that he thinks of his building, upper levels as well as lower ones, as an extension of the public space, circulation, and verdure of the campus. Central to this idea is the ramp (fig. 88). The ramp serves to link the streets on each side of the site and to bind the building into communal cooperation: it is the organizing artery of the building's own various parts, but it also connects each of these parts to the public life. Programmatically, as well as

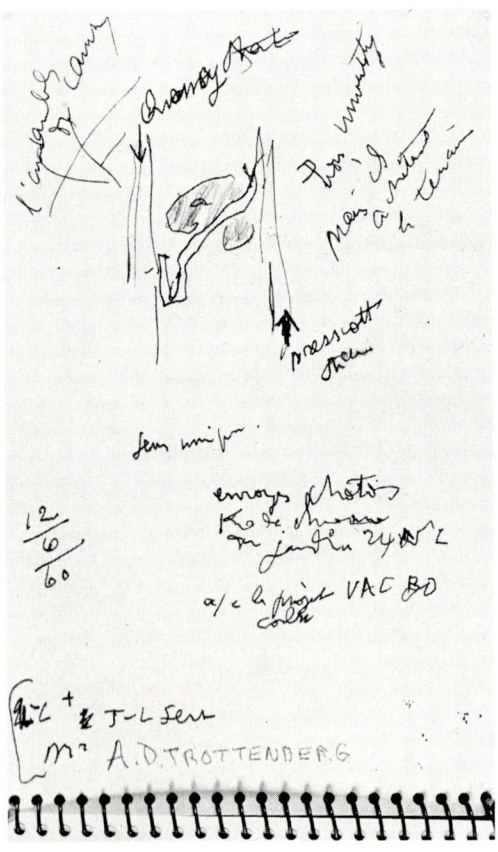

88. *Sketch of visual arts center and its surroundings, Le Corbusier, notebook P61, June 12, 1960. (Small scale; 17.5 × 11 cm; ink on paper.) Le Corbusier's sketch recalls the inspirational idea of the building as a sinuous continuation of the paths of the Yard. He draws the paths to the top left and indicates future expansion of the university beyond Prescott Street to the right. He also marks the one-way directions of the streets.*

"l'ensemble du campus"	("the ensemble of the campus")
"Quency Street"	("Quincy Street")
"Presscott Street"	("Prescott Street")
"hors University mais ils achetent le terrain"	("outside the university but they are buying the land")
"Sens unique"	("one way")

The other notes on this page refer to people Le Corbusier must have met during his visit or to odd fragments of conversation.

formally, the ramp is the central and unifying feature of the concept.

Essentially Le Corbusier had packed a piece of countryside into the trabeated structure of a concrete building—a "terrain construit" ("constructed site") through which it was possible to walk by means of a street in the air.[8] The functional spaces to either side provided swaying sculptural volumes and direct contact with terraces or interior gardens—the canonical urbanistic notion of "activités joyeuses . . . dans le déroulement de la journée de 24 heures" ("joyous activities . . . unfolding throughout the twenty-four hour day") was thus made possible, and signified symbolically, by the S-ramp. The workshop spaces, served by vertical circulation towers, were closed off from the elements by an envelope of glass protected from the sun and punctured in places for adjustable ventilation so that "les moyens necessaires des villes modernes" ("the necessary means for modern cities")—concrete and steel reinforcing techniques—were thus directed to their correct ends, the harmony of circulation and built form, the provision of "essential joys."

Everybody at the dinner party reacted favorably to the building. During the ensuing few weeks the powers at Harvard were unable to resist the attraction of Le Corbusier's design. Arthur Trottenberg was inspired to write to Eduard Sekler only a few days after the presentation: "I think there is almost universal opinion that this will be one of the best things he has done . . . The 'old man' . . . has performed even better than we had all expected, and all of us here in Cambridge are in a state of euphoria" (6-20-60).

Professor John Coolidge, an architectural historian from the Fine Arts Department and a member of the Committee for the Practice of the Visual Arts, described the situation some years later as follows: "I don't know what we expected—some spidery drawings, some intricate diagrams—but we were quite unprepared for the breathtaking beauty of the first project. It silenced serious criticism."[9] Speaking here was the very same person who had expressed concern over Le Corbusier's possible lack of "urbanity" three months before the June 1960 presentation. His recollection continues, outlining something of the usual Harvard procedure for reviewing a project of this kind: "Suggestions are made by independent committees, working in isolation. Visual Arts, Buildings and Grounds, Corporation, Overseers. Each one reacted—'of course I recognize the astonishing quality of this proposal but will X ever accept it?' We were all astonished that everyone bought it without any question. Criticism was overwhelmed by beauty."[10] This is not to suggest there were no criticisms of Le Corbusier's visual arts center. As early as the dinner party presentation, the ramp, which understandably made the greatest impression, was also the cause of alarm. Pusey said he thought it inappropriate to the New England winter: it would be slippery and cause drafts at access. Le Corbusier answered with nothing but a memorable image: the ends of the ramp "acted like wings, lifting the building off the ground."[11]

Pusey further suggested emphasis on the ground floor entrance. Le Corbusier's notebook (fig. 89) contains the brief reminder, "le Président désire accès: transversale des étudiants (du dehors) = p. aller au restaurant" ("the President wants a side entrance from the exterior for the students—to go to the restaurant")—the first of a series of claims for transversal circulation at ground floor level. Put simply, Le Corbusier wished to keep the center of gravity of the program and main events of circulation at the third level where they would be vitally served by the ramp; Pusey tended to think of the building in conventional terms, entered at ground floor level. He even wished to move the administrative offices down to the ground floor where the program had asked for them: Le Corbusier had placed them at the third. This was a threat to the idea of the building as an ascending visit or continued walk. Nor was the accommodation of a new transversal direction of circulation at ninety degrees to the old just a matter of punching holes in the envelope at the right places. Some response seems to have been necessary in the actual structure as well: the notebook was illustrated by a light sketch of a grid of pilotis supporting heavy longitudinal beams running with the main axis of the circulation, crossed at ninety degrees by smaller ones signaling the new direction. The long distance between the columns was 7 meters, the short, 3.66 meters.

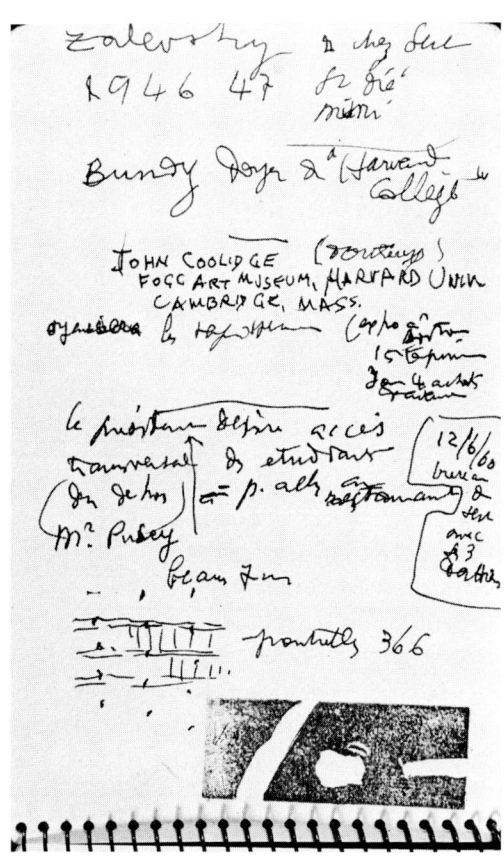

89. *Jottings from Le Corbusier's second Cambridge trip, June 1960, notebook P61. (Small scale; 17.5 × 11 cm; ink on paper.) To the bottom of the page appears a sketch plan of structure showing pilotis and beams, and an imprint of Le Corbusier's Boston mark.*

"Zalevsky chez Sert 1946 47 St. Dié [?]"	("Zalevsky at Sert's 1946/47 St. Dié [?]")
"Bundy doyen de Harvard College"	("Bundy Dean of Harvard College")
"John Coolidge, Fogg Art Museum, Harvard Univ, Cambridge, Mass. organisiera les tapisseries expo a Boston 15 tapisseries 3 ou 4 achats [?] (douteux)"	("John Coolidge, Fogg Art Museum, Harvard Univ, Cambridge, Mass. will organize the tapestries exhibit at Boston 15 tapestries 3 or 4 purchases [?] [doubtful]")
"Le President desire access transversal des etudiants (du dehors) p. aller au Restaurant"	("The President wants a side entrance from the exterior for the students to go to the restaurant")
"Mr. Pusey"	("Mr. Pusey")
"12/6/60 bureau Sert avec ses trois dattiers"	("12/6/60 Sert's office with his three date palms")
"beams 7m. poutrelles 366"	("beams 7 meters, crossbeams 366")

What is most striking about the building which Le Corbusier presented at the dinner party, aside from the sculptural dynamism in plan, is the mass of Corbusian devices in it, especially in the elevation treatment. With the various angles and distances of the brise-soleil, the rhythms of the ondulatoires and the irregular placements of aérateurs in aluminum, the potentials of that major point of Corbusian doctrine, "the free facade," were not simply employed but rhetorically exploited and fluidly expressed. The fenestration solution was so packed with devices that it ended in clashes and inadequacies. Not only did the brise-soleil block the effects of the ondulatoires, but the remedy for this—wider spacing of the brise-soleil—made the ondulatoires vulnerable to the sun: hence the need for curtains.[12] Moreover, the combination was too difficult to construct (he did qualify his ondulatoires with "probably") and tended to clutter the building edge, so compromising the sculptural integrity of the building's bounding planes. Combined with his standards for "éclairage" ("lighting"), "aération" ("ventilation"), and "protection du soleil" ("sun protection"), there were typical devices: a pilotis/slab skeleton, roof gardens, and a ramp allowing vantage points for interior and exterior study of all the other elements.

The same held true for another one of his Five Points of Architecture,[13] the "free plan," which in the twenties was demonstrated by placing curved, manifestly nonweight-bearing partitions down among the grid of point supports. His visual arts center had its partitions certainly, but the independence of floor arrangements was surely being demonstrated here by the thorough independence of one curved floor from another in the curves on the exterior of the building, each layer swaying out and back, oblivious structurally of the layers below and above it. In Le Corbusier's structures of the twenties the free plan was scarcely legible from outside because it was discretely hidden from view by the lightweight exterior box of the buildings; in this case, though, a rectangle was at the center of the composition with the curves rippling freely outwards from it. The positions, speaking purely formalistically, had been reversed.[14]

Of those present perhaps only Sert was really qualified to recognize the didactic intentions of his fellow architect. As codesigner, Jullian was fully aware of the meaning: in the atelier they referred to the curve jutting out over Quincy Street as the "coup de poing" or "punch" when they were designing it. This was the side that could most easily be seen in its entirety from the Yard, and the metaphor does certainly describe the lunging of the studio to that side. Evidently, though, this phrase was also intended to convey the architect's desire to produce a manifesto of his own solutions to correctly identified single problems: support, ventilation, lighting, and so on—solutions he believed to have the same authority in architecture as the wheel in transport on the ground, the wing in the air.

Maybe the metaphor of the "punch" was appropriate for other reasons. It was, in a way, a show of aggressive confidence to the "timid people," if not a stern reprimand for the United Nations building, which followed his idea in general outline but infuriated him in elevation by being a sleek, mechanistic, air-conditioned glass box.[15] This general American address was, I believe, uppermost in the architect's mind,[16] but the local context added point to his demonstration. The neo-Georgian buildings provided a classic contrast to which he had resorted on paper many years before:[17] that between traditional wall-bearing structures and the liberated plan and facade of modern pilotis/slab structures in reinforced concrete. Against the traditional buildings he set a symbolic, abstract sculpture that emanated its qualities into the surrounding environment and incorporated his "points of architecture." The older buildings were set on the routine axes of the Beaux Arts he so despised; his was on the living axis of the sun and could really be walked along. They were dead, his was living. "One is discussing a matter of life or death when one speaks of exterior movements, the life or death of architectural experience, the life or death of feelings." It is no accident that this passage, which makes the point explicit, can be found in a book entitled *Talks with Students,* where Le Corbusier also states: "Good architecture is 'walked through' and 'traversed' . . . the classical era baited the trap for the total destruction of architecture . . . our own man . . . equipped with his own two eyes and looking straight ahead . . . walks about and changes position, applies himself to his pursuits, moving in the midst of a succession of architectural realities. He re-experiences the intense feeling that has come from that sequence of movements. This is so true that architecture can be judged as dead or living by the degree to which the rule of *movement* has been disregarded or brilliantly exploited."[18]

Even to the observer standing still there was inner force in the forms, movement in the curves, the suggestion of pressure, weight, resistance, and other habitual bodily experiences. But the observer was rarely static, and as he passed in a car, walked along Quincy Street, burrowed beneath the pilotis, or ascended the curving ramp, the ondulatoires would ripple into motion, each level differently, the perspectives of columns would slip by, brise-soleil would shift, vistas would open and close again, spaces enlarge or compress, sliding elements realign.

> Unceremoniously, a living being is sometimes called a "digestive tract." Let us speak just as plainly and say that architecture is internal circulation, and this not just in the functional sense . . . Architecture is interior circulation more particularly for emotional reasons: the various aspects of the work—a symphony whose music never leaves us—are comprehensible in proportion to the steps that place us there, permitting our eyes to feast on the walls or the perspectives beyond them, offering up the anticipation or surprise of doors which reveal unexpected space; or a chiaroscuro pattern of shadows designed by the sun as it streams through windows or bays; or the views of distant prospects, whether built up or still virginal . . . The quality of interior circulation is the biological discipline of the work, for the organisation of the building is bound up with the building's essential purpose.[19]

Thus the first design for the visual arts center combined the most personal, irrational elements (a walk through an "Ubu" poised on stilts, though not a "white whale") with the fruits of Le Corbusier's "recherche patiente" ("patient research"): his rational standards of architecture for worldwide use. The fact that it was a large-scale abstract sculpture imbued with the formal and metaphorical devices of twentieth century art made it a fitting metaphor for the institution it was to house. The symbolism of its primary forms (cube, freehand curves, and S-ramp) made it a minor demonstration of the "correct" use of modern techniques in urban planning, perhaps a vicarious statement addressed to the New York he would have re-planned completely. Its vital, sculptural quality and the fact that it could be walked through made it a paragon of "good" architecture, a true teaching building—but a paragon that was not to be built.

5. A CONFERENCE AT SERT'S

Architecture c'est avec des matériaux bruts, établir des rapports émouvants.

Le Corbusier

On the morning of June 13, 1960, Le Corbusier arrived at Sert's office wearing his usual suit and bow tie. He installed himself in the conference room, put on his horn-rimmed spectacles, and began to explain his building in more detail. The meeting was pleasantly low-keyed. The ticky-tacky presentation model that had been thrown together at the last minute was supplemented by a flow of jokes, reproofs of people who fail to date drawings ("to be executed in the guardroom"), reminiscences of cacti found on holiday, discussions of architectural elements in the making, and the information that was supposed to guide Sert in assembling the building.

It is tempting to see this meeting in terms of a contrast between a unique avant-garde European architect with a lyrical attitude to building techniques and American technicians abreast of the more recent sophistications of the trade. At least Sert's office manager, John Nickols, tended to see it in this way,[1] and he may have been well able to judge because he discussed technical matters with Le Corbusier in detail and was probably less awed by the personnage than anyone else. On some points of technical knowledge he found Le Corbusier to be surprisingly nonchalant.[2]

The question of Le Corbusier's precise notions of building technology is a tract of as yet unwritten history. Here the intention is to throw some light on his attitude to materials, not to reveal his technical limitations. A number of extreme positions can be stated in this connection. The first might be Le Corbusier the "abstract formalist," concerned exclusively with the impact of the overall lines of a design. The second might be Le Corbusier the engineering rationalist, concerned with the performance and laws of materials. The third might be Le Corbusier the combined craftsman-artist, as deeply involved with the materials of the building craft as he was with the majority of twentieth-century artistic movements in painting and sculpture which could guide materials aesthetically to their places in a design. Fortunately he was rich enough to include all such crude categories and more. He was even able to employ irony in confronting them with one another.

At the conference he began by discussing the structural frame. The presentation drawings had shown slabs and pilotis without beams. Nickols believes Le Corbusier was unaware of the spanning capacity of a smooth slab. In any event, he discussed a number of possible ceiling solutions including unidirectional beams, suspended ceilings, and a set of small transversal Catalan vaults set in between larger longitudinal sleepers. In his notebook he drew a similar arrangement with small transversal beams instead of vaults (fig. 89). Beams of any kind turned out to be untenable in combination with this building's forms; they were also unnecessary, but Le Corbusier either did not know this or else he did not care. Beams widened the field of his aesthetic experimentation, and, at one later stage, aesthetic experimentation even made beams a temporary necessity.

At the party he had told Paul Krueger, the eventual job captain at Sert's, that he intended to use standard steel forms for casting his concrete because he felt that standardized techniques should be employed, especially in the United States. He also said he hoped that his aluminum aérateur doors might be mass produced, and he referred to them as "airplane wings." To be sure, his brise-soleil blades (which he envisaged as possibly being made in aluminum as well) also bear resemblance to flaps, and Le Corbusier's notebooks make frequent reference to the alloy components of aircraft he traveled in. Andreini has explained that the material also fascinated the architect as a machine age contrast to concrete, which was regarded as a natural material.[3]

At the conference, Le Corbusier said a good deal about concrete finishes—for example, that it should never be painted on exteriors and that in this building it should be left bare on columns and ribs. He told Paul Krueger that he had just received detailed photographs of the Tokyo Museum and that he was surprised at the roughness Sert intended for the Holyoke Center; in fact, he said he was surprised Sert was using concrete at all. The visual arts center's concrete should be smooth, he said, a point he stressed again later. While he talked, he sketched (fig. 90). Alongside a perspective of a typical interior with unidirectional beams, he drew a column in plan and in perspective, indicating the steel formwork. On the same sheet he drew a typical floor solution with rectangles of terrazzo, through the center of which passed the columns. The terrazzo was to be rough in quality, divided by metal strips: "Use large rectangles with black and white and different colors in the squares."[4] Alongside the smooth, gray, concrete walls, the terrazzo floor would have made a dazzling contrast, as it would with, say, Catalan vaults in the ceiling. It is intriguing to speculate about the associations terrazzo floors may have had in his mind. He specified that the metal separation strips were to be aluminum or brass. The result would have resembled certain Art Deco floors he may have seen in Paris of the late twenties and in the skyscrapers of New York that he visited in 1935.[5] In his late notebooks there are a number of references to Raymond Hood, who designed some of these skyscrapers. Furthermore, Le Corbusier had admired the highlife of Rio de Janeiro in the thirties where he specifically noted black and white marble pavements.[6] Whatever his source, the point should be clear: the floor was another category —just as the brise-soleil and aérateurs were categories—into which a new material might be inserted. Its juxtaposition with the materials around,

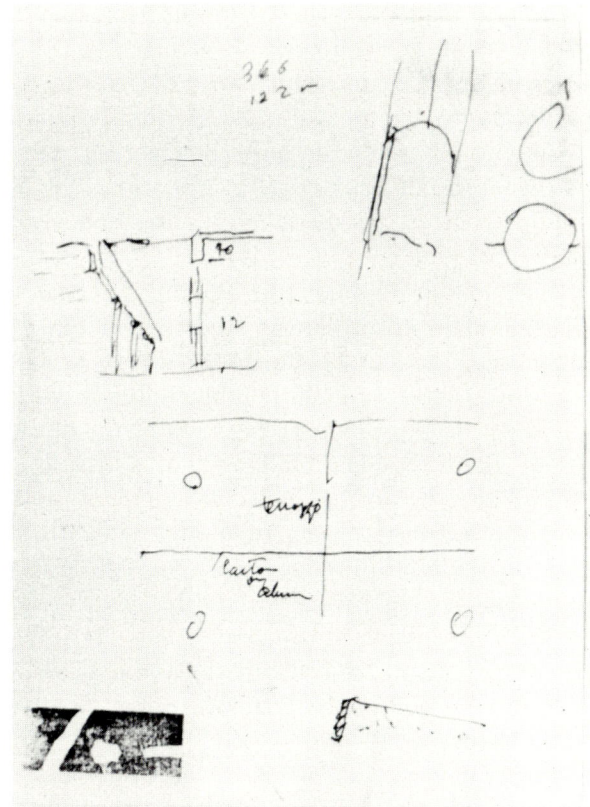

90. *Sketches of pilotis, slabs, and beams, Le Corbusier, morning of June 13, 1960. (No definite scale; 28 × 21.5 cm; ink on paper.) These drawings were made while conferring at the office of José Luis Sert. Top right, piloti formed from steel formwork; top left, an interior section/perspective of structure with unidirectional beams; bottom, a floor plan showing terrazzo rectangles separated by brass or aluminum strips. The sketch to the bottom right may be of a concrete beam while the hieroglyph to the bottom left is Le Corbusier's Boston mark. The spidery drawing style is typical of Le Corbusier's late years.*

91. *Sketches of ramp, Le Corbusier, morning of June 13, 1960. (No definite scale; 28 × 21.5 cm; ink on paper.) A suggestion for heating the ramp appears to the top left. In the center, the ramp is drawn with its groove and with patterns incised according to the Modulor. At the bottom right Le Corbusier betrays his source for the groove idea: the Suleymaniye mosque, observed in 1911 during his trip to the Near East, the "Voyage d'Orient." The drawing is stamped at the top right with his Boston mark.*

each in its own functional category, could lead to heightened textural, coloristic, and metaphorical tensions. In my opinion, the placement of an opulent floor in a studio space held up by "naturalistic" concrete columns, with aluminum flaps drawn directly from the world of aeroengineering, and narrow panes of glass set in between concrete struts in proportion—each material, each category rich in associations and enriched in relationship to the others—has the quality of the best Cubist collage.[7]

Discussion then switched to the ramp. At the dinner party, Le Corbusier had shrugged off President Pusey's suggestion that the slope would be slippery in winter ice. Now the architect suggested that a groove be made down the center of the ramp and that salt water be poured on the snow and ice; "the salt water can then run down and we can have sea fish."[8] On one sheet he drew the source of his idea for the groove: the system of access ramps to the Suleymaniye Mosque in Istanbul which he had observed during his "Voyage d'Orient" (fig. 91). He wrote the name of the mosque alongside the sketch and dated it 1910. A figure in a turban was shown standing alongside the parapet, recalling a sketch done nearly fifty years before.[9] And down the center of the visual arts center ramp, done in

103

another drawing, he drew the groove and specified that the concrete be rough "opus optimum" with striated pattern marks "au Modulor." The question of heating the ramp was raised, but no decision taken; and there is no documentary source for its ever being mentioned again. In the meantime Sert stated that the entries and exits were "all right" (thus glossing over what was to emerge as a problematic feature), while Le Corbusier devoted some time to a description of possible reliefs in the concrete "with camels," like those at Chandigarh.

John Nickols asked Le Corbusier to authenticate his sketches, so the latter asked for a penknife and eraser. He dug out a shape on the flat surface of the eraser, asked for ink, and stamped his mark (figs. 90–93) on all the sketches and on the page in his notebook relevant to his trip. He was in the habit of inventing a new symbol for each trip he made.

Discussion then turned to fenestration, as Nickols records. "He described his idea for varying the spacing of the mullions and the introduction of ventilating panels." (In other words, he outlined the principles of ondulatoires and aérateurs.) "Corbu spoke in detail of the placement of the mullions and the fins. He sketched a section showing column, man, glass, slabs and the fins."[10]

The sketch in question (fig. 93) was an exact repeat in reverse of one of the structural studies of May 1, 1960 (fig. 65). Although Nickols states "he spoke in detail," he did not speak in enough detail, clearly, for working drawings to be produced. Le Corbusier had to promise to make more detailed drawings of ondulatoire fixings, a promise he was ultimately unable to keep. He did make reference to the Chandigarh ondulatoires and aérateurs, even including a little sketch of an interior (fig. 93), but there the practical problems of fixing were less complicated. Here the brise-soleil had to be held by the same extremity of thin slab as held the ondulatoires. Although this arrangement was never constructed, his description did give a sense of the reality of stretches of glass, blades of aluminum, and flowing struts. He also spoke of the curtains behind, which would enliven the building as they were moved into different positions. The aesthetic effects of the fenestration may not have been Le Corbusier's prime concern, however. A primary theoretical matter was at stake when he spoke of "the death of the window"[11] and referred to secretaries in Brooklyn shivering in the drafts of ordinary windows. There was, in Le Corbusier's mind, something inherently unsatisfactory about a normal window acting as ventilator and source of light simultaneously, especially when exposed to the full glare of the sun.

From early conception, the building had been a "paysage dans un paysage" ("landscape in a landscape"),[12] and what Le Corbusier had to say of verdure on and around the building reinforced this guiding concept. A little has been said of the desire to put countryside in a building and its urbanistic implications. Part of Le Corbusier's answer to suburban sprawl was to bring greenery into the town and use modern techniques to lift it up to the sky, instead of having people invade the countryside for their own patch of greenery.[13] Suburban, decentralized life was, in Le Corbusier's view, responsible for the hell of the tramway and commuter traffic congestion—wasted time which he saw having its daily toll in New York, where he believed it responsible for a severe disruption of social life. The visual arts center, with its S-ramp and rustic roof gardens brought into intimate contact with the "built cube," may be understood as a microcosm of this ideal city where greenery is valued. It is not surprising that, when asked how he would like his photo taken (his "American" photo), he said, "with verdure" (fig. 76).[14]

At the conference he stressed that he wanted the visual arts center's roof gardens to run wild and referred to his own roof garden at the rue Nungesser et Coli in Paris. Some years before he had said that his garden was "allowed to run wild . . . the rosebushes have become large eglantines; the winds, the bees have brought seeds; a laburnum has grown; a sycamore; lavendar bushes have spread out. The turf has become coarse grass. The wind and sun control the composition, half man and half nature."[15]

His intentions for planting the visual arts center's roof gardens were similarly romantic (fig. 92). He seems to have envisaged an almost picturesque disarray of wild grasses, crawling and climbing shrubs. He made it quite clear that he did not want men to interfere with the processes of nature: "No

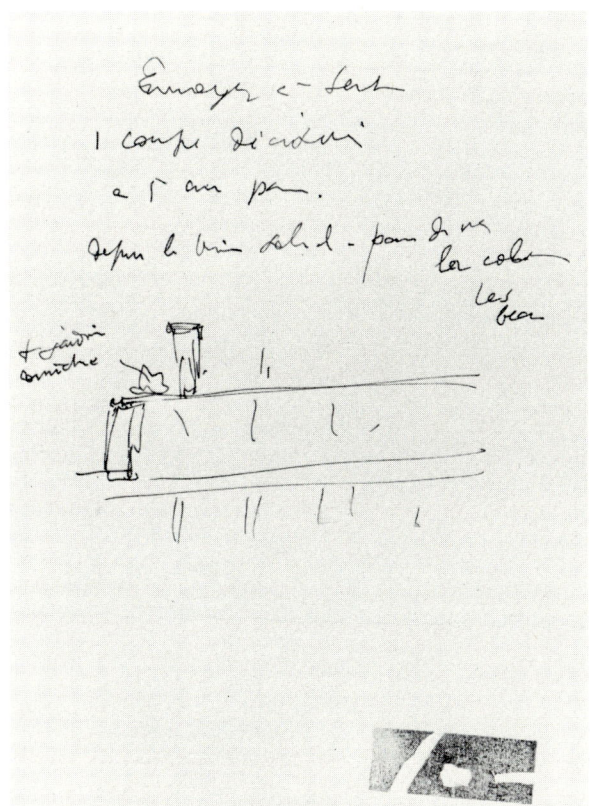 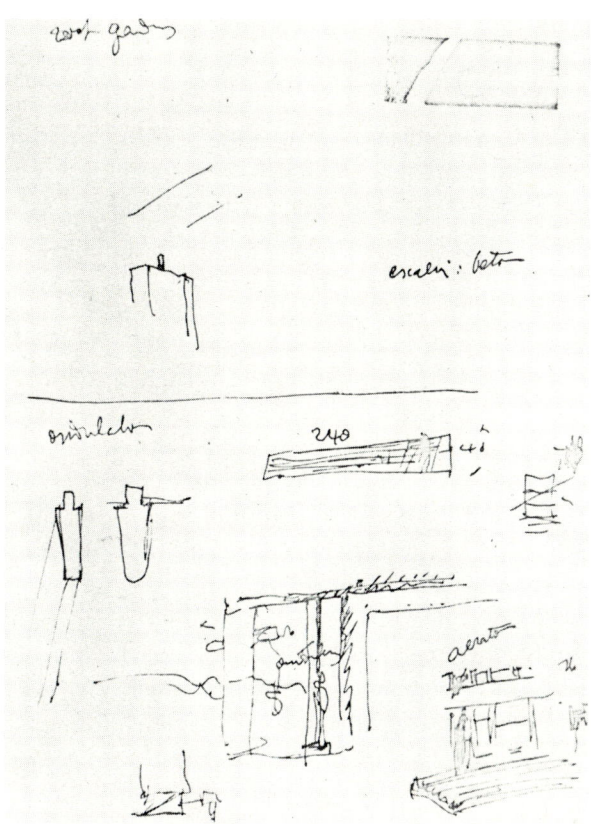

92. *Sketch of "jardin corniche" ("garden cornice"), Le Corbusier, morning of June 13, 1960. (No definite scale; 28 × 21.5 cm; ink on paper.) The architect's intention that verdure should be visible outside the building is here demonstrated.*

93. *Sketch of fenestration showing section through brise-soleil, ondulatoires, slab and beam (bottom center), and details of ondulatoire struts (left and top), Le Corbusier, morning of June 13, 1960. (No definite scale; 28 × 21.5 cm; ink on paper.) To the far right is a building section with the sun's light penetrating it at an angle; to the bottom right a sketch of an interior.*

gardeners, nature will do it." This was followed by a denunciation of the large axial gardens of Louis XIV at Versailles ("he started it") and the apotheosis of natural selection with special reference to a yucca collected in Spain in 1931, of which he even supplied a sketch. "In Spain I used Yucca. I returned to Paris and cleaned out my car and put the Yucca in pots . . . has been there 30 years, a splendid Yucca with flowers on it. I never made a gesture in this garden, only the rain. In thirty years I have put no fertilizer."[16]

He reemphasized that he wanted no landscape architect to work on the grounds surrounding the visual arts center, that only trees and shrubs requiring no attention should be planted, that these should seed themselves: "The plants that cannot survive, they die, others take their place." He then drew a section of the building showing brise-soleil, fenestration, an elevator tower in the background, and a little clump of greenery at the extreme edge (fig. 92), which was entitled, significantly, "jardin corniche" ("garden cornice").

Whereas in his buildings of the "first machine age" the top was defined by a rigorous straight line with mechanical associations, here the edge was to be a freehand curve, supplemented by the fuzzy, ragged outline of straggles of greenery: a natural "corniche." Le Corbusier seems to have been concerned that the wild countryside and the earthworks on top of his building should be visible, even from below. Greenery was an emblematic adjunct to the other elements in the "punch"; he seems to have thought of it as a building material in its own right, to be brought into contrast with machine materials, glass, and aluminum. Again, I think the collage principle is at work in this contrast of materials and functions: industrial glass meeting aluminum brise-soleil and aérateurs, and colliding with the qualities of "naturalistic" concrete[17] and natural greenery. The sheer visual richness of the building edge where these qualities collide is indisputable.

Finally the meeting turned to practical issues such as dates, budget, and so on. The members agreed that no publicity would be permitted until plans were complete, and Le Corbusier said these would be done on a large scale by November. He also suggested that coordination between Cambridge and Paris should continue from September till November 15, when he said he would be going to Chandigarh. Oddly enough, though, at another point in the meeting he also indicated that he would be coming to Cambridge with "large scale plans" at that time. It was stated that Bundy and Trottenberg would look over the plans on behalf of the university in November; that heating proposals would be studied; and that Le Corbusier would approve Sert's working drawings. An estimate was made that the building would be completed by June 1962.

Then Le Corbusier and Sert stood up to take their leave of Nickols and of the "dattiers" Gourley, Jackson, and Zalewski, and as he left the master said: "Le projet est fini" ("the project is finished").

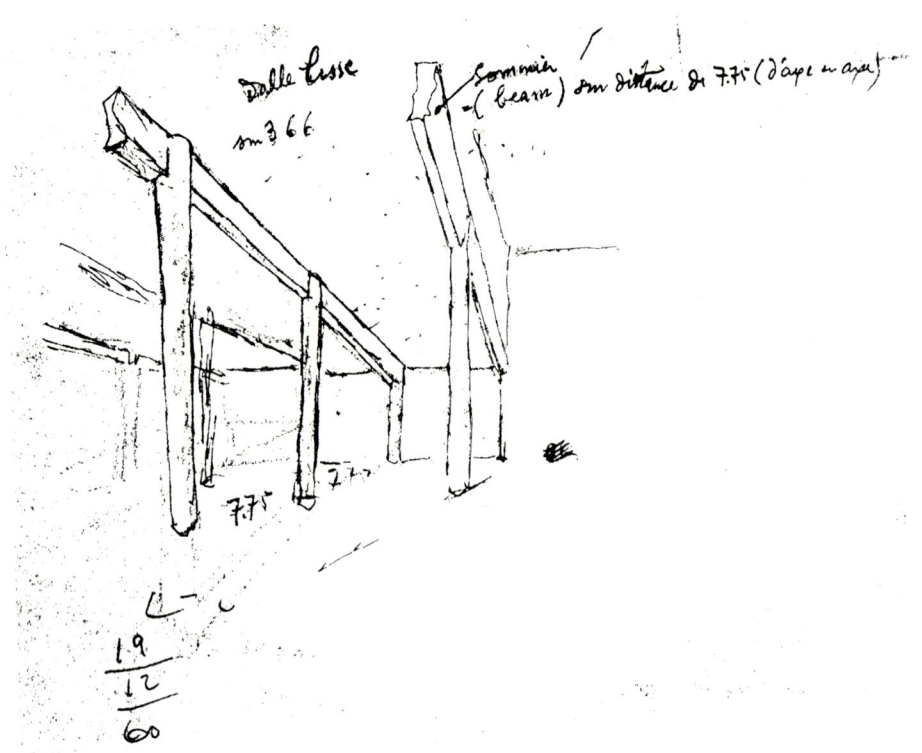

6. CONFLICTS IN THE DESIGN

This combination whose rules have emerged at the moment of creation, have developed, affirmed themselves, becoming commanding.

Le Corbusier

While Le Corbusier was spending his summer next to the Mediterranean at Cap Martin and Jullian was away on holiday, Sert was suffering from overwork in Cambridge and the university was busy collecting reactions from everybody reasonably concerned. The report of these findings was sent to Sert on August 10, 1960. The contrast was remarkable between the practical requirements and precise requests it contained and the vague statements of intent preceding the arrival of Le Corbusier's model.

Perhaps Le Corbusier had understood the somewhat provisional nature of his project, had known from the outset that modifications could be expected. There was always an element of risk in his projects because he used each one as another step in his own "recherche patiente" ("patient research"). But, between them, he and Jullian had devoted very little time to the design; if it was his aim to design loosely to avoid disruption of a tightly worked out plan and later to accommodate clients' modifications and tighten up his project, his strategy backfired somewhat. It is quite clear from the order of ensuing events that Le Corbusier and Jullian had avoided facing many technical realities of their project. The story of the advent of the second project is the gradual forcing of technical, functional, and legal requirements on the architect's attention, and the realization of weaknesses inherent in the first design—the obverse, in some ways, of the development of the first project, where pure plastic ideas were allowed to take a course of their own. It was these weaknesses, not the client's changes, that forced a second project.

The university's criticisms were that the building too amply filled the site, that the Quincy Street end of the ramp encroached on the Faculty Club lawn, and that more emphasis should be given to access from the Faculty Club side (8-10-60). In a floor-by-floor analysis, it was recommended that the basement be used for the auditorium, television, photographic, and film facilities, that the first floor contain a general lobby and exhibition space, and that the administrative offices be moved from their previous position on the third floor to one near the access door on the Faculty Club side. The first point, the placement of the auditorium in the basement, was a reassertion of the client's original program suggestion; and subsequent thinking led to the suggestion that extra space required for Light and Communications also be created there. Le Corbusier had placed the administrative offices at the third level, the building's heart, as an inducement to use the ramp. The client now requested that this major node of activity be placed on the ground floor (as suggested in the program)—and with some good reason, for Le Corbusier had placed the offices next to a noisy workshop and in the path of the freight lift. Finally, pressure from conservative elements in the administration, and probably in the Fogg, resulted in the request that the architect use that most sacred of Old Boston materials, red brick.

These points, and many more detailed ones, were relayed by Sert to Le Corbusier with some practical hints and cushioning remarks (8-31-60; appendix 10; 9-1-60). Having explained that the size of the building needed reducing, shown that the ramp required modification, and implied a decrease in importance of the ramp through the new emphasis on the ground floor level, he wrote: "The only changes of consequence requested were on the ground floor. These result in greater freedom here, which should make it possible to do something very handsome with this space. Moreover, since the changes in the upper floors are so minor, the volumes and forms which you now have need not be altered" (8-31-60; appendix 10). How to regard Sert's breezy attitude in this case is not clear. After all, the removal of the administrative offices to the ground level seriously threatened the usefulness of the ramp, and a reduction in size was also a change of "consequence," so consequential in fact as to be quite unacceptable to Le Corbusier. It would have upset the proportion of heights to widths, and even if this were compensated by an overall reduction in the height of the building, the absolute measurements of the building would nonetheless have been thrown off the Modulor scale. Was Sert playing down the problem to mute impact or simply failing to recognize it as a problem at all? As far as the "volumes and forms" were concerned he was right: the client's changes did not threaten anything other than dimensions; general sculptural relationships could remain untouched.

In Paris this was just what they wanted to hear. Le Corbusier and Jullian continued with their June presentation plans as a basic outline, packing into it new details, shifting about the parts like the pieces in a puzzle, until at last they understood: either the pieces had been cut wrong or else they were in the wrong box and the old box must be broken open.

Difficulties with Fenestration

The first problem to which Jullian addressed himself after the summer vacation was the fenestration, in particular the ways in which brise-soleil and ondulatoires might be combined. In the first project all glass was treated with ondulatoires, the glass between the jambs being replaced occasionally by vertical pivoting doors (aérateurs) for natural cross ventilation. To this basic facade brise-soleil were tacked on quite separately: they were fitted in between canted extensions of the slabs above and below the glazed areas (no details of joints being given). These slab extensions were gradually tapered towards their ends in section, with odd results in places where brise-soleil were needed above one another, especially on curved parts of the building. The brise-soleil were to be made of either concrete or aluminum—another hint that the architects anticipated weight problems—and the overall effect of the building would have been lightweight, temporary, and somewhat makeshift; whatever their aesthetic value, the brise-soleil tended to obscure the ondulatoires behind.

It may not have been just technical difficulties, then, which on September 9 prompted Jullian to make two small cardboard models of specification facades (fig. 94). In these the brise-soleil were recessed under the normal floor slab, their outer end made flush with both floor end and ondulatoires. The slab extensions, now redundant, were done away with, so the facade plane was preserved. The result on the interior was that fins of brise-soleil jutted back between ondulatoires into the rooms. To exploit the plastic qualities of this effect, and to distinguish between the brise-soleil and ondulatoires on the exterior, Jullian had the ingenious idea of bringing some of the ondulatoires back a couple of feet making their *inside* edges flush with the inside edges of the intruding brise-soleil. Far more than in the first project the elements became plastic adjuncts, integrated as a system, and the structural problems also seemed to be reduced. He did not stop there. In places horizontal brise-soleil were thought necessary, cutting the vertical ones into upper and lower registers. He decided therefore to treat upper and lower compartments independently of one another, applying all that has just been described to each level. The sinuously textured result would have been the ultimate in what Giedion might have described as "the revitalisation of the wall."[1]

These were ideas doomed to eventual rejection. Nevertheless, it must be borne in mind that a system of this kind was assumed, though not drawn onto plans, for two months to follow. The sight of slabs of brise-soleil through the slats of ondulatoires on interiors must be considered the visual accompaniment of structural modifications hypothesized during the period up until late November—in particular, the frequent replacement of cylindrical pilotis supports by thin, vertical rectangular slabs—henceforth referred to as "piers."

Sert's Harvard modifications were delayed in the mail and did not arrive from America until September 15. Jullian's researches had occurred

94. *Cardboard model experimenting with combination of recessed brise-soleil and ondulatoires, Jullian, September 9, 1960. (1:50; 15.2 × 21.0 × 10.2 cm.) This solution was attempted in response to the problems of fixing and combining these elements in the first project, but Jullian's device confuses the conceptual distinction of the elements and gives too much visual weight to the facade.*

independently before that date. He was pleased with his device: on one model he wrote a note referring to its spatial qualities.[2] He was not liable to let his idea go easily.

Provision of the New Basement

On the 15th Jullian produced two plans from prints of the June project, one of the first floor, the other of the recently demanded new basement (fig. 95). The outline of the basement was simply derived by tracing out the first floor plan. In it he set aside a space for the auditorium beneath the old first floor auditorium of June, but enlarged slightly to the Quincy Street end. Its ceiling slab was to be borne by piers placed around the edges of the room instead of the confused pilotis arrangement of the old one that had hampered the space and restricted projection. Access from the first floor down to the new basement was by means of a ramp placed transversally.

The first floor plan of the same date showed that this ramp was approached from and aligned with the entrance from the Faculty Club side—emphasis enough for Pusey, one might think—but

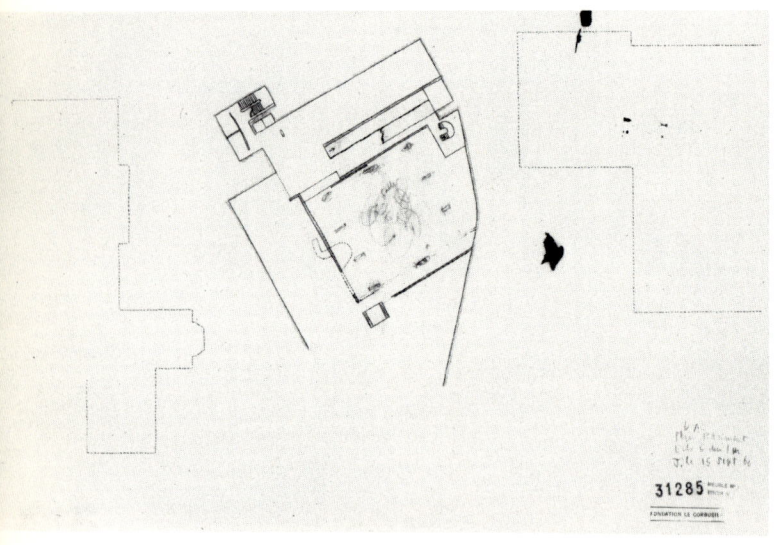

95. *Plan of new basement auditorium, Jullian, September 15, 1960. (1:200; 41 × 56 cm; thick tracing paper.) The idea of putting the auditorium here was the client's. A transversal ramp appears opposite the side entrance and there is also the tentative suggestion of pier supports instead of cylindrical pilotis.*

96. *Plan of level 1, Jullian, September 16, 1960. (1:200; 30 × 38 cm; onion skin.) Red transversal piers are shown all over the building.*

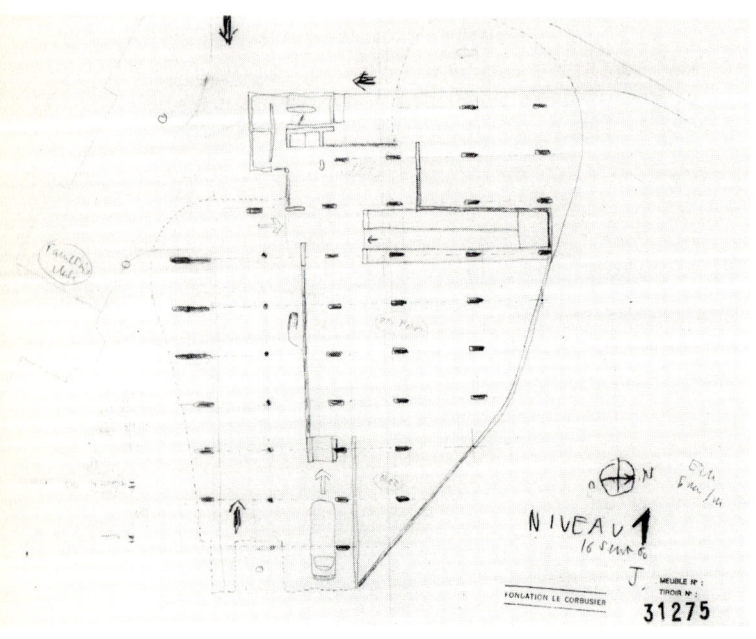

Jullian was also envisaging the use of piers on his first floor, as in the auditorium beneath. These were placed transversally, like the ramp: he was evidently thinking of the directional emphasis a pier provided which a cylindrical piloti did not. The entrance lobby in his plan would have had a hall-like feeling directed between the Faculty Club and the gate into the Yard on Quincy Street. A door was punched through the old fabric at the northwest corner of the lobby, fulfilling the promise of the June notebook that an extra entrance would be provided to one side, allowing a transversal route at ground level for students.[3]

The Faculty Club exit was clearly marked in the plan Jullian drew the next day. Remembering that the project still had "portiques" ("porticoes")—three piers in the covered garden to the north side on the second floor—one realizes that his plans of the 15th would have resulted in three floors with piers. The next day, he went the whole way and placed piers all the way up the building (fig. 96). Transversal streaks in red crayon appeared like so many wounds across the old structure. He appeared willing to use pilotis only where the flow was definitely along the east–west axis, as by the main ramp, the route between the streets next to the Faculty Club, or the interior ramp to the fourth floor.

Le Corbusier does not seem to have been so wildly enthusiastic about this system which, while it undoubtedly had excellent and necessary structural characteristics—for example, it reduced the moments in extending curved slab-ends—was probably rooted in Jullian's aesthetic preferences[4] and in his desire to make the interior structure support the visual strength and actual weight of his new undulating facade. On the 16th, Le Corbusier entered into the proceedings with two sketches of the first floor and basement (figs. 97, 98) showing piers of fatter size than Jullian's, their axis running at ninety degrees to Jullian's. The direction implied by the structural supports and the placement of the ramp down to the basement in a longitudinal position make it clear he was concerned to preserve the main longitudinal spine of the building. But here he ran into a difficulty: his new interior ramp blocked the lift access. The remedy adopted was to move the freight lift out to one side

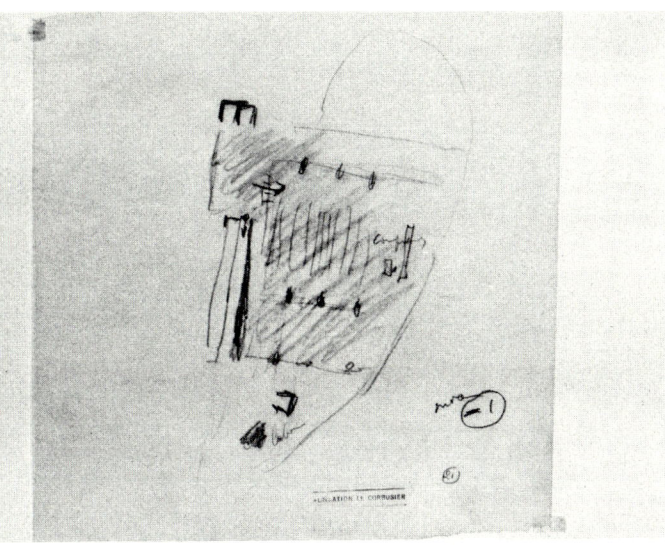 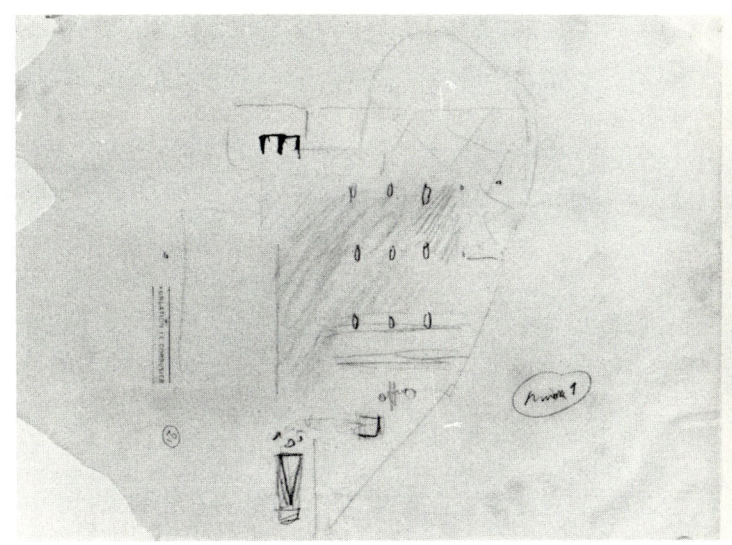

97. *Basement plan, Le Corbusier, September 16, 1960. (1:200; 30 × 34 cm; onion skin.) The interior ramp is placed longitudinally but this has the unfortunate effect of blocking the freight lift entrance. As a temporary remedy the lift is moved out of the rear of the building and switched through ninety degrees. This could not be regarded as a real solution, and there would be no easy solution.*

98. *Plan of level 1, Le Corbusier, September 16, 1960. (1:200; 30 × 38 cm; onion skin.) The shifted lift now rises oddly through office space.*

and to turn the lift ninety degrees. But this was not a real remedy because it would have forced those using the lift on the ground floor to pass through the open air—hardly desirable in the New England winters. The shift of orientation and position would have had bad effects on the other floors too, but for the moment these were ignored.

Experiments with Piers

The next few days were devoted instead to a detailed study of the structural proposals of Jullian's drawings. In all, eleven sections were drawn, eight transverse, three longitudinal (figs. 99, 100). These were drawn to analyze the structure of piers hypothesized in Jullian's plans. Transversal beams were included all over the building, giving much needed support to the profusion of piers, some of which were structurally unnecessary. On some floors piers were inserted for visual consistency, but their considerable weight led to the need for piers or beams on lower floors, especially where pilotis had once been envisaged. Overall, the structure was snowballing.

Moreover, the new visual effects clashed with the earlier sensitivities between structural directions and main circulation directions. Viewed from one angle, the piers gave an elephantine quality to the building (fig. 100). Jullian's facade idea was likewise very heavy visually. Through this increasing visual weight the project was departing from the earlier conception with its stress on transparency and slender tectonic supports.

On September 21 Le Corbusier set aside considerations of superfluous structure and focused on the essential span of the basement auditorium (fig. 101). As Sert had said, the new placement would not require major formal rearrangement, but it did require some structural rethinking. In the first project the span had been bridged by the "portiques" ("porticoes"), the three piers in the covered second floor garden, which acted as a lattice beam. Assuming a surrounding piloti/slab system, Le Corbusier now brought these porticoes down into the entrance lobby where they spanned three bays. They required that a thick support be provided at the back of the auditorium beneath.

On the same sheet of paper, Le Corbusier hypothesized a free span for the basement of three normal bays plus the main ramp bay—the whole distance, without the intermediary support, being

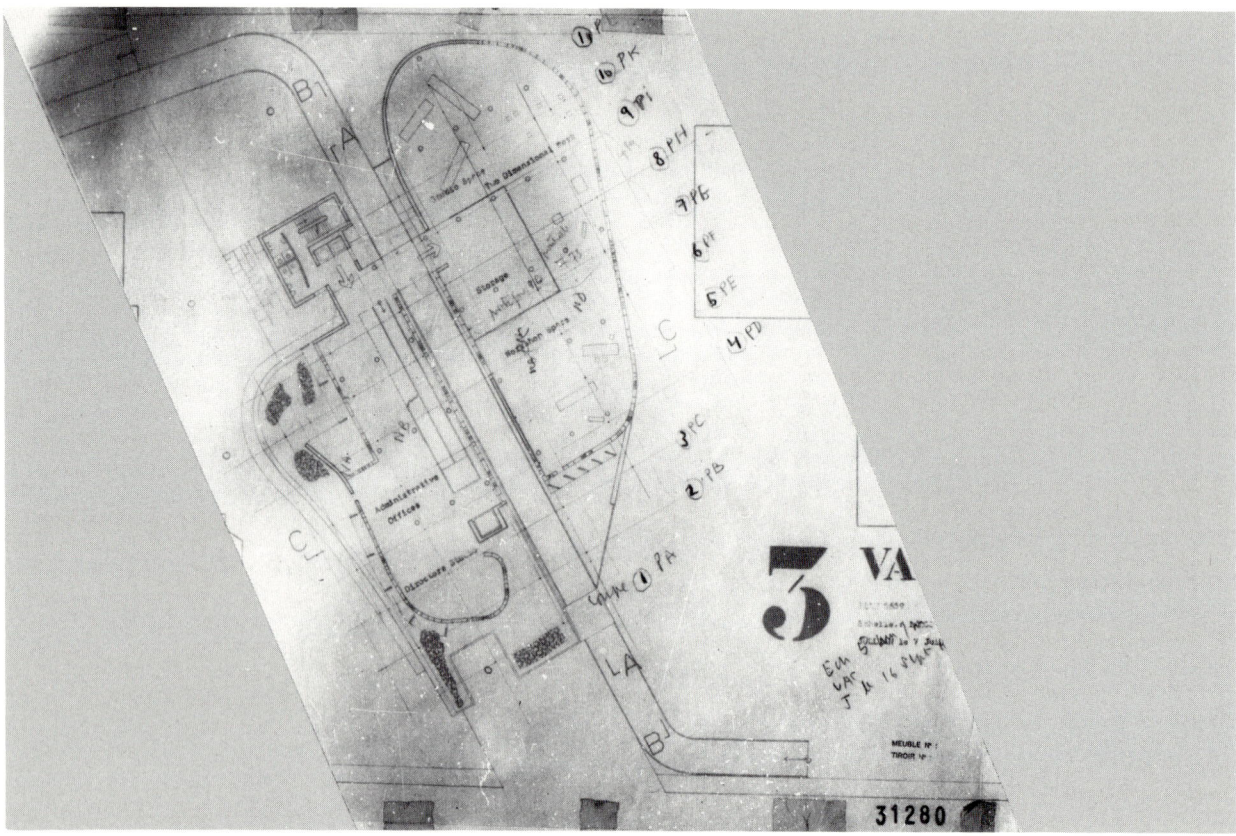

99. *Plan of level 3 with overlay of sectional cuts, Jullian, September 16, 1960. (1:200; 42 × 50 cm; onion skin attached to print.)*

something in the order of 18.5 meters. Over two-thirds of the first floor structure now became a sort of extended lattice beam. At the ramp gallery, the reinforcing spread into the second level. Small people were drawn in for scale.

On another small sheet, Le Corbusier tried a second solution (fig. 102). He traced the bay dimensions from Jullian's section PE done a couple of days before (fig. 100). This time the auditorium span was much less (two normal bays, a little over 7 meters), but as the porticoes were composed of reduced bays (each two-thirds of a normal one), a pier from the normal structural grid now arrived at the midpoint of a span of the porticoes, above a gap.

These three drawings summed up an attempt to liberate the basement space from structural supports, to allow free planning and unobstructed projection; they also represent the opposing structural reality, the limitation of concrete spans. Le Corbusier seems still to have been concerned about the strong transversal emphasis these structural necessities gave the building. A section drawn by Jullian the same day placed a large doorway in the glazing just to the south of the main ramp at second level, so providing a means of access from studio to terrace for even large objects. Le Corbusier's presence over Jullian's shoulder was affirmed by a small sketch on another Jullian section the same day, which showed pilotis surmounted by beams in both directions (fig. 103). Le Corbusier was probably now aiming to compromise between structural realities and earlier aesthetic values: to avoid piers, preserve pilotis, but still be structurally realistic. Alongside his light pencil sketch he wrote "nefs" —"naves."

Conflicts between Elevator and Interior Ramp

During the next week Jullian concentrated on the third floor in the region of the ramps. Only days before he had been willing to use pilotis in this

100. *Three sections PG, PF, PE, Jullian, September 17–20, 1960. (1:200; 56 × 48 cm; thick tracing paper.) These three drawings (part of a strip of eight) show clearly the elephantine effect of Jullian's transversal piers and the placement of fat piers over slender pilotis. The transversal ramp to the basement is visible in the top section.*

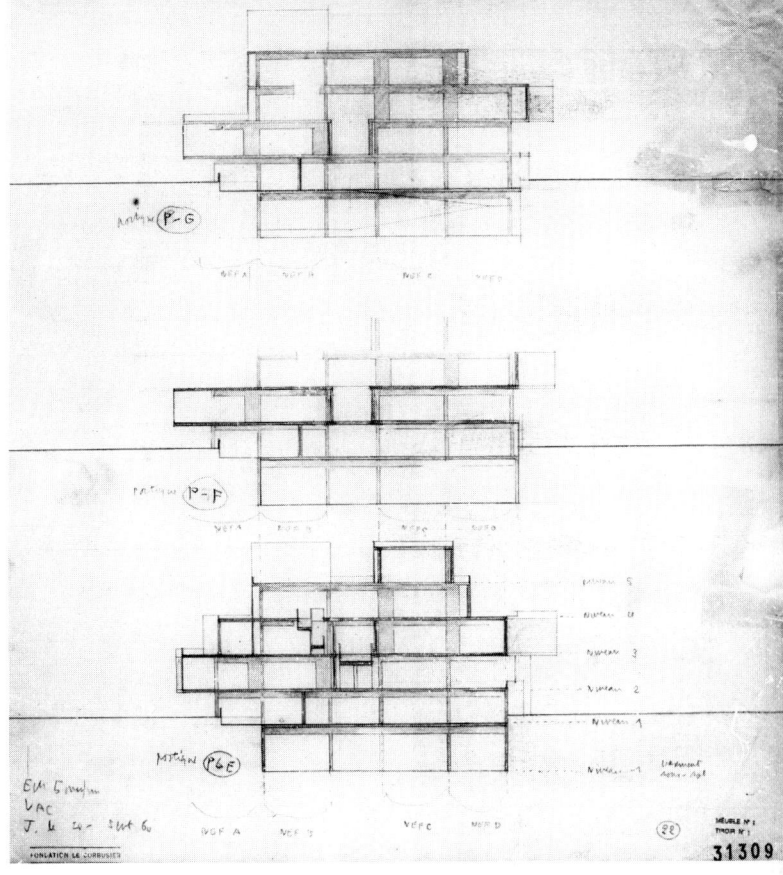

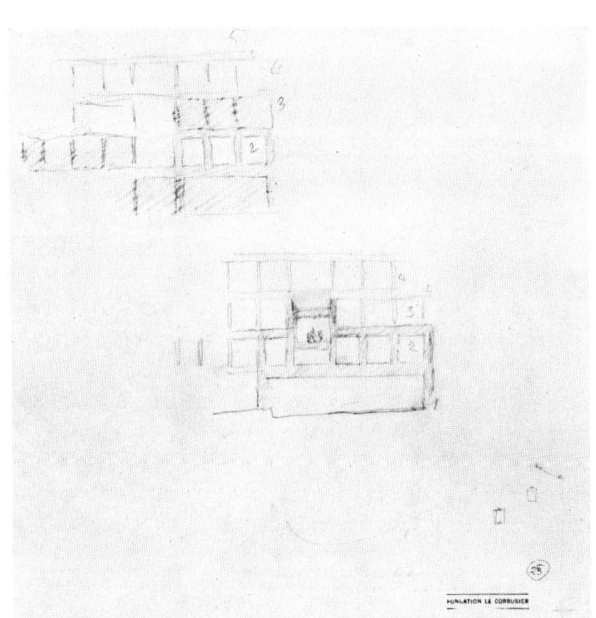

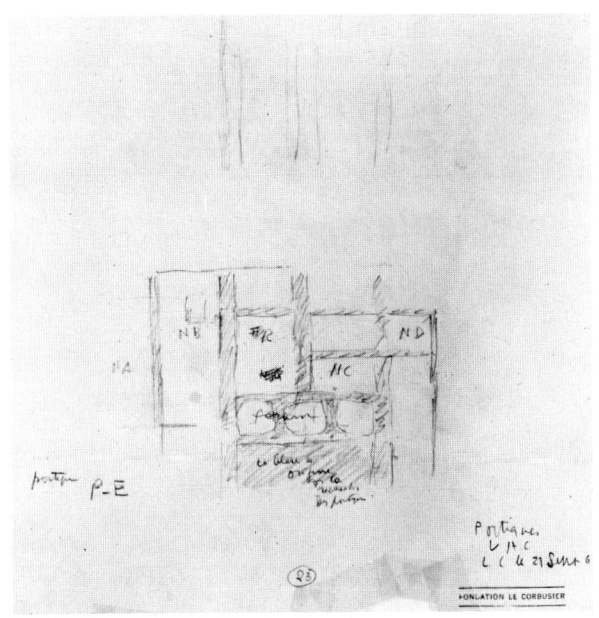

101. *Structural sketches, Le Corbusier, September 21, 1960. (1:200; 38 × 40 cm; onion skin.) Various solutions are tried for bridging the basement auditorium. At the bottom of the sheet is a light sketch of a suspension structure.*

102. *Structural study, Le Corbusier, September 21, 1960. (1:200; 56 × 48 cm; thick tracing paper.) The concrete truss is christened "les portiques" ("the porticoes") and the public area at level 1, the "forum." This section was traced from one of Jullian's of September 17–20.*

115

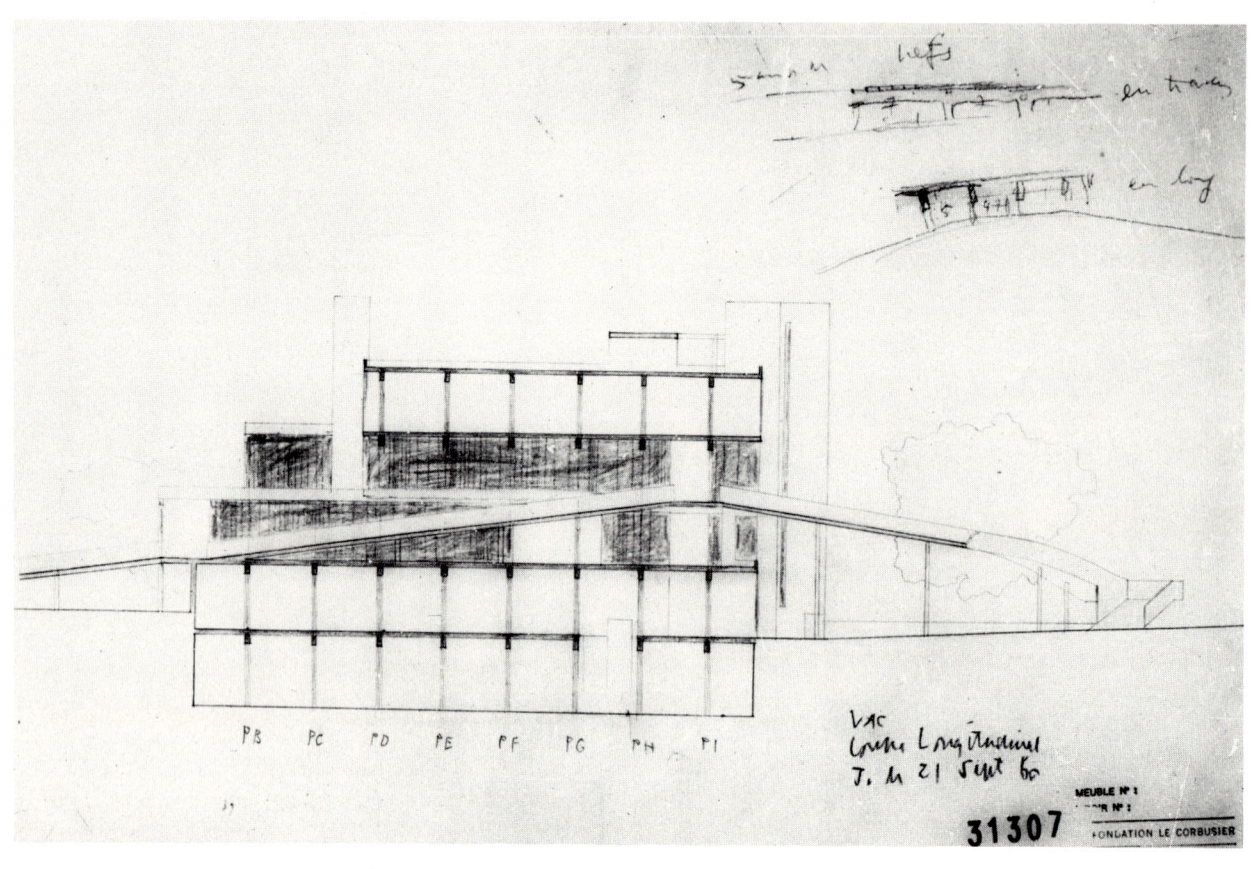

103. *Longitudinal section, Jullian, September 21, 1960. (1:200; 30 × 64 cm; onion skin.) In contrast to the transversal sections of September 17–20, this gives a slender appearance. At the top right Le Corbusier sketched pilotis surmounted by beams in both directions.*

area. Now, on September 22, he became totally uncompromising and, on one sketch, drew thick piers in red. On another sketch the same day he made the startling move of unfixing the interior ramp that ran up to the exhibition space and setting it down astride the main ramp gallery as a transversal bridge (fig. 104). In the process it presumably became an external ramp itself.

This might be regarded as a sensationalist display of circulation, but it was in fact a drastic measure for dealing with a difficult problem inherent in the organization of the first project. Jullian had come to realize what had been anticipated in the basement earlier in the month: that interior ramp landings blocked access from the freight elevator for all but the smallest objects. In the next few days Jullian attempted to solve this problem for the third level in a variety of ways, starting with a series of rearrangements of the interior ramp. The nature of each hypothesis and the difficulties each in turn created show clearly in the drawings (figs. 104, 105).

Realizing that his gambits for the third level had for the moment failed, on September 28 Jullian again shifted attention to the lower parts of the building. His basement plan outlined the required functions in more detail than previously and switched the direction of the auditorium projection through ninety degrees (fig. 106). He used prints of an earlier plan (paper cutouts) marked with "storage" or "lockers" to help him arrange the functions correctly and on a ground level plan drew in longitudinal piers in the main entrance lobby; these acted as a lattice beam to span the space beneath. He christened them "les ponts" ("the bridges") and in sections the same day queried whether or not 18 meters without intermediate support would be possible. The same drawings drew attention to other structural queries (fig. 107). The joining of fenestration to a skeleton with beams was not resolved either. Indeed, a solution would only be found when both skeleton and fenestration were modified.

Jullian's return to the lower levels could not continue for long without his reencountering the ramp/lift clash at basement and first level, and the plans of September 28 show him shifting the other term in the problem: the entrance to the freight lift

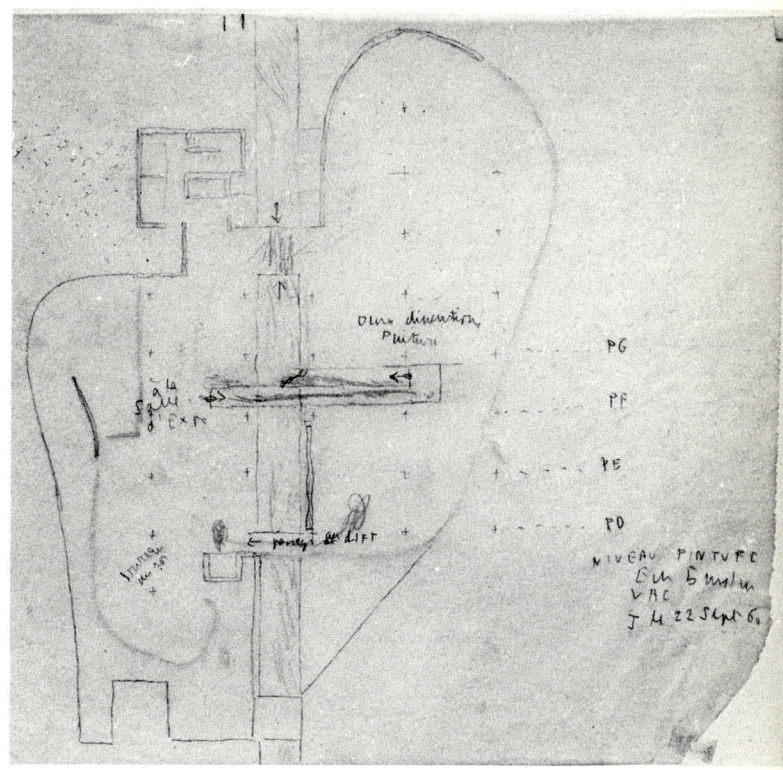

104. *Plan of level 3, Jullian, September 22, 1960. (1:200; 30 × 44 cm; onion skin.) The third level ramp was switched through ninety degrees and dropped over the main ramp gallery as a bridge. Another smaller bridge is created to the rear close to the freight lift. Jullian was attempting to avoid the blockage of the lift by the interior ramp landing at level 3. The client had also been concerned about the way the painting studio (to the right) had been neglected by the lift: hence the new rear bridge marked "passage au lift" ("passage to the lift"). But the interior transversal ramp would require protection from the weather and would also disrupt the previous longitudinal spine of the building, so transgressing one of the building's guiding "laws."*

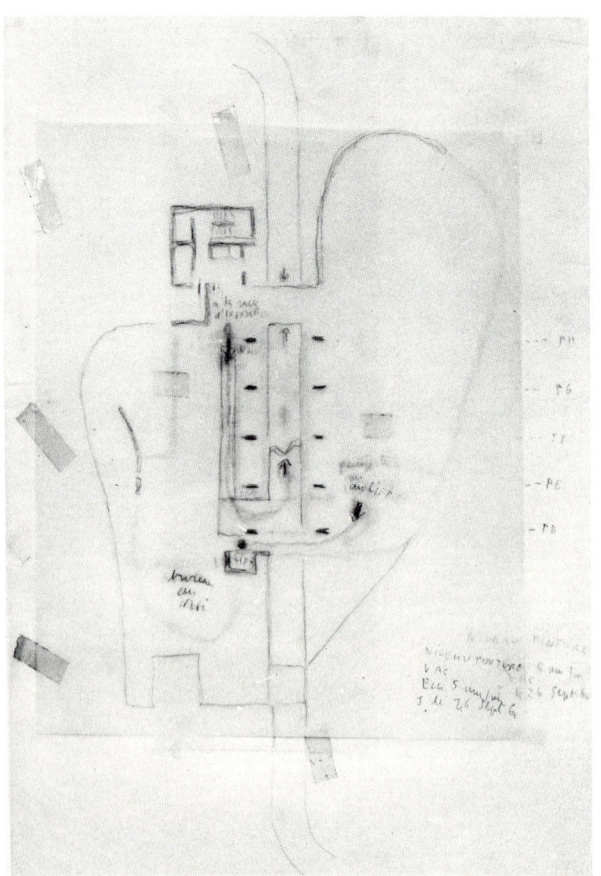

105. *Plan of level 3, Jullian, September 26, 1960. (1:200; 30 × 46 cm; onion skin.) In another attempt to alleviate the clash between interior ramp and freight lift, the base of the ramp is shifted as far away from the lift as possible so that its landing will be higher at the point where encroachment previously occurred. The internal ramp then continues above the main ramp to ascend to the fourth level.*

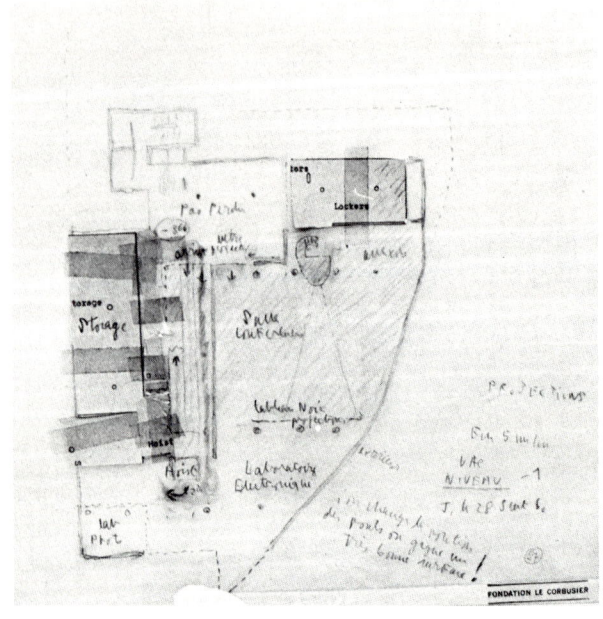

106. *Basement plan, Jullian, September 28, 1960. (1:200; 30 × 52 cm; onion skin.) The drawing shows projection in a longitudinal direction, as well as a typical atelier method: the use of old prints and tape when attempting functional hypotheses. The freight lift (here marked "hoist") has been turned through 180 degrees, so creating a small maneuvering space to the rear. Considerable smudging on the sheet bears witness to some confusion and the figure 2-26 indicates that there is something of a squeeze even now. Jullian is probably thinking of a freight lift with doors on both sides for the higher levels. The effect of this shift on level 1 would have been to force users of the lift outside in all weathers.*

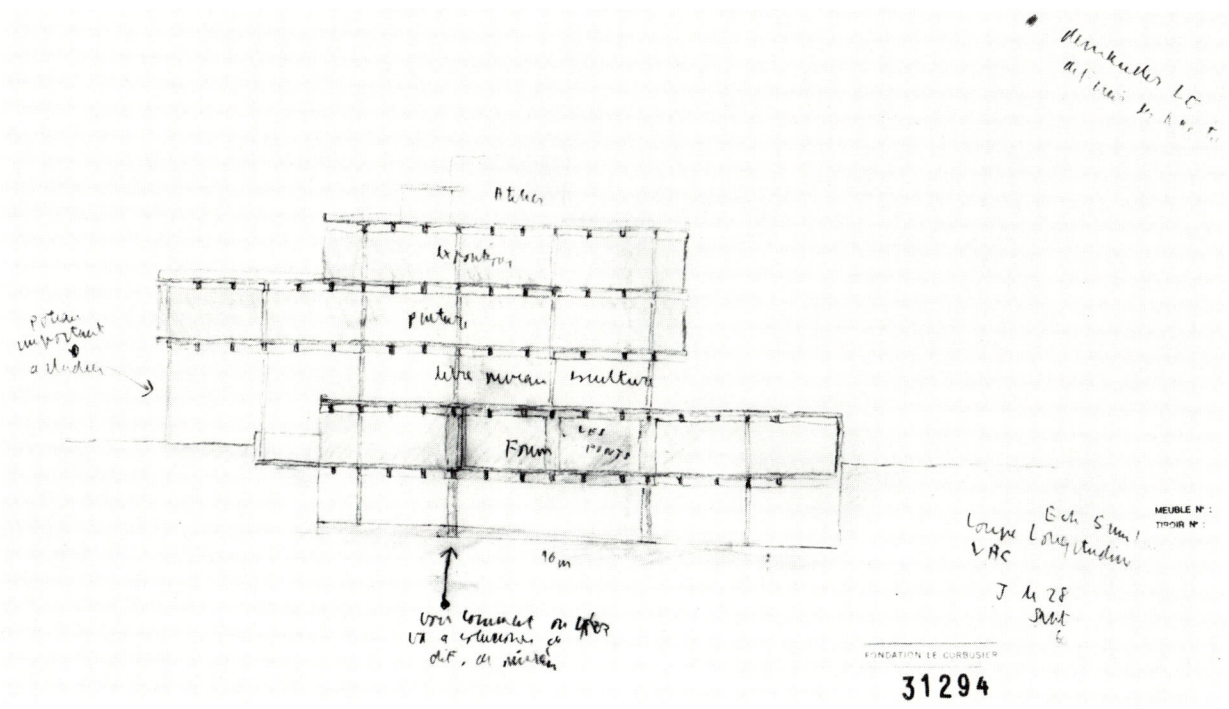

107. *Longitudinal section, Jullian, September 28, 1960. (1:200; 30 × 53 cm; onion skin) Here the structure has crystallized (temporarily) into a piloti/slab system with beams running in both directions, except for the "ponts" ("bridges") at ground level. To the left a column rises two stories on the outer edge of the building and is marked by Jullian "poteau à étudier" ("column to be studied")—with some reason, considering the extent of the curved volume to be supported. To the top right he writes a reminder, "Demander L-C de faire des aérateurs" ("Ask L-C to make aérateurs"). He is also concerned about the vast width of the span in the basement and wonders if an intermediate support will be necessary.*

(fig. 106). It was switched through 180 degrees and resulted in the need to pass out of doors: an impossible suggestion for New England winter climate. This was no solution.

Five days later, on October 3, Jullian threw all his weight into trying to solve the ramp/lift problem. He attempted a variety of solutions such as moving the ramps or moving the lift at the third level and basement. On one drawing he succeeded in removing the interior ramp landing from the lift entrance by making the lower part of the third level ramp longer than the top part, but the same could not be done for the ground-floor/basement interior ramp without blocking the side entrance (fig. 108). He reconsidered a 180 degree switch for the lift entrance, going so far as to create a special covered maneuvering area to the rear, but this would have interfered with the spatial qualities of the rear of the building. He considered shifting the lift laterally more than twenty feet along the rear side of the Prescott Street facade, but this too constituted a major interference with overall formal properties (fig. 109). Next he made an exterior passageway at the rear of the building as a sort of

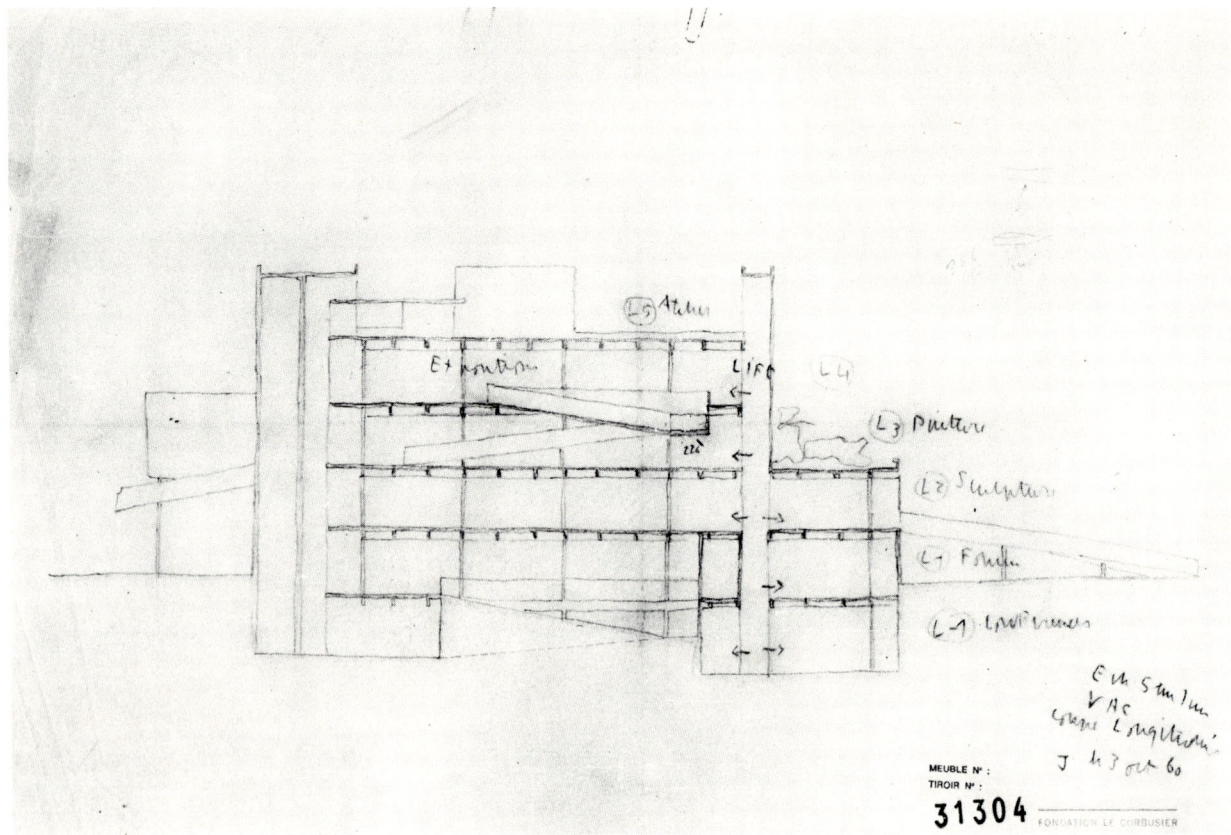

bridge over the main ramp (fig. 110). When this too ran into difficulties, Jullian tried moving the lift longitudinally three or four feet (fig. 110, 111). Again this seriously disrupted the formal harmony of the building.

At this point it is perhaps pertinent to inquire why Le Corbusier did not drop the idea of an interior ramp altogether and think of another way up. He seems to have attached enormous importance to this element as a means of joining the levels, especially in a building whose very conception implied the notion of an ascending "promenade" visit. Here was one of those "rules" of the building: sacrosanct features to be disrupted on no account. When the ramp was eventually dropped, removal stemmed from the request of a client concerned about money and wasted space. By then, too, the ramp had ceased to be a problem because its context—the building as a whole—had changed considerably.

It is probably worth stepping back from the project to consider the architects' working methods.

108. *Longitudinal section, Jullian, October 3, 1960. (1:200; 30 × 46 cm; onion skin.) This section dramatically advertises the conflict of the freight lift with the interior ramp at level 3 and at the lower levels, and shows Jullian's various attempts to find a solution. At level 3 he has made the bottom slope of the internal ramp extend a long way to the west (left) end of the building, allowing the landing to be 2.26 meters high, and a considerable distance away from the lift entrance. At level 4 this also creates a wider maneuvering space than previously between the entrance and the void created by the interior ramp. No such resolution exists for the lower level, though, where Jullian again resorts to a 180 degree shift of the lift entrance and creates a curved undercroft for sheltered passage, destroying completely the spatial effect of the cantilever and disrupting the whole Prescott Street side of the building. Jullian has also resorted to a double door lift in the basement and at level 2. But such an elevator was not allowable and anyway Jullian's overall hypothesis was here clearly untenable because of its general interference with the building.*

120

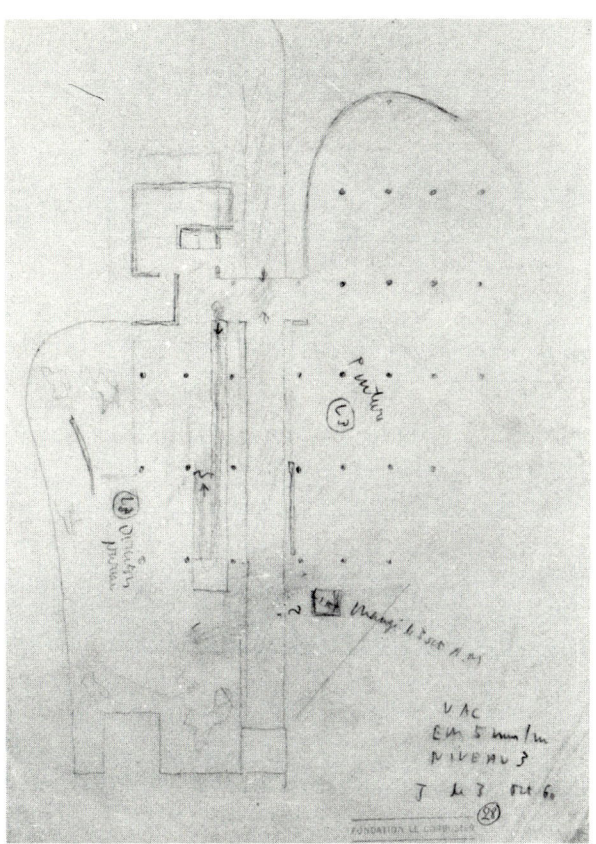

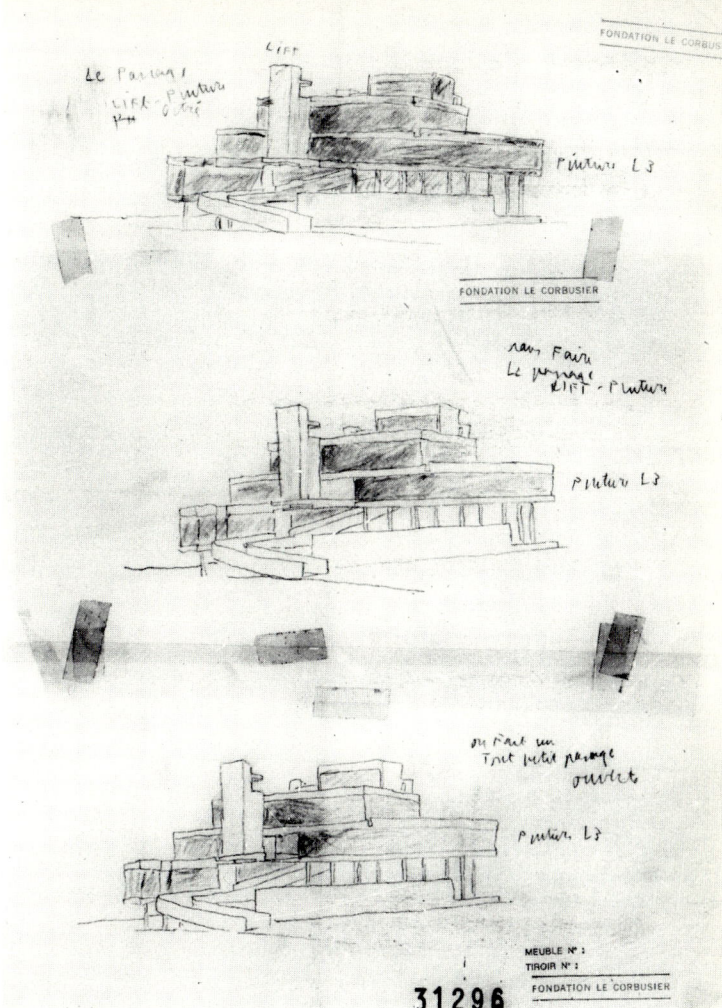

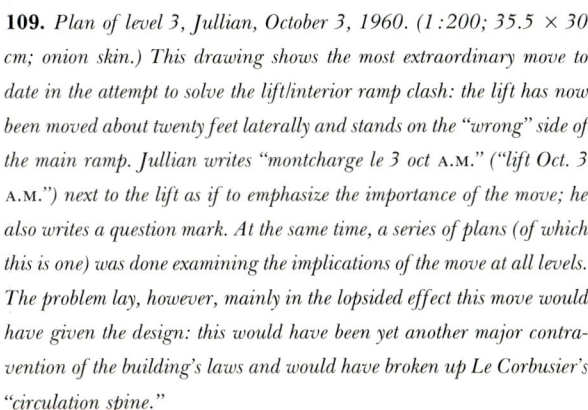

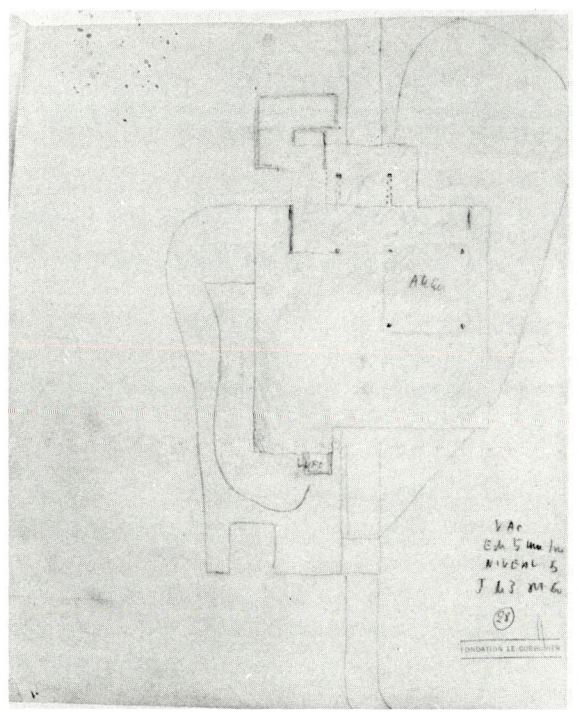

109. *Plan of level 3, Jullian, October 3, 1960. (1:200; 35.5 × 30 cm; onion skin.)* This drawing shows the most extraordinary move to date in the attempt to solve the lift/interior ramp clash: the lift has now been moved about twenty feet laterally and stands on the "wrong" side of the main ramp. Jullian writes "montcharge le 3 oct A.M." ("lift Oct. 3 A.M.") next to the lift as if to emphasize the importance of the move; he also writes a question mark. At the same time, a series of plans (of which this is one) was done examining the implications of the move at all levels. The problem lay, however, mainly in the lopsided effect this move would have given the design: this would have been yet another major contravention of the building's laws and would have broken up Le Corbusier's "circulation spine."

110. *Three perspectives of Prescott Street facade, Jullian, October 3, 1960. (1:200; 43 × 27 cm; onion skin.)* They show another ingenious attempt at solving the lift/ramp clash: the lift (now back on the "correct" side) has been shifted out a few feet along its longitudinal axis, so presenting a large flank of side wall, but relieving the squeeze inside the building against the interior ramp landing. The perspectives were made from a tracing over a photograph of the model.

111. *Plan (and aerial view) of level 5, Jullian, October 3, 1960. (1:200; 35.5 × 30 cm; onion skin.)* The effects of a longitudinal lift shift are shown. The fourth floor is no longer a single rectangle, but has an ungainly projection.

Jullian seems to have been able to pursue a single hypothesis to its logical, and sometimes preposterous, conclusion. On other occasions he grasped the significance of a cluster of features, proceeding with a single leap. Most of the time till Christmas was spent singling out problems for discrete consideration and, as it were, clipping one solution alongside the next. Le Corbusier entered this process at many points, setting a general direction by means of a rapid sketch or stray remark and returning to examine the idea when it was clarified. Sometimes, as with the plans of the first project, he drew with such assurance that Jullian's role became entirely subsidiary. On other occasions Jullian took the initiative, and Le Corbusier's presence was only hinted at by small sketches or humorous doodles. He would go to the atelier in the afternoons, after a morning's painting, and glance over his colleagues' shoulders at the morning's work. Those who knew them say that Le Corbusier and his team were well suited to one another in his last years and that Jullian and he in particular had a marked mutual sympathy.[5]

Serts' Clarification of the Basement and Level 1

On his basement plan of October 3, Jullian had scrawled the note, "demander précisions J-L Sert" ("ask J-L Sert for details"). By coincidence, the same day in Cambridge Sert was preparing a package of practical details which—and this is typical of the lurching fashion in which the project proceeded—were to make half the preceding month's work, both problems and solutions, irrelevant. The mixed blessing was sent off on October 4, arriving innocently at the rue de Sèvres on October 15. Sert's letter read "I am . . . enclosing herewith some prints showing possible basement and first floor layouts, which would meet the requirements of the program as listed in the letter of August 10th, sent to me by Dean Trottenberg—a copy of which I previously sent you" (10-4-60; figs. 112, 113). If there had been any doubt about Harvard's intentions before the arrival of this parcel, there could be no doubt of them after. Species of trees, water table levels, rooms to be specially insulated, local regulations—all were painstakingly indicated in a small neat hand on carefully colored prints. Sert concentrated on three principal features: the functions of the basement (fig. 112), those of the first floor (fig. 113), and the gradients of the ramps, which by law had to be ten percent or less (fig. 114). Sert expanded in some detail on this last point, indicating that there was a lateral limit for the main ramp at a set-back line 7 feet 6 inches from the main property line. To deal with the gradient inside the limits set by this, Sert suggested turning the ramp back on itself at both ends. The extremities of the main ramp now both faced inwards towards the building. Little did he know that his colleagues in Paris had been battling with a similar problem of horizontal limits, but for the inside ramp, not the main one.

Of course, Sert knew nothing at all of the quagmire of problems into which the dinner party building was sinking. As Jullian had confidently done a month before, he simply traced around the first floor for the plan of the new basement (fig. 112). But where Jullian had only dealt with the auditorium and some flexible spaces for Light and Communication, Sert had stuffed his plan full of the most detailed requirements; and where the Paris architects had used a ramp down, the more pragmatic Sert took the space-saving measure of a small curving staircase.

Certainly the Committee for the Practice of the Visual Arts and Robert Gardner, the projected coordinator of Light and Communication, had put their heads together. The basement contained storage spaces, a workshop, toilets, a darkroom, recording space, a cutting room, and film vaults, as well as spaces for documentary film making and for animation, and a place for television control and projection. The first floor had been tackled with similar thoroughness.

But it is Sert's auditorium that stands out. He made it double height, with its floor in the basement and its ceiling under the second floor. In this way he accommodated the tall studio gear that would occasionally be used there and still avoided the extremely high water table.

Alongside the top half of the auditorium, on the first floor (fig. 113), he placed a seminar room with views down to the screens below. His swift practicality, fast eye for functional contingencies, and pragmatism were in marked contrast to the structural poetics at the rue de Sèvres. One wonders if

112. *Basement plan, Sert, Jackson and Gourley, October 3, 1960. (1:200; 43 × 70 cm; print.) Light and Communications accommodations for this level are outlined in great detail. The plan is a print made after the presentation set.*

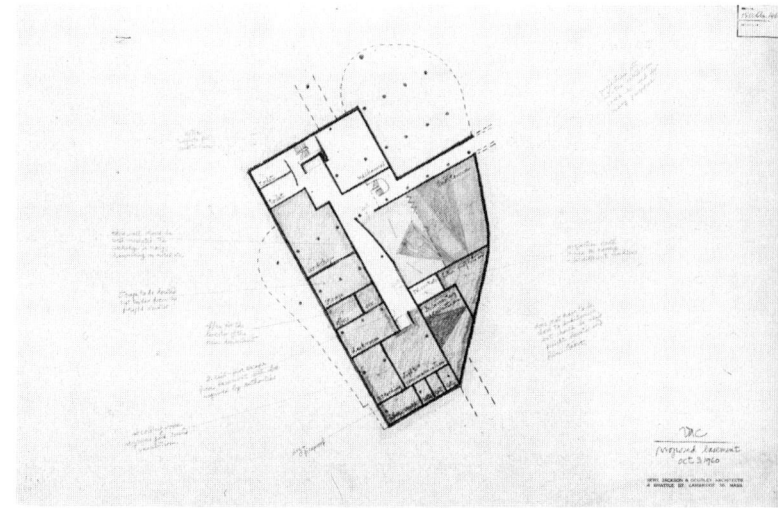

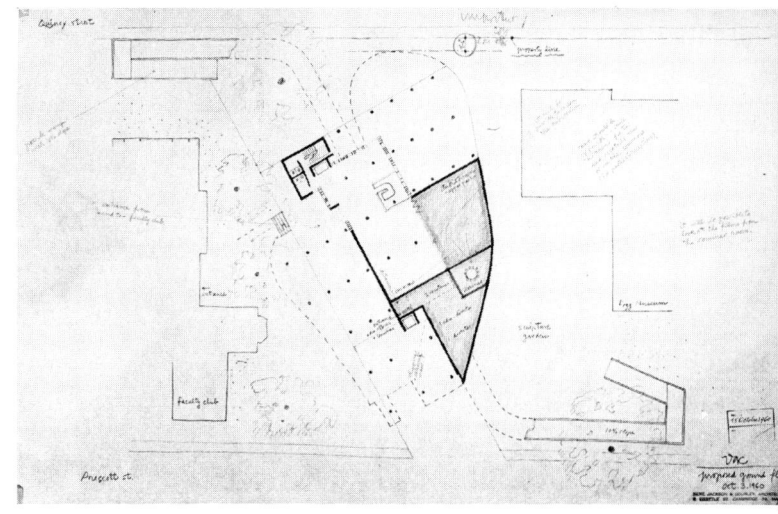

113. *Plan of level 1, Sert, Jackson and Gourley, October 3, 1960. (1:200; 43 × 70 cm; print.) This plan suggests the arrangement of functions and shows that the double height auditorium was originally Sert's idea. To the top Sert demonstrates how the visual arts center must be kept within the building line 7 feet 6 inches from Quincy Street.*

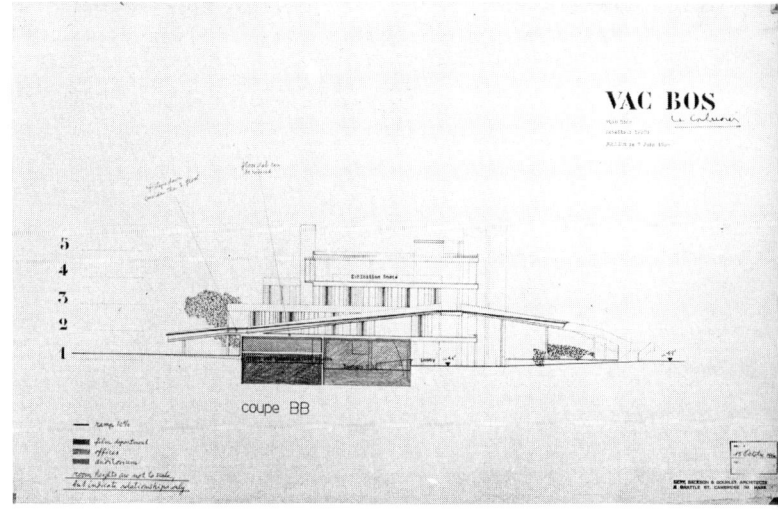

114. *Longitudinal section BB, Sert, Jackson and Gourley, October 3, 1960. (1:200; 43 × 70 cm; print.) The need for a ten percent gradient for the ramp is stressed. The double height "lecture hall" shows clearly.*

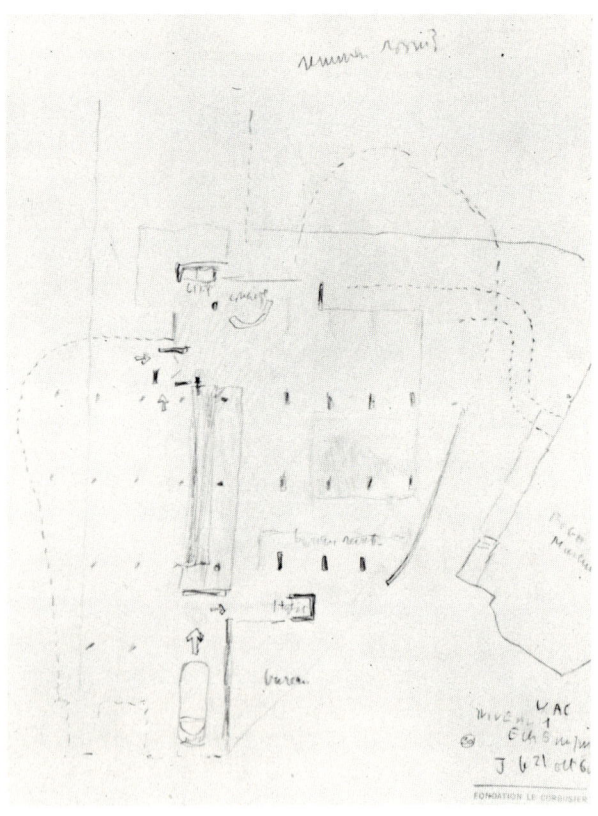

115. *Plan of level 1, Jullian, October 21, 1960. (1:200; 37.5 × 35 cm; onion skin.) In light hatching Jullian reacts to Sert's double height auditorium suggestion, and in an inscription ("seminar room?") demonstrates his puzzlement over one detail of Sert's level 1 plan. The lift is still on the wrong side.*

Sert had an idea what problems the Paris architects were encountering. He must surely have expected the final plans with their "forms unchanged" within a few weeks—or just as long as it took Paris to juggle the basement functions as they wanted them and to make the most of that "handsome space," the first floor entrance lobby (8-31-60; appendix 10).

Jullian's response to this brisk intrusion was to produce three plans on October 21 (fig. 115). The prints had arrived with something of the stunning novelty of messages from another planet. Not only were the annotations in English but the plans themselves seemed to speak a different architectural language. On top of two sheets Jullian wrote the query "seminar room?" but otherwise the implications of Sert's prints were plain. The ramp to the basement was earmarked for elimination, and with it went its problems. Then the freight lift shifted to the wrong (that is, north) side again, for no obvious reason other than an empty gesture at the recalled problem of ramp and lift four floors above. Then, apart from the most minor rearrangements, the basement functions were planned substantially as Sert had suggested; indeed, Jullian has since confirmed that the basement was designed by Sert "except for the auditorium." But the double-height auditorium was certainly Sert's invention (although his use of sectional arrangements is traceable in the long run to Le Corbusier), whatever later details of its design were undertaken in Paris. The new auditorium also made Jullian's "ponts" ("bridges") irrelevant and moved the problem of bridging the span back to the "portiques," where it had started. Indeed, without the plans of the preceding five weeks, it would be difficult to say anything at all had happened. Only the lift position hinted that something was wrong. The designers had taken their building into a number of cul-de-sacs but had returned to the main line of development with a much clearer idea of its problems if not the means for solving them. The client's changes had been incorporated (except for the reduction in size). It was the building's inherent weaknesses that now needed attacking.

It does not seem to have occurred to the university that the basement would cost them extra until after it had been designed, in early November.

The original objections to its size had to do with encroachment on the Faculty Club, not with finances. At the beginning of November, Bundy wrote to Pusey that Sert's studies had revealed "that on the basis of our current plans the cost will be about $2,100,000, as against an original budget of $1,500,000." There were "contingencies" but "the main reason for the increased cost is quite simply that we have added 10,000 feet of basement to the design . . . Aside from the basement the building is not unreasonable, and the construction cost estimate from Vappi and Company per square foot, are a shade under the $30 figure that was used for planning before we ever had a design from Le Corbusier. So it is not the building that is extravagant, it is, in a sense, we ourselves" (11-2-60).[6]

What size was the building Vappi and Company's study was based upon? Since Le Corbusier's plans were not known, and since it was certainly not known that he had so far ignored the instruction to reduce the size, one must assume that the calculations were based on the June floor area plus the extra amount that Sert's basement print of October had suggested. It is odd, in that case, that the list of proposed remedies did not include insistance that Le Corbusier reduce the overall size. Bundy thought of everything else: delving into other funds, consulting the Carpenters, abandoning the basement. It was not they alone who were being extravagant, but also, for certain, their architect.

At the time, Le Corbusier was in Chandigarh, and his absence from the rue de Sèvres corresponded with a lull in the project. His notebook of the trip[7] was filled with the usual jottings of cloud formations, reminiscences and ex cathedra pronouncements—an extreme contrast with the stern realities being faced in Cambridge. During his absence there were sparse communications from Sert to Jullian indicating the need for fire escapes (with the suggestion that a stair be provided in the vicinity of the freight lift), clarifying the director's studio space needs at the third level with the aid of a sketch, and confirming that the legal stipulation of ten percent for ramps applied to interior ones as well as exterior ones (11-15-60; 11-16-60). With this legal barrier, the third floor reached an impasse, for an increase in slope might have delivered him from his predicament. Moreover, an extremely detailed specification for the type of elevator desired (written by Huson Jackson, Sert's partner) made it clear that a minimum diagonal length of eight feet was necessary for the transport of large materials. Shrinkage of the elevator could not therefore be used to increase the space between itself and the ramp. Jackson further pointed out that an elevator with doors at both ends would have to be even larger, would then cost more, and would not be acceptable for open air access at ground level on account of the "severe winters." This effectively jammed all Jullian's proposed solutions of early October. The third floor "puzzle" reached a deadlock.

Changes in the Fenestration

The oddest of these communications from Sert's office concerned ondulatoires and must have arrived just before Le Corbusier's departure, for there is a "note to Jullian's attention" dated October 14: "I am giving you below a paragraph concerning you in a letter from Mr. José-Luis Sert of October 11th, 1960: 'I suppose that you received my letter and the diagrams of the basement. We are still *waiting* for the sections and glazing details of the ondulatoires that you promised in June.'"

Now, it is important to note that Le Corbusier was reminded of his promise before he went. Not only does the promise made in June help to explain why attention was so swiftly turned to the fenestration after the vacation—which, in turn, suggests Le Corbusier quickly realized his June solution could not stand close scrutiny—but the fact that Le Corbusier did not reply to Sert till *after* his return from India on November 25, six weeks later, suggests that the ondulatoires were far from resolved on his departure. In fact, the embarrassment was so acute that Le Corbusier later denied having made such a promise at all (12-3-60; appendix 11).

Confirmation that it was on his mind comes from the notebook he was carrying with him in India. Among some sketches of the Assembly at Chandigarh, he wrote:

125

Attention! retrouver *fiches* papier a lettre ochre du croquis fait 3 Nov à L'Assembly—petits offices avec brise soleil sans ondulatoire formant 4e mur observés ici pour emploi a Boston.[8]

Attention! to find again the scrap of paper with ochre lettering of the sketch made November 3 at the Assembly—little offices with brise soleil without ondulatoire forming fourth wall observed here for use in Boston.

The extent of the emergency is indicated by the phrase "without ondulatoire." It meant he was abandoning his first idea for "ondulatoires partout" ("ondulatoires everywhere"). One motive for the change was the desire for transparency—paradoxical because ondulatoires could normally have provided it. But views would have been impossible from the interior of one of Jullian's rooms with their atypical obstructing slats (fig. 94). Moreover, Jullian's system resulted in a multiplicity of joints and elements, an incorrect mixture of aluminum and concrete,[9] a system too weighty visually for the structure Le Corbusier desired, and considerable curtailment of useable studio space. Also, in places where the brise-soleil jutted inwards from the glass, the sun's glare might have been excluded, but not its heat, since rays could touch the panes. Jullian's was not a typical solution—Le Corbusier may have wished to show his usual language—and there was no assurance the system would work on a curved plan: Jullian's researches had been with rectangular rooms. Finally, there was the special problem of jointing any system of curved extremity to a rectangular grid of beams.

Ideally Le Corbusier needed a brise-soleil that was the opposite of most of these things. This meant dropping ondulatoires to begin with. Then it meant choosing from the limited range of his preexisting brise-soleil one which would allow views, was simple to construct, avoided confusions of material, and would work on a curved plan without interfering with visual and tectonic subtleties, internal and external. There was at least one element in his repertoire that could do all these things, and the mention of the "4e mur" ("fourth wall") at Chandigarh is a hint to his intention. Moreover, this fenestration problem was an excellent miniature illustration, I believe, of the architect's dilemma of intention. Was he to impress the United States with an innovatory building, or one which contained a barrage of typical solutions "de façon Corbu" ("in the Corbusian manner")? There was no question at all about the impact of the sculptural plan: the problem lay in the elevation treatment. From that point on, the "axis of intention" was singular: innovations might have produced some permanent lessons for the "recherche patiente," but they were set about with hazards; henceforth he would take typical solutions with their well-tried technical certainty and familiarity. The confusions of the previous weeks can only have confirmed him in his beliefs about the certainty of "solutions-types" ("type solutions"). But there was one other condition that was left aside a moment ago: jointing with beams. None of his solutions for brise-soleil could joint with them on a curved slab-end. Although he may not have realized it, the sentence of beams was as good as read.

An elevation study made in late November (fig. 117) was the only drawing giving an idea of what Jullian's system worked up in September's model would have looked like over a whole facade. It was suggestive rather than exact, and to one side were some sketches by Le Corbusier addressed to fixing or viewing problems. But this first drawing was also the last, and a set of elevations done in the same month had unspecified fenestration treatment (figs. 118, 119).

The November Elevations and Sections

Some wishful thinking must account for these elevations, as if the architects were trying to convince themselves that the end was in sight. One letter from Sert awaiting Le Corbusier on his return on November 25 mentioned the "intention" the latter had expressed of sending "finished drawings" "before the end of November" (11-3-60).[10] Le Corbusier wrote back implying to Sert that he would have his plans soon (12-3-60; appendix 11). But the project was not resolved. The ramp and lift problems of the third floor defied solution, and the problems of jointing skeleton to fenestration awaited it.

As abstract compositions the drawings were superb, however. They were overall planar studies of

116. *Plan of level 3, Le Corbusier, May 1, 1960. (1:200; 38 × 23 cm; onion skin.) Administrative offices are to the left with the director's studio; the painting studio is to the right. Notice the color code and the placement of the sun and arrow with a query next to it at the rear of the interior ramp. Red indicates fenestration exposed directly to the midday sun; orange indicates fenestration exposed only to early morning sun; blue indicates fenestration never touched by direct rays; black represents walls. Drawings like this plan invite comparisons with Le Corbusier's painting and sculptures.*

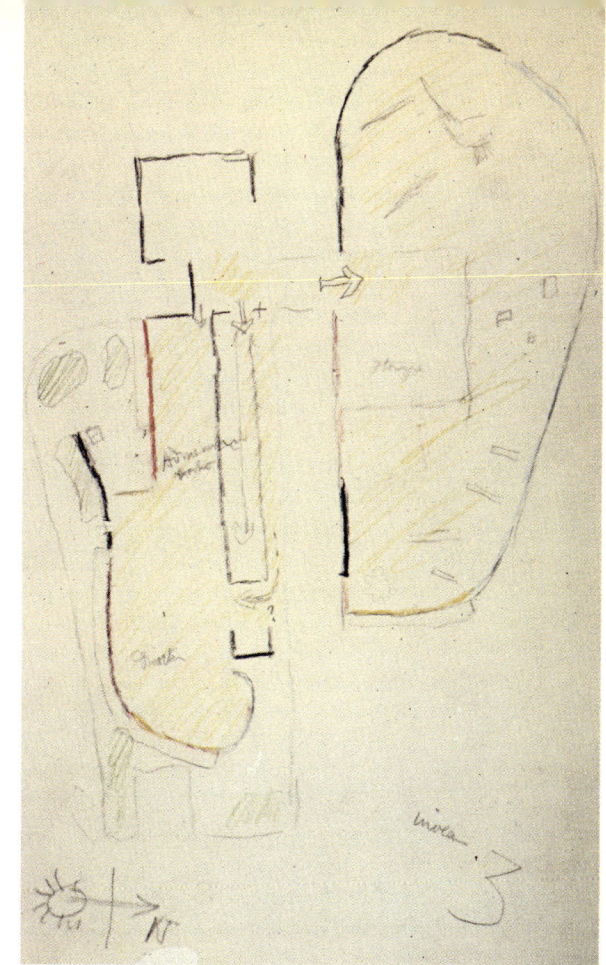

117. *Prescott Street elevation, Jullian, November 1960. (1:50; 55 × 102 cm; onion skin.) This drawing shows the effect that Jullian's September 9 fenestration ideas for mixing brise-soleil and ondulatoires in two horizontal registers might have had on the exterior. Small men appear for scale. To the bottom right are sketches experimenting with the fenestration in section: these may be by Le Corbusier.*

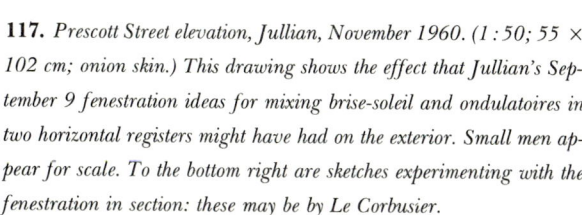

the relationship of concrete to glass. Pale blue-gray and pearly forms were floated in delicate crayon onto the hard tracing paper surface, while pastel shading effects were achieved, in part, by placing rough blue hatched card beneath the semi-translucent skin of paper. Pilotis were shaded, bathed in a weird, otherworldly light; the ramps were lemon yellow, the bold main rectangles of the building were battleship gray tinted with ochre. They were dotted with small black Modulor men: here one standing on a ramp, there one peeping over a parapet, silhouetted against the sky. They gave the drawings an uncanny presence, as if they were populated with metaphysical spectators. Solitary observers in a mathematical scheme, they recall those manikins in Surrealist townscapes, only there the light was less glowering, more warm—an excerpt from De Chirico.

As drawings and poetic evocations they provided a foretaste of the final presentation facades, which the architect regarded as ideal visualizations or "dessins-types" ("type drawings"). As a species of transcendental imagery they recall the Platonizing aesthetics of the twenties and lend a compelling appearance to the pursuit of perfection in purified forms. In terms of the down-to-earth development of the building, they really represented the culmination of the first project in the grandest possible manner and indicated a simplification it was increasingly clear should occur. Not that the architects saw these drawings as tombstones over the first project at the time, or that they yet entertained the notion "first" project at all. They continued along the planning route without realizing it was a dead end and discovered some useful aesthetic refinements. In early December Jullian produced a set of sections on the same scale as the elevations (2 centimeters per meter) and in the same mode; they were bathed in the same pearly, abstract light, but where columns were silver-gray and white, slabs were crimson, ramps and beams pale orange (figs. 120, 121). Light blue shading gave a tangible, liquid quality to interior space. The Modulor men were there guarding the entrances, standing on the ramps, positioned among pilotis—custodians of the absolute. And the interior ramp was still there, supported at its easternmost end by a piloti in front of the lift access, but now the pilotis were carefully graded cylinders, thick at the bottom of the building, reduced in size to the top of it, according to an arithmetical progression. Beams ran longitudinally (Le Corbusier had already seen fit to eliminate transversal ones) and were of constant thickness throughout. Thus, in the lower stories where the pilotis were fat, the beams notched into the tops of pilotis leaving curved flanks to either side, while at the top of the building, where the pilotis were of dwindled diameter, they notched into the underside of the beams, whose sides ran uninterrupted from one end to the other. But not quite uninterrupted: they were taken only as far as the ultimate piloti. The slab alone continued to meet the problems of junction with the brise-soleil.

118. *Quincy Street elevation, Jullian, November 10, 1960. (1:50; 61 × 114 cm; thick tracing paper.) The overall relationship of volumes, surfaces, and lines, especially those provided by slab, pilotis, and openings, are investigated. Proportion regulates the parts (the black ink Modulor men bear witness to this).*

119. *Prescott Street elevation, Jullian, November 1960. (1:50; 60 × 114 cm; thick tracing paper.) Again, overall massing is studied. Like figure 118, this is of technical interest too: the whole is done on thick tracing paper, pilotis being drawn and shaded in pencil, gray areas (touched with ochre) being formed from card attached to the verso with tape. The result has greater depth and subtlety than would a normal drawing.*

Further Conflicts with the Interior Ramp

While Jullian had been concentrating on the troublesome east end of the ramp near the freight lift, he had neglected to acknowledge any problems that might have existed at the west end, near the passenger elevator and the access point from the main ramp. It was to this area of the third level that Le Corbusier now directed his attention,

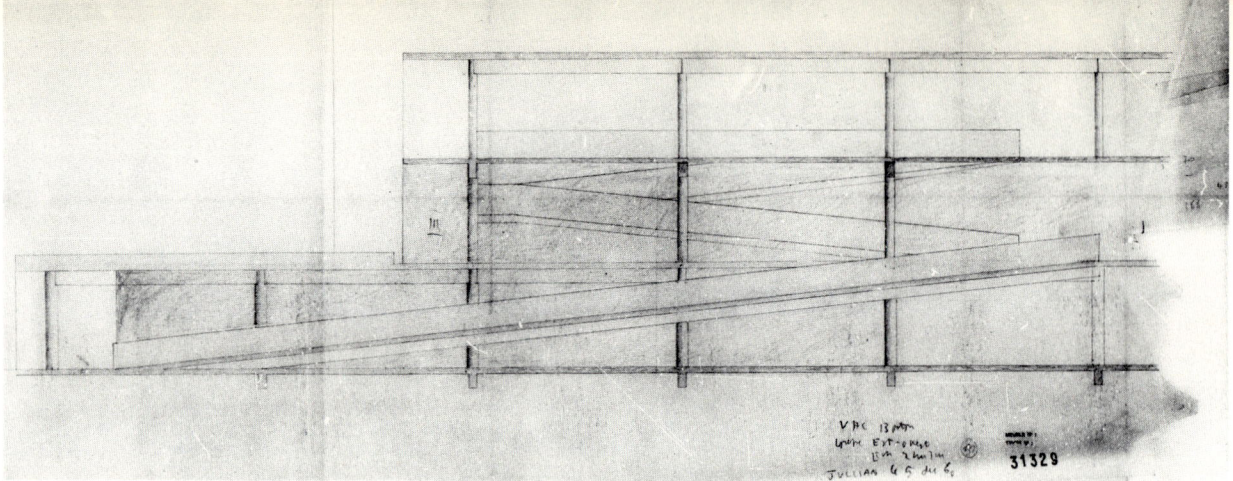

120. *Longitudinal section through interior ramp, Le Corbusier and Jullian, December 1, 1960. (1:50; 40.5 × 130 cm; thick tracing paper.) Shown are visual refinements of the structural skeleton. Smooth pilotis are reduced arithmetically from lower to upper floors according to apparent load; they are surmounted by beams which run in both directions underneath the slab, but are taken only as far as the end columns. This is one of Le Corbusier's most refined and idealized structures—a Purist work of art in pastel colors.*

121. *Transversal section of skeleton and ramps, Jullian, December 1, 1960. (1:50; 61.5 × 116 cm; thick tracing paper.) The study reveals visual refinements of structure and diminishing pilotis diameters. The lattice truss above the auditorium and the relationship of the ramps can also be seen. To the top left are calculations concerning pilotis sizes.*

identifying it as a trouble spot and attempting improvement (fig. 122).

The first project plans of June 1960 showed quite a casual and relaxed attitude to the entrances from the main ramp, treating them as simple openings. Le Corbusier now realized that a set of double doors would be necessary to cope with the drafts and chill winds of New England winter. The frames of these doors would have to encroach on the open space at the top of the ramp, on the landing in the stair tower, or a combination of the two. Two little concrete boxes at the top of the ramp, one of the key focal points of the building where the ramp passed through, were obviously not acceptable. But, as the drawing shows (fig. 122), the interior encroachment was just as serious, because it would have blocked the passenger elevators (which are no longer shown). The same drawing demonstrates that Le Corbusier had found it necessary to enlarge the area of the entire stair tower to fit both lavatories and stairs in.

Sert's letter of November 16 had said that a single passenger elevator was sufficient, and Le Corbusier's drawing shows him to have reduced the number to one and to have shifted his single elevator diagonally back to the outer wall where it was safely tucked out of the way. This lodged the elevator in the notch which had previously supplied a legible differentiation between the vertical circulation tower and the areas it served. As the shift of the freight lift had done, it drastically altered the external form of the building.

Nor was this all. There was still the question of where to place the stairs. The architect had placed a high premium on the first view of the studio spaces immediately after stepping out of the elevators. Now that the elevator was in its new flanking position, facing the wrong way, such a view was desirable from the top of the stairs, and to achieve it he put the stairs on the side of the tower nearest the main ramp (fig. 123). This likewise allowed the stairs to be seen. If they were placed on the outside of the tower, away from the main ramp, the view to and from was blocked by the new elevator position (fig. 122). But either way he was stumped, because the double doors were still encroaching, as they had with elevators; there was no apparent way out of his dilemma. The architect also examined the

122. *Plan, west end of level 3, Le Corbusier and Jullian, December 15, 1960. (1:50; 44 × 30 cm; onion skin.) This end of the floor is identified as another trouble spot. A double door is shown giving access to the ramp but this has so encroached on the previous position of the elevators (now containing lavatories) that the number of elevators has been reduced to one, which has been shifted to a point diagonally opposite the old position. It now blocks the view from the top of the stairs into the administration offices and studio and fills a previous notch in the plan, so interfering with overall forms. The whole landing has been widened, too, and results in a piloti rising through a sheet of glass (with "?" next to it). Another question mark appears on the stairs as Le Corbusier wonders which flight should stand on which side.*

131

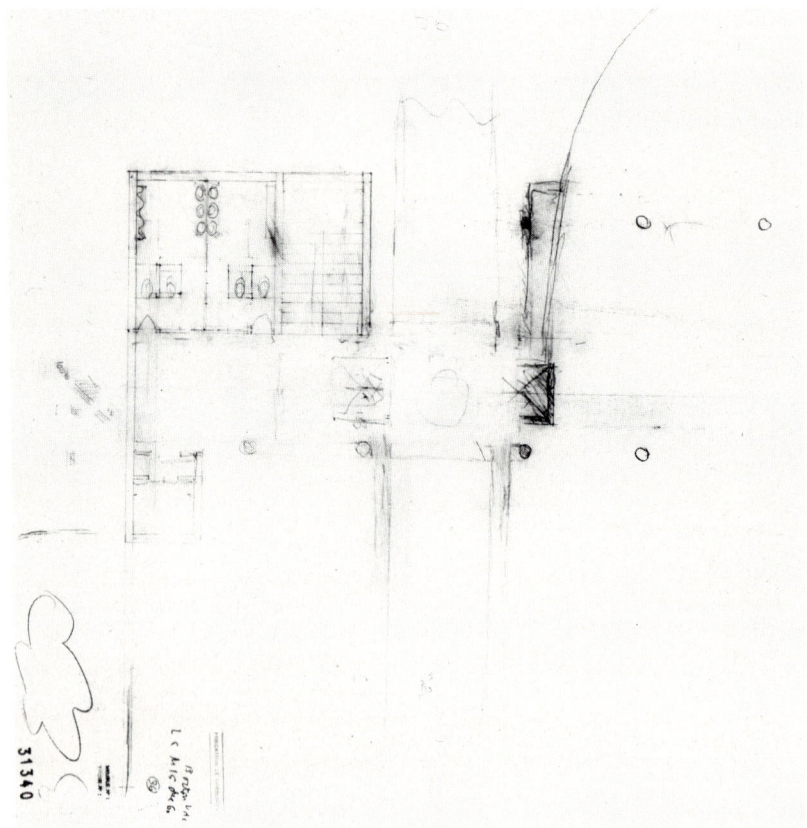

effects of these alternatives at ground level, with similar problematic results (fig. 124).

Two more problems were identified in these drawings. A piloti on the side towards the Faculty Club was bisected by a sheet of glass in the fenestration—a problem which arose from the triple need to light and support the new small area he had just created while still respecting the piloti grid (fig. 122)—and the interior ramp, it now seemed clear, was as seriously cramped by the newly placed elevator as its other end had been by the freight lift (fig. 125). But it was not the egress from the elevator that was blocked, nor the base of the ramp: it was the entrance to the third level studio. And these were both problems which were generated by the most recent "remedies."

Even the clean sweep of removing the interior ramp altogether could not now obviate the problems that Le Corbusier had identified, although it could certainly have reduced them. Anyway, this was not a notion that either architect would entertain. The ramp was fundamental to their circulation system. Any solution put forward had some-

123. *Plan of level 3, Le Corbusier and Jullian, December 15, 1960. (1:50; 55 × 58 cm; onion skin.) Double doors to each side of the ramp block the stairs, which are here set on the side of the stair tower nearest the ramp.*

132

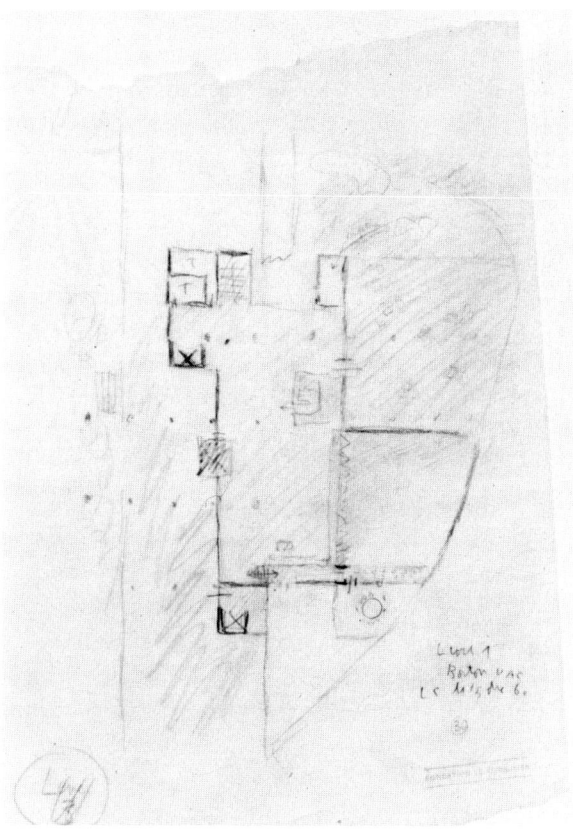 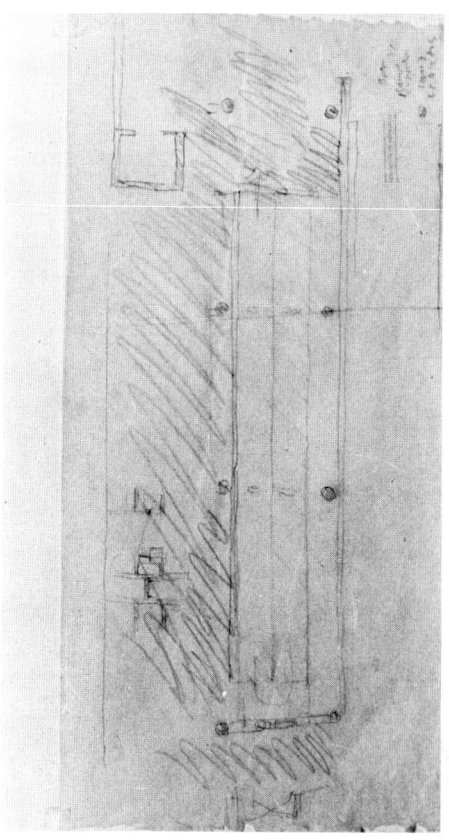

124. *Plan of level 1, Le Corbusier, December 15, 1960. (1:200; 39 × 30 cm; onion skin.) The recent moves on the third level are examined for their effect on the ground floor.*

125. *Plan of level 3, Le Corbusier, December 15, 1960. (1:50; 61 × 30 cm; onion skin.) The way between the shifted passenger elevator and the interior ramp is discovered to be seriously constricted. The freight lift, with its own history of clashes with the interior ramp, is just visible at the bottom.*

how to accommodate it and set right all the other problems as well.

A Change in the Floor-to-Ceiling Height

It comes as a bit of a shock to discover Le Corbusier writing to Sert on December 19, only four days after these plans were done, the day before the Christmas vacation, in the following recklessly optimistic terms.

> Nous avons établi les plans et coupes 2 centimètres par mètre. Tout le jeu des escaliers, ascenseurs et rampes est désormais en ordre. . . . Par ailleurs, j'estime que je ne viendrai pas moi-même à Boston. Tu viendras, toi, à Paris prendre connaissance de tous les dossiers, ayant ici à disposition les éléments de questions et réponses utiles. La dépense sera la même que si je venais moi-même à Boston et j'estime que pour cette étape de mise au point définitive du plan architectural, la discussion se situerait mieux à Paris.

> We have established plans and sections at 2 centimeters per meter. Henceforth, the whole play of stairs, elevators, and ramps is in order . . .
> As for other matters, I think that I will not come to Boston myself. You will come to Paris—to acquaint yourself with all the files, having here the ingredients of useful questions and answers. The expense will be the same as if I came to Boston and I estimate that for this stage of putting the building scheme in final shape, the discussion would be better placed in Paris. (12-19-60; appendix 12)

Since the faculty, committee, and President had been led to expect final plans in November, this was probably good estimation on Le Corbusier's part, given the state the building was in.[10] The phrase "to put the building scheme in its final shape" allowed him a little extra leeway: if the job was not complete when Sert visited—and who could say what other problems lurked?—Sert had at least been warned. If Le Corbusier had agreed to go to Cambridge it would have been tantamount to setting himself a deadline: he could not possibly have gone without final presentation drawings.

Under the circumstances, some queries by Le Corbusier concerning floor heights are of great interest, as they indicate that his confidence may have been partially grounded in a recent change. They occur in the same letter, and it is a good thing Le Corbusier made his inquiries when he did, especially for the future of his problematic beams.

> Pour qu'il n'y ait pas de confusion, je t'envoie un calque (d'étude) no. 5707 VAC Boston, échelle 5 cm/m, Jullian le 18 dec. 1960 montrant les cotes admises jusqu'ici par moi, c'est à dire:
> A/ dalles de 12 pieds (3m 66) de plancher à plancher
> B/ dalle lisse de 20 centimètres d'épaisseur sur les portés (environ 3m 90 de portée entre les sommiers)
> C/ sommier franchissant les portées de 7 m 75 (d'axe en axe) entre colonnes.
>
> Ma question est celle-ci: Etes-vous d'accord avec les hauteurs *de vide* de 3m46 ou double hauteur de 3m66 + 3m46 = 7m12. Il s'agit de tous les locaux de travail: administration, peinture, sculpture.
>
> So that there will not be any confusion, I am sending you a tracing (study) no. 5707 VAC Boston, scale 5cm/m, Jullian Dec. 18, 1960 showing the dimensions allowed until now by me, that is to say:
> A/ slabs of 12 feet (3m66) from floor to floor
> B/ smooth slab 20 centimeters thickness over the bays (around 3m90 carried between the beams)
> C/ beam crossing spans of 7m 75 (axis to axis) between the columns.

My question is this: are you in agreement with the *clear* heights 3m46 or the double height of 3m66 + 3m46 = 7m12. It concerns all the areas of work: administration, painting, sculpture. (12-19-60; appendix 12)

What is most striking about this passage is the 20 centimeter reduction in floor-to-ceiling heights, a drastic modification, given the architect's protective attitude towards his building's proportions. Admittedly he retained the 3.66 meter Modulor dimension (twice the 1.83 meter height of a six foot man) as his floor-to-floor height, but the measure was taken in response to an otherwise insoluble problem: the third floor interior ramp. Now the ramp might reach its vertical destination inside less lateral distance, leaving room beyond the landing for access to the lift. At the same time the main ramp was made legal, less than ten percent.

Of course, this in no way removed the recently mentioned problems at the west end of the third level and, obviously, in no way logically resulted in a reduction of overall size. But it is easy to understand how someone reading the letter in Cambridge who assumed such a reduction to have taken place could see the reduction in height as befitting it. The perspective and section enclosed with the letter showed the same bay dimensions as June, but showed only a few bays in the abstract, unrelated to a dimensioned plan (figs. 126, 127). Nor did they show the jointing of beams to curved elevations. Le Corbusier had not reduced the building's area: perhaps this contributed to his squeamishness at going to Cambridge.

Actually the height reduction was to prove only temporarily valuable. There had never been anything very positive, or assertive, about the letter suggesting its implementation in any case.

> On pourrait peut-être déclarer ces hauteurs trop faibles, mais leur modification réagirait très difficilement sur les rampes.
>
> One could possibly declare these heights to be too weak but their modification would react with great difficulty on the ramps. (12-19-60; appendix 12)

He later stated he "thought the VAC was destined for work approaching the real conditions of life" and added that the spaces "would give a fine aspect"—both effects attainable, surely, in rooms twenty centimeters higher.

When the drawings and letter arrived in Cambridge they fell into the lap of Huson Jackson, Sert's partner—a man who had already shown his ability to sympathize with the problems of the design then taking place in Paris and to supply it with readily available American solutions. He raised the issue in a letter to Sert, at that time spending the New Year holidays in Rome. It was not a purely structural matter but nonetheless was to have important repercussions on the structure; he refers to the letter just quoted from, received in Cambridge a few days before.

> I have a thought regarding his proposals which deserves some consideration and discussion when you see him. He proposes a thin slab spanning about 3m90 between columns and establishes the floor to floor height at 3m66. There is no indication in his sketch of any means of distributing heating or ventilation to the perimeters of the building in the slab system and no chance to bring it up from below because of the building design. Mechanical ventilation is a requirement for classrooms. The "Airfloor" system would, I believe, be a most compatible way of introducing ventilation into Le Corbusier's design. It consists of a structural slab on top of which Is [sic] placed metal domes creating passages for the air supply and topped with a finished floor (see catalog enclosed). The overall depth of such a construction would have to be about 12" including the structural slab, which would not fit the floor to floor height of 3m66 unless the floor to ceiling height could be reduced to 3m36. I think it is important to the concept of this building to provide now for some spaces for air circulation and for heating pipes. With the open stories below it will be very difficult to work them out if they are not given advanced consideration. Adding spaces for the mechanicals later would spoil much that Corbu wants to achieve. I hope you can solve this when you see him in Paris. (12-28-60)

126. *Section detail of structural frame, Le Corbusier, December 18, 1960. (1:200; 50 × 75 cm; print.) Heights: floor to beam, 3.0 meters; floor to ceiling, 3.46 meters; floor to floor, 3.66 meters; double height floor to ceiling, 7.12 meters.*

127. *Perspective of interior structure, Le Corbusier, December 19, 1960. (1:100; 21 × 27 cm; print.) The skeleton will have longitudinal bays (axis to axis) of 7.75 meters, transversal bays of 3.66 meters.*

Le Corbusier's attitude to the "mechanicals" was such that he rarely considered them until late in the design process, when he would pack them in as best he could. In his late buildings too he tended not to romanticize machine elements, and usually tried to hide them away.

Instead of "mechanicals," he preferred to use those twin devices of his own invention for environmental management: the brise-soleil and the aérateur. This was fine for equable climates and for cultures whose clients were not educated to expect humid air at the touch of a switch. It probably took an American architect working in the Corbusian tradition to recognize a probable incompatibility between Le Corbusier's sublime structural ideals and the mundane demands of ventilating pipes and ducts. Sert's and Jackson's own experience of American clientele and climate had forced them to face up to realities like plant rooms, grill intakes, cooling towers, and exhausts: these are facts that play an identifiable role in the massing of Sert's designs. Jackson was providing a valuable solution to a legal ventilation requirement and, as it turned out, an option for the problem of the beams as well. But he was doing more: he was throwing into high relief Le Corbusier's extremely idealistic practice at the rue de Sèvres, and highlighting an issue of key importance to the future history of the building: mechanical environmental control.

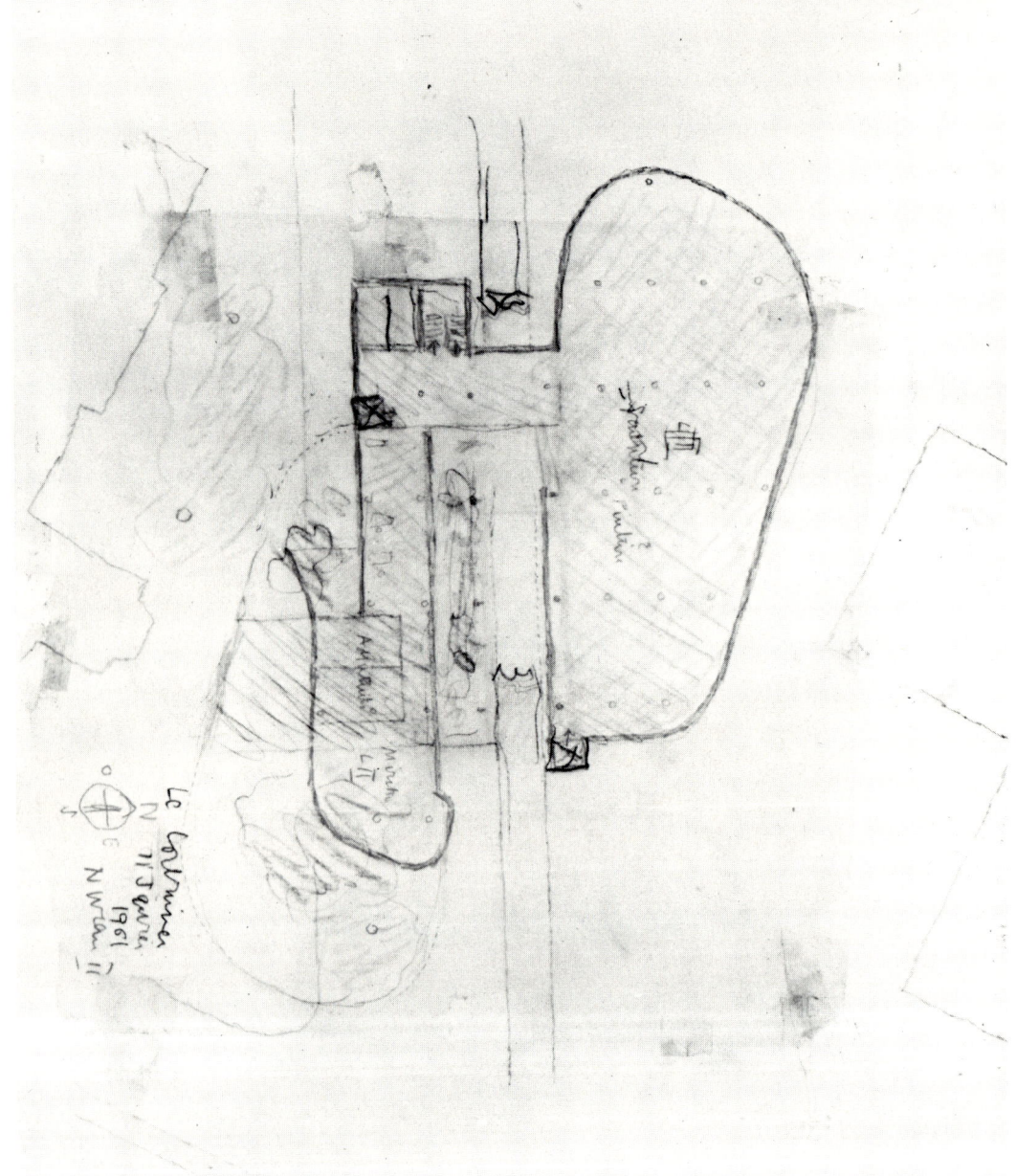

7. THE DAY OF CRISIS: THE SECOND PROJECT

Tout a été ramené à une très grande simplification.

Le Corbusier

It was an odd situation then, that Christmas of 1960. On the one hand Le Corbusier knew he was not as advanced as he was pretending to Sert, on the other there were factors Sert knew about that could even more disrupt Le Corbusier's design. The situation was worse than any one could know or would admit.

After Christmas Le Corbusier returned from Switzerland to tackle the third floor problems, arriving back in the studio on January 4, and turning attention to the visual arts center on the 9th.[1] The stairs, elevators, and ramps about which he had spoken to Sert in his letter before the vacation were still far from being in order: they threatened to burst the project open at the seams. The pressure was now intense, for Sert had arranged to visit the atelier in Paris on the 20th of the month. On the 9th the inevitable began to happen: the major forms of the building began to change.

Dissolution of the First Project

To solve the bisected piloti problem on the Faculty Club facade, Le Corbusier joggled the wall over a foot or two and let the piloti rise through the

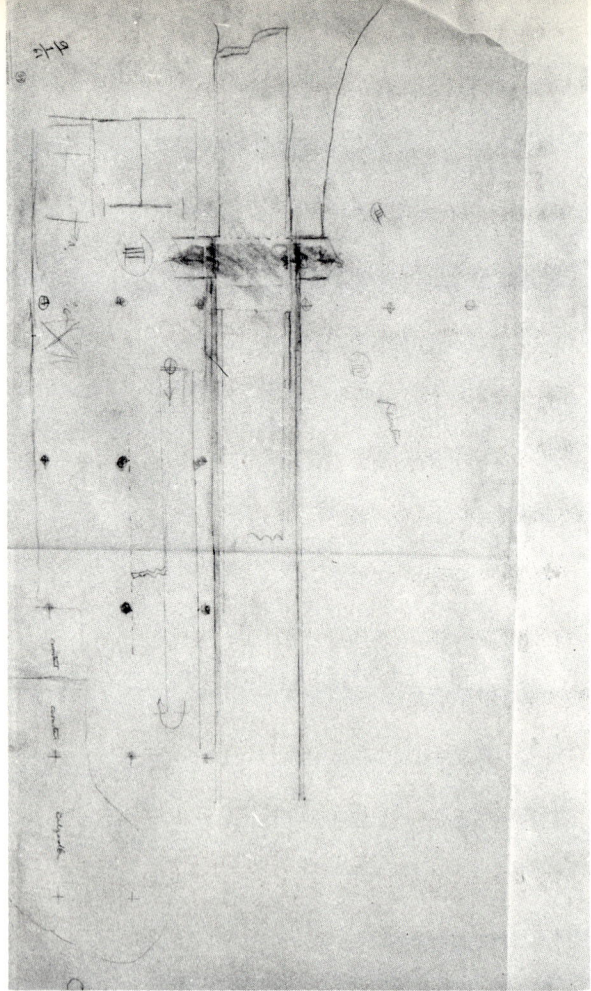

128. *Plan of level 3, south side, Le Corbusier, January 9, 1961. (1:50; 115 × 55 cm; onion skin.) To alleviate the clash of a pilotis and the glazing in the south wall, the latter has been joggled outwards. This also has the happy effect of relieving the encroachment of elevator and ramp, but begins seriously to distort the building's south edge.*

interior. On the same drawing (January 9) the director's studio was lightly drawn at the rear of the building (fig. 128). The straightened southern edge now ran back three longitudinal bays and cut into the curves of the assistants' studio areas.

On the 10th he drew four plans on a strip of tracing paper in soft pencil with pink, green, mauve, and yellow shading (figs. 129–132). The nebulous and mollified forms seem to be a direct graphic equivalent to the flux of his thinking. The side of the third floor curved director's studio was cropped completely in favor of a straight line running from the front of the building to the back, in other words continuing the flank of the elevator tower. This was highly unsatisfactory because it completed the muting of the separateness of that element begun by filling the notch with the eleva-

129. *Plan of level 1, Le Corbusier, January 10, 1961. (1:200; on strip measuring 182 × 30 cm; onion skin.) The new south wall is dotted in and the freight lift is back on the wrong side. The tree to the rear is clearly marked. Figures 129–136 show portions of a continuous strip of drawings.*

130. *Plan of level 2, Le Corbusier, January 10, 1961. (1:200; on strip measuring 182 × 30 cm; onion skin.) The previous level 3 has here found its way down to level 2, except for the lift, which has switched sides. The designation "peinture" appears twice.*

131. *Plan of level 3, Le Corbusier, January 10, 1961. (1:200; on strip measuring 182 × 30 cm; onion skin.) The new level 3 retains the Quincy Street curve which had existed before, but has now developed an entirely rectangular south side. The interior ramp has shifted sides but so has the freight lift; thus the old problem is recreated.*

132. *Plan of level 4, Le Corbusier, January 10, 1961. (1:200; on strip measuring 182 × 30 cm; onion skin.) The exhibition space remains at this level but the freight lift is on the wrong side and the south side has lost the notch by the stair tower.*

133. *Plan of level 1, Jullian, January 11, 1961. (1:200; on strip measuring 37.5 × 135 cm; onion skin.) The lift is on the wrong side and the passenger elevator entrance faces in a transversal direction. The offices are shown on the south side.*

134. *Plan of level 2, with superimposed tracing of new level 3, Le Corbusier, January 11, 1961. (1:200; on strip measuring 37.5 × 135 cm; onion skin.) Here the new forms of the second project are established. The south side curve has been made by tracing the Quincy Street curve and reproducing it diagonally opposite. A double bay, double height space begins to form around the ramp.*

135. *Plan of the new level 3, Jullian, January 11, 1961. (1:200; on strip measuring 37.5 × 135 cm; onion skin.) The major relationships of the new building are easily discernible. The ramp gallery has crystallized and now the interior ramp is to the north side in a rectangular space. The freight lift is also to the north side and again clashes with the ramp. A roof terrace appears above the Quincy Street curve.*

136. *Plan of level 2, Jullian, January 11, 1960. (1:200; on strip measuring 38 × 100 cm; onion skin.) Now that level 3 has been clarified, level 2 is refined by making the once curved south side into a rectangular L-shape. Attached plastic arrows indicate public and student circulation.*

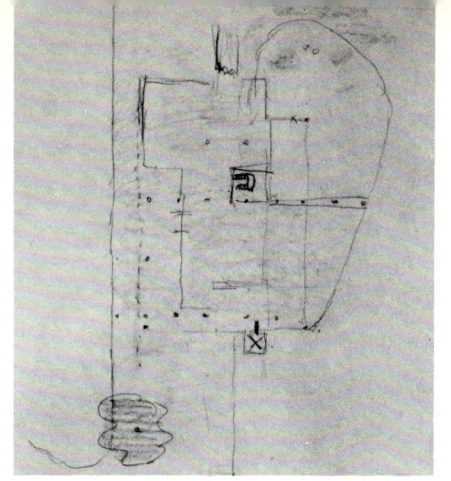
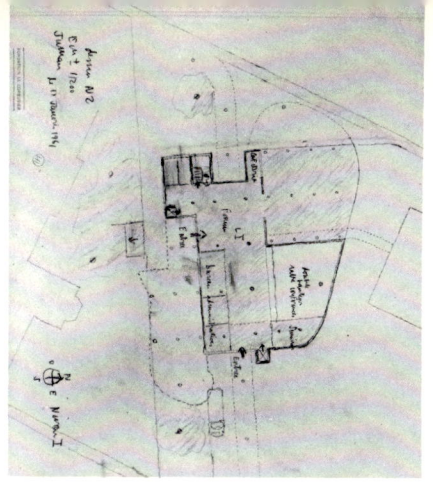
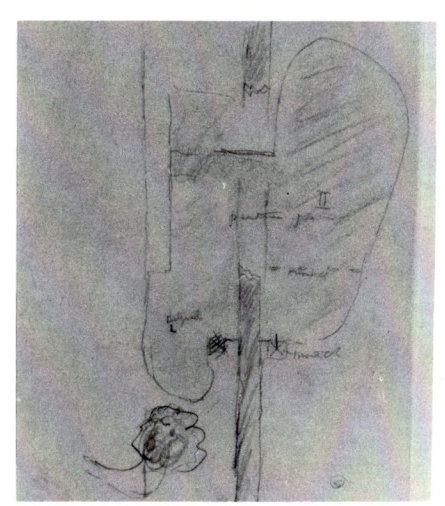
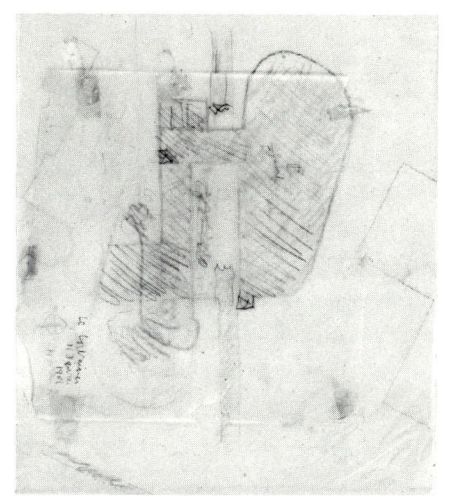
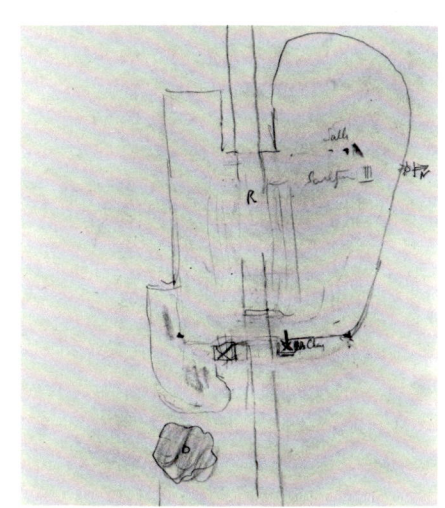
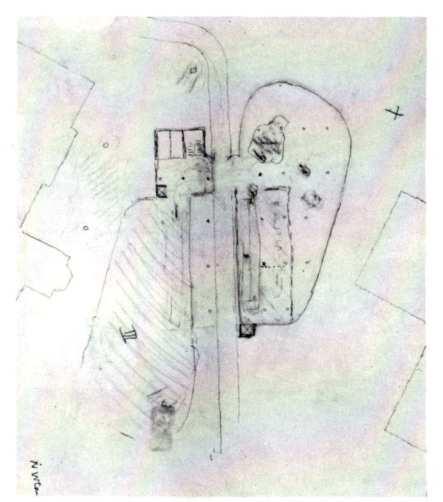
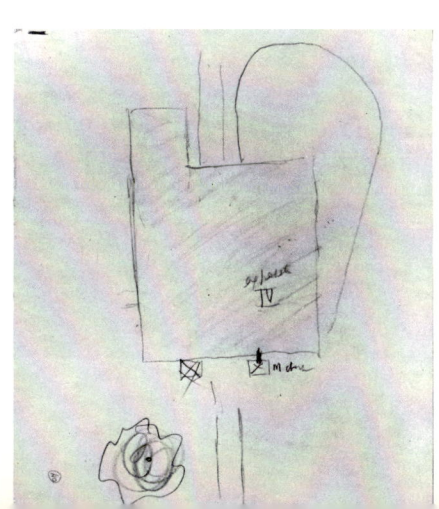
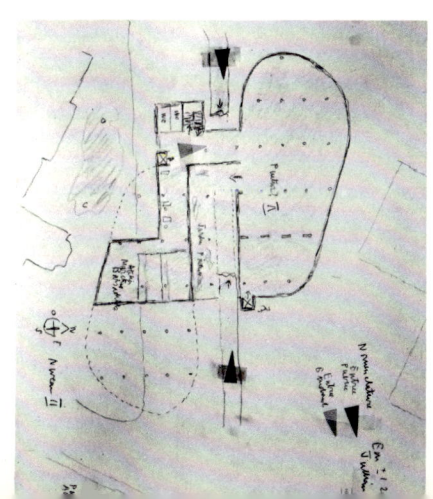

tor tower and obliterated the play of curves on the third level to that side. It also obliterated the home of "le roi" ("the king"), but Le Corbusier's measures seem to have been formal rather than functional in emphasis. He attempted to save the situation and counterbalance the lopsided design by moving the freight lift across to the wrong side of the main ramp—a desperate measure, since Jullian had already demonstrated its futility. On the 10th, too, he switched the interior ramp to the other side, thus creating a mirror image of the old problem. A second floor plan done that afternoon showed the functions beginning to reshuffle, the designation "peinture" ("painting") appearing twice, but at the second level, not the third, and on the Quincy Street side where the covered garden had been. A third floor plan showed sculpture replacing painting, and a literal reconstruction of the building now gave two large studios of similar curvature stacked one on top of the other over Quincy Street. However these drawings probably did not represent terminations but the process of change itself: planning, self-questioning, and proffering tentative solutions. He examined the implications of the straightened southern wall at first and fourth levels. By the evening of the 10th, the first project lay in ruins.

Creation of the Final Project, "VAC BOS"

The building had to be raised up again in nine days, as Sert was expected on the 20th. January 11, 1961, has since been referred to by Jullian as "la journée de la crise" ("the day of crisis").[2] But there is something so smooth and effective about his drawing and Le Corbusier's rearrangement of the main forms that day that the word "crisis" seems scarcely applicable.

Jullian worked on a long strip of tracing paper, one floor per fold (figs. 133–136). He carried on from Le Corbusier's suggestions of the previous day, beginning, therefore, with the transference of all third floor functions to the second level. That is, he brought down the small director's studio and the painting atelier where the interior ramp would have been if it too had been moved down, and he placed a garden next to the main ramp. On the second level he now had the director's studio to the south of the ramp, by the Faculty Club, and the large curved two-dimensional studio to the north, jutting out towards Quincy Street.

This move displaced the large three-dimensional studio and the covered garden opposite it, its "complementary open space"—two elements that were now joined by a third, the interior ramp, as "floating elements," to be slid into place in some combination or another at the third level. Such recombination had to consider one new condition arising from the move down: the garden down alongside the ramp would have to have room to breathe, a monumental space two floors high and a bay wide. The rearrangement of the third level took place around this rectangular fillet of space jutting up into it, and of course around the main ramp.

One immediate result was that the interior ramp could not be put back in the place it had occupied, except for occasional excursions, since its birth. Not that for a moment Jullian intended placing it back there after all the trouble it had caused him due to its position: he began by placing the ramp on the north side, opposite the main ramp, as Le Corbusier had suggested the day before (figs. 134, 135). This recreated his old obstruction problem with the freight lift (the lift was back on the wrong side), but relative to the problems at hand this could be regarded as a nicety; despite the fact that it had caused months of worry, it could be overlooked as insignificant alongside the major metamorphosis the building was undergoing.

Around this ramp, which was sitting above the large curved studio looking down on Quincy Street, he now placed a small rectangular enclosure with a glass front and an opening allowing easy access to the base of the interior ramp from the main one; around the enclosure he made a roof garden. The second of his "floating elements," the "complementary open space," was thus disposed. What now became of its complement, the three-dimensional studio?

This, the third and final floating element, had to be placed somehow over the narrow and recently shifted director's studio to the south side of the main ramp next to the Faculty Club. The solution was simple, beautiful, and expensive, as it entailed the creation of an extra longitudinal bay in the southeast/northwest direction. Le Corbusier stepped in and made the decision. He simply made a tracing on a loose sheet of the large curved studio facing Quincy Street, flipped the form over on its end and tucked it alongside the main ramp facing Prescott Street (fig. 134). Unfortunately his extra bay entailed the destruction of the elm tree that had figured so strongly in his drawings of January 10 and which had been preserved in the first project by the notch to the rear of the building.

From the air the building was now greatly simplified (figs. 134, 135, 146): one curved form straining towards Quincy Street, its replica straining diagonally in the opposite direction; the ramp curve pulling one way, passing through, and pulling the other; the elevator tower to one corner, the freight lift towards the other. This was in fact a system of counterpoints, but held in check by an assertive central rectangle.

From the ground as well it was obvious that the relationships had altered completely. The bulk of the studio over Quincy Street was now low down, at the second level, while that on the Prescott Street side was high up, on the third. This reversed the decision taken early in the planning, and made the basis of the decision clear. The site sloped so steeply from Quincy Street that the extremity of the studio to that side was close to being earthbound.

Refinements followed. Not completely happy with the way his new second and third floors related on the south side, the architect lopped off the bulbous end of the director's studio (fig. 136). On the interior this seriously constricted the assistants' studios. On the exterior it gave further emphasis to the central rectangular core. In plan there were now strong cross-bracing alignments, as if the curves and the rectangular parts had all been drawn in one movement of the pencil without stopping. There was a square in the center with the two tear drops abutting it and the S-ramp running between them; this naturally recalls the early phases of the project, the central "built cube," but the simple final image was not achieved, as one myth would have it, by Le Corbusier beginning with a square and then departing from it in the simplest way. The curves came first, the square was placed among them (first project); the square was then lost in the rearrangement of the curves, only to be replaced among them after they were rear-

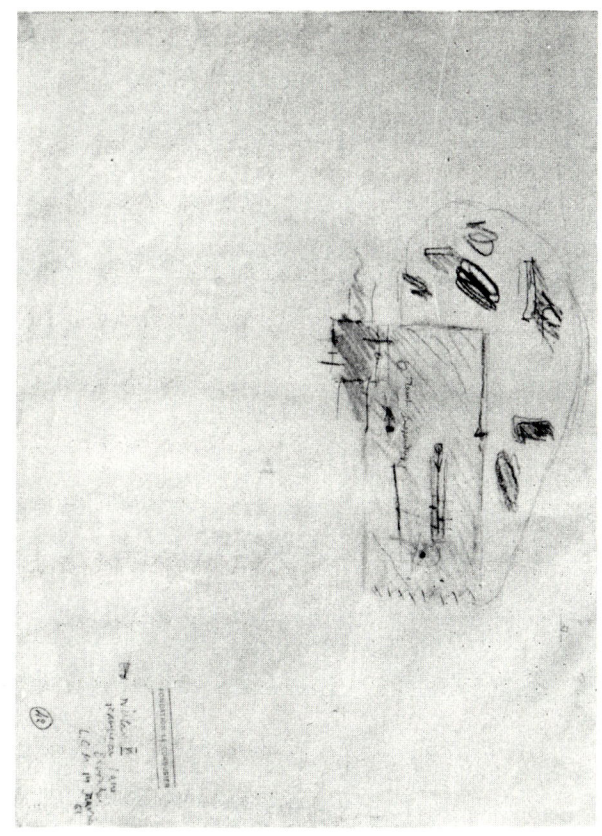

137. Plan (overlay) of level 3, north side, Le Corbusier, January 14, 1961. (1:200; 42.5 × 37.5 cm; onion skin.) Curved interior ramp and brise-soleil appear tentatively to the rear.

ranged. Now that the curves of the terraces were equal in size, and placed diagonally opposite one another to serve both the circulation of the S-ramp and the built cubical volume, the building as a whole, seen from the air, took on a simple, generalized image and form. Here we see the general formal relationships of the finished building.

But there was still the interior ramp, and in a stroke Le Corbusier alleviated the problem (fig. 137). He enlarged the rectangular space that had just been created above the Quincy Street studio and gave it glass on three sides, brise-soleil on the fourth. Within this nearly transparent box he bent the ramp around in an ascending curve. The brise-soleil, making their first reappearance for months, were the recessed fin type he had used at Ahmedabad in the Millowners' Building and in the Parliament Building at Chandigarh.[3] They were compact with the structure, gave the "fourth wall"

143

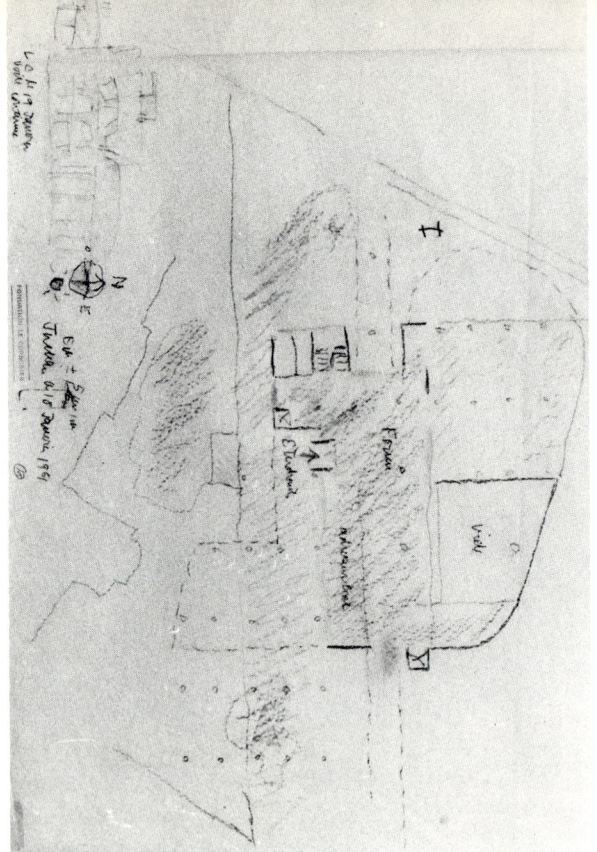 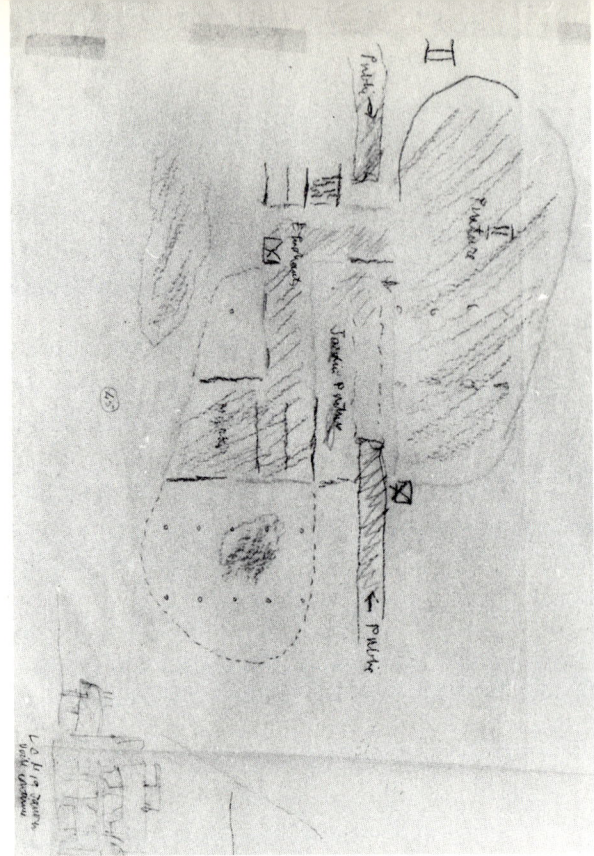

138. *Plan of level 1, Jullian, January 18, 1961. (1:200; on strip measuring 38 × 176 cm; onion skin.) To the left, in a tiny sketch, is an "Ubu"-like south elevation of the building by Le Corbusier.*

139. *Plan of level 2, Jullian, January 18, 1961. (1:200; on strip measuring 38 × 176 cm; onion skin.) The lower part of the two story and two bay ramp gallery is entitled "jardin peinture" ("painting garden"). The lift is still on the wrong side.*

effect he was after, and considerably solidified the external appearance of the building. A monumental, denser sculptural treatment of the exterior tended to replace the membrane-like effects of the first project.

Admittedly some good features of the first project had been lost. For example, the gardens were no longer, properly speaking, "complementary open spaces" but entirely separate entities, and the interior one, next to the ramp, was a poor substitute for the views and sun the painters and plants might have enjoyed: it was too dark for work or growth. In the same way the elements of the earliest idea, the walk and greenery, the ramp and the roof gardens, had been split apart and the earthbound Quincy Street studio was only partially alleviated by cutting into the ground beneath it: a solution that created one of the deadest spaces of the finished building. But some change of the major forms had been unavoidable, and of the various possibilities, Le Corbusier had chosen a solution of overall formal elegance which obliterated the pressing combination of interior puzzles that had forced the change. Whatever the retrospective observer may think of his choice or of other possible solutions, it must be borne in mind that Le Corbusier had allowed himself to get into a situation where some rapid solution was required.

On January 18, 1961, two days before Sert's visit, plans and sections were drawn (figs. 138–143). As had been most of the drawings of the previous four weeks' researches, these were at a scale 5 centimeters per meter, unelaborate sketches to give simple information to Sert about structure, functional spaces, and circulation. The usual code was employed: yellow for circulation, red for structure, green for greenery, and blue for glass. The large space on the fourth floor was given over to exhibitions. The freight lift remained on the "wrong" side; the passenger elevator was

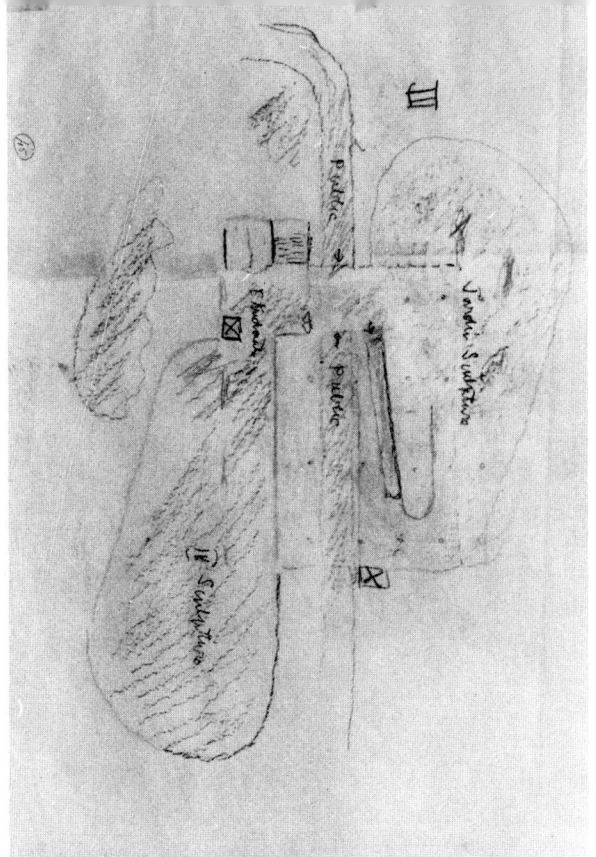

140. *Plan of level 3, Jullian, January 18, 1961. (1:200; on strip measuring 38 × 176 cm; onion skin.) The integral relationship of curves, the circulation, and the new interior ramp show clearly. The adjacent terrace is called "jardin sculpture" ("sculpture garden"). The main ramp is marked "public," the side entrance "étudiants" ("students").*

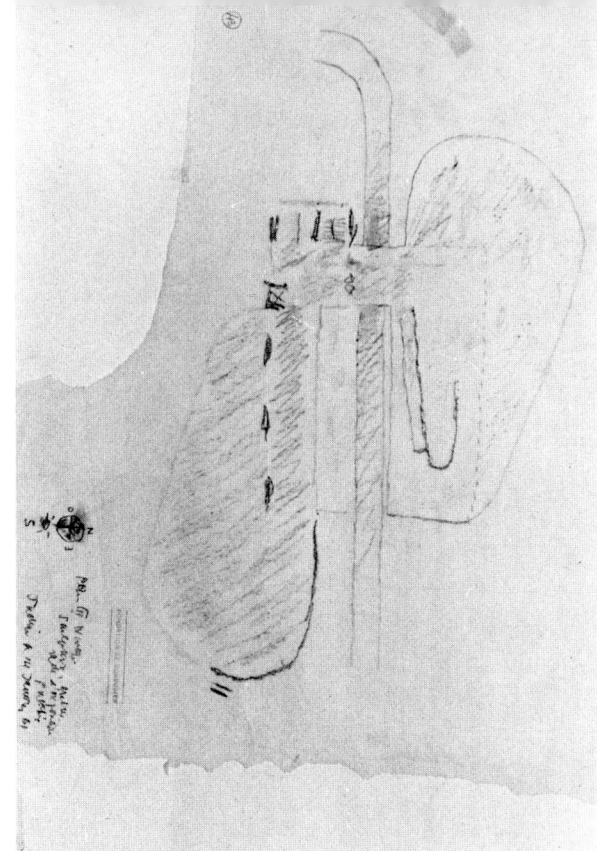

141. *Plan of level 3, Jullian, January 18, 1961. (1:200; on strip measuring 38 × 176 cm; onion skin.) The possibility of three piers on the south side is examined.*

transversally oriented. On the ground floor the administrative offices were laid in a strip next to the entrance. At the third level piers were created to partition off a passageway from the freight lift to the front of the building—a way for materials to be transported to the painting studio. The main ramp no longer touched at the second level, and Jullian wrote "public" next to it in contradistinction to the "student" circulation areas such as the side entrance. The access value of the ramp was thus cut still further.

The pressure was off; the breakthrough had been made. Only minor problems of readjustment remained. The architects probably were pleased with themselves and the next day, the 19th, they eagerly made a tracing of the new building over the old and some comparative cardboard cutouts of the two projects (figs. 144, 145). This latter method of comparison was ingenious (you simply took the one piece of cardboard and laid it over the other), but the aerial view of the third levels was more flattering to the second project than to the first.

The Airfloor

The sections done on the 18th showed no beams, only smooth slabs and pilotis. For two months the structure had had beams running longitudinally as far as the end columns. This was not a happy solution. It caused a ragged edge just inside the fenestration where the slab continued on its own, especially as the extension of the smooth slab varied from bay to bay according to the curvature of the plan, and the axial emphasis of beams seemed inappropriate in the new building with its quasi-centralized plan. But the columns still required some reinforcement at the head just beneath the slab, and on the longitudinal section of January 18 there was a tiny sketch in red crayon of a mushroom support—a solution that was as unsatisfactory to Le Corbusier aesthetically in a building of this size as it was necessary, he thought,

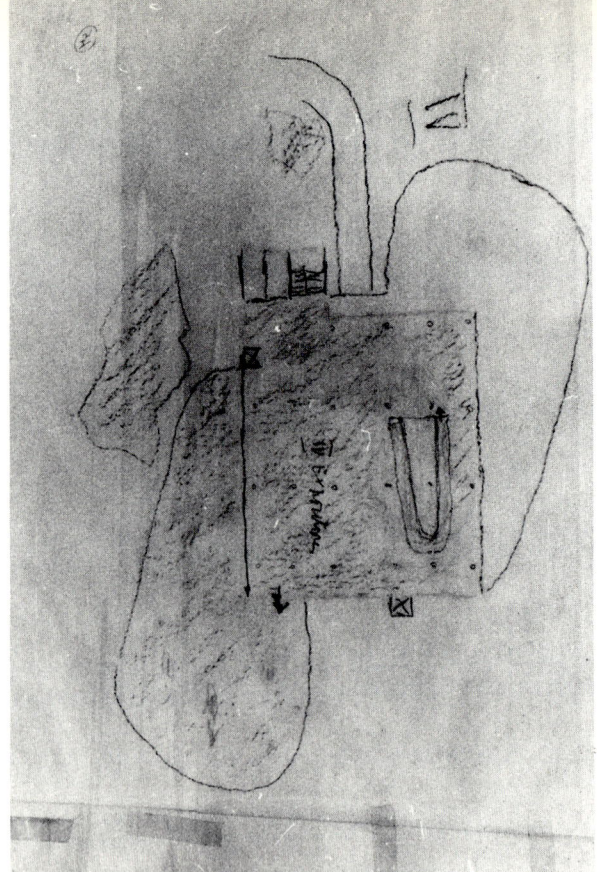

142. *Plan of level 4, Jullian, January 18, 1961. (1:200; on strip measuring 38 × 176 cm; onion skin.) The interior ramp is inside the exhibition space.*

143. *Longitudinal section, Jullian, January 18, 1961. (1:200; 31 × 55 cm; onion skin.) This drawing captures the unified quality of the new relationships and the way in which circulation is integral to the conception.*

to the structure. Of course he used mushroom capitals in the Parliament Building at Chandigarh but there they were on a monumental scale. Here at least two objections to mushroom capitals could be raised. They would have wedded badly with the freehand curves of the plan, and—more serious—they would have halted the aspiring thrust of the pilotis through the full height of the building by disrupting the vertical continuity. The vertical structure would then have been broken down into particulate elements and the horizontal slabs would no longer have behaved as hovering planes.

News of the ventilation requirement arrived two days later with Sert. There was no way out of the requirement, and Jackson's carefully pondered remedy was the best solution at hand. Admittedly it forced Le Corbusier to fatten up his slabs a few centimeters, throwing them out of the Modulor scale and making the rooms even lower, but then, in a flash, it was clear this was a blessing. The "airfloor" (fig. 147) came as a godsend, because it made what only two days before had been a graphic illusion, smooth slabs, an attainable reality: it solved the problem of what to do with capitals by allowing extra room for their recession into the slab. This extra space was acquired without the expense of overbearing weight (much of the extra was airfloor air), and it also served to mask reinforcements at cantilever edges where reinforcing was most urgently required.

The extra depth amounted to some fifteen centimeters, which brought down the ceiling height to 3.31 meters. The architects decided this was really too low. Now that the inside ramp had plenty of room for maneuver and the main ramp touched the building at only one point (previously it had touched at two), it was possible to alter floor-to-ceiling heights without reacting unfavorably on the ramp gradients. They therefore returned to a floor-to-ceiling height of 3.66 meters.[4]

On January 20, then, the former pupil visited the atelier to cast his eye over his former master's plans. Then Sert returned to the United States and just over a week later he wrote from Cambridge to say that he had told President Pusey the work was "very advanced" (1-30-61). The original projected date for the opening of the center, September

1961, was now out of the question, and Huson Jackson even expressed his doubts that working drawings and construction could be completed by the fall of 1962 (1-11-61).

Composition of External Elements

Through February the work dragged on: elevations, plans, and sections "at a large scale," "the definitive expression of the structure," as Le Corbusier called them, "that is to say, the nature of the slabs and the columns, all the definitive, exact dimensions of the building" (figs. 148–154; 2-4-61). Indeed, it seemed in some ways as if it was no longer the building that was being thought of primarily but the drawings themselves; Jullian has said that Le Corbusier told him, "Do these plans so that they will think I am a real architect."[5] There were a few outstanding planning decisions, it is true. The lift was shifted back and to it were abutted the necessary escape stairs. Piers were introduced on the south side of the building, as had been suggested in the tiny Le Corbusier sketch, and studied in a model that was made of the project (fig. 146). Pilotis were abandoned at the points of maximum cantilever on the curve. A covered passageway was made from the top of the passenger elevator to the studio at the fifth level and entailed the introduction of an extra piloti standing free in space with its beam running back into the roof. Brise-soleil angles were calculated and the fins integrated with the curves of the building to concur with its main sculptural tensions. And through the month of February 1961 Le Corbusier's letters changed in tone from the easy familiarity of his earlier communications and took on a more elevated tone, beginning with the following annotations scrawled along the bottom of one of them:

> Tout s'achève avec précision. Il y a une douzaine de plans . . . Chacun de ces plans (d'environ 2 metres de coté) donne le structure définitive, le totalité du béton, les dimensions exactes des locaux et circulations etc.
>
> Ils apportent une solution (peut-être valable, en tout cas pleine de ressources) des surfaces, volumes *éclairés* avec *imagination*—Un aboutissement de la recherche Corbu.

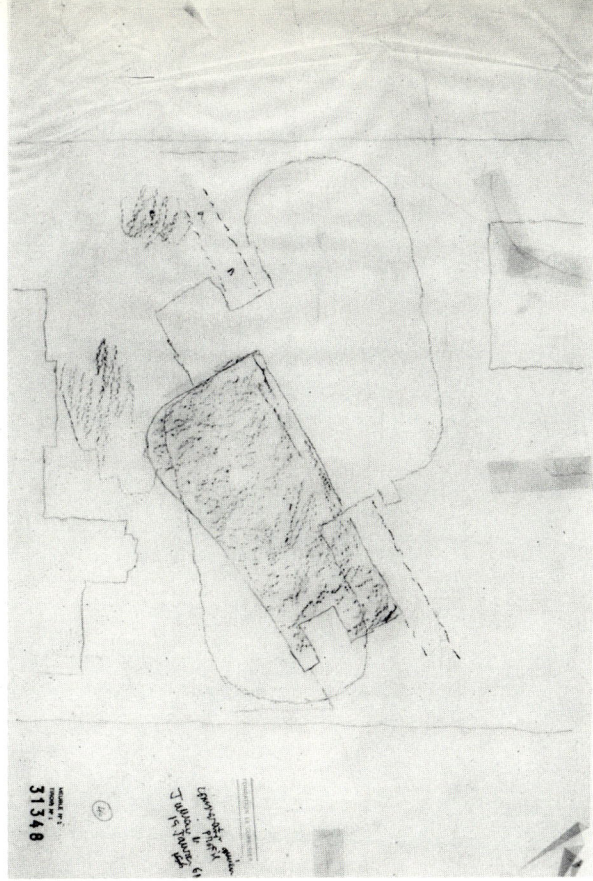

144. *Building outlines at level 3 of projects one and two, Jullian, January 18, 1961. (1:200; 55 × 38 cm; onion skin.) The relative silhouettes of new and old are compared.*

145. *Cardboard cutouts of the first and second projects, Jullian, January 19, 1961. (1:200; each cutout 35 × 25 cm, approximately.)*

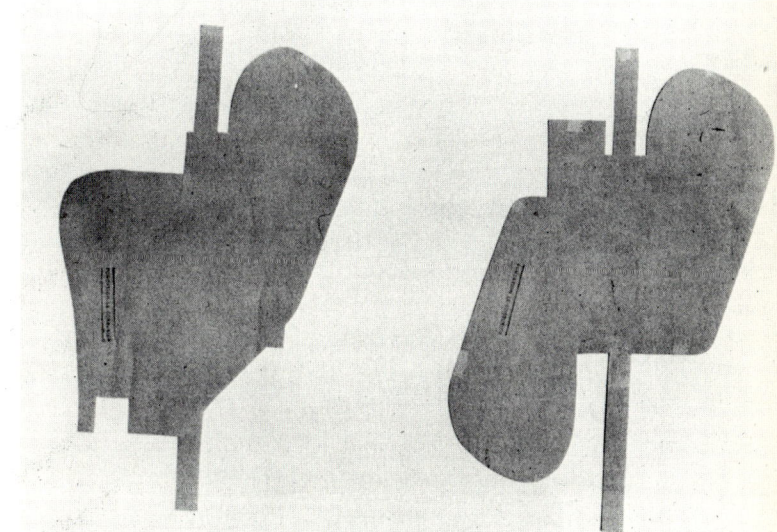

147

Everything is being achieved with precision. There are a dozen plans . . . Each of these plans (about 2 meters a side) gives the definitive structure, the totality of the concrete, the exact dimensions of the localities and circulation etc.

They bring a solution (perhaps valid, in any case full of resources) of surfaces, volumes *lit* with *imagination*—A final goal of Corbu's research. (2-18-61)

The reservation implied by "perhaps valid" was soon to disappear in a series of imperious letters on the results of "Corbu's research."

But for the moment attention turned to the "surfaces" and "lighted volumes," to visual refinements and alignments—in a word, to composition. The building's silhouette and size were determined. The principal visual facts on the exterior, aside from walls, slab-ends, and visible pilotis, were concrete brise-soleil and plates of glass. These needed fitting into the prescribed frame in a sculpturally unified fashion. The methods that Le Corbusier and Jullian employed to do this offer

146. *Model of the second project, Le Corbusier and Jullian, January–February 1961. (Scale and size unknown.) Ondulatoires and brise-soleil are shown.*

148

intriguing insights into the way the plastic, proportional, and aesthetic effects of the building's final exterior forms were achieved. As is suggested by Le Corbusier's phrase, "a final goal of Corbu's research," the drawings also demonstrate the way some of the architect's lifelong researches and discoveries found their way onto the drawing board through an active process of compositional trial and error, of refined visual choices and judgments.

Jullian started the process on January 31 with an elevation study of the Prescott Street facade (fig. 148). This was the first elevation of the second project; the only previous elevations had been of the first project and done the previous November. Jullian's facade was delicately drawn and shaded with ochre for concrete, blue for glass, and shadows on pilotis or in recesses shown by pencil hatching. Light was shown coming from above, probably as if mid-to-late morning around midsummer, and Modulor men were stamped in black ink.

The brise-soleil were set out within the overall frame of the elevation so that they were all angled diagonally inwards towards the ramp gallery and so that they were all exactly aligned vertically. All were also made to run exactly to the northeast corner so that their tips actually formed the vertical corner edge of the building. They were then repeated right to left across the facade at equal intervals such that the small slots of glass between them were just visible to an observer at a position perpendicular to the facade plane. This led to an odd meeting at the fourth level next to the freight lift tower where a little extra space was left over, but the brise-soleil of the lower three levels terminated neatly at the ramp gallery, forming a flush vertical edge. The extra space at fourth level could well serve for an exit onto the required fire escape, so in due course Le Corbusier superimposed a slim vertical sheet of tracing paper, hypothesizing an open stair just next to the freight lift tower (fig. 149). Meanwhile the curved Prescott Street studio was shown with blank fenestration, as was the barely visible rear of the Quincy Street curved studio.

The next day, February 1, the architects studied the brise-soleil in more detail. The first elevation seems to have been a sort of compositional leap in

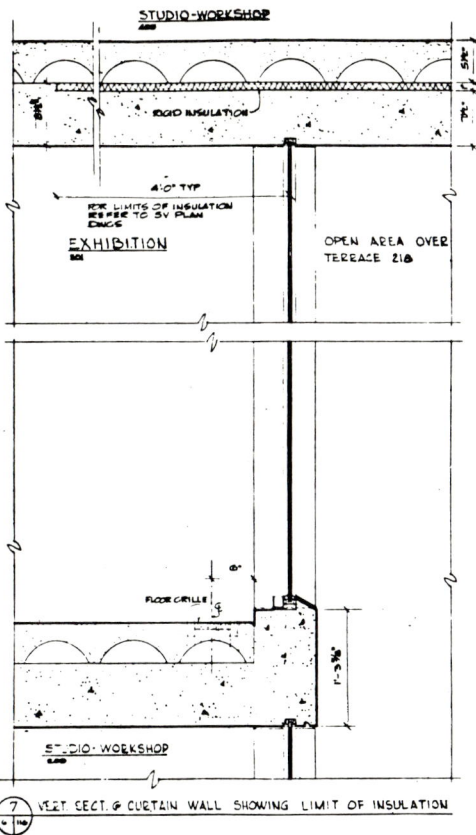

147. *Section showing arrangement of airfloor, part of working drawing, Sert, Jackson and Gourley, March 27, 1962. On top of the carrying slabs of the third and fourth floor semicircular airducts are visible. Near the window one of the outlets for warm air is indicated.*

the dark to assess the external appearance of this kind of brise-soleil in this particular building, and to fix the ideal bay proportions articulating the facade plane (that is, floor-to-ceiling height equal to the distance from fin-tip to fin-tip). The result had been quite beautiful. The problem was now to project the brise-soleil onto a plan. Jullian concentrated on the fourth level, which he began by drawing in outline (fig. 150). The diagonal orientation of the brise-soleil the previous day had not been exactly calculated, so Jullian began by calculating the critical limits of angles and fin lengths, given the distance fin-tip to fin-tip he had decided on the previous day, the climatic data for Cambridge, and the orientation of his facade. When the range of angles had been chosen on one sheet, he fixed a diagonal and then traced on another sheet a series of brise-soleil over this determining geometry. He was now working inside the constraints of

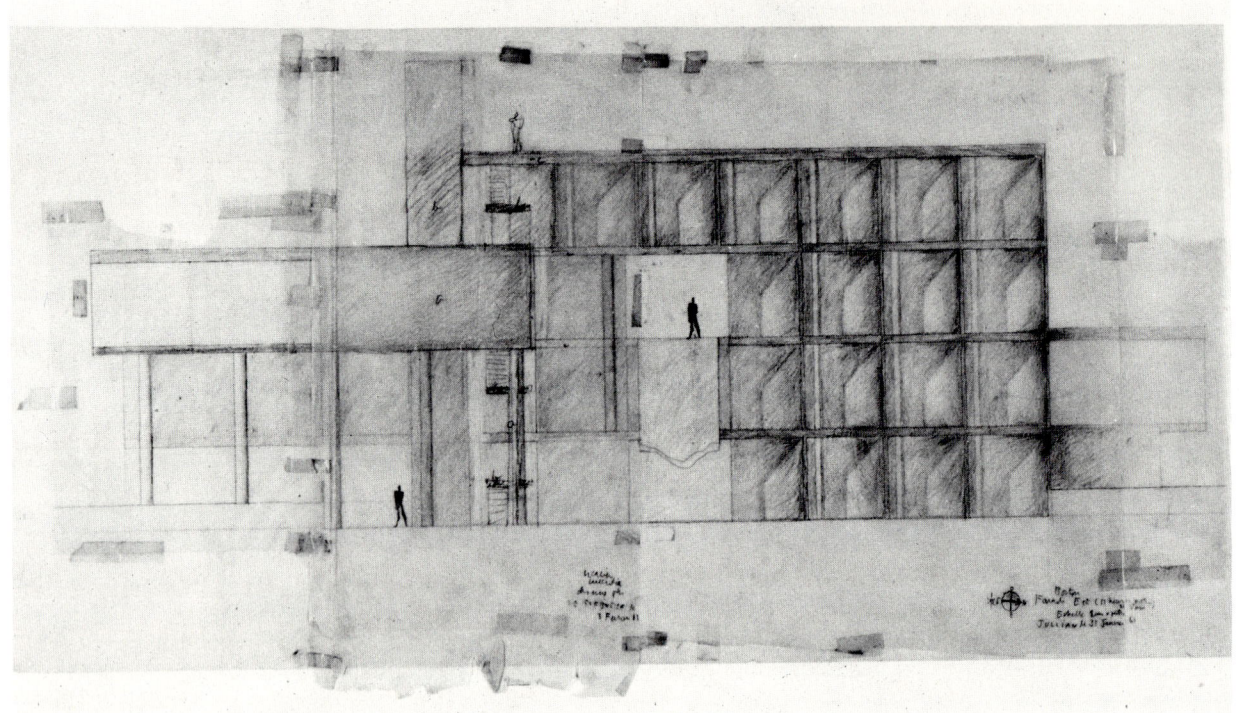

148. *Prescott Street elevation, Jullian, January 31, 1961. (1:50; 55 × 111 cm; thick tracing paper.) Modulor men and light angled as if sun were at solstice in the morning (11 A.M.) are shown. Brise-soleil of the recessed, diagonal fin type are in position except on the curved studio to the left which has not yet been studied. The ochre coloring for concrete is typical of this series of elevations.*

149. *Fire escape design, Prescott Street elevation, Le Corbusier and Jullian, February 3, 1961. (1:50; 55 × 31 cm; onion skin.) The new detail is drawn on a thin, transparent onion skin and then set in place over a Prescott Street elevation.*

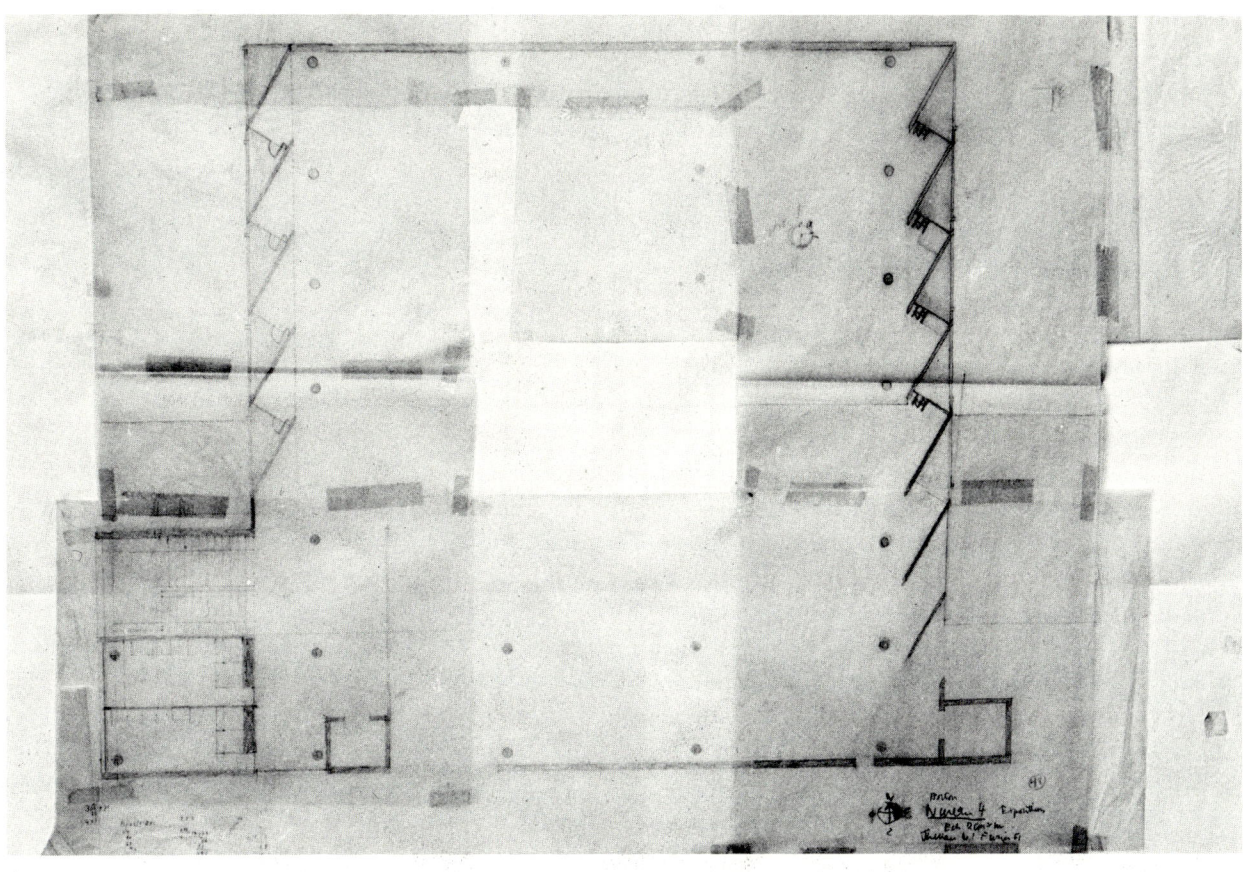

150. *Plan of level 4, Jullian, February 1, 1961. (1:50; 92 × 84 cm; onion skin.) Diagonal brise-soleil are in place, parallel to one another on both the Quincy and Prescott Street facades. Aérateurs and exact glazing positions are not yet fixed but will be calculated on overlays of tracing paper. The use of red crayon to indicate pilotis and brise-soleil and blue to indicate glass is typical of this series of plans.*

an aesthetically and mathematically conditioned bay size and a calculated angle of fin such that the early morning sun would just fail to touch the glass.

This left two principal variable areas for continued experiment and definition: the fin lengths and the position of the glass panes, which were to be set normal to the diagonal fins. On two imposed onion skins (fig. 150) he experimented with these two variables and discovered that he could not make his fins too long if he wanted to avoid impinging on the structural grid, and that he could not make them too short without letting in too much light and without leaving too little brise-soleil surface for the joint with the glass panes. A solution was eventually found which also satisfied another requirement—that the brise-soleil surface area should harmonize with the overall proportional scheme of the building. He fixed this area so that it exactly equaled the bay area. It was as if a flat wall had been simply pivoted inwards to create the brise-soleil. Next he fixed the glass panes in place,

151

coloring them blue; he then colored his brise-soleil and pilotis red.

But the studio still needed ventilating, so there was now the problem of situating the aérateurs. A final onion skin was taped in place over the by now fairly thick wad of tracing paper that constituted the fourth level plan. With a little experimentation, the aérateurs were drawn in place.

Thus the shape, spacing, and angles of the brise-soleil were discovered for the whole of the rectangular part of the building facing Prescott Street: naturally the fourth level angles and sizes applied to the whole elevation. On the same plan of February 1 (fig. 150), Jullian drew a set of aligned and exactly parallel fins at fourth level on the Quincy Street facade. Since it seemed necessary to examine the effect of this further, the Quincy Street elevation was completely drawn, with brise-soleil in position, on the 2nd and 3rd of February (fig. 159).

The same color conventions were used as in the earlier elevation and with similarly beautiful results. These elevation studies recall Le Corbusier's overriding concerns for an architecture of pure, primary, geometrical forms composed into intensely pleasing plastic compositions. The Quincy Street facade drawing illustrates the artist's method of accentuating these overall forms. One has first of all to imagine the facade with only walls and openings laid out according to the planar positions determined by the plan. The major sculptural forces of the facade even in such a blank state would be the curve at second level and the ramp, converging dynamically towards the entry at third level. Now there were also the brise-soleil just created at fourth level on which Jullian concentrated. He placed a horizontal brise-soleil exactly half way up to complement the directionality of the diagonals and to lock this level horizontally to the stair tower: as a whole the fourth level now unified and bridged the upper part of the building and answered horizontal forces lower down. Probably after discussion with Le Corbusier, he then did another version of the fourth level with the horizontal brise-soleil moved up to 2.26 meters, with even more satisfactory results (fig. 159).

Surely, though, one of the oddest features of this facade is the presence of brise-soleil immediately below and above unprotected pans-de-verre. Naturally this tempts one to inquire whether the brise-soleil were redundant or the pans-de-verre inadequate, and to further inquire why the combination was made. In fact curtains have to be used behind the pans-de-verre for the last hour or two of a sunny day.[6] It is the unprotected glass which needs explaining, and this may be done only by hypothesizing the architect's thought processes, his own evaluation of the possibilities and alternatives facing him. It is highly likely (Jullian has said as much) that it was one of Le Corbusier's aims to preserve views over the Yard, especially from the top of the ramp. Then, clearly, an isolated strip of brise-soleil at fourth level could give a strong sculptural accent (both in terms of density and strongly right-directed movement), whose effectiveness would probably have been far less had other brise-soleil been included, or another combination chosen. Surely too the architect was aware of the rhetorical pointedness given the display of his free facade elements by such isolation and immediate juxtaposition of them and contrast of their visual qualities and functional meanings.

How was the glazing immediately below the brise-soleil, at third level, to be treated? This was a problem to which Le Corbusier turned on a tiny sheet of tracing paper which he simply slid into place over Jullian's large-scale drawing (fig. 151). In it Le Corbusier aligned four aérateurs with slots of glass in the brise-soleil above. This led to an unsatisfactory coincidence of aérateur and glazed corner by the ramp at third level. Eventually this corner was left with glass meeting glass and the aérateurs were shifted slightly to the left to align with the brise-soleil fins. The same sketch shows concrete at the fourth level between the stair tower and the last fin to the right—eventually this too was dematerialized by being left open, as occurs in similar incongruent meetings at Chandigarh.[7]

Similar refinements were now made on the right-hand side of Jullian's Quincy Street elevation using another scrap of tracing paper as an overlay. Brise-soleil were definitely needed on this, the south side, so Le Corbusier sketched some in as they might appear to someone approaching the side entrance from Quincy Street. He drew a horizontal brise-soleil exactly half way up (an extremely subtle decision). Then, the next day (February 4) this new horizontal stress was examined for its repercussions on the Prescott Street facade where the same brise-soleil terminated (fig. 152). The result was successful and accepted.

Visual, tectonic tensions were obviously a major consideration on the curves, and the Prescott Street one required sun protection. On February 5 a number of separate studies (fig. 153) were made in plan of different numbers and spacings of fins. The fins were kept parallel to each other but out of line with the pilotis grid. With these drawings of February 5, 1961, most of the major decisions for the external composition of the visual arts center were complete. These discoveries were now anchored in place on a series of plans for the whole building (fig. 154). "Facts" were thus manipulated on plan and in elevation; "accidents," the effect of lighting, color, tone, density, were examined in elevation alone.

151. *Overlay tracing, Quincy Street brise-soleil, Le Corbusier, February 1961. (1:50; 30 × 49 cm; onion skin.) This was inserted in place over figure 159 to establish relationships of fin-tips to aérateurs below.*

152. *Prescott Street elevation, Jullian, February 4, 1961. (1:50; 50 × 109 cm; onion skin.) This drawing, rapidly traced from figure 148, experiments compositionally with a horizontal brise-soleil stiffener midway up the void to the far left.*

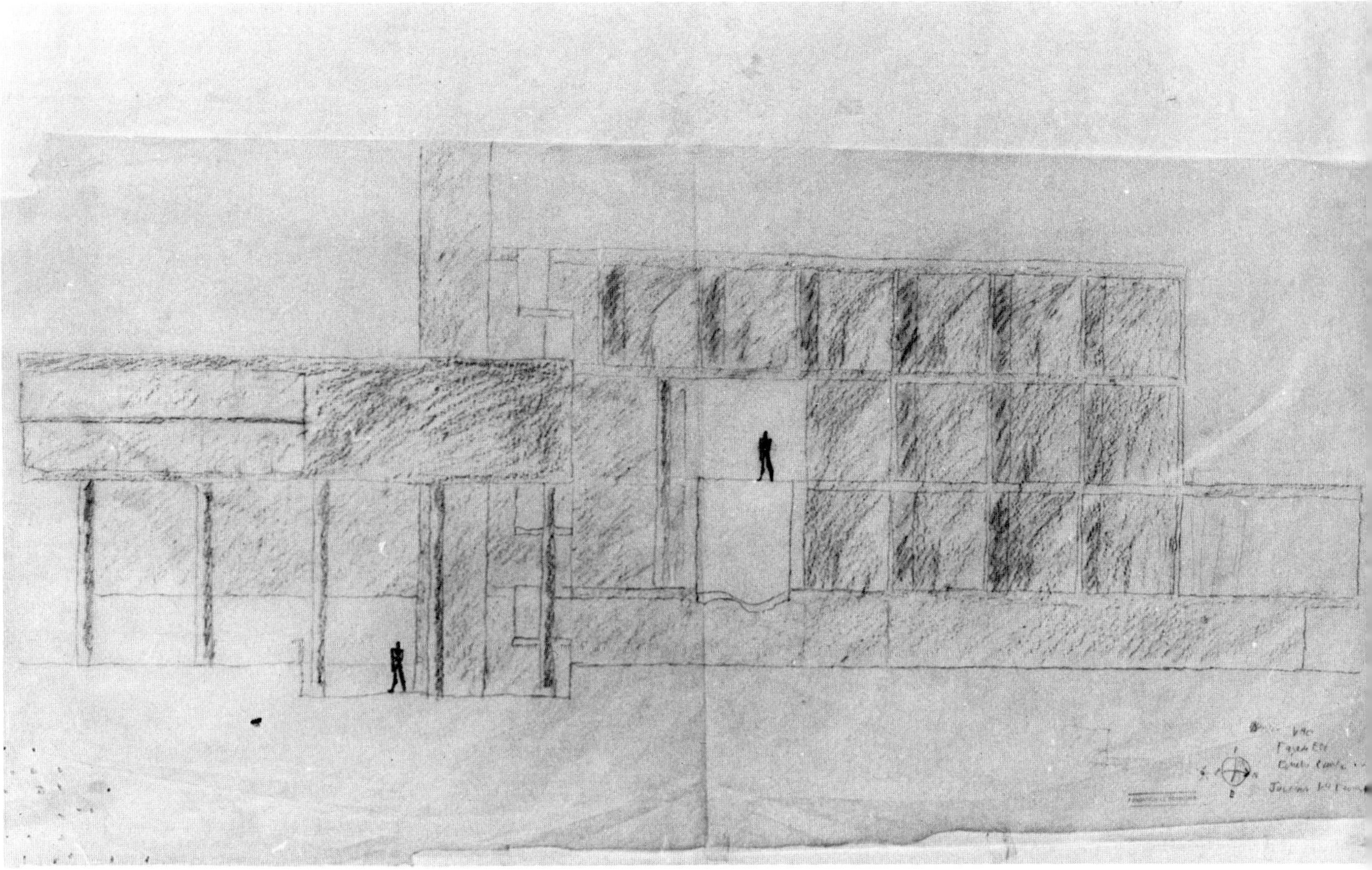

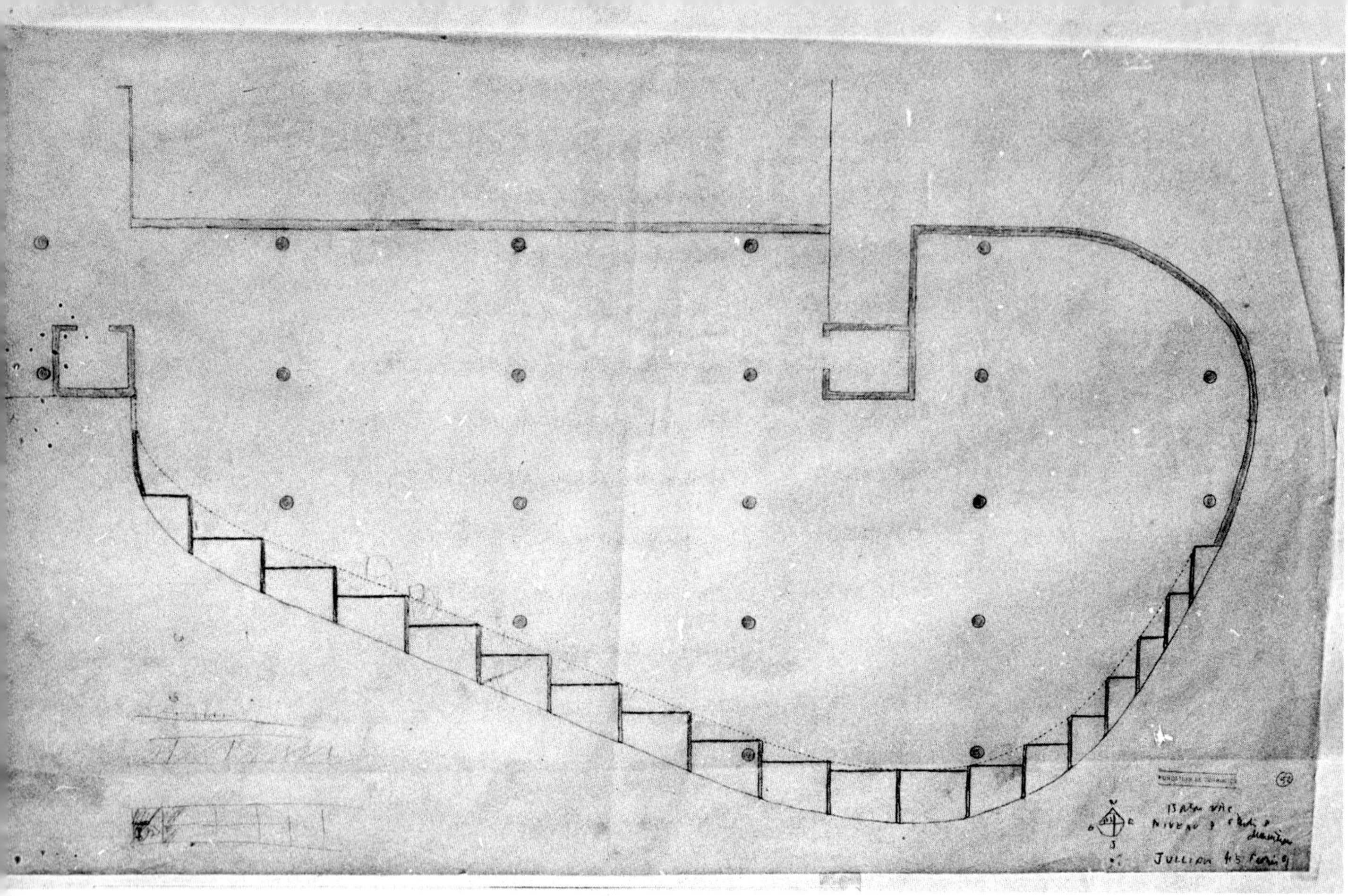

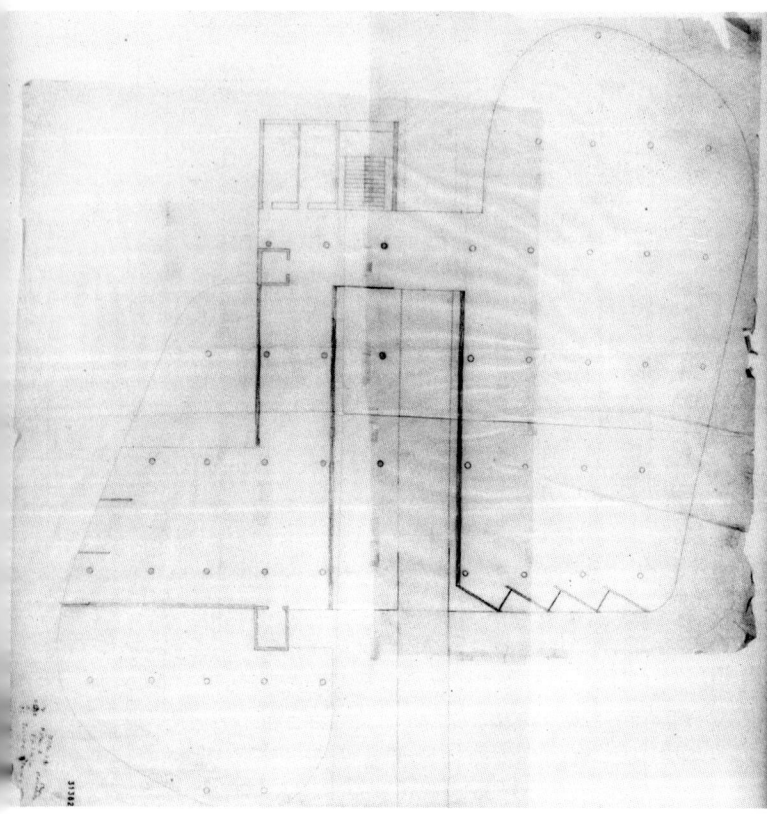

153. *Plan of level 3, south side, Jullian, February 5, 1961. (1:50; 55 × 90 cm; onion skin.) Positioning of brise-soleil on the curve is demonstrated: here the constraints are that the fins be parallel with each other but off the line of the structural grid, that spacings fit the Modulor, and that inside tips present an uninterrupted curve when a line was drawn through them. The solution was hard found, but the result has a taut, incremental quality which accentuates the overall form.*

154. *Plan of level 2, Jullian, February 7, 1961. (1:50; 106 × 105 cm; onion skin.) One of a series of "tidying up" plans done in the second week of February.*

These visual researches show Le Corbusier, the master of form, at work; they also demonstrate Jullian's assimilation and understanding of Le Corbusier's language. With their diagonal shadows, pale pilotis, static pastel forms, simple geometries, and Modulor men, the elevations have something of the timeless quality of the November 1960 studies. But this time the project was in no cul-de-sac. Through the sharply ruled, crystalline images in pencil and colored crayon we may begin to discern the final forms in concrete and glass.

The plans were tidied up in the second week of February and color coded with thin blue lines for glass, pale red for the structure, and yellow for circulation; they were to culminate in the presentation drawings, which Le Corbusier later referred to as his crystallization of the drawings of his epoch. And when, in his letter of transmission, he discusses the smooth slab/pilotis system as the "key to the solution for reinforced concrete," it becomes clear once more that his intentions and attitudes are rather special in his only American building.

8. LE CORBUSIER'S DEFINITION OF REINFORCED CONCRETE

We must aim at the fixing of standards in order to face the problem of perfection.

Le Corbusier

The first set of drawings of the second project (figs. 155–158, 160–163) arrived in Cambridge in early March accompanied by the aforementioned note from Le Corbusier and by a short letter from Jullian. At the time they were sent, Le Corbusier was headed in the other direction, towards India. His part of the agreed contract had almost reached completion; all that remained was to finish the elevations and to send them on. At the rue de Sèvres they decided not to do this till Le Corbusier's return in April. With the arrival of this second set of drawings in Cambridge his legal obligations were complete. At the office of Sert, Jackson, and Gourley Associates, the code for the visual arts center ceased to be VAC BOS and became job number 5911.

All bidding for contractors and decisions to be made prior to the commencement of construction had to be rushed if ground was to be broken by summer 1961—any later and the center's opening would have to be postponed beyond 1962. The project was already a year behind schedule. Le Corbusier was consulted on every decision concerning details through this period, which added

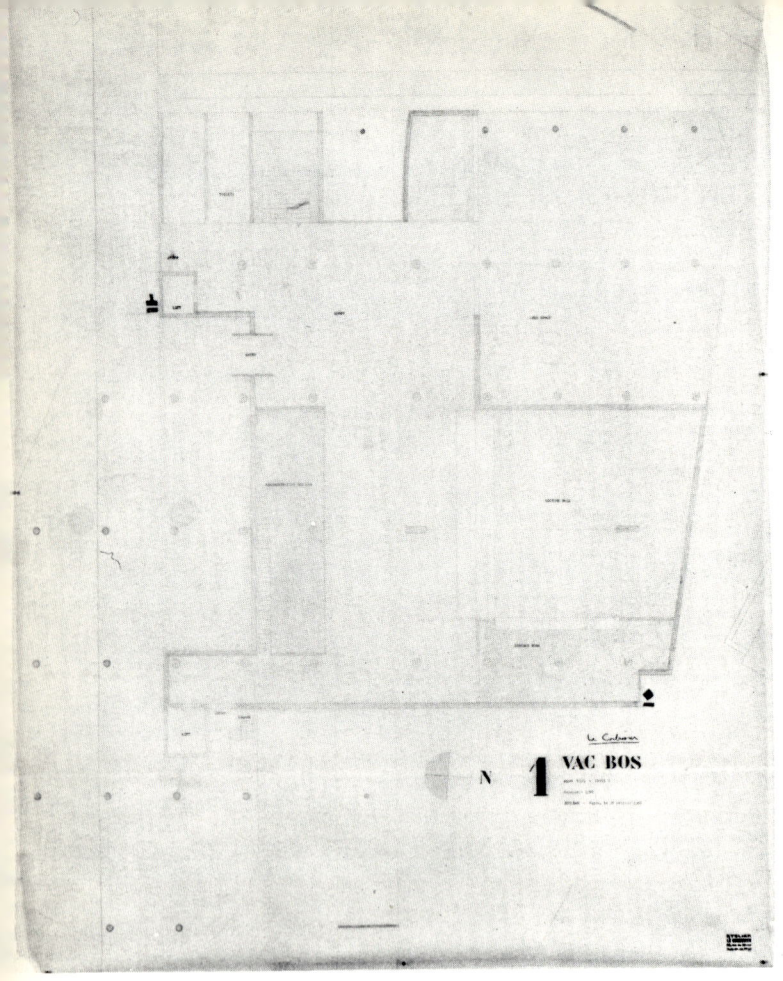
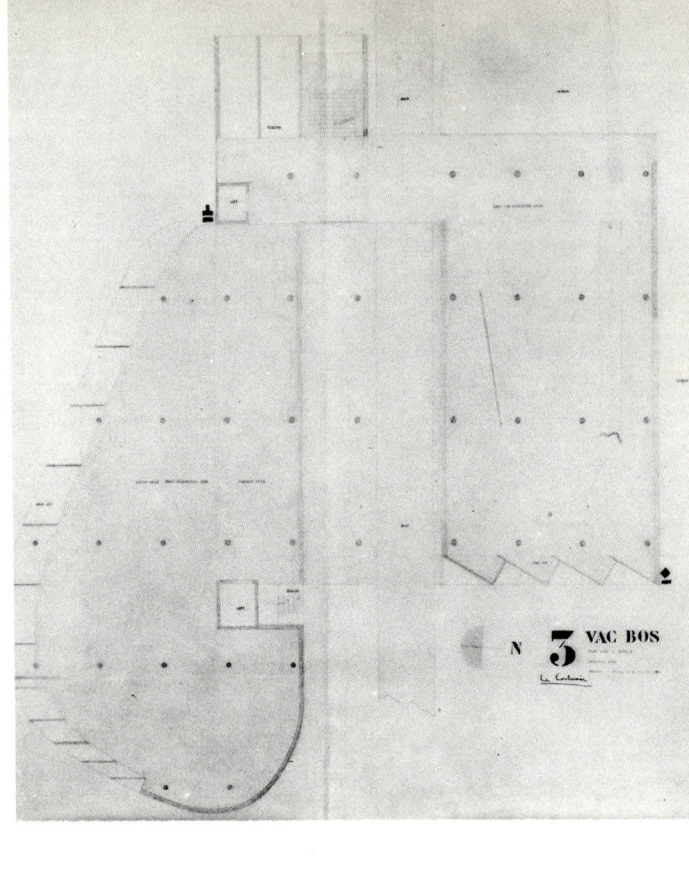

155. *Presentation plan of level 1, second project, Le Corbusier and Jullian, February 25, 1961. (1:50; 117 × 91 cm; thick tracing paper.)*

156. *Presentation plan of level 3, second project, Le Corbusier and Jullian, February 25, 1961. (1:50; 117 × 98.5 cm; thick tracing paper: "vellum.")*

to the delay. And to the extent that Sert was helpful, Le Corbusier seems to have become dogmatic. Sert naturally welcomed the idea that the building should be executed exactly according to Le Corbusier's intentions. The correspondence between Cambridge and Paris from 1961 to 1962 is so valuable precisely because it documents Le Corbusier's intentions on matters as diverse as concrete finishes and mosquito screens, air-conditioning and proportions. In these letters his principles and prejudices are revealed outside the arena of public discourse and publications through which they are ordinarily known. The rhetorical guard is let slip somewhat, the architectural heart laid bare, the intimate intentions underlying the design are partially revealed.

The Presentation Drawings

Even without accompanying documentation, it was clear that the drawings were something special (figs. 155–163). Executed in pencil on vellum with ochre crayon hatchings for concrete, red for section cuts and blue for glass, the drawings had obviously been prepared with great care; they had, in fact, taken weeks of work. As in the drawings of late November, those "tombstones" of the first project, Modulor men were shown at entrances and exits. The Modulor was not used exclusively in relating the parts, but salient features such as brise-soleil distances, floor-to-floor heights, bay distances, and column thicknesses were all keyed into the system. Later on, when details such as shuttering marks, wooden panels, and steel railings had to be incorporated, they were also scaled according to the Modulor.

Without dimensioning of any kind and with only the slightest annotations of the main spaces, the drawings made impressive unified images, giving, as the architect put it, "la sensation architecturale pure et simple" ("the pure and simple

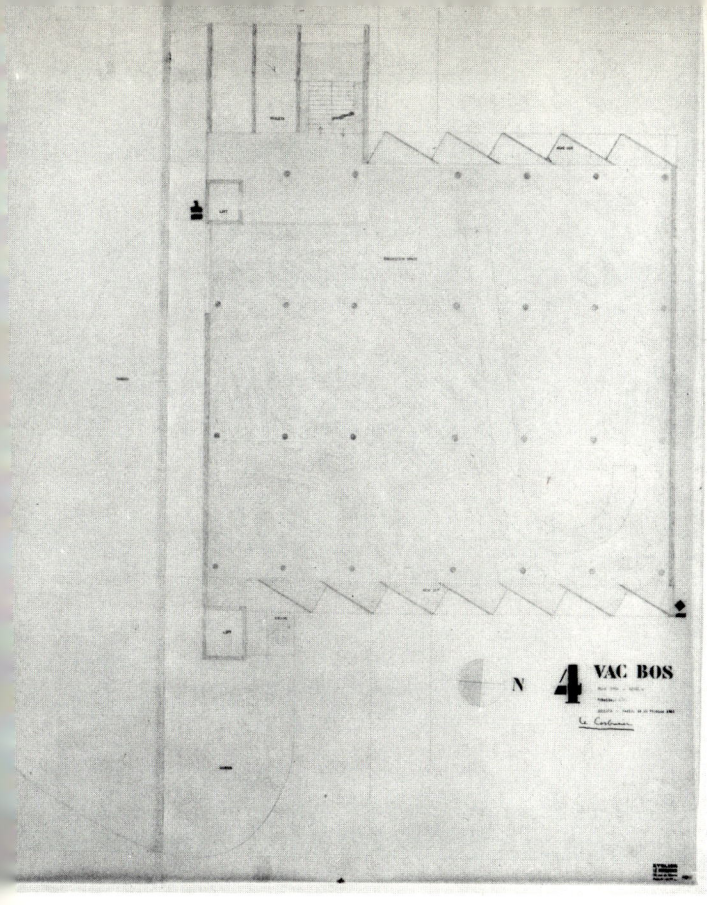

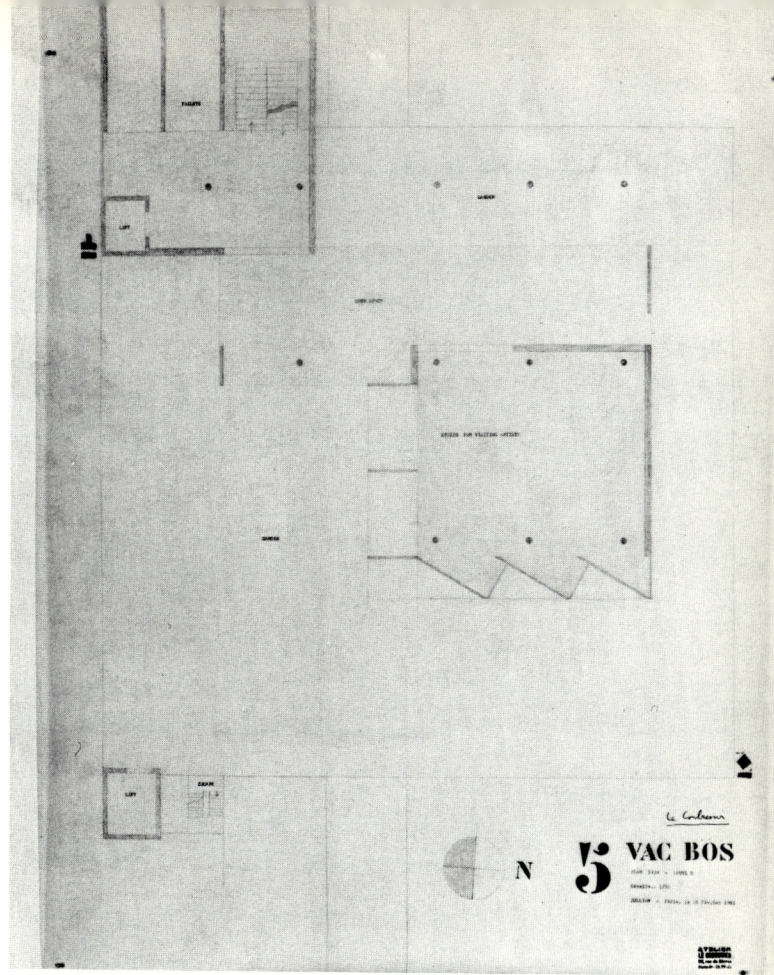

157. *Presentation plan of level 4, second project, Le Corbusier and Jullian, February 25, 1961. (1:50; 108 × 91 cm; thick tracing paper: "vellum.")*

158. *Presentation plan of level 5, second project, Le Corbusier and Jullian, February 25, 1961. (1:50; 108 × 91 cm; thick tracing paper: "vellum.")*

architectural sensation"; 5-29-61; appendix 16). Rigorously drawn, proportionally regulated, composed of the simplest curved and rectangular elements, they call to mind the Purist pictures of bottles, violins, and other objects that Le Corbusier and Amédée Ozenfant painted in the twenties. These were also disposed parallel to the picture plane (they showed plans and sections of bottles, glasses, pipes, and other everyday objects) and were also composed for maximum formal effect. And just as the Purist pictures were a distillation of Cubism, cleansed of the Cubist forerunners' accidental blemishes and visual mistakes, so, evidently, were the Cambridge drawings quintessential presentation drawings of the modern era, since Le Corbusier explicitly stated in reference to a set of prints made from them,

> [ces tirages] sont le résultat d'une mise au point de mes idées relatives aux dessins d'architecte à notre époque.

[these prints] are the result of a crystallization of my relative ideas concerning the architectural drawings in our epoch.[1] (5-29-61; appendix 16)

The elevations showed the main proportional configurations of lines, planes, and forms, suggested the materials by color, and described the fall of light. This was no Cambridge, Massachusetts, light as it had been on one January elevation study showing shadows exactly as they would have appeared at 11 a.m. on a cloudless midsummer day; it was an abstract, drawing board light, above local and particular conditions (fig. 161). The columns were bathed evenly from an imprecise light source off to one side of the building; but whereas columns to the other side of elevator towers or walls should have been obscured or darkened, on the contrary, they too were evenly lit, but from the *other* side, implying two light sources at one hundred and eighty degrees. And although elevation brise-soleil bore no diagonal shadows, one section dramatically sifted light into the interior of the building from above. Abstract configurations, without any indication of shuttering marks, greenery, or ondulatoires, they tended to be ideal visualizations, perennially frozen at the "minute of high proportion."[2] They were, perhaps, visual equivalents to such abstract definitions of architecture as "le volume et la surface sont les éléments par quoi se manifeste l'architecture" ("volume and surface are the elements through which architecture manifests itself") or the better known "l'architecture est le jeu savant, correct et magnifique des volumes assemblés sous la lumière" ("architecture is the magnificent, knowledgeable, and correct play of volumes brought together in light") from *Vers une architecture*.[3]

These drawings should act as a reminder that, even in Le Corbusier's late works where the material facts of glass, béton brut, brick, greenery, and so on figure so robustly in the actual experience of the finished work, design nonetheless passes through a phase of abstract, formal visualization. In one letter, Le Corbusier implied a division between the establishment of a satisfactory matrix—the "most perfect possible perfection of proportions" (5-29-61; appendix 16)—and the befitting "typical materials" to be inserted at some other time. The stress on an underlying framework of immutable proportional relationships, on simplified geometry, on ideal form, and on types reminds us of the strong Neoplatonic ingredient in Le Corbusier's thought.

The omission of detailed annotations and dimensions played its part by leaving the ideal forms inviolate, preserving their perceptual purity, allowing them better to "touch the heart"[4] but had the extra property of disallowing anyone unarmed with a scale (members of the Harvard Committee for the Practice of the Visual Arts, for example) from working out the dimensions:

> Nous avons fait tous les plans à grande échelle: 2 centimètres par mètre, plans et coupes, de façon à ce que toutes *les solutions* en plans et coupes soient impeccables.
>
> A vrai dire, les plans et coupes soumis ici, n'ont pas besoin de commentaires. Les dimen-

159. *Quincy Street elevation, Jullian, February 2–3, 1961. (1:50; 53 × 115 cm; onion skin over white card.) Overlays were used in establishing brise-soleil designs. The final version with the horizontal brise-soleil at 2.26 meters is illustrated.*

160. *Presentation longitudinal section BB, second project, Le Corbusier and Jullian, February 25, 1961. (1:50; 56 × 121 cm; thick tracing paper: "vellum.") This section shows clearly the architect's "clef de la solution de béton armé," the Purist pilotis/slab skeleton in its ultimate refinement.*

161. *Prescott Street (east side) presentation elevation, second project, Le Corbusier and Jullian, April 7, 1961. (1:50; 54 × 108 cm; thick tracing paper: "vellum.")*

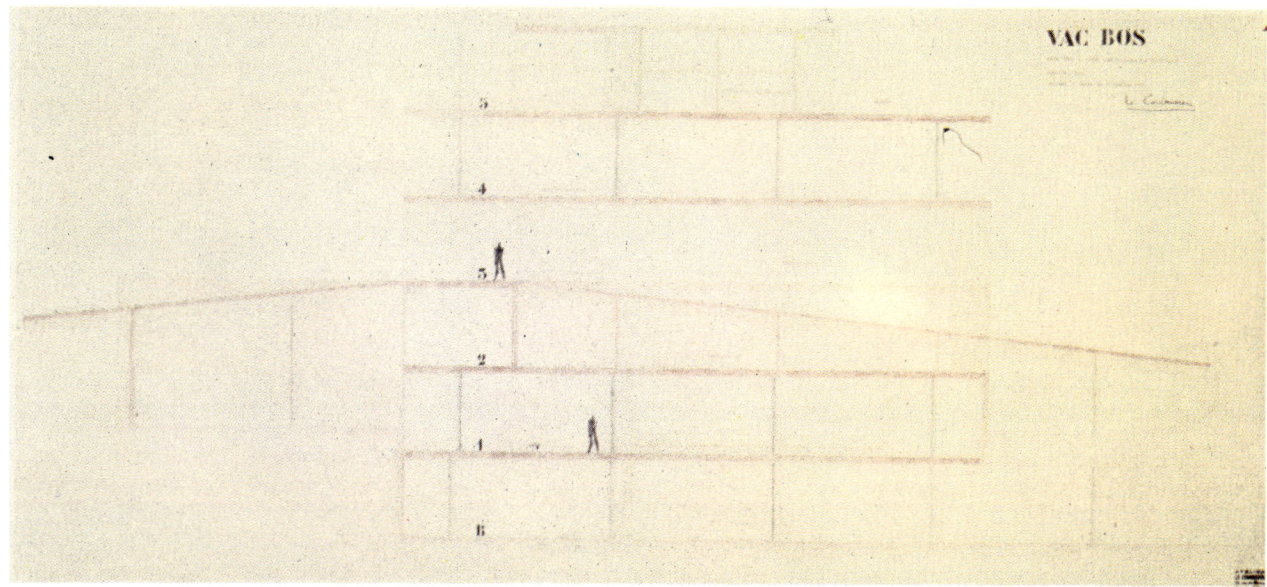

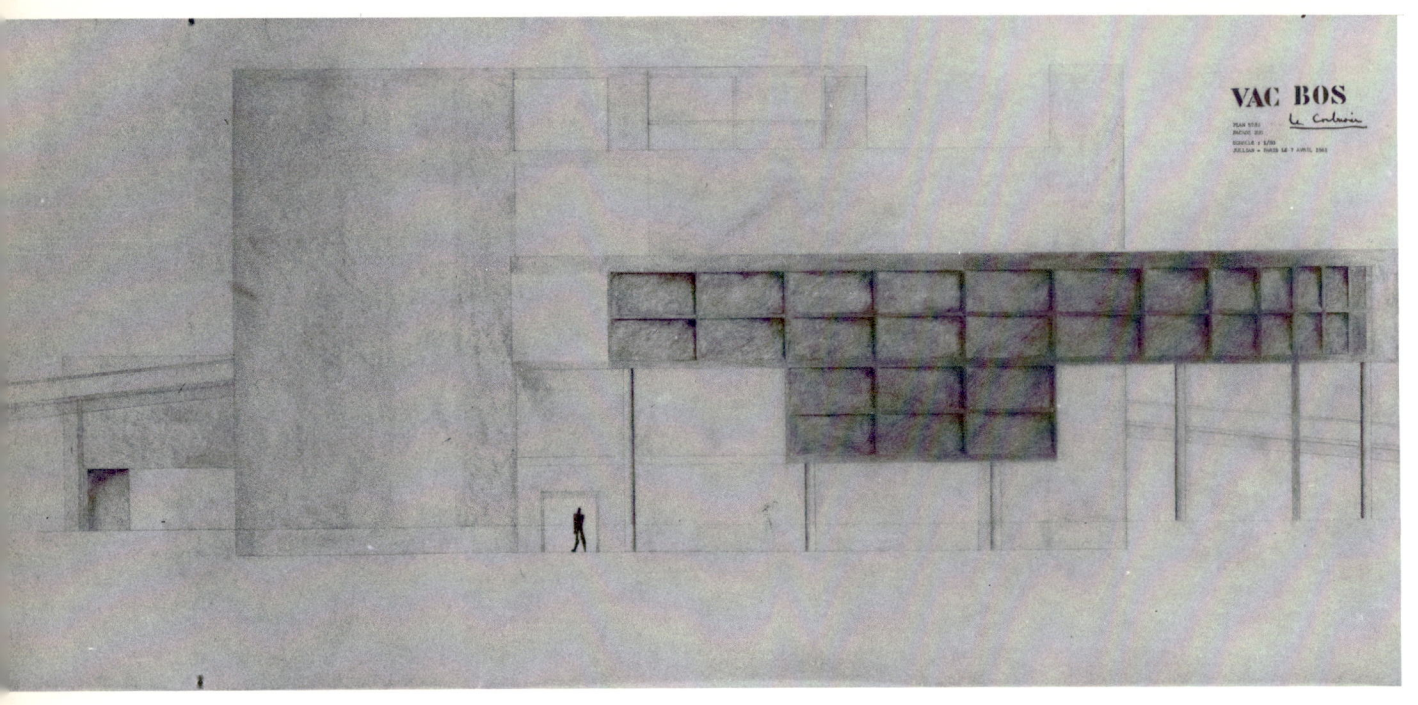

162. *South side presentation elevation, second project, Le Corbusier and Jullian, April 7, 1961. (1:50; 56 × 125 cm; thick tracing paper: "vellum.")*

163. *Quincy Street (west side) presentation elevation, second project, Le Corbusier and Jullian, April 7, 1961. (1:50; 58 × 108 cm; thick tracing paper: "vellum.")*

sions sont toutes rigoureusement dessinées exactement. Elles peuvent être prises avec le "kutch."

We have made all the plans at a large scale: 2 centimeters per meter, plans and sections, so that all *the solutions* in plan and section are impeccable.

To tell the truth, the plans and sections submitted here do not need commentary. The dimensions are all rigorously drawn exactly. They can be measured with the "scale." (2-28-61; appendix 13)

In a later letter, Le Corbusier further elaborated his conception of the ideal arrangement regarding architectural drawings:

J'ai décidé de séparer deux natures de plans:
a) les dessins donnant en plans et en élévations la sensation architecturale pure et simple très lisibles
b) de charger le 'Service d'Exécution' des plans nécessaires pour le chantier, c'est à dire des plans côtés, annotés autant que possible, remplis d'explications, etc, etc. . . .
Grâce au Modulor (employé pas forcément exclusivement) les cotes sont faciles à mesurer avec le kutch et à apprécier au Modulor.
⎰ De cette façon l'architecte voit l'*architecture*.
⎨ Le chantier reçoit les ordres dessinés et chiffrés.
⎱ Résultat: on y voit clair et c'est capital.

I decided to separate two species of plan:
a) drawings giving the pure and simple architectural sensation, in plans and elevations, very readable
b) to charge the 'Service of Execution' with the working drawings necessary for the site, that is, dimensioned plans, annotated as much as possible, full of explanations, etc., etc. . . .
Thanks to the Modulor (not employed compulsively throughout) the dimensions are easy to measure with the scale and to appreciate according to the Modulor.
⎰ Thus the architect sees the *architecture*.
⎨ The site receives orders drawn and numbered.
⎱ Result: one sees clearly and this is great.
(5-29-61; appendix 16)

Certainly, the second building was seen much more clearly, in every sense of the term: on the outside the building was neatly packed into a silhouette, the wall plane respected by the recessed brise-soleil fins now that the old clutter had been shaved away (fig. 18). To Le Corbusier, this no doubt meant that purer sensations were emitted; it certainly made the elements that much easier to read. On the inside, beams had been purged from slabs, and in plan the spine of longitudinal circulation had been satisfactorily reconciled with the centralizing tendency; altogether the second building presented a more compact and circumscribed image than had the first.

The second building was also much heavier visually. It was less poised especially on the Quincy Street side, where the studio was now low down, so that at its extremity it was scarcely more than two meters above the highest part of the site (fig. 3). The ramp still ran to the third level, but the visual effect of uplifting the Quincy Street studio was lost. To counteract this loss of height, Jullian suggested that a flat-bottomed trench be dug under the studio so that there would be at least one floor-to-ceiling height of space, and piloti would retain their intellectual dignity by being uncropped (3-8-61; appendix 14).

The facades were much denser as well. The aluminum blades of the first project's brise-soleil might have engendered a floating effect, especially in combination with all the glass. The effect of transparency had been lost, though the light admitted to the interior was only cut slightly by the different type of brise-soleil. And these brise-soleil were not like attached mechanisms at all; rather they were integral sculptural elements, set in place between the architraves of the slab-ends, tips flush with them on the exterior plane.[5]

The Skeleton

The exterior was articulated by floor slab-ends, brise-soleil tips, ondulatoires, and aérateurs. The interior space, especially viewed from the ramp, was subdivided by pure cylindrical pilotis of varying sizes, receding in perspective, bathed in many different qualities of light (figs. 160, 161). The structural system's simplicity, however, was largely a surface affair; and not just because the treatment of the columns had been specified as *"lisse"* (smooth). Jullian asserted that the column thicknesses varied according to "the weight born," a principle which, if consistently exercised, would have resulted in dozens of diameters (3-8-61; appendix 14). In fact, the columns were sized according to the *apparent* load that they carried, the column becoming an increment thicker for each additional floor supported. In some cases (figs. 161, 162, 163, 26) this system resulted in slender columns rising unbraced through clear space for two stories. These had to be so packed with steel reinforcing that concrete could not be poured but had to be crammed manually. The diminishing column sizes were not equal to standard formwork dimensions, and standardized reinforcing solutions were found to be impossible, too. The reason for this, of course, was that weights above were actually varying, even when the column size did not acknowledge it. Columns of the same size would often require totally different reinforcing solutions from the engineer despite the assertion of the architect that they were "bearing the same weight."

And if the plans (or the finished building) are examined carefully, it will be seen that the large curved studios bulging out towards the streets and creating cantilevers of continuously varying extensions were supported at the ends by emergency measures: the Quincy Street one by a curved wall for some twenty feet, disastrously tranquilizing the play of curves and ondulatoires above by anchoring them to the ground (figs. 163, 3), the Prescott Street one by a brise-soleil extended downwards to become a pier (fig. 22), which the architect christened "a strange tree in the forest of firs which is the pilotis" (3-8-61; appendix 14). These, the areas of greatest cantilever, had always been a trouble spot in the design that, it had optimistically been supposed, would be solved in some other way. It is possible to see this plane among the cylinders as a rich contradiction, or a spatial rudder; the wall is inescapably an inelegant expediency.[6]

Aside from quibbling of this kind, the structural skeleton was extremely elegant (figs. 33, 34), a purist recasting of the rationalist dream, a structure gauged according to load, but with obvious parallels further back in time—the tectonic hierarchy (slim at the top, fat at the bottom) of the classical orders used in combination, or even (since the architect himself spoke of a "forest of firs") the diminution toward the top of trees. The smooth slab/piloti system was probably the "key to the solution of reinforced concrete" because it was a plastic system in tune with Le Corbusier's aesthetic prejudices: reflecting the logic of support and supported in the simplest possible way—"so pure as to give almost the feeling of the natural," as Le Corbusier wrote of the Doric system he so admired.[7] So pure as to reflect, too, the harmony of ideal forms: cylinders were among the beautiful absolute forms singled out for special attention in *Vers une architecture*, especially when made smooth. Made smooth, they became more beautiful because this made them so much easier to see.[8]

> Tout a été ramené à une très grande simplification. La construction est limitée à des poteaux ronds, d'épaisseur variable, portant des dalles

parasol *sans chapiteau*. C'est la clef de la solution de béton armé. La disposition des poteaux se prête à cette solution.

De cette manière, le bâtiment est fait de dalles avec plafonds lisses, sans chapiteaux et sans "beams".

Everything has been very greatly simplified. The structure is limited to round columns, of variable thickness, bearing parasol slabs *without capitals*. It is the key to the solution for reinforced concrete. The disposition of the columns lends itself to this solution.

In this manner, the building is made of slabs, their ceilings smooth, without capitals and without beams. (2-28-61; appendix 13)

This was not true representation of the structural facts of the matter, for, as was said before, the equivalent of capitals were there, only recessed out of sight in the slab alongside the "airfloor."

When Le Corbusier speaks in the above passage of "the key to the solution to reinforced concrete," he implies much more than the indisputable suitability of a smooth slab/pilotis solution to this particular building; he implies *the* absolute solution for the material, and indicates his rationalist view that each material has an exclusive, "correct" theoretical and formal definition. He seems to mean that the visual arts center skeleton should be regarded as a quintessential statement in reinforced concrete, a crystallization of forms which the material itself inherently desired.

Concrete: "Béton Brut"

To go with his final word on architectural drawings and his ideal solution for the frame, Le Corbusier proposed a grammar for the facade that was discussed as if it too had some absolute sanction. Appropriate to the gravity of their message, Le Corbusier's letters were frequently tabulated with underlined headings and written in clipped dogmatic prose. The theme was introduced thus:

Les façades sont soit aveugles, soit munies de contrôle du soleil (brise-soleil).

Le "4ème mur de la chambre" se trouve ainsi réalisé. Ce ne sont pas des fenêtres, c'est un système double d'éclairage solaire par des panneaux de verre nettoyables dedans et dehors et munis d'aérateurs assurant la "trans-aération" selon les expériences concluantes faites aux Indes, à Paris et au Couvent de la Tourette.

Un troisième genre d'éclairage existe: les "ondulatoires" de chaque côté de la rampe qui traverse le bâtiment.

The facades are either blank or provided with sun control (brise-soleil).

The "fourth wall of the room" is thus achieved. These are not windows, it is a double system of sunlighting using glass panes which can be cleaned inside and out, and supplied with aérateurs assuring "cross ventilation," after the conclusive experiences had in India, Paris, and at the Monastery of La Tourette.

A third type of lighting exists: the "ondulatoires" to each side of the ramp which runs through the building. (2-28-61; appendix 13)

Ondulatoires in the ramp gallery were later abandoned in favor of plain glass for easy viewing, but they were retained on the curved Quincy Street studio where they were most effective. The elevations were thus composed of four main elements: brise-soleil, aérateurs, ondulatoires, and concrete walls (figs. 4, 18).

The concrete walls were of two kinds: flat or curved (figs. 4a, 7). These were referred to by Jullian as "the skin."

Les façades sont en béton coulé dans des coffrages standards de tôle (en principe) et pour les plus grandes surfaces éventuellement en Isorel ou en contre-plaqué ou en lames de bois pour les surfaces courbes (voliges) . . . Les lames de bois pour les parois courbes seront de dimensions plus réduites qu'il n'est coutume de le faire. Nervi l'a réalisé à l'UNESCO et au grand bâtiment italien du Centenaire 1861–1961 à Turin. Ces coffrages de béton sont extrêmement élégants et très propres.

The facades are of concrete poured into standard steel forms (in principle) and for the largest surfaces, eventually, of Isorel or of plywood or wooden strips for the curved surfaces (battens) . . . The wood strips for the curved surfaces are in smaller dimension than is customary. Nervi realized it at UNESCO and in the large Italian building for the 1861–1961 Centennial in Turin. Those forms for the concrete are extremely elegant and very clean. (5-29-61; appendix 16)

This attitude toward the concrete envelope is in marked contrast to what might be expected from the author of the Marseilles Unité block, where rough shuttering marks and rugged edges led to the coinage of the term "béton brut." Even though husky brick and rubble during the thirties presaged the Marseilles development, there is evidence that the roughness at Marseilles was forced upon him: an instructive postscript scrawled along the bottom of a letter to Sert in 1962 (when the visual arts center was under construction) refers to Claudius Petit, the man who made Marseilles possible, and to the use of concrete in the visual arts center.[9]

> P. S. Je fais pour Claudius Petit "La Maison de la Jeunesse et de la Culture" à Firminy. Hier il s'est mis en colère (pas devant moi, mais devant les dessinateurs) disant que nous avions fait du béton uni (coffrage en contreplaqué), que c'est une trahison, que cela devait être en béton brut—avec bois visible.
>
> Le béton brut est né de l'Unité d'Habitation de Marseille où il y avait 80 entrepreneurs et un tel massacre de béton qu'il ne fallait pas rêver de faire des raccords utiles par les enduits. J'avais décidé: laissons tout cela brut. J'appelais cela du béton brut. Les Anglais ont immédiatement sauté sur le morceau et m'ont traité (Ronchamp et le Couvent de la Tourette) de "Brutal",—béton brutal;—en fin de compte, la brute c'est Corbu. Ils ont appelé cela "the new brutality". Mes amis et admirateurs me tiennent pour le brute du béton brutal!
>
> Veux-tu être assez gentil, toi "qui a beaucoup de temps libre!" de passer un mot à Claudius et de lui dire que le Visual Art Center, que nous faisons ensemble au Centre de l'Université de Harvard, est en béton brut, mais lisse, et ceci dans un esprit de perfection qui t'anime toi-même aussi bien que moi. J'envoie d'ailleurs à Claudius copie de cette lettre.

> P.S. I am doing for Claudius Petit "La Maison de la Jeunesse et de la Culture" at Firminy. Yesterday he flew into a rage (not in front of me, but in front of the draftsmen) saying that we had made unified concrete (formwork of plywood), that it is treachery, that it was supposed to be béton brut—with wood showing.
>
> Béton brut was born at the Unité d'Habitation at Marseilles where there were 80 contractors and such a massacre of concrete that one simply could not dream of making useful transitions by means of grouting. I decided: let us leave all that brute. I called it "béton brut" ["bare concrete"]. The English immediately jumped on the piece and treated me (Ronchamp and the Monastery of la Tourette) as "Brutal"—béton brutal—all things considered, the brute is Corbu. They called that "the new brutality." My friends and admirers take me for the brute of the brutal concrete!
>
> Will you be so nice, you "who have a lot of free time!" to drop a line to Claudius and tell him that the Visual Arts Center, that we are doing together at the center of Harvard University, is in béton brut, but smooth, and this in a spirit of perfection which animates you as well as me. And I am sending Claudius a copy of this letter too.[10] (5-26-62; appendix 20)

Admittedly Le Corbusier made virtuoso concrete articulation out of the rough concrete he had to use at Marseilles, but these highly textured effects were not compulsory aesthetic usage, as they eventually became for almost a decade of other architects.

Sert wrote to Claudius Petit dutifully supporting Le Corbusier's point of view, adding the qualification that rough concrete should only be used in special circumstances. Although he remained vague about the boundaries of permissiveness, the gist may be understood from the following excerpt.

Les parties finies ont une precision qui va très bien avec le caractère de ce bâtiment. Ici on fait beaucoup de beton avec des formes finies en matière plastique pour obtenir des surfaces presque polies. Ceci doit etre plus facile en France où vous avez plus d'expèrience avec le beton et ou le climat est moins dure. Je suis d'accord avec Corbu qu'il est dangereux de tomber dans quelque chose qui a l'air artisanal sans l'être, ici comme ailleurs il-y-a une tendance dangéreuse et romantique parmi quelques jeunes.

Finished sections have a precision which is entirely in character with this building. Here we do a lot of concrete with finished forms of plastic material to obtain almost polished surfaces. This must be much easier in France where you have more experience with concrete and where the climate is less hard. I agree with Corbu that it is dangerous to fall into something which has the craft feeling without being such, here, as elsewhere there is a dangerous and romantic tendency among some of the young. (6-13-62)

Perhaps Le Corbusier would not himself have gone quite so far as to moralize about his concrete finishes, but he certainly appreciated that it would have been "false primitivism" to have cultivated rough effects of the material "in the center of Harvard," especially with one of the best contractors to be had in the United States; he did not like the contrived roughness of Sert's contemporary Holyoke Center.[11] However, Le Corbusier was not averse to using local "trades" to achieve the "nontrade" feeling of elegant finish—indeed, one of the things he avowedly liked about the material was its flexibility, because poured into molds, in fitting the local situation and local technical methods. Nova Scotia shipbuilders were eventually employed to make the formwork for the awkward curves, a regionalist touch that he must have enjoyed;[12] and the elegant plankwork of New England buildings had been a cause for comment among many of his architectural friends.[13]

Le Corbusier's smooth finish for the visual arts center was not supposed to be "expressive of the American machine age" (as one reviewer put it),[14] but to be an essay in the correct appearance and articulation of surface for béton brut. He spoke of it as a "new stereotomy for reinforced concrete," adding that béton brut was not béton "d'une brute" ("the concrete of a brute"), but simply concrete coming directly from the formwork (5-29-61; appendix 16). According to Andreini, Le Corbusier thought of concrete as a "natural material." In finish as in form, he felt that concrete had inherent qualities that should not be betrayed by fanciful shuttering or incorrectly placed joints.[15] Even so, he seems to have allowed witty references to other substances through analogies with two natural materials frequently associated with reinforced concrete by its pioneers: wood, in vertical planks on the curves, and stone on the flat portions (figs. 5, 6). If such allusions were intended, they are appropriate to the large primary forms of which they are part—the stone to the cubical volume at the center, the wood to the free-form curves. They enhance the meanings of larger forms as well as responding to technical factors.

"Correct" Fenestration Elements in Concrete

Into the openings in the concrete walls of the visual arts center were inserted, in various combinations, the other three elements described by Le Corbusier in his letter of February 28, 1961: brise-soleil, aérateurs, and ondulatoires (figs. 2, 18). At a later date some of the ondulatoires were dispensed with, leaving plain pans-de-verre. Of the three elements, brise-soleil and ondulatoires were the only ones incompatible with one another, as was well demonstrated in the first project where even brise-soleil specially designed for the job failed to match. The others could be intermixed; both brise-soleil and aérateurs and ondulatoires and aérateurs were actually wedded to one another by a common constituent element, the vertical concrete strut. When these two elements were combined, as on the Quincy Street studio (fig. 3), Le Corbusier's belief in the ultimate derivation of his elevation elements from reinforced concrete was most easy to understand. The struts there were very like the individual vertical striations in the shuttering marks to either side: it was as if the concrete wall had simply been discontinued in places, here for a plate of glass, there for a vertical pivoting aluminum door, here an aperture for light, there an aperture for air.

This was the way the architect thought of all his elements:

> Après avoir assuré au bâtiment une perfection la plus parfaite possible de proportions, mon intention est de choisir des matériaux qui, après cinquante années de recherche, deviennent les matériaux types du béton armé.
> Ainsi les vitrages sont-ils fixés, scellés dans le béton: ils sont là pour éclairer exclusivement.
> Les aérateurs sont là pour apporter l'air frais par les moyens physiques d'échange par gravité et par orientation.

> Having assured the most perfect perfection of proportions possible for the building, my intention is to choose materials which, after fifty years of research, become the typical materials for reinforced concrete.
> Thus the panes are fixed, sealed in the concrete: they are there exclusively to light.
> The aérateurs are there to supply fresh air by physical means of exchange through gravity and orientation. (5-29-61; appendix 16)

The meaning of these two elements was in their exclusiveness; where the normal window would let in light and air, Le Corbusier invented a separate form for each function—a "solution-type" for each characteristic. And both were formed by machine materials in contrast with the "natural" concrete to either side; opaque aluminum let in no light, sealed glass, no air. Such a tendency to individualize had a long history, dating back in his own career to the "separation des pouvoirs" ("separation of powers") of the Dom-Ino system, where much was made of the way the point support, supported slab, and nonsupporting wall were manifestly separate elements. It might be christened the "atomic tendency": the need, at all costs, to individuate the elements of architecture according to discrete, indivisible functions. There it was applied to structural parts, here to environmental ones.[16]

Another element "typical" to reinforced concrete was the brise-soleil (figs. 2, 18), whose function was to keep out the direct rays of the sun. In the letter quoted above, aérateurs and brise-soleil, the specifically environmental elements of the facade, were related to air-conditioning:

> *Aérateurs:* j'ai prévu des aérateurs semblables à des de Chandigarh (ou differents si vous faites une proposition). Ces aérateurs vont du plancher au plafond. Vous me répondrez: "Nous faisons de l'air conditionné". Je vous réponds: "Je ne vous en félicite qu'à moitié (sinusite, etc . . . et condition artificielle périlleuse: Dr Alexis Carrel)."
> Je propose fermement d'employer les aérateurs qui pourront fonctionner dans l'air libre aux saisons favorables. ll sera possible d'installer votre air conditionné contre le froid, mais je pense qu'à Boston il est superflu de l'installer contre le chaud puisque tous les vitrages du VAC ont leur soleil contrôlé.

> *Aérateurs:* I have planned aérateurs similar to the ones at Chandigarh (or different, if you make a proposal). These aérateurs go from floor to ceiling. You will reply: "We are air-conditioning." I reply to you: "I only half congratulate you on it (sinus troubles, etc. . . . and artificial, perilous condition: Dr. Alexis Carrel)."
> I firmly propose to employ aérateurs which will be able to function in free air during favorable seasons. It will be possible to install your air-conditioning against the cold but I think that in Boston it is superfluous to install it against the heat since all the glazing of the VAC is sun-controlled.[17] (5-29-61; appendix 16)

This was written on the morning of May 29. That afternoon he had his doubts (quite rightly) about the superfluity of air-conditioning in the sticky Boston summers and admitted that it might, after all, be of value as a complement to the sun-controlled facades. But that afternoon, when he wrote the rest of his letter, his tone was laconic, his attitude to air-conditioning censorious nonetheless.

L'air conditionné cher aux Americains et à leurs sinusites devenues traditionnelles, pourra fort bien fonctionner pendant les périodes de froid, mais je pense qu'on peut aérer les locaux avec l'air du dehors sans mécanisme d'air pulsé au moment où le printemps rayonne à l'extérieur. L'air conditionné peut intervenir à nouveau pendant la période des chaleurs (si vos MMrs ne se trouvent pas tout nus à Cape Cod.)

Air conditioning, dear to Americans with their by now traditional sinus conditions, will certainly be able to function during cold periods, but I think that the spaces can be ventilated with fresh air from the outside without mechanical exchange, when spring shines on the exterior. Air-conditioning can intervene again in the hot periods (if you sirs are not found completely naked on Cape Cod). (5-29-61; appendix 16)

It is amusing to find Le Corbusier turning the sinus condition into a sort of "maladie-type" ("typical illness") of America, traceable to the American luxury, air-conditioning, in much the same way that French liver conditions are traced to their luxury, cuisine. And it seems important to distinguish air-conditioning from the "heating and ventilating" system Le Corbusier was forced to use by law. This contained no humidity control and no cooling apparatus. Air-conditioning was eventually used in the basement and ground floor because natural ventilation was not sufficient, in the basement for the additional reason that film required special conditions of humidity.

Le Corbusier's position on mechanical environmental control had shifted considerably since the early thirties when he first used his device "respiration exacte," fitted the hermetic Maison de Refuge with the device and with a curtain wall facade of acres of glass but without a single opening, and interpreted notices in American buildings requesting that windows not be opened to avoid disruption of the air-conditioning as a sign of a more advanced culture.[18]

By the same token his position was no longer in keeping with the sealed curtain wall solution of the United States' skyscrapers contemporary with his visual arts center design, which he mischievously characterized as "aprés U.N." (The United Nations building itself infuriated him in that its environmental solution was a closed glass box.) Yet at the same time he did not approve of the traditional hole-in-the-wall window, which did not let in enough light and confused the concepts of lighting and ventilating; in Cambridge Le Corbusier had stated that his fenestration system marked "the death of the window."[19] It held the special status of the "correct" solution for a building's adjustment to climate because, as he wrote to Sert, "toute l'architecture moderne a pour mission de s'occuper du soleil" ("it is the mission of all modern architecture to concern itself with the sun"; 11-9-61; appendix 18).

The plan forms of the visual arts center seem to have been determined in part by Le Corbusier's polemical intentions in his only American building. Evidently the building's presentation drawings and architectural elements were propelled by similar intentions and were conceived as correct and absolute definitions: the results of Le Corbusier's lifelong quest for principles. The piloti, brise-soleil, ondulatoire, and other parts of the architect's language in concrete were here given their essential form and organized so that they could be seen inside and out—for the ramp was a way to inspect the architecture as much as the contents of the building. Moreover, all elements were combined as a single demonstration in the Quincy Street facade, where they were presented to the life of Harvard Yard, the architecture school, and the United States beyond. Arranged in proportion and in a moving, plastic composition like the elements of the Greek temple in *Vers une architecture,* these elements ceased to be just "standards"—in the sense of mere functional solutions to well-defined problems—but became elevated to the level of architecture (fig. 2).[20]

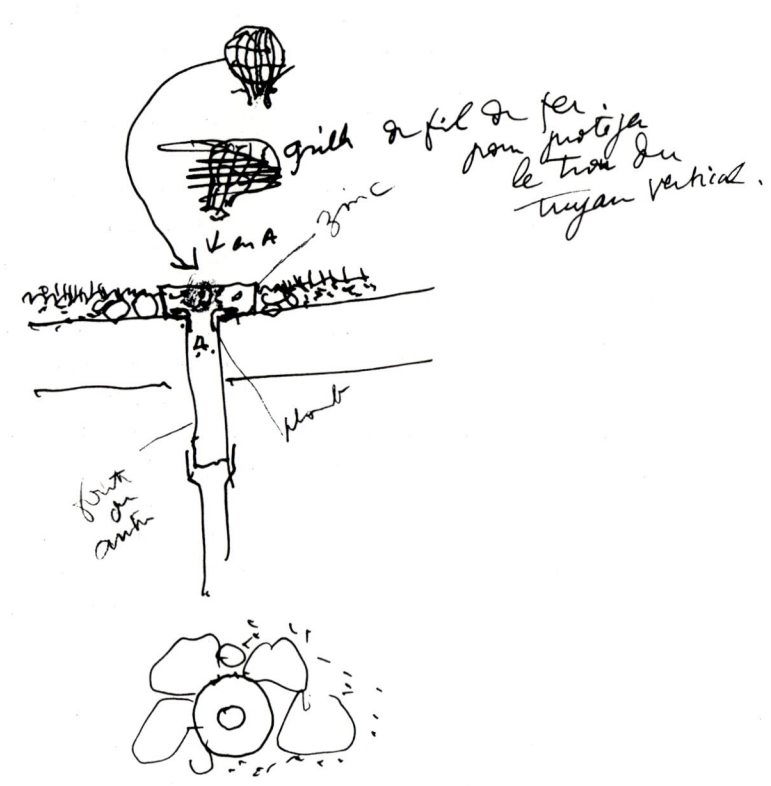

9. TRANSATLANTIC DETAILS AND THE MODULOR

The man in question is an architect and painter, who for the past forty-five years has practiced an art in which all is measured.

Le Corbusier

Le Corbusier delivered the visual arts center ex cathedra from the rue de Sèvres in the spring of 1961, and Sert, his partners, and assistants now saw it as their business to comply rigorously with Le Corbusier's intentions. Every other arrangement would be tried to avoid the slightest rearrangement of Le Corbusier's conception and proportions—whether juggling the budget, shifting the reinforcing bars, or rescheduling the personnel. Those changes in the building that were unavoidable would always be referred to Paris for the final word.

The Building's Size

The university was far less concerned with proportions initially than with dimensions, because dimensions were affecting the budget. The modifications of the Prescott Street studio on January 11 had entailed the addition of a structural bay, the creation of expensive extra space not specified in the program. Superb as were the formal characteristics of the change, it had still been a crash measure. The second building had really been designed in the few days following January 10, the architects attaching functional tags somewhat randomly to spaces created under extreme pressure when niceties such as area requirements were far from their minds (to which they may never have been very close).

When, on March 24, 1961, Trottenberg wrote to Sert that he was "a little bit worried about the entire situation," he was certainly understating. He had had only a quick glance at the plans and had noticed more encroachment on the Fogg garden, the wastefulness and redundancy of the interior ramp, an overabundance of unasked-for exhibition space, and the inadequacy of the ground floor offices. At that stage, though, he was apparently unaware how much bigger the building had grown (appendix 15).

Sert was fully aware. He knew that Le Corbusier had never done anything at all to reduce the size of the first project, and he knew that the second project resulted in a building both too big and too expensive. What is more, by mid-April, Le Corbusier also knew these things, for Sert sent him a memorandum outlining the budgetary situation (4-7-61). The extra bay enlarged the building 13 feet longitudinally, but the total excess area over the most recent program was 5,000 square feet. This resulted in an additional $150,000 over the *excess* budgeted in November. As if things were not bad enough, the Faculty Club began to complain again: they were worried about the way the new convex third floor south side bulged close to their projecting wing. So Sert suggested to Le Corbusier a reduction in size.

In Sert's mind a reduction in size through a simple overall reduction of dimensions seemed an obvious solution. He suggested a slight lessening of column spacing, leaving twelve feet clear space longitudinally between them, and a slight reduction in the other axis, with heights remaining the same. The shrinkage in the northwest–southeast direction would have been five feet—enough to reduce the squeeze up against the Faculty Club. With the same aim in mind, the university insisted on a reduction in the width of the ramps. Sert knew quite well that Le Corbusier would object to these changes because they would throw off the Modulor and tamper with the fine proportions, but he must have realized that it was political to bow to university demands. Events had reached a point where, if he did not, construction might not begin at all, or start so late that the center's opening might be postponed another year. Sert's other propositions to Le Corbusier, floor by floor, were mostly minor modifications compared with the drastic suggestion of a size change. But the list did include the stipulation that the interior ramp be removed (Trottenberg felt it wasted space), and this may be seen as a further clash between practicality and the building's guiding ideas.

Ironically, this cutback also eliminated one of those factors that had forced the change from first to second projects. Two other such features that had caused weeks of concern previously were also removed without much ado: the passenger elevator, which the university felt could be dispensed with, and the winter doors for the ramp. No substitute was found for the latter, with effects that are felt in the finished building.[1] The passenger elevator shaft became a vertical duct for electrical and mechanical conduits, and the lavatory on the top floor was turned over to heating and ventilating equipment—one wonders where Le Corbusier would have put these ducts and machines if the university had not taken the initiative.

The interior ramp was never very satisfactory in its new position, and even Le Corbusier had his doubts about it structurally.[2] Other significant changes were these: the elimination of the pilotis at the northern end of the lecture hall; the transference of the offices on the ground floor to the northeast corner (Pusey was continuing his trend—he wished the handsome space of the lobby to open towards the Faculty Club and the move meant that the stairs down to the basement could be enlarged); the elimination of partitions in the studio spaces; the reversal of the functions of the three- and two-dimensional studios; and the enclosure of the link between the stair tower and the fifth floor studios. Escape stairs were also required in some unusual places by the Massachusetts fire laws, one outstanding case being from the terrace above Quincy Street, which would have wrecked the effect of the ondulatoires (fortunately these stairs were argued out of the design later).

On April 29 Le Corbusier was in America again, receiving an American Institute of Architects gold medal, and Sert went to New York to meet him. Le Corbusier agreed to all the major points raised by the university except the placement of the machine rooms on the roof (5-1-61). An extra point concerned the main staircase: Le Corbusier wished the landings to be set in 70 centimeters from the outside wall, and the wall of the tower to be partly of glass brick.

The April elevations were examined by the university in May. The fact that to their maker they were crystallizations of his ideas on the architectural drawings of the epoch did not guarantee them a warm reception. The *Harvard Crimson* of May 23 carried the headline: "Fellows refuse to pass proposed Art Building,"[3] beneath which was printed: "There was no comment from the Administration on the Corporation's reaction to the artistic and architectural features." To enlighten the majority of the faculty and all the students who were gasping for news (not even the first project was published) there was only the negative characterization of one official who stated, "It sure ain't Georgian," as unintentionally incisive a judgment as it was uninformative.

No wonder the matter was handled with secrecy. The figures of early May had reported a total budget of $2,345,100, an increase of $150,000 on the November figure, close to one and a half times the available sum. The situation was becoming desperate, and Sert and his team set to work finding more cutbacks. On June 2 a "revised project budget estimate" was produced: "The building is virtually the same volume as that covered in the May estimate, but a number of changes of materials and revisions in the scope of the heating and ventilation system have been adopted to reduce cost." There were also modifications in contracts and a host of details like changing the glass used in the exterior or omitting the tunnel to the Fogg. These appear to have accounted for a reduction of over $625,000. Finally, on June 26, 1961, the university corporation voted to build.

Two days after this decision was made, Sert was in Paris with Le Corbusier discussing detailed proposals. The set of prints used for these discussions was evidently made up from Sert's earliest working drawings, including plans and sections of the entire building reduced according to the size modification of April (fig. 164). But on every plan can be found the following inscription in black ink signed by Le Corbusier:

Ces plans ne sont pas valables. *Il faut revenir aux dimensions de notre* serie N5719 à 5727. Décision de M. Le Corbusier et M. Sert à Paris le 28 Juin 1961.

These plans are not valid. *It is necessary to return to the dimensions of our* series N5719 to 5727. Decision of Mr. Le Corbusier and Mr. Sert in Paris, 28 June 1961.

In other words, Le Corbusier had done nothing whatever to change the size of the building, had no intention of doing so, and was endorsed in his decision by Sert.

There had been a prelude to this in late May 1961 when Le Corbusier had received some drawings sent by Joseph Zalewski from Sert's office in Cambridge showing the building at reduced dimensions.[4] Sert had evidently thought the reduction would allow the use of the highest quality materials—he had an eye on the budget.[5] Le Corbusier was furious and wrote back the same day that he had "the greatest reservations" and that Sert would "understand immediately" when he received Le Corbusier's prints.

29 Mai, 13h
Recu à l'instant les 7 feuilles de plans VAC BOS envoyés par Joseph Zalewski le 26 Mai 1961. Je fais les plus grands réserves. *Tu comprendras* immédiatement *en recevant les dessins de façades et coupes,* échelle *1:50,* colorés, que je t'expédirai par avion demain. Ces façades ont pris des semaines de travail. Elles sont dessinées rigoureusement au Modulor . . . C'est la minute de la haute proportion; "le moment où la partie se gagne ou se perd" "Marius" (= Raimu). C'est très grave. Ici, je deviens impérieux et impératif et je demande à Boston de bien vouloir admettre que ce sont mes dessins qui déterminent la construction.

May 29, 1 p.m.
Received just this minute the seven sheets of VAC BOS plans sent by Joseph Zalewski. I have the

173

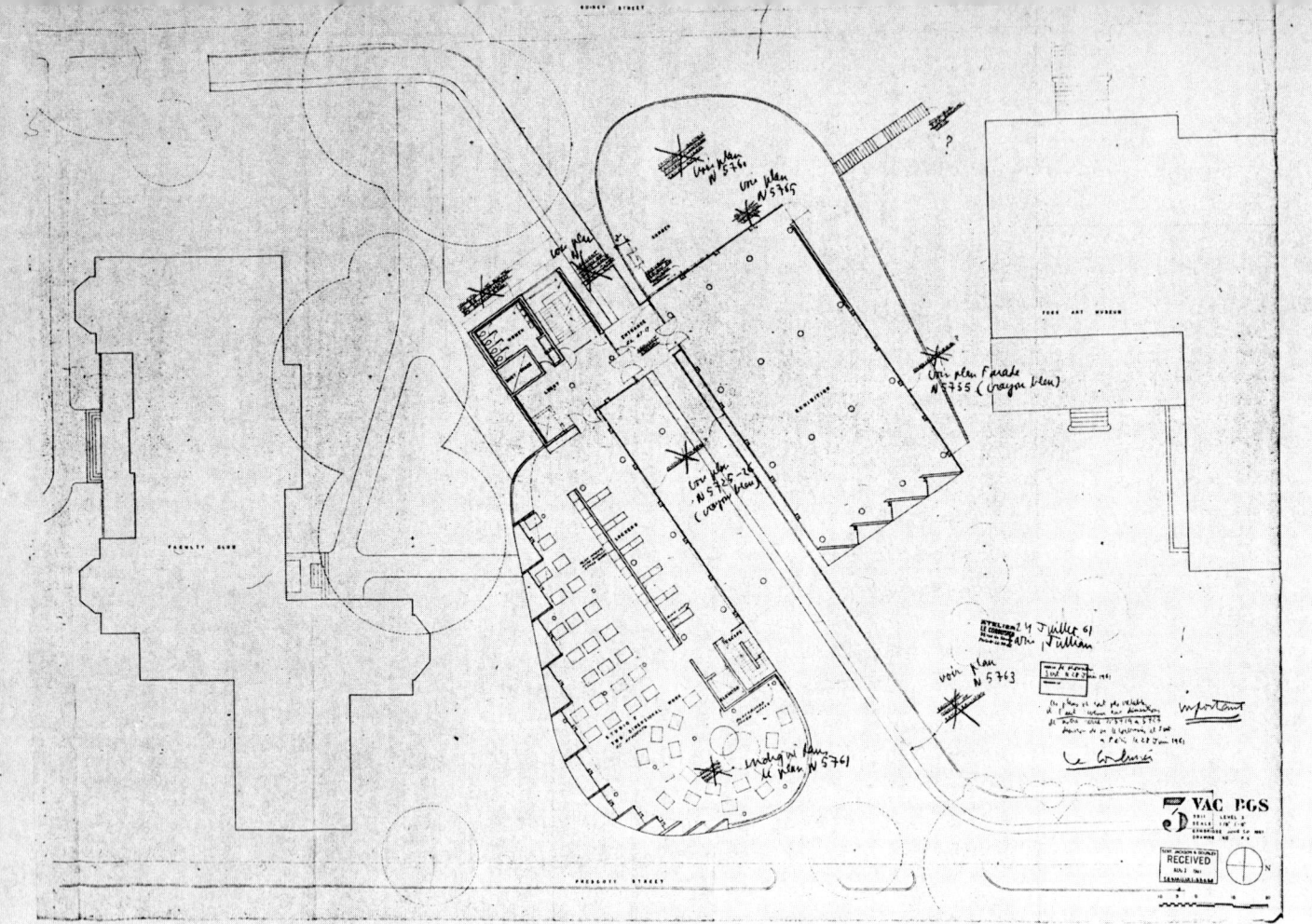

greatest reservations. *You will understand immediately on receiving the drawn elevations and sections, scale 1:50, colored, which I shall send off to you by plane tomorrow. These facades have taken weeks of work. They are drawn rigorously to the Modulor . . . It is the minute of high proportion; "the moment when the game is won or lost" "Marius" (= Raimu). This is very serious. Here, I become imperious and imperative and demand that Boston admit that it is my drawings which determine the building (appendix 16).*

The facade drawings that Le Corbusier enclosed furnished the exact dimensions of window bays, the placement and exact dimensions of the aérateurs, the shutterings of the facades. In short, the letter constituted a broadside in defense of the Modulor. And it worked because Sert complied: the absolute dimensions of Le Corbusier's ideal proportional system won the day against practical and budgetary considerations.

164. *Plan level 3, Sert, Jackson and Gourley, spring 1961. (1:96; 46 × 60 cm; print.) This working drawing shows the building at reduced size (the extra breathing space between it, its neighbors, and the streets is evident) and was one of a set taken to Paris by Sert in late July 1961. To the bottom right is the inscription by Le Corbusier beginning "ces plans ne sont pas valables" ("these plans are not valid"), a complaint about the size reduction. The print is typical of the method of transatlantic querying that continued through 1961: inscriptions like "request skylight design" were answered by "indiqué dans le plan N–" ("indicated in plan N–"), the detail in question being sent later by mail.*

The size came to light in February 1962, long after the structure had been examined by the structural engineer, drawn up by Sert's office, piped and ducted on drawings by the contractors, and pegged out by the construction firm. In fact the first floor had already been formed, and it was too late to do anything about it when Sert explained what had happened.

In March 1961, Le Corbusier sent his final preliminary plans. To facilitate certain problems of placing the building and the ramps on the site, our office proposed a slight reduction in bay dimensions amounting to five inches on the north–south column spacing and ten inches in the east–west spacing. This modification was discussed with Le Corbusier during his visit to the United States in April, and he seemed to agree to it at that time. Accordingly the reduced dimensions were incorporated in the drawings on which the estimates were taken in May. As these first cost estimates were too high, further estimates were made in early June; also on drawings with these same dimensions, and these formed the basis for budget approval. In late June, I visited Le Corbusier in Paris and learned then that after careful study of the plans he had decided to keep the original column spacing shown on his preliminary plans, because the proposed changes would modify the proportions of the building as he had conceived it. These spacings, which resulted in an area increase of 2599 square feet, were then used for the working drawings.

It should be recognized that when building under this kind of contract changes are unavoidable in the transformation from preliminary studies to final drawings. (2-14-62)

When he referred to this incident, quietly smiling, Sert once invoked the Catalan saying, "No matter if the devil produces the miracle, as long as the miracle occurs." Sert's action seems entirely praiseworthy: if he had given way to short-term pressures and let the building be constructed as money dictated, nothing could have been done later to restore the building to Le Corbusier's original conception. Instead, there occurred a brief scrambling for funds and cutbacks on such matters as roof planting which, after ten years, still need putting right. But these are at least features that *can* be put right.

Even so, Le Corbusier remained suspicious of any tampering with his dimensions and in late September 1961, when Sert's working drawings had been converted into feet and inches by the members of Sert's office, he went so far as to insist that he be sent the drawings to approve them, being afraid, apparently, that the reduction demands might have been slipped in under cover of conversion (9-23-61).

To clarify the problem of the building's size it has been necessary to telescope the events of nearly a year, for by the time the Sert explanation was made, construction was already underway. During the preceding year, architects, clients, and contractors were all aiming at the earliest possible realization of the building; however, unfinished jobs, weather conditions, a steel shortage, and the inevitable unforeseen technical problems and revisions caused kinks in this ideal linear development. These were either accentuated or flattened out by a continual bombardment of letters from Paris.

Sert's job was to translate Le Corbusier's pastel presentation drawings of 1961 into working drawings and to produce a detailed specification geared to the American building industry. The many details required to do so were supplied by Le Corbusier through 1961 in the form of rapidly drawn sketches and annotated prints—a species of evidence that might not have been produced had this project not been split between preliminary design and working drawing phases. The drawings tell us more of Le Corbusier's theories about the aesthetics of detailing, construction, and proportion and of his ideas on mechanical servicing and acoustics. The accompanying correspondence sheds further light on the elements of his architectural language and indicates his technical intentions for them at the level of mosquito screens, rubber gaskets, and glazing joints. Le Corbusier the technician emerges in these letters: a man with a lifetime's experience of locksmiths tucked away in odd arrondissements, or of some of France's greatest acousticians.

As soon as the sections arrived in March 1961,

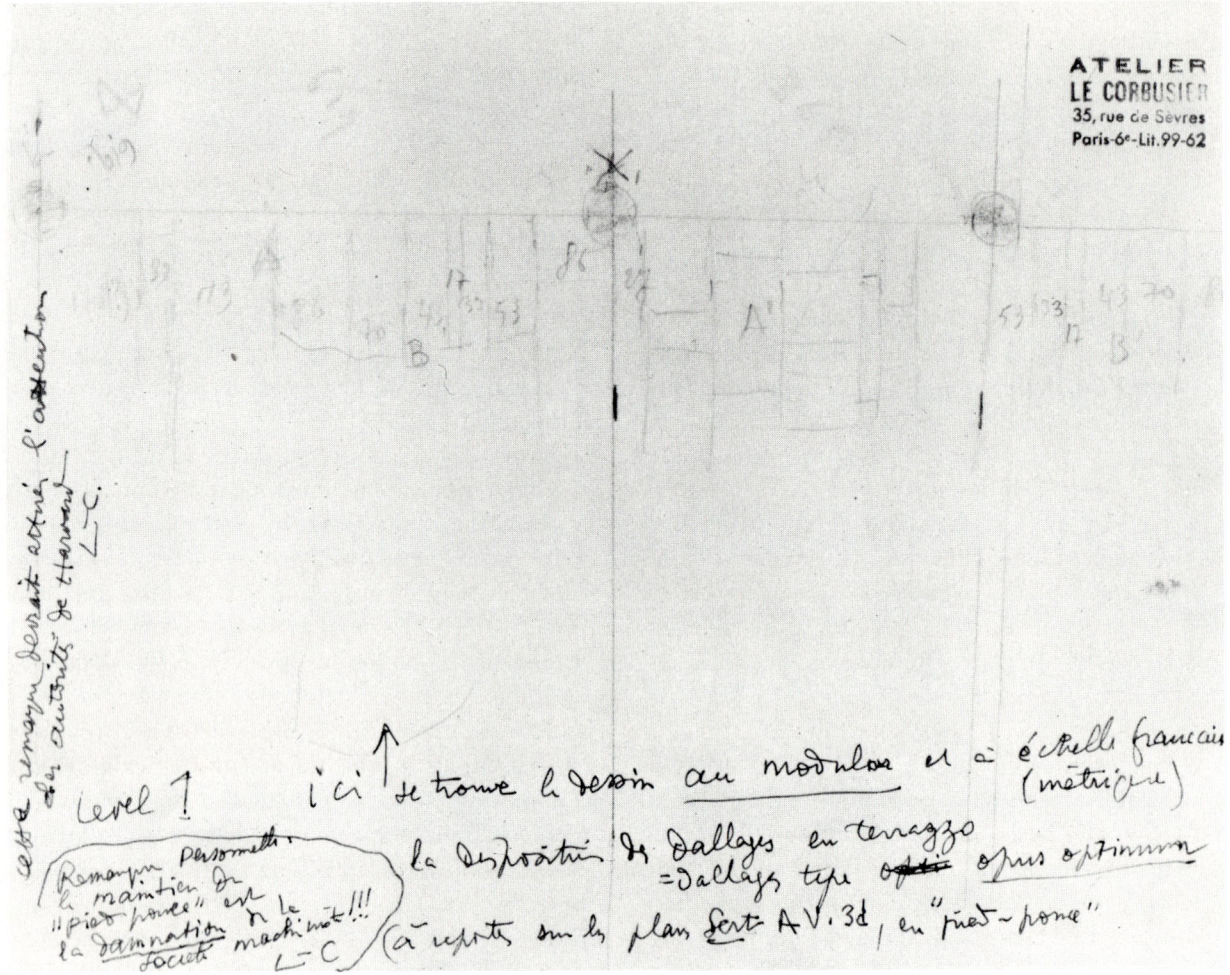

conversion from meters to feet and inches began. Modulor measurements, which are integers in the metric system, often caused complex fractions when converted. On one plan of floor articulation heavily annotated with Modulor dimensions in centimeters (fig. 165), Le Corbusier wrote that a "mechanistic society" such as America would be damned if it did not turn metric. By the summer months there may have been tired members of Paul Krueger's team at Sert's who would agree with this. Le Corbusier requested that his view be forwarded to "the Harvard authorities."

The sections were referred to the structural engineer William Le Messurier, who stated on immediate inspection that the volumes as shown were quite feasible but that ten inches must be allowed for a minimum thickness in weight-bearing walls (to mask reinforcement) and fourteen inches for floors "especially at cantilever edges." This was

165. *Design of floor rectangles, "Opus optimum au Modulor," Le Corbusier, 1961. (Small scale; 21.5 × 28 cm.) The detail is divided into typical sequences of dimensions and is scrawled over with dogmatic statements by the architect on the absurdity of feet and inches ("the damnation of machine age society!!!") which he recommends be "drawn to the attention of the authorities of Harvard."*

166. *Detail of Prescott Street end of ramp (N5806), Le Corbusier, September 21, 1961. (1:96; 87 × 117 cm; ozalid print.) A pathway proceeding from the sidewalk, under the ramp, and around to the ramp base is shown. To the bottom right Le Corbusier insists on a grass bank and not a concrete wall immediately adjacent to the end of the ramp. A wall was eventually built.*

to lead to a battle between ideal proportions and structural pragmatics. Another theme of this kind was to be the impossibility of standardizing, and difficulty of constructing, elements whose design was partly informed by a symbolic intent of standardization. Thus, a year later, when construction was at last under way, the main contractor pointed to a divergence of intention and means when he stated "this particular structure does not lend itself, both from an economic and quality basis, to mass production" (4-26-62).[6]

The construction contract was awarded to George A. Fuller Co. on July 28, 1961. The job was never let out for competitive bidding. There was not the time and Fuller was known to be reliable and of high standards. The new Fogg library extension, which had been recently designed by Sert, was negotiated on the same contract. To the northeast of the site, this extension had the unfortunate effect of stopping the Prescott Street end of the ramp from descending to the sidewalk. Instead, the ramp was forced to peter out on a terrace above the new extension. It was yet another university nail in the coffin of Le Corbusier's ramp—this time stopping it from being a viable way between the streets. Le Corbusier made an emphatic drawing two months later (fig. 166) showing a grassy slope down to the street instead of a concrete wall, but this could only be done if the library was cut back; the decision not to do this was extremely shortsighted and ran counter to Le Corbusier's basic circulation concept.[7] Here again was a clash between the architect's intention and contingent realities in Cambridge.

Le Corbusier had been more than willing to accompany his presentation drawings with grave statements of general architectural philosophy, but obtaining detailed information was not so easy. It may be, as Huson Jackson has suggested, that Le Corbusier was "not going to break his neck for the USA" on such matters.[8] It therefore fell to Sert to clarify what details were needed from Paris, and from spring 1961 till the summer vacation his time was spent doing this: lists were duly dispatched for escape stairs, roof gardens, brise-soleil, standard glazing solutions, aérateurs, the ramp, the floors, even details of roof garden drains and staircase railings. These were scrawled with "urgent" or "otherwise we risk misunderstandings that will be difficult to correct." Like a barometer responding to changes of weather, Paris produced a new batch of drawings for each list of requests. Le Corbusier and Jullian worked steadily for the last three weeks of July and then on the 29th the atelier closed down for the summer holiday.

Roof Gardens

Among the July drawings, five concern a matter of special importance to Le Corbusier in this project, the roof gardens (figs. 167–170). Plan N5760, drawn by Le Corbusier himself, showed the most prominent of these, the third level garden on top of the Quincy Street curved studio (fig. 167). Grass and bushes were placed close to the edge of the curve and a shrub was shown in a cement cylinder 86 centimeters high. Adjacent to the front of the exhibition space a concrete terrace with a re-entrant outline was partially defined by concrete benches. "Sliding door" was written over the exit onto the terrace, also marked with an arrow, and the concrete area was incised with Modulor rectangles ("opus optimum au Modulor"), as was the first floor in the early project (reference was made to this earlier design in an inscription on the drawing). Most dimensions of the terrace were according to the Modulor, resulting in a striking contrast between man-made geometry and the surrounding disarray of nature. Benches were marked in detail and were of two kinds: without backs ("bench simple") and with backs ("bench with back"). To the bottom right-hand corner of the sheet Le Corbusier drew a section with a man seated on one of the latter resembling some of the architect's diagrams presenting the Modulor in publications.[9]

On July 24, Jullian drew a detailed section of a portion of the same roof garden showing the slab terminating at the outside edge and turning up to form a cornice rim (fig. 168). Between the rim and the low wall holding back soil was a pedestrian way with a concrete floor 55 centimeters wide. Jullian showed a layer of "béton de protection" ("protective concrete") immediately above the roof surface, on top of which was a thick layer of soil surmounted by tufts of grass. To the right the soil banked steeply into the beginnings of a hill. Above the slope Jullian wrote "time to time one hill"—a delightful reassertion of Le Corbusier's intention, from the time he first saw the site, to put countryside in his one United States building. The hills (some of them eventually proposed as five and six feet high) necessitated extreme reinforcements in the roofs, of which Jullian gave no hint in this sketch.

There was no sign in Jullian's section of grading or drains or, for that matter, of adequate insulation. From July 22 to 24, Le Corbusier gave the problem the only thought it was to get from his end with a curious little sketch section of a lead and zinc drain set into the grass and fitted with a wire grill cover (fig. 169).[10] Also, Le Corbusier sketched the fifth level garden around the visiting artist's studio (fig. 170), and the covered terrace at the base of the ramp gallery, adding an inscription that realistically assessed the position of the garden by saying (in English): "no flowers."

Aérateurs

While Le Corbusier was planning the future wild gardens of the visual arts center, Jullian was concentrating on another one of Le Corbusier's elements: the aérateur. First on July 22, he defined the typical element in the abstract on plan and in section (drawing N5765; fig. 171). The plan was at 1:1 scale and showed adjacent glass panes jointing without frames into the vertical struts (shown temporarily in aluminum) to left and right.[11] In the middle was the ventilating opening with a door set into it on a plane somewhat closer to the interior than the neighboring glazing. The door was marked "aluminium" and vertically pivoted assymmetrically to insure that when open it did not snarl on the "fixed flyproof wire gauze" set across the entrance. The width of the whole, inside edge to inside edge, was marked 43 centimeters, the depth of the struts half this precisely. At its edges the door was sealed with simple rubber stops.

The section showed the top and bottom joints of the element with ceiling and floor slabs and concentrated on the embedding in concrete of steel pivots at each end of the vertical door (fig. 171). Inscriptions were in English and recommendations were made to the millimeter. For example, the steel bracket into which the pivots were to fit was shown with a tiny gap between itself and the concrete to which Jullian drew attention with the words "clearance between steel plate and concrete"; this drawing reflected the firm knowledge derived from experiment with the same element at Chandigarh.

Having defined the element in the abstract, Jullian then set about inserting it in the places where it

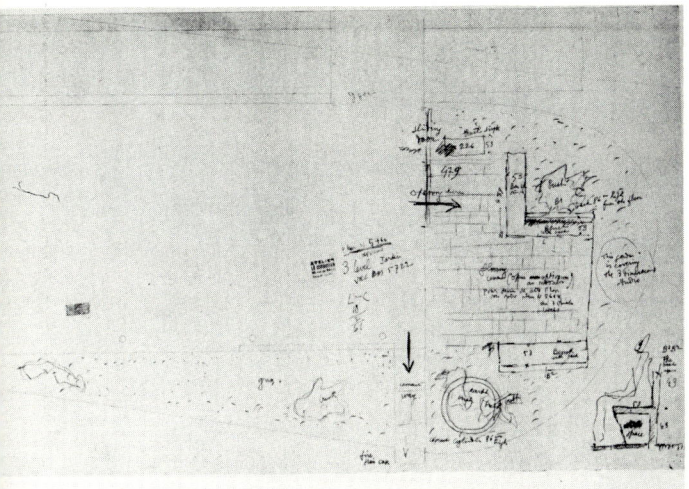 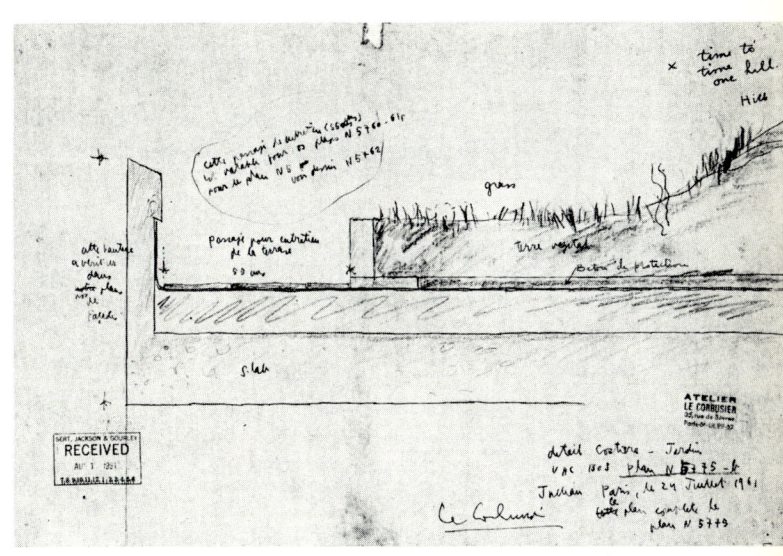

167. *Plan of level 3, Quincy Street roof terrace (N5760), Le Corbusier, July 18, 1961. (1:50; 52 × 90 cm; ozalid print.) Modulor dimensions are used and indicated.*

168. *Section detail of level 3, Quincy Street roof garden (N5775b), Jullian and Le Corbusier, July 24, 1961. (Scale unknown; 30 × 46 cm; ozalid print). Shown are part of a "hill" and the inscription "time to time one hill."*

169. *Detail of roof drain, Le Corbusier, July 22–24, 1961. (Scale unknown; 21.5 × 28 cm; photocopy.) The style is inimitably Le Corbusier's: it was details like this (whose usefulness was questionable) which were christened by Paul Krueger "cartoons."*

170. *Plan of level 5 roof garden (N5762), Le Corbusier, July 23, 1961. (1:50; 68 × 89 cm; ozalid print.) A "paysage" of small hills and bushes is set about with benches and Modulor terraces; the mounds, which should have been covered with wild grass and weeds, have not yet been built.*

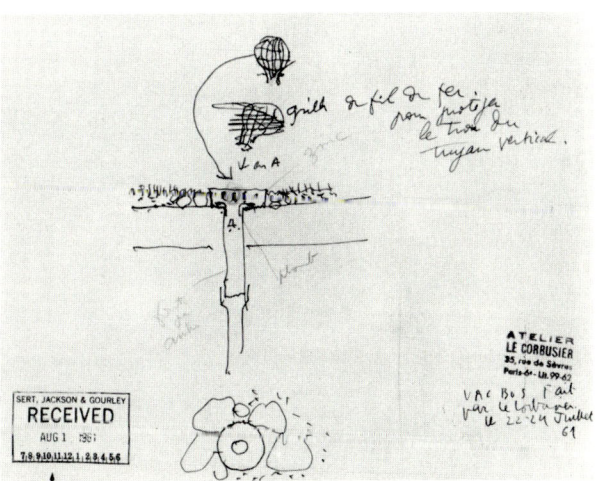 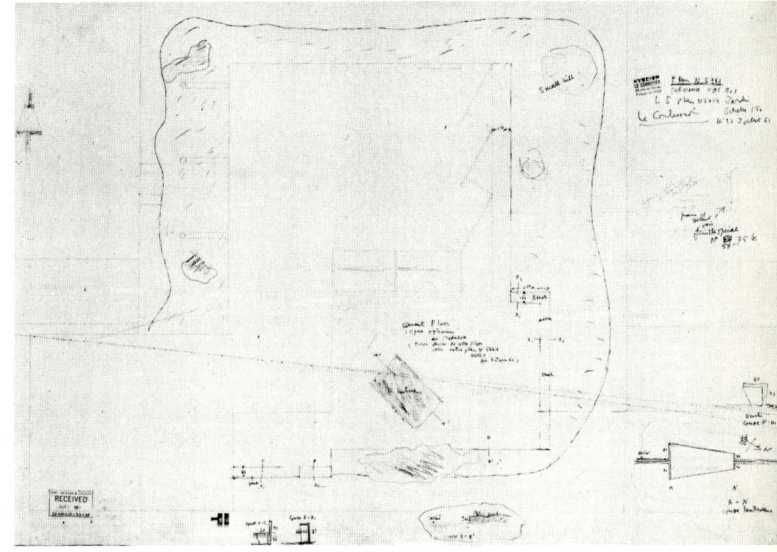

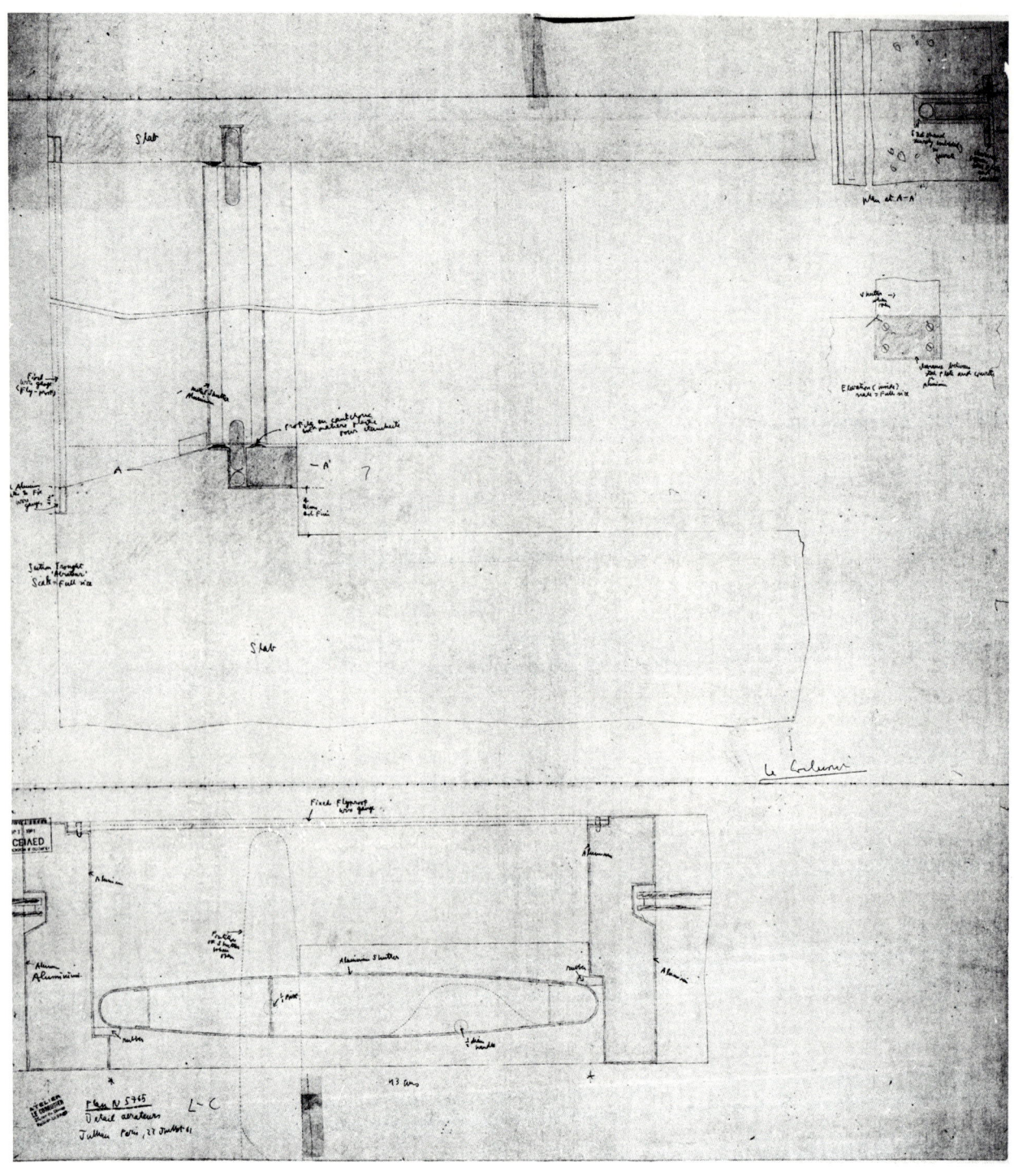

171. *Plan and section of typical aérateur (N5765), Le Corbusier and Jullian, July 22, 1961. (1:1; 100 × 91 cm; ozalid print.) Here the architect defines one of his standard elements down to the millimeter. The plan is below and shows a pivoting door between ondulatoire struts with glass just visible to each side; the section is above and concentrates on top and bottom joints of the pivots into ceiling and upturned floor slabs. Note the "fly-proof wire gauze."*

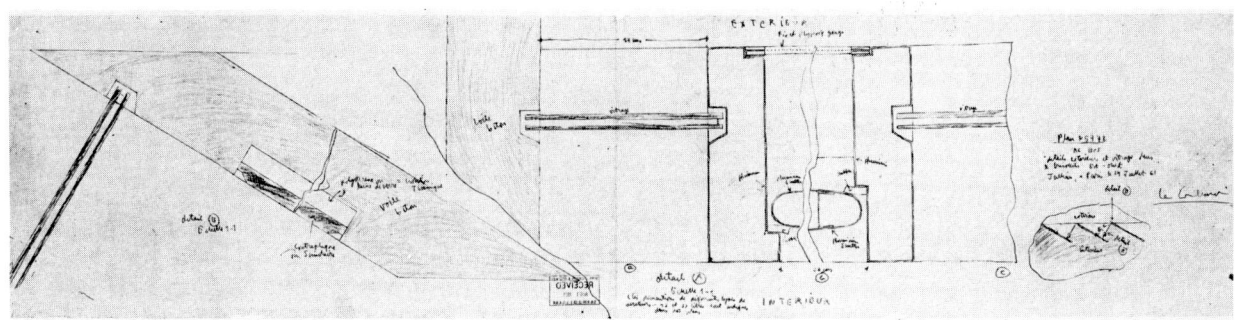

172. *Plan details of typical glazing and aérateur joints between diagonal brise-soleil (N5778), Le Corbusier and Jullian, July 24, 1961. (1:1; 31 × 128 cm; ozalid print.)*

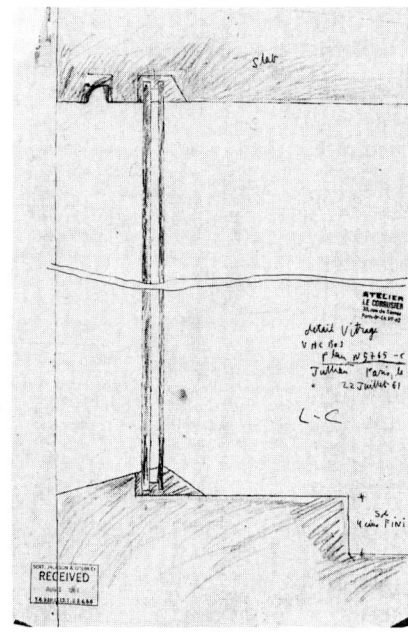

173. *Section detail of typical joint of glazing and slabs (N5765c), Le Corbusier and Jullian, July 22, 1961. (Scale unknown; 47 × 30 cm; ozalid print.)*

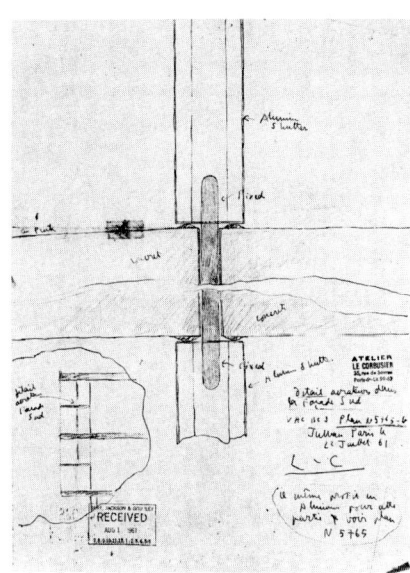

174. *Section detail of typical joint of aérateur to horizontal brise-soleil, Le Corbusier and Jullian, July 22, 1961. (Scale unknown; 60 × 30 cm; ozalid print.)*

was required in the elevations as designed the previous February. On July 24, 1961, on a long strip, he started with a full-scale detail for the aérateurs between the diagonal brise-soleil of the Prescott Street facade (fig. 172). To the bottom right was a small inset at scale 1:50 of a range of diagonal brise-soleil. This inset was inscribed "detail A" and "detail B." Drawn full scale to the center of the sheet, detail A concentrated on the fixing of the aérateur in the plate of glass and the jointing of the plate of glass into the adjacent brise-soleil fins. Detail B concentrated on the most exposed glazing joint on the brise-soleil, which was shown thermally insulated.

Another drawing (fig. 173) showed the typical joint for all normal glazing, with soffits and floors below and the pans-de-verre above (so far details of joints had shown only the junction with lateral edges of panes). And a further detail (fig. 174) showed what was to happen in places where a horizontal brise-soleil bisected the aérateurs (as on the south side curve at level three). The solution was quite simply to reproduce the standard pivot detail below and above the horizontal of concrete. As on all these trans-Atlantic prints, the sketch was approved with the letters "L-C" beneath Jullian's signature and the date.

Ramp and Stairs

Among the pre–summer vacation prints were some showing details of circulation elements such as the stairways and ramp. The ramp, of course, was another "typical element" of Le Corbusier's language in reinforced concrete and was conceptually the very backbone of this particular building; for this reason alone it would deserve special attention. But the ramp is doubly important because the drawings made of it also reveal most clearly Le Corbusier's practice of ruling the intervals and sizes of detailed parts of his building according to Modulor relationships so that their dimensions attune with the larger volumes, surfaces, and intervals of the main forms.

It was singularly appropriate that a system relating to the human scale and dimensions should have been so extensively applied in the sizing of elements accommodating the hand and foot of man, supporting him in leaning, standing, walking, and sitting positions. Bearing in mind the polemical nature of the visual arts center, it is further appropriate that one of the most canonical of Le Corbusier's inventions, the Modulor, should have been applied on the ramp for everyone to see.

Plan 5763 showed all the main ramp dimensions (fig. 175). Its total width was set at 3.66 meters, twice the height of the six foot standard man, and the same dimension as transversal bays and brise-soleil openings, ondulatoire, aérateur, pan-de-verre, and brise-soleil heights, and floor-to-ceiling distances (which equal the majority of pilotis lengths). One gains the impression that Le Corbusier regarded 3.66 meters as a sort of "typical dimension" for his standard elements.

From the inside edge of the parapet on one side to the inside edge of the ramp railing on the other measured 3.01 meters while the groove for drainage was set at 1.83 meters (6 feet) from one side, 1.18 meters from the other. The floor was marked "dallage Modulor" or "opus optimum": both typical Le Corbusier methods of providing concrete floors with Modulor rectangles of many standard sizes. The parapet was made 70 centimeters high on the inside edge, 86 centimeters on the outside, so that the flat portion on top was inclined inwards to make a sloping seat. These two dimensions were those specified by Le Corbusier for a man sitting and a man standing up and leaning on his hands;[12] the steel rail, meanwhile, was made 1.18 meters, the height of an upright man leaning on his elbows (or the height of his navel above the ground); the same dimension was used for railings throughout the building.

The dimensioning of the ramp thus incorporated a sort of visible essay on the "mathematics of the human body."[13] To experience the "promenade architecturale," with the ramp grooves, intervals, and ratios of pilotis and other elements slipping by was also directly to perceive the kinaesthetic spatial rhythms of an architectural music—the bars and notes of Le Corbusier's "architecture acoustique." It was singularly appropriate that this particular demonstration of Le Corbusier's proportional system should have been incised on a ramp whose overall symbolic shape and metaphorical context implied a message of urban harmony for the machine age: a precisely similar concern pervades

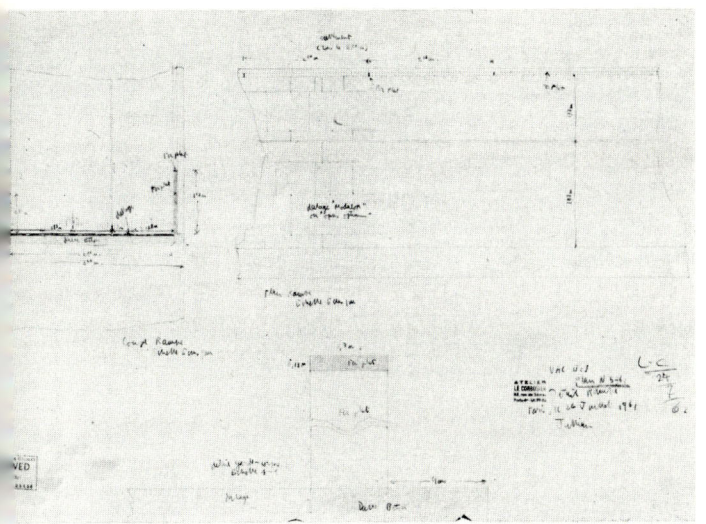

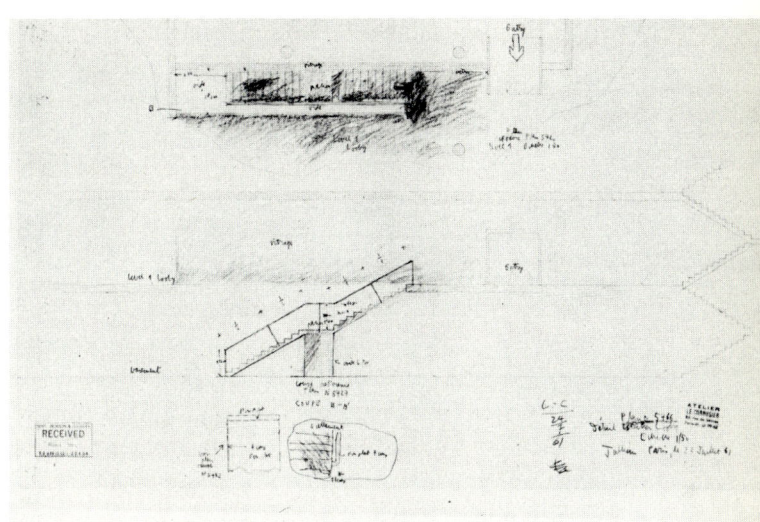

175. *Plan, section, and detail of ramp (N5763), Le Corbusier and Jullian, July 22, 1961. (1:50; 45 × 68 cm; ozalid print.)*

176. *Plan and elevation of internal stairway from level 1 to basement (N5766), Le Corbusier and Jullian, July 22–24, 1961. (1:50; 40 × 73 cm; ozalid print.) Modulor dimensions are shown.*

177. *Elevation and plan of fire stair, Prescott Street facade (N5764), Le Corbusier and Jullian, July 22–24, 1961, showing inset details of steps and railings to far right. (1:50; 47 × 25 cm; ozalid print.)*

many of Le Corbusier's discussions of the Modulor, a system he had tried to deliver to United States industry as a dimensioning and harmonizing tool of standardization in the same period, the late forties, when he delivered the S to Americans.[14]

Stairway dimensions were tackled with similar thoroughness. Plan 5766 showed the stair down to the basement to the immediate right of the side entrance (fig. 176). On plan, the width of the gap into which the stairs were inserted was fixed at 1.83 meters (the height of the standard 6 foot Modulor man), the stair steps themselves at 1.40 meters wide, 17 centimeters high, and 33 centimeters deep. The distance from the bottom step to the wall opposite it was set at 2.26 meters (the height of the upraised arm of the Modulor man). Mostly these dimensions were from the "blue scale," though some were from the "red scale."[15] But the Modulor was not used slavishly in this or other details. Railings, for example, were indicated at 7 centimeters wide, a non-Modulor dimension. (These were also marked "fer plat"—"flat iron.") The height from railing to step was 1.13 meters and care was taken to show that the vertical railings should be inclined diagonally halfway down each flight, and placed vertically at top, bottom, and middle landings. The architects even showed the joint of iron with an 11 centimeter space between

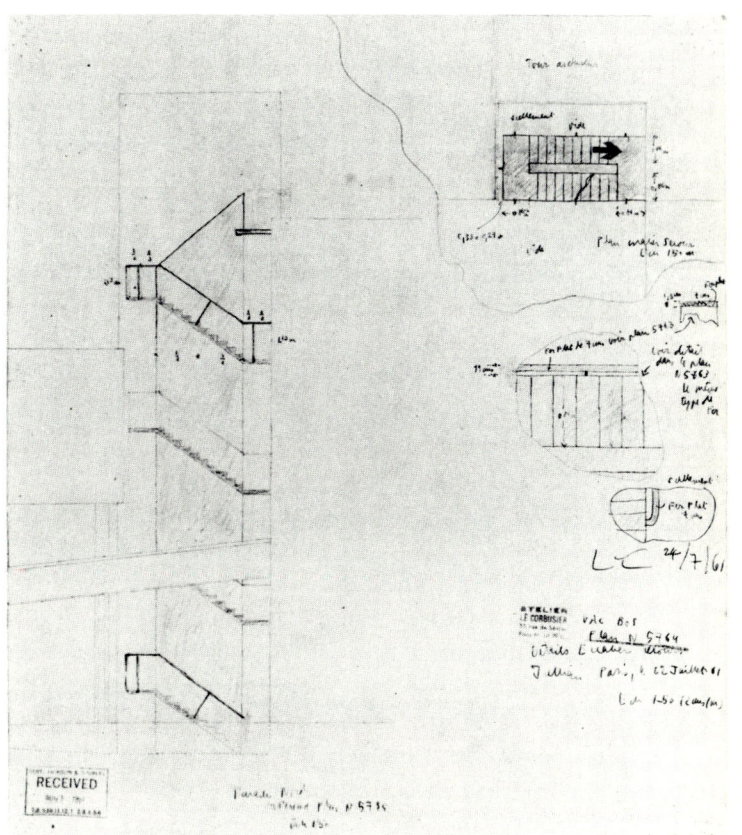

the bottom of the iron and the underside edge of the concrete stairs. With similar care, Jullian tackled details of the fire escape and main stairway (fig. 177).

Mechanical Services

In August, the site for the visual arts center was cleared. Ground was broken on the twentieth of the month and Sert's draftsmen began to produce detailed working drawings.[16] In September, Sert himself returned from Europe and wrote to Le Corbusier, "You may rest assured that all your instructions will be followed closely and that this office will pay the greatest attention and care in carrying out your plans" (8-30-61).

September was a month of more decisions and detailed designs, especially those concerning mechanical services. Sert wished Le Corbusier to approve the first plumbing, electrical, and ventilating designs—an urgent matter since sleeves had to be left in the concrete for ducts and circuitry. Air-conditioning was scheduled for the basement and first floors only—a decision that had been taken as early as June 1960, though one Harvard faction had not thought it wise to neglect the upper stories. They knew quite well that not everyone would be "basking naked on Cape Cod" in the close Boston summer and that the Summer School would use the visual arts center. There is no evidence Le Corbusier was told about this faction's wishes; Sert had told him in March 1960 that air-conditioning would not be required. Le Corbusier's harangues on the subject, therefore, were not in response to a local threat. He invented such a threat ("you will tell me 'We are air conditioning'") to justify a sermon on the subject, a subject of general architectural and American importance (5-29-61; appendix 16).

In the basement, a dust-free, humidity-controlled environment was essential for film storage, and the aesthetic objections to exposed ductwork ceased to exist, as there were no views of structure or surroundings to be interfered with. In fact ductwork, colored in bright Léger or tractor reds or greens, could be a happy articulation of the closed-in underground spaces. Two units were envisaged for the task: a single zone one for the auditorium, a multizone one for the remainder of the basement and the first floor. To cut down on ductwork in the heating and ventilating system, spaces upstairs were locally served. The airfloor was a system of channels cut in the slab with openings around the edges in the topside of it. The units and their water piping were therefore the only visible elements. The pipes were unavoidably visible in places and were painted in bright green; but Le Corbusier's office proceeded to find ways of disguising the units, except where they seemed amenable to the "workshop aesthetic" (on the second floor, south side, for example) or where they had unavoidably to be clamped onto the underside of the slab. Otherwise they were packed away in cupboards or hidden behind blackboards to the sides of the rooms.

The system of lighting was also designed with the purity of the structure, especially the plain underside of the slab, in mind. A print of October 25 shows that Le Corbusier had by then decided to paint the undersides of the slab white, employing it as a reflector: it was lit by a trough diffusing upwards onto the ceiling, like the one used at the Villa Savoye in Poissy over thirty years before, but made discontinuous, and not styled in chromium-plated fixtures. Since some direct lighting was also needed, spotlights were planned to be attached to the same rail that supported the troughs. The rail and its suspended lights were placed longitudinally in the rooms midway in the column spacings.

The Quincy Street studio made a masterly light sculpture at night, but in the day the movement of the forms was threatened by the curved wall which had been invented to hold the studio up. In September Le Corbusier called attention to this wall and tried to cut down its size.[17] At the same time he and Jullian designed a fire escape stairway down from the terrace to the lawn next to the Fogg; it came disastrously close to the ondulatoires scheduled for the second level curve and threatened their effects. The wall had to stay, but the escape required by law was later supplied by a small metal stair from the other side of the terrace onto the main ramp just below the highest point. Le Corbusier had also scheduled a space on the main stair tower for a relief in concrete by his old friend the sculptor Nivola, who lived on Long Island. This was then projected to go onto the large escape stair, but when the stair was canceled, the sculpture idea went with it. Small Le Corbusier relief sculptures like the ones in India, scheduled for imprint in various walls, were not referred to again either.

Interior Finishes and Colors

At the end of the month Sert forwarded a schedule of construction that was highly optimistic: "The building will be completed for occupancy by September 1962. The basement foundations would be poured by November 1st 1961, and remaining concrete floors would be poured in place by April 1962. Consequently, it becomes quite necessary to establish at an early date the problems relating to the building design, partitions, etc" (9-29-61). Thus in October attention focused almost exclusively on interior finishes, though on the same set of prints (annotated on October 25, 1961) Le Corbusier gave some thought to the way approaches to the building at ground level were to be treated.

Le Corbusier had been giving these problems careful thought since before the first presentation. For the second project (and therefore the final building) the architect in the main stuck to his earlier proposals, but in the October 25 prints Le Corbusier expanded considerably on the way he wanted materials fixed, arranged, and colored (fig. 178). He indicated his color choices by means of colored crayon blobs or touches of enamel paint. Finely scrawled inscriptions in black pen provided supplementary explanation. These are the externalized, material traces of an architect who could achieve astonishing precision in the visualization of a space and its details even as he worked with a working drawing print.

As before, Le Corbusier indicated that all pilotis were to be left unpainted, smooth béton brut. Ceilings were to be painted white, floors finished in "opus optimum" concrete or terrazzo, and walls painted in various colors, left bare concrete, paneled with wood sheets, or covered with blackboards. For the entrance lobby floor he specified "opus optimum au Modulor": fairly smooth concrete articulated like the ramp with a variety of Modulor dimensions, all in all resembling a series of ladders laid side by side with different rung widths and spacings. For the second floor, which was visible from the ramp, he suggested that black terrazzo be laid out in squares separated from each other by thin strips of brass and arranged so that columns passed through the center of each square (as in the first project). A similar geometrical arrangement in the same material was proposed for the third level but in white; white terrazzo (with its strong light reflecting qualities) was also planned for fourth and fifth floors.

Terrazzo was expensive and probably would not have stood the wear of studio work too well, but the effect of his second and third floors as seen simultaneously from the ramp would have been quite dazzling. The choice of different floor colors for both levels indicates his intention to treat the visible double floor height as a unit and to exploit it for effects of contrast, recession, depth, vibration, illusion, and transparency. The effect would have been perhaps too vivacious.

At this point, Le Corbusier the painter joined forces with Le Corbusier the "plastician": it was as if he were instructing Savina, the Breton cabinetmaker who carved his sculptures for him, to paint the inside, rather than the outside, of a much enlarged "Ubu" sculpture. Perhaps one can gauge the full impact of the ramp view as it might have been from the much more sober ramp view as it is. To the dense complexities of coloristic and material effects would have been added tiny fragments of exterior reality (sprigs of ivy, red-brick walls), people at work, reflections. Colored sound absorbent curtains glimpsed through glass, moving here and there on rails, would have added a further suggestion of time, accident, flux—not unlike some of the flanges of color in Le Corbusier's paintings. And as the viewer moved up the ramp, all these facets slipped into motion—introducing another element of time and relativity.

Naturally much of the impact was to result from the walls. Walls to Le Corbusier were not simply barriers between interior and exterior, but were also a conceptual part of his structural vocabulary and the primary bearers of aesthetic sensations through the play of light. Because of the visual arts center's function and the degree to which its architecture was designed to be looked at as well as used, choices of an aesthetic nature were certainly crucial: but Le Corbusier's stipulations on wall fin-

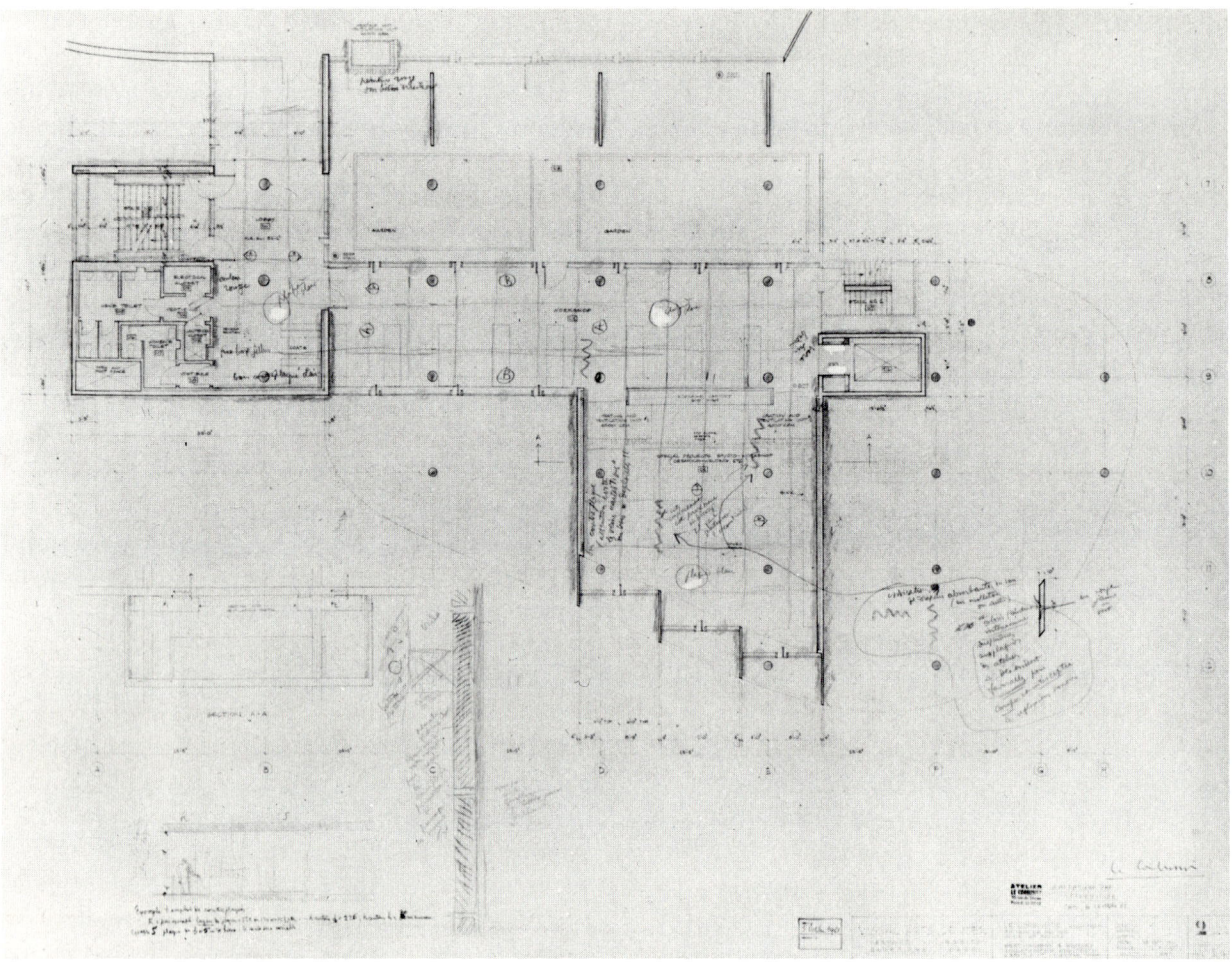

ishes also show his thorough understanding of what it is to work in a studio space (as one would expect from a man who spent about half his life in ateliers). Where color was applied to walls it was directly onto the concrete without a layer of plaster. His colors were bright, bold, festive—as in his paintings, enamels, tapestries, and sculptures. There were no gradations across a surface and there was no toning down. Green, yellow, red, black, and white were scheduled for walls up and down the building and marked in with colored crayon lines, blobs, and dots. Blue was allowed to appear in only two places: on the proposed enameled door into the sunken plaza at ground level and on the folding partition between foyer and auditorium. In most places he intended wood; even the brise-soleil were generally planned with wooden "contre-plaqués" ("attached panels") fixed

178. *Working drawing print of level 2, Sert, Jackson and Gourley, Le Corbusier and Jullian, October 25, 1961. (¼":1'0"; 91 × 123 cm; print.) Colors and finishes are indicated.*

to them. Like the paneling scheduled for most studio walls, these were to be made of oak, but oak with a very fine grain: "Attention éviter les veines artistiques du bois = déplorable" ("Careful to avoid artistic veins in the wood = awful").

There was nothing random about the placement and jointing of these panels, however: they were fixed in proportion. Le Corbusier suggested a system of different sized Modulor rectangles side to side, reminiscent of his proposal for the ramp or ground floor. Naturally some kind of incremental division of the wood was necessary in curved portions of the building. The effect might have been slightly distracting except that Le Corbusier emphasized the necessity of a very fine line between each panel. To provide a neutral dark surface and a place for drawing and demonstrations, he suggested blackboards in some places.

On matters of interior finish, as on everything else so far mentioned, Le Corbusier had strong views. A letter written on October 26 to accompany the prints opened with no endearments and ended with no "bien amicalement" ("best wishes"). Nor were there any apologies for being businesslike. It was simply headed

Principe Fondamental L-C

Je ne veux en *aucun cas* avoir des *"cement-blocks"* apparents dans l'intérieur des locaux.

On adoptera, à volonté, les "cement" ou "typical" blocks pour construire les cloisons, mais le revêtement intérieur de ces parois sera soit:

    a) à la choix peints de forts couleurs
        ou de blanc
        ou de noir

ou b) de revêtements en bois contreplaqué permettant de fixer avec les punaises (tacs) des feuilles de papier, des dessins, des photos etc. (ces documents pouvant être changer souvent.)—Ces contreplaqués seront le *plus uni* possible (*Evitez* les veines du bois "artistiques" qui sont *prétentieuses!!!*) Les joints seront le plus simple possible . . . ainsi donnera-t-on de la diversité aux locaux.

                              L-C

Fundamental Principle L-C

In *no circumstances* do I wish *"cement blocks"* to be visible on interiors.

Certainly one may use "cement" or "typical" blocks to construct the partitions but the inner sheathing of these walls will be either:

    a) painted in strong colors according to choice
        or in white
        or in black

or b) of attached plywood sheets allowing the fixing with thumbtacks of sheets of paper, of drawings, photos, etc. (those documents able to be changed often)—These plywood sheets will be the *most uniform* possible (*Avoid* the "artistic" grain of the wood which is *pretentious!!!*) The joints will be the simplest possible . . . so diversity will be given to the localities.

                              L-C

A small sketch was scrawled on his letter of his ideal joint for paneling; the effect on the inside would have been similar to the fine line articulation of the exterior flat concrete surfaces—as if the formwork had been detached when the concrete was dry and then tacked onto the inside walls it had just created. On one of the prints of October 25, Le Corbusier drew a detailed section of an entire wall thickness at a large scale next to a detail of a typical interior panel elevation at a much smaller scale (fig. 178). The section shows the concrete wall separated from a layer of insulation on the inside of a plywood sheet by a gap of a few centimeters. Wooden chocks fix the wood skin to the inside of the wall and provision is made for dampproofing (on the concrete surface) and soundproofing (on the inside of the ply).

Acoustics and Insulation

Soundproofing was another consideration that awaited detailed resolution. At the end of his letter (10-26-61) Le Corbusier wrote: "Question. Avez-vous pensé aux bruits à travers les parois?" ("Question. Have you thought about the noise that will cross these walls?") Indeed, one wonders when Le Corbusier first gave thought to echoing concrete studios with hammer taps and seminar sounds running through them. His first project had nonchalantly placed administrative offices alongside a workshop without even intervening partitions. Sound does not seem to have been a matter of primary importance in Le Corbusier's design processes unless formal addresses (in chapels and auditoriums) were expected, in which case he would even argue that acoustics were determinant.[18] At the bottom of his letter he wrote an "examination of the constraints of the problem."

Acoustique—Isolation phonique
pour Sert: As-tu pensé aux bruit?
      "   "   " l'isolation
         phonique?
Examin des constraints du probleme:
les *SOLS:*
les *plafonds*
les *parois*
le *passage du son à travers les cloisons.*

Acoustics—Sound Isolation
for Sert: have you thought of noise?
        have you thought of sound isolation?
Examination of the constraints of the problem:
the *floors*
the *ceilings*
the *walls*
the *passage of sound through the partitions.*
(10-26-61)

There is evidence that Le Corbusier had thought about these constraints the day before. On the prints he suggested purple curtains to be hung in places where they were needed around the studio. This, he felt, would muffle the echoes: to be sure, his "architecture acoustique" was perfectly shaped to rocket the sounds around the walls. But it did not do much to muffle floor-to-floor sounds, and curtains were liable to rot with dust and not stand up to student wear and tear. Seminar rooms were not adequately served by the curtains; much sound was also generated by mechanical equipment. This, Le Corbusier metaphorically as well as literally "tucked in a cupboard": it was the consultants Bolt, Beranek, and Newman (who had examined the "constraints" at Krueger's and Sert's request six weeks before) who developed ingenious slings and rubber washers to reduce the mechanical vibrations. Bolt, Beranek, and Newman were aware of the primacy of the structural effects, just as Jackson had been when he thought of the airfloor, and they suggested an analogous solution which also took care of some of the constraints that Le Corbusier ignored: the placement of Tectum boards *within* the structure and of antivibration devices *in* the airfloor. Considerations of this kind led Le Corbusier temporarily to abandon his exclusive views on where paint could be applied and to allow the use of acoustic tempered hardboard in places that were to be painted over—but he later retracted.

The auditorium was a different matter, as a certain degree of sound reflection was desirable there, combined with a degree of echo control. The consultants suggested a slightly zigzag wall, a reduction of nearly 10 feet in the extension of the balcony formed by the first floor lobby, the placement of reflecting boards above the speaking position, and some sound mufflers on the east wall. These were examined and approved by Bernhardt, the great French acoustician. They were the determinants of the auditorium's shape. Le Corbusier's only contribution was the cross projection which, he noted with excitement, had been inspired by the Philipps Pavilion (Poème Electronique). He also suggested that the side wall (the one eventually zigzagged) be painted white. Of course the zigzag gave a slanting surface and a later solution was temporarily adopted of holding screens normal to projection on frames.

Finally the prints of October 25 showed what Le Corbusier had in mind for the ground level approaches to the visual arts center. In the pavement in front of the side entrance (by now one should really be referring to it as the main entrance) he indicated brick, as he did in the sunken piazza beneath the Quincy Street studio. In other areas he showed tarmacadam or sand. In August 1960 the overseers had requested the use of brick in the lower parts of the building, and the solution of a brick pavement had seemed a good way of answering the plea while still avoiding disruption of Le Corbusier's concrete work. Eventually Le Corbusier rejected the idea; this coincided all too conveniently with a need for cutbacks, and so the material was rejected, concrete being placed in its stead. The client was failing to understand a remark Le Corbusier had made when he first visited the site in 1959 and stated that the Fogg would be "his wall": transparency allowed visual inclusion of the brick structures to either side, making brick in the center itself unnecessary.

By November 1961 final working drawings had been completed for the plumbing and for electrical and mechanical services; attention was again turned to the imminent realities of concrete casting and concrete finishes.

Concrete and the Modulor

Correspondence exchanged at this time sheds further light on the nature, underlying ideas, and "correct" finish of the remaining "éléments-types" in béton brut employed by the architect in this building: walls, ondulatoires, brise-soleil, pilotis, and slabs. In the presentation drawings, the exterior concrete fabric was shown by light ochre crayon hatching. The earliest indication of formwork design was supplied in May 1961 on a set of colored prints which have, unfortunately, been lost. It is at least known that these drawings were made according to the Modulor, and an extant print of September 1961 (fig. 179) enables us to reconstruct how formwork lines and standard panel sizes were decided for flat walls throughout the visual arts center and were made to conform to the building's overall proportional scheme. The drawing in question shows only the front plane of the stair tower, but it typifies the manner in which flat portions of the rest of the building were determined.

Le Corbusier was seeking an extremely smooth finish. Had the spring 1961 presentation facades been built as drawn, the walls would have been sheer, shiny planes without texture. The question facing Le Corbusier in November was to decide how these flat surfaces of concrete should be articulated. The problem had been outlined in *Vers une architecture*, where the architect had spoken of the necessity of controlled "modénature" of a composition achieved in its general lines, so that "the outward aspect" would be made "radiant."[19] In this phase of a design, articulation was capable of enhancing or destroying earlier proportional sensitivities; success in such an operation, where free

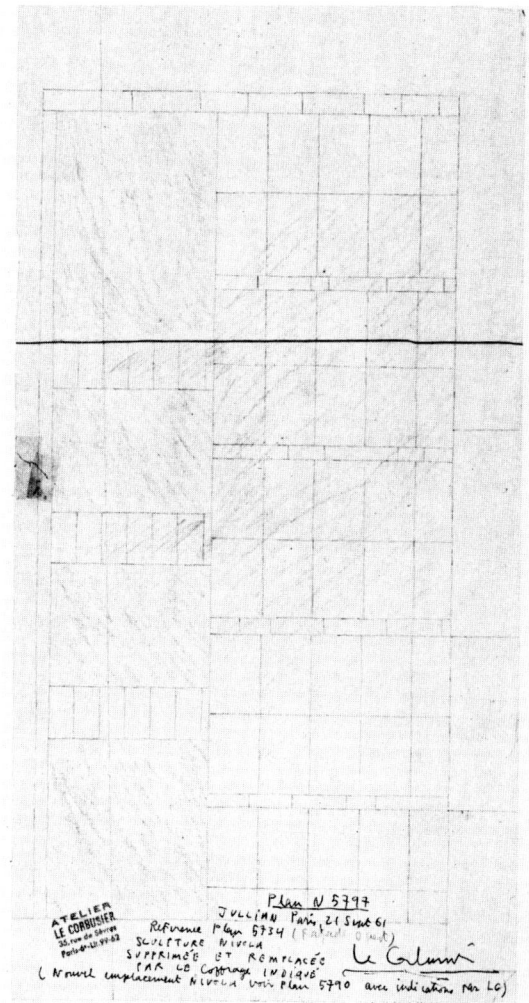

179. *Elevation of stair tower showing formwork design (N5797), Le Corbusier and Jullian, September 21, 1961. (1:50; 46 × 24 cm; ozalid print.) This is the only extant drawing revealing the process of formwork design for flat parts of the visual arts center. Transcription: "Reference plan 5734 (façade Ouest) Sculpture Nivola supprimée et remplacée par le coffrage indiqué (Nouvel emplacement Nivola voir plan 5790 avec indications par Le Corbusier)" ("Reference plan 5734 [west facade] Nivola Sculpture replaced by the indicated formwork [for new position of Nivola see plan 5790 with indications by Le Corbusier"]).*

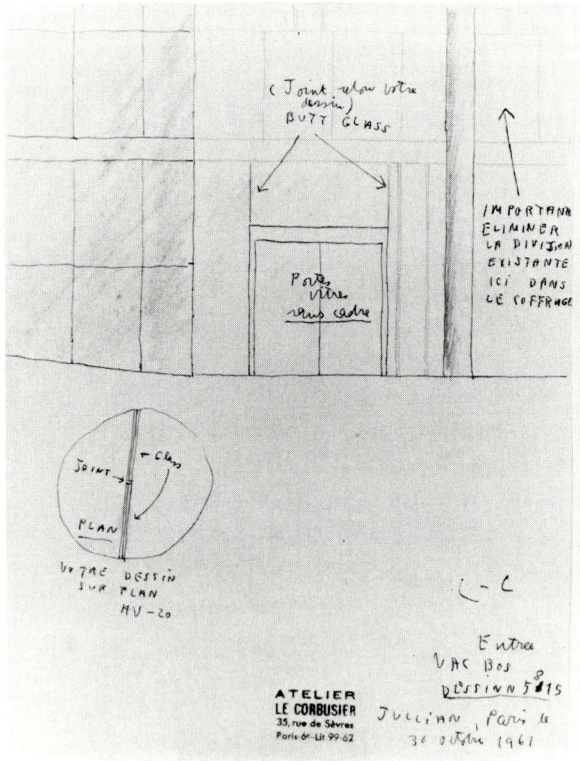

180. *Elevation detail of south side entrance (N5815), Le Corbusier and Jullian, October 31, 1961. (Scale unknown; 28 × 21.5 cm; photocopy.)*

aesthetic choice counted most, was the mark of the good architect.

However, even for Le Corbusier's highly refined compositional sense, intuition alone was not enough to solve this perennial architectural problem. Proportional schemes to eliminate caprice were evidently also required.

This is demonstrated by the use of Modulor dimensions in the stair tower drawing, which shows fine formwork division lines in place (fig. 179). The basic format (or "blank canvass," since he might have been composing a picture) was provided by the rectangular contour of the tower and by the position and size of concrete floor and stair landing slab-ends. Between the former have been marked a series of rectangles of vertical proportion whose height is half the 3.66 meter floor-to-ceiling dimension (1.83 meters) and whose width is one-third (1.22 meters). The rectangular divisions were lined up with the left-hand edge of the wall and disposed side by side to the right, with the result that a smaller sized rectangle was left to the extreme right of the tower on all floors. Shuttering lines were placed carefully on the slabs so as *not* to align with the wall panels and were set at varying distances according to the Modulor, thus emphasizing the conceptual distinctness of the slabs by an implied visual movement in the horizontal direction. Meanwhile the stair landing terminations were detailed in a smaller repeated module which was also drawn from left to right.

The same formwork scheme was drawn for the wall above the side entrance, where the door was placed in a concrete box extending through the glass without a frame (fig. 180). By such means the narrow net of lines without which concrete can become dull and overbearing was chosen and regulated according to mathematical proportions and the human scale. Le Corbusier's emphasis on "disegno"—drawn lines, crisp and distinct, without hazy transition between one part of the structure and the next—is apparent here, and serves further to remind us of the deep interrelationship between his architecture and his painting. The same effort at achieving firm distinctions and clear edges can be found in many detail designs for the visual arts center: for example, the design for the ondulatoires at second level, made in September 1961.

Ondulatoire Proportions

The south side curve articulation by means of brise-soleil had been achieved early in 1961. The north curve, hovering out towards Quincy Street and the Yard, is perhaps the part of the building most often seen during the day and night (fig. 181). In any case the strip of fenestration at this level is most instrumental in conveying the curved form's dynamics to a ground-level viewer.

Although the presentation elevation (fig. 163) showed only a blue crayon void for this opening, the curve had always been scheduled for ondulatoires and was safely out of range of the direct rays of the sun. The mental processes behind ondulatoire placement resemble those for shuttering mark design. But here it was a case of articulating an opening rather than a solid, a curve rather than a flat surface in concrete and glass. As with earlier brise-soleil design, it was a case of respecting—and enhancing—the "accusing" and "generating" lines of the major primary forms.

To the top right of the sheet Jullian drew a typical ondulatoire to full scale with glass jointing into it (fig. 181). The exterior surface was made flush with the building edge and in all respects the detail repeated the aérateur strut of July (fig. 171), including the temporary use of aluminum. In the left-hand upper portion of the sheet, he drew an elevation of the curve as viewed from the north side that included part of the north concrete wall to the left and extended to the extremity of the curve close to Quincy Street to the right. The second level glazing was divided off into six unequal parts by means of aérateurs—part A, part B, and so on, through to part F on the extreme left. The right-hand four parts (A–D) were inscribed "ondulatoires," the left hand two, "without ondulatoires": in other words, parts E and F, to the east end, were to be left plain pans-de-verre.

Immediately below the elevation Jullian faintly drew a plan of the curve. This was to help him gauge more precisely the full surface to be glazed—a matter on which the elevation was totally deceptive because of the accelerating curvature to the right: parts A and B were actually much larger than the others though the elevation gave the illusion that they were about the same size.

Below the curve Jullian did another drawing projecting the full curved facade onto a two-dimensional plane. This resulted in a long strip which was then inscribed with the various parts (A–F) and annotated with the inscription "aérateurs" in appropriate places. The drawing as a whole was entitled "Development Facade 'ondulatoires.'" Parts F and E were left blank, part D nearly so, and parts C, B, and A (working from left to right) were articulated with various numbers of struts at varying intervals; they numbered thirteen, eleven, and sixteen respectively for these bays if one includes the strut to each side of the aérateurs. The composition was extremely subtle so that, passing from the pans-de-verre to the left, the eye was pushed into rhythms that increased slowly, then accelerated to a climax as the point of maximum curvature was reached. All this calls to mind the behavior and composition of the brise-soleil on the other curve, except that there, fin lengths varied with everything else; here, ondulatoire struts remained of constant depth. A repeating cadence was also introduced into the fenestration rhythm by the aérateurs whose width stayed at 43 centimeters whenever the element occurred.

Jullian's intuitive exploitation of the kinesthetic potentials of the curve was not in itself enough; the Modulor had to be involved to give his intervals the required rigorous mathematical sanction. Struts were laid out using both red and blue series of the Modulor, exactly as specified in Le Corbusier's publication *Modulor 2* for this kind of fenestration.[20] In the following passage from the same book, Le Corbusier outlines his thinking on ondulatoires: "Our last invention has been to equip the palace of the Ministries in the Capital of Chandigarh and the Convent of La Tourette at Lyons with glazed panels called 'musical,' the most rational solution of modern glasswork, governed by a rule which for a long time past has governed music."[21] Late in the same chapter he quotes Xenakis the musician who helped design the La Tourette glazing: "The idea of the Modulor has created a narrow structural link between time and sound."[22] In the visual arts center, then, struts and glass of the second level glazing do not simply represent the "death of the window" and the conceptual distinction of the basic functions of fenestration in concrete: they also seem to represent, in

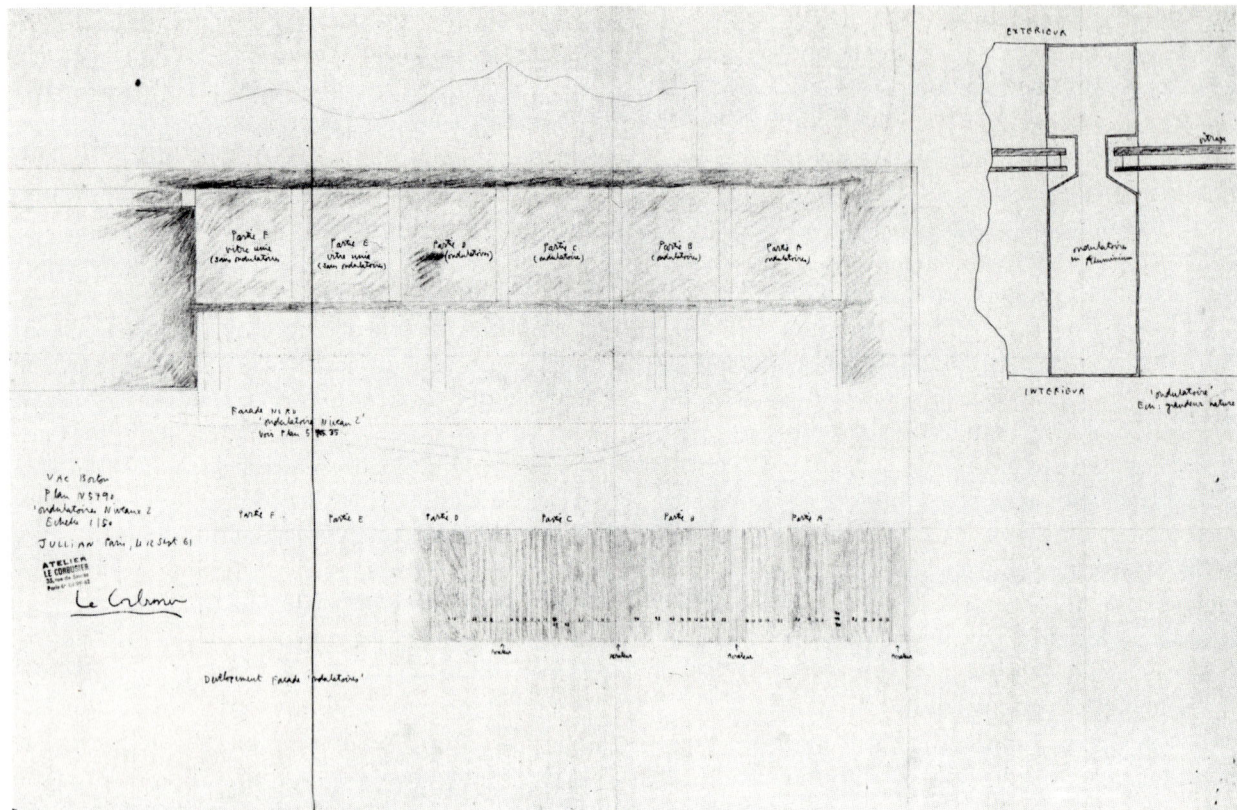

their dimensioning and abstract proportional content, an attempt at representing a ribbon of "space-time."[23] As such, the ondulatoires take their place in a long intellectual history of attempts at infusing metaphysical content into architectural form through reference to a world of pure abstract numerical relations by means of harmonic proportions.

It must be emphasized that strict proportioning of such a dynamic composition as that for the ondulatoires would hardly have been possible before the invention of the Modulor with its great numerical flexibility. One might even go so far as to suggest that the Modulor encouraged Le Corbusier's greater sculptural freedom in his late works.[24]

Definition of the Brise-soleil

The tectonic complement, in the fenestration treatment, to the lightweight glass band of visualized music on the curve was the much heavier brise-soleil. The overall shape and dimensions of typical brise-soleil fins had been determined in one

181. *Elevation, detail, and plan showing calculation of ondulatoire proportions for the Quincy Street curve (N5790), Le Corbusier and Jullian, September 12, 1961. (1:50; 53 × 83 cm; ozalid print.) The fenestration area to be filled is to the top, the curved plan is traced just beneath it, and to the bottom are the ondulatoires and aérateurs in a lateral strip, dimensioned according to blue and red scales of the Modulor. To the top right is a typical ondulatoire strut with glazing inserted to either side.*

of the July drawings (fig. 172). Further details followed, showing the diagonal fin with a wooden panel attached to its inside (fig. 182) and the typical arrangement for the third floor south side curved studio elements with inside tips made flush with the curved interior extremity of the horizontal brise-soleil. In November, to help later work, a trial brise-soleil unit was cast and laid down next to the sidewalk of Quincy Street where it became known (affectionately and otherwise) as the "mousetrap" (fig. 183). The complete unit included two parallel brise-soleil fins and slab-ends below and above. Drain pipes were incorporated and a horizontal brise-soleil fin (cum stiffener) was placed half way up. Although the arrangement of the unit was not exactly as at any point in the building design, the trial version was excellent for experimentation with formwork of different materials, grain, and textures. Once cast and dry, the "mousetrap" was photographed in great detail to show the finishes, drainage, and angles of the tips. The latter were a special concern because a knife-edge tip could easily be bitten away by frost. The solution adopted was a beveled tip of half an inch, thin enough not to be seen at a distance.

These photographs were sent off to Le Corbusier on November 3 by Sert, who referred to the brise-soleil in his letter as a "sun baffle." The reply came bouncing straight back.

> Le béton des architraves et des montants est parfait (y compris les bulles d'air). Le "drain pipe" ne devrait pas être en "tile" (terre cuite = trop fragile), mais en *éternit* (sur le document 28/8/ on semble voir que le "pipe" a une doublure de metal. ATTENTION à la rouille! Ce serait très dangereux à cause de la rouille qui ferait éclater l'enveloppe).
>
> *Coffrage des brise-soleil* (sun-breaker) (Je désire que pour ce bâtiment, on emploie ce terme de "sun-breaker" et non pas celui de "baffle" que ne veut rien dire. Toute l'architecture moderne a pour mission de s'occuper du soleil. Le *brise-soleil,* par consequent est le terme le plus correct).

The concrete of the architraves and vertical elements is perfect (including the air bubbles).

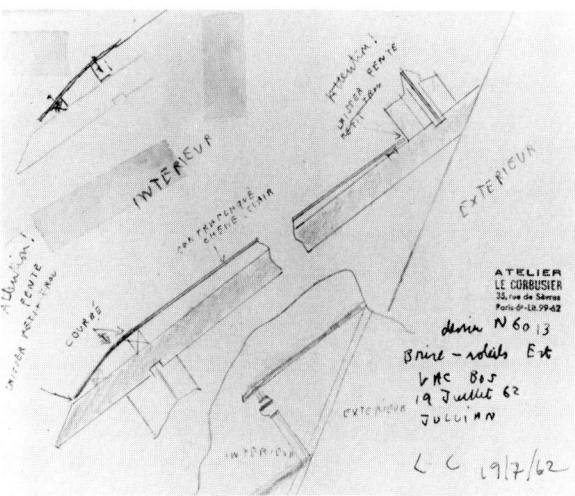

182. *Plan of typical diagonal brise-soleil fin with attached contre-plaqué in wood (N6013), Le Corbusier and Jullian, July 19, 1962. (Photocopy.)*

183. *Trial casting of brise-soleil unit, November 1961, standing to one side of the site. The unit includes two brise-soleil fins, the slab-end below and above, drain pipes, and a horizontal brise-soleil stiffener halfway up. Different wood graining qualities from various formwork patterns are visible: Le Corbusier chose the smoothest. The casting became known locally as "the mousetrap."*

The "drain pipe" should not be in "tile" (terra cotta = too fragile), but in *éternit* (on document 28/8/ it seems that the "pipe" has a metal lining. BE CAREFUL of rust! That would be dangerous because rust would burst the envelope).

Formwork of the brise-soleil (sun breaker) (I wish for this building that the term "sun breaker" be used, not "baffle" which means nothing. All modern architecture has a mission to occupy itself with the sun. *Brise-soleil* is therefore the most correct term.) (11-9-61; appendix 18)

The insistence on the correct term for the correct element seems to concur with the architect's intentions outlined in the last chapter. There was also a question here of the correct finish; of the various samples of formwork, Le Corbusier chose the plywood with the smoothest effect and even suggested the use of Isorel for a smoother finish still. In the same letter, Le Corbusier included a sketch of three tiny formwork joints (fig. 184). The Isorel formwork was shown in place over the concrete. Between adjacent sheets different joints were indicated: with parallel sided opening, with a pointed V, and with a shallow V. This was to be the method of achieving the articulation lines on the concrete. The shallow V was the joint eventually used and was obtained by beveling the formwork edges, so giving a raised, inverted V of about 1 centimeter height on the smooth surface of the concrete which could be picked out by the light and which resembled, from a distance, a pen line on paper (fig. 179). Le Corbusier recommended the same Isorel formwork with the same joints for all the flat walls of the visual arts center and emphasized that the joint should be "simply a visible line without being a design" (11-9-61; appendix 18).

Smooth Pilotis

The appearance of the piloti, a central element of Le Corbusier's architectural language in this particular structure (whose skeleton was hailed as "a new stereotomy for reinforced concrete"), was of paramount importance. In the same letter, Le Corbusier referred to "la douceur des colonnes" ("the softness of the columns") and included a sketch of a column produced from a steel form, re-

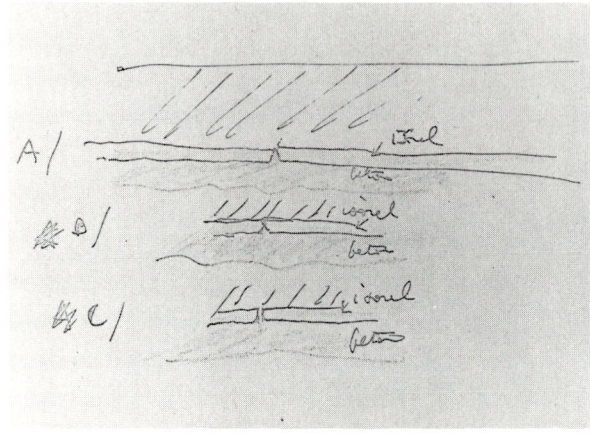

184. *Sketches of three formwork joints from Le Corbusier's letter to Sert of November 9, 1961. They indicate his method for achieving "a visible line without being a design": he suggests the use of smooth, grainless "Isorel" formwork, cut with one of the three incisions suggested to leave a mounted V on the surface able to be picked out by light. Such a detail lay very close to his ideal intentions for the visual arts center's concrete work: "une nouvelle stéréotomie" ("a new stereotomy").*

calling the earlier sketch done in Cambridge at Sert's office in June 1960. Alongside the column stood a man with his arms folded and across the top of the sheet was scrawled a curious "confession" to Lucien Hervé (who took many of the photographs for the late volumes of *Oeuvre complète*) on the "smooth quality of the columns, indispensable to obtain" (fig. 185).

Hervé
    Colonnes de béton armé dits "cuisses de femmes" coulées dans demi-coffrage de *tole* (à joints croisés) le béton est si lisse, si séduisant, "qu'on y met la main" (dites la désignation ci dessus n'est pas officielle).

Hervé
    Columns of reinforced concrete called "women's thighs" poured in half forms of *metal* (with crossed joints) the concrete is so smooth, so seductive "that one puts one's hand there" (say the above designation is not official). (11-9-61; appendix 18)

Presumably the man with his arms folded was engaged in a battle of self-restraint. As for the metal forms, by that time they were out of use in that part of the United States. Sert explained this to Le Corbusier, telling him the customary method was with Sonotube cardboard forms which were much cheaper (12-8-61). A month after the Hervé confession, Le Corbusier examined a photograph of a Sonotube casting from a prospectus.

> "Sonotube": les photographies du prospectus sont difficiles à lire. On voit apparaître une spirale qui nous inquiète beaucoup. Peux-tu nous envoyer une photographie donnant une vision claire de la surface acquise? Il semble évident que si la spirale apparaissait sur les colonnes ce serait très gênant étant donné que celles-ci jouent le rôle éminent dans ce bâtiment.

> "Sonotube": the prospectus photographs are difficult to read. There is a visible spiral and that worries us a lot. Can you send me a photograph giving a clear view of the acquired surface? It seems evident that if the spiral appeared on the columns it would be very annoying given that they play the eminent role in this building. (12-19-61)

And playing the eminent role in Le Corbusier's one American building, the columns had to obey all the rules: they had to be "pure forms"—cylinders—emitting the purest sensations, ideal forms unsullied by spirals or blemishes of any kind.

In the late fall, trial castings were also made of a flat wall and of a piloti using a cylinder of small vertical slats of the size proposed for the curved wall. The latter was a composite method—like the trial brise-soleil casting—of gauging a number of qualities in one go. This method for casting columns (which would have resembled some of Auguste Perret's work) was superseded by the Sonotube method. As for slabs, they too were to be absolutely smooth, though on top, of course, they were to be given the various floor treatments described earlier in this chapter. The job of designing the formwork for smooth ceilings was left to Sert.

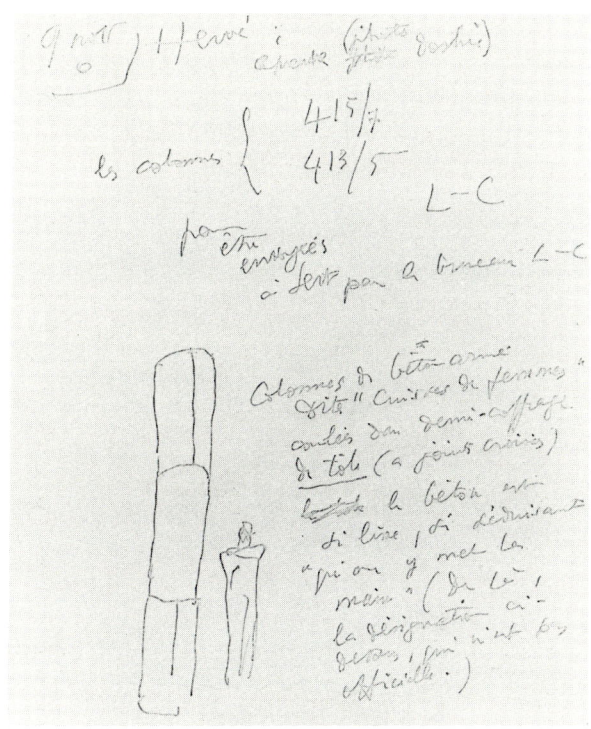

185. *Sketch from Le Corbusier's letter to Sert, November 9, 1961, specifying formwork and quality of finish for pilotis. The sketch shows quartered steel formwork with slight cross joints (similar to those decided at the Sert conference, June 1960).*

The Aérateurs

Before moving on to the history of construction of the visual arts center, there is one sequence of correspondence that highlights perfectly Le Corbusier's absolutism with regard to the very details of one of his "typical solutions." The element in question is the aérateur and the argument (which has the quality of a trans-Atlantic debate some of the time and of a one-way sermon for the rest) concerns the protection of men from mosquitoes.

It all began in late October when Sert's office elaborated the detail of the aérateur made by Le Corbusier in late July. This detail was a relatively simple affair: centrally pivoting wooden door cased in aluminum; rudimentary handle and lock; uncomplicated rubber stops; a thin wire gauze set across the entrance to keep out insects. Sert's office's design eliminated the insect screen, "since they are not required for this kind of building in Cambridge conditions and are not used on similar buildings of the University" (10-20-61),[25] reversed the rubber gaskets to secure the door in the closed position, widened the metal sill at the base to standardize the sills, and introduced a "friction stay arm" with an internal cam fastener for locking. A warning signal came from Jullian by return post:

. . . vous supprimez les moustiquaires, Le Corbusier n'est pas d'accord parce que c'est une partie essentielle de son invention.

. . . you take off the mosquito screens, Le Corbusier is not in accord because that is an essential part of his invention. (10-30-61)

But the full blast came from the inventor himself the following week in what he termed "an imperative letter."

2e/ Je conteste les dessins des "aérateurs" faits par votre firme americaine. Le bâtiment n'est pas de l'automobile! Tous ces luxes de caoutchouc seront bouffés par la poussière, les cacas de mouche, etc. . . . la sécheresse, la pluie. Si un peu d'air passait, personne ne s'en trouverait plus mal, au contraire. Par contre, votre constructeur propose froidement de supprimer les moustiquaires. Est-ce qu'il devient fou? J'ai créé les "aérateurs" pour respirer dans les bâtiments et vaincre une fois pour toutes les moustiques sous n'importe quelle latitude. Aux moustiques, on peut ajouter les mouches, les guêpes, les papillons de nuit qui viennent encombrer les lieux éclairés la nuit. J'ai créé les "aérateurs" à Cap Martin ou j'ai eu deux moustiques en dix années et j'ai mis quatre mille employés au Secrétariat de Chandigarh où il n'y a pas eu un seul moustique à l'intérieur des locaux.

2nd/I contest the drawings of "aérateurs" done by your American firm. The building is not supposed to have the qualities of an automobile! All these rubber luxuries will be eaten away by dust, fly shit, etc. . . . drying out, rain. If a little air creeps in, nobody will be the worse for it, on the contrary. On the other hand your builder coldly proposes to do away with the mosquito screens. Has he gone crazy? I created the "aérateurs" to allow one to breathe in buildings and beat mosquitoes once and for all, at no matter what latitude. To mosquitoes, one can add flies, gnats, night moths, which come to clutter up places lit at night. I created the "aérateurs" at Cap Martin where I have had two mosquitoes in ten years and I put four thousand employees into the Secretariat at Chandigarh where there has not been one sole mosquito in the interior spaces. (11-6-61; appendix 17)

From the author of *Vers une architecture*, who elaborated the automobile/building analogy to its fullest, the author of the Citroen/Citrohan pun, the rejoinder "le batiment n'est pas de l'automobile" comes as something of a shock. But there is much else besides, in this passage, which indicates a change of heart since the days of mechanistic enthusiasm when, for example, he stood over the Ford production line in amazement or addressed panegyrics to American elevators.[26] For, in his mechanical days, he had praised his "respiration exacte" ("air-conditioning") in very similar terms—"breathing at no matter what latitude": "The buildings of Russia, Paris, Suez or Buenos Aires, the steamer crossing the Equator, will be hermetically closed. In winter warmed, in summer cooled, which means that pure controlled air at 18 degrees centigrade circulates within for ever."[27] Against this was now set the aérateur, which kept the mosquitoes out but let in the air, rather as the brise-soleil kept out the glare while letting in the light. Jullian had been right: the essence of an invention was at stake, and the aérateur, essential solution to ventilation, was above the local and particular requirements of Cambridge, Massachusetts; it was a universal solution.

Je *réclame donc, impérativement,* que l'on se dispense des caoutchoucs somptuaires prévus par vos aérateurs et que l'on installe le moustiquaire absolument indispensable à chacun des aérateurs.

J'ajoute que la toile metallique des moustiquaires doit être en cuivre (probablement) et d'une maille suffisamment forte pour laisser passer l'air tout en interceptant les moustiques. On m'a fait, récemment, un moustiquaire à Paris où la toile était si fine que les moustiques restaient dehors, mais l'air également! (Je pense qu'une maille de toile métallique d'un millimetre ne laisse pas entrer un moustique à moins qu'il n'appartienne au 2ème Bureau ou au bureau secrèt du frère de Mr Foster Dulles.)

I make this imperative claim then, that the sumptuous rubber projected for your aérateurs be dispensed with and that the mosquito screens be installed, absolutely indispensible to each of the aerateurs.

I add that the metal of mosquito screens should be copper (probably) and of a strong enough netting to let in the air while intercepting the mosquitoes. Someone made me a mosquito screen recently in Paris where the web of the screen was so fine that the mosquitoes stayed outside but so did the air! (I think that a metal web screen of 1 mm will not let mosquitoes in—at least, so long as they do not belong to the 2nd Bureau or to the secret service of Mr. Foster Dulles' brother.) (11-6-61; appendix 17)

The correct specification of the aérateur was outlined in the new year of 1962.

> Je t'ai envoyé le 26 juillet 1961 le plan L-C No 5765. Aérateur details, Jullian July 22, 1961.
> Un "aérateur comporte:
>   a) le volet pivotant verticalement
>   b) les deux montants formant "bâtis"
> En ce qui concerne:
>   a) Notre plan était tres simple. Il pouvait être fait aux prix X . . . et fourni dans un délai Y . . .
>   b) Je pense que les "bâtis" peuvent être fabriqués en Amérique puisqu'ils serviront pour faire tous les "ondulatoires".

> I sent to you on July 26 the plan L-C No. 5765. Aérateur details, Jullian July 22, 1961.
> An aérateur consists of:
>   a) the vertical pivoting wing
>   b) the two mullions/mountings forming "struts"
> Concerning:
>   a) Our plan was very simple. It could be made for price X . . . and furnished after a delay Y . . .
>   b) I think the struts can be fabricated in America since they will serve to do all the "ondulatoires."[28] (1-8-62)

Sert had discovered that aérateurs were going to be expensive in America and had asked Le Corbusier if he knew a firm in France (10-30-61). For "the finishing of the vertical pivoting wing," Le Corbusier now delved into the underworld of Paris hardware manufacturers and came up with "Monsieur Dujourdy, Entrepreneur de Serrurerie" ("locksmith"; 1-8-62). The latter gave a quotation that improved on the American price, though three months were needed for delivery. But, as Le Corbusier noted on January 11,

> "l'entrepreneur parisien . . . est tombé exactement dans le travers de vos spécialistes américains, c'est à dire poursuivre un idéal d'exécution parfaitement inutile et dépenser un argent fou.

> the Parisian contractor . . . has fallen exactly in the way of your American specialists, pursuing an ideal of execution, perfectly useless, and costing a crazy sum. (1-11-62; appendix 19)

This lamentation on the locksmiths of the West was followed by a panegyric on the Chandigarh fenestration, achieved with miserable budgets (1-11-62; appendix 19).

> J'ai pu faire au Secrétariat de Chandigarh, le palais du Parlement avec les ondulatoires que j'ai inventés à cette occasion et qui m'ont permis, contre tout le monde là-bas, d'atteindre des prix minimum acceptables par les budgets misérables de l'Inde.
> Dix mille pièces de 3m 66 ont été coulés au sol, montées jusqu'a 40m de haut, étalés sur 240m de large (facade est) et sur 240m de large (facade ouest); 100% de verre comprenant tous les 3 m. environ des "aérateurs" avec transaération soit à travers les corridors des bureaux, soit à travers les bureaux eux-mêmes (24 m. de large).

Nehru était dans un état complet d'enthousiasme quand il a visité (dixit Pierre Jeanneret). Il n'y a pas un moustique sur le nez des 4,000 employés. Il n'y a pas un rayon de soleil qui touche le verre à partir de l'équinoxe de printemps jusqu'à l'équinoxe d'automne.

Je viens de mettre au point pour Chandigarh le "Laboratoire de Décision Scientifique" (Government House); facade est: 100% de verre; facade ouest: 100% de verre = contrôle du soleil impeccable, grandeur architecturale qui commence à être impressionnante.

Mon cher Sert, voici mon idée: "l'aérateur" peut être fait d'une feuille pliée d'aluminium d'une seule face avec poignée à l'intérieur . . .

At the Secretariat of Chandigarh, I was able to supply the Parliamentary Palace with ondulatoires that I invented on that occasion and which allowed me against everyone there to achieve the minimum acceptable prices for the miserable budgets of India.

Ten thousand pieces 3m 66 long were poured on the ground, lifted 40m into the air, spread out over 240m width (east facade) and 240m breadth (west facade): 100% glass incorporating every three meters or so, "aérateurs," with transaeration across the office corridors or across the offices themselves (24m wide).

Nehru was in a state of complete enthusiasm when he visited (dixit Pierre Jeanneret). Not a mosquito on the nose of 4000 employees, not a ray of sun touching the glass from spring to autumn equinoxes.

For Chandigarh I have just put in shape the "Laboratory of Scientific Decision" (Government House); east facade: 100% glass; west facade: 100% glass = impeccable control of the sun, architectural size which begins to be impressive.

My dear Sert, here is my idea: "the aérateur" can be made of a single folded aluminum leaf with the handle on the inside . . .[29]

The sketches Le Corbusier included were decoded at Sert's when they arrived and turned into detailed working drawings.[30] Evidently they were reworkings of details from Firminy and La Tourette. Slightly confused by the material to be used for the bâtis, or struts, to either side, and thinking that wood was allowable, Sert suggested that wood be used. He argued that wood would be easier to construct and to fashion, given the high quality of local craftsmanship in the material.[31] Le Corbusier's reply indicated that the vertical concrete strut was an essential and shared "constituent element" of the aérateur and the ondulatoire. Meanwhile, Sert had demonstrated that an aluminum pivoting wing was liable to stick in ice and had suggested plain wood for that part of the device as well.

J'accepte de faire *le* 'volet' en bois, mais je *n'accepte pas* que les montants (ondulatoires) gauche et droit soient en bois; ils doivent être en béton comme tous les autres ondulatoires.

I accept that *the wing* be made of wood, but I *do not accept* that uprights (ondulatoires) left and right be of wood; they must be of concrete like all the other ondulatoires. (2-5-62)

Thus the aérateur was resolved. It had a wooden door but concrete struts to either side and so remained a typical element of reinforced concrete. Sert's suggestion for wood, like his permissiveness over the Sonotube spiral on columns or his idea for painting them (which he occasionally does in his own work), gives a valuable insight into the differences between the two architects: the one with a pragmatic, loose, and somewhat colorful attitude to building fabrics, the other, sternly absolutist, severely constrained in the rigor of his own structural language. The aérateur remained "du chantier" ("of the site"), as Le Corbusier put it, not "de la Cadillac" ("of the Cadillac"); it retained the rough-hewn qualities of country carpentry and did not have the whispering precision of a watch mechanism or modern American car. If some drafts passed, that did not matter. The aérateurs were not "pièces de musée" ("museum pieces"; 1-11-62; appendix 19). And by the time he made this remark in January 1962, the building that had begun its life as a tiny sketch in a notebook was at last on the way up.

10. CONSTRUCTION

That looks like very difficult work.

Pier Luigi Nervi (at the Carpenter Center)

186. *The cleared site and excavation viewed from Prescott Street, winter 1961–1962. In the background are the side wall of the Fogg Museum, the "mousetrap" brise-soleil trial casting, and the spire of Memorial Church in Harvard Yard.*

By the end of 1961 the image of the visual arts center was complete down to the tiniest details, but only on paper. For the craftsmen and contractors to do their essential work, many complicated decisions still had to be made in the minds of a great many men over a relatively short span of time, be it Sert and his architects, administrators at Harvard, engineering consultants, or an individual formwork carpenter faced with the responsibility of cutting the mold of one of Le Corbusier's standard elements.

Before the building as drawing could become intelligible for construction, Le Corbusier's trans-Atlantic prints had to be much amplified. Many of the sketches were virtually useless as they stood (though their historical value is indisputable). Paul Krueger, the job captain, even went so far as to call some of them "cartoons"[1]—a remark that pithily assesses their drawing style, but points also to the hours of labor under extreme pressure that Sert's men went through to make them into useful working drawings. But if the visual arts center demanded blood and sweat as well as managerial ability, it also evoked dedication. Job 5911 was special, and all concerned knew it. It was a test involving enormous prestige and for some it became a labor of love. A major event in the life of a great architect and the history of an institution, it now intersected many other "histories," from the biographies of professionals and manual laborers to the histories of American contracting firms.

The first link in the process towards realization was, naturally, the executant architect, Sert. Members of his office spent the last eight months of 1961 building the visual arts center up in all its details on paper, then breaking it down again into the separate kinds of information needed by different contractors according to the various chapter headings of the eventual building specification. Aside from the recurring theme of collision between the easiest or cheapest way of doing things and the unshakeable ideals and intentions of Le Corbusier (as in the saga of the aérateur), a number of other patterns may be perceived. There was too little money, too little time, and too little precise practical information from Paris. There was the constant problem of translating from metric to feet and inches and the further difficulty of decoding French: where the nomenclature of Le Corbusier's elements was concerned, the lack of time even led to the incorporation of the original titles in French in the actual specification. At times, too, it was necessary to consult late volumes of the *Oeuvre complète* to clarify a detail; and after the detail was understood it had, where possible, to be designed into a form amenable to American building customs. Naturally Sert's special experience of Le Corbusier's work and American ways was a great help in this phase, but there were some instances of specifically Corbusian devices that the Cambridge architects had not had to unravel before.

An example of this was the roof garden over the Quincy Street studio.[2] Krueger received drawings of the roof garden (figs. 167–170) in July 1961. It was immediately obvious that the designation "time to time one hill" would mean unusual strengthening of the roof in *all* places, since no particular hill sitings were given. Krueger consulted Emil Hervol of Le Messurier associates who agreed that reinforcing must be increased; calculations were therefore made for large loads of soil.

Jullian's section (fig. 168) showed a level slab top that was obviously untenable as it provided no run-off gradient for draining. It might have been a case of simply making slopes in the concrete, but the load on the pilotis supporting the garden was coming close to critical with all the extra weight of reinforcing for hills, so structural necessities had somehow to be put to good use. It then became clear that in the solution for reinforcing the column heads with recessed capitals lay the seed of a solution for drainage. For whereas column heads were buried in the airfloor *inside* the building, on the outside (as on the terrace), a little hump was made at each pilotis top. Krueger and his consultant therefore decided to put this structural profile to drainage use and made contour drawings (½ inch height per contour) using the tops of the humps as an upper datum level. Eventually it proved possible by a sort of geographical ingenuity to mold and sculpt the concrete roof in such a way that water would run off to the drains that had to be run down through the interior in places. Months later, anyone passing the visual arts center on Quincy Street was treated to the sight of Fuller's men on hands and knees patting down the wet concrete to fit the contours into a mini-terrain, as if making sandcastles on the beach.

Le Corbusier's plan of the garden (fig. 167) had shown a concrete terrace "au Modulor." Now Krueger had to face budgetary constraints, cancel the concrete, and put gravel in its stead. This compounded the drainage problem. Most of Sert, Jackson and Gourley's experience with roof gardens at that time had been with large pots, not with great mounds of soil and gravel resting directly on the roof surface. Fortunately the Fogg library job (on the same contract) also required roof terracing and offered the opportunity for experiment. Having consulted various other firms, Krueger decided on a dense asphalt compound for the roofs called "brewery floor" because of its beer resistant qualities in the scuppers and floors of breweries. On top of this, where Jullian had written "béton de protection" ("protective concrete"), he placed a level of fiberglass filter. It so happened that Sert could not remember Le Corbusier's method for insulating (though he did recall that in Mediterranean countries cow dung was sometimes used), so the entire definition of the roof terrace required original research, considerable time, and the advice of about a dozen professionals. Once the thinking was correct, drawings could be prepared, but those required the skill and patience of a cartographer on account of the contours. All these deliberations preceded any consideration of the actual plants to be placed in the garden.

The Building Specification: Contractors and Subcontractors

The building specification for the visual arts center was produced throughout 1961 and into the early part of 1962, some revisions to it occurring in spring 1961 due to the change in the building's size.[3] In all there were thirty-one separate sections under such headings as "concrete work," "pre-cast concrete work," "metal windows," "glass, glazing and glazed doors," "lawns and planting"—technical titles to prosaic texts in which one may recognize the parts and elements of Le Corbusier's Olympian architectural language and his detailed orders for the building. Thus Le Corbusier's invocation that glass should joint directly into concrete without frames becomes translated, in terms of procedure and effect, as:

b) *Glazing into concrete and in aluminium jambs—*
1.) Prime faces of concrete rabbet with Pecora P-53 primer. Surfaces shall be clean and dry before application.
2.) Set inside and outside wedge shaped neoprene shims, 3″ long, approximately 18″ o.c. If glass is less than 18″ provide two spacers.
3.) Set glass in reglet. Provide 80 durometer setting locks at quarter points.
4.) Insert neoprene spacers between glass face and neoprene shims specified above taking care to centre glass in reglet. Spacers and shims shall be 40 to 50 durameter.
5.) Fill rabbet with butyl caulking compound BC 158 as manufactured by Pecora as shown.
6.) Face exterior with head of polysulfide sealant, synthacalk, GC-5, gray, non sagging, soft curing, as manufactured by Pecora.[4]

Each item was let out for competitive bidding and by Christmas 1961 most subcontractors had been chosen, though not all of them had been legally bound; most parts of the building had also been defined in writing from the point of view of manufacture, material, technical and structural procedure in a way similar to the above quotation. However, it was to take till mid-1962 for this hybrid abstraction combining technical jargon and Le Corbusier's ideal architectural drawings to emerge as a fully built concrete structure and till the new year of 1963 for it to be finished and furnished on the interior.

In this period of the building's history, overseeing protagonists included Fuller's men on the site. Their job was to insure that plans and specifications were translated correctly on schedule and that all subcontractors fulfilled their agreed roles. Such orchestration was unusually complicated. Kenneth Leach and Norman Whiting, two of Fuller's managerial staff on the job, have recalled the colossal pressures as, on some occasions, details were rushed to Quincy Street from Sert's office (where a twelve hour a day "charette" was in progress) with minutes to spare before a pour was due to take place.[5] Each contracting job proceeds according to its own laws to some extent, with ad hoc discoveries leading to improvements of method later in the process, and the contractor himself anticipating what further details might be necessary. This seems to have been the case with the visual arts center, though as much preplanning as possible was done.

Leach recalls most clearly the "incomplete drawings" from Paris (he had some of Le Corbusier's "cartoons" on site in his cabin); the battles with cost limits; the demand for the highest possible quality of finish; the "tricky structural concept"; and the unpragmatic nature of some of Le Corbusier's solutions, "particularly the vertical harmonic struts" (ondulatoires).[6] He recognized the extraordinary nature of Le Corbusier's building and characterized the architect as "an unusual man . . . a theoretician . . . not a true practising architect."

By late fall 1961 a huge hole was in existence next to the Fogg Museum and the pouring of foundations had begun (fig. 186). The designs for the foundations had been made by Sert's men with the help of William Le Messurier, the engineering consultant.[7] An unusual solution was adopted to cope with the extremely high water table. In effect, the main body of the building was "floated" (on what is known technically as a "floated" or "reinforced mat" foundation). Thus the basement zone was formed from a sunken concrete "boat" that sealed out water to the sides as well as from below. The pilotis of the center part of the building were cast directly onto the floor of this boat. To counteract the huge upward pressures of water that would seep down beneath the floor, a sump pump was inserted which could release small amounts at a time and thus avert the tendency of the water to break through the relatively thin concrete. Pilotis to the outside extremities of the building came down to earth beyond lateral edges of the foundation, so were cast each with its own massive footing. Deep piles were not used.

Construction

From December onwards there was a race between the recognition of further necessary details that could affect or be affected by the structure and the forming and pouring of the floors. The tangible miracle of the building at last began to rise in Cambridge, but in Paris the pressure of concern seems to have subsided, apart from a few more trans-Atlantic details and points on interior finish. There was an amusing incident at the end of the year when an American architectural magazine published a distended view of the building covered with little speckles, which prompted Le Corbusier's sarcastic characterization, "Façon Corbu à la noix de coco" ("the Corbu coconut style"), but aside from flashes of interest of this kind, the Paris end was quietly anticlimactic.[8] The last stages of the creation of the visual arts center were played out where it began: at Harvard.

By 1962, all excavations had been completed, foundations nearly completed, and a trial casting of a wall, using Masonite forms, made and approved. Glass blocks were chosen for the stair tower, concrete (instead of the more vulnerable and expensive terrazzo) agreed upon for the floors, and by February the first floor was being formed.

On the ground floor a nonstructural column was placed to the southwest corner. Provision was made for an enameled door from the lobby into the semicovered coffee place under the Quincy Street studio. The escape stair from the third floor terrace above Quincy Street was argued away, egress being placed instead from the terrace onto the main ramp. At the third level, glass was projected to cover the entire entrance into the third level studio, which had caused all the difficulties in the design; this dealt with the fire code and cut down the drafts with which the troublesome double doors had been supposed to deal. Skylights were designed with double plastic domes instead of Le Corbusier's original flat glass. But by March little progress had been made forming the structure, on account of the winter storms, and this allowed a little leeway for the details. By March, as the weather improved, the contractors prepared themselves to bridge the auditorium. When the "ponts" ("bridges") of the first project disappeared over a year previously, with the breakthrough to the second building, Le Corbusier designed a system mixing pilotis, two piers, and a single beam running under the first floor ceiling transversally, from the lobby into the auditorium space. This was not a feasible arrangement, so Le Messurier designed a system with three steel beams crossing the auditorium from side to side (longitudinally in terms of the whole building), supported at the ends by a total of six staunch pilotis that lay just beyond the confines of the auditorium: three running up through the basement film facilities to the first floor administrative offices, three in the semicovered space by Quincy Street, running down into the photography section.[9] These beams had to deal with a span of fifty-one feet *and* support a superimposed load of four stories on pilotis at their midpoints. The beams created handy pockets of space for electrical services, but were restricted by a height requirement and the need to see the screens from the lobby. The beams were thus forced to be so shallow that they would bend as successive loads were placed above. Bit by bit, as extra floors were formed, the beam would have bowed, cracking the lower floors which had set.

The solution was to predeflect: that is, to simulate the total load, and keep stress constant by reducing the simulated loads as the real ones were applied. In fact, when the balcony was cut back by the acoustician and the height requirement relaxed, the beams could be made deep enough to avoid bending. But since the expensive anchors of the predeflection mechanism had already been cast into the foundations, the engineers decided to go ahead and experiment. They used a deep beam nonetheless, but lighter, and the experiment proved successful (fig. 187).

This was not the only part of the structure where cracks were a worry. The engineers were afraid that the airfloor would dry the slab too quickly. In order to control the cracking of the concrete topping over the channels, the engineers recommended that a scoring pattern of control joints be made at two feet on center in each direction. When they eventually replied to this suggestion in July, Jullian and Le Corbusier asked that Le Corbusier's scoring system be preserved on some floors.

> Ça serait une bonne leçon pour les étudiants d'Architecture qui se rendront compte de comment se produisent les ruptures (s'il s'en produit?) dans les têtes des poteaux.

> That would be a good lesson for architecture students who would then learn how cracks occur (if they occur?) at the heads of the columns. (7-31-62)

In the absence of a reply, the engineers proceeded with their proposed control joints on most floors.[10]

By the end of April, the weather was clear and it was time to face the problems of the visible, above ground slabs and pilotis (fig. 188). On the average it took about three weeks to cast each floor—a long time given the size of the building—but, as was said before, the construction was not amenable to much standardization and an unusual premium was set on precision finish. The visual arts center, for all its ideological intent of standardization, was strictly a "one-off" building, requiring the highest level of handicraft. The same architect who in the early 1920s had had a studio window custom-made to look like an industrialized, mass-produced factory one,[11] encountered the country whose mass-

187. *One of the three steel beams over the auditorium is lowered into place, March 1962.*

production techniques he had always admired on entirely his own formal terms forty years later: aérateurs had to be specially made, ondulatoires were elaborately precast off site, formwork for walls was reused minimally for fear of staining, and even the Sonotube of the cylindrical pilotis had to be made specially to Le Corbusier's dimensions.

The solutions to structural reinforcing were also highly complex. Le Corbusier's grand absolute, "the key to the solution for reinforced concrete" —the pure slab/piloti idea in its essence—emerges, in the light of conversations with those who had to construct it, as a practical nightmare.[12] Its structural purity and tectonic finesse were illusory and produced tremendous inner sheer. Emil Hervol of William Le Messurier Associates, the engineering consultant, designed an ingenious system of an

188. *Forming the floor of level 3, Prescott Street side, May 1962.*

inverted drop panel over each head as a kind of recessed capital, which extended to about two feet off each column axis (fig. 189). At this point, where panels met airfloor, some cracking was expected, but at least the method insured the smoothness of profile and ninety-degree joint of horizontal and vertical, Le Corbusier's ideal trabeation.

Another general problem of the structural skeleton was the varying cantilever of the curved slabs. In some places steel hangers had to be set into walls to suspend the slab (a solution adopted, for example, over the side entrance). On the curves where walls caused a serious weight problem, the walls themselves could also be made to compensate by being employed as stiffeners.

Hervol has said that the visual arts center job was "not a particularly happy one,"[13] but in saying this he was not referring to the complexities of the structure (which he seems to have regarded as a routine example of architectural muddleheadedness), but to the management problems following from the difficulty of obtaining precise information. Even when floors were about to be cast (the fourth, for example) details for them were sometimes lacking.

He remembered that the job description was made for the building at its reduced size. The use of Le Corbusier's original, larger dimensions led to such great increases in area and moments on cantilevers that the steel necessary for what was after all only a minor visual adjustment amounted to an increase of twenty percent. Also on the subject of the structural skeleton, Hervol recalled a number of interesting collisions between "the simplest way to do the job" and Le Corbusier's architectural philosophy. For example, he suggested an optimal slab thickness in the overhanging areas which Sert disallowed "because of Corbu's blue system or something" (Hervol here means Le Corbusier's blue Modulor scale). And when everyone was confronted with the problem of the auditorium span, Hervol suggested that the span be reduced by the placement of hidden columns in the auditorium's side walls—a suggestion that was greeted with horror by the Cambridge architects who felt it was dishonest and anyway broke the grid. But when Hervol left out the redundant column next to the weight-bearing stair wall to save cost, he was chided: evidently the architects preferred structural dishonesty to breaking the grid.

Even though Le Corbusier was not seeking to adulate American technique in his one building for that country, he did see fit to use the high local standards for a precisely controlled articulation of surfaces impossible at, for example, Chandigarh. His "new stereotomy" for concrete required careful thought on the part of Sert and his partners and an entire, long section of the specification was devoted to concrete work.[14] This covers matters as diverse as conveying, depositing, curing, cold weather requirements, proportions of mixture, reinforcing sizes, formwork, size of aggregate, and time of casting. The aggregate for Le Corbusier's "béton brut lisse" was specified "not larger than one fifth of the narrowest dimension between forms of the member for which the concrete is to be used, nor larger than three-fourths of the minimum clear spacing between reinforcing bars." The usual strict instructions were also given

189. *Prescott Street facade, level 3, showing brise-soleil diagonals sunk and recessed into the floor.*

for mixing the concrete: "The concrete shall be mixed until there is a uniform distribution of the materials and shall be discharged completely before the mixer is re-charged."[15] Concerning formwork and finishes: "ALL CONCRETE FORMS AND FINISHES shall be as determined by the Architect. Many of the decisions will be made only after a suitable combination of form materials and workmanship has been achieved in the form of mockups."[16] These mock-ups had a crucial role in assuring the realization of Le Corbusier's precise intentions for the material he had adopted as his own.

Whereas Hervol saw the visual arts center's concrete in terms of its structural behavior, Tucker of Tucker Concrete (Boston) realized that he had to do with a refined essay in concrete *appearance*.[17] It was his job to design and make the wooden formwork and to supervise, with Fuller's men, the actual pouring. His firm had considerable experience of the material and its various Modern Movement aesthetic usages having worked previously for both José Luis Sert and Walter Gropius. Tucker was fully aware that much of his business relied on Le Corbusier's architectural "rediscovery" of bare concrete at Marseilles in the 1950s and he recognized that the visual arts center was a "major catch" for which he even risked slight financial loss in his bidding.

For him Le Corbusier's building became a test of his firm's craftsmanship. At all moments when pouring occurred he was on site himself checking and rechecking dimensions, insuring that the color of aggregate did not vary, and seeing to it that chipped formwork was discarded to avoid blemishes. Only a limited reuse of formwork was possible because eventually the wood absorbed chemicals from the wet concrete which in turn led to slight changes of color if the same panel were reemployed too often. Every single piece of wood had to be approved by the architect. Sert, Krueger,

190. *Formwork for the Quincy Street curve hoisted into place, April 1962.*

and Tucker took Le Corbusier's Modulor dimensions into every stage of every wall and brise-soleil. And throughout, enormous care was taken with the alignment of linear imprints, especially on the exterior.

Tucker had a remarkably simple and apt characterization of the structural concept: "This building was columns, slabs, and walls" (figs. 188, 194).[18] He recalled that the job was enormously complicated, particularly the brise-soleil (fig. 189), because on them, as on all flat walls, there was a tendency for the inverted Vs that formed the drawn line separating the rectangles to blur and chip. Accordingly some recasts were necessary. Another problem was the varying pilotis sizes. Tucker carried around with him in a pocket notebook a diagram of the pilotis grid for each level with color-coded dots indicating the different grades of the cylinders. Even with this aid some mistakes were made and had to be rectified by recasting. In places, too, the cardboard tubes stuck to the solidified concrete, discoloring them slightly.

In the early spring the spiral steel column reinforcements and long floor reinforcing bars scattered about the site were accompanied by a peculiar construction not unlike a part of a large boat: the time had come to cast the curves (fig. 190).

The genesis of the curves began in April 1960 with Andreini's freehand outline of the Quincy Street studio, which was then repeated diagonally opposite by Le Corbusier in the second project in January 1961. Because these curves were not amenable to a simple mathematical formula, they were laid out according to coordinates in feet and inches.[19] Expecting colossal difficulties in transferring these dimensions into full-scale formwork, Krueger was pleasantly surprised by Tucker's ingenious method of formwork design. A grid was laid out on the floor of a large warehouse to full scale, and the curve was then "plotted." At full size it was found to have some kinks and waves, so Tucker laid out a long length of rubber hose between the points, which he and Krueger than adjusted by an inch or two to give an even though irregular curve. Next, templates were cut to fit the curves. Formwork was then made by Nova Scotia shipbuilders specially taken on for this job. When the forms were precise and correct they were reconstructed on site and hoisted into place (figs. 190, 191). The curves were made from a series of vertical planks laid side to side forming a series of chords sufficiently slender for a pure curve to be the apparent result. To avoid any buckling or movement, strong horizontal stiffeners were applied lengthwise while pouring took place. Slight, scarcely visible buckling occurred in only one place. Thus the curves—always antimechanistic in association—were constructed by pure handicraft methods.

By May, construction had reached the third level. Anyone inspecting the building from adjacent upper level windows looking down on it (figs. 192, 193) was greeted with a completely unprecedented architectural experience: two large curves of equal dimension pulling away from the spine of the ramp, a version, hundreds of times enlarged, of forms discovered a little over a year before in colored crayon on tracing paper in Paris (fig. 134).

191. *Part of the curved formwork for the Prescott Street studio adjacent to the stair tower, May 1962.*

From the ground, meanwhile, the forms in space recalled the presentation drawings (figs. 155–163), composed of overall geometries of solids and voids. As yet, though, there was no S-ramp, no central cube, and no glass (figs. 193, 194).

As the structure continued to rise, its makers turned their thoughts to Le Corbusier's ondulatoires—and, by implication, to the aérateurs composed from vertical concrete struts or bâtis (fig. 195). The subcontractor responsible for these was Cambridge Cement Stone Company, who, immediately on receiving the specification and dimensions, realized the likelihood of bowing and recommended the use of wood.[20] But even if the bâtis posed constructional problems, on the ideal plane of architectural theory they *had* to be in concrete. The difficulty was that a groove of great depth had to be made into one side of each strut to allow room for maneuvering each plate of glass into position; this meant that the reinforcing bars had to be placed asymmetrically, resulting in unequal torsion and eventual bending.

192. *The site viewed from an upper window of the Fogg Museum, April 1962. The building has reached level 2. The bottom of the Quincy Street curve shows to the right.*

193. *The site viewed from the Fogg Museum, May 1962. The building has reached level 3, and both curves are visible (the bottom of the Prescott Street studio to the left, the top of the Quincy Street one to the right).*

The bâtis were cast using a fine aggregate matching in all respects the work already in place, for which Cambridge Cement was also the supplier. Absolute smoothness to match Tucker's was insured by birch ply forms treated with urethane varnish. The struts were then transported to the site and hoisted into place, fixed at the bases, and jointed at the top by means of a galvanized slipped connection allowing play for expansion and contraction. Those bâtis serving as ondulatoires on the Quincy Street curve were then inserted in their respective harmonically proportioned places (fig. 195); the brise-soleil on the other curve, also carefully proportioned, were of course cast in place.

Once the bâtis were fixed, aérateur doors and glass panes (pans-de-verre) had to be inserted. The latter posed special problems, too. A thick and heavy glass was used, requiring the help of large cranes in places. Receiving grooves at lateral edges in concrete were sometimes so large that a compound normally used for cathedral glazing was used to caulk and seal the huge incisions. The glass bricks, meanwhile, presented no particular difficulties.

With four months to go till the September deadline, the construction was cutting very close; a schedule prepared at the end of April envisaged July 13 as the finishing date for the roof. Through June attention focused on the square fourth floor and the ramp curves: by the end of the month an aerial view would almost have given the final outline (fig. 1). The fourth floor was more or less routine; the ramp, however, posed some new questions. The engineers found that the column spacing on Le Corbusier's plans was not adequate structurally at the curves and suggested either the widening of the beam under the ramp at that point or the addition of a column at each curve. The latter solution was approved, so giving Tucker another headache: the joining of a curving beam with the notched top of a piloti. Meanwhile scoring for the ramp surface ("opus optimum au Modulor") was based on the pattern of the ramp of the Mill-owners' Building in India that Le Corbusier instructed Sert to copy from the *Oeuvre complète 1952–1957* (9-6-62). The concrete for the ramp surface was made more textured by the use of a rough aggregate.

With the final forms of the building all but visible (figs. 194, 195, 196), the site received one afternoon an unexpected visitor, who had also involved himself lifelong with the "correct" formal definition of reinforced concrete, but had come out with quite different results from Le Corbusier because he tended to let concrete have more of its own way. Tucker noticed a foreigner inspecting the work who turned out to be Pier Luigi Nervi, the Italian engineer, who had just received an honorary degree from Harvard. "That," said Nervi, "looks like very difficult work."[21]

Interior Finishes, Furnishing, Landscaping

By mid-June, enough had been built for thoughts to return to the subject of interior finishes. Sert did not think the concrete was clean enough to be left bare and recommended the painting of the columns and exposed wall surfaces, "perhaps a light grey keeping the same value as the original concrete colour." He also pointed out that it had been necessary to fatten the brise-soleil fins in the course of construction and that Le Corbusier's attached wooden panels now made the element too thick. He suggested that the contreplaques be removed. Le Corbusier did not approve of this at all, but Jackson explained to him that it was now too late to retract, and that the budget cuts meant that for the moment wood should be left off the brise-soleil (5-30-62; 7-19-62). In May Le Corbusier had agreed to the use of "tempered hardboard," for acoustics so long as it was painted and so long as as much plain, unpainted plywood as possible was used elsewhere. He now retracted his decision, drew a sketch of plywood panels according to the Modulor, and delivered his last imperative letter. Plain plywood must be kept to give smooth plain surfaces on which the light could play.

Très important: retablir le bois contreplaqué chêne uni dans tous les endroits que vous l'avez remplacé par "tempered hardboard."
Pour l'acoustique insister pour la solution des "draperies" indiqué dans les "annotations" de Le Corbusier du 25 Octobre 1961.
Ces draperies ont l'avantage décisif de pouvoir être deplacées (pour chaque draperie) au long d'un *"rideau-rail"* appliqué au plafond ou suspendues à une certaine distance du plafond.
Les tissus de ces draperies doivent être absorbants (pas en laine, à cause des mites).
Ces draperies de belles couleurs pourraient être *violet* intense (si le teinturier peut assurer la durée du coloris). On placerait les draperies momentanement selon les sources accidentelles des bruits (les lieux ou se feront les bruits, métal, bois, pistolets, etc. . . .). C'est là l'avantage des draperies.
Les "tempered hardboard" sont d'une tristesse totale, tandis que les draperies illumineront l'espace.

Very important that uniform oak plywood sheets be reestablished in all places you have replaced it with "tempered hardboard."
For acoustics insist on the solution of "draperies" indicated among Le Corbusier's "annotations" 25 October 1961.
These draperies have the decisive advantage of each being movable along a "curtain rail" attached to the ceiling or suspended a little way from it.
The cloth of these draperies should be absorbent (not wool because of mites).
These draperies, in beautiful colors, could be intense *purple* (if the dyer can assure the fastness of the colors). One would place the draperies here and there to deal with accidental noise sources (places where noises will be made, metal, wood, pistols, etc. . . .). That is the advantage of the draperies.
The "tempered hardboards" are of a total sadness, whereas the draperies will light up the space.[22] (7-18-62)

Le Corbusier saw to it that these points were not just made in a letter. They were illustrated and emphasized in a full set of working drawing prints so that there would be no doubt at all as to his intentions. The set had actually been sent by Krueger in June, marked with a handful of queries on last minute details, and had been copied from the earlier set of finished prints of October 25, 1961. In bold red crayon, with an arrow pointing to the interior paneling on the third level Prescott Street

194. *Detail of the northeast corner, June 1962: the straightforward expression of construction and voids. As Tucker put it, "This building was columns, slabs, and walls."*

curve interior (marked in brown to indicate ply paneling as on the 1961 print), Krueger had written: "changed to tempered hardboard as per accoustical engineer. What color?" The reply was direct. Jullian took a piece of sticky white paper, stuck it firmly in place over the disputed curve, and printed in large black letters: "TRES IMPORTANT, RETABLIR LE BOIS CONTRAPLAQUE COMME INDIQUE DANS LA LETTRE DE LE CORBUSIER" ("*very important*, to reestablish wooden paneling as indicated in the letter of Le Corbusier"). Intense violet curtains were also assertively zigzagged across the studio spaces and a small sketch was included, also by Le Corbusier, of the assorted rainbow colors of the proposed folding partition at ground level. Wherever Jullian made an inscription, he made a purple ink arrow next to it from a rubber stamp so that no point would be missed.

Where paint was to be applied, Le Corbusier insisted again that it be applied directly to the concrete and not onto plaster as Sert's details had indicated. Asked a year earlier for his color choices, he had told Sert to "do the building first," that he might come to Cambridge himself to place the correct hues and values when the formal, planar, and lighting characteristics of the design could be experienced firsthand (7-27-61). In the end, though, he never visited the building, and all his choices were made by mail ("which is much more difficult to do") (7-27-61). In the circumstances, although it may have been more difficult to predict the way colors would look from a trans-Atlantic vantagepoint, it was perhaps easier for Le Corbusier to assert his intentions through the mail. The impression one has from people at the Cambridge end is of something close to panic as each new set of directions arrived from Paris, often contradicting earlier ones.[23] Perhaps out of annoyance over the suggestion for painting columns, he demanded that the slabs too remain unpainted; fortunately for the lighting conditions of the studios, he was too late: the job had already been done. Then he asked for terrazzo on floors again only to *re*-retract and agree on concrete. He instructed that brick be eliminated from the pavement in front of the side entrance, which Sert accepted willingly as a much needed cost cutback, and was told by the acoustic consultants that the folding colored partition

195. *The Quincy Street facade, June 1962. Large openings are filled with Le Corbusier's standard fenestration elements in concrete but are awaiting glass and aérateur doors. The ramp has not yet been cast and the glass bricks have not yet been inserted in the stair tower.*

196. *Prescott Street facade, July 1962. The ramp has reached the bottom of its straight incline, the roof above the fifth level studio is on, and the fire escape is being cast. The early morning light shows that only some of the drain pipes on the brise-soleil have been inserted.*

between lobby and auditorium was impractical and should be eliminated—to which he agreed. He sent designs of concrete benches with leather cushions for the lobby and was told that the rest of the furniture would be built by the students.

Furniture was eventually chosen by Sert and Krueger, however. Here the budget was a paramount consideration, so they turned to catalogues of extremely utilitarian furniture of the kind used by industry, and of the kind Le Corbusier had often praised in earlier years. Indeed, Krueger has since said that the selections were made with the vision of the *Oeuvre complète* in mind.[24]

Late in 1962 yet another set of coloring prints was sent to Cambridge, this time including color choices for the aérateur doors (which repeated the range chosen for walls) and incorporating some last minute dogma on béton brut: "béton brut naturel" was written for ceiling slabs, but, again, Le Corbusier was too late (fig. 197).

One of the plans, that for the south side curved studio, had two little sketches attached to it (fig. 197). To the bottom left was a detailed section of the brise-soleil showing clearly the horizontal part of the element at 1.83 meters. Just inside the fenestration was a giant whose height was marked 6 feet 6 inches. Between the giant and the brise-soleil (on which he seemed in danger of knocking his head), Le Corbusier placed a small railing. To one side he explained that his drawing was of an "American" who had outgrown the Modulor. On the other corner of the sheet he sketched the sun's path in the equinox and the solstice. Typically, his last "drawings" for his American building included a joke about Americans and an Olympian pronouncement on the path of the sun.

In Cambridge, meanwhile, the visual arts center stood apparently complete and empty, an abstract sculpture bathed by thin December sunlight and encrusted with January ice, the roof gardens vacant, the sealer holding the glass still soft. Only the plumbers and electricians entered, inserting essential services in the "ideal" structure. Sleeves had been argued in place for the main services at the working drawing stage, and the insertion of ducts and conduitry, heating and ventilating machinery posed no special problems. Two of the main concentrations were in the basement (a huge machine room) and at the top of the stair tower (containing the cooling equipment for air-conditioning). Services were made a routine matter by a combination of what Krueger has called Le Corbusier's "warehouse aesthetic,"[25] gaps left between plywood paneling and walls, and cupboards constructed to house some of the heating and ventilating machines.

Landscaping was not so straightforward, though. The positioning of the building on the site with Le Corbusier's details for parapets and low walls necessitated steep grading and landscape irregularities in places. Krueger, who was a registered landscape architect, did the drawings for the landscaping with advice from Sasaki Associates on technical details. The most problematic areas were between the building and its neighbors. Thus, in order to make the ramp retain a reasonable gradient, a little hillock was made at the Quincy Street end, and to stick to Le Corbusier's design for the zone around the entrance, an extremely steep bank of soil was created up to the side door of the Faculty Club. Of course the setting of the building had involved considerable burrowing below the grade of the preexisting site in the first place.

Except for the tree just inside the Quincy Street curve of the ramp, verdure close to the building had had to be destroyed to create the basement. On the edges of the site, though, original trees were retained. In other places Krueger chose plants that would not clash with the scale of the building or the surroundings. Evergreens were considered essential to mute the meeting of the Quincy Street curve with the Fogg Museum all the year around and to disguise the hump under the Quincy Street ramp end, which is now set about with a clump of yew bushes. Pathways were set in tarmacadam following Le Corbusier's drawings.

Budgetary pressure allowed the planting of only the Quincy Street roof terrace. For this Krueger followed Le Corbusier's rustic prescriptions quite closely, even going to some lengths to seed the area with wild raspberries. Evidently, though, the architect's taste for a ragged "verdure corniche" ("greenery cornice") did not coincide with the university's tidier, New England pastoralism, and the garden today is carefully trimmed, set about with grass and small sprigs of yew.

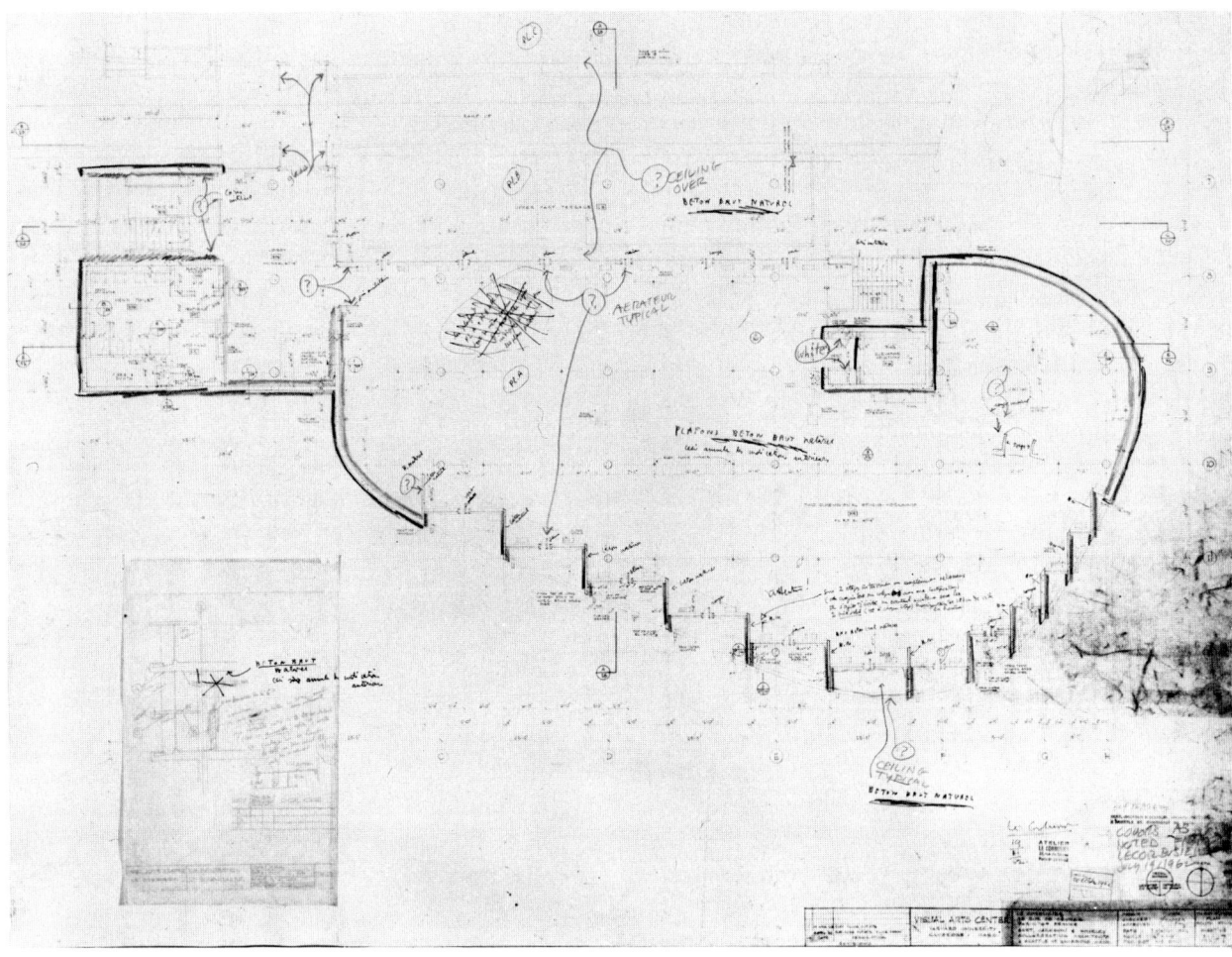

197. *Annotated working drawing of level 3, south studio, Sert, Jackson and Gourley, Le Corbusier, and Jullian. The architect again insists on bare concrete for brise-soleil and ceilings: "Plafond béton brut naturel." To the bottom left is a section of the brise-soleil showing a huge American who has outgrown the Modulor; to the top right in faint pencil is the diagram of the solstices.*

The visual arts center cost more than was originally anticipated. The extra cost was borne by St. Vrain Carpenter and, in a loose sense, by Sert and his subcontractors: as Krueger put it, "nobody made a killing," and nobody had that motive. He suggests that most of the subcontractors bid low deliberately to be involved with a prestige job. They were content if they could break even.

Le Corbusier's Reaction to the Finished Building

February was out of the question for the opening, so the date was moved on to the end of the spring semester in May. Sert wrote in October asking Le Corbusier if he would like to send some material for an exhibition to coincide with the opening, and if he would like to be present himself. With his letter he included photographs of the finished structure. As soon as he received them Le Corbusier wrote back

Mon cher Sert,

Bravo pour le "sabbat"! Veux-tu m'en vendre la moitié?

Donc, tu seras loin au début de février. En janvier, je serai aux Indes pour inaugurer le Parlement. Pourquoi ne serais tu pas là avec Moncha? (mais je vois que tu ne quittes Cambridge que début février!!!). Une inauguration sans toi "est une journee san soleil". Tant pis pour l'inauguration! Nous avons travaillé ensemble, tous deux, avec amitié et efficacité, et le travail semble avoir été bien fait d'après tes photographies. J'aime autant un bâtiment bien fait qu'un bâtiment mal foutu. Mais Marseille est la démonstration que, meme mal fichu, un bâtiment bien pensé peut vivre.

My dear Sert,

Bravo for the "Sabbatical"! Will you sell me half of it?

So you will be away at the beginning of February. In January I shall be in India to inaugurate the Parliament. Why can you not be there with Moncha? (but I see you do not leave Cambridge till the beginning of February!!!). An inauguration without you is a day without sun! Too bad for the inauguration! We have worked together the two of us, in friendship and effectively, and the work seems to have been well done from your photographs. I'd rather have a building well done than a building badly fouled up. But Marseilles is the demonstration that, even fouled up, a building well thought out can live. (10-15-62; appendix 21)

Later he retracted even this complimentary evaluation of the building's execution and stated that the concrete work was "trop stérile" ("too sterile").[26] As for photographs, he requested that construction shots be withheld "even from Boesiger" (editor of the *Oeuvre complète*).

Ce n'est pas la peine de faire pleurer les ânes! Il faut que l'ensemble soit visible, la rue montante, etc. etc. . . .

It isn't worth the trouble to make asses cry! It is necessary that the whole be visible, the climbing street, etc. etc. . . .[27]

And at a later date he instructed that winter shots also be prohibited, obviously wishing that the "ensemble" be known worldwide in the conditions of sun and greenery that had so informed the conceptual genesis of the design.

As to an exhibition: yes, he would agree.[28] But as far as going to Cambridge himself was concerned, he had his doubts:

Impossible d'aller de Chandigarh à Boston et Paris, à mon age, à 10.000 mètres d'altitude, en Boeing, et en quatre ou cinq jours.

Impossible to go from Chandigarh to Boston and Paris at my age at 10,000 meters altitude, in a Boeing, and in four or five days.

He continued ominously:

La vie devient infernale et j'ai quelques choses encore à faire dans mon travail, même en dehors de l'architecture.

Life becomes infernal and I have several things yet to do in my work, even outside of architecture.

And closed strangely:

Mille regrets! Ma lettre est tout ce qu'il y a de vaseuse car il m'est impossible de donner des précisions.

A thousand regrets! My letter is just as hazy as can be for it is impossible for me to be precise. (10-15-62; appendix 21)

At Harvard at the insistence of President Pusey they decided to call the building the Carpenter Center for the Visual Arts instead of the Carpenter Center for Visual Studies, as the Committee for the Practice of the Visual Arts had requested (10-18-62), and in the spring of 1963, exactly three years after the first sketch, Pusey sent Le Corbusier an official invitation to the opening. He promised a "family party" rather than a formal affair "the afternoon of May 27th, and I write to express our earnest hope that you will be able to arrange your schedule in order to be in the United States for this occasion" (4-1-63).²⁹

Le Corbusier wrote back:

Dear Sir,

I have received your friendly letter of the first of April concerning the opening of your Carpenter Center.

My doctor forbids me hurried trips. I am 75 years old (and I still do not yet have crutches!) but I must all the same be careful. I am therefore unable to assure you of my presence on the twenty seventh of May; I regret this keenly.

I pray you to believe . . .

Le Corbusier
(4-5-63; appendix 22)

He did not make it to the opening, and he may have regretted it keenly. He missed the opportunity to meet the protagonists of the building idea (fig. 198) who drank his health, admired his paintings, and splashed champagne on the ramp. The opening of the Parliament Building in Chandigarh, of course, was quite another matter. And although too much should not be made of his failure to attend the opening, it may be seen as emblematic. Time and again India and America came up together; time and again they were opposed—with the aérateurs, with the concrete finishes, with an enamel door for the visual arts center ("I have just done one for Chandigarh free . . . but America is not India"; 5-26-62; appendix 20), in the notebooks, and in the final piece he wrote, a month before his death,

India:
Chandigarh: possible contact with the essential delights of Hindu philosophy; fraternity between the cosmos and living beings: stars, all of nature, sacred animals, birds, monkeys and cows, and in the village, the children and the adults, and the still active old people, the pond and the mangroves, everything has an absolute presence and smiles; everything is miserably poor but well proportioned.

America:
U.S.A. In New York 15 million inhabitants, the horror of an affluent society without aim or reason. On Long Island, my friend Nivola, son of a mason, cultivates vegetables between blank space determining walls. U.S.A.: the women, psychoanalysis everywhere, act without resonance, without goal. Days passed without sequel, except to go through them. People work for twenty four hours, without forecasts of the future, without wisdom, without any plans, without meaningful stages. New York! This city is atrocious towering into the sky, hairy, lacking courtesy, every man for himself . . . ³⁰

As Le Corbusier flew away from New York after the first presentation of the visual arts center in June 1960, he looked down from the window of his Boeing. Far below he could see the island of Manhattan, sinking into the haze—that "fairy catastrophe" that had raised his hopes but dashed them. And as his eyes passed over the avenues one by one, crossed Central Park and wove among the skyscrapers, they settled on the recent steel and glass prisms.

Les modernes, les après l'UN, lisse, nettes, triste, bête, énorme, nue . . . gigantesque et multiplié d'ésprit vide. Ce gens qui ne sentent rien ils vivent "moderne", une vie abrutissant.

The modern ones, the post UN, smooth, neat sad, stupid, enormous, naked . . . gigantic and multiplied of empty spirit. This people who feel nothing, they live "modern," a beastly life.³¹

This tiny fragment of experience, captured in Le Corbusier's notebook, is resonant with a history of personal disappointment and is a fitting place for this chronicle to close. For if this building is Harvard University's Carpenter Center for the Visual Arts, it is also the symbol of one man's relationship with a continent. In an uncanny way the architect's experience at the airplane window recalls his first experience of the United States in 1935 when he stood at the rail of his ship in a different frame of mind, amazed and inspired by the approaching vision of Manhattan rising into the early morning light. In his few months in New York the artist's dream of "the city of the new times" was touched by external reality to an unprecedented degree. The Americans had all the tools and the technical ingenuity at their disposal: the frame-constructed skyscrapers, the freeways on stilts, the parkways, the factories for mass production; here, of all places, the "radiant city" dream seemed a real possibility. But Le Corbusier's ideas were not accepted and even the opportunity of the United Nations building (a fragment of the radiant city in that it was a skyscraper surrounded by greenery) was wrested from him.

Looking down on Manhattan from his airplane, Le Corbusier must have felt disillusioned at the sight of mechanistic chaos and horror beneath him, which to him undoubtedly betokened a machine-age society gone mad. For, I feel sure, he *did* essentially see his role towards America as a "savior" and "redeemer," those terms he had used in an exasperated letter to Sert—as the provider of the guiding hand, who could usher in the promised land of the "deuxième ère machiniste" ("second machine age") using the equipment of the first machine age which in the United States was so abundant (6-25-29; appendix 7). If one recognizes Le Corbusier's role as self-appointed urbanist/utopian, the way is then open, I believe, to an understanding of the meaning of his one American building as an urbanistic, reformist message couched in symbolic form.

198. *Champagne on the ramp at the building's opening, May 27, 1963. Left to right: first person unidentified, President Nathan Pusey, Mrs. St. Vrain Carpenter, Mr. St. Vrain Carpenter, Dean José Luis Sert, Mrs. Sert. "I think of this building as opening the door of future and present enjoyment to those who pass lightly through" (St. Vrain Carpenter, April 15, 1960).*

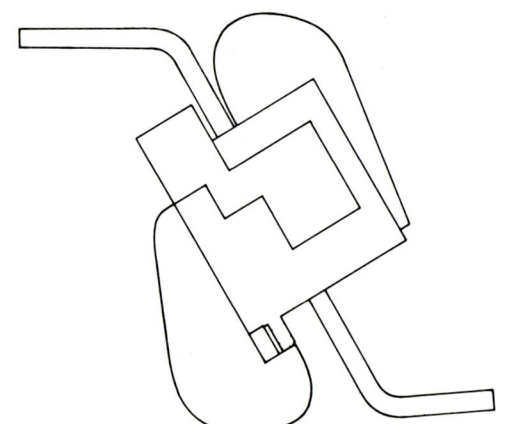

11. THE IMAGE AND IDEA OF THE BUILDING

The events of history are never mere phenomena but things which the historian looks, not at, but through to discern the thought within them.

R. G. Collingwood

A central aim of this account of Le Corbusier's Carpenter Center has been to trace the process of decisions, actions, thoughts, images, and accidents leading up to the creation and construction of the building in its final form. Analysis of this process has necessarily involved investigation of the values behind the program and the reasons for choosing Le Corbusier as architect. Drawings and documents have indicated the architect's method of conceptualizing then solving the many practical and aesthetic problems of an architectural task and may even have revealed typical planning strategies and studio methods. Certainly, they have made it possible to observe the architect's principles, architectural language, and instinctive sense of form in action.

The drawings also bring us closer to the patterns of thought and imagery of a great architectural mind. They may be thought of as ciphers to a rich mental world of informing ideas. They offer vital clues to the artist's intentions, to the meaning of this building, and to Le Corbusier's way of structuring his ideas in form.

Le Corbusier's architecture involved the use and

reuse of standard elements in new contexts, and it is this, in part, which lends consistency to his oeuvre. The elements of the Carpenter Center and its overall forms are deeply rooted in the artist's earlier solutions and in his experience of nature and artistic tradition. But it would be wrong to see the building as a mechanical reassemblage of old Le Corbusier bits stuck together to house this program and to fit this site. Rather, the architect's formulae were transcended and vitalized by intentions and emotions unique to this case. The authenticity of the result resides in part in Le Corbusier's ability to respond to the mythical dimensions of the problem: cliché is avoided because of the artist's sense of form, but also because the form embodies metaphors attuned to Le Corbusier's sense of the building as his one American demonstration. Part of the artist's task was to dig deep into the private fund of imagery, then to abstract these images in an evolving building system of standard solutions.

Typical of this situation is the case of the ramp. In part a response to the client's stipulation that the new center should encourage the other departments of the university to pass through, it seems also to have referred to Le Corbusier's experience of the students passing along the paths of the Yard, to have matched his intention of providing a "promenade architecturale" showcase of his elements, and to have accommodated the combined metaphor of American freeway and S-shaped cosmogram. Many levels of meaning were thus coded into old forms arranged in a new configuration.

Le Corbusier's method for finding the core concepts of a design—intensive unconscious gestation in his "little machine" prior to the production of the first sketch—may be held in part responsible for such a successful fusion of ideas, functions, and forms, of a priori solutions and freshly observed phenomena—the discovery of the "laws" of the particular project. When reviewing the meaning of the finished building one is obviously concerned with kernel concepts which lived all the way through and with those secondary laws that found their way into the project at some later stage of design. An example of the first kind might be the ramp idea or the symbolism of the overall forms, which do not seem to have altered in the change from the first project to the second. An example of the second kind would be the switch to well-tried reinforced concrete fenestration "éléments-type" in the second project, from an experimental attempt, no less demonstrative and polemical, to incorporate a new combination of vocabulary employing aluminum, in the first.

But the primary intention seems not to have changed. This intention was, as the *Oeuvre complète* suggests, to make a demonstration of Le Corbusier's guiding theories, incorporating many of his inventions.[1] Carpenter Center ushered from a retrospective state of mind. The American problem seems to have drawn forth a synthesis of Le Corbusier's architectural, urbanistic, and artistic themes.

A Demonstration in Reinforced Concrete

The evidence is conclusive that the building was intended as a sort of summa of what Le Corbusier felt were the correct elements for reinforced concrete. He went to great pains to insure the exact and correct expression of these elements and even told Jullian that he wanted to make a demonstration of all his principles in one building: it was to be an inclusive polemic.[2] Carpenter Center is remarkable for containing pilotis of various sizes, smooth slabs, walls, pans-de-verre, ondulatoires, aérateurs, roof gardens, and ramp—each of them his specific and quintessential solutions to particular problems of support, lighting, ventilation, circulation, and so on. The building is also remarkable for the clear way in which each of these elements is demonstrated for its specific potentials and its various possibilities of interrelationship with the others.

With the help of Turner's insights on the early formation of Le Corbusier's ideas, it has been possible to recreate something of the theoretical framework of these elements.[3] This seems to blend idealist thinking with a species of rationalism. Le Corbusier appears to have believed in something like Plato's universe of "forms" and "ideas" for architectural elements, as if there existed an ideal set of "function-ideas" for which one and only one material formal expression should exist.[4] Moreover, these forms should (following the tenets of Viollet-Le-Duc and, to some extent, Perret) be rooted in the specific characteristics and structural potentials of the material employed.

The material for which Le Corbusier was trying to find the quintessential forms was reinforced concrete. Concrete can take many forms, but to Le Corbusier the trabeated skeleton with slabs extending into the surroundings was the prototypical expression. "C'est la clef de la solution de béton armé" ("It is the key to the solution of reinforced concrete") was his verdict on the Carpenter Center skeleton.[5] And the other elements fitting into that skeleton were each in turn regarded as the "key" to the separate parts of a concrete system.

When the discrete parts of Le Corbusier's language of elements had been defined, they still needed relating to each other. Certain classes of relationship in any building using the language would arise from the plan shapes and such factors as orientation to the sun and interior use. Other classes of relationship were "grammatically" conditioned by abstract laws of his structurally based system. I am referring to the fact that Carpenter Center represents a mature extension of the premises of his earlier "five points of a new architecture": the piloti, the roof terrace, the free plan, the free facade, and the long window. The building relies on these principles but also demonstrates their spatial and sculptural potentials. At the same time it updates the earlier system by including the pan-de-verre, the ondulatoire, the aérateur, the brise-soleil, and béton brut. In turn the system rests on Le Corbusier's seminal discovery, the Dom-Ino skeleton of 1914.[6]

Thus Carpenter Center represents another step in Le Corbusier's quest for an authentic, modern architectural language based on reinforced concrete in which technique was to be raised to the level of "construction spirituelle" ("spiritual construction").[7] The Modulor was a help in this transcending process as it was able to provide an ideal set of proportions and dimensions. For Le Corbusier, as for the Renaissance architect, elements of individual symbolic significance had to be composed not merely through personal aesthetic taste, nor simply by reference to utilitarian demands, but in response to an ordering framework of prescribed mathematical relationships. The Modulor could simultaneously combine such Corbusian concerns as human scale, "scientific" laws of perception, the golden section, musical ratios, and an ideology of harmonic standardization for the machine age.

As well as the idea and form, the finish of the *éléments-types* was crucial in this building. Clearly it was one of the architect's intentions to leave behind him a demonstration of how the "Le Corbusier vocabulary" *should* be done—a corpus of "correct" usages. This aim involved battles against budgetary constraints, against the attempted reductions in size, and against pragmatic suggestions like that for wooden ondulatoires. Yet, the essay was completed in almost all respects as the creator wanted it done. At Carpenter Center we have the detailed prescriptions of a man who invented his own vocabulary, employed it over a lifetime, and extended it into various tasks and modes of aesthetic expression to refine it towards the end.

In a wider context, the elements of Carpenter Center—the Le Corbusier grammar and language—constituted an attempt at recreating the certainties of, say, the classical orders. The various parts have the status almost of natural facts—unobtrusive, with a quiet beauty and sense of inevitability. It is not hard to forget that they were inventions—"pure creations of the mind." Yet the mind to which they provide a partial index was dissatisfied with anything less than universal aspirations.

Carpenter Center as Urbanistic Metaphor

A further theme that has endured throughout the design history concerns the symbolism of the overall forms: in particular, the meaning of the plan shapes. The grammar and language of elements just discussed provide the means through which the image at the heart of the design is made visible, but this image is generated by the shape of the plan. I have suggested already that fixing a plan involved more for Le Corbusier than just organizing local functional problems or inviting in old forms: it also involved the projection of ideas and the crystallization of appropriate metaphors. Fixing a plan was "to have had ideas," to register "the impulse of an intention," to create an abstraction "containing an enormous quantity of ideas."[8] A plan would thus become an ideogram rich in symbolic qualities.

Chief among the ideas of the Carpenter Center may have been one of his central "idées directrices" and one he felt to be particularly relevant to the United States, that of the ideal city, the "ville radieuse." My suggestion has been that the primary forms of VAC BOS can be correctly read on one level as an urbanistic metaphor. The switch from the first to the second project in no way alters the thrust of the argument that: the S-ramp is a mixed metaphor for the harmonizing of machine civilization with the sun's rhythms and for the freed circulation of the radiant city; that the "cube" at the center refers to the built parts of the city; that the freehand curves bearing the side roof gardens refer to countryside brought to the heart of the city; that the combination of these symbolic shapes in this context refers to the principles of Le Corbusier's urbanism, epitomized in his ville radieuse polemics towards the United States.

The detailed arguments for this symbolic interpretation have been presented earlier in connection with Le Corbusier's trip to the United States of 1935. Here let me reiterate that it was America of all places he felt was capable, through its machinery and tools, of creating the ideal city, and that most of his dialogue with the U.S.A. in the post war period still engaged, above all other problems, that of the high density urbanism according to radiant city principles as a counterforce to the "socially disastrous" suburbs. For Le Corbusier this was a matter of pressing priority: to the incorrectly planned city he traced many of the ills of American society.

The corollary was that the right plan could, and would, promote the "good" society, and in this Le Corbusier was not innocent of determinist thinking. "Cities of hope and hopeless cities at the same time" had been his verdict on the metropolitan areas of the United States in 1935, and hope lay in the combination of indigenous technical ingenuity with the correct formal and conceptual guidance that Le Corbusier felt able to provide.[9] I would find it strange if the architect had failed, in what he had decided would be his one American opportunity, to refer to that missionary urbanistic quest that had occupied so much of his attention toward the United States till that moment. But "the small commission from such a large country" forced him to make his point once removed, so to speak, in the realm of symbolism. There is poignancy to his achievement in metaphor of what he had aspired to in fact: the introduction of the parkway to the center of the American city grid and the application of the controlling rule of the daily solar rhythms.[10]

The Synthesis of the Major Arts

Nor does reference to his ideal city attune oddly with the purposes of Carpenter Center as Le Corbusier understood them. Harmonious urbanism and the integration of the arts with each other and society through the unification of painting, sculpture, architecture, and town planning were overlapping themes in his utopian vision. The program of the building corresponded, as the *Oeuvre complète* says, to "the most important social goal of Le Corbusier": this was an architect for whom the arts should play, ideally, a quasisacral role in social life. Seeking a suitable framework for this high vision, he seems to have found it in the wedding of the "synthèse des arts majeurs" and the ideal city, both of them directed, in the final analysis, to the creation of the ideal society in the ideal physical setting: the city as a work of art.

So integrated are these themes that it becomes difficult to say where one leaves off and the other begins. If the building is an architectural demonstration, it is also an urbanistic one—but when does it cease to be these things and begin to become a sculpture? And as has been suggested already, the forms of Carpenter Center are rooted utterly in Le Corbusier's experiments as a painter: how right the client had been in his introductory letter to the architect when the suggestion was made that the project would be specially interesting to Le Corbusier in his capacities as architect, painter, and sculptor (4-23-59; appendix 4).

Simply as architecture, Carpenter Center is a demonstration of doctrine. To wander over the building with *Vers une architecture* in hand is to realize how thoroughly the emergent talent of the twenties could anticipate his life's work and a building completed forty years later. The three reminders to architects (mass, surface, plan), the claim for inherently beautiful primary forms, the definition of architecture as emotive sculpture in light, the plea for proportion and for an architecture rooted in the concerns of the modern epoch—in so many ways Carpenter Center bears the stamp of the architect's theoretical concerns. So, to some extent, do all his buildings, but the richness of expression and self-conscious clarity of presentation are surely exceptional in this case.

As sculpture Carpenter Center is resonant with many of the major movements of the twentieth century; so, too, as painting, but the plastic qualities of the building must be regarded as outstanding, even in the oeuvre of an architect whose architectural premises were so implicitly *sculptural,* who could compare himself across time with Phidias and Michelangelo. On another level, that of the Modulor, Carpenter Center might also be said to include music—at least the kinesthetic rhythms and harmonic intervals of that art. Had the original idea for electronic emissions of sound been incorporated, the "synthèse des arts majeurs" would have been complete.

An Emblem for "Idées Directrices"

It must be clear that Le Corbusier chose to do a great deal with his one American building, on the little site on Quincy Street. Perhaps he would have chosen some other opportunity to produce a personal emblem of such inclusiveness. We cannot know. The fact is that the combination of Harvard's program and of Le Corbusier's age and attitude toward the United States happily coincided with the request from Harvard University for an arts center which arrived neither too late—nor too soon.

A demonstration of formal basics, of architectural principles, of a supposed universal language of elements, a codification of urbanistic doctrine and cultural idealism concerning the unity and harmony of the arts—Carpenter Center seems to be all of these things. For Le Corbusier these were related themes and thoroughly interdependent ones. They were important matters to him because they had a central bearing on a question he continually posed, "How to live?" It was a question of ethical as well as aesthetic dimensions, which he tried to answer by a quest for architectural certainties. It involved him continually in a battle of opposites, and VAC BOS contains many of them in a state of dynamic synthesis—artificial and natural, city and country, thought and feeling, rectangular and curved, material and ideal—disparate forces in his makeup which he aimed to contain in harmony.

Le Corbusier was an innovator but he was also a traditionalist. Obsessed with the notion of a spirit of the times, he invested his utopian aspirations with anticipation of the future, but was no less concerned to enter dialogue with the architectural statements of the past. The architecture towards which *Vers une architecture* was directed was an architecture whose principles were to extend fundamentals of the art.

At Carpenter Center one recognizes the resonance across time of old ideas—the rule of geometry, the city of the sun, the ideal balance of natural and man-made. Surely, too, in those colored crayon "ciphers" which are the plans and aerial views of the visual arts center and in the olympian detachment of the artist high up in his airplane one can glimpse the specter of an ancient attitude: the idea of the architect as a sort of philosopher-king, who intuits then reveals the model of the ideal state by painting it on a bare canvas: Plato's "painter of constitutions"[11] whose city form reflects "the law" and "the truth" in its plan.

INTERPRETATION AND EVALUATION

Eduard F. Sekler
Rudolph Arnheim
Barbara Norfleet

THE CARPENTER CENTER IN LE CORBUSIER'S OEUVRE: AN ASSESSMENT

Eduard F. Sekler

C'est une ouverture sur demain.

Le Corbusier about the Carpenter Center

The crucial period of planning for the Carpenter Center—from late 1959 through early 1961—coincides with the middle of the last decade of Le Corbusier's creative activity. At the beginning of these ten years the physiognomy of his architecture had been delineated unmistakably by a series of works that upon completion attracted worldwide attention: Ronchamp, the High Court in Chandigarh, the Shodhan, Sarabhai and Jaoul houses. During the following years, immediately preceding the planning of the Carpenter Center, the Millowners' Building in Ahmedabad and the Secretariat in Chandigarh were finished and La Tourette was planned and built, as were the museums in Ahmedabad and Tokyo, and the Brazilian Pavilion in the Cité Universitaire in Paris.

These works by Le Corbusier should be seen in the context of their period which, on the whole, was one of optimism and, as far as architecture was concerned, apparently one of fulfillment and triumph for the Modern Movement, even if some signs of incipient change were recognizable. In the field of housing, Roehampton, Park Hill Sheffield, and the Halen Estate, each in its way, seemed promising steps in a right direction—and each owed something to Le Corbusier. Late works by "old masters" of the Modern Movement—Seagram Building, Guggenheim Museum, United States Embassy in Athens—were still being produced and discussed, while a group of younger men such as Philip Johnson, Paul Rudolph, Eero Saarinen, and their peers aimed to broaden the restrictive canons of Modern Movement orthodoxy by engaging in formal and formalistic explorations in many directions. At the same time Louis Kahn's University of Pennsylvania Medical Research Building made its strong impact, as did the first major works of Kenzo Tange.

But the strongest indications of momentous changes to come originated from small, organized avant-garde groups such as the Japanese Metabolists, the English Archigram group, and above all Team 10, a group of determined younger members of CIAM who had been entrusted with its reorganization and instead destroyed it. The reasons for such action were personal and ideological differences between two generations. Le Corbusier belonged to the older generation, but to those in search of new beginnings he, in his later works, still had most to offer; Team 10 after all included a number of architects who originally had worked in his studio.

During the decade under discussion Le Corbusier was justified in considering himself an admired world leader in architecture. He must have felt more than ever the obligation to remain both innovative and exemplary. Consequently he was faced with a double problem in his studio: on the one hand he had to shun a design routine that would lead to unduly repetitive, predictable results; on the other hand the validity of his earlier architectural solutions had to be reaffirmed.

The consequence was a striving to extract new formal and spatial results from a vocabulary that had started evolving as far back as 1914 and that was informed by strong convictions about the "correct" treatment of most of the key constituents of architecture, convictions that made it possible for forms to become in his mind typical, if not archetypal, formulations.

Self-quotations, often modified from earlier unbuilt projects or from nonarchitectural works, fitted well into this pattern. They were as much corroborations as references for a man who, once he had discovered the "axis" of his existence, consciously aimed to shape life and work together as a consistent demonstration of method—a method that enabled him to utilize previous experience in an orderly fashion without detriment to the freedom of new intuitive synthesis.

If we wish to view the Carpenter Center as a typical result or even demonstration of Le Corbusier's creative method, we must first attempt to understand this method. Some of its tenets can be established clearly from his writings:[1] for example his "rationalism" in classifying the components of a problem in order to arrive at a "correct" formulation that already implied a solution. It is less easy to unravel his method for arriving at visual "solutions" because like many artists he did not care or was unable to reveal fully what went on in the private world of the studio, where he followed the self-imposed rules of his "game." But he has given sufficient indications concerning two fundamental matters: that he regarded his architecture and painting as strictly interdependent and governed by the same underlying geometrical order, and that he felt it was desirable to take up the same visual motif more than once in order to explore it fully.

That Le Corbusier should have relied on an interaction of forms between painting and architecture should not come as a surprise in an artist who, ever since his student days, was convinced of the existence of something like a general morphology of art and nature.[2] One of his paintings from 1945 carries the telltale title *The islands are bodies of women half immersed who hold boats in their arms,* and it was entirely in keeping with his way of looking at the world that he compared the forms of man and his habitation to trees and stones, rivers, and clouds, not unlike Rodin, who stated: "When I have a beautiful woman's body as a model, the drawings I make also give me pictures of insects, birds and fishes . . . A woman, a mountain, or a horse are formed according to the same principles."[3] Moreover, Le Corbusier on several occasions spoke of painting as his most direct access to that poetry of life that he conceived as the aim and justification of existence; during his liberating dialogue with the canvas, so he seemed to feel, he was closest to the roots of his creativity. If one tries to understand Le Corbusier's architecture, one cannot ignore such convictions as are summed up in the following statements:[4]

> Je pense que si l'on accorde quelque signification à mon oeuvre d'architecte, c'est à ce labeur secret qu'il faut en attribuer la valeur profonde. (1948)
>
> I think if one accords some significance to my work as an architect, one must attribute its profound value to this secret labor [painting].
>
> Je n'ai jamais cessé de dessiner et de peindre cherchant, où je pouvais les trouver, les secrets de la forme. Il ne faut pas chercher ailleurs la clef de mes travaux et de mes recherches. (1965)
>
> I have never ceased to draw and to paint, searching for the secrets of form where I could find them. One must not search elsewhere for the key to my labors and to my research.

But the "key" suggested by Le Corbusier is not one that can be grasped easily, and the analysis of relations between his painting and architecture raises questions about parallelism of stylistic change and transferences of form and compositional method between the media. It is obvious that Le Corbusier did not design the visual arts center or any other building by a process of piecing together forms consciously lifted from his own paintings—though, once he had decided on a curved outline, suitable curve segments from a painting might well be utilized. Yet he must have been so thoroughly imbued with a vocabulary of shapes derived from his own paintings and drawings that he could not help but produce intuitively forms directly related to those in the paintings. The importance of outlines in his work is corroborated by his own statement: "To him it is the outline of things which explains their volume."[5] It is also indicative of his feeling for the overriding importance of form as the common denominator that he never hesitated to exhibit black and white photographs of both his buildings and his paintings side by side.

In fact, through pictorial juxtapositions in books and exhibitions Le Corbusier often gave direct hints about the way in which he himself saw the connection of his paintings and architectural works, usually beginning with paintings from the Purist period. "Those were years of extreme intensity," he remarked in retrospect, "during which, with very simple themes (the La Roche house and other houses, or bottles and glasses on canvases) I tried passionately to find certitudes."[6] In order to understand the design of the Carpenter Center as fully as possible it will be useful to try to find out what "certitudes" Purism can provide.

The Purist paintings[7] of Jeanneret (Le Corbusier's family name, which he used to sign his paintings and drawings before 1928) were renditions of a deliberately limited selection of constituent elements: objects of daily use, carefully arranged so as to display their most telling formal aspects, preferably in outline. They had been chosen partly as a matter of tradition—Cubist tradition—and partly for theoretical and polemical reasons explained in the writings that accompanied the Purist production. They were preferred because they were "objets-types" ennobled and familiarized through daily human use and often mass-produced by the machine.

These objects—glasses, bottles, pitchers, books, and musical instruments, among other things—frequently viewed from a very elevated vantage point in a kind of bird's eye view, formed the objective points of departure for sophisticated compositions, disciplined by an underlying system of geometrical order. Distortion, modeling, and textural effects were avoided or reduced to a minimum. Realistic perspective and lighting were eschewed in favor of a mixture of isometric and orthogonal projections evenly and flatly lit and built up in overlapping layers. The limited gamut of color included mostly hues flattened or muted into pastel shades by an admixture of dark or light grays, although after 1925 stronger unbroken hues also appear. One can speak of a tendency to flatten out and to geometrize, but on the other hand one can equally note the use of strong contrasts both in form and color, such as crowding versus emptiness, curves versus straight lines, dark versus light, cold versus warm color.

231

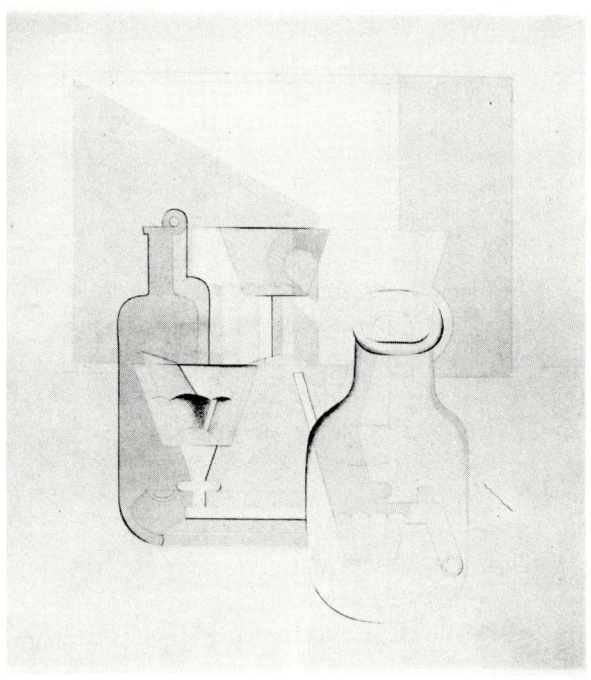

199. *Nature morte aux bouteilles et verres, water color, 1922. Typical Purist composition stressing lightness, transparency, and visual ambiguity. The device of shared outlines is amply used. A stemmed faceted glass is visible in front of a dark bottle.*

Much is made of visual ambiguity as a source of pictorial tension and of dematerialization: shared contours between contiguous forms, misleading alignments, overlappings with ensuing figure–ground relationships all occur together with transparency in all its manifestations. There is an ample use of virtual, pictorial transparency, as well as a wealth of actual transparency pertaining to the depicted objects, such as glass containers half filled with liquid; sometimes there is a bewildering variety of optical effects of refraction (creating dislocation of contours) and reflection, and some works abound with so much transparency that they appear almost insubstantial (fig. 199).[8] If one is willing to make a considerable effort and is sufficiently familiar with Purist works and with their naturalistic preparatory sketches, one can unravel all objective points of departure in these works where familiar objects may undergo strange changes through dislocation, elision, inversion, and continued modification in the direction of sign-like simplicity. Despite the striving for precision and clarity of outline, a conscious hermeticism prevails.

Correspondences between painting and architecture begin to emerge very soon in Le Corbusier's architecture from the early twenties. However it was only around the middle of the decade that, according to his own judgement, he arrived for the first time at a complete integration of forms from painting into his architecture. As he put it:

> En 1925, l'étape était franchie. Entre les formes architecturales, nées du béton armé et de ses adjuvents, et celles de sa peinture, la simultanéité est alors complète. L'esprit des formes anime ses tableaux comme son architecture, et même son urbanisme.[9]

> In 1925 the stage [of development] was over. Between the architectural forms, born from reinforced concrete and its adjuvants, and those of his painting, simultaneity is now complete. The spirit of form animates his paintings like his architecture, and even his urbanism.

Like the paintings the resulting architecture, culminating in the paradigmatic villas—Stein at Garches, Savoye at Poissy—is also based on a deliberately limited selection of constituent elements; in this case standard architectural elements and components such as the piloti and the ribbon window metaphorically take the place of "objets-types." The overall composition is often contained within a simple geometric form and disciplined by geometric order, but there are strong contrasts within the unifying framework—contrasts between volume and void, narrow corridors and spacious rooms, dark areas and dramatically lit ones, straight and curved forms. The architect usually draws at least one isometric or perspective view of his building seen from the same high vantage point that is typical for Purist still lifes.

In this architecture, textural effects are avoided in favor of a unifying smoothness, and colors used in the buildings resemble those found in the paintings. Plans may recall configurations of outlines from Purist drawings; this is strikingly true, for example, in the case of the top floor of the Villa Savoye in the first version of the design (1929), a composition that relies very much on the interaction of straight lines and curves (fig. 211). One

room, at the corner between boudoir and bureau, has a curving wall whose combination of different curvatures and straight segments in plan appears like an early precursor of the free-form curves in the Carpenter Center.

While formal and semantic considerations (such as nautical allusions) were of overriding importance in the creation of the curved elements atop the Villa Savoye, the architect nevertheless felt the need to justify them on rational grounds. He wrote: "les formes courbes résistent à la poussée des vents et apportent un élément architectural très riche"[10] ("the curved forms resist wind pressure and contribute a very rich architectural element"). It would be too simplistic to classify the statement about resistance to wind pressure just as a post-factum rationalization; rather, as on many other occasions,

200. Nature morte aux nombreux objets, Indépendants, *oil on canvas, 1923. The many elements of this elaborate Purist composition include two superimposed stemmed glasses close to the right margin in the lower half of the painting.*

233

201. Nature morte de l'Esprit Nouveau, *linecut, 1924. A pair of superimposed stemmed glasses comparable to those in figure 200 is shown in a prominent central position in the upper third of the composition.*

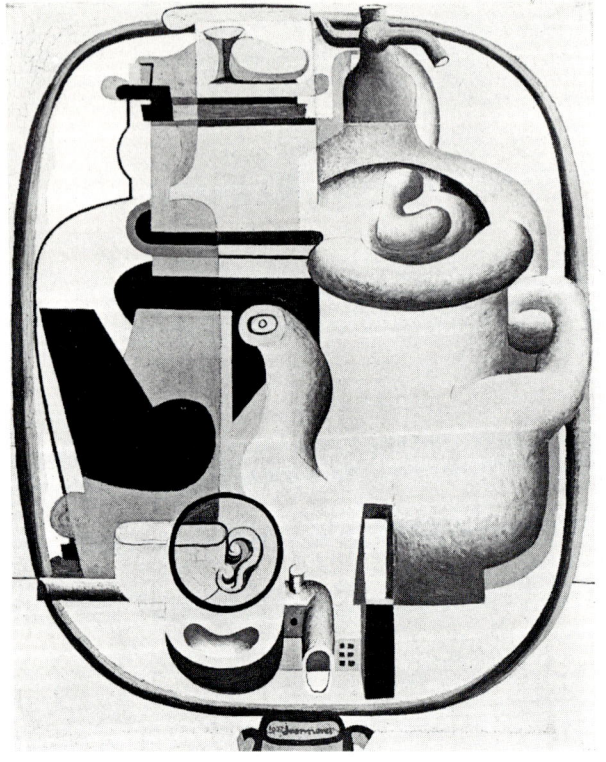

202. Nature morte, *oil on canvas, 1927. The pictorial handling of two coffee pots and a siphon bottle on an oval table indicates a change in Jeanneret's style. The artist now is interested in nongeometric forms, complex modeling, and the sensuous qualities of color and texture.*

we have here a typical instance of two levels of thinking about a design which the architect was aiming to synthesize: one dealing with rational, the other with visual aspects. In this manner it was possible for the visual form to become symbolic of, among other things, engineering rationality; the designer could consider it an authentic form because, in the framework of his thought, its symbolic claim was capable of practical validation.

Flat or curved planes in this architecture often appear insubstantial or screenlike because their thin section is revealed; an effect of extreme lightness is also achieved by the use of very slender supports both under the building itself and under built-in table-slabs, which appear almost to hover. At the Villa Savoye the staircase is a real tour-de-force in the way it seems to hang from a thread—a thin black steel tube. Effects of transparency and reflection further help to dematerialize the bulk of the building.[11] Naturally they also create ambiguities that may be compared to those in the paintings. In the floor-to-ceiling faceted envelope of glass on the ground floor of the Villa Savoye, the surrounding landscape is mirrored and distorted while fragments of the interior may be seen; the total effect is one of dematerialization in contrast to the clearly defined volume of the second floor. But with all its clear definition by outline, the second floor too is rich in ambiguities due to transparency: there are glazed and unglazed openings that make it possible to look through the building from one end to the other and beyond, and one is led to wonder what is "inside" and what is "outside." The aligned bottles and glasses with shared contours in Purist paintings made it equally difficult to determine their exact spatial locations. But Purist painting had come to an end by the time the Villa Savoye was being designed.

In 1927, the year of the League of Nations competition, a distinctive change of style became noticeable in Jeanneret's paintings. An interest in organic forms and in the sensuous qualities of color, texture, and complex modeling is characteristic for the artist's new direction. It is well exemplified in his *Nature morte* with two coffeepots and a siphon-bottle (fig. 202).[12] Even the selection and presentation of these objects is indicative of change: two objects with very complicated outlines are made the central feature and are presented on an oval rather than a straight table, thus making for a complex total interaction of curves. The prevailing hues are very different from those found in such paintings of the previous year as *Le dé violet* or *Table bouteille et livre*[13] and the total effect is muted, almost somber. There is much reliance on modeling through shading, with color applied so as to achieve a textural effect. Where paintings from the previous years had succeeded to bestow on familiar household objects a machinelike geometric, abstract character and a certain flat insubstantiality, this work almost manages to impart to a coffeepot the sensuous qualities of organic form, as if it were not a machine-made object but a very substantial product of natural growth.

It comes as no surprise to find that in paintings from the next year, 1928, the soft, richly molded forms of heavy gloves are introduced in a prominent position[14] and female figures begin to appear on the canvases. They are heavily modeled and clearly invite comparison with some of Picasso's post-1920 compositions of nudes in the "colossal" (Alfred Barr) style. Female figures had already been the subject of Jeanneret drawings in 1927 and earlier, though in retrospect the artist designated 1928 as the year when he "threw open a window on the human figure."[15]

After 1928 he no longer signed his paintings Jeanneret but rather Le Corbusier, another indication of fundamental change. This change does not mean that familiar motifs from the Purist period disappear entirely from his repertoire. They are taken up and modified time and again, but the use of line, color, and texture in their rendition becomes different,[16] and eventually even their pictorial frame of reference begins to change; they are no longer presented purely within a self-contained pictorial unit of a single scale but become juxtaposed with references to the surrounding world and with objects of an entirely different order of magnitude.[17] In the *Déjeuner au phare*, 1928 (fig. 203), a rocky coast with light house is seen below the still life, as if one were looking through underneath a table at a distant landscape; in the *Sculpture et vue*, 1929, a fragment of a bone, a wine glass, and a nude appear side by side at the same size (fig. 204).[18] The artist himself deemed the *Objets à ré-*

action poétique ("objects evoking poetic reactions"), displayed in the Pavillon de l'Esprit Nouveau of 1925, important clues in connection with these changes in his paintings.[19] But this indication only shifts the need for explanation a step further.

There may have been personal, psychological reasons for adding to the machine-made objects in the repertoire of his paintings shells, bones, eroded stones, and, increasingly, the female figure, but these will remain elusive unless more evidence becomes available from letters and sketchbooks. Even then it will be difficult to establish direct links between the artist's mental life and his artistic production, since not all moods and concerns of an artist lead equally to pictorial realizations and often the logic of visual thinking remains but loosely linked to nonvisual emotions and phenomena. One could also adduce the strong impressions from journeys in the late twenties (to Spain, Russia, North Africa, South America) as causes for certain changes in Jeanneret's paintings. There would be truth in such an assertion, but the explanation would still call for additional clarification because it would leave open the question, why were some new stimuli absorbed and not others that were equally available?

By contrast, if one looks at avant-garde painting of 1925–1927 in Paris—the scene against which Jeanneret measured his own production—it becomes quickly apparent that, even without any outside stimuli, an artist sensitive to new directions in the mainstream of artistic life would have felt under considerable pressure to make just such changes as we find in Jeanneret's paintings. The year 1925 marked the end of Cubism as an active movement and, most importantly for our purpose, brought the first Surrealist exhibition. The offerings of Surrealism must have found a sympathetic echo in Jeanneret because throughout his career he utilized the device of free association as an important means of personal expression, often in enigmatic or highly surprising juxtapositions—whether in writing, or in paintings and drawings.

In 1926 Picasso, with whom Jeanneret kept closer contact after his break with Ozenfant,[20] began a series of strongly distorted curvilinear metamorphic works whose full impact on Jeanneret was felt only in the thirties. Léger, who had been on friendly terms with Jeanneret since 1920 and whose *Le balustre* in 1925 had hung next to the architect's own still life in the Pavillon de l'Esprit Nouveau, had started in 1923–1924 to paint canvases with—in his own words—"des objets isolés de toute atmosphère et de tous rapports communs" ("objects isolated from all atmosphere and from all common relationships"). In the following years Léger was elaborating his discovery of objects isolated in space by the inclusion of leaves, shells, and stones (including silex, a favorite topic of Jeanneret's).[21]

Finally, Ozenfant himself, co-founder and for many years co-champion of Purism, in 1926–1927 for the first time "after a decade of still-lifes"[22] turned again to the human figure in a major work, his *La femme à la fontaine*. Clearly for Jeanneret too the time must have appeared ripe for change. But despite the addition of new subject matter to his stock of motifs and despite striking changes in his modes of pictorial rendition, he remained faithful to one fundamental principle of his method as a painter: he continued to take up old motifs in new contexts, forever exploiting their visual potential afresh. This is indicated by the many paintings that carry several dates, sometimes separated by long intervals of time, a fact that is deeply significant.

Long after the Purist period had ended, motifs from one painting are sometimes repeated and modified over and over again in other works and reappear in connection with the most varied pictorial themes or topics. It was not just a question of making several versions of one and the same theme—a tradition as old as painting—but of reworking a single element and using it like a sign or character, apparently without consideration of its original derivation and possible significance. The "purified," highly selective renderings of objects characteristic for Purist works were often based on numerous reworkings of studies that began as fairly realistic sketches from nature. In this process Le Corbusier utilized a well-known architectural drafting technique: many of his Purist drawings—and some later sketches—are on transparent onion skin paper, which permits easy copying and compositional experimentation

203. Le déjeuner au phare, *oil on canvas, 1928. In this painting as in the* Nature morte, *1927 (fig. 202), the artist obviously has moved a long way from the geometric simplicity and luminous transparency of his Purist phase.*

204. Sculpture et vue, *pencil and watercolor, 1929. Side by side with a stemmed glass appear a fragment of a bone, a match box, and a nude: objects of an entirely different order of magnitude. The orderly world of Purism has been left behind for one filled with startling juxtapositions and "objets à réaction poétique."*

205. Composition, *oil on canvas, 1926. A pair of interlocking stemmed glasses, hardly recognizable as such unless one knows their antecedents (see figs. 200, 201), is related to two carafes and a dark bottle.*

206. Composition, *colored crayon on tracing paper, probably 1926–1927. Dealing with the same motifs as figure 205, this work has been erroneously described as "Accordéon et carafe" because the zigzag shapes were not recognized as glass facets.*

by superimposing and moving several overlays, as was done later in the Carpenter Center designs.

A typical example of the transformation and survival of a pictorial element is a motif that was still used in 1963 in a lithograph of the Unité series but that first appeared in 1923 in Jeanneret's paintings, while his fellow Purist Ozenfant seems to have used it even earlier.[23] It consists of a standing stemmed glass (of the type seen by itself in figure 199), placed in front of another one in such a way that one of them is upside down, resting on its rim as in figures 200, 201; often the pair of glasses is further related to a third, taller object (bottle, carafe) that appears below them in approximate alignment with their axes. This configuration had the potential for amply fulfilling the Purist compositional ideal of "la liaison des éléments en vue de créer dans le tableau un objet unique . . . par des agencements organiques" ("the conjunction of elements with a view to creating in the painting a unique object . . . by organic arrangements").[24] It also lent itself easily to the creation of visual ambiguity.

We find the pair of glasses close to the right margin in the lower half of the *Nature morte aux nombreux objets, Indépendants,* 1923 (fig. 200),[25] while in the *Nature morte de l'Esprit Nouveau,* 1924, and in its linear version (fig. 201)[26] the glasses have moved into a prominent central position at the top of the composition, though their relation to objects below and in front is not very outspoken.

This is changed in the *Composition,* 1926 (fig. 205),[27] where the pair of glasses interlocks visually with a large carafe below, that in turn interacts with a pipe, dice, and a single faceted glass.[28] The pair of glasses by now has become a highly abstract constellation of two transparent, overlapping, excentrically placed forms that are approximately trapezoidal in outline. The carafe in the center is accompanied by two more large glass containers:

a tall dark bottle on the right and a large carafe with faceted bottom part and strongly curving shoulder on the left. A colored crayon sketch (fig. 206)[29] of the same composition reads more easily than the painting because it concentrates on what the artist considered the essential features.

In the following years numerous variations on the theme of *Composition,* 1926, were done by the artist and among these the *Composition spirale logarithmique,* 1929 (fig. 207),[30] is most interesting in our context because it shows how, by Le Corbusier's method, certain original elements might be modified drastically, yet not lose their identity completely. The pair of glasses on top has been simplified and stylized to such a degree that one would not be able to recognize it if one did not know the preceding stages of the design; it has been formalized into a sign and as such occurs in numerous later works.[31] The humps or shoulders of bottles and carafes have been accentuated and simplified into two balancing, irregularly curved forms that invite comparison to the outline of the Carpenter Center plan in its first version when both curved studios faced the same way (figs. 64, 65, 84).

In the upper third of the painting, the simplified rendering of a mask that Le Corbusier owned naturally encourages an anthropomorphic interpretation, despite the fact that dice and a faceted glass still are essential parts of the composition. In the 1940s the whole theme was taken up again in an exploration of its sculptural potential,[32] and finally an actual piece of sculpture was carved by Savina (fig. 208). The strong shapes in this work and in its preparatory drawings look purely abstract, except for the head (fig. 208). If one compares them with the simple glasses and carafes from which they originated, one realizes that in this instance Le Corbusier certainly lived up to the ideal of his friend Lèger who had wanted artists not to imitate but to derive from the objects of daily life forms that would be stronger than the originals. Over a period of four decades, a constellation of objects had become a topos, no longer related to any original figurative meaning. Similar transformations from "Modest Pictorial Themes, 1918–27"[33] to esoteric looking late works could be traced in detail for other motifs, chief among them

207. Composition spirale logarithmique, *oil on canvas, 1929. Motifs from figures 205 and 206 are further developed and given a new, anthropomorphic meaning by the addition of a head (mask) atop the composition.*

the Ubu series and the Taureau series, and in either case direct formal relations to the Carpenter Center could be pointed out. But for our purpose one example should be sufficient since in all cases the findings are similar: each time, a slow metamorphosis takes place in which certain initial elements are used, juxtaposed and modified in an ever varying context.

The process is well described by the artist himself when he explains:

> Le Corbusier porte en lui et avec lui des idées de nature plastique qui remontent à dix, quinze, vingt années, ou davantage: ce sont des croquis, des esquisses qui remplissent des tiroirs chez lui et dont il emporte certains en voyage, de telle sorte que le contact est instantanément repris d'une étape nouvelle avec une étape antérieure.[34]

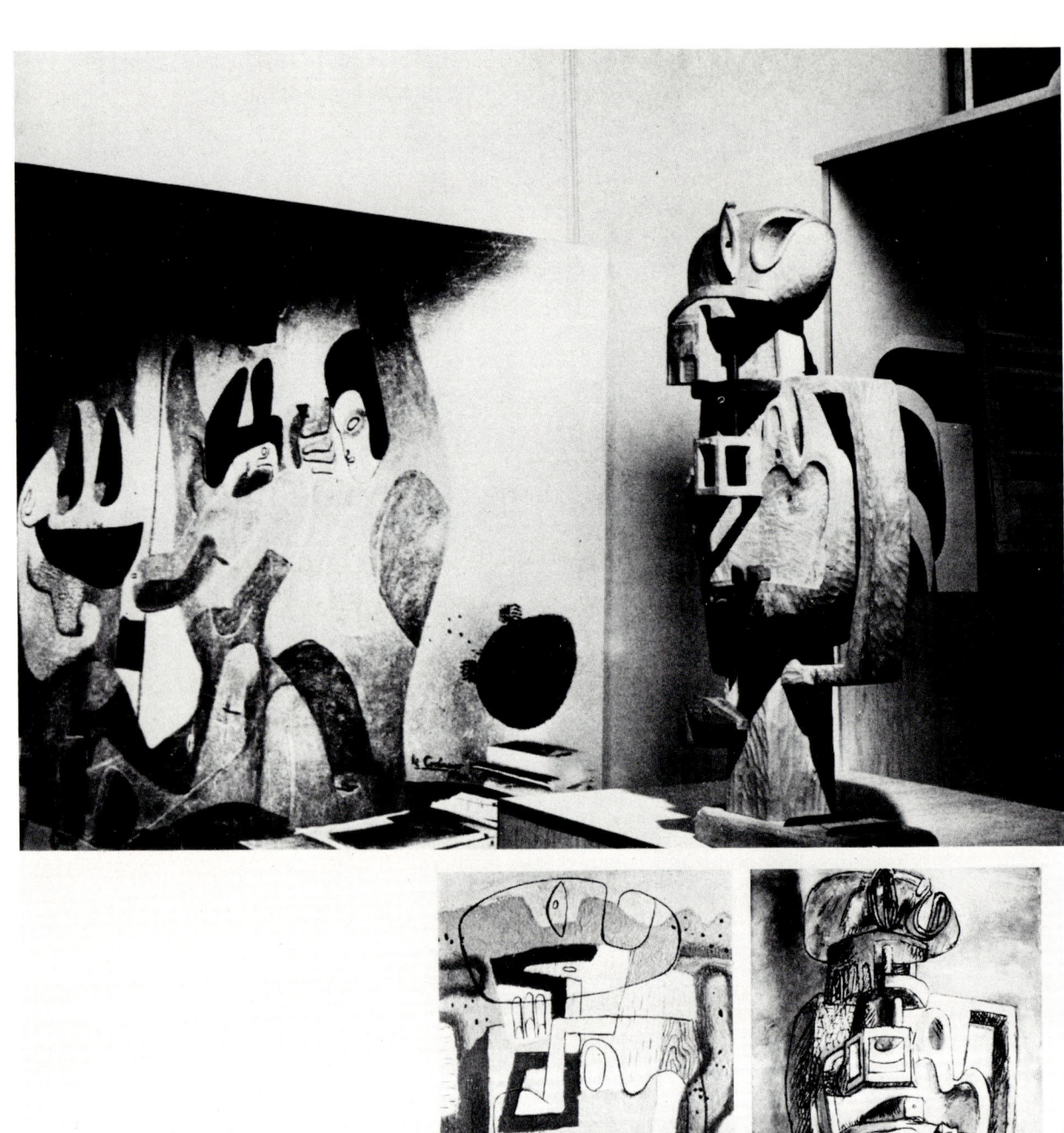

208. *Reproduction of page 247 from* Creation Is a Patient Search, *illustrating the metamorphosis of* Composition spirale logarithmique *(see fig. 207) into a sculpture entitled* Totem.

240

Le Corbusier carries inside himself and with himself ideas of a pictorial ("plastique") nature that go back ten, fifteen, twenty years or more: they are drawings, sketches which fill drawers at his home and some of which he takes along on journeys in such a manner that contact is instantly reestablished from a new stage [of development] to a preceding stage.

In plate 75 of the *Poème de l'angle droit* there is, for example, a telling description of how, by dint of repeated drawing, certain "objets à réaction poétique"—pieces of dead wood and pebbles—were metamorphized into a bull:

Les éléments d'une vision se rassemblent. La clef est une souche de bois mort et un galet ramassés tous les deux dans un chemin creux des Pyrénées. Des boeufs de labour passaient tout le jour devant ma fenêtre. A force d'être dessiné et redessiné le boeuf—de galet et de racine devint taureau.

The elements of a vision come together. The key is a stump of dead wood and a pebble, both of them picked up in a hollow gulley of the Pyrenees. Some working oxen were passing all day in front of my window. By dint of being drawn and redrawn the ox, from the pebble and from the root, became a bull.

The use and imaginative reuse of comparatively few pictorial elements must be seen in the light of Le Corbusier's verbal statements about painting in order to fully appreciate its significance. Early in his career he wrote: "Je suggère l'existence de 'mots plastiques' le sens de ces mots plastiques n'est pas de nature descriptive" ("I suggest the existence of 'pictorial words' the sense of these pictorial words is not descriptive in nature").[35] Later, in his most thoughtful, extensive essay on painting, he specifically compared a picture to a

parole prononcée, entendue, comprise.
Une parole, donc une phrase faite de mots, de mots qui portent un sens—si loin que l'hermétisme puisse en retarder volontairement l'entendement.

Les 'mots' de la peinture ne peuvent être que massifs . . . exprimant plus une notion qu'une qualité . . . de tels mots-notions, on en mettra deux ou dix ensemble. De leur présence, de leurs diverses contiguités naîtra un rapport. Ce rapport . . . c'est précisément cela que découvre l'artiste.[36]

statement pronounced, heard, understood.
A statement, therefore a sentence made from words, words which carry a meaning—so far that hermeticism could deliberately delay its comprehension.
The words of painting can only be massive . . . expressing more a notion than a quality . . . of such words-notions two or ten may be put together. From their presence, from their diverse contiguities a relationship will be born. This relationship . . . is precisely what the artist discovers.

It is clear from this and similar pronouncements and from the evidence of analyzed works what Le Corbusier's "patient search" meant in painting: a method of selective adoption, reuse, and modification of a limited number of elements that were fundamental in nature and originally recognizable as such. The artist found it necessary in his process of work to establish a vocabulary of signs intelligible to him—typical forms in painting—and a set of syntactic rules and ordering principles with which to operate in order to arrive at "precise solutions"; what counted for Le Corbusier, as for Léger, was thorough preparation, not improvisation.

It is not surprising that the same habit of mind—"manière de penser"—that was at work in painting should also have been operative in Le Corbusier's writing. His vast output as an author was facilitated by his manner of reusing creatively and often in modified form key portions from earlier works in order to reinforce what one is tempted to call his "arguments-type."

In view of recent concern with the application of linguistic method to architecture and the visual arts, the preceding observations would be interesting in themselves because they show an artist thinking of painting as language in a quite literal, technical sense. For our purpose they assume added importance because Le Corbusier thought of architecture in similar terms. After he had visited a Romanesque monastery, he wrote: "Bands, vaulting stones of arch and vault . . . the shafts of columns . . . plinth and capital . . . such are the words and phrases of architecture."[37]

As in painting so in architecture, Le Corbusier invented or adopted a set of prototypical sign-like elements for use as a vocabulary that was amenable to gradual modification and from which a great variety of statements could be constructed. For the composition of these statements he operated with a system of geometrical ordering and with syntactic rules he defined for himself. One such set of rules is described in the well known diagrammatic sketches of 1929, which refer to four possible ways of architectural composition: loose connection of individual parts (La Roche), all-encompassing prismatic regularity (Garches), freedom within a regular delimiting structural system (Tunis), and within a regular enclosing shell (Savoye, Poissy).[38]

The visual arts center, in its final version, is too tightly organized around a central regular figure to qualify for inclusion in category one, and, though it has many affinities to buildings in category three, it probably warrants description in a category of its own. This group would be characterized by peripheral free forms more or less closely related to the geometric regularity of a main volume; other members would include La Tourette with its free-form annex to the church and the project for Olivetti at Rho in Italy.

If, as a composition or organization of forms and spaces, the Carpenter Center belongs in a small group of its own, its elements certainly have a clear ancestry. Indeed, having just seen that it was Le Corbusier's method to combine creatively a comparatively small number of basic visual "words-notions," one would be surprised if the architectural components of the Carpenter Center did not have precedents in the storehouse of his experience and visual memory, among the images from his own projects and paintings and those accumulated during travels and studies, including the observations of form and structure in nature.

Some of these antecedents can be found at the very beginning of the architect's career: when he first utilized the "Dom-Ino" system of columns and floor slabs, which permitted the non-load-bearing envelope with its numerous variations; when he discovered the potential of ramps, or the attractions of glass brick. At other times elements will be found to stem from more recent works: the ondulatoires and skylights from La Tourette, the "fourth wall" from Chandigarh, the zigzagging fire escape stairs from the observation tower at the Kembs-Niffer sluice (fig. 221), and so on. Yet with all its reliance on elements found in earlier buildings, the Carpenter Center is more than a mere compendium of old devices, because of the way elements are treated as signs and as such organized and transformed in their new context.

Le Corbusier had never done a building before in which a ramp went all the way across from one side to the other, though the idea appears in the project for an exhibition pavilion in San Francisco or Liège of 1939 (fig. 209).[39] Otherwise ramps were always used as routes of access from one side only, or as a means of internal communication and "promenade."

If one disregards the fact that the ramp at the Carpenter Center crosses the building completely, the closest parallel to the vertical organization in the first project of the visual arts center one may find is the Millowners' Building in Ahmedabad (fig. 212), and, in a more general sense, La Tourette. In both cases the main point of access and distribution is placed on an upper level of a multilevel building. At La Tourette this was a solution appropriate to the placement of the building on a steep slope, and no ramp was needed. In contrast, Ahmedabad and the visual arts center have their main access at an upper level, not because of a sloping site but because it seemed desirable for other reasons: a ramp to an upper level made a kind of effortless smooth movement possible that affected one's perception of space in a special way—"un escalier sépare . . . une rampe relie" ("a staircase separates . . . a ramp connects").[40] It also could assume symbolic significance, and finally it enabled people to reach all levels in a building with less climbing of stairs than did ground floor access. No wonder that the idea was

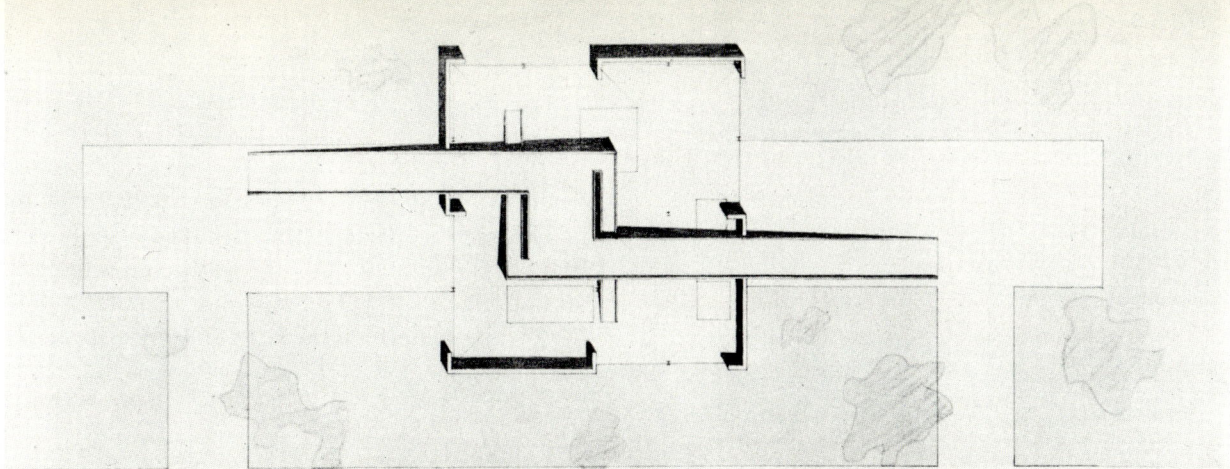

209. *Plan of design for an exhibition pavilion organized around a central ramp and implying pinwheel motion.*

taken up again later in, among others, the 1964 project for the Congress Palace at Strasbourg, where a wide ramp leads to the main lobby on the third level.[41] In the first project of the visual arts center, a second ramp would have mounted from the third level to the exhibition room above. At Strasbourg the main ramp from the third level continues in a curve round the main block of the building to its upper levels. Its spiraling movement recalls Le Corbusier's earliest intentions for the Carpenter Center.

Virtual rotation and the spiral movement of growth frequently occur in Le Corbusier's oeuvre. In drawings and paintings they may appear directly, as in the *Composition spirale logarithmique* (fig. 207) and on other occasions when such objects as shells, coils of rope, and scrolls are depicted; they may also make their presence felt in a less literal but not less visually effective manner through compositional devices that generate virtual torsion; the motif of two excentrically arranged overlapping glasses in figures 200, 205, and 207 is a good case in point. In his architecture the best known example of a plan implying spiral movement is that of a museum capable of endless growth but there are other less obvious cases, among them the design for the exhibition pavilion for Liège (fig. 209). A comparable kind of visual pinwheel motion is inherent in the side facade and section of the original project for a villa at Carthage, Tunis (fig. 210).[42]

Actually, nowhere is virtual torsion as evident as in the final plan for the visual arts center, where it is engendered by the eccentrical and centrifugal arrangement of free-form shapes on either side of the stable central square. The torque, however, remains a phenomenon only perceived in plan, or by looking at the building from a high vantage point. It does not affect the experience of space inside the building, since the two free-form studios are on different levels and their spaces cannot be comprehended together even if visual connections are made from one to the other. It also does not affect a viewer of the building from the outside because the rotational relationship of volumes cannot be perceived from any normally accessible viewpoint.

210. *Villa at Carthage, Tunis, first project; a virtual pinwheel motion is implied in the lateral facade.*

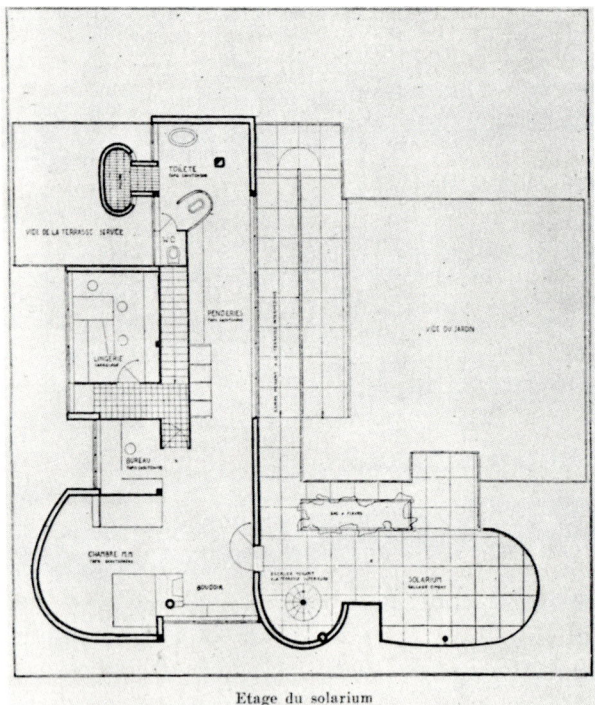

211. *Villa Savoye, first project, 1929. Plan of top floor, showing composite curves that appear like precursors of the free-form curves of the Carpenter Center.*

Though the torsional effect was absent in the first version of the design, Le Corbusier had considered a spiraling ramp in a preliminary sketch (April 7, 1960; fig. 44), and earlier he had even hinted at a building that in its upper parts would be cylindrical in form (notebook sketch, April 1, 1960; fig. 43). He soon realized that the visual arts center did not lend itself to a spiral or cylindrical design, though a distant reference to such a solution may be detected in certain views of the east and west facades when the cylindrical portions of the free-form studios assume major importance in one's field of vision. To find a whole building in cylindrical shape other than the abortive schemes for Strasbourg and Meaux we have to wait for the chancellery of the French Embassy for Brasilia, 1964.

Next to the ramp the free-form studios on either side of the central cubical volume are the most striking compositional elements of the Carpenter Center. Le Corbusier had never used the contrast between prismatic volumes and "ear" or "mandoline" shapes as major external containers of space before; free-shape or similar volumes on the outside of buildings either occurred as part of an entirely free-shape complex (Ronchamp) or as minor adjuncts (La Tourette) and enclosures for circulation elements—ramps and stairs.

Le Corbusier's free-form volumes and spaces cannot be classified unequivocally according to the uses to which they were put. While it is possible to point to the frequent use of free-form envelopes for toilets and bathrooms, presumably because considerations of "biology"[43] entered here, not to mention the practical advantages of ease for cleaning, there are many other instances of curved interior spaces where possible practical reasons for the free form are less clearly apparent. When it comes to exteriors, even omitting Ronchamp as a special case, there is an even greater variety of uses to which a curved envelope of space may be put.

In the Carpenter Center the ear-shaped free-form enclosures of space serve as studios, but in housing planned with the Millowners' Building, Ahmedabad, similar shapes on a minute scale were destined to be toilet annexes (fig. 212).[44] In the first project for the Erlenbach Art Center, free forms were given to workshops and depots, at the Chandigarh museum they were to enclose archives, at the Ahmedabad museum (second project) a lecture hall. In the project for an Olivetti factory at Rho, Italy, free-form shapes would have served all functions that were nonrepetitive and involved the movement of people, leaving only the office wings and assembly halls in regular, rectangular shapes.

At times the question of semantic appropriateness must have been considered together with that of functionality for use; when ramps and stairs are housed in curving envelopes, these can be considered expressive of the flowing movement they contain. In addition, irregular curves in architecture and urbanism could be linked to an obvious symbolism of biological growth and harmony. But what emerges more clearly than any pattern of semantic or functional correlation in the use of curved volumes is, as on many other occasions, a pattern of visual, compositional logic. Regular or irregular curved volumes are usually contrasted to

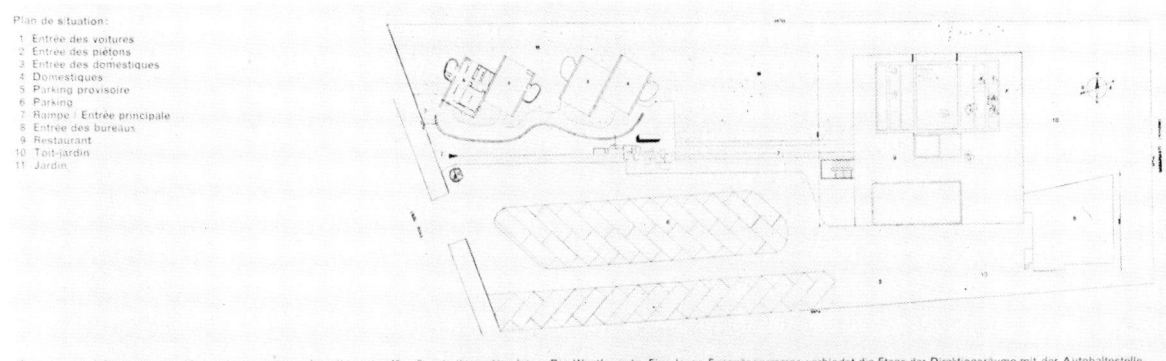

212. *Site plan and west facade, Millowners' Association Building, Ahmedabad, finished 1957.*

great advantage with prismatic ones: a simple syntactic rule is observed that is applicable under the most varied semantic conditions. After all, when Le Corbusier began designing houses for La Chaux-de-Fonds prior to and during World War I, his work clearly fitted into a tradition of design that included the use of curved components as an integral part of a traditional, syntactic "art of composition." It is not surprising therefore to find in these buildings round, apse-like bays, shallow segmental niches, and curves as aids in turning corners. Curved elements are not only used for compositional reasons, however, but in these early buildings may also serve such practical ends as saving space, easing traffic-flow, and avoiding re-entrant angles that are difficult to keep clean.

Curves in the early works are generated from segments of circles, resulting in cylindrical volumes in contradistinction to the more complex irregular curvatures found in later work.

In the villa at Vaucresson (1922), curves enclosing the bathroom are used to facilitate a spatial transition to the bedroom; in a preliminary design the staircase would also have been enclosed in a cylindrical volume, but this feature, which would have been conspicuous on the outside, disappeared when the position of the staircase was changed in plan. In the studio-house for Ozenfant, concave envelopes of space and their corollaries, curved volumes bulging out into space, play an important role inside the building but, as at Vaucresson, the outside presents itself as a prismatic volume only. We have to wait for the La Roche–Jeanneret houses to find a cylinder segment (housing appropriately a ramp) appearing prominently in the facade, with another curved volume appearing on the roof level.

At Pessac cylindrical shapes on the ground floor serve as storage bins in realization of an idea that had already been present in the Citrohan project; in the first project for Madame Meyer an oval volume was to enclose the staircase in dramatic contrast to the sheer prism of the body of the house; in the Cook house one enters through a semicylindrical "parloir" visible under the overhang of the first floor, somewhat like the curved storage bin under the garden terrace at Garches. But at Garches, in 1927, this curved, elongated volume has a more complex shape than the comparable storage bin at Pessac, just as the use of curves in the interior is more complex than anything done before. We have a premonition here of the composite curves atop the Villa Savoye project in its first version of 1929 (fig. 211).

In view of the interrelation between Le Corbusier's architecture and painting, the period 1927–1929 seems very plausible for a turning toward greater complexity in architecture. The year 1927, as we have seen, marked a stylistic turning point in painting, and one would expect the changes in architecture to be in the same direction as those in painting: towards more sensuous, textural, freely modeled and complex compositions.[45] Since it had taken some time, however, for the forms of Purist painting to find their full correspondence in architecture, it seems reasonable to expect that changes occurring in later painting would also reverberate in architecture, with some delay. A scrutiny of some projects and buildings from the crucial years bears out these expectations, beginning conveniently with a comparison of two large projects with similar programs: the League of Nations Palace of 1927 and the Palace of the Centrosoyus, third project, 1929 (figs. 213, 214).[46]

Though their formal architectural vocabulary is very similar, the layout of these great groupings shows significant differences. What we see in plan and bird's eye view of the Geneva palace is not unlike the transparent planarity and comparatively simple geometry that characterized the additive conjunctions of forms and the layering of virtual space in a Purist painting; a similar mood and mode prevail. There is a comparable layering of architectural space[47] and a certain looseness in the manner of creating spatial tension by additive juxtaposition of predominantly prismatic volumes. It was this compositional looseness that made it possible in 1929 to modify the project for another site without difficulty. Curved shapes, except for the apse-like projection of the library and the president's pavilion, play a negligible role.

213. *League of Nations Palace, project of 1927. Bird's-eye view.*

214. *Palace of the Centrosoyus, third project, 1928-1929. Air view of model showing the greater complexity and substantiality of visual organization in comparison to figure 213.*

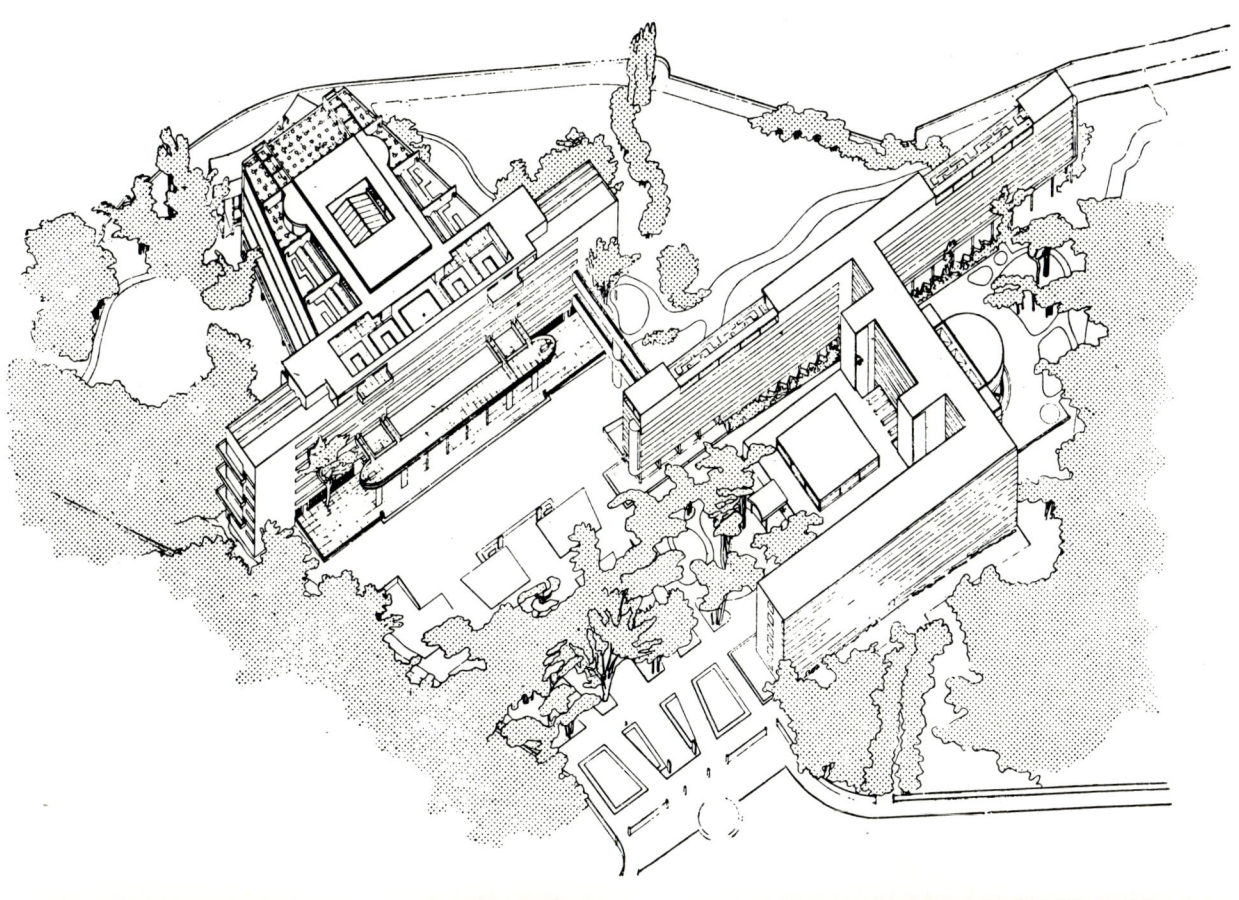
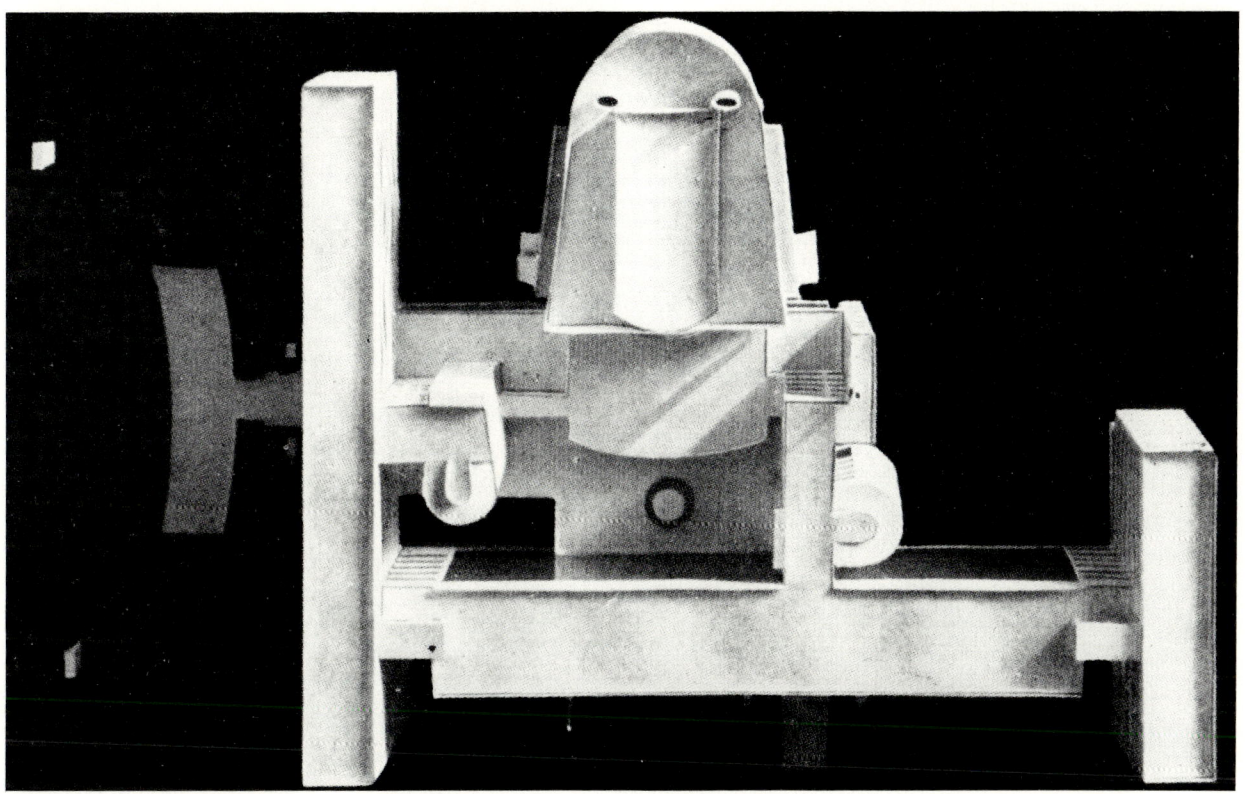

By comparison the plan and airview (photograph of model) of the Centrosoyus display a greater complexity and substantiality of visual organization, achieved through a reliance on the tight interlocking of straight and curved volumes. Especially the wedge-shaped, curved ramp towers at crucial points of the total composition serve as strong plastic accents. The same constituent elements are assembled here as at Geneva, but the mode of their coexistence is as different as that found in two paintings—still lifes with identical objects—from 1926 and 1928.

It is precisely in the spirit of such a comparison with paintings that Le Corbusier himself presented the two buildings in one of his typical autobiographical recapitulations. In *New World of Space* (1948) he placed the Centrosoyus building after a painting of 1928, *Le déjeuner au phare* (fig. 203), and the League of Nations Palace after *Composition, 1926* (fig. 205), which also serves as a comparison for the Villa Stein at Garches. The *Composition, 1926*, is the same painting discussed earlier (p. 238) as a typical example of Purist compositional method.

The tendency, noted at the Centrosoyus, toward greater concentration, complexity, and substantiality including a reliance on strongly curved shapes is even more striking in the Swiss Pavilion of the Cité Universitaire of 1930–1932. Here a whole wing of a building is not only treated as a modeled volume but also given a richly textured wall;[48] additional curved shapes occur that are not generated by spaces they enclose but, in a radical new move, through pure modeling of solid mass. The supports on ground level no longer appear in the geometrically simple cylinder shapes typical for all earlier pilotis but as strongly sculptural forms. As in the curving solarium enclosure at the Villa Savoye, different realms of reasoning here entered the design process. The architect made a point of explaining that the form of these sensuously curving supports was dictated by foundation difficulties of the site, and no doubt this is the truth;[49] but it is not the whole truth since obviously simpler, less modeled forms could have performed the same technical job. However they would not have produced the same visual richness and density.

At the same period in which the Swiss Pavilion was built, the project "A" or plan *Obus* for Algiers showed long stretches of apartment housing arranged in free curves on hilly terrain.[50] They illustrate what Le Corbusier meant in the statement quoted above: "the spirit of form animates his paintings like his architecture, and even his urbanism."

Between the early thirties and the early fifties Le Corbusier did little actual building, but a few houses from the midthirties and later unexecuted projects (for example, the Algiers skyscraper) indicate the same tendency we have noted at the Swiss Pavilion. There is a clear movement toward increased intensity and substantiality by means of modeling (the curved ceilings of the little weekend house of 1935) and unbroken expanses of textured wall. The scale of texturing becomes bigger with the introduction of the brise-soleil, but the tendency remains unchanged until Marseille, Ronchamp, and the first buildings in Chandigarh eventually make it evident how far the architect has moved in the direction of maximum intensity in the modulation of form and space, color and texture. But while it is easy in retrospect to recognize the road that led from the Swiss Pavilion, the little weekend house, and the Algiers projects to the Marseille apartment block, some of the Indian work, and the Jaoul houses, the chapel at Ronchamp would still come as an enormous surprise to anyone who tried to understand Le Corbusier's development from a study of his architecture alone; the curved volumes and dramatically modeled and lit spaces of this church were more explicitly foretold in paintings and sculptures than in buildings.

In painting, the two decades that had passed since the first major change in Le Corbusier's style had been marked by significant developments. What resulted can well be judged by looking at two works from 1953, the year the artist had a great retrospective one-man exhibition at the Musée d'Art Moderne in Paris. One is the series of lithographs entitled *Poème de l'angle droit* (1947–1953, published in 1955) and the other the *Nature morte aux nombreux objets,* 1953 (fig. 215),[51] a painting which took up not just a motif but a whole composition from thirty years earlier: the *Nature morte*

aux nombreux objets, Indépendants, 1923 (fig. 200).[52]

The *Nature morte* of 1923 is a harmonious composition in pleasant predominantly bluish, greenish, and brownish mild pastel tones, displaying Purist characteristics that were discussed earlier in this chapter. In the revised version of 1953 the composition is simplified and strengthened through the omission of some elements; the chromatic effect is enhanced through the use of highly saturated unbroken colors, including contrasting complementaries (red and green) and large areas of black; there is some modeling in color and some through the textural effect of hatching; the geometrically disciplined curves of 1923 are replaced by freer ones that convey a more organic feeling and there is ample use of flowing black outlines. In its total effect, the later work seems more strident and uninhibited, more clearly articulated

215. Nature morte aux nombreux objets, *oil on canvas, 1923–1953. A reworked version of a Purist painting (see fig. 200) which permits revealing comparisons between point of departure and final result. The later work differs from the earlier one in the use of free flowing curves, highly saturated unbroken colors, large areas of black, and other devices that make for stronger articulation and greater overall freedom.*

in its total organization, and more strongly pulled together.

The same comments could be made about other paintings from the same period, notably the Taureau series. These variations on a theme based partly on the imagery of the bull are interesting in connection with Le Corbusier's architecture because the characteristic horn shapes that are invariably found in them have their three-dimensional echo in the upturned roof of the Chandigarh Assembly Building. They prove that Le Corbusier still used painting as a laboratory for the invention of new forms in architecture.

The *Poème de l'angle droit* took up a theme of the early years in Le Corbusier's career: the praise of the right angle, as it had already been sung in the pages of *l'Esprit Nouveau* (no. 18) in 1924. In the *Poème*, which took six years to prepare, the author passes in review the concerns and images that had moved him during his lifetime. He evokes the structuring forces of nature outside and inside himself, how they are to be mastered through the power of intellect, feeling, character—everything finally expressed in the decisive gesture of intersecting the vertical with the horizontal. Le Corbusier recalls his major conceptual contributions: the Modulor, the five points of a new architecture, the unité d'habitation, the brise-soleil. He then turns to an evocation of the sources for his most profound emotions: the experiences of love and fighting, the sheer exhilaration of action and of being an architect.

It is a poetic scanning of the four horizons of his life, and the images needed to support it are created by the same method we have observed at work before: they are modified versions or recurrences in a new context of major motifs from the totality of his past work as a painter. We find segments from Purist still lifes, including the pair of stemmed glasses discussed earlier; objets à réaction poétique; the beloved beaches with boats, ropes, and bathers; women in many roles, among them musicians, dancers, amazons; the mythical world of Minotaur and unicorn; Ubu and Taureau. But most frequent of all we find the human hand, often in symbolic gesture. It seems almost inevitable that two of the strongest, most successful color lithographs of the entire series should deal with hands: there is the "Open Hand" as it was planned for Chandigarh, and, at the very end of the volume as concluding image, the artist's hand engaged in drawing a cross of rectangular coordinates. The two straight lines, at right angles to each other, are contrasted with a subtly curved open-ended line around them and with two algebraic symbols below them in a visual statement of such strength and simplicity that it assumes the sign-like quality of an ancient pictograph.

Altogether the formal treatment of images in the *Poème* tends toward directness and strength, with color used in the service of this tendency; strong contrasts are aimed for. In several plates a black background is used which intensifies the hues that are set against it like a dark night sky. The hues themselves are often restricted to primary colors, or to primaries with one additional tone. In the best instances there is great mastery in the way linear patterns are made to interact with areas of color, and the device of divorcing form and color from each other is used successfully to strengthen the total composition. Figure–ground effects occur frequently and strikingly, for example, in the title page. They call to mind the parallel use of figure–ground relations in buildings that are perforated in the middle (the Carpenter Center, Kembs-Niffer) or where solid and glazed stretches of curved wall interact so as to create ambiguities between positive and negative shapes (Brazilian Pavilion).

Although partly due, no doubt, to the lithographic process, flowing lines that convey a feeling of great spontaneity abound in the *Poème*; having seen this work, one feels it would have been surprising if free-form curves had not occurred in architecture at the same time. Many outlines resemble closely those found in the plans of the visual arts center, as for example in an Ubu drawing or in the ear-like shape that protrudes from the lower part of a Taureau line drawing on plate 149 (fig. 216).

The presence of an ear-shaped handle in this drawing is less surprising if one remembers Le Corbusier's own revelation that the formal motivation for the Taureau series, in a very typical fashion, came from resketching an earlier still life and turning it by ninety degrees in the process (fig.

216. Taureau, *line drawing from the* Poème de l'angle droit, *pl. 149. The earlike protruding shape in the lower part resembles the curving outline found in plans for the visual arts center.*

217. *Reproduction of page 232 from* Creation Is a Patient Search, *illustrating Le Corbusier's explanation about the genesis of the Taureau motif.*

217).[53] The two round forms under the bull's head for example are modifications of an ear-shaped handle from the original still life. In Jeanneret's Purist still lifes there were several handle shapes that are reasonably similar to the outline of the free-form studios of the visual arts center. At the same time one can also discover many instances of the small, bottle-like carafe that is commonly used to serve wine in a French bistro. It can be seen for example on the wash drawing related to the *Nature morte au grand livre* of 1928[54] or in the outline drawing of the *Nature morte de l'Esprit Nouveau*, illustrated in *Peinture moderne,* page 169 (fig. 201). The outline of this carafe deserves our attention because it may well be an ancestor of the third floor south studio of the first version of the visual arts center (fig. 116), just as the ear-shaped handles may be precursors of the curved studios of the second version.

The pictorial production of the period coinciding with and subsequent to Le Corbusier's actual involvement with the visual arts center follows the directions heralded in the *Poème*. On the technical side there is a shift of emphasis away from oil paintings to lithographs, collages, tapestries, paintings in enamel. In the best works of the period, such as *Les dés sont jetés,* 1959, and *Deux têtes,* 1960,[55] there is a further reduction of form and color to essentials and an impressive combination of formal clarity with visual tension through ambiguity. The organic (flowing curves) and the coincidental (torn fringes of pasted papers) now have a place in an order that is more comprehensive than that of the pristine configurations of Purism. Instead of painstaking elaboration there is now a roughness and nonchalance of execution that can hardly be unintentional. In comparison one is tempted to think of the way roughness and imperfections are exploited in the "béton brut" of a number of buildings from the same period. But in the very last lithographs, from 1964, and engravings such as *Le taureau* dated February 28,

251

218. Le taureau, *engraving, 1965. This is one of Le Corbusier's last graphic works. Its sparseness and linear precision are striking.*

219. *Chandigarh Assembly Building, entrance hall.*

1965 (fig. 218),[56] there is something else: a sparseness and linear precision that seems to indicate another "recall to order."

The architecture of Le Corbusier's last years shows a similar trend toward economy of formal means and a self-imposed restriction to very simple and strong statements, tempered however by an unabated mastery in applying the compositional syntax in the creation of subtly balanced visual tensions.

Attention has been usually focused more on the strikingly complex and richly articulated works of the period just preceding the final years such as La Tourette or the Chandigarh Assembly Building (opened at the same time as the Carpenter Center) with its "horned" portico and bold roofscape. But even in these buildings the trend towards simplicity can already be detected: the Assembly Building has facades of highly ordered tranquillity and an entrance hall so simple in its monumentality that a revolutionary classicist like Gilly would have appreciated it (fig. 219). A similar restraint and return to the very fundamentals of pier-and-lintel architecture characterizes the boat club at Chandigarh (fig. 220).

On another level we find great simplicity in the open-ended system of planning with individually reticent repetitive units that governed both the art school in Chandigarh and the Venice hospital design. The design for the French Embassy in Brasilia also manifests great simplicity in the selection of its basic geometric volumes—prism and cylinder—but handles their surfaces in a complex way with strong visual tensions through ambiguity especially in the cylindrical building.[57] In a similar manner the youth center at Firminy, though striking in overall shape, is as simple in volumetric form as it is ambiguous in the possibilities for perceptual interpretations offered by its slanting facades; it also displays considerable precision in the treatment of its concrete surfaces—a characteristic owed to a deliberate decision on the part of its designer and shared with other buildings, including the sluice house and control tower at Kembs-Niffer (fig. 221) and, of course, the Carpenter Center.

The complex of the Kembs-Niffer sluice was designed and built at almost the same time as the Carpenter Center. A presentation drawing for it,

220. *Chandigarh, boat club.*

numbered 5731 (fig. 221)[58] and drawn by Taves in March or April of 1961, looks very similar in its drafting style (including the printed Modulor men) to the set of presentation facades of the visual arts center that Jullian drew. It seems reasonable to assume that together Kembs-Niffer and the Carpenter Center can well serve to illustrate a prevailing mode of formal treatment in Le Corbusier's studio at the time.

As long as one regards only the overall geometry of its plan, the sluice house at Kembs-Niffer seems to be extremely simple, but this simplicity reveals itself as deceptive when one considers the spatial and volumetric ambiguities created by the ruled surface of the roof and by its extensions on both sides of the building. There is also a figure–ground effect resulting from the striking visual penetration of the building by an open passage near its center, next to a small curved volume that resembles a diminutive relative of the visual arts center's free-form studios. Equally striking is the ambiguity dominating the design of the control tower, with its staircase that—harking back to the Plainex house of 1927—is identical to the fire escape stairs in the Carpenter Center. The plan of this tower plays a sophisticated game with the juxtaposition of right angle and triangle. In principle, its intersection of straight and oblique movement is not unlike that inherent in the plan of the visual arts center.

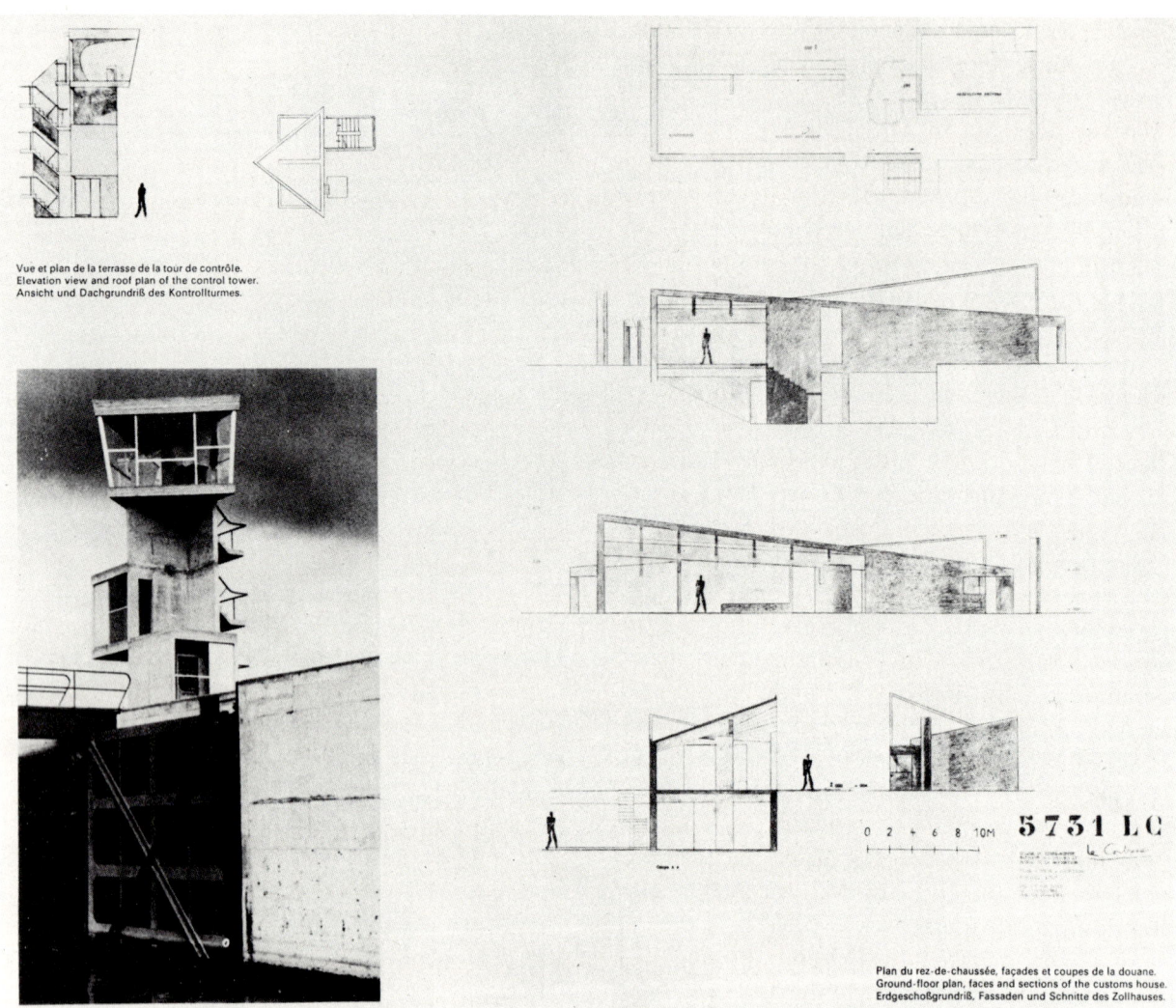

221. *Reproduction of page 45 from* Last Works *showing the presentation of the sluice house and control tower of Kembs-Niffer.*

In order to determine more precisely to what extent the characteristics that Kembs-Niffer shares with the Carpenter Center may represent a trend, it will be useful to compare the latter with some of its predecessors, provided we keep in mind the obvious limitations imposed on architectural comparisons between buildings with nonidentical purposes.

Some purposes will affect form more strongly than others. This is evident from Le Corbusier's museum designs, which all are derived from the "museum capable of unlimited growth" and consequently have square, blocklike shapes and unbroken walls (Tokyo, Ahmedabad, Chandigarh). Fortunately three buildings exist that were sufficiently indeterminate formally, though not in pro-

254

gram, and are close enough in date to the Carpenter Center to permit a meaningful comparison: the Millowners' Building in Ahmedabad, the monastery of La Tourette, and the Brazilian Pavilion in the Cité Universitaire, Paris. They even have in common at least one point of program: all three had to provide for the gathering of small and large groups of people for a common purpose within an institutional framework, though the degree of implied formality varied. All three buildings were also expected to make a strong positive impression on outsiders and perhaps to stimulate or otherwise positively affect users.

A comparison between the Carpenter Center and the Millowners' Building in Ahmedabad, finished in 1957 (fig. 212), seems particularly apt because the two buildings are very similar in size: the central square is 89 by 89 feet at Ahmedabad, 92 by 92 feet at the Carpenter Center. Also, at least one detail of the visual arts center, the scoring of the ramp, was directly taken from Ahmedabad (according to an office memorandum from Sert dated October 9, 1962, and approved by Le Corbusier). Both buildings are organized according to the same syntactic principle of contrast between prismatic and curved volumes in relation to a neutral grid of supports, though at Ahmedabad just as at the Chandigarh Assembly Building the juxtaposition takes place inside the building, while at the Carpenter Center it occurs outside. Both buildings also create visual ambiguity by means of opening up an important view into and across the building, and by treating the east and west facades (with brise-soleil) differently from the north and south facades. In both buildings a ramp with an outside staircase next to it plays an important role.

However, a further comparison between the entrance facade of Ahmedabad (fig. 212) and the Prescott Street facade—admittedly not the main entrance to the Carpenter Center (figs. 21a, 21b)—reveals a very significant difference in visual and textural weight. The Millowners' Building appears more robust, more articulated rhythmically. This is so because its floorslabs are expressed externally by a higher ledge of concrete than those of the Carpenter Center and because the horizontal upper delimitation is more powerful owing to a concrete parapet that visually serves the function of a tall cornice. In addition the open spaces defined by the floor slabs and the brise-soleil invite a reading as slender subdivided rectangles, while at the Carpenter Center the comparable spaces are square. A facade that consists chiefly of square compartments and has no strong horizontal crowning feature obviously is less dynamic than one in which strongly expressed horizontal bands and a heavy upper feature contrast with rhythmically subdivided vertical slots of space.

Similarly the outside fire escape staircase at the Carpenter Center is a much less conspicuously modeled volume than the staircase at Ahmedabad, which has an unbroken parapet all the way up where the Carpenter Center has thin metal railings. Even in a small detail, the triangular supports for the handrail of the ramp, the same kind of contrast can be observed. At the Carpenter Center they are made entirely of steel and appear linear, immaterial. At Ahmedabad the bases of the triangle take the shape of a heavy block of concrete—a volume instead of a linear or planar element. Whereas the visual arts center works with tension between planar elements, Ahmedabad has tension between volumes.

La Tourette and the Brazilian Pavilion in Paris (designed with Lucio Costa) were both begun in 1957, the year when Ahmedabad was finished. They share with it, and with the buildings of the Chandigarh Capitol, the kind of insistence on strongly articulated volume, weight, and texture that in the Swiss Pavilion indicated the first change in Le Corbusier's mode of handling his own vocabulary. Compared to the Brazilian Pavilion, the Carpenter Center appears definitely lighter visually because it is more broken up as a volume, has smoother surfaces, and is supported by slender pilotis. Similarly, without going into detailed comparisons, one realizes that La Tourette is treated much more richly and roughly than the Carpenter Center. Though in the south facade of the center there is as much boldness in cantilevering a higher story over a lower one as at La Tourette, the monastery otherwise combines a greater variety of different, exciting forms in a manner that would be anarchic were it not for the overriding discipline of geometric simplicity that governs the main concept.

At Ahmedabad some of the effects of greater heaviness and textural richness may owe their existence simply to the designer's awareness of the climatic, cultural, and technological conditions he had to reckon with, but such an explanation cannot be adduced for the other buildings in our comparison, where he would have been free to employ lighter forms and less textured surfaces. Inversely, in designing the Carpenter Center he could have placed concrete parapets where there are none, he could have aimed for different proportions of the brise-soleil areas, and he would have been more than welcome to use brick in conjunction with concrete, had he wanted to create such strong textural effects in the visual arts center as he had at Ahmedabad, La Tourette, the Brazilian Pavilion, and in the Sarabhai and Jaoul houses.

It is tempting to ascribe Le Corbusier's insistence on precision of detailing and smoothness of concrete at the Carpenter Center and at Kembs-Niffer to an awareness not only of the available potential for first rate execution but also of the technological context into which these buildings fit. Kembs-Niffer serves a technological purpose in a highly industrialized part of western Europe; the Carpenter Center stands in a country that is renowned for its technological prowess. But because Le Corbusier's feelings towards United States technology and its consequences were ambivalent, it might also have made sense for him to place a very antitechnological building—rough, individualistic in detail—on American soil.

However, one can also look at the visual arts center in a different light and see it as a reaffirmation of ideals from the early, formative years, a demonstration of fundamental principles that were established at the beginning of Le Corbusier's career. He saw the final presentation drawings as a summing up, a "crystallization," and they had various characteristics in common with architectural drawings of the Purist period. It is striking that so many of the initial elevation and section drawings of the Carpenter Center appeared in the *Oeuvre complète*—more than from any other project of Le Corbusier's later years. Carefully labeled "plan d'étude," their function was in part to establish for posterity what had been the architect's ideal intentions before changes were made in response to university demands. But they may have been published also because they truly embodied an ideal of their author—not only of draftsmanship but also of an attitude toward form, and toward his own past. He returned to a fundamental simplicity, to an "impeccable order," in all his last works, whether they were pictorial or architectural; it was as if he tried to summon back the victorious clarity of his early works that had made them appear as the genuine embodiments of a "new spirit." Perhaps he felt that the messages of Ronchamp (termed Baroque by some critics, to the architect's great annoyance), Jaoul, and La Tourette were being misinterpreted by the "romantic young" and that a visual "word of clarification" was in order. Keeping the complexity and substantiality of his late work, he returned to the order and simplicity of earlier work but on a different level. In this sense the Carpenter Center may illuminate in part the meaning of one of his most carefully worded final statements:

Evidemment le problème est, à travers les complexités, d'atteindre à la simplicité. A travers les destructions de la vie, de poursuivre un rêve éperdu: non pas celui de rester jeune, mais celui de devenir jeune.[59]

Obviously the problem is to reach simplicity across the complexities. Across the destructions of life to pursue a crazy dream: not that of remaining young but that of becoming young.

On May 27, 1963, the Carpenter Center was handed over to its users. It was greeted with enthusiasm by most architects,[60] artists, and critics, and by those members of the university community who were in sympathy with art movements of the time; others received it with mixed feelings and with criticism, claiming it was misplaced, disruptive, incomprehensible. In 1976 President Pusey at the dedication of the library named after him recalled: "Most of them didn't like it [the Carpenter Center] and said very unpleasant things . . . you will remember the overseers who wanted to take up a collection to get ivy to cover it as quickly as they could, and all the rest of it. But one comment that bothered me was the fact that many people said they liked the building but they did not like it on that site. And the trouble with that comment was that there is not a line or feature of that building that is not what it is because of where the building is."

Sensitive observers have agreed with him, calling the building "a very good neighbor" (Fello Atkinson) and "respectful urbanism, and excellent for the street" (Vincent Scully), but the single most popular criticism voiced about the Carpenter Center still remains that it does not sit well between its neighbors. This comment is based on an ideal of conformity that would welcome nothing but directly matching materials and forms, and on a lack of recognition for the way in which the center, by its careful scaling as well as its modulation of surrounding space, relates very positively to its neighbors. From my own observations and the evidence of the design history I find that the building has drawn the greatest possible advantage from its admittedly cramped site and illustrates Le Corbusier's contention: "Le terrain biscornu absorbe toutes les facultés créatrices de l'architecte et épuise son homme. L'oeuvre qui en resulte est hermétique par définition, solution hermétique ne rejouissant que celui qui en connait les dessous."[61] ("The irregular site absorbs all creative faculties of the architect and exhausts its man. The work which results from it is by definition hermetic, a hermetic solution which only gives pleasure to somebody who knows what underlies it.")

Undeniably, however, the way the building meets the ground is unhappy—the group of pilotis facing Quincy Street visually half-buried in a sunken pit and some excessively low pilotis standing in an unkempt no man's land under portions of the south studio are the most unsuccessful aspects of the building. They perpetuate a capitulation in front of—perhaps insurmountable—difficulties of levels around the site, difficulties that also contributed to make the approach to the main entrance slippery in winter and unconvincing to the eye. Le Corbusier is not entirely responsible for all this; certain arrangements regarding the levels were forced on the architect in the process of the change from the first to the second project, just as the unfortunate devaluation of the ramp as a genuine means of approach and entry was due to later changes and events no longer under his control.

The Carpenter Center conveys many messages implicitly; here Le Corbusier once more broached all major concerns of his career. At times when facing this comparatively small building one may even wonder if perhaps the size of the chosen vessel inherently was not too limited for the content it was made to hold, if the architect's decision to convey here so many significant formal messages did not endanger the clarity of transmission for some of them. Yet there can be no doubt that explicitly the center conveys the message the client had entrusted to his architect; it superbly announces the presence of the visual arts at Harvard University. At the same time it serves well the quickly changing needs of its users (appendix 24)—whether students or teachers—and by its mere presence challenges their creativity and sense of quality.

Visually and spatially the Carpenter Center is a powerful statement of contrasts held in balance by unifying devices, in conformity with Le Corbusier's ideal, "unité dans le détail, tumulte dans l'ensemble" ("unity in detail, tumult in the ensemble").[62]

Contrasts exist between straight and curved elements, between fields of spatial tension and very massive volumes, between parts of the building that imply virtual movement and others that are extremely static, between portions that seem to hover above ground and others that are firmly anchored to it, between zones that invite and zones that repulse, between high and low spaces, between unbroken and perforated, flat or space-holding surfaces. The way light is modulated and exploited, both during the day and at night, tends to enhance existing contrasts and to create additional ones. If the planting on the roof terraces had been carried out as intended by the architect, this would have provided another important textural and symbolic contrast.

Unifying factors in detail are the presence of only a few materials throughout the building (chief among them concrete and glass), the consistent use of very few colors, the relative visual consistency of the tectonic statement (the few occasions when stiffening concrete walls are used instead of pilotis add a welcome touch of complexity without destroying the overall unity of the structural system). Space is treated very consistently as a measured continuum, activated and defined by elements at its boundaries but never entirely encased, rarely prevented from acting as an agent of dematerialization.

If there is one place in the building where a visual coup has not been carried off with complete success, it is in that part of the Prescott Street facade where the coming together of fire escape stairs, brise-soleil, and enclosure of the high ramp space appears too additive and somewhat unresolved (figs. 18, 21a). A similar problem of composition is more masterfully handled at Ahmedabad.

Side by side with tension of contrasts held in balance by unifying factors, the typical Corbusian tension through visual ambiguity prevails. From certain viewpoints, for example, it is possible to look through the entire depth of the building across rooms and through several panes of glass; consequently zones of lightness and darkness as well as actual and reflected images intermingle in a bewildering manner. What in one moment is experienced as a dark hole punched through a surface of concrete, the next moment may turn into a shimmering, reflecting rectangle as light as the surrounding concrete if not lighter. Similarly the reading of a facade made up of slanting brise-soleil fins becomes ambiguous to an observer who moves parallel to the facade, since concrete eventually is replaced by glass in his field of vision.

It is striking that "ambiguity in the means of configuration" is one of the four crucial elements Werner Hofmann enumerated in 1969, when he characterized the "decisive artistic event" of the twentieth century. The other elements are "intermixture of degrees of reality, disturbance (alienation) of form, equivalence between positive and negative forms."[63] All these occur in the architecture of the Carpenter Center, even the varying degrees of reality—between portions that are primarily perceived as image and others that primarily act on the level of three-dimensional palpable presence. The fact that Hofmann is talking of elements of anti-illusionism employed in painting, while in our case they are found in architecture, is all the more significant as he sees the nature of the "decisive artistic event" in "the effort to abolish the barriers and differences of degree between artistic categories and to pave the way for an elemental quality of transition in the occurrence of form which will no longer give recognition to architecture, sculpture, and painting as distinct species." Similar observations led to my suggestion in 1965 that it would be appropriate for our time to vary Walter Pater's dictum, "All art aspires to the condition of music," to "All art aspires to the condition of environmental art."[64]

It is clear that with his commitment to painting, Le Corbusier among all architects of his generation was predestined to create works that in architecture would display characteristics also applicable to paintings; after all, he gave continuous architectural demonstrations of the "synthesis of the major arts"—not in the sense of a superficial resemblance or coordination but in the sense of a fundamental identity of method and consequently of inner structure. In this sense the Carpenter Center—a building for the arts—has as important a message as any of the other most momentous buildings of its designer, from the Villa Savoye to Ronchamp and the Jaoul houses. It is a message that has yet to be fully appreciated if we are to judge from its direct or indirect influence on architectural production so far.

Instead of a grappling with the problem of Le Corbusier's motivating concepts in their interrelationship with expressive forms, or of a genuine transmutation of these forms, an eclecticism seems to prevail that deals with the Carpenter Center chiefly on a level of purely formal preoccupation. But elements in the visual arts center that for Le Corbusier may have been meaningful and evocative of rejuvenation through a return to his own roots also anchor the building all the more strongly to a past that, as far as providing forms for the future is concerned, must be treated with caution.

What remains valid is principle and method alone because they can generate new forms in new contexts. Le Corbusier shortly before his death warned "rien n'est transmissible que la pensée"[65] ("nothing is transmissible but thought"). It was solely as a contribution to the better understanding of his *manière de penser* that the present study was undertaken.

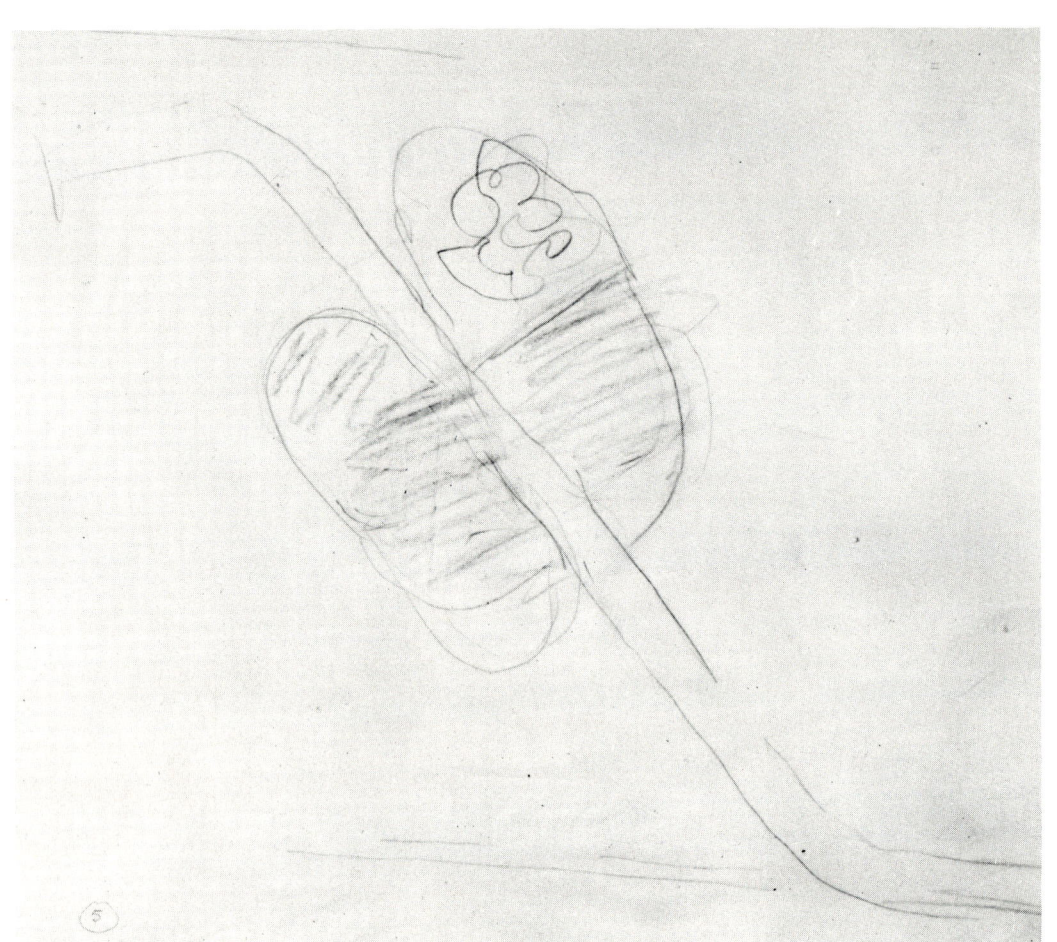

NOTES ON CREATIVE INVENTION

Rudolf Arnheim

The case history of an architectural project is bound to attract the attention of the psychologist. As creativity is increasingly threatened by the mechanization of production and conduct, we take an almost frantic interest in the conditions of human invention. Although not reducible to machine operations, creative thought proceeds according to principles that can be identified. These rules do not fully describe the process of problem solving in any particular example but they offer generalizations on typical strategies of the inventive mind—strategies that are remarkably similar in different human activities, even though their applications vary. To be sure, it makes a difference whether the target is a physical object, such as a building, a machine, or a piece of sculpture, or whether it is a poem or a scientific law. Also the variety of purposes which inventions must meet has a bearing on the nature of the solutions to be sought. Nevertheless, the striking similarities of procedure preempt our interest.

By the nature of their subject, pronouncements on creativity tend to be lofty. The examination of individual cases serves to counterbalance this temptation by warning the explorer of the complexity prevailing under practical conditions and by providing tangible illustrations that give flesh and blood to theory. Therefore the opportunity offered by the detailed biography of a work of architectural genius should not be missed. The following remarks formulate some of my first observations in response to the rich material collected in the present volume.

One safe generalization has it that every creative invention develops from a relatively simple kernel. The nature of this nuclear conception could be described fairly easily if, like the biological embryo, it resembled the final creature in all essential aspects. Some products of the mind meet this simple condition approximately. A musical idea commonly resembles the final composition in kind. Both are patterns of sound. But a piece of sculpture may spring from the "idea" of representing peace or justice, in which case a nonsculptural and perhaps nonvisual conception is the initial item.

What does the first idea of an architectural project look like? Is it a little image of a building? Sometimes, but not often. More typically the program given to the architect enumerates functions or describes desirable qualities by words such as "intimate," "monumental," "simple." However, the discrepancy between the nonvisual specifications and the germinal architectural form is not as great as it may appear in theory. All thought is based on imagery, much of it visual. Even the most elementary consideration of what, for example, "a school of art" shall be like will come forward with statements such as: "There should be facilities for the teaching of two-dimensional and three-dimensional design, and space will be needed for exhibitions and for administration." Almost automatically, the visual equivalent of such an enumeration will be an aggregate of containers, stacked vertically or assembled horizontally, but certainly characterized as a sum of distinct entities. There is an imperceptible shift from the spatial arrangement of the list of requirements submitted by the client on a piece of paper to its translation into a most elementary group of spatial volumes. Where does the architecture begin? There is so much intercommunication between program and architectural design that if, for example, at an advanced stage of the planning the architect wonders whether the studio areas for painting and sculpture should really remain separate or should combine or overlap in some way, this spatial consideration directly modifies the educational program of the school to be housed in the building.

The earliest shapes occupying the minds of planners are so simple that one hesitates to call them shapes at all. The search for a proper site, for example, is surely a visual task, but what is being moved around on the map may as yet have no defined outline and therefore be represented by a circular patch, which stands for mere "thingness." However, not only the location but also the approximate size of the building may be indicated by that first noncommittal circle. Beyond that, its roundness, taken more literally, may state that the building will differ in shape from the surrounding cubes, and it may also express compactness—a volume gathered around its center rather than stretched out along a line.

A circle, though elementary, has a tangible shape. Some of the most concrete aspects of early conception may be even less corporeal. It is evident that Le Corbusier's decisive impulses were in part purely dynamic. The very modern notion that the building, although solid, should be permeable conveys the idea of a perforation, of bridges or tunnels, without connotations of particular shape. In fact, the bare paradox of a permeable solid can present itself with great precision but without palpable geometry of any kind.

The same can be said about the theme of aggressive intrusion, the diagonal imposed upon the checkerboard of traditional cubes. The diagonal solves the problem of how to obtain the greatest extension in a rectangular area, but it is also the spontaneous symbol of deviance, of nonconformism. It exerts this function as a mere direction, just as the gesture of the *coup de poing* aimed at the fenced-in, rigidly angular heartland of the Yard can remain disembodied for some time without lacking concreteness and precision. Muscular sensations, reported Albert Einstein, were important elements of his thought, and according to the somewhat impetuous thesis propounded in Heinrich Wölfflin's doctoral dissertation, muscular sensations are the base of all architectural expression.

The story of the Carpenter Center offers many illustrations of the development from simple to complex patterns in the process of creative invention. For example, early conceptions tend to cling to symmetry. As a rule, this is less evident in the work of seasoned professionals, but it is strikingly demonstrated nevertheless in Le Corbusier's sketches which present the building as a pair of kidney-shaped volumes attached to the stem of the ramp, which at first is a straight central spine rather than an S-curve. The psychologist watches with interest how the initial simplicity of this pattern is gradually modified under the pressure of functional demands, which impose different conditions on the two halves of the building, only to return to a compelling, though more sophisticated symmetry in the final plan. Simplicity is an early and also a final condition of successful problem solving, but whereas early simplicity is still innocent of the vicissitudes to come, final simplicity is admirable for having tackled them all and prevailing nevertheless.[1] The simplicity of the underlying theme remains perceivable in the final composition. Under the simplifying influence of memory the implicit symmetries and elementary shapes emerge from the mature complexity of the actual building.

Another instance of a guiding symmetry is the image of the stair tower as the central stem toward which the ramp rises and from which it descends (fig. 52). Again this centrality will be overruled by later demands, but the stair tower remains a dominant vertical even in its final eccentric position and shares the function of a supporting spine with the cubic core of the building, which, although invisible from the outside, plays the central role originally envisaged for the tower. Here again the final complexity preserves the original theme in a more differentiated version.

Parallelism of shape, but also of direction, is another feature of early conception. Thus the two halves of the building point at first in the same direction (fig. 61), supporting a simple distinction between a front side and a back side. Le Corbusier's dramatic flipping of the shapes transforms this parallelism of direction into an antagonism of rotational symmetry, with the two volumes pointing now in opposite directions. Beyond parallelism, the right angle is the simplest spatial relation the mind can conceive. Examples are provided by the rectangular element connecting the two halves of the building across the central ramp in figure 56 and the curious attempt to arrange them at right angles in figure 55.

The tidiness of early conceptions shuns the mutual interference brought about by overlapping. Each element preserves its territorial integrity. There is at first a clear distinction in plan between the curved lateral areas and the rectangular core in the center. Only later can the mind face the risk of the confusion resulting from the superposition of shapes invading each other. The final solution intertwines curved and angular spaces, creating a sophisticated complexity that would have been inconceivable without the neat distinction preceding it. Similarly, in the vertical dimension it takes some boldness to break through the orderly stacking of floors, each assigned to a different function. To think of ramps crossing the horizontal arrangements of the floors obliquely taxes the spatial imagination. Similarly, the thought of letting the auditorium reach through two floors introduces a vertical connection that must overcome the conservative resistance of a mind committed to the simple system of layers.

Even the complexity of the final design respects certain distinctions, which give manifest appearance to the structural order. For example, one need only compare figures 65 and 130 to share the architect's uneasiness about the fusion of the stair tower with the contour of the southern wing. In fact, the completed building preserves very skillfully the visual integrity of the tower while at the same time protecting it from isolation by various lateral connections.

One of the most helpful basic distinctions is that between inside and outside. Two common types of architectural solution clearly differ as to their level of sophistication in this respect—even though buildings of great beauty may derive from either principle. At a simpler level of problem solving the outside of the building conforms to a geometrical volume which envelops it with an unbroken skin. This container surrounds the various spaces fulfilling the functions of the building. There is a clear separation—although no lack of correspondence

—between outside and inside. This is easy on the mind's power of spatial organization. Renaissance palaces may serve as an example of this approach. The second type of building is conceived as an aggregate of volumes, which reach all the way through its inside and whose nature can only be inferred from the partial shapes they exhibit on the outside. Overriding the distinction between inside and outside, this sort of conception strains spatial imagination. The Carpenter Center belongs in this category. It involves a truly three-dimensional complexity, which cannot be fully grasped by either plan or section.

The distinction between inside and outside affects also the relation between the building and its environment. When Le Corbusier observes that a living being is sometimes called a digestive tract and goes on to assert that "architecture is internal circulation," he may have in mind the biological conception of the "milieu intérieur" ("internal environment") proposed by Claude Bernard.[2] There is, in evolution, an increasing sophistication of nature, rather similar to that observed in human problem solving. One such development transfers the outer environment of the aquatic animal to the chemical ingredients of the liquids circulating inside the body of the terrestrial mammal. Le Corbusier's vision of people moving not only toward and away from, as well as within, the building but right through it is another breach of the conceptual barrier between inside and outside, and so is the internalized landscape of plants and rocks on the terraces. Also the internal windows through which the exhibition space, the auditorium, and the studios can be viewed from the ramp or the lounge differentiate the originally simple distinction between in and out.

This draws our attention to the related phenomenon of how and when extrinsic factors are adapted to the nuclear conception. I referred earlier to the way in which forms emerge initially in response to functional demands of the program. However, once established, the developing architectural shape easily yields to the temptation of developing autonomously as though it were an abstract crystal growing in empty space, and the functional conditions to be observed assume the role of external modifiers, whose demands are heeded when they can no longer be ignored. It is surely significant for the way of thinking and thereby for the style of an architect which functional dimensions are considered from the beginning as being of the essence—circulation is one of them in Le Corbusier's case—and which others seem to be viewed more nearly as alien intruders, whose demands are met through secondary modifications of the otherwise autonomous conception. Among the examples that come to mind is the slope of the terrain, which led to the digging of the pit—clearly an afterthought, not adopted for its positive virtues but resorted to negatively in order to create a breathing space beneath the protruding north studio. Other such factors are the reduction of the building's scale to meet the budget and to keep it away from its neighbors, the orientation with regard to the positions of the sun, the adaptation to the grid of structural supports, the thickening of the floors for the accommodation of heating and ventilation ducts, and so forth.

In addition to the gradual differentiation leading from simple to complex patterns, one notices other principles equally typical for processes of creative invention. Not only in architecture but in other areas of problem solving as well, the initial situation contains a number of constituent elements that are rather clearly defined in themselves but are afloat, devoid of any final anchoring to one another. Various locations and combinations are tried out, each revealing its particular advantages and disadvantages. But they fall decisively into place only when the particular location or combination is convincingly confirmed by the total layout, not just by an acceptable arrangement of some details; and in turn they help to complete that total arrangement. When the stair tower finds its place in the southwest corner of the building, it acts like a keystone completing an arch by giving actuality to the skeleton of the plan as a whole. Local conflicts, such as that between the ramp and the elevator, are not ironed out until the particular relation between the two elements can be understood in the total context. Redundancy also, such as that leading to the elimination of the secondary ramp, can be diagnosed only by criteria derived from the whole design.

For the purpose of such arrangement and

rearrangement, the constituent elements are treated essentially as coordinated equals. Cardboard cutouts are moved about on a board. Inevitably, however, the search for the proper configuration is also an attempt to establish a suitable hierarchy. The various components carry different weights, although these weights may be readjusted in the process. In Le Corbusier's early conception, the main emphasis was given to the third level, which was therefore slated to accommodate not only the exhibition space but also the administrative offices. When this solution, based on the symbolism of ascent, was vetoed for practical reasons, it was not possible to accompany the shift of the hierarchic accent to the groundfloor with a corresponding restructuring of the whole building. The position of the ramp, which spelled out the original conception, was no longer negotiable. Consequently, in the final realization the architectural gesture pointed to a functionally weakened center on the third floor and by its power prevented any other floor level from establishing an alternative dominance. The example not only shows how an inconclusive compromise between coordination and subordination leaves the visitor suspended in his quest for guidance, but also illustrates the typical process of gradual hardening by which more and more elements and relations lose their initial flexibility and become constraints, limiting the degrees of freedom available for further readjustment.

This gradual consolidation is indispensable for the progress toward a stable solution. When, however, the design has hardened in a way not conducive to a viable solution, forceful restructuring must take the place of gradual modification. The conditions that call for such a revolution as well as the boldness needed to undertake it are illustrated by the telling episode in the history of the Carpenter Center when Le Corbusier "made a tracing on a loose sheet of the large curved studio facing Quincy Street, flipped the form over on its end and tucked it alongside the main ramp facing Prescott Street." This revolutionary move not only took care of a number of practical problems, but also gave the architectural solution the kind of elegance that makes for beauty.

It has often been observed that ugliness is a revealing characteristic of a situation suffering from an unsolved problem. The lack of proportion and unity characterizing such a situation is not only visual, though it does show up in drawings like figures 65 and 130. Looked at by themselves, there is nothing wrong with the shapes assigned to the south and southeast areas of the building. In fact, the outline indicated in figures 65 and 84 was sanctioned by associations with the shape of bottles and the human figure. But when one considers the plan in retrospect one sees that the two halves of the design were not balanced. The northern wing was overpoweringly strong not only because of its large area but also because of the compelling beauty of its solid and dynamic shape. By repeating this pattern on the south side the architect replaced a weak form with a stronger one. What is more, he gave his building a new simplicity, which pulled everything together in a unified shape. The solution convinces us immediately as a valid addition to our store of significant shapes and thereby acquires a permanence more durable than carefully poured concrete.

THE HAND AND THE HEAD AT THE CARPENTER CENTER

Barbara Norfleet

Even at birth the Carpenter Center was thought to be different from any other building. It gives you a vision of quality. It assaults the senses. It is a work of high art, a piece of sculpture; it is a building that is clearly not just a means to an end, but a building that is an end in itself. You cannot be indifferent to it. You are encouraged to look closely, study its forms, take in the changing lights and shadows, analyze, and make judgments.

What is it like to work in a building whose presence is so felt? It does not lie around waiting to be used, to serve its function. It relentlessly reminds you of its first-rateness. It mocks your own little creations with its greatness.

In the spring of 1973 a sample of half the faculty and some students and staff were interviewed to get their feelings about the building and about working in it. One faculty member could find no fault and was inspired and renewed daily by just being there, and one condemned each and every piece of concrete and sliver of winking glass. Reactions to the Carpenter Center tended to be just as complex as the building itself: there was often a love–hate relationship, with all the closeness, fondness, and frustration it entails. Each Carpenter Center inhabitant had some unique attitudes about the ways the building affected his own work and the work of his students, but a majority seemed to agree about the building's dual impact. It is almost as if the building has a split personality: when people spoke of the forms, of the light and of the space, they were ecstatic; when they spoke of the texture, the noise, and the somberness, they were glum. One individual said, "I like it in winter. It is so lovely upstairs with light and air all around. It is like being enclosed above ground but like being all open. You look across and up and down. It's lovely." The same person then added, "I'm not sure what I would prefer to the Carpenter Center, but I think of wooden frame houses with wood floors and old staircases. I think of soft sounds and no echoes. It would smell different—of pipe tobacco and of rugs, not of concrete."

A visiting artist had a project that took him all over the building. "I climbed through and all over the building. I had the right keys to get on terraces, bays, and roofs. Here was a truly cubistic space in the finest sense which I was only able to see in one, at best two dimensions ordinarily. It opened up the complexity and excitement of the penetration and spacial variations in that complex. Moving from interior space to tunnel-like protected space was extremely exciting and made you feel you were in the middle of a building the way Corbu meant you to be. He permitted so much of the outside world into it. Once I got outside it helped me invent vigorous, inventive exploration of space in my own work. Suddenly the grayness, the hardness, the bad feel of the whole color–texture–noise–smell of the building was replaced by the notion of high quality, of a big statement."

Perhaps one student was also getting at this inside–outside view when he said, "It is beautiful from the outside, a real center of the visual arts, playful and impressive all at once. From the inside it is less pleasing. I guess it appears more functional than it really is." It is interesting that this student spent all of his time in the basement, which he found to be inhuman, noisy, hard on the feet.

There was much joking from almost all the interviewees about the building having been designed for a different time and place. One artist told me the rumor that it had been designed for Baghdad and by mistake the package came to Boston. An architect said he was sure it was meant for Marseille. He went on to say that Le Corbusier had "no feel for cold weather and the need to psychologically keep it out." Another staff member was sure it was meant to be in Rome where the "grey concrete, the huge quantities of glass, the hardness, would have been cooling, not cold." "When the sun is out, this building is twinkling and festive, but it's usually the smog that's out," sadly stated one student. No one interviewed liked the outside sunken, enclosed area under the overhang of the second floor. It was called the cave, the cellar, the swimming pool, the snake pit. One person said he was going to make a point of visiting the center on the hottest day of August so that he could say he had once used it. It was the unused snake pit that made people think Le Corbusier had no understanding of the New England climate.

"You get to know everybody here, not just because it is a small department, but because of the lobby. I almost think one should choose a college major on the basis of whether the department has a lobby. Of course there are lobbies and lobbies. The one in William James Hall doesn't work. It's isolated, separated from the flow of people," said one student. Most people liked the Carpenter Center's lobby once rugs, tables, and leather cushions were there. "Things happen in the lobby. I like to see it changed by student work. It lends itself to all kinds of imaginative activities, ranging from great parties, to quiet discussions, to changed visual environments," stated one faculty member. "The lobby is immediate. All exhibits should be there," said another. "The fact that we all wander around the lobby is very friendly, even if we do have slightly schizoid conversations with no beginnings or endings. You sort of walk in and out and have glancing circular encounters, and at the same time are close to everyone. It's a little like a family. Maybe that is the one thing we gained by locking off the other umpteen entrances." "I can even take my naps there," said one student. They also thought the coffee and cake that was served there in the late afternoon was a wonderful kind of luxury. "It encouraged you to stay late and work hard."

Harvard is an enormous and diversified institution. Becoming a concentrator in a small department like Visual Studies is one way to combat this hugeness, but even a small department needs a place for all to gather, to wander through, to sit and rest. The lobby works because it encourages intimacy and a sense of community.

The interviews were filled with attitudes about the unused and locked away terraces, roofs, and ramps. There was great sadness that these spaces were there to see, but no longer there to be part of everyday living in the Carpenter Center. Again, numerous people brought up the myth that the building had been designed for a sunnier climate. Many reported that various doors are now always locked. "Corbu thought we were all brothers; he didn't know we were all thieves."

Like the visiting artist mentioned above, the fortunate few who have sneaked out onto roofs and terraces all spoke of how wonderful it was: "The few times I have been illegally on the roof it was lovely." "I think 'sundeck' the whole time I'm typing down here." "Yesterday both doors onto the ramp were open and suddenly the exhibition room became a wonderful space and I was tempted to go into it, and I went." "Corbu should have given us a concierge to guard each door of the building so we could use it the way he meant it to be used." "I met architecture head on through this building when I was once allowed to crawl all over it." "The animation is destroyed by all the locked doors."

People felt the exhibition hall lacked the warmth and intimacy of the lobby. The general idea was expressed by one instructor: "The exhibition hall is too separate, both in space and content. It is not part of us. I guess I think of it as a public gallery which happens to be at Harvard and happens to be here." "The exhibition space should be a classroom or studio. We don't need a museum here," said another.

The general feeling was not against having exhibitions or against the exhibition space itself; most people found the space beautiful and coveted it for their own use. "The exhibition hall is away by itself and private. It should be a studio for advanced students." "I'd like to see the exhibition hall space exchanged with one of the studios. The studios should have some privacy, but exhibitions gain from a lot of hustle and bustle." "The exhibitions should be in a spot where you have to go by, where you have to stop and see them. That is why I like shows in the lobby. You see them every day and after a week you begin to see them differently." "The location of the exhibition hall made sense when the ramp drew people into the architecture and filled people's minds with our visual experiments, but with all the locked doors the ramp ceased to be the backbone of the building."

Many of the people quoted above played architect. "We should glass in the cross-over from the third floor, right across the ramp, and then the exhibition hall would be part of the building." "Any exhibition here must compete with the whole building. The building and the student's work are both on show. It is doubly necessary to make the exhibitions accessible. Maybe we should move the whole administration up there and have the whole first floor exhibition space." Several people suggested that the "snake pit" be glassed in and made into an exhibition room and that the door between the lobby and it should be kept open.

It is interesting how private these attitudes are. Only one person took cognizance of the deliberate attempt to have exhibitions serve the whole Harvard and Cambridge community, not just those who use the Carpenter Center daily. He said, "The exhibition hall is a necessary part of the life of this place. It is one of the things that makes the building special. It is the only place where we deliberately display works and that is very important." It would be interesting to know how the outside public feels about the space. They do use the ramp to get to it, and so they experience this part of the building as Le Corbusier meant it to be experienced.

People who work in the center resent the intrusion of the public into their private world, and some feel that the use of the exhibition room for shows encourages this intrusion. Quietness, isolation, and removal from the bustle and business of everyday life is the traditional vision of the academic scholar's world. This nineteenth century romantic image of the lonely creator pleases the artist as well. In spite of the intrusion of the telephone, the mushrooming of committee work, the huge grants for multistaffed projects, the faculty forays to the outside world for exposure and supplementary income, there still exists the notion that creativity is antithetical to worldliness and the intermingling of people.

Although both students and faculty want to protect their world from unsought contacts with the "real" world, they are usually unaware of how cleverly the building does protect them. The public must get to the most public space, the exhibition hall, using a ramp that is totally outside the building. The ramp leads to only one open and unlocked door and that door is to the exhibition room. The exhibition room leads only back to the ramp. If casual passersby enter the lobby, the one other public space, they do not fare much better. They may look at the exhibitions there, but there is no place else to wander. They may go up and down stairways, but if they do they are met by signs on every door leading out of the stairwell stating, "No Visitors in Workshops." They are confined to the stairwell. For the most part, the visitors heed the signs. They do not wander about classrooms and studios. They may gawk with curiosity through the thick glass walls, but they are separated by many feet from the students who are working and they cannot be heard nor can they interfere. It is the public who are frustrated and ask plaintively if there is any place they may go or if the building is *ever* opened up. Obviously the building was designed primarily for teaching and studio work and not for public viewing. Its neighbor, the Fogg Art Museum, is a museum first and a teaching department second. The Fogg has a public feel about it that is totally absent from the Carpenter Center; somehow, Carpenter turns in on itself in spite of all its glass. If doors were unlocked, crossways glassed over, exhibitions put into areas within the main-building, this brilliant separation of public and private spaces would be destroyed. It is astonishing how little the public intrudes in Harvard's most famous building.

The ambivalence of students towards the public was made clear after space in Sever Hall was acquired by the department. Students were encouraged to exhibit their work in the gloomy and spacious hall of Sever, but there was almost no desire to do this. The students wanted the lobby of the Carpenter Center or the exhibition hall because they wanted the public to see their work and the public did not wander through Sever. Protecting one's privacy while exposing one's wares is never easy. It is just as difficult for the Carpenter Center as a department to establish communication and understanding with other parts of the university while it maintains its sense of privacy and intimacy. Nevertheless, it is clear that Le Corbusier wanted the ramp to draw the whole university and the public into the Carpenter Center.

Several faculty members felt the building in its greatness overpowered a student's work and made it hard for any student to do anything as good as the building itself. Not one student felt this way. The students were inspired by the building. One student said that "far from being oppressive, the very greatness of this building makes me want to do something big." Another student said, "You can't think small in a building like this." Two other students said that the building itself had inspired them to become architects. Another said he knew he was going to this special place to do special work.

Even though neither faculty nor student saw any real communication among the different floors or activities of the center, several students felt that the building represented an intellectual model of visual expression and that they would somehow seek and find the key to it all. One very perceptive student mentioned that "the stairwell isolates you because of the large landings and closed doors. You have to be filled with purpose and determination to enter any studio on the other side. It does not invite you to be curious and casual." Many students said, "The building begged to be played with, to be opened up, to be transformed."

The students in the basement, however, spoke about the crowded darkrooms and the need for more space. They wanted to spend more time in the building, twenty-four hours a day, in fact, but this was mostly to be able to use the equipment under less crowded conditions. In contrast an upstairs student said, "It is so expanding to do studio work here." Still, the upstairs students, too, desire more privacy. "I feel like a celebrity, but sometimes I want to be alone and contemplative with my work and that's impossible in studios."

The greatest complaint the students had about the building was that it was treated like a precious object, as if Le Corbusier was sacred and so was his building. "You can't slop, you can't hang things," complained one student. "The building is a showroom. It only becomes alive when it is cluttered and spilled upon, but you can't do that," said a faculty member. "We can't slop because everything is expensive and polished. The Carpenter Center is paranoid about hurting Corbu's building. The great thing about this building is that it could take it." "The building is more important than the sum of its parts. Even when you are creating a work of art, you must protect the whole building, and you are punished if you manage to forget this restriction. It is not healthy to be so neat when you are making things." "I hunger for mess." These were the opinions of the people working upstairs. Faculty and students in the basement film and photography rooms recognize that dirt and dust are their enemies and they want neatness and strict punishment of the slovenly.

The faculty, even while stating that they found it impossible to get any of their own work done in the building because of a lack of space and privacy, wished that this was not so. They wanted to spend more time there. It is interesting that only one could think of a specific building he would rather be in, and that building had to do with sunsets and rivers. All the others said that they would not want to be in any other Harvard building, although one longed for "a large void, an old boathouse, a loft, a warehouse, something I could live in and transform." This would appear to be a private dream rather than a demand on Harvard's resources.

The faculty who used the studios on the upper floors loved them. Most of the comments about the building as a stimulus to creative work refer to work in the studios. They have lots of glass, fascinating views across interior spaces to other parts of the building. They are the inspiration that Le Corbusier intended them to be.

The basement is another story. Le Corbusier planned that the film and photography area would be on the first floor. It was shifted to the basement, and not everyone likes it. "There is no sense of space in the basement at all. I just don't count the basement when I think of the building." "I constantly want to be out of it. It's not even seasonal down here; it's a gopher hole." "The basement is about dampness, about being enclosed, about not seeing around corners, about no perspective. It is the antithesis of the rest of the building." "One is a mole." "I am under the pyramids." "The basement is at its best when you get out of it and walk to Harvard Square." These are the opinions of those who worked in the basement.

The upstairs people, however, who admitted they had a luxurious feeling of spaciousness, envied the basement people because they were "so close to one another, a real community," "in a no-nonsense work place," "packed and crowded and stacked up," and "filled with constant ant-like intense and lively activity." They also envied the basement people because they do not have to handle constant intrusions from the outside world. One instructor with a studio easily seen from the ramp said, "There is no distinction here between the public and private. People take pictures of us as if we were birds. The high school troops through." Another teacher said, "People stare at us all the time from the ramp. Finally my students put up big signs that said, 'You look funny too!'" But these same people spoke of how great it was to "look out and see beyond the place you were working, to look beyond the immediate environment. You can hang things on the ramp, in natural light, and see them from afar."

Perhaps this kind of ambivalence was best expressed by a visiting artist. He started out in the basement which he found to be gray, austere, noisy, hard, and cold. At the same time he saw the building as "an immediate and great piece" and the people in the basement as "doing fascinating things and involved in diverse and different projects, and I liked it and them and found the atmosphere exciting."

Carpenter Center began as a great space to fill, but became overcrowded as the department expanded. Overflow space was then provided, first in Hunt Hall, and later in Sever Hall, and the crowding problem subsided. As one student said in 1976, "Carpenter Center has a sense of grand loneliness—it is a pleasant place to work because it is so generous with space. Sever is for the sloppy overflow. It is nice having the two atmospheres."

Perhaps one faculty member described the Carpenter Center best. He said, "The kind of space in which you do things is very important. If I were in another Harvard building, the difference would be fantastic for me. I've been spoiled. I would feel I was in a chicken coop, compared with the generosity of our building here. Here I have large halls to walk through and no walls hemming me in. There is a difference in my whole stance. My self-image as a member of Harvard University is influenced by being in this Roman sort of building, and not being tucked away some place. I have the feeling of royalty."

LIST OF CORRESPONDENCE AND DOCUMENTS

The design and construction of the Carpenter Center produced many documents. The following is a list of those that are referred to by date in this volume. The nature of each is briefly indicated, as well as its location. The majority of letters marked "Fondation Le Corbusier" exist as original carbon copies either in J. L. Sert's possession or in the Carpenter Center archives.

Appendix 1; Report of the Committee on the Practice of the Visual Arts, 1957–58: Educational and Building Programs; Carpenter Center archives.

6-26-58; J. L. Sert to M. Bundy; Carpenter Center archives.

7-3-58; M. Bundy to J. L. Sert; possession of J. L. Sert.

7-11-58; M. Bundy to H. Carpenter; Carpenter Center archives.

7-21-58; appendix 2; A. St. Vrain Carpenter to M. Bundy; Carpenter Center archives.

10-16-58; J. L. Sert to Le Corbusier; Fondation Le Corbusier.

10-27-58; appendix 3; Le Corbusier to J. L. Sert; possession of J. L. Sert.

11-14-58; J. L. Sert to Le Corbusier; Fondation Le Corbusier.

4-23-59; appendix 4; E. Reynolds to Le Corbusier; Fondation Le Corbusier.

4-28-59; J. L. Sert to Le Corbusier; Fondation Le Corbusier.

275

5-12-59; appendix 5; Le Corbusier to J. L. Sert; possession of J. L. Sert.

5-14-59; appendix 6; Le Corbusier to J. L. Sert; possession of J. L. Sert.

5-27-59; J. L. Sert to Le Corbusier; Fondation Le Corbusier.

6-25-59; appendix 7; Le Corbusier to J. L. Sert; possession of J. L. Sert.

7-9-59; Sigfried Giedion to J. L. Sert; possession of J. L. Sert.

7-59; Le Corbusier, notes during interview with J. L. Sert, Paris; Fondation Le Corbusier.

10-6-59; J. L. Sert to Le Corbusier; Fondation Le Corbusier.

10-6-59; E. Reynolds to Le Corbusier; Fondation Le Corbusier.

10-19-59; Le Corbusier to J. L. Sert; possession of J. L. Sert.

10-19-59; Le Corbusier to E. Reynolds; Fondation Le Corbusier.

10-30-59; E. Reynolds to Le Corbusier; Fondation Le Corbusier.

11-1-59; J. L. Sert to Le Corbusier; Fondation Le Corbusier.

11-5-59; appendix 8; Le Corbusier to J. L. Sert; possession of J. L. Sert.

11-24-59; A. St. Vrain Carpenter to N. Pusey; Carpenter Center archives.

12-2-59; A. St. Vrain Carpenter to A. D. Trottenberg; Carpenter Center archives.

12-2-59; N. Pusey to Mr. and Mrs. St. Vrain Carpenter; possession of Mrs. Carpenter.

2-9-60; J. L. Sert to Le Corbusier; Fondation Le Corbusier.

2-15-60; Le Corbusier to J. L. Sert; possession of J. L. Sert.

3-14-60; J. L. Sert to Le Corbusier; Fondation Le Corbusier.

3-60; J. Coolidge, notes in reaction to building program; copy in Carpenter Center archives.

4-11-60; A. D. Trottenberg to Le Corbusier; Fondation Le Corbusier.

4-15-60; appendix 9; A. St. Vrain Carpenter to A. D. Trottenberg; Carpenter Center archives.

5-27-60; Le Corbusier to J. L. Sert; possession of J. L. Sert.

6-7-60; Le Corbusier to J. L. Sert; possession of J. L. Sert.

6-20-60; A. D. Trottenberg to E. F. Sekler; possession of E. F. Sekler.

8-10-60; A. D. Trottenberg to J. L. Sert; possession of J. L. Sert.

8-12-60; A. D. Trottenberg to J. L. Sert; possession of J. L. Sert.

8-31-60; appendix 10; J. L. Sert to Le Corbusier; Fondation Le Corbusier.

9-1-60; J. L. Sert to Le Corbusier; Fondation Le Corbusier.

9-14-60; Le Corbusier to J. L. Sert; possession of J. L. Sert.

10-4-60; J. L. Sert to Le Corbusier; Fondation Le Corbusier.

10-12-60; J. L. Sert to Le Corbusier; Fondation Le Corbusier.

10-27-60; budgetary figures, first project, J. C. Deveney; Carpenter Center archives.

10-2-60; M. Bundy to N. Pusey; Carpenter Center archives.

10-8-60; Jullian de la Fuente to J. L. Sert; possession of J. L. Sert.

11-3-60; J. L. Sert to Le Corbusier; Fondation Le Corbusier.

11-15-60; J. L. Sert to Jullian de la Fuente; Fondation Le Corbusier.

11-16-60; H. Jackson to Jullian de la Fuente; Fondation Le Corbusier.

12-3-60; Le Corbusier to J. L. Sert; possession of J. L. Sert.

12-3-60; appendix 11; Le Corbusier to J. L. Sert; possession of J. L. Sert.

12-19-60; appendix 12; Le Corbusier to J. L. Sert; possession of J. L. Sert.

12-28-60; H. Jackson to J. L. Sert; possession of J. L. Sert.

1-11-61; H. Jackson to J. L. Sert; possession of J. L. Sert.

1-30-61; J. L. Sert to Le Corbusier; Fondation Le Corbusier.

2-4-61; Le Corbusier to J. L. Sert; possession of J. L. Sert.

2-18-61; Le Corbusier to J. L. Sert; possession of J. L. Sert.

2-27-61; Le Corbusier to J. L. Sert; possession of J. L. Sert.

2-28-61; appendix 13; Le Corbusier to J. L. Sert; possession of J. L. Sert.

3-8-61; appendix 14; Jullian de la Fuente to J. L. Sert; possession of J. L. Sert.

3-24-61; A. D. Trottenberg to N. Pusey; Carpenter Center archives.

3-24-61; appendix 15; A. D. Trottenberg to J. L. Sert; possession of J. L. Sert.

4-6-61; W. Le Messurier to Sert, Jackson and Gourley; possession of J. L. Sert.

4-7-61; Sert, Jackson and Gourley to Le Corbusier; Fondation Le Corbusier.

5-1-61; report of New York conference between J. L. Sert and Le Corbusier, 4-29-61; possession of J. L. Sert.

5-12-61; J. C. Deveney to L. G. Wiggins; Carpenter Center archives.

5-29-61; appendix 16; Le Corbusier to J. L. Sert; possession of J. L. Sert.

5-31-61; Jullian de la Fuente to J. L. Sert; possession of J. L. Sert.

6-2-61; J. C. Deveney to L. G. Wiggins; Carpenter Center archives.

6-20-61; memorandum, Sert, Jackson and Gourley; possession

of J. L. Sert.

6-26-61; N. Pusey to A. D. Trottenberg; Carpenter Center archives.

7-3-61; J. L. Sert to Le Corbusier; Fondation Le Corbusier.

7-27-61; Le Corbusier to J. L. Sert; possession of J. L. Sert.

8-30-61; J. L. Sert to Le Corbusier; Fondation Le Corbusier.

9-6-61; Bolt, Beranek and Newman to P. Krueger; possession of J. L. Sert.

9-23-61; Le Corbusier to J. L. Sert; possession of J. L. Sert.

9-29-61; J. L. Sert to Le Corbusier; Fondation Le Corbusier.

10-20-61; memorandum, Sert, Jackson and Gourley; possession of J. L. Sert.

10-23-61; J. L. Sert to Le Corbusier; Fondation Le Corbusier.

10-26-61; Le Corbusier to J. L. Sert; possession of J. L. Sert.

10-30-61; Jullian de la Fuente to J. L. Sert; possession of J. L. Sert.

11-3-61; memorandum on concrete, Sert, Jackson and Gourley; possession of J. L. Sert.

11-6-61; appendix 17; Le Corbusier to J. L. Sert; possession of J. L. Sert.

11-8-61; Le Corbusier to J. L. Sert; possession of J. L. Sert.

11-9-61; appendix 18; Le Corbusier to J. L. Sert; possession of J. L. Sert.

12-8-61; J. L. Sert to Le Corbusier; Fondation Le Corbusier.

12-12-61; J. L. Sert to Le Corbusier; Fondation Le Corbusier.

12-19-61; Le Corbusier to J. L. Sert; possession of J. L. Sert.

12-29-61; Le Corbusier to J. L. Sert; possession of J. L. Sert.

1-8-62; Le Corbusier to J. L. Sert; possession of J. L. Sert.

1-10-62; Le Corbusier to J. L. Sert; possession of J. L. Sert.

1-11-62; appendix 19; Le Corbusier to J. L. Sert; possession of J. L. Sert.

1-30-62; J. L. Sert to Le Corbusier; Fondation Le Corbusier.

2-5-62; Le Corbusier to J. L. Sert; possession of J. L. Sert.

2-14-62; memorandum on budget and building size, Sert, Jackson and Gourley; possession of J. L. Sert.

2-15-62; A. D. Trottenberg to L. G. Wiggins; Carpenter Center archives.

2-21-62; Bolt, Beranek and Newman to Paul Krueger; possession of J. L. Sert.

3-5-62; memorandum L. G. Wiggins to N. Pusey; Carpenter Center archives.

4-10-62; J. L. Sert to Le Corbusier; Fondation Le Corbusier.

4-23-62; J. L. Sert to Le Corbusier; Fondation Le Corbusier.

4-26-62; K. Leach to Sert, Jackson and Gourley; possession of J. L. Sert.

5-26-62; appendix 20; Le Corbusier to J. L. Sert; possession of J. L. Sert.

5-30-62; Jullian de la Fuente to J. L. Sert; possession of J. L. Sert.

6-13-62; J. L. Sert to J. Petit; possession of J. L. Sert.

7-18-62; Le Corbusier to H. Jackson; possession of J. L. Sert.

7-19-62; H. Jackson to Jullian de la Fuente; Fondation Le Corbusier.

7-31-62; Le Corbusier to H. Jackson; possession of J. L. Sert.

8-62; H. Jackson to Jullian de la Fuente; Fondation Le Corbusier.

9-6-62; Jullian de la Fuente to H. Jackson; possession of J. L. Sert.

10-9-62; J. L. Sert to Le Corbusier; Fondation Le Corbusier.

10-11-62; F. Ford to A. D. Trottenberg; Carpenter Center archives.

10-15-62; F. Ford to A. D. Trottenberg; Carpenter Center archives.

10-15-62; appendix 21; Le Corbusier to J. L. Sert; possession of J. L. Sert.

10-18-62; N. Pusey to F. Ford; Carpenter Center archives.

4-1-63; N. Pusey to Le Corbusier; Fondation Le Corbusier.

4-5-63; appendix 22; Le Corbusier to N. Pusey; Carpenter Center archives.

4-9-63; N. Pusey to Le Corbusier; Fondation Le Corbusier.

Appendix 23; list of consultants, contractors, and members of the office of Sert, Jackson and Gourley who worked on the Carpenter Center.

Appendix 24; building adaptations from 1962 through 1976.

APPENDICES

Appendix 1

REPORT OF THE COMMITTEE ON THE PRACTICE OF THE VISUAL ARTS

FOR THE YEAR 1957–58

Almost immediately after the appointment of the Committee on the Practice of the Visual Arts, the generous gift of Mr. and Mrs. Alfred St. Vrain Carpenter was announced. Being thus confronted by the availability of $1,500,000 for construction of a Design Center for the Visual Arts, the Committee felt that recommendations regarding this building must constitute its most urgent task.

As a first step in this direction, the Committee undertook to formulate a preliminary statement of a basic policy for its own activities and for the conduct of practice in the visual arts under its general guidance. By unanimous vote a *General Statement of Policy* was adopted (see *Appendix A*).

Next the Committee attempted to analyze how, in terms of space requirements, the basic policy might best be implemented in a new Design Center. The Committee early realized that any accurate estimate as to the probable number of participating students both in course work and in extracurricular activity, would be virtually impossible. On the basis, however, of the present enrollment of some 150 students in the temporary Design Center on Memorial Drive, and of the sketchy figures obtainable from other institutions, the Committee decided to estimate space requirements in two versions: one for 500 students, and another for 750 students (see *Appendix B, Versions I and II*).

It developed, on study of Version II, for 750 students, that a building to accommodate them, estimated at roughly $20 per square foot, would cost about $1,227,500—in excess of the $1,000,000 that the Committee presumed might be assignable to capital construction expenditure. Version I, however, might be estimated to accommodate 500 students for an outlay of slightly over $1,000,000.

A study of floor assignments was accordingly made on the basis of Version I only. From this study (see *Appendix C*) it was estimated that a building of three stories and basement, each 12,600 square feet in area, would suffice.

The Committee then proceeded to a study of possible sites within the University complex. First consideration was given to the general area now occupied by the temporary Design Center on Memorial Drive, beyond Dunster House. Experience during the past year demonstrates that this site, while happily workable for present experimental purposes under present limitations, would not be the best site for the permanent Design Center. It is too far outside the normal flow of College pedestrian traffic, is prohibitively far from Radcliffe, and would better be held for ultimate occupancy by high-rise apartment buildings.

The Committee next considered a site between Quincy and Prescott Streets, south of the Fogg Museum (see sheet entitled "*Farlow House Site*"). This site, however, is questionable on grounds of limited area, requiring for full workability the destruction not only of Farlow House but of the Faculty Club as well. In any event there would be encroachment on the parking space needed for the Faculty Club, and there would be no room whatever for possible future expansion.

Next in order of study was the site of present Hunt Hall (see sheet entitled "*Hunt Hall Site*"). Despite certain advantages as to location well within the normal flow of pedestrian traffic of the College, this site is questionable principally because of the necessity of according proper respect to the Memorial Church, involving possible compromises as to the architectural character of the Design Center and the likelihood that the use of the Center, especially on weekends, would interfere at least psychologically with the atmosphere appropriate to services in the Church. Hunt Hall would of course need to be demolished; but the Committee feels that, in the event of such demolition, the site would better be occupied by a smaller and more neutral building, such as a lecture hall.

The Committee then considered several sites on Kirkland Street. The first of these, involving demolition of the present Printing Office (see sheet entitled "*Corner Divinity Avenue and Kirkland Street*"), was dropped from further consideration because the Committee understands from Dean Bundy that much of this area is already earmarked for other purposes.

The next site studied on Kirkland Street was that west of the corner of Oxford Street, where Peabody House now stands (see sheet entitled "*Peabody House Site*"). A major consideration for questioning this is the projected plan for a new School of Education, which would severely limit both the area available for the Design Center and the possibility of future extension. Otherwise, assuming that Peabody House could be demolished, this site would have much to recommend it.

The last site examined on Kirkland Street was that between the New Lecture Hall and the Busch-Reisinger Museum (see sheet entitled "*Kirkland Street next New Lecture Hall*"). On all counts, the Committee is unanimous in recommending this as the best available site for the permanent Design Center. In the Committee's judgment, the New Lecture Hall is not destined to have a very long life of usefulness. As a first step, therefore, the Committee recommends demolition of the New Lecture Hall and the construction of a thoroughly up-to-date lecture hall on the site of the present Hunt Hall, which would be a perfect location for a building so generally used by the College body as a non-departmental lecture hall of adequate proportions. Nor would such a building, by virtue of its character and use, interfere in any way with the atmosphere appropriate to the immediate vicinity of the Memorial Church. The space now used in Hunt Hall by the Graduate School of Design could be provided in an extension of the new Design Center, which could then extend from the west side of the Busch-Reisinger Museum all the way to Oxford Street, including the site of the present New Lecture Hall.

Even if, for the present, the New Lecture Hall could not be removed, the Committee would still recommend this site above all others for the Design Center. The Scott House, if saving it is deemed desirable, could well be moved bodily (as was the Dana-Palmer House) to a location far better adapted to residential purposes. Service access to the Design Center would be available from the rear, through Frisby Place. The highly desirable outdoor exhibition space for the Design Center could on occasion extend into the garden of the Busch-Reisinger Museum. The site is well situated in relation to the normal pedestrian flow of the College population (especially if the site of the New Lecture Hall could be made available at the outset).

Attached hereto, as integral parts of this report, are the following documents:

Appendix A: General Statement of Policy
Appendix B: Preliminary program of approximate space requirements, Version I, for 500 students.
Appendix B: Preliminary program of approximate space requirements, Version II, for 750 students.
Appendix C: Suggested distribution of required space in four stories, including basement.
Appendix : Map of Old Cambridge in the vicinity of Harvard University, with possible sites indicated.

[Not included:]
Appendix : Sheet entitled "Farlow House Site."
Appendix : Sheet entitled "Hunt Hall Site."
Appendix : Sheet entitled "Corner Divinity Avenue and Kirkland Street."
Appendix : Sheet entitled "Peabody House Site."
Appendix : Sheet entitled "Kirkland Street next New Lecture Hall."

Mirko Basaldella
John P. Coolidge
Wilbur K. Jordan
Francis Keppel
Norman T. Newton
Ivor A. Richards
Eduard F. Sekler
José Luis Sert, Chairman

APPENDIX A

COMMITTEE ON THE PRACTICE OF THE VISUAL ARTS

General Statement of Policy

1. *Types of Committee activity*

The Committee on the Practice of the Visual Arts (CPVA) will pursue three lines of action:

   a. Encouraging independent creative projects in studio space provided for the purpose in each of the Houses;
   b. Sponsoring extracurricular activity on the part of individuals and of organized groups in the Design Center;
   c. Offering courses for credit in the Design Center.

2. *Activities in the Design Center*

The CPVA will determine what projects and courses are to be conducted in the Design Center.* Specific space will be allocated there for approved extracurricular activities, and every effort will be made to provide such coaching or guidance as may prove advisable.

Courses for credit will be offered either by a Department or by the CPVA itself:

   a. Departmental courses, consisting of: (1) courses, existing or future, offered by a Department and approved by the CPVA for inclusion in the program of the Design Center; and (2) any new courses suggested to Departments by the CPVA and given in the Design Center by mutual consent as departmental offerings;
   b. Committee courses: if the CPVA finds a new course desirable, but no Department feels prepared to offer it immediately, then this course may be offered in the Design Center by the CPVA itself, at least on an experimental basis, with the thought that a Department will later wish to assume responsibility for the course.

---

* NOTE: In accordance with the Faculty vote of May 21, 1957, Departments will continue to have freedom to propose their own courses independently of the CPVA. If any of these courses, in the judgment of either the Department or the CPVA, would not form an appropriate part of the Design

Center's program, then such courses will be conducted in space outside the Center.

3. *Studio courses*

The major course-offerings in the Design Center will be studio or workshop courses in the practice of the visual arts. Their primary aim will be to immerse the student deeply in his own creative processes by actual contact with materials, encouraging him thereby to develop within himself, in visual rather than verbal terms, a grasp of the sensory values involved in his total experience. His ability to feel and to use such phenomena as form, texture, color, proportion, and scale will be accepted as more important than his ability to talk about them. The student will be induced to judge his progress and his product in relation to the potentials inherent in himself, in the materials, and in the task at hand; the main emphasis must be on his own work and on the future, rather than on the work of others and on the past.

For basic purposes existing Departmental courses, conducted in accordance with the primary aims stated above, will be continued on their present non-professional levels. These courses will presumably continue with relatively large enrollments. For further experimentation with specialized visual media, such as typography, photography, ceramics, etching, cinema, television, and any other aspects of visual communication, there might well be new courses with small selected enrollments.

4. *Lecture courses, seminars, and symposia*

Lecture courses and seminars given under the auspices of the CPVA are intended principally to complement the studio courses in the practice of the visual arts; they are to be strongly reinforced with field trips and with the best available films and other visual materials. Here again the major aim will be the student's personal involvement to the greatest possible degree in genuinely felt experiences. Every effort must be made to arouse and sharpen his sensory awareness of the world about him, to release his latent creative faculties, and to develop his capacity for visual communication.

In addition to the scheduled courses and seminars there will be symposia or groups for free discussion. Whenever possible these will be conducted in the studios or otherwise in the actual presence of what is being discussed. Some of these discussions might well be led by qualified advanced students, especially by those interested in the eventual teaching of the practice of the visual arts; for them such an experience should prove far more valuable than the more customary service as section men in large lecture courses.

5. *Exhibitions*

Space will be provided in the Design Center for a wide range of exhibitions, including a continual showing of the current work of students. Arranging such exhibits will be an integral part of the students' workshop experience. It is hoped that the training thus received will encourage students to participate actively in the arrangement of other exhibitions throughout the University.

6. *Personnel in the Design Center*

The Design Center will be under the charge of three highly competent men, equal in rank and all responsible to the CPVA. Two of these, like the present Director of the Design Workshop, will be professional creative artists. In order that they may concentrate their energies on creative work and on instruction, the physical plant of the Design Center will be under the general operational charge of the third man; though not necessarily a creative artist, he should have a sympathetic understanding of the visual arts. Additional personnel, on the staff of the CPVA itself or on those of Departments, will need to be provided as circumstances require.

The three chief officers should be appointed members of the Faculty of Arts and Sciences; the CPVA believes further that the program of the Design Center would gain if the officers and the members of their staffs were invited to be members of the Department of Architectural Sciences or the Department of Fine Arts or both.

There should be in the Design Center a studio for a continuing series of Artists-in-Residence, one of whom would always be on the scene. The active presence of such artists would be an invaluable stimulus to student growth.

The CPVA should also have from time to time, from outside the University, the advice and counsel of appropriate persons of stature in the world of the visual arts.

APPENDIX B

DESIGN CENTER   VERSION I

Preliminary program of approximate space requirements assuming 500 students in 2 shifts of 250
(4 studios of ca. 60 students each)

(1) Lobby or vestibule (all-purpose room)   Sq. Ft.
    for social functions, informal meetings etc. 2,000
    in close visual relation to (2)

    connected with it: checking room for coats,
                           toilets. . . . .
                           reading room, (20–30
                           people), close to secretarial
                           offices. 400
                           refreshments. 300

(2) Exhibition area: indoor. 6,000
                     outdoor. . . . .

(3) Studio space for 2-dimensional work
    120 students/60 sq. ft.. 7,200

    Studio space for 3-dimensional work
    120 students/60 sq. ft.. 7,200

    Free, experimental studio for students. 1,200

    2 studios of visiting artists
    (with little office, toilet). . . . . 1,000+

    Studio of director's assistants(?). 500

    Studio of director. 600

    Light and Communication studio, incl. T.V.,
    with special equipment connected to . . . . . . 1,000+
                        Photo Lab.. 300

    Workshop space, flexible, with some permanent
    facilities, such as a kiln. 4,000

    Lockerrooms and toilets. 1,500

(4) Lecture Hall with film equipment; movable stacking chairs for 200 people (15 sq. ft./person) . . . 3,000

    Seminar and meeting room (30 people?). 300

(5) Administrative offices, incl. director. 1,000

(6) Service, heating and air conditioning, and storage
    of equipment and materials. 3,000
                                                 40,500
    Circulation, including freight elevator, etc.,
    approx. 25%. 10,125
                             TOTAL 50,625

DESIGN CENTER   VERSION II

Preliminary program of space-requirements assuming 750 students in 2 shifts of 375
(4 studios of ca. 90 students each).

(1) Lobby or vestibule (all-purpose room)   Sq. Ft.
    for social functions, informal meetings etc.. 2,500
    in close visual relation to (2)

    connected with it: toilets . . . .
                           reading room, (20–30
                           people). 400
                           refreshments (?). 300

(2) Exhibition area: indoor. 6,000
                     outdoor. . . . .

(3) Studio space for 2-dimensional work
    180 students/60 sq. ft.. 10,800

    Studio space for 3-dimensional work
    180 students/60 sq. ft.. 10,800

    Free, experimental studio for students. 1,200

    2 studios of 2 visiting artists
    (with little office, toilet). 1,000

                                                  Sq. Ft.
    Studio of director. 600

    Studio of director's assistants (?). 500

    Light and Communication studio, incl. T.V.,
    with special equipment, connected to 1,000
                        Photo-Lab.. 400

Workshop space, flexible, with some
permanent facilities, such as a kiln   4,500

Lockerrooms and toilets.   1,800

(4) Lecture Hall with film equipment for 200 people . .   3,000

Seminar and meeting room (30 people?).   300

(5) Administrative offices, incl. director.   1,000

(6) Service and storage. 3,000
                                                            49,100
Circulation, etc., approximately 25% 12,275
                                      TOTAL 63,375

APPENDIX C

DESIGN CENTER

Assuming 500 students in 2 shifts
(4 studios of ca. 60 students each)

Suggested distribution of required spaces in four stories (incl. basement)

	Area in Sq. Ft.	Area of Story	Total Area
BASEMENT			
Storage of equipment & materials, and Service (incl. mech. equip.)	3,000		
Lecture Hall (movable stacking chairs)	3,000		
Workshop space	4,000		
Toilets and lockers	400		
Circulation, etc.	2,200	12,600	
FIRST FLOOR			
Lobby with	2,000		
Reading room, refreshments, checking rm.	700		
Exhibition area, indoor	6,000		
Administrative offices	1,000		
Seminar room	400		
Toilets	300		
Circulation and storage, etc.	2,200	12,600	
SECOND FLOOR			
Studio space for 3-dim. work	7,200		
Studio space for visiting artists	1,200		
Light and communication studio with	1,200		
Photo lab	400		
Toilets and lockers	400		
Circulation and storage, etc.	2,200	12,600	
THIRD FLOOR			
Studio space for 2-dim. work	7,200		
Experimental studios for students	1,200		
Studios for director and assistants	1,200		
Meeting room	400		
Toilets and lockers	400		
Circulation and storage, etc.	2,200	12,600	50,400

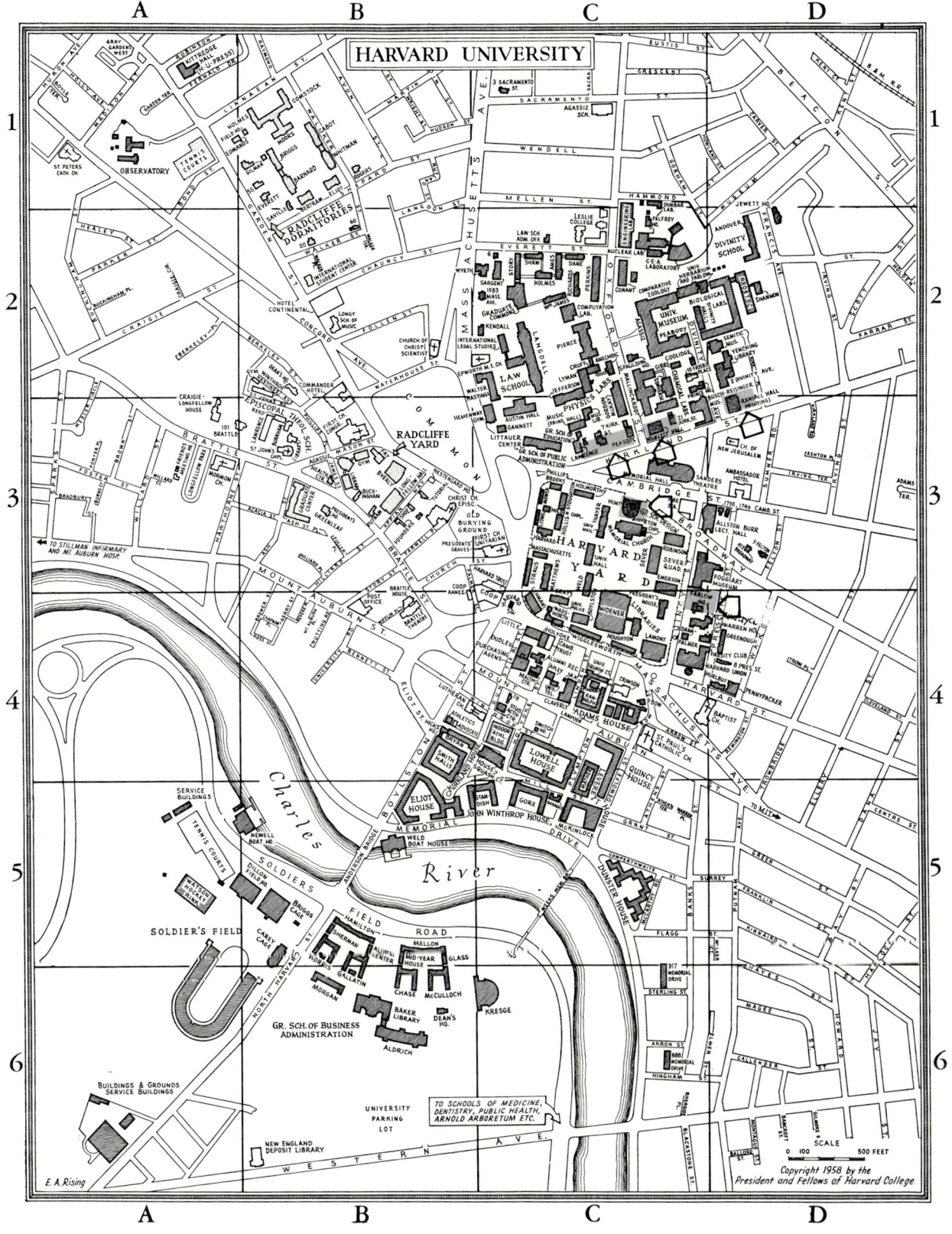

Appendix 2

Alfred S. V. Carpenter
Topsides
Medford, Oregon

July 21, 1958

Dean McGeorge Bundy
Harvard College
Cambridge, Massachusetts

Dear Dean Bundy:

Thank you for the copy of the report of the Committee for Visual Arts. Mrs. Carpenter and I read it with great interest and also your letter to Harlow. We hope that you will be able to obtain the service of Le Corbusier to do the architectural planning of the building. We think that the building should be on a large enough site to allow room for considerable area of trees, shrubs and flowers. Unfortunately the only section of Cambridge which has any senic value is that which borders the Charles and I understand from your report that no site on the banks of the River is satisfactory to President Pusey. It is my thought that Visual Arts must have their foundation in mountains, hills, streams, forests and trees, shrubs and flowers, pastures and fields. And as these are not available in Cambridge, I suggest some room be provided for these in the site of the building. I even had the thought that a study might be made to find out if it were feasible to have a conservatory and a court where students and others might sit and have luncheon or other meals.

We had a letter from Harlow after he had your letter and he seemed very pleased with the idea of having Le Corbusier for the architect.

Please remember us to President and Mrs. Pusey.

I trust that you are getting some sort of a vacation and are not shut up in Cambridge for the summer.

Sincerely yours,

Alfred St. V. Carpenter

Appendix 3

Le Corbusier
35, Rue de Sèvres
Paris (6e)
Tel.: Littré 99–62

Paris, le 27 Octobre 1958

Mr. José Luis Sert
Office of the Dean
Graduate School of Design
Harvard University
Cambridge 38, Massachusetts

Mon cher Sert,

J'ai reçu le 20 octobre ta lettre du 16 octobre 1958. Je suis actuellement débordé mais la proposition qu'elle contient (Visual Art Center) m'intéresse. Je t'écris aujourd'hui pour te le dire et surtout pour te signaler qu'on ne devrait pas acheter définitivement le terrain sans m'avoir soumis le plan de cadastre car certaines dimensions peuvent être hostiles au projet.

Une telle chose pourrait se faire si l'on admettait par exemple, que Jacques Michel soit chargé d'une participation dans l'exécution (avec les Américains) tandis que je ne ferai moi-même que les plans "à la française". Ainsi ai-je agi pour le "Musée National des Beaux Arts de l'Occident" à Tokio où les transcriptions en méthodes, matériaux et moyens de mesure et écritures sur les plans ont été faites par Mayekawa, Sakakura et Taka.

Autre question: Quels sont les honoraires que je suis en droit de demander? Je l'ignore complètement, mon rôle restant de fournir les plans nécessaires et suffisants pour l'exécution du bâtiment par les Américains. Les budgets ne sont pas très gros dans votre affaire.

Bien amicalement à toi et mes amitiés à Muncha.

LE CORBUSIER

Appendix 4

Harvard University
Cambridge 38, Massachusetts
Administrative Vice President
Massachusetts Hall

le 23 avril 1959

Monsieur Le Corbusier
35 rue de Sèvres
Paris VI, France

Monsieur,

Nous sommes heureux d'apprendre de Monsieur le doyen Sert que vous voulez bien accepter de dessiner le futur Visual Arts Center de l'Université de Harvard.

Ce projet est en effet pour nous de première importance et fera l'objet des soins et de l'intérêt non seulement de l'Université mais aussi du grand public.

Ce bâtiment ne doit pas tant son importance à ses dimensions,—limitées comme vous le savez au cadre d'un budget de 1.200.000 dollars, mais à sa signification et à la fonction qui lui est assignée.

Des étudiants venus de tous les points du globe y étudieront, et votre architecture sera pour eux une source constante d'inspiration et d'encouragement. C'est pourquoi nous avons pensé qu'il vous revenait de le dessiner, et aussi que les possibilités créatrices qui s'y attachent pouvaient intéresser en vous aussi bien l'architecte, le peintre, et le sculpteur.

C'est donc à la fois en raison de sa signification architecturale et de l'influence déterminante qu'il aura sur notre important programme d'études que nous serons heureux si vous voulez bien entreprendre la création de cet édifice.

Nous comprenons que vous voulez porter le dessin du nouveau bâtiment jusqu'à l'achèvement des plans préliminaires. Si tel est votre désir, nous nous ferons un plaisir d'entrer en relations avec une société d'architectes locale qui travaillera selon vos directives. Nous sommes heureux d'annoncer que Monsieur Sert est tout disposé à travailler en collaboration avec vous et à mettre ses bureaux à votre disposition, si cela vous est agréable. C'est à lui qu'il reviendrait alors de préparer les plans de travail de détail nécessaires pour la réalisation de votre projet et la surveillance des travaux. Nous savons que Monsieur Sert et ses assistants ont toutes les qualités requises pour ce genre de travail.

Dans cette lettre, vous trouverez également un mémoire relatif aux conditions financières de notre accord, et aussi un contrat établi selon les règles de l'American Institute of Architects, qui expose les conditions de rémunération que nous sommes prêts à vous offrir. Nous espérons tous que cette offre vous conviendra et que vous voudrez bien nous le faire savoir dès qu'il vous sera possible. Dans l'affirmative, nous pourrons alors décider ensemble de la date prochaine de votre première visite à Cambridge, et commencer d'assembler les éléments nécessaires, tels que le plan de situation, les photographies de l'environnement, etc. Au cas où une certaine date vous conviendrait, soyez assez aimable pour nous le faire savoir.

En attendant le plaisir de faire votre connaissance et de recevoir votre visite, veuillez agréer Monsieur, l'expression de ma haute considération.

Edward Reynolds
Vice-président Administratif

Appendix 5 (facsimile)

LE CORBUSIER					Paris, le 12 Mai 1959

						Mr Jose Luis SERT
						Office of the Dean
						Graduate School of Design
						Harvard University
						CAMBRIDGE 38, Mass.

Mon cher Sert,

J'ai reçu ta carte de New York.

Je suis rentré d'un voyage aux Indes et d'un second voyage à Bagdad. J'ai reçu la proposition concernant le futur "Visual Arts Center". Les conditions sont à examiner très sérieusement; je le ferai bientôt. Quoiqu'il en soit, il ne faut pas compter que je vienne cet été à Boston étant donné que ma santé ne me permet pas d'accumuler tant de déplacements. Les choses doivent se faire dans le calme et non pas dans la précipitation. Le problème m'intéresse, bien entendu.

Bien cordialement à toi.

						LE CORBUSIER

P.S. Sois assez gentil pour communiquer le contenu de cette lettre à Mr Edward Reynolds.

Ce serait gentil de vous voir ici à Paris

L-C

35, RUE DE SÈVRES · PARIS (6e)
TÉL.: LITTRÉ 99-62

Appendix 6 (facsimile)

LE CORBUSIER Paris, le 14 Mai 1959

Mr Jose Luis SERT
4 Brattle Street
CAMBRIDGE 38, Mass.

MAY 18 1959

Mon cher Sert,

Serais-tu assez gentil pour me faire envoyer, par retour du courrier, les dimensions des petites armoires standard américaines qui sont placées sur les lavabos des hôtels: dimensions, profondeur, rayonnage intérieur, miroir. Prière de faire tes observations si tu as des objections au sujet de ce standard.

2º/ Affaire "Visual Arts Center" : J'ai lu attentivement la proposition qui m'est faite. Je ne suis pas d'accord sur le chiffre qui m'est offert; j'en parlerai avec toi à ton passage à Paris. Pour l'exécution, je serais enchanté de faire ce travail avec toi, bien entendu.

Bien cordialement à toi.

LE CORBUSIER

35, RUE DE SÈVRES · PARIS (6º)
TÉL.: LITTRÉ 99-62

Appendix 7

Le Corbusier
35, Rue de Sèvres
Paris (6e)
Tél.: Littré 99–62

Paris, le 25 Juin 1959

Mr José Luis Sert
4 Brattle Street
Cambridge 38, Massachusetts

Mon cher Sert,

J'ai ta lettre du 16 juin. Je retiens que tu seras disponible entre le 22 et le 25 juillet à Paris ou entre le 17 et le 21 août à Cap Martin. Le numéro de téléphone de l'Etoile de Mer est: le 29-2-31 à Roquebrune. Tu ne pourras me joindre *qu'avant 8h 30 du matin,* sinon je suis à l'eau et, le reste de la journée, je suis dans des lieux indéterminés.

J'aurai le plus vif plaisir à vous voir, bien entendu. Il est bien temps qu'on se voie un peu après tant d'années de séparation! Le problème américain, dont le Capitaine Giedion m'a parlé hier matin, au téléphone, d'un ton comminatoire et dictatorial, est, paraît-il, dramatique! Qu'est-ce que tu veux que cela me foute de devenir le sauveur ou le sauveteur; il faudra que ceux qui m'emploient *"payent"*. Mille regrets d'être aussi goujat, mais je rends la monnaie de la pièce. Mais, encore une fois, avec toi et Muuncha, nous pourrons examiner tout cela avec le sourire aux lèvres et le verre de pastis à la main. Et comme vous êtes deux nageurs, genre clefs, je ne vous engage pas à vous aventurer dans les profondeurs aquatiques et les rocailles qui voisinent l'Etoile de Mer.

Amicalement.

LE CORBUSIER

J'embrasse Mouncha.

Appendix 8 (from a transcript)

Le Corbusier

Paris, le 5 Novembre 1959

Mr. José Luis Sert
Sert, Jackson and Gourley, Arch.
4 Brattle Street
Cambridge 38, Massachusetts

Mon cher Sert,

Inclus copie de ma lettre à Mr. Reynolds.

A bon entendeur salut, tu as pris des engagements solennels et sacrés lorsque vous exposâtes les "Taureaux" dans votre Universi*tâte;* seulement le soleil se couche sur ces bonnes intentions! . . . . .

Et Sweeney est rentré sous sa tente, comme Achille, courageusement, et il a inauguré ces jours-ci le monument "up to date" des temps modernes avec la peinture de ces Messieurs et Dames des temps modernes! Le Corbusier n'avait pas l'honneur de la cimaise dans ce cénacle aristocratique et courageux! Vive l'Amérique! Vivent les musées! etc, etc. . . . Tout cela, sans la moindre rancune.

Sweeney, en entrant chez moi, m'a proposé un chèque de 20.000 dollars pour emporter sous son bras un Braque de 1911; et; rentrant à New York, il m'a, d'avion, écrit pour me demander de lui vendre le Lipchitz que celui-ci m'avait donné à la suite de circonstances dans lesquelles je n'avais pas été précisément crétin!

Amitiés.

LE CORBUSIER

Je suis enchanté, ravi de passer quelques heures avec vous: Moncha et toi. Tu occupes une place privilegiée dans mon petit coeur depuis cette première rencontre, quai de la gare de Barcelone 1927 ou 28. Tu te dressais au milieu de ta troupe: tous au niveau < 1m 56!

L-C

Appendix 9

Alfred S. V. Carpenter
Topsides
Medford, Oregon

April 15, 1960

Dear Mr. Trottenberg:

Thank you for your letter of April 15th. and the "extra work" I must undertake to understand a little what is being planned. I am convinced that many and better minds are working on this project than mine but I hope that it won't become so difficult for the simple minded student to enjoy the advantages of having a moderate knowledge of "Visual Arts". I think of the building as opening the door of future and present enjoyment to those who pass lightly through. I see no need of making it the exclusive path for those who are going to spend their lives in some one of the branches of Visual Arts.

To my way of thinking the United States is about to or maybe is entering, the greatest period of prosperity that has ever been and thus the greatest period of leisure for its citizens. If I am correct then I feel that the universities should assume and direct the proper way that this leisure should be used. Harvard in the past has had other obligations to the Nation to undertake. Now we have accomplished some of them and here today is the best one ever presented.

We shall be delighted to see you if and when we come to Boston. I have the thought that it might be wiser for us to come to see President Pusey and other people who are interested in the Visual Arts Building toward the end of May instead of at the time of Commencement. Let me know what you think of this idea.

Sincerely yours,

Alfred St. V. Carpenter

Appendix 10

August 31, 1960

M. Le Corbusier
35, Rue de Sèvres
Paris VIe, France

Mon cher Corbu:

I am enclosing a letter from Dean Trottenberg which summarizes the comments of the various people who have reviewed the plans for the Visual Arts Center at Harvard. To these I would add the following remarks:

a. The President and Corporation, as well as certain other persons, are concerned that the building too amply fills the site. It has also been remarked that the total area is now somewhat too large, and may increase further as a result of the suggestions contained in the letter. I believe that a certain reduction in size of the building is possible without injury to the conception, but this will be up to you to arrange. The local laws require a distance of not less than 7.5 feet from the property lines on both Quincy Street and Prescott Street. This can easily be accomplished if the building is shifted slightly towards Prescott Street.

b. The design of the ramp of the Quincy Street end where it comes in front of the Faculty Club is a serious concern to many. I believe that if the ramp could be straightened and made parallel to the sidewalk of Quincy Street, most of the objections would disappear. The ramp may also be shortened because the elevation of the ground where it would terminate is about six feet higher than the elevation of the ground at the building. Since many students are expected to approach the building along Quincy Street from the south, a ramp extending in this direction would be most useful. We are sending you separately a marked print showing the ramp in this position and also marking the five foot setback lines mentioned above.

c. Regarding the request for the use of some brick in the building, you might like to consider employing brick in the sidewalks and terraces. Brick is widely used as a paving material in Cambridge.

d. The University is very much interested in enlarging the useful areas of the basement by placing the lecture hall, seminar room and light and communications studios here. As there is a plan to use the lecture hall for a television studio, it requires a clear ceiling height of sixteen feet. This may be arranged by placing the lecture hall at some lesser depth, such as twelve feet below the ground floor, possibly, with offices on a raised mezzanine floor above. The rest of the basement area will be used for storage and workshops, but the detailed program for this will not be available until later when Mirko has returned from Italy. Air-conditioning will be required for the lecture hall, seminar room, and light and communications studio and similar spaces in the basement. It is not planned to air-condition the rest of the building, but some form of mechanical ventilation is required by law for classrooms.

e. The University people feel that the administration offices must definitely be on the ground floor in order to be readily accessible for visitors to the building, but this would not mean locating studios for the Director and Assistant Director here. They should remain where you placed them on the third floor, but the other administrative offices could occupy some of the space freed by the removal of the lecture hall, etc., from this area. They also stress the Common Room as an attractive space which would help to animate the ground floor. An ample space for shipping and receiving, linking the truck quay and the service elevator, is also considered necessary. You are familiar with the desire of President Pusey for an approach to the side door of the Faculty Club through the ground floor terrace of the Visual Arts Building. There will be a considerable number of people approaching both buildings from the north along Quincy Street—probably as many people coming from the north as the south.

f. No important changes are requested on the upper floors, except for the moving of the administrative offices from the third to the ground floor, and the substitution of one large studio for a visiting artist in residence in place of two smaller studios. The director's and assistant director's studios must be larger than you showed them, hence the general size and perimeter of this floor can remain as you designed it with only partition changes.

g. With regard to the requested tunnel connection to the Fogg Museum, we will indicate on the plan which we are sending to you the possible location at which connection may be made to this building.

In summary, I would point out that your building was very well received and much admired. The only changes of consequence requested were on the ground floor. These result in greater freedom here, which should make it possible to do something very handsome with this space. Moreover, since the changes in the upper floors are so minor, the volumes and forms which you now have need not be altered.

My partners and I look forward to your further studies. Please count on us for all the cooperation which you may need.

Sincerely,

J.L.S.

Appendix 11 (from a transcript)

Le Corbusier
35, Rue de Sèvres
Paris (6e)
Tel.: Littré 99–62

Paris, le 3 Decembre 1960

Mr. José Luis Sert
Architect-Town Planner
4 Brattle Street
Cambridge 38, Massachusetts

Mon cher Sert,

Je suis rentré des Indes le 25 novembre ayant passé un mois à Chandigarh. Pendant ce temps l'atelier a avancé très fortement le projet. Nous avons fait tous les plans et coupes à échelle 2 cm/m. Lundi je commencerai la cristallisation finale. Les choses iront assez vite. Nous n'avons pas perdu un instant jusqu'à présent.

Jullian a reçu tes communications successives.

Dans ta lettre du 13.XI.60 tu me dis: "Avant ton départ de Cambridge au mois de juin tu avais promis d'envoyer des coupes du bâtiment à plus grande échelle et des détails du pan de verre ondulatoire avant les vacances". Je doute beaucoup d'avoir fait une promesse pareille car elle était hors des réalités possibles. Mon travail se fait de telle façon qu'il ne peut pas être bousculé par embauche de personnel supplémentaire. Ceci ne conduit à rien du tout. Mais rassure toi; vous aurez vos plans bientôt. J'ai toujours précisé qu'il ne m'était pas possible d'accepter des délais incontrôlables.

Sois certain que je fais au mieux.

Amitiés a Montcha, à toi et à tous les amis.

LE CORBUSIER

Appendix 12

Le Corbusier
35, Rue de Sèvres
Paris (6e)
Tel.: Littré 99–62

Paris, le 19 Decembre 1960

Mr. José Luis Sert
Architect-Town Planner
4 Brattle Street
Cambridge 38, Massachusetts

OBJET: *Visual Arts Center*

Mon cher Sert,

Nous avons établi les plans et coupes 2 centimètres par mètre. Tout le jeu des escaliers, ascenseurs et rampes est désormais en ordre.

Pour qu'il n'y ait pas de confusion, je t'envoie un calque (d'étude) no 5707 VAC Boston, échelle 5 cm/m, Jullian le 18 dec, 1960 montrant les cotes admises jusqu'ici par moi, c'est à dire:

A/ dalles de 12 pieds (3m 66) de plancher à plancher

B/ dalle lisse de 20 centimètres d'épaisseur sur les portées (environ 3m 90 de portée entre les sommiers)

C/ sommier franchissant les portées de 7m 75 (d'axe en axe) entre colonnes.

Ma question est celle-ci: Etes-vous d'accord avec les hauteurs *de vide* de 3m 46 ou double hauteur de 3m 66 + 3m 46 = 7m 12. Il s'agit de tous les locaux de travail: administration, peinture, sculpture.

On pourrait peut-être déclarer ces hauteurs trop faibles, mais leur modification réagirait très difficilement sur les rampes. J'ai pensé que le VAC était destiné à du travail se rapprochant des conditions réelles de la vie, par conséquent j'ai évité d'avoir des hauteurs de plafond démesurées. J'ai pensé que 3m 46 de vide sous les dalles unies pourrait donner un très bel aspect. Je désire toutefois avoir votre impression et votre confirmation.

Par ailleurs, j'estime que je ne viendrai pas moi-même à Boston. Tu viendras, toi, à Paris prendre connaissance de tous les dossiers, ayant ici à disposition les éléments de questions et réponses utiles.

La dépense sera la même que si je venais moi-même à Boston et j'estime que pour cette étape de mise au point définitive du plan architectural, la discussion se situerait mieux à Paris.

Bien amicalement à toi.

LE CORBUSIER

P.J.: 1

Appendix 13

Le Corbusier
35, Rue de Sèvres
Paris (6e)
Tel.: Littré 99–62

Paris, le 28 Février 1961

Note relative au Plan d'Exécution du
VISUAL ARTS CENTER BOSTON: Mr Sert

Le plan a été entièrement revu tenant compte des observations faites par Boston. Les dessins ont été également revus à Paris par Mr Sert lors de son passage le 20 janvier 1961.

Tout a été ramené à une très grande simplification. La construction est limitée à des poteaux ronds, d'épaisseur variable, portant des dalles parasol *sans chapiteau*. C'est la clef de la solution de béton armé. La disposition des poteaux se prête à cette solution.

De cette manière, le bâtiment est fait de dalles avec plafonds lisses, sans chapiteaux et sans "beams".

Les façades sont soit aveugles,
soit munies de contrôle du soleil (brise-soleil).

Le "4ème mur de la chambre" se trouve ainsi réalisé. Ce ne sont pas des fenêtres, c'est un système double d'éclairage solaire par des panneaux de verre nettoyables dedans et dehors et munis d'aérateurs assurant la "trans-aération" selon les expériences concluantes faites aux Indes, à Paris et au Couvent de la Tourette.

Un troisième genre d'éclairage existe: les "ondulatoires" de chaque côté de la rampe qui traverse le bâtiment.

. . . .

Nous avons fait tous les plans à grande échelle: 2 centimètres par mètre, plans et coupes, de façon à ce que toutes *les solutions* en plans et coupes soient impeccables.

A vrai dire, les plans et coupes soumis ici, n'ont pas besoin de commentaires. Les dimensions sont toutes rigoureusement dessinées exactement. Elles peuvent être prises avec le "kutch".

Nous désignerons sur les plans la nature des finitions:
en béton brut
parois enduit lisse
plafond béton
plafond enduit lisse
sol à déterminer d'accord avec vous, pour des raisons d'acoustique ou d'usage des locaux.

Voici la liste des plans à 2 centimètres par mètre que Jullian va vous envoyer; il s'agit des originaux, en couleur, de façon à vous permettre de faire des tirages à volonté:

No 5719 VAC Boston Basement	Echelle: 1/50
No 5720 VAC Level 1	Echelle: 1/50
No 5721 VAC Level 2	Echelle: 1/50
No 5722 VAC Level 3	Echelle: 1/50
No 5723 VAC Level 4	Echelle: 1/50
No 5724 VAC Level 5	Echelle: 1/50
No 5725 VAC Coupe transversale Nord-Sud	Echelle: 1/50
No 5726 VAC Coupe longitudinale Ouest-Est	Echelle: 1/50
No 5728 VAC Coupe longitudinale Est-Ouest	Echelle: 1/50

Vous recevrez sous peu les façades à même échelle de 2 cm par mètre. Ainsi il n'y aura pas de dessins faits à 1 cm par mètre ou de 5 mm par mètre. Tout sera de 2 cm par mètre.

Nous vous enverrons les plans par avion.

Jullian terminera ses dessins complémentaires (façades et aménagement du terrain) pendant mon absence aux Indes. Je les corrigerai à ma rentrée le 5 avril.

Ainsi seront terminés ce que notre convention appelle "the preliminary plans" et vous serez gentil à ce moment là de me faire parvenir le solde des honoraires prévu au paragraphe 5. b.

LE CORBUSIER

Appendix 14

Le Corbusier
35, Rue de Sèvres
Paris (6e)
Tel.: Littré 99–62

Paris, le 8 Mars 1961

Mr. José Luis Sert
Office of the Dean
Graduate School of Design
Harvard University
Cambridge 38, Massachusetts
U.S.A.

OBJET: *Visual Arts Center*

Cher Monsieur Sert,

Je vous envoie par avion le "Squelette" de VAC-BOS. Je crois que ces plans vous suffiront pour les premières études que feront les Ingénieurs. Comme M. Le Corbusier vous l'a écrit, ils sont rigoureusement exacts et vous pouvez prendre sur eux les mesures nécessaires. J'ai défini dans les plans pour votre information, la qualité des éléments qui constitueront la "peau" du bâtiment; l'ubication est exacte, et dans le prochain envoi, au retour de M. Le Corbusier des Indes, seront les mesures et les natures définitives du 4ème mur.

Je vous donne les mesures de base qui ont servi à déterminer les dessins. Dans l'horizontal, dans le niveau 1 la trame qui forme les poteaux est de 7 m 75 (entre axe) dans la grande distance et dans la petite distance 3 m 66 entre les poteaux, plus 0 m 55 qui correspondent au diamètre de certains d'entre eux (si les poteaux sont moins gros on conserve quand même cette mesure).

Comme vous le verrez sur les plans, nous avons établi des diamètres différents selon les charges que les poteaux doivent porter, ceci fera une differenciation qui sera d'une certaine richesse.

Dans la verticale nous avons changé les hauteurs entre planchers qu'on vous avait donné dernièrement. Cette fois la rampe ne donne pas au niveau 2 ce qui nous laisse libre de choisir la plus convenable. Cette hauteur est de 3 m 66 libre de plancher à plancher, plus 0 m 35 pour l'épaisseur de la dalle (inclus le revêtement de sol).

Il n'y aura pas de poutre, le système sera formé de poteaux et dalles.

Niveau 1—Dans ce niveau nous avons prévu un espace ouvert en creux de 1 m 13 sous le niveau du sol (au même niveau Forum), cette cote pourra servir de base pour implanter le bâtiment dans le terrain, de cette façon nous gagnons sur le côté dans lequel la rampe est moins favorisée pour se développer.

Niveau 2—La rampe s'appuiera au moyen des voiles sur ce niveau. Ces voiles seront troués.

Dans le côté Ouest de la salle une partie du mur extérieur se prolongera jusqu'au niveau plus bas pour soutenir la dalle en cantilever. Nous trouvons ici comme dans les niveaux 3, 4 et 5 le 4ème mur Est dont vous recevrez plus tard les dessins définitifs.

Niveau 3—Dans le studio de 3 dimensions, on trouve le 4ème mur Nord, je vous ai dessiné le sens et la place qu'aura le pan de verre. Dans le côté Est de la salle, j'ai prévu un prolongement jusqu'au niveau plus bas de un des voiles du 4ème mur pour soutenir une partie de la dalle, ça sera "un étrange arbre dans la Forêt de sapin que sont les poteaux" (L-C). Je vous ai indiqué aussi la rampe d'accès à la salle d'exposition. Ce n'est pas définitif, L-C n'était pas content de ça, de toute façon cela vous servira pour déterminer avec les Ingénieurs le poids nécessaire à prévoir.

Je vous ai envoyé aussi la rampe incomplète. Les départs de celle-ci je vous les enverrai au retour de L-C avec les plans d'aménagement du terrain.

Toutes les canalisations (chauffage, électricité, eaux, etc. . .) seront laissées visibles.

J'aimerai beaucoup que vous puissiez m'envoyer les plans de vos Ingénieurs avant l'arrivée de M. Le Corbusier pour prévoir dans les plans que je prépare les modifications que vous pourriez proposer.

Avec un salut amical.

JULLIAN

P.S. Je joins à cette lettre quelques photographies de la maquette que vous avez vu à l'atelier.

Dans les niveaux 1, 2 et 3 je vous ai indiqué en pointillé une ligne qui va entre les deux ascenseurs; on prévoit à cet endroit un mur qui ne sera pas porteur. Vous pourrez le voir dans les photographies de la maquette. Vous recevrez le dessin avec les autres.

P.J. 10

Appendix 15

A. D. Trottenberg
Assistant Dean
Harvard University
Faculty of Arts and Sciences
8 Weld Hall
Cambridge 38, Massachusetts

March 24, 1961

Dean José Luis Sert
4 Brattle Street
Cambridge 38, Massachusetts

Dear José Luis:

Since I have had absolutely no opportunity to really study the new plans by Corbu these are perhaps not very intelligent comments. In the few minutes I have had to spend with them, however, I am disturbed by a number of things. One is the expansion of the first floor of the building so that it quite literally eliminates the garden space between Fogg Museum and the Visual Arts Center. I think this is wrong both aesthetically and functionally. I am worried, too, about the narrow slot designed for office space. I did not have an opportunity to actually measure it and see whether it would work, but my first glance depressed me. I also think the inside ramp leading from the third to the fourth floor is both unnecessary and wasteful. It makes a mess of the available floor space and makes a large portion of two floors semi-usable. I would also question whether we actually need additional exhibition space. We did not ask for it either in the original program or in the modifications we sent him at a later time. I will admit, however, that it could be used as auxiliary studio space.

I am a little bit worried about the entire situation. It seems to me that in some ways we are making little progress and that we don't seem to be getting our needs clear to Corbu. I will be away for a week and will call you immediately when I return. I am wondering whether a trip to Paris by you or any of us might not be helpful.

Sincerely yours,

A. D. Trottenberg

Appendix 16

Le Corbusier
35, Rue de Sèvres
Paris (6e)
Tel.: Littré 99–62

Paris, le 29 Mai 1961

Mr. José Luis Sert
Architect-Town Planner
4 Brattle Street
Cambridge 38, Massachusetts

OBJET: *Visual Arts Center Harvard University*

Mon cher Sert,

Vitrages: ceux-ci seront en glace posés entre les bétons coulés. S'il est nécessaire les joints des glaces pourront être jointifs.

La question vous est posée à vous, de Boston: les cadres recevant la place dans le béton seront-ils en aluminium ou purement et simplement supprimés?

J'ai donné les possibilités de nettoyage par l'extérieur (il faut rendre l'extérieur des vitrages accessible. La corniche des bâtiments pourrait contenir un dispositif permettant d'accrocher la passerelle des laveurs de carreaux).

Aérateurs: j'ai prévu des aérateurs semblables à des de Chandigarh (ou différents si vous faites un proposition). Ces aérateurs vont du plancher au plafond. Vous me répondrez: "Nous faisons de l'air conditionné". Je vous réponds: "je ne vous en félicite qu'à moitié (sinusite, etc. . . et condition artificielle périlleuse: Dr. Alexis Carrel)"

Je propose fermement d'employer les aérateurs qui pourront fonctionner dans l'air libre aux saisons favorables. Il sera possible d'installer votre air conditionné contre le froid, mais je pense qu'à Boston il est superflu de l'installer contre le chaud puisque tous les vitrages du VAC ont leur soleil contrôlé.

29 Mai, 13 h.

Reçu á l'instant les 7 feuilles de plans VAC BOS envoyés par Joseph Zalewski le 26 Mai 1961. Je fais les plus grandes réserves. *Tu comprendras* immédiatement *en recevant les dessins de façades et coupes*, échelle *1:50, colorés*, que je t'expédierai par avion demain. Ces façades ont pris des semaines de travail. Elles sont dessinées rigoureusement au Modulor. Les cotes sont à prendre avec un kutch. C'est la minute de la haute proportion; "le moment où la partie se gagne ou se perd" "Marius" (= Raimu). C'est très grave. Ici, je deviens impérieux et impératif et je demande à Boston de bien vouloir admettre que ce sont mes dessins qui déterminent la construction du bâtiment étant entendu que des applications constructives peuvent être discutées sur vos propres propositions.

Les dessins de façades et coupes fournissent:

a) les dimensions exactes des baies vitrées
b) la situation et dimensions exactes des aérateurs
c) les shutterings des façades.

Les façades sont en béton coulé dans des coffrages standards de tôle (en principe) et pour les plus grandes surfaces éventuellement en Isorel ou en contre-plaqué ou en lames de bois pour les surfaces courbes. (voliges)

Il s'agit ici d'une nouvelle "stéréotomie" du béton armé. Le béton brut n'est pas le béton "d'une brute"; c'est simplement le béton sortant directement des moules.

Les lames de bois pour les parois courbes seront de dimensions plus réduites qu'il n'est coutume de le faire. Nervi l'a réalisé à l'UNESCO et au grand bâtiment italien du Centenaire 1861–1961 à Turin. Ces coffrages de béton sont extrêmement élégants et très propres.

Après avoir assuré au bâtiment une perfection la plus parfaite possible de proportions, mon intention est de choisir des matériaux qui, après cinquante années de recherche, deviennent les matériaux types du béton armé.

Ainsi les vitrages sont-ils fixes, scellés dans le béton: ils sont là pour éclairer exclusivement.

Les aérateurs sont là pour apporter l'air frais par les moyens physiques d'échange par gravité et par orientation. L'air conditionné cher aux Américains et à leurs sinusites devenues traditionnelles, pourra fort bien fonctionner pendant les périodes de froid, mais je pense qu'on peut aérer les locaux avec l'air du dehors sans mécanisme d'air pulsé au moment où le printemps rayonne à l'extérieur. L'air conditionné peut intervenir à nouveau pendant la période des chaleurs (si vos MMrs ne se trouvent pas tout nus à Cape Cod.)

Dans le béton de temps en temps seront insérées des sculptures moulées petites et inattendues provenant de planches sculptées très simplement telles que j'en ai installées à Chandigarh au Parlement.

Je profite de cette incidence pour dire que j'ai réservé pour Nivola l'emplacement d'une sculpture de sable qui pourra être à son gré, mais pas en rond-de-bosse.

. . . .

Autre chose: les tirages que vous recevez, *colorés en bleu pour les fenêtres*, sont le résultat d'une mise au point de mes idées relatives aux dessins d'architecte à notre époque. En effet, les dessins d'architecte munis de lignes de cotes et de chiffres rendent la lecture des plans à peu près impossible pour l'architecte lui-même et pour le client également.

J'ai décidé de séparer deux natures de plans:
a) les dessins donnant en plans et en élévations la sensation architecturale pure et simple très lisibles

b) de charger le "Service d'Exécution" des plans nécessaires pour le chantier, c'est à dire des plans cotés, annotés autant que possible, remplis d'explications, etc, etc. . .

Grâce au Modulor (employé pas forcément exclusivement) les cotes sont faciles à mesurer avec le kutch et à apprécier au Modulor. De cette façon l'architecte voit l'*architecture*.

Le chantier reçoit les ordres dessinés et chiffrés.

Résultat: on y voit clair et c'est capital.

. . . .

Bien amicalement.

LE CORBUSIER

P.S. Ci-joint, en retour, les deux bordereaux du 25 et du 26 mai 1961 envoyés par Joseph Zalewski qui j'ai signés.

L-C

Appendix 17

Le Corbusier
35, Rue de Sèvres
Paris (6e)
Tel.: Littré 99–62

Paris, le 6 Novembre 1961

Mr. José Luis Sert
Sert, Jackson and Gourley, Architects
4, Brattle Street
Cambridge 38, Massachusetts

Mon cher Sert,

J'ai fait expédier les plans revus par nous très sérieusement (ci-joint bordereau).

Je tiens à t'écrire une lettre impérative sur trois points:

1° Je refuse absolument les "cement blocs" à l'intérieur du bâtiment; c'est horrible!

2° Je conteste les dessins des "aérateurs" faits par votre firme américaine. Le bâtiment n'est pas de l'automobile! Tous ces luxes de caoutchouc seront bouffés par la poussière, les cacas de mouche, etc. . ., la sécheresse, la pluie. Si un peu d'air passait, personne ne s'en trouverait plus mal, au contraire. Par contre, votre constructeur propose froidement de supprimer les moustiquaires. Est-ce qu'il devient fou? J'ai créé les "aérateurs" pour respirer dans les bâtiments et vaincre une fois pour toutes les moustiques sous n'importe quelle latitude. Aux moustiques, on peut ajouter les mouches, les guêpes, les papillons de nuit qui viennent encombrer les lieux éclairés la nuit. J'ai créé les "aérateurs" à Cap Martin où j'ai eu deux moustiques en dix années et j'ai mis quatre mille employés au Secretariat de Chandigarh où il n'y a pas eu un seul moustique à l'intérieur des locaux.

Je *réclame donc, impérativement,* que l'on se dispense des caoutchoucs somptuaires prévus par vos aérateurs et que l'on installe le moustiquaire absolument indispensable à chacun des aérateurs.

J'ajoute que la toile métallique des moustiquaires doit être en cuivre (probablement) et d'une maille suffisament forte pour laisser passer l'air tout en interceptant les moustiques. On m'a fait, récemment, un moustiquaire à Paris où la toile était si fine que les moustiques restaient dehors, mais l'air également! (Je pense qu'une maille de toile métallique d'un millimètre ne laisse pas entrer un moustique à moins qu'il n'appartienne au 2ème Bureau ou au bureau secret du frère de Mr Foster Dulles).

3° J'ai installé le plus possible des tableaux noirs en peinture d'ardoise peints sur les contreplaqués qui remplacent les "cement blocs". J'attire votre attention sur le danger qu'il y aurait à employer des contreplaqués à veines artistiques pour faire des décorations prétentieuses. Il faut adopter pour les contreplaqués apparents, du chêne, ou du frêne, ou de l'acajou, etc. . . ou tout autre bois *sans veine artistique*. (Ceci pour les contre-plaqués qu'on laissera *naturels*).

Bien amicalement à toi.

LE CORBUSIER

P.J.: 1 bordereau

Appendix 18

Le Corbusier
35, Rue de Sèvres
Paris (6e)
Tel.: Littré 99–62

Paris, le 9 Novembre 1961

Mr. José Luis Sert
Sert, Jackson & Gourley
4, Brattle Street
Cambridge 38, Massachusetts

Mon cher Sert,

Reçu ta lettre du 3 novembre 1961 relative à l'échantillon de coffrage grandeur naturelle exécuté sur place par l'entrepreneur de ciment.

Cette démonstration est très utile. Voici ce que je propose:

1° Nu des façades

Documents 28/9, 28/11 et 28/6: le béton des architraves et des montants est parfait (y compris les bulles d'air). Le "drain pipe" ne devrait pas être en "tile" (terre cuite = trop fragile), mais en *éternit* (sur le document 28/8/ on semble voir que le "pipe" a une doublure de métal. ATTENTION à la rouille! Ce serait très dangereux à cause de la rouille qui ferait éclater l'enveloppe.
Coffrage des brise-soleil (sun-breaker) (Je désire que pour ce bâtiment, on emploie ce terme de "sun-breaker" et non pas celui de "baffle" qui ne veut rien dire. Toute l'architecture moderne a pour mission de s'occuper du soleil. Le brise-soleil, par conséquent, est le terme le plus correct.)

Le document 28/9 montre le "smooth plywood"

Le document 28/6 donne le détail de ce revêtement en "smooth plywood". Ce coffrage me paraît le meilleur pour les surfaces planes de vos brise-soleil (Observation: Nous employons souvent, en Europe, le coffrage en Isorel lisse comprimé qui donne d'excellents résultats. Ce pourrait être mieux encore que le "smooth plywood".)

Sont inacceptables, les coffrages des documents 26/1 ou 7 (?), 26/12, 27/10, 26/11, 28/5.

2° *Les parois arrondies*

Le document 27/9/ (ou 21/9 (? ! ! !) est acceptable

3° *Les arêtes verticales des brise-soleil*

Les documents 28/17, 28/15 et 28/18 (square corner) fournissent une arête acceptable. Il semble que le document 28/17 fournit une plus petite arête qui serait mieux que celle du document 28/15.

Les documents 27/16 et 27/19 montrent la nécessité de trouver une solution pour l'arête. On pourrait, éventuellement, arrondire cette arête avec le ciseau et le carborundum.??

4° *Colonnes*

Inclus un croquis destiné a Lucien Hervé avec une confession de L-C sur la douceur des colonnes rondes.

Les photos 415/7 et 413/5 de Hervé (que vous allez recevoir dans deux ou trois jours) montrent la qualité lisse des colonnes indispensable à obtenir.

Votre document 27/9 *ne convient pas* pour les *colonnes* mais seulement pour les parties rondes.

5° *OBSERVATION:* Les parties pleines du bâtiment doivent suivre les joints indiqués sur les plans des façades. Le coffrage sera fait, de préférence, en Isorel lisse comprimé. Les joints A, B et C (croquis ci-joint) sont différents. Il ne faut pas que le béton produise une arête trop vive. Mis je pense que si cette arête est un petit peu fracassée, ce ne sera pas grave. Il faut que le joint soit tout simplement une ligne visible sans être un dessin.

Bien amicalement.

LE CORBUSIER

Appendix 19

Le Corbusier
35, Rue de Sèvres
Paris (6e)
Tel.: Littré 99–62

Paris, le 11 Janvier 1962

Mr. José Luis Sert
Sert, Jackson & Gourley, Architects
4 Brattle Street
Cambridge 38, Massachusetts

OBJET: *VAC "Aérateurs"*

Mon cher Sert,

Je te donne (ma lettre du 10 janvier 1962) le résultat de l'entrepreneur parisien qui est tombé exactement dans le travers de vos spécialistes américains, c'est à dire poursuivre un idéal d'exécution parfaitement inutile et dépenser un argent fou.

J'ai pu faire au Secrétariat de Chandigarh, le palais du Parlement avec les ondulatoires que j'ai inventés à cette occasion et qui m'ont permis, contre tout le monde là-bas, d'atteindre des prix minimum acceptables par les budgets misérables de l'Inde.

Dix mille pièces de 3m 66 ont été coulés au sol, montées jusqu'à 40m. de haut, étalés sur 240 m. de large (façade est) et sur 240 m. de large (façade ouest); 100% de verre comprenant tous les 3 m. environ des "aérateurs" avec trans-aération soit à travers les corridors des bureaux, soit à travers les bureaux eux-mêmes (24 m. de large).

Nehru était dans un état complet d'enthousiasme quand il a visité (dixit Pierre Jeanneret). Il n'y a pas un moustique sur le nez des 4,000 employés. Il n'y a pas un rayon de soleil qui touche le verre à partir de l'équinoxe de printemps jusqu'à l'équinoxe d'automne.

Je viens de mettre au point pour Chandigarh le "Laboratoire de Decision Scientifique" (Government House); façade est: 100% de verre; façade ouest: 100% de verre = contrôle du soleil impeccable, grandeur architecturale qui commence à être impressionnante.

Mon cher Sert, voici mon idée: "l'aérateur" peut être fait d'une feuille pliée d'aluminium d'une seule face avec poignée à l'intérieur (voir croquis A).

Le croquis B montre une chose plus parfaite, c'est à dire un élément tubulaire général.

Le croquis C représente une plaque basse et une plaque haute destinées à fixer l'écartment des "bâtis". Par conséquent on peut poser les "bâtis" et ces deux plaques pendant le chantier dans votre délai de planning et vous pouvez venir après placer le volet de l'aérateur, 27, 33 ou 43.

Le croquis D
no. 1: ondulatoires en béton (les Japonais ont fait cela admirablement au Musée de Tokio).
no. 2: ondulatoires en aluminum (pas en tôle d'acier) à poser pendant le chantier dans votre délai de planning.

Ma conclusion: c'est de la folie de vouloir faire de l'horlogerie de précision avec ces "aérateurs" qui doivent rester *"du chantier"* et non pas devenir des pièces de musée ou alors il faut avoir beaucoup d'argent.

Mes conseils: il faut suivre à Harvard les solutions proposées par mes croquis A, B, C, D, datés du 11.1.1962, qui sont des solutions de "chantier".

Tu avais reçu le 30 octobre (par Jullian) l'aération de Chandigarh légèrement transformée. Encore une fois, c'etait du "chantier" et non pas de la "Cadillac".

Je t'expédie ceci en hâte. J'avais renoncé plusieurs fois à Dujourdy. Il est arrivé hier avec des profils semblables à ceux de tés Américains de Harvard et cela coûte des prix insensés.

Bien amicalement à toi.

pour M. LE CORBUSIER

Jullian

Note indicative: Gardien de chez nous a employé à la Maison du Brésil des "aérateurs" de 27 ou 33 qui coutaient 18.000 ou 14.000 francs c'est à dire dix fois moins. Je te ferai envoyer un ozalide ces jours-ci.

C'est à toi de choisir. Fais cela sur place.

J'ose affirmer qu'on ne pourrait pas obtenir une solution de grande série. Mais on n'obtient pas une grande série sans des délais, des essais, des programmes et des commandes.

Appendix 20

Le Corbusier
35, Rue de Sèvres
Paris (6e)
Tel.: Littré 99–62

Paris, le 26 Mai 1962

Mr. José Luis Sert
Sert, Jackson & Gourley
4 Brattle Street, Cambridge 38, Massachusetts
U.S.A.

Mon cher Sert,

Porte d'émail du VAC: je veux bien me charger de peindre cette porte d'émail à un moment donné, quand j'aurai le temps. On pourrait combiner, toi et moi, le processus d'accrochage des plaques. Il s'agit, peut-être, de 8 plaques par face de porte. Question: y aura-t-il *émail* recto verso?

Combien cela coûte ma peinture? A vous de me fixer un prix américain. Je viens de faire gratuitement la porte d'émail du Parlement de Chandigarh, mais l'Amérique n'est pas l'Inde! Je te laisse me faire une proposition utile et si je ne suis pas d'accord, on donnera un beau ton uni à la porte et ce sera peut-être la meilleure solution.

Bien amicalement à toi et à Muncha.

LE CORBUSIER

P.S. Je fais pour Claudius Petit "La Maison de la Jeunesse et de la Culture" à Firminy. Hier il s'est mis en colère (pas devant moi, mais devant les dessinateurs) disant que nous avions fait du béton uni (coffrage en contreplaqué), que c'est une trahison, que cela devrait être en béton brut: avec bois visible.

Le béton brut est né de l'Unité d'Habitation de Marseille où il y avait 80 entrepreneurs et un tel massacre de béton qu'il ne fallait pas rêver de faire des raccords utiles par des enduits. J'avais décidé: laissons tout cela brut. J'appelais cela du béton brut. Les Anglais ont immédiatement sauté sur le morceau et m'ont traité (Ronchamp et le Couvent de La Tourette) de "Brutal",—béton brutal;—en fin de compte, la brute c'est Corbu. Ils ont appelé cela "the new brutality". Mes amis et admirateurs me tiennent pour le brute du béton brutal!

Veux-tu être assez gentil, toi "qui a beaucoup de temps libre!" de passer un mot à Claudius et de lui dire que le Visual Art Center, que nous faisons ensemble au Centre de l'Université de Harvard, est en béton brut, mais lisse, et ceci dans un esprit de perfection qui t'anime toi-même aussi bien que moi. J'envoie d'ailleurs à Claudius copie de cette lettre.

Les Anglais disent: "Life is difficult" (mais je crois bien que c'est moi qui ai inventé cette affirmation).

L-C

Je serais heureux de te voir à
votre passage à Paris en juin
(m'avertir S. V. P.)

Appendix 21 (facsimile)

Expédiée le 17 Octobre 1962

Paris, le 15 Octobre 1962

Mr José Luis SERT
Sert, Jackson & Gourley, Architects
4 Brattle Street
CAMBRIDGE 38, Mass.

Mon cher Sert,

Bravo pour le "sabbat" ! Veux-tu m'en vendre la moitié ?

Donc, tu seras loin au début de février. En janvier, je serai aux Indes pour inaugurer le Parlement. Pourquoi ne serais tu pas là avec Moncha ? (mais je vois que tu ne quittes Cambridge que début février !!!). Une inauguration sans toi "est une journée sans soleil". Tant pis pour l'inauguration ! Nous avons travaillé ensemble, tous deux, avec amitié et efficacité, et le travail semble avoir été bien fait d'après tes photographies. J'aime autant un bâtiment bien fait qu'un bâtiment mal foutu. Mais Marseille est la démonstration que, même mal fichu, un bâtiment bien pensé peut vivre.

Je ne désire pas que l'on donne des photographies de ce bâtiment, en cours de chantier, même chez Boesiger. Ce n'est pas la peine de faire pleurer les ânes ! Il faut que l'ensemble soit visible, la rue montante, etc, etc ...

Si jamais tu rencontres Pierre Jeanneret durant ton "sabbat", tu lui diras ce que je t'écris ici: j'ai demandé à Sert quelques photographies de ma construction. Il m'a envoyé quatorze magnifiques photographies de haute qualité professionnelle presque par retour de courrier. Moi, je suis actuellement sans photographies valables de mes constructions de Chandigarh malgré mes supplications, mes sommations, etc... Pierre habite juste en face du Capitol. Il n'a que la rue à traverser. Tu le remercieras de ma part, si tu le rencontres.

Exposition Corbu: paintings, prints, models, dans le nouveau bâtiment du VAC. J'avais noté:(inauguration avec ma présence là-bas: point interrogatif)

Impossible d'aller de Chandigarh à Boston et Paris, à mon âge, à 10.000 mètres d'altitude, en Boeing, et en quatre ou cinq jours. Je renonce à peu près totalement à prendre des rendez-vous à distance. La vie devient infernale et j'ai quelques choses encore à faire dans mon travail, même en dehors de l'architecture.

...

- 2 -

Cette exposition pourrait s'organiser. On verra.

Mille regrets ! Ma lettre est tout ce qu'il y a de vaseuse car il m'est impossible de donner des précisions.

Bien amicalement à toi.

LE CORBUSIER

P.S. Ci-joint photo-copie de ton MEMORANDUM du 9 octobre 1962 avec mes annotations manuscrites.

Appendix 22

Le Corbusier

Paris, April 5, 1963

Mr. Nathan M. Pusey
President
Harvard University
Cambridge 38, Massachusetts

Dear Sir,

I have received your friendly letter of the first of April concerning the opening of your Carpenter Center.

My doctor forbids me hurried trips. I am 75 years old (and I still do not yet have crutches!) but I must all the same pay attention. I am therefore unable to assure you of my presence on the twenty-seventh of May; I regret this keenly.

I pray you to believe, dear sir, in the assurance of my best sentiments.

LE CORBUSIER

Appendix 23

Consultants and Contractors
Structural engineer: William LeMessurier and Associates
Mechanical engineers: Delbrook Engineering Company
Plumbing engineers: Tiot Engineering Company
Electrical engineers: Thompson Engineering Company
Acoustical consultant: Bolt, Beranek and Newman
Specification writer: Mario Pfaff
Landscape architects: Sasaki, Walker and Associates
General contractor: George A. Fuller Construction Company
Subcontractor for concrete form work: Tucker Concrete Form Company
Subcontractor for precast concrete: Cambridge Cement Stone Company

Members of the office of Sert, Jackson and Gourley who worked on the Carpenter Center
Paul H. Krueger (Job Captain)
Jerome Lindsay
Gerald Howes
Knud Bastlund
David Leonard
R. Stephen Newark
Giles Barbey
Richard Mullin
Robert Kramer
Allen Cooper
R. Wendell Phillips
Jean-Claude Steinegger
Maria Rupp
Alan Balsbaugh
Theodore Monacelli
Mario Schack
Russell B. Brown
Francisco Ramirez
Frank H. Richards, III
Ozdemir M. Erginsaw
William Lindemuller
John McKenzie
Eugene Lew
Minoru Takayama
Kenneth DiNisco
Thomas D. Ward
Arnold Koerte
Andrew C. Filoso
Nicholas Quennel
David Allen

Appendix 24

Building adaptations from 1962 through 1976

Prior to any alterations, the finished building had 56,903 sq. ft.; construction cost was $1,564,534; project cost (including all fees) was $1,868,645.

Basement
Partitions were inserted on either side of the western portion of the central lobby so as to create additional darkroom accommodation. The large area east of the lecture hall was subdivided into a number of rooms in accordance with the technical needs of documentary film making and animation; as needs changed several new adaptations were carried through.

Groundfloor
A small area in the southwest corner of the lobby was partitioned off to gain additional office space.

Second and Third Floor
On each floor a small area at the southern end of the lobby was partitioned off to gain additional office space.

Fifth Floor
The penthouse studio was subdivided into a large studio of three bays and a smaller area next to the entrance from the roof terrace; from the smaller area another little office was partitioned off.

All alterations were designed to blend as completely as possible with the existing building through compatible formal treatment and the use of identical colors and textures. Alterations were necessitated by the fact that the original building program underestimated the need for small offices. It also failed to foresee the dramatic growth of student interest in photography and film making or, for that matter, in the entire program of Visual and Environmental Studies housed in the Carpenter Center. By the end of the sixties additional accommodation had to be found in other buildings including Hunt Hall and, after its demolition, Sever Hall.

BIBLIOGRAPHY

To date the best general bibliographies on Le Corbusier are found in the following three works:

L'Opera di Le Corbusier, Mostra in Palazzo Strozzi. Exhibition Catalogue. Florence, 1963.

Petit, Jean. *Le Corbusier lui-même.* Geneva: Rousseau, 1970.

Serenyi, Peter, ed. *Le Corbusier in Perspective.* Englewood Cliffs, N.J.: Prentice-Hall, 1975.

The following bibliography is restricted to publications that deal with the Carpenter Center exclusively or to works that have a more than cursory mention of the center.

Ambler, Peter. "Visual Arts Centre, Harvard University." *Architectural Review,* December 1963.

Atkinson, Fello. "Le Corbusier in America." *The Listener,* 69 (May 16, 1963).

"Big Change on the Campus: Carpenter Center for the Visual Arts." *Architectural Forum,* March 1963.

Boesiger, W., ed. *Oeuvre complète 1957–1965.* Zurich: Editions Girsberger, 1965.

"Carpenter Centre." *The Architect and Building News,* January 1, 1964.

Casati, Cesare. "Il primo edificio de Le Corbusier negli Stati Uniti per l'Università di Harvard." *Domus,* July 1963.

"Centre d'étude d'arts visuels à Harvard, États-Unis: Le Corbusier." *Aujourd'hui,* April 1964.

"Centro Carpenter per le arti figurative dell'Università de Harvard." *Architettura,* August 1963.

"Corbu's Center Rises at Harvard." *Progressive Architecture,* December 1962.

"Corbu's First U.S. Building: Harvard's Visual Arts Center." *Progressive Architecture,* December 1961.

Czagan, Friedrich. "Fantazie a vněyšé svět." *Československý Architekt,* 13 (May 3, 1968).

Donat, John, ed. *World Architecture One.* London: Studio Vista 1964.

Eldredge, Joseph. "Vision in Concrete." *Boston Globe,* July 8, 1966.

"First U.S. Building by Corbusier Completed." *Architectural Record,* March 1963.

Futagawa, Yokio, ed. *Global Architecture 37, Le Corbusier.* Tokyo: A.D.A. Edita, 1975.

Giedion, S. "Das Carpenter Center der Harvard Universitaet." *Bauen und Wohnen,* August 1964.

Giedion, S. "New Ventures in University Building (Le Corbusier, Sert)." *Zodiac,* 16 (1966).

Giedion, S. *Space, Time and Architecture,* 5th ed. Cambridge: Harvard University Press, 1967.

Hejduk, John. "Out of Time and into Space." *Cable,* n.s., 1 (1969).

Hitchcock, Henry R. "Le Corbusier and the U.S." *Zodiac,* 16 (1966).

Huxtable, Ada L. "Bold Harvard Structure." *The New York Times,* May 28, 1963.

Johnson, C. A. "VAC: A Layman's Second Look at the Visual Arts Center." *Harvard Bulletin,* 75 (May 1973).

"Le Corbusier at Harvard: A Disaster or a Bold Step Forward?" *Architectural Forum,* October 1963.

"Le Corbusier Builds at Harvard: New Visual Arts Center." *Architectural Forum,* December 1961.

"Le Corbusier Designs for Harvard." *Architectural Record,* April 1963.

"Le Corbusier in Amerika: Das Visual Arts Center in Cambridge." *Das Werk,* April 1964.

"Le Corbusier Smooths His Style for U.S. Debut at Harvard." *Engineering News Record,* April 4, 1963.

"Le Corbusier: Visual Arts Center, Harvard University," *Arts and Architecture,* December 1961.

Lyndon, Donlyn, "Filologia dell' architecttura Americana." *Casabella Continuità,* November 1963.

Monk, A. J. "The Carpenter Center for the Visual Arts." *RIBA Journal,* May 1963.

Morris, J. S. "Corbusier at Harvard." *RIBA Journal,* August 1966.

Saltzman, Cynthia. "Carpenter Center Asks the Question." *Harvard Bulletin,* 74 (May 1972).

Scully, Vincent. *American Architecture and Urbanism,* New York: Praeger, 1969.

Sekler, E. F. "Carpenter Center for the Visual Arts, Le Corbusier's Building." *Connection,* December 1963.

Shlugar, E. "Centro Carpenter di Artes Visuals." *Arquiteto,* 3, no. 23.

von Moos, Stanislaus. *Le Corbusier, Elemente einer Synthese,* Frauenfeld und Stuttgart: Verlag Huber, 1968.

Wells-Thorpe, J. A. "Harvard's Tribute to Le Corbusier." *Architectural Review,* January 1966.

NOTES

Introduction

1. "The Development by Le Corbusier of the Design for l'Eglise de Firminy, etc.," *Student Publications of the School of Design of the University of North Carolina,* 14, no. 2 (1964).

2. Jean Petit, *Le Corbusier lui-même* (Geneva: Rousseau, 1970), p. 125.

3. Mary Patricia May Sekler, *The Early Drawings of Charles-Edouard Jeanneret (Le Corbusier) 1902–1908* (New York: Garland, 1977).

4. Some examples are: H. Weber, *Walter Gropius und das Faguswerk* (Munich: Callwey, 1961); Eduard Sekler, "The Stoclet House by Josef Hoffmann," *Essays Presented to Rudolf Wittkower* (London: Phaidon, 1967), pp. 228ff; Kenneth Frampton, "Maison de Verre," *Perspecta,* 12 (1969), 77ff; William H. Jordy, *American Buildings and Their Architects,* 2 vols. (Garden City, N.Y.: Doubleday, 1972).

5. See note 2, above.

6. Kermit Vanderbilt, *Charles Eliot Norton* (Cambridge: Harvard University Press, 1959), p. 124.

7. Moore published several books that indicate the nature and orientation of his instruction. In one volume, *Examples of Elementary Practice in Delineation* (Boston: Houghton Mifflin, 1884), he reproduced outline drawings, especially of plant forms, to be copied by beginning students; in a

second volume, *Facsimiles of Examples in Delineation Selected from the Masters* (Boston: Moses King, n.d.), he included for copying by advanced students works by, among others, Holbein, Dürer, Leonardo, Turner, and Ruskin. From the last he also quoted on several occasions in the text of both volumes. See also Frank J. Mather, Jr., *Charles Herbert Moore, Landscape Painter* (Princeton: Princeton University Press, 1957); Roger B. Stein, *John Ruskin and Aesthetic Thought in America 1840–1900,* (Cambridge: Harvard University Press, 1967), p. 240.

8. The most important publications are: Denman Waldo Ross, *A Theory of Pure Design* (Boston: Houghton Mifflin, 1907), and *On Drawing and Painting* (Boston: Houghton Mifflin, 1912); Arthur Pope, *An Introduction to the Language of Drawing and Painting,* 2 vols. (Cambridge: Harvard University Press, 1929, 1931).

9. George H. Chase, Chairman of the Department of Fine Arts, in: Samuel E. Morison, ed., *The Development of Harvard University* (Cambridge: Harvard University Press, 1930), pp. 131ff.

10. José Luis Sert around 1970 adopted the Catalan spelling of Josep Lluis for his Christian names. This book follows his usage by keeping the earlier spelling for documents and occurrences before 1970.

11. In his introductory lecture Sir Herbert Read acknowledged his debt to, among others, Konrad Fiedler.

12. "Report of the Committee on the Visual Arts at Harvard University" (1956). Members of the committee were: J. N. Brown, F. Keppel, D. Oenslager, C. H. Sawyer, W. Stechow, G. Wald, J. Walker, with S. L. Faison, Jr., as executive secretary.

13. Members of the committee during its first five years of existence were: J. L. Sert, Chairman, F. Keppel, E. F. Sekler, M. Balsadella, I. A. Richards, W. K. Jordan (1957–1960), N. Newton, S. Slive (1959–1962), A. D. Trottenberg (1959–1962), S. J. Freedberg (1959–1961), and R. G. Gardner (1959–1962).

History of the Design
1. Outline of the Task

1. The arrival of the Modern Movement at Harvard was encouraged by Dean Hudnut's invitation to Walter Gropius to teach at the Architecture School in 1937. In the late forties, Gropius and his firm, The Architects' Collaborative (TAC), were commissioned to design the Harvard Graduate Center, a group of buildings north of Harvard Yard. The majority of other buildings at Harvard, even those built as late as the thirties, were in the neo-Georgian and neo-Classical styles. Red brick is the local building material most frequently used.

2. Confusingly, the art history department bears the title Fine Arts Department, though it is not a practical art school.

3. "Report of the Committee on the Visual Arts at Harvard University," pp. 114, 115. (See above, Introduction, n. 12.)

4. According to Eduard Sekler, former Director of the Carpenter Center, who was a member of the Committee.

5. The "client" was, strictly speaking, the Harvard Corporation, which made its opinions known via President Pusey, Dean McGeorge Bundy, and Assistant Dean Arthur Trottenberg. Trottenberg played the central role among the Harvard personalities in this project. However, the functions of "client" in the widest sense were divided among the committee, St. Vrain Carpenter, Sert, and others.

6. Dates in parentheses refer to the chronological list of correspondence and other documents at the back of this volume, where the present location of each document is indicated.

7. President Pusey's determination was confirmed by A. D. Trottenberg in discussion with Eduard Sekler, March 1972.

8. Possibly influenced by nineteenth-century rationalist theories like those of Auguste Choisy, Le Corbusier frequently upheld the notion that "correct" solutions would follow from "correct" analyses of problems. For the influence of Choisy on modern architecture see R. Banham, *Theory and Design in the First Machine Age* (London: Architectural Press, 1960), pp. 23ff.

2. Captain Giedion's American Problem

1. Details of the effect on Le Corbusier of his wife's death were given by José Luis Sert in an interview June 2, 1971, and supported by Andreini, a member of Le Corbusier's atelier in an interview March 4, 1972. Both implied that the death of his wife had a harrowing effect on the architect and that he was never quite the same again.

2. Andreini, with whom Le Corbusier frequently discussed matters, felt certain that without mediation from José Luis Sert, Le Corbusier would not have designed a building in

the United States at all, as a result of his bitterness over the United Nations Building.

3. In interview June 2, 1971, Sert stressed the internationalism, saying that this aspect was especially appealing to Le Corbusier and important in averting his American grumbles. For the flavor of this internationalism, see his introduction to *When the Cathedrals Were White*, trans. Francis E. Hyslop, Jr. (New York: Reynal and Hitchcock, 1947), p. 30: "I have felt myself become more and more a man of everywhere"; "I shall do my best to avoid the conceptions 'France,' 'Germany,' 'America,' 'USSR,' etc." Internationalism was always integral to the branch of the Modern Movement to which both Sert and Le Corbusier belonged, and that is why, for example, Nazi regionalists attacked the "International Style." And the title CIAM (Congrès Internationaux de l'Architecture Moderne) reflects this concern. For further internationalist innuendoes see reports of various post–World War II CIAM meetings. "La synthèse des Arts majeurs" is dealt with explicitly by Le Corbusier in *Le livre de Ronchamp* (Paris: Les Cahiers Forces Vives, 1961), p. 17.

4. Author's translation. Drafts of this letter in English existed for some months prior to the final version, which was in French. They reflect a gradual identification (presumably with the help of Sert) of Le Corbusier's "soft spots."

5. Throughout this history Le Corbusier's French has been preserved in its original form, including his spelling and grammatical mistakes and his occasional idiosyncratic usages. In those rare cases where Le Corbusier's language or construction completely obscures the meaning, it has been silently corrected.

The "troupe" were fellow students of Sert's to whom Le Corbusier lectured subsequent to Sert's discovery of *Vers une architecture* in a Paris bookshop in 1926. After his studies, Sert was invited to the atelier at 35 rue de Sèvres, where he collaborated with Le Corbusier on the second stage of the League of Nations and Mundaneum projects. They worked together on a town plan for Barcelona during the thirties and met with Walter Gropius and Sigfried Giedion (both of whom had posts and influence at Harvard long prior to Le Corbusier's appointment as architect). Sert later wrote the urbanistic handbook of the congress, *Can Our Cities Survive?* (Cambridge: Harvard University Press, 1942), and later still became the last President of CIAM. After World War II, when he was living in New York as a practicing and teaching architect, he supported Le Corbusier through the United Nations fracas. From time to time they met on the shores of the Mediterranean during vacations. These details of the relationship were summarized by Sert in interview June 2, 1971. See also note written at the time of Le Corbusier's death by Sert, "Le Corbusier and the Younger Generation," *Harvard Graduate School of Design Association*, 12, no. 1 (November 1965), 1–4.

6. The mention of "saviour or redeemer" ("sauveur ou sauveteur") is ironical since this, in essence, was the way Le Corbusier was to understand his role as regards the United States in this building. There is a strong messianic ingredient in Le Corbusier's career generally. See for example, Le Corbusier, *Croisade, ou, le crépuscule des académies* (Paris: Crès, 1933). The title "Crusade" is in itself significant, and on page 71 an illustration of Le Corbusier preaching his urbanism at Algiers is juxtaposed with an illustration of prophetic leaders of the past, including Christ. Recent scholarship has revealed more clearly a strong eschatological strain in Le Corbusier's and other modern architects' visions: see for example N. K. Smith, "Millenary Folly," *Art and Architecture in the Modern World* (Victoria, B.C.: University of Victoria Press, 1971), and Colin Rowe, introductory essay to *Five Architects* (New York: Wittenborn, 1972).

7. To the United Nations experience (when Le Corbusier accused certain American architects of stealing his project in its suitcase and denounced Americans as "gangsters"), one must add the rows that appear to have occurred in 1935 between himself and the Museum of Modern Art, which helped with his trip and paid him what he seems to have thought was too small a fee.

8. Sert recalled the phrase in interview June 2, 1971. Most information in this paragraph is from the same source.

9. Explicit revulsion at American materialism occurs in a letter to Sigfried Giedion written by Le Corbusier May 21–23, 1948, at the time of the publication of Giedion's *Mechanisation Takes Command*. The letter is reproduced in facsimile in *Hommage a Giedion, Profile seiner Persönlichkeit*, eds. Paul Hofer and Ulrich Stucky (Basel and Stuttgart: Birkhäuser Verlag, 1971), p. 50. In his letter Le Corbusier jokingly suggests a second volume to come out in 1950 with the title "Epanouissement du machinisme: L'homme a repris les commandes" ("Flowering of Machinism: Man Has Taken Command Again"). He refers to the Americans, "Mon Dieu que les Américains savent peu vivre!" ("Good God how little the Americans know how to live!") but says that they are "le laboratoire" ("the laboratory").

He also states that "les oeuvres de la 1ère ère machiniste devront être balayées comme de la merde" ("the works of the first machine age should be swept away like shit"), and refers to the need to harmonize the cities.

10. For CIAM ideals see José Luis Sert, *Can Our Cities Survive?*, and Sigfried Giedion, *Architecture, You and Me* (Cambridge: Harvard University Press, 1958). The tenor of the philosophy may be gleaned from numerous Le Corbusier writings, and was referred to in connection with this building by Sert and E. Sekler (interviews 1971–1972). Both took part in CIAM and both were members of the Committee for the Practice of the Visual Arts. "The essential joys" ("les joies essentielles") is Le Corbusier's term for the provision of light, space, and greenery in his discussions of the "ville radieuse" ("radiant city"); it recurs frequently in his urbanistic writings.

11. Giedion, *Architecture, You and Me,* p. 84.

12. Interestingly, the same day, on the same page, Le Corbusier remarked that he was wearing a necktie that Yvonne, his wife, had given him at the time of the United Nations project. He also remarked that it was the first time he had worn this tie since her death in 1957.

13. These notes were made on a loose sheet—not in his "sketchbook." The point is of some interest for it may be that he had a hierarchy of his rough notes and ideas, and in that case the sketchbooks (or notebooks as they are called in this study) were certainly being preserved for posterity, however "spontaneous" they may appear to be: they bear some uncanny resemblance to Leonardo da Vinci's notes, on occasion. Le Corbusier had three kinds of notebooks: the sketchbook he always carried with him, a blue book in the atelier for more detailed ideas, and a book next to the atelier telephone.

14. Author's translation. Sert's awareness of the value of careful timing when writing to Le Corbusier was confirmed by Paul Krueger, a member of Sert's office, in interview June 1972.

15. The term is McGeorge Bundy's.

16. The site inspection recalled in detail by Sert in interview February 6, 1971.

17. Le Corbusier, *When the Cathedrals Were White*, pp. 134–135. Le Corbusier reacted to Central Park in New York with similar enthusiasm and from much the same point of view.

18. The reader may wish to compare an aerial view of the yard, figure 1, with an aerial view drawing of the residential quarter of the radiant city in Le Corbusier, *La ville radieuse* (Paris: Editions de l'Architecture d'Aujourd'hui,

(Notes to Pages 48–52)

1933), p. 163.

19. Notebook N57, p. 49, in a section entitled "Carolum Eduardum Le Corbusier." His own sentiments were not so straightforward. He seems to have had a mixed attitude toward academic acclaim, being flattered by it on the one hand, rejecting it as meaningless on the other.

20. Recalled by President Pusey in discussion with Eduard Sekler, 1971.

21. Recalled by Eduard Sekler, who was present.

22. "Notes à l'attention" ("notes to the attention") were left on the drawing boards of members of the atelier as conceptual guides or as indications as to which sketch in a notebook should be consulted. Jeanne, the atelier secretary, was guardian of the notebooks.

23. For Le Corbusier's heightened vision there may not have been an "ordinary." However, one notes throughout his career the use of "facts" around him (grain siloes, factory windows, automobiles, airplanes, pebbles, seashells, test-tracks, country paths, and so on) as points of departure for architectural ideas.

24. *Le poème électronique Le Corbusier* (Paris: Editions de Minuit, 1958).

25. Le Corbusier, *Le livre de Ronchamp,* pp. 17–18. The idea for electronically produced sounds was an afterthought at Ronchamp.

26. Le Corbusier, *New World of Space* (New York: Reynal and Hitchcock and the Institute of Contemporary Art, Boston, 1948), p. 8.

27. Cited by Stanislaus von Moos, *Le Corbusier, Elemente einer Synthese* (Frauenfeld and Stuttgart: Verlag Huber, 1968), ill. 68.

28. Le Corbusier, *U.N. Headquarters* (New York: Reinhold, 1947), p. 39.

29. In most jobs it was a case of the individual constraints of the problem and Le Corbusier's preexisting type solutions meeting about halfway. Here he may have been responding all too literally to the vicarious United Nations opportunity that the visual arts center provided, in the provision of a spiral *museum*. Indeed, he may have been scoring points against his American rival, Frank Lloyd Wright, whose spiral Guggenheim Museum was the object of caustic remarks in a letter one week earlier. Le Corbusier's spiral museum presumably would be an antidote to Wright's, as it was the other way up and based on a square spiral.

30. The term "dattier" is an abbreviation, according to An-

dreini, of "dattier royale"—royal date palm. This was a term of very high praise, meaning, roughly, "fine fellow." Le Corbusier first used the term in India when riding a mule under palm trees.

The events of his stay are reconstructed from his Boston notebook (P59) which has some fifteen pages of jottings made during his visit, from personal recollections by Sert and Sekler, and from the diary of John Nickols, Sert's office manager.

31. Notebook P59, pp. 5,13.
32. "Voyage au pays des timides" ("Journey to the Country of the Timid") was the subtitle of *When the Cathedrals Were White*. The student party is recalled in the last edition of Sigfried Giedion *Space, Time and Architecture*, 5th ed. (Cambridge: Harvard University Press, 1967), pp. 556–563.
33. Paul Krueger of Sert's office says a pair of huge cardboard glasses mimicking Le Corbusier's hornrimmed spectacles was also constructed by the students. Le Corbusier was impressed by the mural. He got the artist to write his name on a loose leaf that was placed between the pages of notebook P59.
34. Arthur D. Trottenberg at that time was also Assistant Dean for Resources and Planning of the Faculty of Arts and Sciences. A dynamic and personable man, he took a great interest in the arts and especially in the Carpenter Center project, which owes much to his sympathetic understanding, tact, and managerial skill.
35. Nickol's diary of Le Corbusier's stay recalls that Le Corbusier looked out of the window of Sert's office at a brick building and said, "Brick is handsome," on November 14, 1959. The next day he wrote in his Boston notebook, "Il y a du granit gris" ("There is gray granite"). It should be emphasized that he had no inherent dislike of brick (as would be clear, in any case, from the Maisons Jaoul) but that the devices of the Corbusian language were specifically reinforced concrete.

3. Finding the Building's Form

1. Recalled by Eduard Sekler, who was present.
2. Jerzy Soltan, who passed through the atelier in the late forties, has stated that Le Corbusier was "essentially a poet." His ideas were frequently first exercised in writing, as in this case.
3. These cutouts have all disappeared.
4. See Le Corbusier, *Le livre de Ronchamp*, p. 17. See also *Student Publications of the School of Design of the University of North Carolina,* 14, no. 2 (1964), on the genesis of Firminy. Le Corbusier's statement reads: "When a task is entrusted to me, I am accustomed to place it *inside my memory,* that is, to allow myself to make no sketch for several months. The human head is so made that it possesses a certain independence. It is a box into which one can pour pell-mell the bits of a problem. Let it float, 'marinate,' 'ferment.' Then one day out of a spontaneous initiative of the inner being the click is produced. One takes up a pencil, a piece of charcoal, a colored crayon (the color is the key to the course) and one gives birth on the paper: the idea comes forth—the child comes out, it has come into the world, *it is born.* Jose Oubrerie drafted the plans. Paris May 21, 1964, L-C" (author's translation).
5. von Moos, *Le Corbusier, Elemente einer Synthese,* p. 323.
6. Le Corbusier, *When the Cathedrals Were White.* One theme of his book is that New York has the necessary techniques for a new urbanism (for example, steel framing and elevators) but these are as yet in a raw state, requiring the harmony of a guiding hand. There is a great deal in the last few pages of this book (the section entitled "Necessity of Communal Plans") that repeats the subject matter of his lectures on the radiant city given in the United States and concerns such matters as the harnessing of industrial power, the provision of the "essential joys," and respect for the cosmic rhythms. See also Le Corbusier, "What Is the Problem of America?" in *Oeuvre complète 1934–1938,* ed. Max Bill (Zurich: Editions d'Architecture, 1939), pp. 65–68, for his condemnation of United States suburbs.
7. *Oeuvre complète 1957–1965,* ed. W. Boesiger (Zurich: Editions Girsberger, 1965), p. 54, on the visual arts center states: "La construction de béton et de verre est une démonstration des théories de Le Corbusier et de nombreuses idées directrices qui lui sont propres s'y retrouvent: la pénétration reciproque de l'exterieur et de l'interieur, l'emploi de béton brut, la rampe qui relie deux rues par la troisième étage, les pilotis pour chacun des cinqs étages, les brises-soleil." ("The concrete and glass building is a demonstration of Le Corbusier's theories, and many guiding ideas typically his own are to be found in it: the reciprocal penetrating interior and exterior, the use of reinforced concrete, the ramp which links the two streets with the third level, the pilotis on all five floors, the sun baffles.") Andreini, interview March 4, 1972, and Jullian de la Fuente on four separate occasions (March 1971 and March 1972) have both stated that Le Corbusier thought

of the visual arts center as "his only American building." Jullian also said that Le Corbusier therefore told him they would be putting all his devices in this one building.

8. "He sees the reverse logic of every situation," John Summerson, *Heavenly Mansions* (London: Cresset Press, 1949), p. 190.

9. Le Corbusier, *Modulor 2, 1955. (Let the User Speak Next): Continuation of* The Modulor, *1948,* trans. Peter de Francia, Anna Bostock (Cambridge: Harvard University Press, 1955), pp. 321f, for "musical glazed panels." The ondulatoire first appears at La Tourette and was born of a combination of Le Corbusier's interests in musical proportions, sculptural effects, and his notion of the correct logic of fenestration. He was stimulated in his musical interests by the musician Xenakis but also perhaps by Rudolf Wittkower whom he almost certainly met at the Milan Primo Convegno Internazionale sulle Proporzioni nelle arte . . . September 26–29, 1951 (see H. A. Millon, "Rudolf Wittkower, Architectural Principles in the Age of Humanism: Its Influence on the Development and Interpretation of Modern Architecture," *Journal of the Society of Architectural Historians,* 31, no. 2 [May 1972], 83–91, esp. notes on 85). Especially on a curved plan, the ondulatoires allow a direct experience of their rhythm even to the static observer; in the visual arts center, though, the spectator was expected to be moving.

10. Le Corbusier, *When the Cathedrals Were White,* p. 136.

11. Le Corbusier, *Manière de penser l'urbanisme* (Paris: Éditions de l'Architecture d'Aujourd'hui, 1946), pp. 79f, 90–92. On page 91 he speaks of the "esprit de grace, de mariage heureux de la technique et de la nature. Ce parkway de la rive d' Hudson installe une véritable ceinture de splendeur sur le flanc de la ville . . . Dans cet organisme, dans ce corps urbain, qui semblait irrémédiablement condamné à la paralysie, à l'ossification, voici qu'est apparu un nouvel élément biologique; il n'est encore qu'un pourtour . . . mais des embranchements déjà ont établi le contact avec le réseau interieur." ("spirit of grace, of happy marriage between technique and nature. This parkway on the bank of the Hudson introduces a belt of splendor on the side of the city. Here a new biological element has appeared in this organism, this urban body, which seemed condemned to paralysis and ossification; it is only on the edge at present . . . but branches have already established contact with the interior grid.") Thus he sees the parkway as a regenerating device that should, ideally, save the built parts of the city at all points.

Le Corbusier on page 91 also states, "S. Giedion, Européen, dans son histoire de l'architecture: Temps et Espace, écrite ces jours-ci en Amérique . . . page 559: 'Le park-way est l'avantcoureur de la première reforme necessaire au developement des villes de l'avenir: *La suppression de la rue corridor!*'" ("S. Giedion, European, in his history of architecture: Time and Space, written recently in America . . . page 559: 'The parkway is the forerunner of the first reform necessary to the cities of the future: *The suppression of the corridor street!*'"). In the essay "What Is the Problem of America?" *Oeuvre complète 1934–1938,* pp. 67f, Le Corbusier singles out the parkway as a "basic principle of the city of the future." It seems likely, therefore, that the section of freeway surrounded by greenery and rising around the functional spaces of the drawing of April 7, themselves like orbits, and oriented to the sun, constitutes an element of forward-looking urbanistic iconography.

12. J. L. Sert, interview with the author, June 1971.

13. According to Andreini and Jullian de la Fuente.

14. Boston notebook p59, p. 7. A caveolji is a Turkish coffee shop.

15. Le Corbusier, "If I Had to Teach You Architecture," *Focus,* 1 (1938), 3–12.

16. The nature of Le Corbusier's relationship with particular members of his atelier was gathered from discussions at the Fondation Le Corbusier, 1971–1972. His assistant for this job was called simply by the first part of his surname, Jullian.

17. Joseph Zalewski (recalled by John Nickols). For excellent illustration of Le Corbusier's roof garden in an overrun state, see Le Corbusier, *New World of Space,* pp. 116–117.

18. Le Corbusier, *When the Cathedrals Were White,* p. xviii, where the S is illustrated. See also Le Corbusier, "What Is the Problem of America?" pp. 65–68: "New York and Chicago in their present inordinate dimensions have lost all contact with the realities imposed on us by the twenty-four hour day. The cities of America must be reorganized so as to take account of that period of time which controls all our labours and activities, that period of time between the rising and the setting of the sun." The mixed metaphor of circulation and the rhythm of the sun occurs in writing in *Sur les quatres routes* (Paris: Gallimard, 1941), p. 37: "The twenty-four hour cycle, under the influence of twenty or even thirty times higher speeds, suddenly extends our sphere of action; the sun revolves at twenty times slower tempo" (author's translation). By the time he worked on

the visual arts center, Le Corbusier had developed a cosmology of his own. His chief signs were arranged along a processional way at Chandigarh called "La Fosse de Consideration" (see "Les Signes," *Oeuvre complète 1946–1952,* ed. W. Boesinger [Zurich: Editions Girsberger, 1953], p. 149); these were the "open hand," the Modulor spiral, the S of day and night, the curves of the solstices, and so on.

19. Andreini has explained of the phrase "le cube bâti": "It certainly suggests what one would normally call the 'built volume.' Le Corbusier made up his own vocabulary from words and expressions which he thought were closer to the concrete reality of things" (letter to the author, November 1972, author's translation). Eduard Sekler has suggested, in that case, that Le Corbusier's rather special usage may reflect the influence of German architectural usage (perhaps from the time Le Corbusier was in Behren's office) where "Kubatur" means "umbauter Raum," that is, "built volume."

20. Jullian de la Fuente discussed the circle fully with the author in March 1972.

21. Jullian stated that the 0.86 meter slab-plus-beam figure hypothesized at this stage (rather a large amount) was arrived at quite casually.

22. Interview with Andreini, March 4, 1972.

23. Le Corbusier, "Nothing is Transmissible But Thought," *Le Corbusier, Last Works,* ed. W. Boesiger (New York: Praeger, 1970), p. 174.

24. Le Corbusier, *Sur les quatres routes,* pp. 124–125.

25. Interview with the author, March 1971.

26. Le Corbusier, *New World of Space,* p. 23.

27. "Two grand pianos making love"—said to have been coined by a member of the Classics Department.

28. There is some discussion of the straight line and its mechanistic symbolism in Banham, *Theory and Design in the First Machine Age,* p. 121. The corollary, that curved lines are somehow "antimechanistic," "picturesque," or "romantic," cannot necessarily be assumed. But Andreini has asserted that his intentionally freehand curves should be understood according to such a convention. like so much else in this building, they were an antidote to American machine precision.

29. For lungs as a paradigm of the daily circulation of the city (one side light for day, one side dark for night), see the appendix to Le Corbusier's *Urbanisme* (Paris: Crès, 1925). See also Le Corbusier, *La ville radieuse,* pp. 40–41, where lungs are illustrated and the architect states: "Les arbres absorbent l'acide carbonique. Ils rejetent de l'oxygène. L'arbre est le compagnon de l'homme. Il n'y a bientot plus

(Notes to Pages 71–87)

d'arbres dans les villes." ("Trees absorb carbonic acid. They emit oxygen. The tree is the companion of man. *There are almost no trees left in cities.*")

The senses of free air circulation and free traffic circulation are overlapping because the remedies for both were strictly interdependent: the creation of open space in the city through high density building, the introduction of greenery into the space so created, the placement of elevated freeways in the same space among the trees, so avoiding congestion of air and traffic.

30. Le Corbusier, "What Is the Problem of America?." *Oeuvre complète 1934–1938,* pp. 65–68.

31. Le Corbusier, *Vers une architecture,* 1st ed. (Paris: Crès, 1923), p. 145 (author's translation).

4. The Presentation

1. His activities in the early part of 1960 can be reconstructed from notebook P60. He was in India at the end of 1959 and then in Persia. Most of the observations used here were made from the return airplane trip which passed over Cairo and Mont Blanc. On page 37 of P59, written therefore about December 1959 (shortly after his site visit), appears "UN 1947 L-C et Oscar accusé d'etre communistes par la haute presse USA" ("UN 1947 L-C and Oscar accused of being Communists by the high American press").

2. For Le Corbusier's attitude toward aircraft there are numerous references: *Vers une architecture,* of course; *Aircraft* (London: Studio, 1935); *Précisions sur un état présent de l'architecture et de l'urbanisme* (Paris: Crès, 1930); and *Sur les quatres routes.* The notebooks are full of observations made on aircraft while flying in them, and full of sketches of views from them. He frequently became introspective and autobiographical while in flight.

3. Jullian de la Fuente has stated that no special model was made for presentation. The structural working model was simply painted. This is now at the Carpenter Center. Arthur Trottenberg remembered his surprise when he was confronted with such a crude model; from his dealings with other architects he was used to slick presentation models prepared by professional model builders.

4. John Nickols kept a detailed diary of Le Corbusier's visits; the cocktail parties are reconstructed from his notes and with help from his verbal recollections. The other source

for Le Corbusier's presentation visit was J. L. Sert, interview June 2, 1971.
5. Diary of John Nickols, entry for November 1959. The diary is in the possession of Nickols.
6. Diary of John Nickols, entry for June 13, 1960.
7. The translation was made in Paris shortly before Le Corbusier's departure.
8. These terms are all taken from Le Corbusier, *Sur les quatres routes*, pp. 58–88, especially 69f, in which the architect also illustrates the idea of "terrains artificiels" ("artificial sites") with a perspective of one of his Algiers schemes (p. 75). Incidentally this Algiers scheme certainly provides a relevant comparison with the visual arts center: it too has sinuous forms, a freeway, greenery, and living space—all supported by a rudimentary pilotis/slab grid.
9. This quotation from John Coolidge's recollections written to the author in March 1973.
10. Ibid.
11. Recalled in interview with Sert, 1970.
12. See section 6 of Le Corbusier's "Construction of a Visual Arts Center."
13. Le Corbusier, *Oeuvre complète 1910–1929*, ed. O. Stonorov and W. Boesiger (Zurich: Editions d'Architecture, 1929), pp. 126–127. The "five points of a new architecture" are: (1) pilotis, (2) roof garden, (3) free plan, (4) strip window, (5) free facade.
14. When Nickols first saw the model in Sert's office he wrote in his notes that it "was not an innovatory building," that it seemed to be "backward looking," and that it recalled the Villa Savoye at Poissy. The question is not so simple, but his instinctive comparison is instructive.
15. Andreini in an interview March 2, 1972, commented on Le Corbusier's horror of the curtain wall in the late years.
16. Andreini concurred with this opinion. He took more interest in such theoretical matters than Jullian, and Le Corbusier, who rarely discussed such ideas, did divulge his attitudes to Andreini.
17. Le Corbusier, *Précisions*, p. 40, comparing masonry and point support structures. Also *Oeuvre complète 1910–1929*, p. 127.
18. Le Corbusier, *Talks with Students* (New York: Orion Press, 1961), pp. 46–47.
19. Ibid., p. 46.

5. A Conference at Sert's

1. This chapter is composed almost entirely of information from John Nickols' oral and written recollections. I am much indebted to him for the use of the sketches Le Corbusier made at the meeting, which Nickols kept.
2. Le Corbusier's technical flippancy was corroborated by Paul Krueger, job captain at Sert's, who had to deal with Le Corbusier's directives at the working drawing stage (interview June 1972).
3. Andreini (interviews December 15, 1971, and March 3, 1972) recalled an evening on the site at Marseilles when he and Le Corbusier were alone, inspecting the pumping house. Le Corbusier stated that he loved the contrast between the glistening machines and the machine-rolled glass, and the "natural" concrete. The irony of paying homage to American engineering when so much else about the building was deliberately primitivist was raised in discussion with Andreini (March 2, 1972), who smiled at the word "irony" and said "exactly." He went further and said it was specially ironical because "everything else about the building" was intended to be naturalistic. The link between the aluminum aérateurs and brise-soleil and the parts of an aircraft wing are strongly supported by Le Corbusier's remark, made in Cambridge in June 1960, that the aérateurs were airplane wings. The brise-soleil solution should be compared to the illustration of a tail flap from a "scylla" class aircraft: Le Corbusier, *Aircraft*, ill. 43. A frame type brise-soleil was used at St. Dié and on the pavilion on top of the Unité d'Habitation at Marseilles.
4. Words recorded by Nickols in his notes.
5. Le Corbusier records a trip to Rockefeller Center in *When the Cathedrals Were White*, p. 62. While he was put off by the eclecticism of the skyscrapers, he did admire their technical, structural, and communications virtuosity, and the workmanship of their detailing.
6. Le Corbusier, *Sur les quatres routes*, pp. 42–43. Of the Rio de Janeiro pavement he writes: "Les trottoirs mosaique en marbre blanc et noir, sont les promenoirs adorables" ("The mosaic pavements in black and white marble are adorable walkways").
7. Although no direct link is made with collage, there is a valuable discussion of the meaning of Le Corbusier's early work (especially the Ozenfant studio) by W. H. Jordy, "The Symbolic Essence of Modern Architecture of the Twenties and Its Contemporary Influence," *Journal of the Society of Architectural Historians*, 22, no. 3 (October 1963), pp. 177–187.
8. From John Nickols' notes.

9. This information kindly supplied by Patricia M. Sekler, who noted the resemblance.
10. Nickols' notes.
11. Ibid.
12. The actual phrase in the Boston notebook is "une piste de jardins et rocailles dense[?] dans le paysage et formant paysage" ("a track of gardens and dense[?] rockeries in the landscape and forming landscape").
13. This is fully discussed in Le Corbusier, *Sur les quatre routes*, pp. 69f. On page 70 Le Corbusier states: "Nous nous proposons simplement de prolonger la nature hospitalière, par les Quatre Routes, *en ville même*" ("We propose simply to extend the hospitality of nature *into the town itself* by means of the four routes").
14. Recalled by John Nickols in interview March 1972. He took photographs of Le Corbusier and Sert in Harvard Yard.
15. Le Corbusier, *New World of Space*, p. 116, where the quoted statement appears in English. See also *Oeuvre complète 1938–1946*, ed. W. Boesiger (Zurich: Editions d'Architecture, 1946), pp. 140–141, where the garden is also illustrated. He insists later in the passage that the garden be left to run in a wild state and speaks of his preoccupation with the countryside and his idea for "une toiture verte" ("roof of greenery"). For further discussion of countryside in buildings see Le Corbusier, *Sur les quatre routes*, p. 76, and *Talks with Students*, pp. 60–73.
16. All these quotations are from the notes of John Nickols, who seems to have been a highly trained observer, and in the habit (after his experiences in polar regions) of keeping details of temperature and humidity. These are interspersed among the notes.
17. At the opening of Marseilles Le Corbusier spoke of the concrete as "stone."

6. Conflicts in the Design

1. See S. Giedion's introduction to Knud Bastlund, *José Luis Sert* (New York: Praeger, 1967), p. 8.
2. The inscription refers to the use of aluminum and the interpenetration of inside and outside space.
3. Notebook P61.
4. In more recent works Jullian shows a taste for enhancing circulation flows and spatial effects by means of piers (for example, at Brazilia). But the piers supporting La Tourette over the hillside, and the spatial effects of the varied brise-soleil sizes in the projected "Tower of Shadows" for Chandigarh indicate that Jullian may be indebted to Le Corbusier. In this case, however, Le Corbusier was probably placing a high premium on pilotis and their appropriateness to a curved plan.
5. Understood from various discussions at the Fondation Le Corbusier, especially with Andreini.
6. The suggested figure at the time this program was defined was in fact $20 per square foot. See appendix 1.
7. Notebook P62, p. 8.
8. Notebook P62, p.8. See *Oeuvre complète 1957–1965*, p. 88, for plan of the offices to which he refers. The "fourth wall" was formed by angled brise-soleil fins which, from any distance inside a room, offered no views out of the structure (thus appearing as a wall) but let in light. As one approached the "wall" more closely and was enabled to see it diagonally, it dissolved completely, allowing views out.
9. "Incorrect" mixture, I believe, because there was a confusion of elements and materials—some concrete and some aluminum ondulatoires. Le Corbusier would, I believe, have sanctioned the mixture of aluminum and concrete, indeed, would have encouraged it, if each material were confined to each species of element. Jullian's researches were eventually useful: a comparable solution was adopted in the Zurich Exhibition Pavilion: see *Oeuvre complète 1957–1965*, p. 23, for photograph of model.
10. At the Cambridge conference in June, he had said by November 15, 1960.

7. The Day of Crisis—The Second Project

1. His movements are traceable through his notebooks.
2. In conversation March 1971.
3. *Oeuvre complète 1952–1957*, ed. W. Boesiger (Zurich: Editions Girsberger, 1958), pp. 94–101, 144–157. A difference and innovation at the visual arts center is the manner in which glass is placed in between each fin normal to it, so as to be angled to the room.
4. The ramp could now run legally from the third level entrance to Prescott Street. On the Quincy Street side, the gradient problem was exaggerated by the floor height increase, and it became necessary to build a mound of earth at the base of the ramp.
5. Recalled by Jullian in conversation with E. F. Sekler, 1968.
6. In summer the top studio can become unbearably hot by late afternoon even if curtains and aérateurs are used.

The finger of light which can just stream in the brise-soleil on this side on winter's evenings is not a "mistake" but a poetic intention envisaged from the time of earliest experimentation with brise-soleil (see *Oeuvre complète 1938–1946*, pp. 103–109).

7. See Assembly Building, Chandigarh; *Oeuvre complète 1957–1965*, p. 89, for photograph.

8. Le Corbusier's Definition of Reinforced Concrete

1. The prints were made from the presentation drawings and colored in by hand. Unfortunately they have disappeared, but according to Joseph Zalewski they were very close in appearance to the presentation drawings. The main difference seems to have been the registering of formwork positions in the prints. Obviously, being prints of the presentation set, they were the same in overall scale and shape; they were also colored according to the same convention of ochre for concrete, blue for glass.
2. This opportune phrase is Le Corbusier's, and refers in his letter (appendix 16) to the prints mentioned in note 1, above, which were made from the presentation drawings.
3. Le Corbusier, *Vers une architecture*, p. 16.
4. Ibid., p. 165.
5. The term "architrave" is used by Le Corbusier himself when discussing brise-soleil casting (appendix 18).
6. That this measure was not foreseen (Jullian has said it was a last minute job) is surely further evidence of Le Corbusier's technical nonchalance. To have placed a piloti in each of the points of maximum cantilever would have been inadequate structurally. What is more, the pilotis would have broken the structural grid at two conspicuous points of the building. In the model made in January a very fat piloti was shown under the Quincy Street studio, aligned correctly with the grid, but this would have left a precariously large area of soffit unsupported at a point where fenestration immediately above disallowed the use of the curved wall as a stiffener, and would have conflicted with the tectonic system of visual equivalents to visual loads.
7. Le Corbusier, *Vers une architecture*, p. 171. This quote is taken from the subtitle of an illustration of the Parthenon, "si pur qu'on a la sensation du naturel" ("so pure as to give one the feeling of the natural"). He continues to claim that the Doric system is a pure creation of the mind—but "cela crée un fait aussi naturel à notre entendement que le fait 'mer' et le fait 'montagne.' Quelles sont les oeuvres

(Notes to Pages 152–166)

de l'homme qui ont atteint ce degré?" ("that creates a fact as natural, according to our understanding, as the fact 'sea' and the fact 'mountain.' Which creations of man have reached this level?")

8. For the matter of Le Corbusier's attraction to smooth ("lisses") structural frames, see Paul V. Turner, "The Education of Le Corbusier: A Study of the Development of Le Corbusier's Thought, 1900–20" (Ph.D. diss., Harvard, 1971), p. 125: "What is truly Jeanneret's [Le Corbusier's original name] is the uncompromising formal decision to strip the structural elements down to their barest, most generalized, most 'ideal' forms: a pure slab and a pure column . . . The important thing was that the ultimate form should be the simplest, most pure expression of the concepts 'slab' and 'column' . . . in other words the Ideal Slab and the Ideal Column . . . divested of all particularity. The Dom-Ino system, in effect, is philosophical idealism applied to architectural structure."

Turner tends to underplay the pragmatism whereby the simplest forms were thought to be the easiest to mass produce (the Dom-Ino was originally an emergency housing kit), and the Rationalist influence. That there is striving toward ideal form is undoubtedly correct, the more so in the visual arts center with its cylindrical supports.

As well as idealism (in Turner's sense) and the structural-Rationalist expression of diminished sizes for diminished visual loads (which led to impossibly slender columns beneath the third level Prescott Street studio), there was the perceptual argument that cylinders, like cubes and spheres, emitted the purest sensations (*Vers une architecture*). Then there was the aesthetic choice, in this particular case, that beams, mushroom capitals, and so on were inappropriate to a showpiece structure of such stunning spatial properties. Furthermore, the forms of the visual arts center skeleton are the "correct" ones for reinforced concrete. It is important, in such a detailed discussion of the piloti, not to loose sight of its general urbanistic value: in the "radiant city" this element was the quintessential component, supporting both built form and circulation.

9. Claudius Petit was the minister in charge of reconstruction at the time of the opening of Marseilles, at which occasion he presented Le Corbusier with the "Cravate de commandeur de la Legion d'Honneur." Later, Petit was elected Mayor of Firminy. He then commissioned Le Corbusier to

do the Unité, church, and youth center for the city.

10. By the "new brutality," Le Corbusier means the "new brutalism"; see R. Banham, *The New Brutalism, Ethic or Aesthetic?* (New York: Reinhold, 1966) Sert "has a lot of time" because of a sabbatical leave.

11. Le Corbusier's dislike of Holyoke Center's finishes (for which see Bastlund, *José Luis Sert,* pp. 210, 219) was recalled by Paul Krueger and Huson Jackson (interview June 1972). Krueger also stated that they (of Sert's office) had been much interested in the Maison du Brésil finishes (see *Oeuvre complète 1952–1957,* pp. 200–201) when doing the concrete work of Holyoke Center and that carpenters were brought from Nova Scotia for the job. Jackson and Krueger recalled that Le Corbusier was amazed that Sert was not using steel instead of concrete in the United States. His intention of using steel formwork in the visual arts center may possibly be related to these experiences.

12. See Le Corbusier, *Talks with Students,* p. 50, in which he discusses concrete as follows: "the erection of walls, floors, arches, etc. will take its cue from local custom and from materials used locally in timberwork."

13. For example, Walter Gropius, whose house in Lincoln, Massachusetts, was a synthesis of regionalism and standardized building elements.

14. "Le Corbusier Smoothes His Style for U.S. Debut at Harvard," *The Engineering News Record,* 170 (April 4, 1963), 80–82.

15. In interview March 4, 1972. Andréini said that he thought Le Corbusier treated his architectural materials "as painter and sculptor" and stated of Le Corbusier: "Il disait que le béton était un materiél de nature spécifique" ("He said that concrete was a material with a specific nature").

16. Turner, "The Education of Le Corbusier," states in reference to Le Corbusier's earlier language: "Le Corbusier's attitude was one of conceptualising, separately, each structural role in architecture, and then assigning to each a form which, in some dramatic or symbolic way, embodied it and raised it to a generalised and ideal level" (p. 179). Again, "for him, a form ought to be the perfect fulfillment of one function alone." See *Oeuvre complète 1957–1965,* p. 100, where Le Corbusier discusses the Chandigarh fenestration (my translation): "Glazings named 'ondulatoires' have been invented so as to eliminate the expense of hardware of opening windows. At the same time the real problem of the window was posed. To light, to air, to ventilate. To light: by means of clear or translucent glass, which it is not possible to open (sealed in the concrete. See Visual Arts Center, Boston, U.S.A.). To air: installed vertical aérateurs, from the floor to the ceiling, from 27 to 43 cms width and capable of being opened gradually and at will for their entire height, providing an immense natural transaération by virtue of the differences in specific gravity of the air between one facade and the other, according to the position of the sun in the course of the day. To ventilate: during extremely hot periods in the tropics. It is necessary to correct the effect of the heat of air which is more than body temperature by a violent 'Air Current' ensured by fans placed on the floor or suspended from the ceiling. The window is henceforth abolished."

17. This letter is an excellent example of Le Corbusier's instinctive sense of layout for the rhetorical reinforcement of his points; also of his use of Jura slang: "semblable à des de."

18. For the environmental aspects of the Maison de Refuge, see R. Banham, *The Architecture of the Well-Tempered Environment* (London: Architectural Press, 1969), pp. 156–157. For Le Corbusier's discovery of air-conditioning in the United States, see Le Corbusier, *When the Cathedrals Were White,* p. 33.

19. For further discussion of the shortcomings of the traditional window, see Le Corbusier, *When the Cathedrals Were White,* p. 54. Also note that when discussing the aérateurs and ondulatoires of the visual arts center in a letter (appendix 13), Le Corbusier states: "Ce ne sont pas des fenêtres" ("These are not windows").

20. Le Corbusier, *Vers une architecture,* pp. 106–107.

9. Transatlantic Details and the Modulor

1. The ramp entry through the Quincy Street facade acts as a wind tunnel in the final building. The exhibition space to the north is entered through a single set of doors. To the south, a landing is formed at the top of the stairs, which is also entered from the ramp through a single set. Another set of doors stands between the landing and the studio space. Continuity between vertical circulation and the main space served by it is thus severely disrupted. But the Corbusian ideal would have been disrupted in any case by fire codes, which also require a set of doors between the landing and the stairs.

2. On Le Corbusier's drawing of January 14, 1961, which created the space, appears a note in his handwriting doubting the structural feasibility of the interior ramp.

3. *Harvard Crimson,* May 23, 1961. The "officials'" quotation immediately following is from the same source.
4. The drawings that were sent to Sert have, unfortunately, disappeared. They were prints of the presentation drawings colored in crayon and were referred to later as the "crystallization of Le Corbusier's relative ideas of the architectural drawings of our epoch" (May 29, 1961; appendix 16).
5. According to John Nickols, interview March 1972.
6. Probably referring to his idiosyncratic reinforcing solutions and formwork complications.
7. Alan Chimacoff, Michael Dolinski, and Lionel Glendenning, "VAC BOS, The Carpenter Center For the Visual Arts at Harvard University, Le Corbusier" (unpublished M.A. thesis, Harvard, 1969), reveal that José Luis Sert attempted to have a stairway built over the parapet at the Prescott Street end of the ramp. The Fogg Museum objected, saying that the space at the top of these proposed stairs was to be used for an enclosed garden. There is no such garden there today.
8. Jackson (interview June 1972) seems to have sensed Le Corbusier's ambivalence toward the visual arts center and America generally.
9. Le Corbusier, *Le Modulor* (Boulogne-sur-Seine: Éditions de l'Architecture d'Aujourd'hui, 1948), p. 67, where the heights (inches) 27, 43, 70, 86, 113, 140, 183, 226 are all diagrammed with the body in different sitting and standing positions.
10. Drain pipes from *some* of the terraces (for example, the fifth floor northwest side) were eventually run vertically down through the studios. Drainage for the brise-soleil was by small pipes in the architrave onto the ground (or terraces) beneath.
11. The temporary use of aluminum for struts was suggested because delay was anticipated in precast work. Eventually this proposed measure proved unnecessary.
12. Le Corbusier, *Modulor,* p. 67, fig. 26.
13. Ibid., p. 19.
14. Ibid. pp. 46ff, 113–115, for references to the United States and the architect's attempts at delivering his system to United States industry.
15. The red and blue scales of the Modulor are most handily explained in *Oeuvre complète 1946–1952,* pp. 178–179. The diagram presented there is most useful as an accompaniment to the drawings of details in this chapter.
16. See appendix 23 for list of men in Sert's office involved with the visual arts center. I am indebted to Penelope Johnson, Sert's secretary, for this list and for much other help as well.
17. Drawing, September 1961, not included; at present in posession of José Luis Sert.
18. The forms of the auditoriums of his League of Nations and Palace of the Soviets entries were based on acoustic optimization.
19. Le Corbusier, *Vers une architecture,* p. 178.
20. Le Corbusier, *Modulor 2,* p. 324.
21. Ibid., p. 321.
22. Ibid., p. 330.
23. Sigfried Giedion's phrase. See *Space, Time and Architecture,* pp. 350–432.
24. This point is made by Alan Chimacoff, Michael Dolinski, Lionel Glendenning, "VAC BOS, The Carpenter Center for the Visual Arts at Harvard University, Le Corbusier."
25. In fact, insect screens are used on many university buildings. Perhaps Sert foresaw that the screen would not be included in contractor's quotations or that colored painted wooden doors would eventually be used for the aérateurs instead of aluminum and wished not to obscure the colors. (This reason was given by Krueger, interview June 1972.)
26. Le Corbusier, *When the Cathedrals Were White,* pp. 62, 64, 167.
27. Cited and translated by Banham, *The Architecture of the Well-Tempered Environment,* p. 160.
28. "Bâtis" are therefore those ondulatoire struts that form the sides of each aérateur. Andreini (letter to the author, November 13, 1972) explained that the term was commonly used in connection with buildings to refer to the mountings of doors and windows, and that in this case Le Corbusier was applying the generic term to his ondulatoires, which he likened to classical moldings.
29. The idea for the folded aluminum leaf aérateur door recalls Le Corbusier's reference to the doors as "airplane wings."
30. Paul Krueger (interview June 1972) recalls the "decoding" process, involving detailed perusal of La Tourette, and other late buildings' details, in the *Oeuvre complète.*
31. Sert referred casually to the ondulatoire struts as "studs." In his own work, he uses struts that are applied to the facade, not made flush with it, as is the case with Le Corbusier's element. Nickols has explained (interview March 1972) that, early in his stay in the United States Sert converted a stable which had vertical wooden "stud" partitions, rather like Le Corbusier's eventual ondulatoire struts.

10. Construction

(Notes to Pages 201–216)

1. Paul Krueger, interview with the author, January 1, 1974. Much of this chapter is based on this source.
2. These difficulties were recalled by Krueger, January 25, 1974, as was the history of the toit-jardin detail.
3. I am indebted to José Luis Sert and his partners for letting me examine the specification in detail.
4. Building specification, section 12, p. 7. The specification is in the possession of J. L. Sert.
5. Norman Whiting, telephone interview with author, February 26, 1974. Kenneth Leach, telephone interview with author, February 28, 1974.
6. Interview February 28, 1974. All quotations in this paragraph are from the same source.
7. The entire story of the foundation design (with the nomenclature quoted below in this paragraph) was told by Paul Krueger, interview with the author, December 26, 1974.
8. *Architectural Forum,* 115 (December 1961), 108ff. This must have confirmed all of Corbusier's attitudes toward American journalists. The ondulatoires of the ramp gallery had something of the density of a garden fence in the rendering and the structure beneath the curved studio was incorrectly portrayed.
9. Recalled in detail by Emil Hervol of Le Messurier Associates, interview with author, October 10, 1972. Hervol also supplied the information that follows on the predeflection mechanism.
10. Cracks have occurred in places. A structure course of the Graduate School of Design at Harvard set these cracks as a study problem in the spring of 1972. Later in his interview of October 10, 1972, Hervol indicated that where cracking did eventually occur on the ground floor near the entrance, it was caused by the presence of a large, flat, oblong plenum for the air-conditioning system. In a place of maximum structural sheer—the second floor beneath the main ramp—sleeves for heating and ventilating were required next to the glass of the workshops, which was, in turn, close to a range of columns. The problem was to shift the air through the extremely reinforced slab: Hervol cleverly arranged his sheer heads to function as an ad hoc system of air channels. Hervol remembered the brise-soleil and ondulatoires. The former were beveled at the edge on his suggestion. The latter have buckled in places because the concrete was too quick drying and the reinforcement was noncentrally placed. It was Hervol who suggested wood be used instead of concrete.
11. The large glazing of the Ozenfant Studio of 1922.
12. Interviews: Leach, February 28, 1974; Whiting, February 26, 1974; Hervol, October 10, 1972.
13. Interview, Hervol, October 10, 1972.
14. Building specification, section 2 (entitled "Concrete Work"), p. 1.
15. Ibid., p. 5.
16. Ibid., p. 9.
17. Interview between the author and Tucker, February 15, 1974. Most of the details on concrete finish were derived from this discussion.
18. Ibid.
19. These details concerning the construction of the curves came from interviews with Paul Krueger (January 25, 1974) and Tucker (February 15, 1974).
20. Details concerning ondulatoire precasting are from Francis A. Facchetti of Cambridge Cement Stone Company: interview with author, February 27, 1974.
21. Recalled by Tucker, interview February 15, 1974.
22. Curtains were not used and the brise-soleil were not fitted with contreplaqués, but painted. Where hardboard was used, it was mostly painted black. The oak plywood that was used has a fairly distinctive grain. It is not clear whether Le Corbusier means "spray guns" or "pistols" by "pistolets." The more picturesque "pistols" has been used, bearing in mind Le Corbusier's impish sense of humor and his belief that Americans were "gangsters."
23. Interview, Krueger, January 1, 1974.
24. Interview, Krueger, December 26, 1974.
25. Ibid. The following details on landscaping are from the same source.
26. Andreini (interviews December 15, 1971, and March 4, 1972) stated that it was a direct comparison between the concrete work of the main Chandigarh buildings and the visual arts center that prompted Le Corbusier to say the latter was too sterile. It may be that he had become used to allowing for the slightly slipshod work of the laborers at Chandigarh whose traditions, wheelbarrows, wooden scaffolds, and formwork must surely have given him "l'ésprit du chantier" ("the spirit of the worksite") without any special prompting. In the United States, George A. Fuller Co., the contractor, was capable of giving him precisely what he asked for: finishes that are "lisse" (smooth) and "élégant" (elegant). Indeed, in the United States context slick finishes are a virtuous sign of high craftsmanship (precisely "du Cadillac!"): the result is not surprising. I

have to admit that I find the concrete work slightly dead.

27. A survey of what was excluded from the *Oeuvre complète* by Le Corbusier personally would make a useful study. One can only speculate here as to his reasons. Construction shots occur on some rare occasions in the *Oeuvre complète* (see Ronchamp, *Oeuvre complète 1952–1957*, p. 38). Possibly he did not wish to show the complex reinforcing and hanging arrangements necessary to hold up his "key to the solution of reinforced concrete," for clearly the visual arts center skeleton was one of his most polemical structures. (His use of the term "street" in the quoted passage to refer to the ramp should be noted.)

28. Le Corbusier's notebook P61, at the time of his June 1960 visit, contains reference to a possible exhibition of his works. An exhibition was held at the time of the opening.

29. Formal parties were not to Le Corbusier's taste. In the letter from Pusey, he circled the words "family party."

30. From Le Corbusier, *Last Works*, pp. 168f. Le Corbusier put great hope in India because it avoided the troubles of the first era of the machine age: with reference to the "Open Hand" at Chandigarh he wrote in 1954: "'La Main Ouverte' affirmera que la seconde ère de la civilisation machiniste a commencé: l'ère de harmonie." See von Moos, *Le Corbusier, Elemente einer Synthese*, p. 359.

31. Notebook P61, p. 13. One notes a tendency to judge a people's moral qualities by the quality of their architecture. Le Corbusier, I believe, upheld the corollary: "It was as if harmony in matter (architecture) could be expected to bring a social and spiritual harmony with it."

11. The Image and Idea of the Building

1. *Oeuvre complète 1957–1965*, p. 54.
2. Jullian de la Fuente, interview with Eduard Sekler, 1968.
3. Turner, "The Education of Le Corbusier."
4. For some suggestions concerning the influence of idealism, particularly Platonic ideas on Le Corbusier in the period of Purism, see Banham, *Theory and Design in the First Machine Age*, p. 205f, in which the theory of "types" is touched upon. Again, I am indebted to Paul Turner for the thrust of this interpretation.
5. Appendix 13.
6. Le Corbusier, *Oeuvre complète 1910–1929*, p. 23, for the Dom-Ino; p. 129 for the "five points of a new architecture." The following from *Vers une architecture*, p. 127, is relevant to the elements of Le Corbusier's architectural system in concrete: "The establishment of a standard involves exhausting every practical and reasonable possibility, and extracting from them a recognized type conformable to its functions, with a maximum output and minimum of means . . ."
7. Giedion, *Space, Time and Architecture*, p. 519, for the phrase "construction spirituelle." The organization of structural, architectural elements into a gestalt or an organization of significant form is one of the central messages of *Vers une architecture*. "Almost every period of architecture has been linked with research into construction. The conclusion has been drawn that architecture is construction" (p. 200). "This is construction, this is not architecture. Architecture only exists when there is poetic emotion. Architecture is a plastic thing" (pp. 198–199; author's translations).
8. Le Corbusier, *Vers une architecture*, p. 165.
9. Le Corbusier, *When the Cathedrals Were White*, p. 43. See also William Curtis, "Le Corbusier, Manhattan et le Rêve de la Ville Radieuse," *Archithèse*, 17 (March 1976), 23–28.
10. Carpenter Center seems not to be an isolated case of Le Corbusier's incorporating urbanistic doctrine and metaphors in single buildings. For analogous interpretations of Pavillon Suisse, the United Nations Project, the Villa Savoye, and the Unité d'Habitation at Marseilles, see articles by William Curtis in *Archithèse*, 12 (December 1974), 14 (June 1975), and 17 (March 1976); and by S. von Moos, 14. See also William Curtis, "Le Corbusier: The Evolution of His Architectural Language and Its Crystallisation in the Villa Savoye at Poissy," *Le Corbusier/English Architecture 1930's, Units 17/18* (Milton Keynes: Open University Press, 1975), pp. 33–44, esp. pp. 40ff; see also von Moos, *Le Corbusier, Elemente einer Synthese*, p. 140.
11. See Plato, *Republic*, 500d–501a. It seems to me that Le Corbusier's view of the planner (particularly himself) has deep affinities with Plato's view of the philosopher-king, and that the architect was in almost every sense of the word an "essentialist." In the *Republic* the philosopher-king is the founder of the virtuous city; only he can sketch "the ground-plan of the city." "True philosophers" see the original city idea (the divine model), "letting their eyes wander to and fro from the model to the picture, and back from the picture to the model" (501a/b, 484c).

That there is also a case for rooting Le Corbusier's messianic outlook in biblical thought has been suggested by N. K. Smith, *Art and Architecture in the Modern World*. Thus I would suggest that the holistic tendencies of Le Corbusier's utopian outlook must be understood in a context of ideas far older than the ideas of nineteenth-century utopian socialists such as Charles Fourier and St. Simon, though undoubtedly related to these more recent precursors.

The most incisive critique of utopianism has been provided by Karl Popper in *The Open Society and Its Enemies* (London: Routledge and Kegan Paul, 1945), where the author warns that utopian engineering leads rapidly to totalitarianism. See particularly chap. 10 of that work. Such a critique would presumably require adjustment in dealing with metaphors of utopia by artists.

The Carpenter Center in Le Corbusier's Oeuvre: An Assessment

1. Banham, *Theory and Design in the First Machine Age*, section 4; von Moos, *Le Corbusier, Elemente einer Synthese*, chap. 2; Charles Jencks, *Le Corbusier and the Tragic View of Architecture* (Cambridge: Harvard University Press, 1973), pp. 55–84.
2. Turner, "The Education of Le Corbusier"; Sekler, *The Early Drawings of Charles-Edouard Jeanneret*.
3. Quoted by Herbert Read in David Sylvester, ed., *Henry Moore, Sculpture and Drawings 1921–48*, 1 (London: Percy Lund, Humphries, 1957), xii.
4. Le Corbusier, *Creation Is a Patient Search*, trans. James Palmes (New York: Praeger, 1960), p. 197; Le Corbusier, *Dessins* (Geneva: Editions Forces Vives, 1965), introduction. The best discussion so far about the inseparable link between painting and architecture in Le Corbusier's work is by Stanislaus von Moos, "Natur und Geometrie im Werk von Le Corbusier," *Kunstnachrichten*, 2, no. 6 (March 1966).
5. Le Corbusier, *Creation*, p. 245.
6. Le Corbusier, *New World of Space*, p. 13.
7. John Golding and Christopher Green, *Léger and Purist Paris*, exhibition catalogue (London: Tate Gallery, 1971); *Le Corbusier*, exhibition catalogue (New York: Galerie Denise René, 1972). Roberto Gabetti and Carlo Olmo, *Le Corbusier e "L'Esprit Nouveau"* (Turin: Einaudi, 1975) appeared after the conclusion of research for the present study.
8. For example, the still life reproduced on the cover of *Le Corbusier*, exhibition catalogue (New York: Galerie Denise René, 1972), and *Two Bottles on Rose Background*, 1926, reproduced in *L'Opera di Le Corbusier*, exhibition catalogue (Florence: Palazzo Strozzi, 1963), no. 56, color plate 1.

(Notes to Pages 230–238)

9. Le Corbusier, "Plastique et poetique," *Oeuvre complète 1946–1952*, p. 225.
10. *Oeuvre complète 1910–1929*, p. 187.
11. Colin Rowe and Robert Slutzky, "Transparency: Literal and Phenomenal," *Perspecta*, 8 (1963), 45, discuss transparency in connection with the articulation of space. It is important to recognize that cantilevering from the pilotis on two sides of a house occurs first of all as a structural expedient and as a polemical demonstration of the principle of nonloadbearing walls. There is no evidence to indicate that the purpose of cantilevering was to create a layer of "shallow space" between the windows and the concrete columns on the second floor.
12. *Le Corbusier peintre*, exhibition catalogue (Basel: Galerie Beyeler, 1971), no. 16.
13. *Fifty Works by Le Corbusier*, sales catalogue (London: Sotheby, 1969), lots 6 and 7.
14. *Le syphon et le gant*, illustrated in Petit, *Le Corbusier lui-même*, p. 218.
15. Le Corbusier, *New World of Space*, p. 16; for a discussion of earlier renditions of the human figure see Stanislaus von Moos, *Le Corbusier, l'architecte et son mythe* (Paris: Horizons de France, 1971), p. 259.
16. For example, *Deux bouteilles et livre*, 1928, in Beyeler, *Le Corbusier peintre*, no. 19, and *Verre et bouteilles avec vermillon*, 1928, in Sotheby, *Fifty Works*, lot 11.
17. The occurrence of deliberately inconsistent scale in a painting was first discussed by S. Giedion in his introduction to "Le Corbusier (oeuvre plastique) 1919–1937," exhibition catalogue, (Zurich: Kunsthaus, 1938).
18. Petit, *Le Corbusier lui-même*, p. 219.
19. Le Corbusier, *New World of Space*, p. 16; (see also note 9, above).
20. Samir Rafi, "Le Corbusier et 'Les Femmes d'Alger,'" *Revue d'histoire et de civilisation du Maghreb*, 4, no. 1 (January 1968), 55.
21. J. Golding and C. Green, *Léger and Purist Paris*, pp. 21, 80; Maurice Jardot, *Léger dessins* (Paris: Editions des deux mondes, 1953), p. 27. Jean Cassou and Jean Leymarie, *Fernand Léger dessins et gouaches* (Paris: Chêne, 1972), pp. 87, 99, 123.
22. Amédée Ozenfant, *Memoires 1886–1962* (Paris: Seghers, 1968), p. 141.
23. *Still Life with Glass of Red Wine*, 1921, in Maurice Besset, *Who Was Le Corbusier?*, trans. Robin Kemball (Geneva: Skira, 1968), p. 60.

24. Amédée Ozenfant and Charles-Edouard Jeanneret, *La peinture moderne* (Paris: Crès, n.d. [1925]), p. 168.
25. Le Corbusier, *Creation*, p. 225.
26. Besset, *Who Was Le Corbusier?*, p. 61; Ozenfant and Jeanneret, *La peinture moderne*, p. 169.
27. Le Corbusier, *New World of Space*, p. 39. In Petit, *Le Corbusier lui-même*, p. 217, the work is erroneously entitled *Nature morte à l'accordéon* because the zigzagging facets of a glass were misinterpreted as bellows. Such an error is a tribute to Le Corbusier's power of transforming what were originally renditions of objects into pictorial ciphers.
28. The single faceted glass is more easily recognized for what it is in a drawing that belongs to the painting *Le dé violet*, 1926, (see Jardot, *Le Corbusier dessins*, p. 17.); here facets and rim are connected by outlines so as to form a cylindrical glass.
29. Sotheby, *Fifty Works*, lot 9, where an error similar to Petit's (see note 27, above) is made by giving the title *Accordéon et carafe* to something that has nothing to do with an accordion. A related sketch, unnumbered, is illustrated in Galerie Denise René, *Le Corbusier*.
30. Petit, *Le Corbusier lui-même*, p. 219.
31. Some examples are: *Still Life, Vézelay*, 1939 (Petit, *Le Corbusier, lui-même*, p. 225); tapestry, *Nature morte*, 1954 (ibid., p. 242); enamelled plaque, dated 1928–1959 (ibid., p. 239); collage (?), dated 1928–1960, reproduced in color in Le Corbusier, *Creation*, p. 254; several lithographs from the late series. See E. Sekler, "Le Corbusier's Use of a 'Pictorial Word' in His Tapestry *La femme et le moineau*," in M. Henle, ed., *Vision and Artifact* (New York: Springer, 1976) p. 119.
32. Jardot, *Le Corbusier dessins*, p. 64; Le Corbusier, *Creation*, p. 247.
33. This is the title of a pen drawing, Jardot, *Le Corbusier dessins*, p. 22.
34. *Oeuvre complète 1946–1952*, p. 225.
35. *L'Esprit Nouveau*, pp. 1489ff, quoted by von Moos, *Le Corbusier, l'architecte et son mythe* (author's translation).
36. Le Corbusier, *Oeuvre plastique peintures et dessins architecture* (Paris: Éditions Albert Morancé, 1938), introduction (author's translation).
37. François Cali, *Architecture of Truth* (New York: Braziller, 1957), preface by Le Corbusier.
38. *Oeuvre complète 1910–1929*, p. 189.
39. *Oeuvre complète 1934–1938*, p. 173; another exhibition pavilion with a system of ramps was designed for the "Ideal Home" exhibition 1938–1939; *Oeuvre complète 1938–1946*, p. 13.

(*Notes to Pages 238–248*)

40. *Oeuvre complète 1929–1934*, ed. W. Boesiger (Zurich: H. Girsberger, 1935), p. 25.
41. *Oeuvre complète 1957–1965*, p. 153.
42. *Oeuvre complète 1910–1929*, p. 177. In the long facades of the Zurich exhibition pavilion, *Le Corbusier, Last Works*, p. 155, a different kind of movement is implied: the triangular sides of the roof adjacent to each other can be read as if they were two levers ready to move around a central axis, like the arms of an old-fashioned pump or steam engine.
43. At a later date Le Corbusier commented on what he called "an astonishingly complex biology of the house" and explained, "Sometimes as a result of the biological necessity of the plan, curved or oblique partitions are necessary" (Stamo Papadaki, ed., *Le Corbusier* [New York: Macmillan, 1948], p. 144). In 1960 Le Corbusier wrote: "The biology of a plan or section is as necessary and obvious as that of a creature of nature. The introduction of the word 'biology' illuminates all researches in the field of building" (*Creation*, p. 201).
44. *Oeuvre complète 1952–1957*, p. 145. Toilet enclosures with similar shapes had long been used inside buildings. It seems as if Le Corbusier occasionally transferred forms from the inside to the outside of a building at a later moment. For example the curving main wall with its wedge-shaped ending at Ronchamp may well owe something to the curved wall of diminishing thickness that delimits one side of the entrance lobby at Garches.
45. Some of these changes are lucidly discussed by Peter Serenyi, "Le Corbusier's Changing Attitude toward Form," *Journal of the Society of Architectural Historians*, 24, no. 1 (March 1965), 15ff. He considers the years 1928–1929 a turning point in Le Corbusier's style.
46. *Oeuvre complète 1910–1929*, pp. 160ff, 213ff.
47. Rowe and Slutzky, "Transparency"; in their perceptive discussion of the spatial qualities of the League of Nations project, they stress "lateral extension" and refer to the "apportionate slicing of space." It should be noted, however, that "the glazing along the side walls" of the auditorium is not "disturbing the normal focus of the hall upon the presidential box" by "introducing a transverse direction," as they maintain; as explained in *Oeuvre complète 1910–1929*, p. 165, the architect intended to use translucent and not transparent glass which visually would have acted like a solid, though luminous, wall.
48. Texture is a significant indicator of architectural mood.

Several designs by Le Corbusier from the early and mid-thirties show a reliance on varied, rough textures: the gardener's lodge at the Villa Savoye, the Errazuris and de Mandrot houses, the architect's own penthouse studio, and finally the small weekend house and the house at Mathes.

49. *Oeuvre complète 1929–1934,* p. 79.
50. Ibid., p. 140.
51. Sotheby, *Fifty Works,* lot 46.
52. Le Corbusier, *Creation,* p. 225.
53. Ibid., p. 232.
54. Jardot, *Le Corbusier dessins,* p. 23.
55. Le Corbusier, *Oeuvre lithographique* (Zurich: Centre Le Corbusier, n.d.); Beyeler, *Le Corbusier peintre,* no. 91.
56. Sotheby, *Fifty Works,* lot 48.
57. Alan Colquhoun, "Formal and Functional Interactions: A Study of Two Late Projects by Le Corbusier," *Architectural Design,* 36, no. 5 (May 1966), 221ff.
58. *Le Corbusier, Last Works,* p. 45.
59. *Oeuvre complète 1952–1957,* p. 8; another part of the meaning probably is to be understood in very personal terms as is clear from *Entre deux* (Paris: Éditions Forces Vives, 1964).
60. In 1964 the Carpenter Center was awarded the Harleston Parker Medal of the Boston Society of Architects.
61. Le Corbusier, *Urbanisme,* p. 167.
62. *Oeuvre complète 1929–1934,* p. 132.
63. Werner Hofmann, *Turning Points in Twentieth-Century Art: 1890–1917* (New York: Braziller, 1969), p. 238.
64. E. F. Sekler, "The Visual Environment," *The Fine Arts and the University* (Toronto: Macmillan, 1965), p. 82.
65. *Le Corbusier, Last Works,* p. 168.

Notes on Creative Invention

1. In speaking of early and later conceptions I am not necessarily referring to a strict chronological order but rather to an inherent growth from simple to complex patterns. In the actual praxis of the inventive process there is typically a somewhat erratic moving back and forth between the root conception and its elaborations. Aspects of the final shape may show up in early flashes, and at advanced stages there may be check-backs to the simplicity of the beginnings. Thus the development is implicit rather than traceable through an exact logical sequence in time.
2. On Claude Bernard, see Walter B. Cannon, *The Wisdom of the Body* (New York: Norton, 1960), p. 37.

ACKNOWLEDGMENTS

Without the cooperation and active support of many individuals and institutions, this book could not have been written. Initially the Graham Foundation for Advanced Studies in the Visual Arts provided essential funds for research and publication. Later, at the suggestion of Harlow Carpenter, Jr., these were supplemented by a grant authorized by President Bok from the bequest of St. Vrain Carpenter to Harvard University.

The Fondation Le Corbusier, Paris, freely granted access to its collections and permission to publish a great deal of material. Its board of directors under the presidency of André Wogensky and its staff were invariably encouraging and helpful, in particular Roggio Andreini and Françoise de Franclieu, as well as Christian Gimonet and Brian Taylor during the periods of their affiliation with the Fondation. Jullian de la Fuente, Le Corbusier's co-designer for the Carpenter Center project, fortunately had carefully collected and dated all relevant sketches and other material and graciously made all this and his personal memories available to the authors, thus providing an invaluable core of solid documentation.

Josep Lluis Sert not only opened his files and shared his recollections but took time out from pressing professional commitments to write a foreword for this book and continued to be of assistance in many ways, as were his partners and collaborators Huson Jackson, Paul Krueger, Josef Zalewski, and Penelope Johnson. John Nickols very kindly came forth with some important information and photographs from the period of Le Corbusier's visits to Cambridge. Arthur D. Trottenberg provided valuable source material from the period when, as Harvard administrator, he had been closely connected with the project.

Professor Jerzy Soltan, for years a faithful collaborator of Le Corbusier's, never tired of being a source of encouragement and assistance during the long years of this book's preparation. It was a special pleasure to join him in the guidance of a student project in the Graduate School of Design which dealt with the Carpenter Center for the Visual Arts. The resulting unpublished masters thesis by Alan Chimacoff, Michael Dolinski, and Lionel Glendenning contains precious preparatory work for the present book. Accurate plans and sections utilized in their thesis and in this book were prepared under the direction of Professor Werner Seligmann, who kindly permitted their publication. Edward Nilson not only gave useful research and photographic assistance but also specially drew an isometric section of the building as a contribution to the present volume.

Valuable criticism and advice were given by Professors James Ackerman and John Coolidge, colleagues and friends over many years, who with me shared the responsibility of being thesis advisors to William Curtis. He also received support in other ways from the Department of Fine Arts under three consecutive chairmen: Sidney Freedberg, Seymour Slive, and John Rosenfield. Rudolf Arnheim provided much sound advice with great kindness and unfailing good humor. Gyorgy Kepes and Ben Weese helped through their unfaltering belief in the project. The staff of the Carpenter Center over a long period contributed greatly to this book; special thanks go to Roger Brandenberg-Horn, Marjorie Kane, Cynthia von Thüna, Hope Norwood, Jack Lueders-Booth, and above all Todd Stuart, who took and retook many difficult photographs with great skill and patience. Richard S. Field graciously contributed a series of most instructive photographs he had taken as a systematic record of the building's construction.

The Le Corbusier Research Collection of the Frances Loeb Library in Harvard's Graduate School of Design was a precious resource; Caroline Shillaber and her successor as librarian, Angela Giral, and their able staff never failed to be helpful, as were their colleagues in the Fine Arts Library at the Fogg Art Museum. Others to whom a debt of gratitude is owed are the Harvard Planning Office, the university's Department of Buildings and Grounds, the Harvard News Office, the photographers who are acknowledged in the list of illustration credits, and the many individuals, publishers, and galleries who provided information and illustrations as mentioned in the references.

My wife, Patricia, contributed in innumerable ways through patient practical assistance and by her own solid Le Corbusier scholarship. Finally, those many students from the Graduate School of Design must be mentioned who through their searching questions and boundless enthusiasm convinced me that it was worthwhile to persevere in trying to achieve a better understanding of "Corbu."

Eduard F. Sekler

I owe a great deal to my family and to my friends all over the world for their moral support while writing. I wish to dedicate my part of this work to my American friends—particularly C. D., P. T., M. J. R., N. S., and J. F.

William Curtis

LIST OF ILLUSTRATIONS

Frontispiece, Le Corbusier writing in his notebook at Harvard University, June 1960. Photo, Arthur D. Trottenberg.

1. Aerial view of Harvard Yard, early spring 1972. Photo, Aerial Photos of New England, Inc.
2. Oblique view of Carpenter Center from Harvard Yard (Sever Quadrangle) in winter. Photo, Robert Frisbee.
3. View of the building from Quincy Street just outside the Yard. Photo, Robert Frisbee.
4. (a) Quincy Street facade. Photo, Todd Stuart.
4. (b) Quincy Street elevation.
5. Detail of northwest corner at fourth and fifth levels. Photo, Todd Stuart.
6. Detail of Quincy Street curved studio wall after a rainstorm. Photo, Todd Stuart.
7. Winter view along the south side past the stair tower toward the Prescott Street studio and workshop wing. Photo, Harvard News Office.
8. View up the ramp in summer on the Quincy Street side of the building. Photo, Harvard News Office.
9. Isometric section showing the way the ramp penetrates the building. Drawing, Edward Nilson.
10. View into the heart of the building along the ramp toward Prescott Street. Photo, Todd Stuart.

11. View of the ramp gallery toward Prescott Street. Photo, Robert Frisbee.
12. View of the ramp gallery back in the direction of the third level landing with doors to the exhibition gallery. Photo, Todd Stuart.
13. Ramp gallery at night. Photo, Harvard News Office.
14. Second level curved studio (northwest), viewed at night from the ramp. Photo, Todd Stuart.
15. View in the late afternoon from the ramp into the third level studio (southeast) and second level workshops. Photo, Todd Stuart.
16. View, with reflections from the third level studio, across the ramp gallery toward the exhibition room and Prescott Street. Photo, Robert Frisbee.
17. View back toward the Prescott Street facade from approximately halfway up the ramp. Photo, Harvard News Office.
18. East and north facades viewed from Prescott Street. Photo, Todd Stuart.
19. View from the north corner, along the Prescott Street facade. Photo, Robert Frisbee.
20. View along the north side toward Quincy Street. Photo, Todd Stuart.
21. (a) Prescott Street facade from a raised point on the opposite side of the street. Photo, Todd Stuart.
21. (b) Prescott Street elevation.
22. Detail of the Prescott Street curved wing showing brise-soleil. Photo, Todd Stuart.
23. View of the Prescott Street curved studio from southeast. Photo, Robert Frisbee.
24. Prescott Street facade at night. Photo, Robert Frisbee.
25. Quincy Street curved studio at night, showing illuminated glass bricks on the stair tower. Photo, Robert Frisbee.
26. Overall view of south side in winter. Photo, Todd Stuart.
27. Ground floor lobby. Photo, Robert Frisbee.
28. Underside of the ramp seen from the lobby. Photo, Jack Lueders-Booth.
29. Auditorium seen from under the overhang at the rear. Photo, Harvard News Office.
30. View down the stairway toward the glass brick wall. Photo, Todd Stuart.
31. View up, inside stair tower. Photo, Todd Stuart.
32. Second floor landing, with views into machine shop and ramp gallery. Photo, Robert Frisbee.
33. View toward the Yard through ondulatoires of the second level curved studio. Photo, Robert Frisbee.
34. Interior of third level curved studio shortly after completion. Photo, Harvard News Office.
35. Interior of third level curved studio during a class. Photo, Susan Butler.
36. Second level studio during a class. Photo, Susan Butler.
37. Walter Gropius, member of the Visiting Committee, in the second level studio. Photo, Todd Stuart.
38. One of the seminar rooms at level four, with a seminar of I. A. Richards' in progress. Photo, Harvard News Office.
39. View through brise-soleil in third level studio toward Prescott Street. Photo, Todd Stuart.
40. View of the ramp and Quincy Street from the fifth level roof terrace. Photo, Todd Stuart.
41. View from the fifth level studio and adjacent terrace toward the northwest. Photo, Harvard News Office.
42. Notes taken by Le Corbusier during his November 1959 trip to Cambridge at the time of his site visit (notebook P59, p. 7). Fondation Le Corbusier.
43. The first drawn idea of the visual arts center, Le Corbusier, April 1, 1960 (notebook P60, p. 26). Fondation Le Corbusier.
44. Tentative plan of the whole building and its surroundings, Le Corbusier, April 7, 1960. Fondation Le Corbusier.
45. Schematic plan and sections, Le Corbusier, April 7, 1960. Fondation Le Corbusier.
46. Section and sketch plan, Le Corbusier, April 7, 1960. Fondation Le Corbusier.
47. The Hudson Parkway, New York City, related to the "radiant city." Plate from Le Corbusier, *Manière de penser l'urbanisme*, 1947.
48. First exploration by Jullian of Le Corbusier's guiding ideas: ground level schematic plan and circulation study, April 10, 1960. Fondation Le Corbusier.
49. Second level schematic plan, Jullian, April 10, 1960. Fondation Le Corbusier.
50. Transversal section looking from Prescott Street, Jullian, April 10, 1960. Fondation Le Corbusier.
51. Combined elevation, transversal section, Jullian, April 10, 1960. Fondation Le Corbusier.
52. Longitudinal section, Jullian, April 10, 1960. Fondation Le Corbusier.
53. Schematic plan examining position of building on site, Le Corbusier, April 11, 1960. Fondation Le Corbusier.
54. Sketch plan, Le Corbusier, April 11, 1960. Fondation Le Corbusier.
55. Sketch plan examining alternative studio positions, Le Corbusier, April 11, 1960. Fondation Le Corbusier.
56. Sketch plan, Le Corbusier, April 11, 1960. Fondation Le Corbusier.
57. Le Corbusier's S-shaped cosmogram signifying the

rhythms of day and night from *When the Cathedrals Were White*.
58. Ruled longitudinal section along ramp, Jullian, April 12, 1960. Fondation Le Corbusier.
59. Ruled plan of ramp, site, and trees, Jullian, April 12, 1960. Fondation Le Corbusier.
60. Aerial view of the building, Le Corbusier, April 14, 1960. Fondation Le Corbusier.
61. Aerial view of the building, Le Corbusier and Andreini, April 14, 1960. Fondation Le Corbusier.
62. Plan of level 1 (ground floor), Le Corbusier, May 1, 1960. Fondation Le Corbusier.
63. Plan of level 2, Le Corbusier, May 1, 1960. Fondation Le Corbusier.
64. Plan of level 4, Le Corbusier, May 1, 1960. Fondation Le Corbusier.
65. Plan of level 5 (aerial view of the building) and small sketches of details, Le Corbusier, May 1, 1960. Fondation Le Corbusier.
66. Brise-soleil angle calculations, Jullian, May 1, 1960. Fondation Le Corbusier.
67. Ruled plan of level 2, Jullian, May 2, 1960. Fondation Le Corbusier.
68. Ruled plan of level 1, Jullian, May 3, 1960. Fondation Le Corbusier.
69. Longitudinal section along main ramp with attached detail of stair tower, Jullian, May 10, 1960. Fondation Le Corbusier.
70. Longitudinal section BB, Jullian, May 12, 1960. Fondation Le Corbusier.
71. "Ubu" sculpture, Le Corbusier, 1947, which displays affinities with the biological forms of the visual arts center. Fondation Le Corbusier and Mme Savina-Geffroy.
72. A pair of lungs from Le Corbusier's book *Urbanisme* (1925).
73. View of the atelier at 35, rue de Sèvres, early June 1960. Photo, Burri-Magnum.
74. Sketches of clouds from Le Corbusier's notebook P61, which he carried with him in the Boeing from Paris to Boston. Fondation Le Corbusier.
75. Le Corbusier and José Luis Sert in Harvard Yard, June 1960. Photo, John Nickols.
76. Le Corbusier's "American photograph," June 1960. Photo, John Nickols.
77. The visual arts center presentation model, Le Corbusier and Jullian, May–June 1960. Carpenter Center for the Visual Arts.
78. Presentation plan of the basement, Le Corbusier and Jullian, June 7, 1960. Harvard University.
79. Presentation plan of level 1, Le Corbusier and Jullian, June 7, 1960. Harvard University.
80. Presentation plan of level 2, Le Corbusier and Jullian, June 7, 1960. Harvard University.
81. Presentation plan of level 3, Le Corbusier and Jullian, June 7, 1960. Harvard University.
82. Presentation plan of level 4, Le Corbusier and Jullian, June 7, 1960. Harvard University.
83. Presentation plan of level 5, Le Corbusier and Jullian, June 7, 1960. Harvard University.
84. Presentation aerial view, Le Corbusier and Jullian, June 7, 1960. Harvard University.
85. Presentation longitudinal section AA, Le Corbusier and Jullian, June 7, 1960. Harvard University.
86. Presentation longitudinal section BB, Le Corbusier and Jullian, June 7, 1960. Harvard University.
87. Presentation transversal section CC, Le Corbusier and Jullian, June 7, 1960. Harvard University.
88. Sketch of visual arts center and its surroundings, Le Corbusier, notebook P61, June 12, 1960. Fondation Le Corbusier.
89. Jottings from Le Corbusier's second Cambridge trip, June 1960, notebook P61. Fondation Le Corbusier.
90. Sketches of pilotis, slabs, and beams, Le Corbusier, morning of June 13, 1960. Courtesy of John Nickols.
91. Sketches of ramp, Le Corbusier, morning of June 13, 1960. Courtesy of John Nickols.
92. Sketch of "jardin corniche" ("garden cornice"), Le Corbusier, morning of June 13, 1960. Courtesy of John Nickols.
93. Sketch of fenestration showing section through brise-soleil, ondulatoires, slab and beam, and details of ondulatoire struts, Le Corbusier, morning of June 13, 1960. Courtesy of John Nickols.
94. Cardboard model experimenting with combination of recessed brise-soleil and ondulatoires, Jullian, September 9, 1960. Fondation Le Corbusier.
95. Plan of new basement auditorium, Jullian, September 15, 1960. Fondation Le Corbusier.
96. Plan of level 1, Jullian, September 16, 1960. Fondation Le Corbusier.
97. Basement plan, Le Corbusier, September 16, 1960. Fondation Le Corbusier.
98. Plan of level 1, Le Corbusier, September 16, 1960. Fondation Le Corbusier.
99. Plan of level 3, with overlay of sectional cuts, Jullian, September 16, 1960. Fondation Le Corbusier.
100. Three sections PG, PF, PE, Jullian, September 17–20,

1960. Fondation Le Corbusier.
101. Structural sketches, Le Corbusier, September 21, 1960. Fondation Le Corbusier.
102. Structural study, Le Corbusier, September 21, 1960. Fondation Le Corbusier.
103. Longitudinal section, Jullian, September 21, 1960. Fondation Le Corbusier.
104. Plan of level 3, Jullian, September 22, 1960. Fondation Le Corbusier.
105. Plan of level 3, Jullian, September 26, 1960. Fondation Le Corbusier.
106. Basement plan, Jullian, September 28, 1960. Fondation Le Corbusier.
107. Longitudinal section, Jullian, September 28, 1960. Fondation Le Corbusier.
108. Longitudinal section, Jullian, October 3, 1960. Fondation Le Corbusier.
109. Plan of level 3, Jullian, October 3, 1960. Fondation Le Corbusier.
110. Three perspectives of Prescott Street facade, Jullian, October 3, 1960. Fondation Le Corbusier.
111. Plan (and aerial view) of level 5, Jullian, October 3, 1960. Fondation Le Corbusier.
112. Basement plan, Sert, Jackson and Gourley, October 3, 1960. Fondation Le Corbusier.
113. Plan of level 1, Sert, Jackson and Gourley, October 3, 1960. Fondation Le Corbusier.
114. Longitudinal section BB, Sert, Jackson and Gourley, October 3, 1960. Fondation Le Corbusier.
115. Plan of level 1, Jullian, October 21, 1960. Fondation Le Corbusier.
116. Plan of level 3, Le Corbusier, May 1, 1960. Fondation Le Corbusier.
117. Prescott Street elevation, Jullian, November 1960. Fondation Le Corbusier.
118. Quincy Street elevation, Jullian, November 10, 1960. Fondation Le Corbusier.
119. Prescott Street elevation, Jullian, November 1960. Fondation Le Corbusier.
120. Longitudinal section through interior ramp, Le Corbusier and Jullian, December 1, 1960. Fondation Le Corbusier.
121. Transversal section of skeleton and ramps, Jullian, December 1, 1960. Fondation Le Corbusier.
122. Plan, west end of level 3, Le Corbusier and Jullian, December 15, 1960. Fondation Le Corbusier.
123. Plan of level 3, Le Corbusier and Jullian, December 15, 1960. Fondation Le Corbusier.
124. Plan of level 1, Le Corbusier, December 15, 1960. Fondation Le Corbusier.
125. Plan of level 3, Le Corbusier, December 15, 1960. Fondation Le Corbusier.
126. Section detail of structural frame, Le Corbusier, December 18, 1960. Fondation Le Corbusier.
127. Perspective of interior structure, Le Corbusier, December 19, 1960. Fondation Le Corbusier.
128. Plan of level 3, south side, Le Corbusier, January 9, 1961. Fondation Le Corbusier.
129. Plan of level 1, Le Corbusier, January 10, 1961. Fondation Le Corbusier.
130. Plan of level 2, Le Corbusier, January 10, 1961. Fondation Le Corbusier.
131. Plan of level 3, Le Corbusier, January 10, 1961. Fondation Le Corbusier.
132. Plan of level 4, Le Corbusier, January 10, 1961. Fondation Le Corbusier.
133. Plan of level 1, Jullian, January 11, 1961. Fondation Le Corbusier.
134. Plan of level 2, with superimposed tracing of new level 3, Le Corbusier, January 11, 1961. Fondation Le Corbusier.
135. Plan of the new level 3, Jullian, January 11, 1961. Fondation Le Corbusier.
136. Plan of level 2, Jullian, January 11, 1960. Fondation Le Corbusier.
137. Plan (overlay) of level 3, north side, Le Corbusier, January 14, 1961. Fondation Le Corbusier.
138. Plan of level 1, Jullian, January 18, 1961. Fondation Le Corbusier.
139. Plan of level 2, Jullian, January 18, 1961. Fondation Le Corbusier.
140. Plan of level 3, Jullian, January 18, 1961. Fondation Le Corbusier.
141. Plan of level 3, Jullian, January 18, 1961. Fondation Le Corbusier.
142. Plan of level 4, Jullian, January 18, 1961. Fondation Le Corbusier.
143. Longitudinal section, Jullian, January 18, 1961. Fondation Le Corbusier.
144. Building outlines at level 3 of projects one and two, Jullian, January 18, 1961. Fondation Le Corbusier.
145. Cardboard cutouts of the first and second projects, Jullian, January 19, 1961. Fondation Le Corbusier.
146. Model of the second project, Le Corbusier and Jullian, January–February 1961. Location unknown. Photo, Carpenter Center archives.
147. Section showing arrangement of airfloor, Sert, Jackson

and Gourley, March 27, 1962. Courtesy of J. L. Sert.

148. Prescott Street elevation, Jullian, January 31, 1961. Fondation Le Corbusier.

149. Fire escape design, Prescott Street elevation, Le Corbusier and Jullian, February 3, 1961. Fondation Le Corbusier.

150. Plan of level 4, Jullian, February 1, 1961. Fondation Le Corbusier.

151. Overlay tracing, Quincy Street brise-soleil, Le Corbusier, February 1961. Fondation Le Corbusier.

152. Prescott Street elevation, Jullian, February 4, 1961. Fondation Le Corbusier.

153. Plan of level 3, south side, Jullian, February 5, 1961. Fondation Le Corbusier.

154. Plan of level 2, Jullian, February 7, 1961. Fondation Le Corbusier.

155. Presentation plan of level 1, second project, Le Corbusier and Jullian, February 25, 1961. Harvard University.

156. Presentation plan of level 3, second project, Le Corbusier and Jullian, February 25, 1961. Harvard University.

157. Presentation plan of level 4, second project, Le Corbusier and Jullian, February 25, 1961. Harvard University.

158. Presentation plan of level 5, second project, Le Corbusier and Jullian, February 25, 1961. Harvard University.

159. Quincy Street elevation, Jullian, February 2-3, 1961. Fondation Le Corbusier.

160. Presentation longitudinal section BB, second project, Le Corbusier and Jullian, February 25, 1961. Harvard University.

161. Prescott Street (east side) presentation elevation, second project, Le Corbusier and Jullian, April 7, 1961. Harvard University.

162. South side presentation elevation, second project, Le Corbusier and Jullian, April 7, 1961. Harvard University.

163. Quincy Street (west side) presentation elevation, second project, Le Corbusier and Jullian, April 7, 1961. Harvard University.

164. Plan level 3, Sert, Jackson and Gourley, spring 1961. Courtesy of J. L. Sert.

165. Design of floor rectangles, "Opus optimum au Modulor," Le Corbusier, 1961. Courtesy of J. L. Sert.

166. Detail of Prescott Street end of ramp (N5806), Le Corbusier, September 21, 1961. Courtesy of J. L. Sert.

167. Plan of level 3, Quincy Street roof terrace (N5760), Le Corbusier, July 18, 1961. Courtesy of J. L. Sert.

168. Section detail of level 3, Quincy Street roof garden (N5775b), Jullian and Le Corbusier, July 24, 1961. Courtesy of J. L. Sert.

169. Detail of roof drain, Le Corbusier, July 22-24, 1961. Courtesy of J. L. Sert.

170. Plan of level 5, roof garden (N5762), Le Corbusier, July 23, 1961. Courtesy of J. L. Sert.

171. Plan and section of typical aérateur (N5765), Le Corbusier and Jullian, July 22, 1961. Courtesy of J. L. Sert.

172. Plan details of typical glazing and aérateur joints between diagonal brise-soleil (N5778), Le Corbusier and Jullian, July 24, 1961. Courtesy of J. L. Sert.

173. Section detail of typical joint of glazing and slabs (N5765c), Le Corbusier and Jullian, July 22, 1961. Courtesy of J. L. Sert.

174. Section detail of typical joint of aérateur to horizontal brise-soleil, Le Corbusier and Jullian, July 22, 1961. Courtesy of J. L. Sert.

175. Plan, section and detail of ramp (N5763), Le Corbusier and Jullian, July 22, 1961. Courtesy of J. L. Sert.

176. Plan and elevation of internal stairway from level 1 to basement (N5766), Le Corbusier and Jullian, July 22-24, 1961. Courtesy of J. L. Sert.

177. Elevation and plan of fire stair, Prescott Street facade (N5764), Le Corbusier and Jullian, July 22-24, 1961. Courtesy of J. L. Sert.

178. Working drawing print of level 2, Sert, Jackson and Gourley, Le Corbusier, and Jullian, October 25, 1961. Harvard University.

179. Elevation of stair tower showing formwork design (N5797), Le Corbusier and Jullian, September 21, 1961. Courtesy of J. L. Sert.

180. Elevation detail of south side entrance (N5815), Le Corbusier and Jullian, October 31, 1961. Courtesy of J. L. Sert.

181. Elevation, detail, and plan showing calculation of ondulatoire proportions for the Quincy Street curve (N5790), Le Corbusier and Jullian, September 12, 1961. Courtesy of J. L. Sert.

182. Plan of typical diagonal brise-soleil fin with attached contreplaqué in wood (N6013), Le Corbusier and Jullian, July 19, 1962. Courtesy of J. L. Sert.

183. Trial casting of brise-soleil unit, November 1961, standing to one side of the site. Photo, courtesy of Richard S. Field.

184. Sketches of three formwork joints from Le Corbusier's letter to Sert of November 9, 1961. Courtesy of J. L. Sert.

185. Sketch from Le Corbusier's letter to Sert, November 9, 1961, specifying formwork and quality of finish for pilotis. Courtesy of J. L. Sert.

186. The cleared site and excavation viewed from Prescott Street, Winter 1961-1962. Photo, courtesy of Richard S. Field.

187. One of the three steel beams over the auditorium is lowered into place, March 1962. Photo, courtesy of Richard S. Field.
188. Forming the floor of level 3, Prescott Street side, May 1962. Photo, courtesy of Richard S. Field.
189. Prescott Street facade, level 3, showing brise-soleil diagonals sunk and recessed into the floor. Photo, courtesy of Richard S. Field.
190. Formwork for the Quincy Street curve hoisted into place, April 1962. Photo, courtesy of Richard S. Field.
191. Part of the curved formwork for the Prescott Street studio adjacent to the stair tower, May 1962. Photo, courtesy of Richard S. Field.
192. The site viewed from an upper window of the Fogg Museum April 1962. Photo, courtesy of Richard S. Field.
193. The site viewed from the Fogg Museum, May 1962. Photo, courtesy of Richard S. Field.
194. Detail of the northeast corner, June 1962. Photo, courtesy of Richard S. Field.
195. The Quincy Street facade, June 1962. Photo, Harvard News Office.
196. Prescott Street facade in July 1962. Photo, Harvard News Office.
197. Annotated working drawing of level 3, south studio, Sert, Jackson and Gourley, Le Corbusier, and Jullian. Courtesy of Paul Krueger.
198. Champagne on the ramp at the building's opening, May 27, 1963. Photo, Harvard News Office.
199. *Nature morte aux bouteilles et verres,* water color, 1922. Collection Denise René.
200. *Nature morte aux nombreux objets, Indépendants,* oil on canvas, 1923. Musée National d'Art Moderne, Paris; cliché des Musées Nationaux.
201. *Nature morte de l'Esprit Nouveau,* linecut, 1924. Fondation Le Corbusier.
202. *Nature morte,* oil on canvas, 1927. Galerie Beyeler, Bâle.
203. *Le dejeuner au phare,* oil on canvas, 1928. Fondation Le Corbusier.
204. *Sculpture et vue,* pencil and watercolor, 1929. Fondation Le Corbusier.
205. *Composition,* oil on canvas, 1926. Fondation Le Corbusier.
206. *Composition,* colored crayon on tracing paper, probably 1926–1927. Waddington Galleries.
207. *Composition spirale logarithmique,* oil on canvas, 1929. Le Corbusier-Galerie Heidi Weber, Zurich.
208. Reproduction of page 247 from *Creation Is a Patient Search.* Fondation Le Corbusier and Verlag Gerd Hatje.
209. Plan of design for an exhibition pavilion. Fondation Le Corbusier.
210. Villa at Carthage, Tunis, first project. Fondation Le Corbusier and Verlag fur Architektur Artemis.
211. Villa Savoye, first project, 1929. Fondation Le Corbusier and Verlag für Architektur Artemis.
212. Site plan and west facade, Millowners' Association Building. Fondation Le Corbusier and Verlag fur Architektur Artemis.
213. League of Nations Palace, project of 1927. Fondation Le Corbusier and Verlag für Architektur Artemis.
214. Palace of the Centrosoyus, third project, 1928–1929. Fondation Le Corbusier and Verlag für Architektur Artemis.
215. *Nature morte aux nombreux objets,* oil on canvas, 1923–1953. Collection Nehmad, Milan.
216. *Taureau,* line drawing from the *Poème de l'angle droit,* pl. 149. Fondation Le Corbusier.
217. Reproduction of page 232 from *Creation Is a Patient Search.* Fondation Le Corbusier and Verlag Gerd Hatje.
218. *Le taureau,* engraving, 1965. Le Corbusier-Galerie Heidi Weber, Zurich.
219. Chandigarh Assembly Building, entrance hall. Fondation Le Corbusier and Verlag für Architektur Artemis.
220. Chandigarh, boat club. Fondation Le Corbusier and Verlag für Architektur Artemis.
221. Reproduction of page 45 from *Oeuvre complète, Last Works.* Fondation Le Corbusier and Verlag für Architektur Artemis.

PLANS, SECTIONS, AND ELEVATIONS

1. Basement plan.
2. Plan level 1 (ground floor).
3. Plan level 2.
4. Plan level 3 (ramp access).
5. Plan level 4.
6. Plan level 5.
7. Aerial view.
8. Transversal section.
9. Longitudinal section.
10. West elevation, Quincy Street.
11. East elevation, Prescott Street.
12. North elevation, Fogg Museum side.
13. South elevation, Faculty Club side.

INDEX

Acoustics, 50–51, 59, 187–188, 211, 225
Administrative offices, 26, 75, 78, 97, 110, 145, 305
Aérateurs:
    of finished building, 18, 20, 24, 33
    vs. ventilating machines, 32, 66, 136, 297, 298
    in presentation plans, 95, 98, 102, 104, 165, 167
    aluminum for, 98, 102, 168, 178, 191, 301
    Jullian on, 110, 152, 178–182, 191, 196
    screens for, 195–197, 299
    wood for, 198, 209
    construction of, 205, 209–210, 301
    colors for, 214
Aerial view, 9–11, 143
Ahmedabad, 143, 229, 242, 244, 254, 255, 256
Air-conditioning, 25, 27, 32, 66, 184, 292
    machinery for, 135–136, 173, 214
    vs. aérateurs, 168–169
Aircraft, 52, 85–86, 102
Airfloor, 135, 146, 184, 188, 205
Albers, Josef, 4
Algiers, 248
Aluminum, 222
    for aérateurs, 98, 102, 168, 178, 191, 301
    for brise-soleil, 102, 111, 164
Ambiguity, 20, 80, 232, 235, 250, 253, 258
American Institute of Architects (AIA), 46, 172
Andreini, R., 73, 77, 78, 102, 167, 208
Archigram group, 230

Architectural Review, 2
Artists' studios, 28, 35, 66, 72, 73, 75, 95
    garden by, 72, 95, 178
Arts and Crafts Movement, 2
Atkinson, Fello, 257
Atomic tendency, 168
Auditorium, 41, 110, 111, 112, 117, 263
    in finished building, 26, 27–28
    on first floor, 75, 95
    span of, 113, 114, 204
    Sert's plan for, 122, 124
    acoustics for, 188

Barr, Alfred, 52, 253, 281
Basaldella, Mirko, 5, 52
Basement, 41, 110, 111, 113–114, 117, 122, 204
    in finished building, 25, 26–28, 270, 271
    ventilation in, 25, 27, 32, 184, 214
    Sert's plan of, 122–124
    costs of, 124–125
Bâtis, 209–210, 301
Bauhaus, 4
Beams, 102, 114, 126, 129, 134, 136, 210
    in basement, 77, 117, 204–205
    deletion of, 145, 163
Bernard, Claude, 264
Bernhardt, 188
Béton brut, 166–167, 185, 189, 206, 214, 251
Bloom, Hyman, 4
Boesiger, W., 216, 303
Brazilian Pavilion, 229, 250, 255
Brewery floor, 202
Brick, 110, 188–189, 256. *See also* Glass, bricks of
Brise-soleil, 78, 104, 136, 147, 149–153, 163, 165, 248, 255,
    of finished building, 12, 19–24, 32, 33, 258
    concrete, 21, 111, 168, 208, 300
    on Quincy Street side, 24, 143–144, 192–194, 210
    and ondulatoires, 66, 77, 95, 98, 110–111, 125–126, 167
    aluminum, 102, 111, 164; aérateurs between, 182
    wood for, 186–187, 211, 300
    for curves, 191
Brown, John Nicholas, 5, 40
Brown Report, 5, 40, 41, 42
Budget, *see* Finances
Buenos Aires, viii
Building Program, 4, 5, 39–41, 48, 53, 59, 61, 96, 97, 110, 221,
    262, 264, 283
Bulfinch, Charles, 11, 40, 53
Bundy, McGeorge, viii, 42, 106, 125, 286

Cambridge Cement Stone Company, 209, 210, 304
Cambridge University, 49–50
Capitals, 145–146, 165, 206
Carpenter, Harlow, 40, 42, 89, 286

Carpenter, St. Vrain, 40, 42, 43, 66, 89, 215, 279, 286, 291, 304
Carthage, villa at, 243
Ceilings: heights of, 72, 134–135, 146, 164
    paint for, 185
Centrosoyus, Palace of the, 246, 248
Chandigarh, viii, 2, 45, 125–126, 217, 229, 248, 255, 293, 298,
    301–303
    site of, 47
    art school in, 85, 253
    aérateurs at, 104, 152, 178, 196
    ondulatoires at, 104, 191, 197–198
    brise-soleil at, 143, 152
    capitals at, 146
    fourth wall from, 242
    museum at, 244, 254
    Open Hand for, 250
    assembly building at, 250, 253
    boat club at, 253
CIAM, 47, 48, 87, 230
Circles, 72, 262
Circulation, 50–51, 59, 73, 95, 99, 264; and ramps, 22, 59, 63,
    66, 72, 73, 177
    and Harvard Yard, 50, 61, 66, 73
Citrohan, 246
Climate, 14–15, 75, 103, 136, 257, 268, 269
Colors: for finished building, 24, 27, 28, 32, 185–186, 188,
    211–213, 214
    in 1960 plans, 59–61, 75–76, 78, 89, 129
    in 1961 plans, 144, 149, 152, 155, 158
    in Le Corbusier paintings, 231, 235
Columns, *see* Pilotis
Committee on Practice of Visual Arts, 5, 6, 40, 41, 48, 96, 122,
    160, 216, 279
Composition, 238–239, 248
Composition spirale logarithmique, 239, 240, 243
Concrete, 102, 152, 164–165, 222–223, 255–257
    and light, 14–15, 18
    for brise-soleil, 21, 111, 168, 208, 298, 300
    with glass, 21–22, 25–26, 129, 203
    finishes for, 102, 104, 166–167, 189, 194–195, 206–207,
        210, 211, 256, 298, 300, 302
    of ramp, 104, 210
    of walls, 165–167, 298
    for ondulatoires, 167–168, 198
    for ground approaches, 188–189
    for pilotis, 194–195, 294–298, 300
    construction of, 206–207
    for bâtis, 209–210, 301
Congrès Internationaux de l'Architecture Moderne, *see* CIAM
Congress Palace, Strasbourg, 243
Contractors, 175, 177, 202–211, 304
Coolidge, John, 53, 96
Costa, Lucio, 255
Costs, *see* Finances
Cubes, 71, 81, 143, 224, 262
Cubism, 80, 82, 103, 159, 231, 236, 268

cummings, e e, 4
Curtains, 26, 98, 104, 152, 185, 188, 211–213
Curves, 224, 244–246, 248, 250
    of finished building, 12, 14, 22
    in plans, 73, 76, 80, 98, 140–142, 143, 191
    construction of, 206, 208
    of Villa Savoye, 232–233
    of Swiss Pavilion, 248

De Chirico, Giorgio, 129
Deux têtes, 251
Dewey, John, 4
Diagonals, 12, 61, 149, 151, 152, 262
Director's studio, 75, 78, 125, 140, 142, 143
Disegno, 190
Dom-Ino system, 168, 223, 242
Doors, double, 131, 172. *See also* Aérateurs
Doric system, 164

Einstein, Albert, 262
Elevator tower, 22, 63, 66, 72, 140–142, 143
Elevators, passenger, 95, 131–132, 144–145, 147, 172. *See also* Freight lift
Eliot, T. S., 4
Emerson Hall, 12, 61
Entrances, 25–26, 95, 97, 131, 204. *See also* Lobby
Erlenbach Art Center, 244
Exhibition space: level of, 41, 63, 110, 144
    and ramp, 95, 270
    overabundance of, 172
    students' views of, 269
Expenses, *see* Finances

Faculty Club, 11, 22, 50, 61, 63, 67, 68, 139
    ramp view of, 18
    and building size, 41, 42, 110, 125, 172
    and building curves, 73
    exit to, 111–112
    director's studio by, 142
    and landscaping, 214
Farlow House, 41, 42, 50, 57
Fees for Le Corbusier, 46–47, 48–49
Fiedler, Konrad, 4
Filipowski, Richard, 5
Film, 52, 169, 184. *See also* Light and Communication division
Finances, 40–41, 46–49, 124–125, 172, 173, 175, 214–215, 280, 287, 305
Fins, *see* Brise-soleil
Fire escape stairs, 125, 172, 184, 204, 258
    and freight lift, 22, 125, 147, 149
    and Kembs-Niffer sluice, 253
    and Millowners' Building, 255
Firminy, 2, 253

Floor finish, 102–103, 185, 204, 205, 213
Fogg Art Museum, 4, 20, 21, 61, 63, 110
    as wall, 11, 12, 67, 189, 214
    art history department in, 40
    garden of, 50, 87, 172; director of, 53
    tunnel to, 68, 95, 173
    library extension for, 177, 202
    as public building, 270
Fondation Le Corbusier, 2, 275–277
Formalism, 1, 230
Form, 1, 71–72, 222–224, 230–235, 242, 262, 264. *See also* Cubes; Curves; Rectangles; Spirals
Free-form volumes, 242–244
Freight lift, 78, 95, 110, 131, 143, 144, 147, 149
    and ramps, 112–113, 114–120, 124, 125, 132, 134, 142
French Embassy, Brasilia, 244, 253
Fuller (George A.) Company, 177, 202, 203, 304
Furniture, 214

Gallery, ramp, 31, 114, 117, 165
Garches, Villa Stein at, 232, 246, 248
Gardens, *see* Roof gardens
Gardner, Robert, 5, 122
Giedion, Sigfried, 43, 47, 87, 111, 290
Gilly, Friedrich, 219
Glass, 31, 75, 143, 151–152, 168
    viewed from ramp, 16–18, 19–20
    with concrete, 21–22, 25–26, 129, 203, 294, 297–298
    in brise-soleil, 22–24, 182
    bricks of, 24, 173, 204, 210
    for entrances, 25–26, 204
    and greenery, 66
    and aluminum, 164 *See also* Ondulatoires Pans-de-verre
    glasses and bottles, 231–239
Gourley, Ron, 89, 106, 202
Graphics studio, 33
Greenery, 49, 59, 61, 71, 81–82, 104–106, 214. *See also* Roof gardens
Gropius, Walter, 4–5, 40, 43, 207
Guggenheim Museum, 230

Halen Estate, 229
Hand, 89, 94, 250
Harvard Crimson, 173
Harvard University Archives, 4
Harvard Yard, 9, 87, 98, 112, 152, 262
    Sever Quadrangle in, 11–12
    and radiant city, 49, 58
    and circulation, 50, 61, 66, 73
Head, 89, 94
Hervé, Lucien, 194
Hervol, Emil, 202, 205–206, 207
Hoffmann, Josef, 52
Hofmann, Werner, 258

Holyoke Center, 102, 167
Hood, Raymond, 102
Hudnut, Joseph, 4
Hudson Parkway, 61
Hunt, Richard Morris, 40
Hunt Hall, 4, 271, 281, 305

Icarus, viii
"Icon and Idea," 5
Ideas and form, 222–224, 225, 241, 258
Isorel, 194
Itten, Johannes, 4

Jackson, Huson, 87, 106, 147
    and elevator, 125
    and ventilation, 135–136, 146
    on Le Corbusier, 177
    and roof gardens, 202
Jarry, Alfred, 80
Johnson, Philip, 4, 230
Jullian de la Fuente, 48, 77–78, 109, 129, 147–149, 155, 157, 177, 222, 295, 296, 301
    and spiral poem, 50, 64
    and ramps, 66, 67, 68, 129, 142, 145
    and basement, 66, 111–114, 117–122, 124, 125, 129
    and roof gardens, 66, 178, 202
    and circle, 72
    and curves, 73, 80, 98
    and brise-soleil, 75, 110–111, 126, 149–152
    models by, 78, 86, 111, 126, 147
    and ondulatoires, 110–111, 126, 191
    and aérateurs, 110, 152, 178–182, 191, 196
    and piers, 113–117
    and Quincy Street studio, 164
    and columns, 164
    and concrete walls, 165
    and stairways, 184
    and floors, 205
    and wood paneling, 213
    and Kembs-Niffer sluice, 253

Kahn, Louis, 230
Kembs-Niffer sluice, 2, 242, 250, 253–254, 256
Klee, Paul, 4
Krueger, Paul, 102, 176, 188, 214, 304
    and Le Corbusier sketches, 201
    and roof gardens, 202
    and Modulor, 207–208
    and wood paneling, 211–213
    and finances, 215

La Chaux-de-Fonds, 2, 4, 89, 245
La femme à la fontaine, 236
Landscaping, 214

La Tourette, 45, 229, 242, 255, 256, 294
La ville radieuse, 49. See also Radiant city
Leach, Kenneth, 203
League of Nations Palace, 246, 248
Le balustre, 236
Le déjeuner au Phare, 235, 237, 248
Le dé violet, 235
Léger, Fernand, 47, 236, 239, 241
Le Messurier, William, 176, 202, 204, 205, 304
L'Eplattenier, Charles, 58, 85, 94
L'Esprit Nouveau, 234, 236, 238, 250, 251
Les dés sont jetés, 251
Le taureau, 251–253
Levine, Jack, 4
Liège exhibition pavilion, 242, 243
Light, 159–160, 164, 258
    natural, 14–15, 20, 257
    artificial, 24, 32, 184, 257
Light and Communication division, 26–27, 41, 95, 110, 122, 184, 271
Lobby, 27–28, 110, 112, 117, 124, 185, 268–269
Loos, Adolf, 52
Lungs, 81

Machine rooms, 135–136, 173, 214
Maeght, Adrien, 47, 48
Maison de Refuge, 169
Maison La Roche, 72, 246
Manière de penser l'urbanisme, 61
McKim, Charles F., 40, 52
Mead, Larkin G., 40, 52
Memorial Church, 11
Metabolists, 230
Millowners' Building, 143, 210, 229, 242, 244, 255
Miro, Joan, 47
Modern Movement, 20, 43, 207, 229–230
Modulor, 87–89, 110, 158, 163, 176, 214, 223, 298
    and spiral, 51–52
    and cube, 71
    and concrete, 104, 189, 208
    men in plans, 129, 149, 158, 253
    and room height, 134, 146
    and building size, 174
    for roof garden, 178, 202
    and S-ramp, 182–183
    for lobby floor, 185
    in stair tower, 190
    for ondulatoires, 191, 192
    and walls, 208
    for wood panels, 211
    and music, 225
    and brise-soleil, 208
Moholy-Nagy, Laszlo, 4
Mongan, Agnes, 50
Moore, Charles Herbert, 4

Moore, Henry, 50
Musée d'Art Moderne, 248
Museum of Unlimited Growth, 51, 243, 254
Museum of World Culture, 51

Nature morte with two coffeepots, 235
Nature morte au grand livre, 251
Nature morte aux bouteilles et verres, 232
Nature morte aux nombreux objets, 248–249
Nature morte aux nombreux objets, Indépendants, 233, 238, 248–249
Nature morte de l'Esprit Nouveau, 234, 238, 251
Nervi, Pier Luigi, 211, 298
New World of Space, 248
Nickols, John, 87, 89, 101–102, 104, 106
Nivola, Costantino, 5, 184, 217, 298
Norton, Charles Eliot, 4
Norton (Charles Eliot) lectures, 5

Objets à réaction poétique, 235–236
Obus, 248
Oeuvre complète, 2, 222, 224
    photographs for, 194, 216
    and construction plans, 202
    and concrete finish, 210
    and furniture, 214
    Carpenter Center drawings in, 256
Olivetti factory, 242, 244
Ondulatoires, 59, 61, 78, 293, 294, 301
    of finished building, 12, 19, 21, 33
    on Quincy Street side, 19, 21, 165, 191–192
    and brise-soleil, 66, 77, 95, 98, 110–111, 125–126, 167
    and beams, 77, 126
    at Chandigarh, 104, 191, 197–198
    in ramp gallery, 165
    and fire escapes, 184
    material for, 198
    construction of, 205, 209–210
Opening, of Carpenter Center, 215–217, 256
Ozenfant, Amédée, 159, 236, 238, 246

Painting studio, *see* Quincy Street studio
Paintings, of Le Corbusier, 159, 190, 224, 225, 230–251 *passim*, 258
Palace of the Centrosoyus, 246, 248
Paneling, 32, 186–187, 211–213
Pans-de-verre, 59, 152, 167, 182, 191, 294, 297, 301
    in finished building, 21, 33
    insertion of, 210. *See also* Glass
Park Hill Sheffield, 229
Parkways, 61, 224
Parthenon, 51
Pater, Walter, 258
Pavillon de L'Esprit Nouveau, 236
Peabody Museum, 5
Peinture moderne, 251
Perret, Auguste, 85, 195, 222

Pessac, 246
Petit, Claudius, vii, 166
Phillips Pavilion, 51, 188
Photographs, 2, 215–216, 231, 248
Photography, 53. *See also* Light and Communication division
Picasso, Pablo, 235, 236
Piers, 111, 113, 147
    bastard, 22, 164
    above basement, 111–112, 113–114
    on third floor, 117, 145. *See also* Slabs
Pilotis, 58–59, 72, 95, 98, 129, 147, 153, 155, 294, 295, 300
    of finished building, 12, 18–19, 20, 22, 24, 25, 26, 31, 32, 33, 257
    in basement, 26, 111, 112, 114
    in studios, 32, 33
    in first floor, 63
    jointing of, 77, 210
    in models, 78
    and porticoes, 113
    on Faculty Club facade, 132, 139–140
    and beams, 145, 165
    and capitals, 146, 165, 206
    on Quincy Street side, 164, 202, 257
    unpainted, 185
    casting of, 194–195, 205, 208
    and water table, 204
    and Le Corbusier paintings, 232
Plainex house, 253
Poème de l'angle droit, 241, 248, 250–251
"Poème Electronique," 85, 188
Pope, Arthur, 4
Porticoes, 112, 113, 114
Prescott Street studio (sculpture), 41, 63, 67, 75, 95, 142, 143
    brise-soleil on, 19, 22, 149, 164
    curves on, 31, 143
President's House, 61
Private zones, 20, 28, 33, 269, 270
Program for Harvard College, 40
Public zones, 20, 28, 63, 269–270
Purism, 231, 232, 235, 236, 238, 246, 248, 251
    and Cubism, 159, 231
    and Villa Savoye, 235
    Ozenfant and, 236, 238
    and Villa Stein, 248
    and Carpenter Center drawings, 256
Pusey, Nathan M., viii, 102, 111, 125, 146, 291, 304
    and art studies, 5, 40, 94
    and building site, 42, 50
    at presentations, 89, 97
    and entrance, 97, 172
    and opening, 216–217, 256–257

Quand les cathédrals étaient blanches, 49, 68, 71
Quincy Street studio (painting), 41, 63, 73–75, 95, 142–143, 149

Quincy Street studio (painting) (Continued)
    curves on, 12–14, 19, 98, 208
    ondulatoires on, 19, 165, 167
    and stair tower, 24
    and lighting, 32, 184
    roof garden over, 33, 142, 178, 202
    and freight lift, 78, 145
    and interior ramp, 142
    trench beneath, 144, 163–164, 257
    aérateurs with, 167

Radiant city, viii, 49, 58. *See also* Urbanism
Ramp, 66, 72, 73, 95, 111–112, 143, 242, 255, 263, 269, 270
    and freight lift, 112–113, 114–120, 124, 125, 132, 134, 142
    and floor-to-ceiling hights, 146
    deletion of, 172. *See also* S-ramp
Read, Herbert, 5
Rectangles, 68, 71–72, 76, 98, 143, 262
Reynolds, Edward, 49, 73, 287
Richardson, Henry Hobson, 11, 40
Rio de Janeiro, 102
Robinson Hall, 40, 52
Rodin, Auguste, 230
Roehampton, 229
Ronchamp, 47, 51, 58, 229, 248, 256
Roof gardens, 33–35, 98, 104–105, 144, 202–203, 257, 269
    over Quincy Street studio, 33, 142, 178, 202
    and interior ramps, 66
    by artists' studios, 72, 95, 178
    by Prescott Street studio, 75, 113, 142
    and finances, 175
Ross, Denman, 4
Rudolph, Paul, 230
Ruskin, John, 4
Ruskinianism, 2, 4

Saarinen, Eero, 230
St. Dié, 52
San Francisco exhibition pavilion, 242
Sasaki Associates, 214
Savina, J., 185, 239
Scully, Vincent, 257
Sculpture: of Le Corbusier 80, 185, 225, 239
    of Nivola, 184–185
Sculpture et vue, 235
Sculpture studio, *see* Prescott Street studio
Seagram Building, 230
Seminar room, 122, 124
Sert, José Luis, 109, 111, 113, 126, 133–135, 158, 177, 218
    and art studies, 5
    and Le Corbusier choice, 42, 43, 45
    and finances, 46–48, 172, 173, 215
    with Le Corbusier, 49–50, 52, 87, 89, 101, 104, 106
    and site plan, 57
    and "biological" plans, 61
    and correspondence, 275–304 *passim*
    and presentation plans, 86, 89, 98
    staff of, 101, 102, 106, 135, 171, 176, 201–202
    and Holyoke Center, 102, 167
    and building size, 110, 125, 172, 173, 174, 175
    and basement, 122–124
    and elevators, 131
    Paris trip of, 139, 142, 144, 146
    and ventilation, 146, 184
    and concrete, 166–167, 206, 207–208, 210, 211, 213
    and Fogg library extension, 177
    and construction schedule, 185
    and acoustics, 188
    and brise-soleil, 193
    and aérateurs, 195, 197, 198
    and roof gardens, 202
    and furniture, 214
    and opening, 215–216
Sever Hall, 11, 270, 271, 272
Sever Quadrangle, 11–12
Shahn, Ben, 5
"Shape of Content, The," 5
Site, 41, 42–43, 47, 58, 257, 280, 281, 286
Size: building, viii, 41–43, 110, 125, 171–175, 206, 257
    site, 41, 42, 47
Skylights, 32, 204
Slabs, 33, 98, 155, 164
    and jointing, 77, 129
    and beams, 78, 102, 145, 163, 165
    and brise-soleil, 104, 110, 111, 129
    and porticoes, 113
    and ventilation, 135
    and capitals, 146, 165, 206
    smooth, 155, 165, 195, 205–206
    finishes for, 213, 214. *See also* Piers
Sonotube, 195, 205
Sound, 50–51, 59, 187–188, 211, 225
Spiral, 50, 51–52, 59, 243–244
Squares, 71
S-ramp, 15–16, 61, 67–68, 94–96, 122, 142–143, 163, 222, 224
    and studio curves, 12–14
    view from, 18–22, 31, 169, 185, 264
    and circulation, 22, 59, 63, 72, 73, 177, 270
    on Prescott Street side, 22, 177
    and urbanism, 81
    and winter, 97, 102
    concrete for, 104, 210, 255
    dimensions of, 110, 182–183
    limited access to, 145, 270
    and floor-to-ceiling heights, 146
    and spirals, 59, 242–243
S-shape, 71, 263
Staircases, 95, 131, 173, 185, 184, 255, 270. *See also* Fire escape
Stair tower, 28–31, 263, 264
    and Quincy Street studio, 24

enlargement of, 131
  glass brick for, 173, 204
  Modulor in, 190
  machinery in, 214
  centrality of, 263
Stone, 167
Storage areas, 73–75, 122
Studios, 28, 31–33, 66, 186–187, 244, 270–271. *See also* Artists' studios; Director's studio; Prescott Street studio; Quincy Street studio
Suleymaniye Mosque, 63, 103
Sur les quatres routes, 71
Surrealism, 236
Sweeney, James Johnson, 52, 290
Swiss Pavilion, 248, 255

Table bouteille et livre, 235
Talks with Students, 98
Tange, Kenzo, 230
Taureau series, 239, 250
Taves, A., 253
Team 10, 230
Technology, building, 101–102, 110, 175, 256
Television facilities, 110, 122. *See also* Light and Communication division
Terrazzo, 102, 185, 204, 213
Thayer Hall, 50
Tokyo Museum, 102, 229, 254, 286
Transparency, 33, 126, 164, 189, 232, 235
Trottenberg, Arthur D., 52, 89, 96, 106, 122, 172, 297
Tucker, Leonard, 207–208, 210, 211
Tucker Concrete Form Company, 207, 304
Tunnel, to Fogg, 68, 95, 173
Turner, Paul, 222
Tyrwhitt, Jacqueline, 87

Ubu, 80, 185, 239, 250
United Nations building, viii, 45, 51, 98, 169, 218
United States Embassy, Athens, 230
Unités, 45, 80–81, 166, 238, 302

University Hall, viii, 11, 49, 53
University of Pennsylvania Medical Research Building, 230
Urbanism, 61, 68, 71, 80–82, 217–218, 224, 232, 248, 257

Van Brunt, Henry, 40
Vappi and Company, 125
Vaucresson, villa at, 246
Vaults, 102
Venice hospital, 253
Ventilation, 32, 110, 135–136, 172, 214. *See also* Aérateurs; Air-conditioning; Airfloor
Versailles, 105
Vers une architecture, 82, 160, 189, 224, 225
  grain silos in, 47
  cubes in, 71
  and Greek forms, 164, 169
  and automobile building, 196
Villa Savoye, 66, 184, 232–235, 244, 246
Villa Stein, Garches, 232, 242, 246, 248
Viollet-Le-Duc, E. E., 222

Walls, 33, 185–187, 205
Ware, William R., 40
Westchester Parkway, 61
"What Is the Problem of America?", 81
When the Cathedrals Were White, 49, 68, 71
White, Stanford, 40
Whiting, Norman, 203
Windows, *see* Glass; Pans-de-verre
Wölfflin, Heinrich, 262
Wood, 167, 186, 198, 209, 211–213

Xenakis, Yannis, 51, 191

Yanagi, Sori, 52

Zalewski, Joseph, 52, 87, 106, 173, 297, 298

341

PLANS, SECTIONS, AND ELEVATIONS

1. Basement plan.
2. Plan level 1 (ground floor).
3. Plan level 2.
4. Plan level 3 (ramp access).
5. Plan level 4.
6. Plan level 5.
7. Aerial view.
8. Transversal section.
9. Longitudinal section.
10. West elevation, Quincy Street.
11. East elevation, Prescott Street.
12. North elevation, Fogg Museum side.
13. South elevation, Faculty Club side.

1. *Basement plan.*

2. *Plan level 1 (ground floor).*

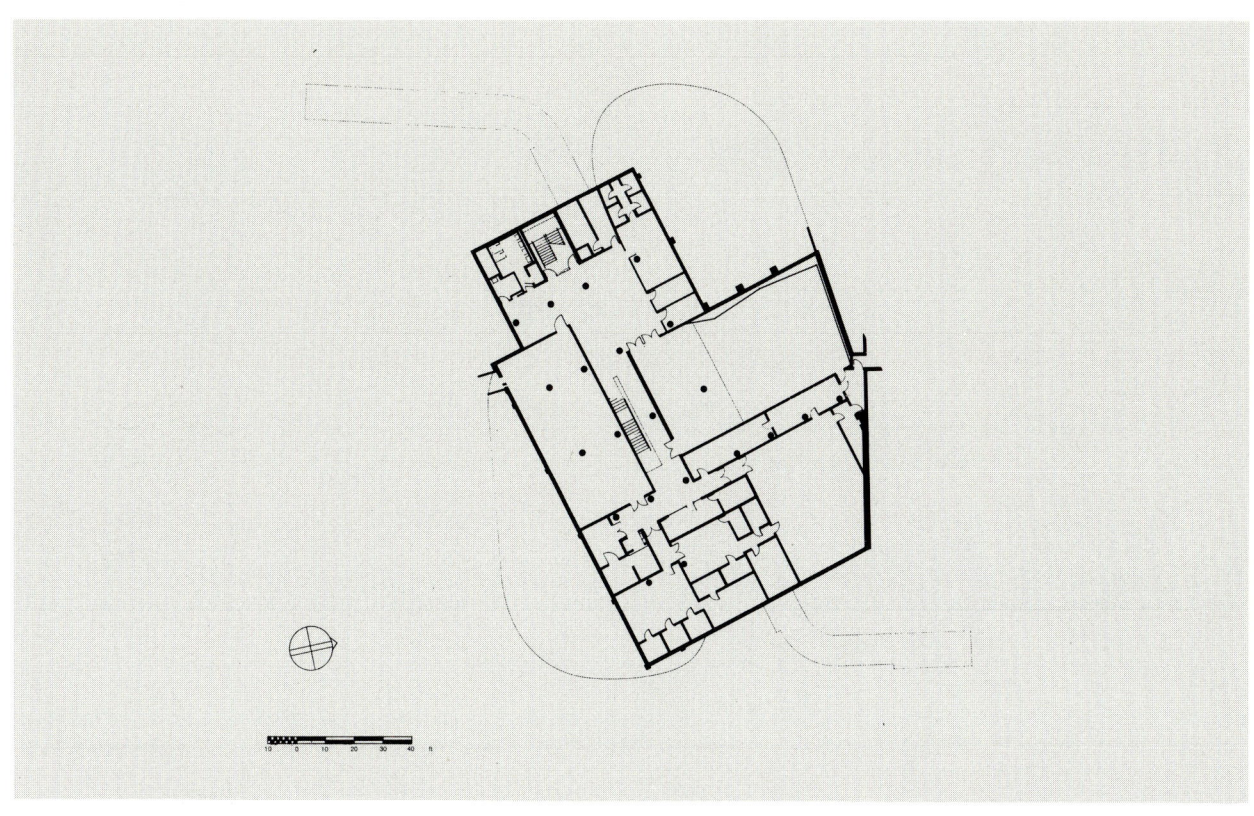

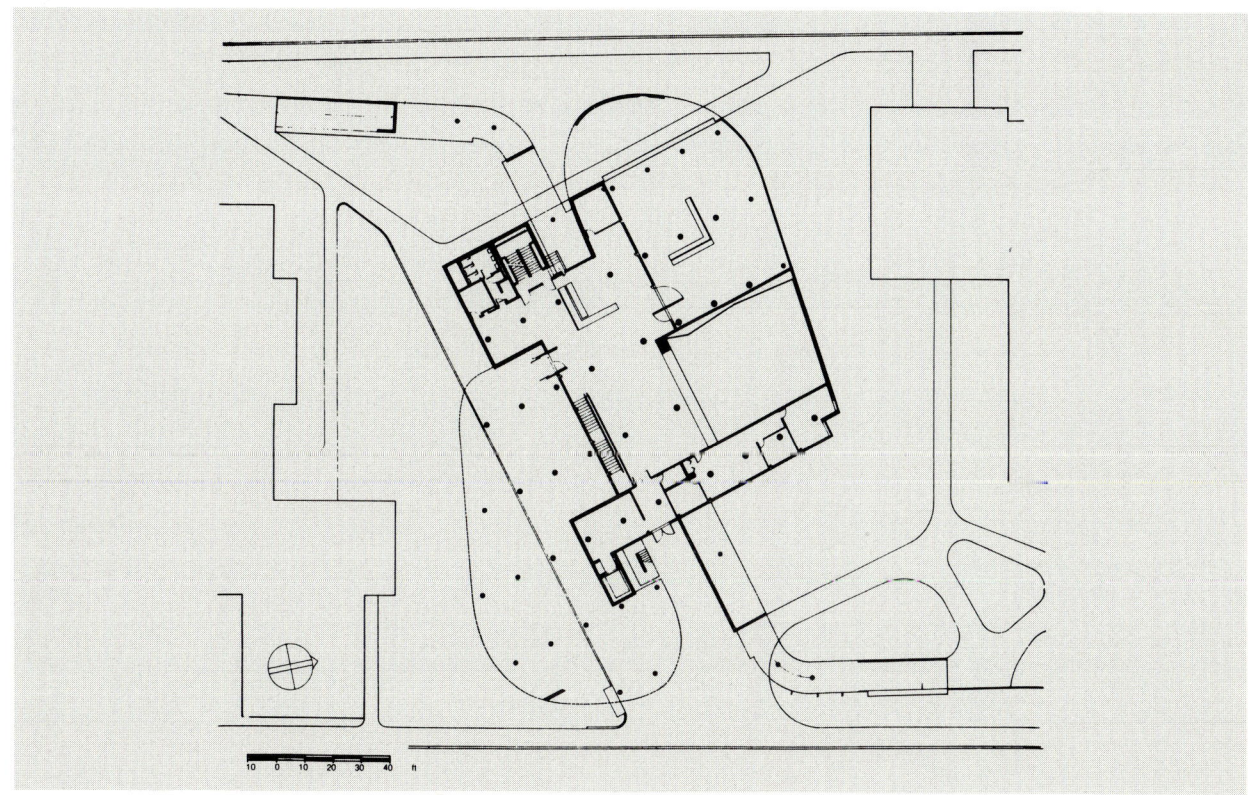

3. *Plan level 2.*

4. *Plan level 3 (ramp access).*

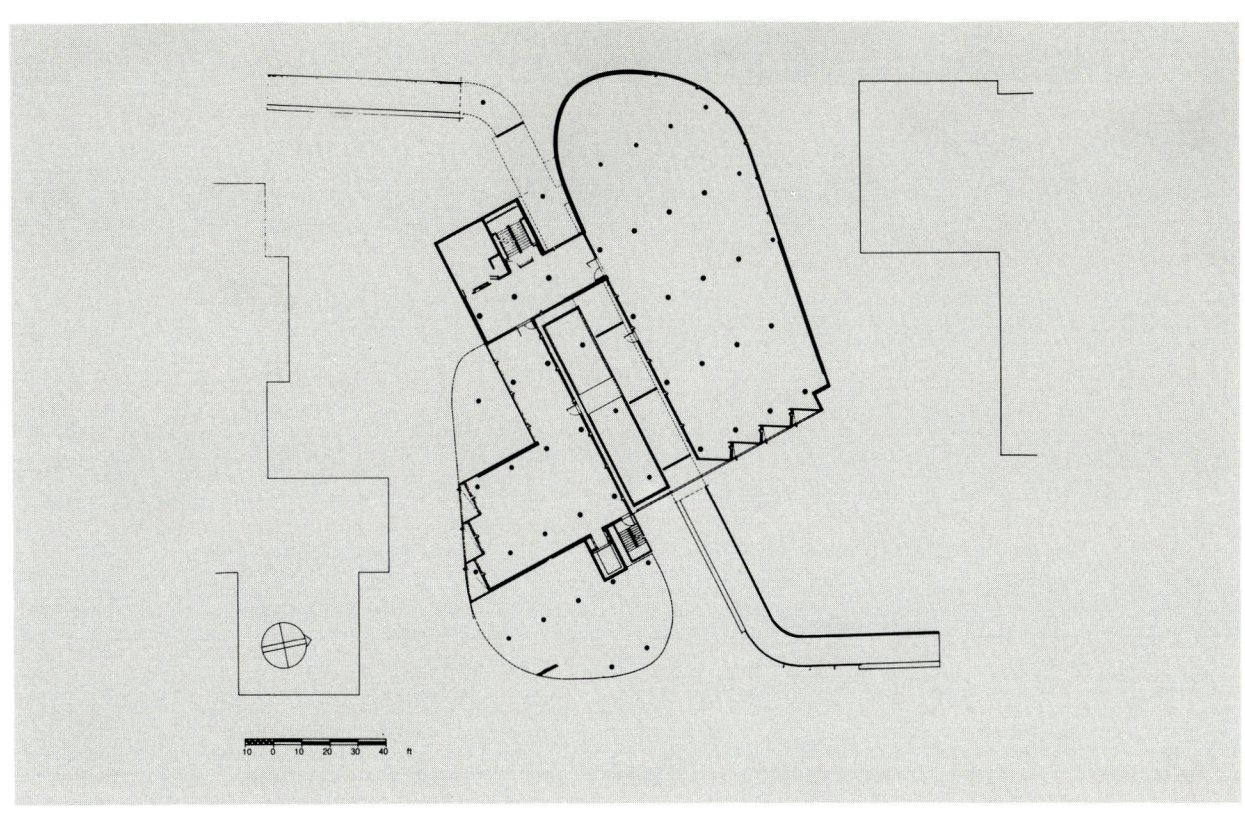
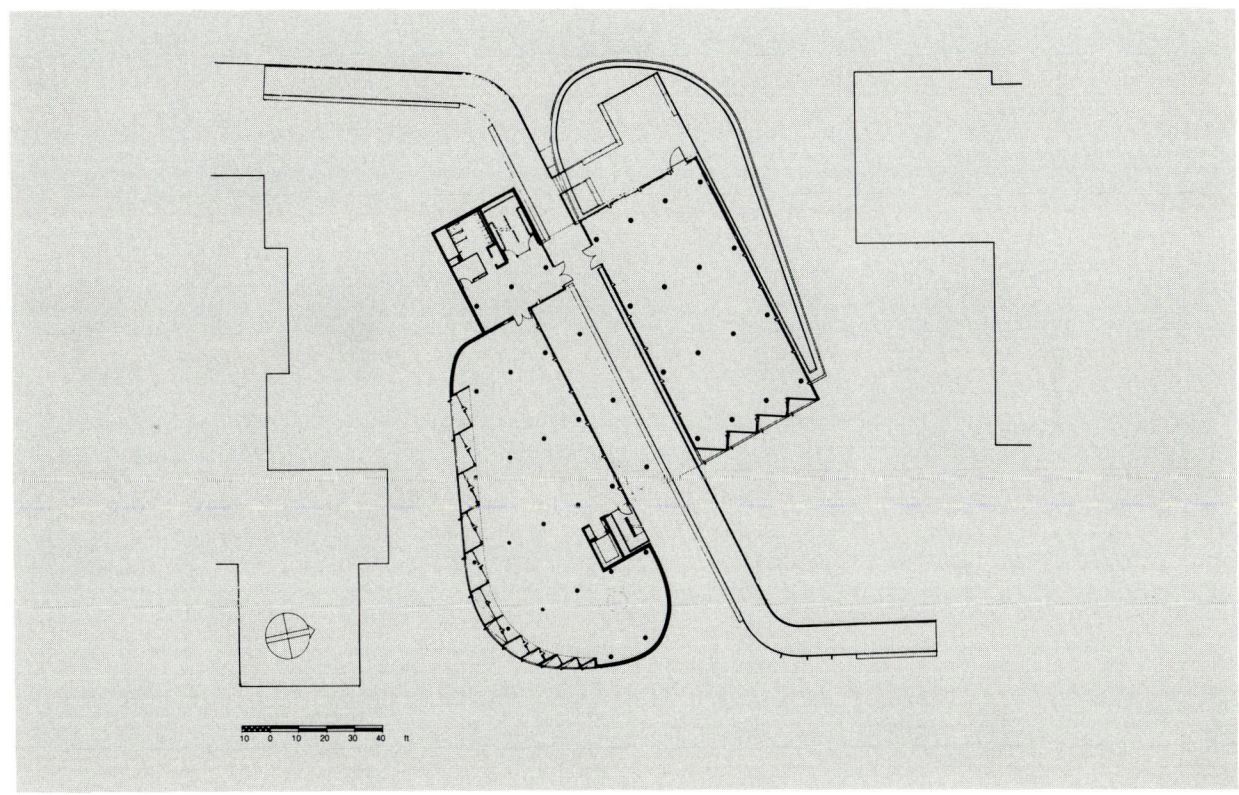

5. *Plan level 4.*

6. *Plan level 5.*

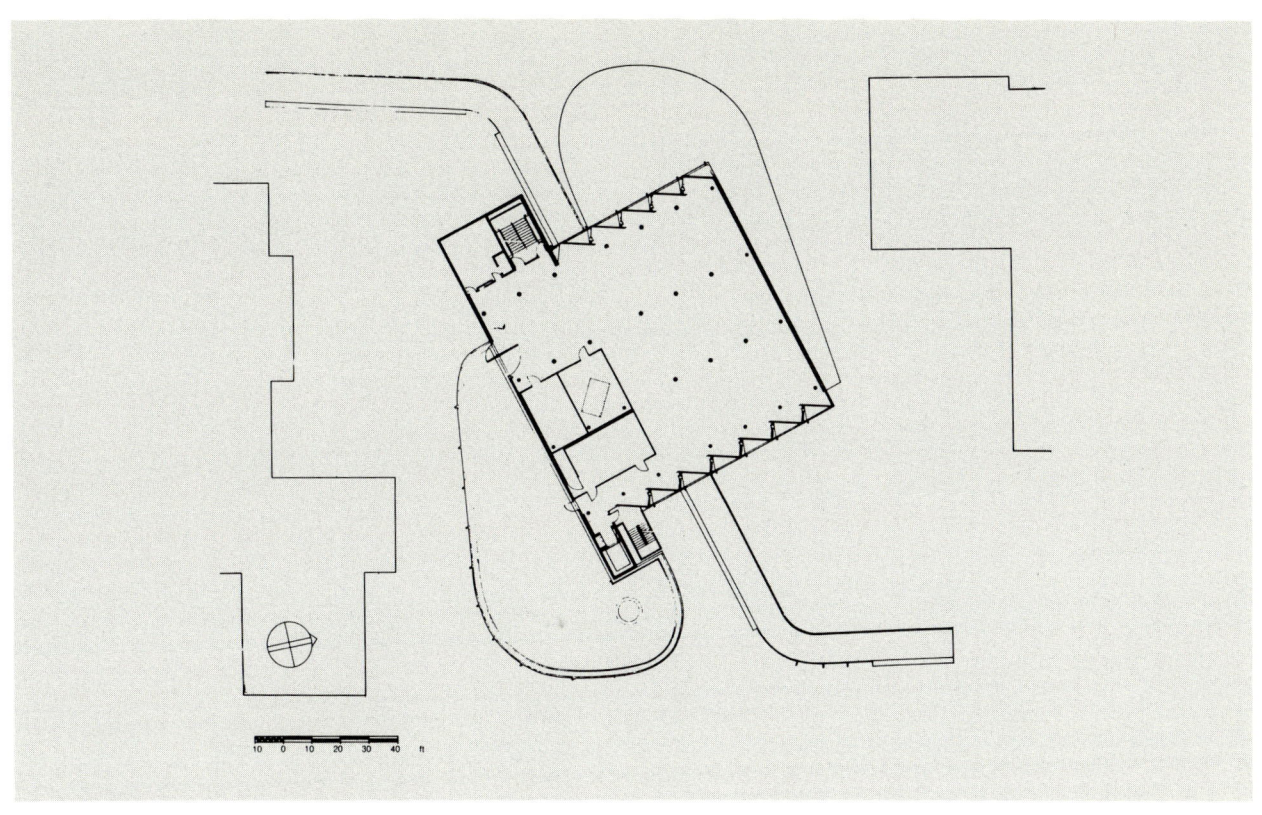

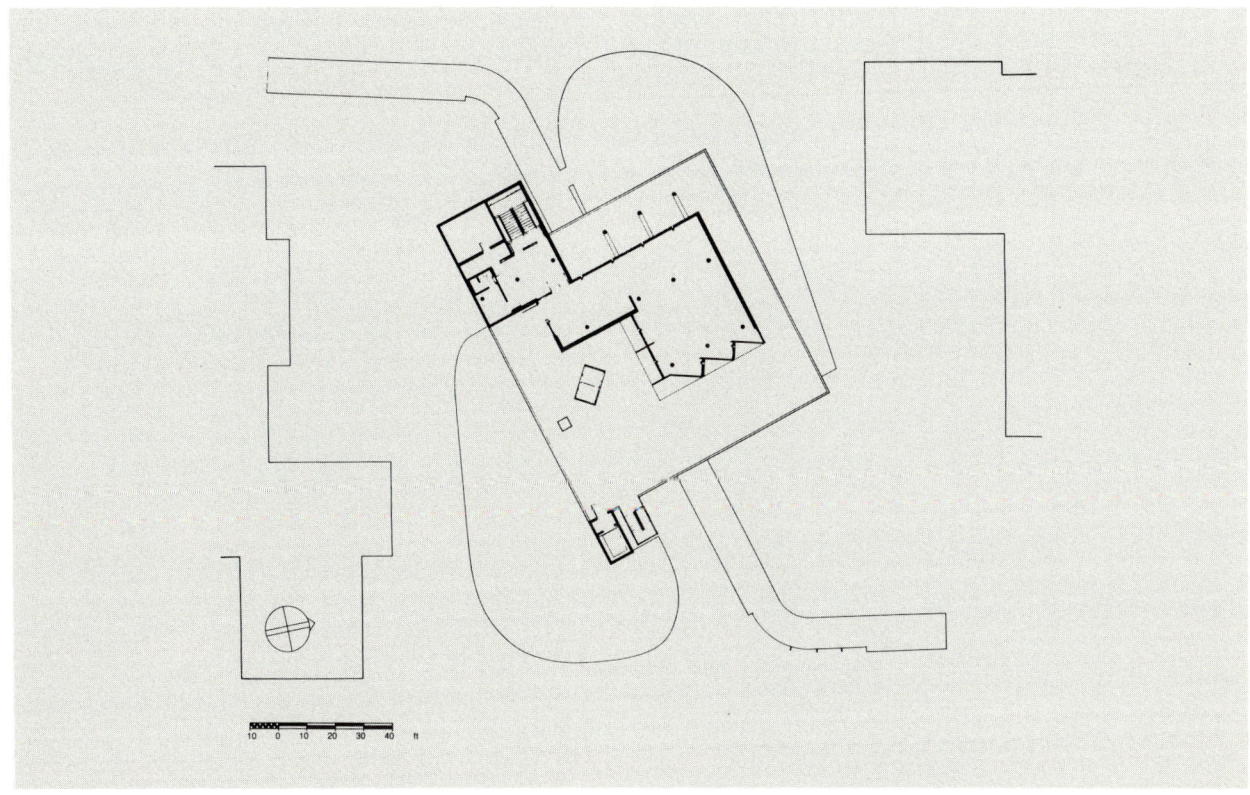

349

7. Aerial view.

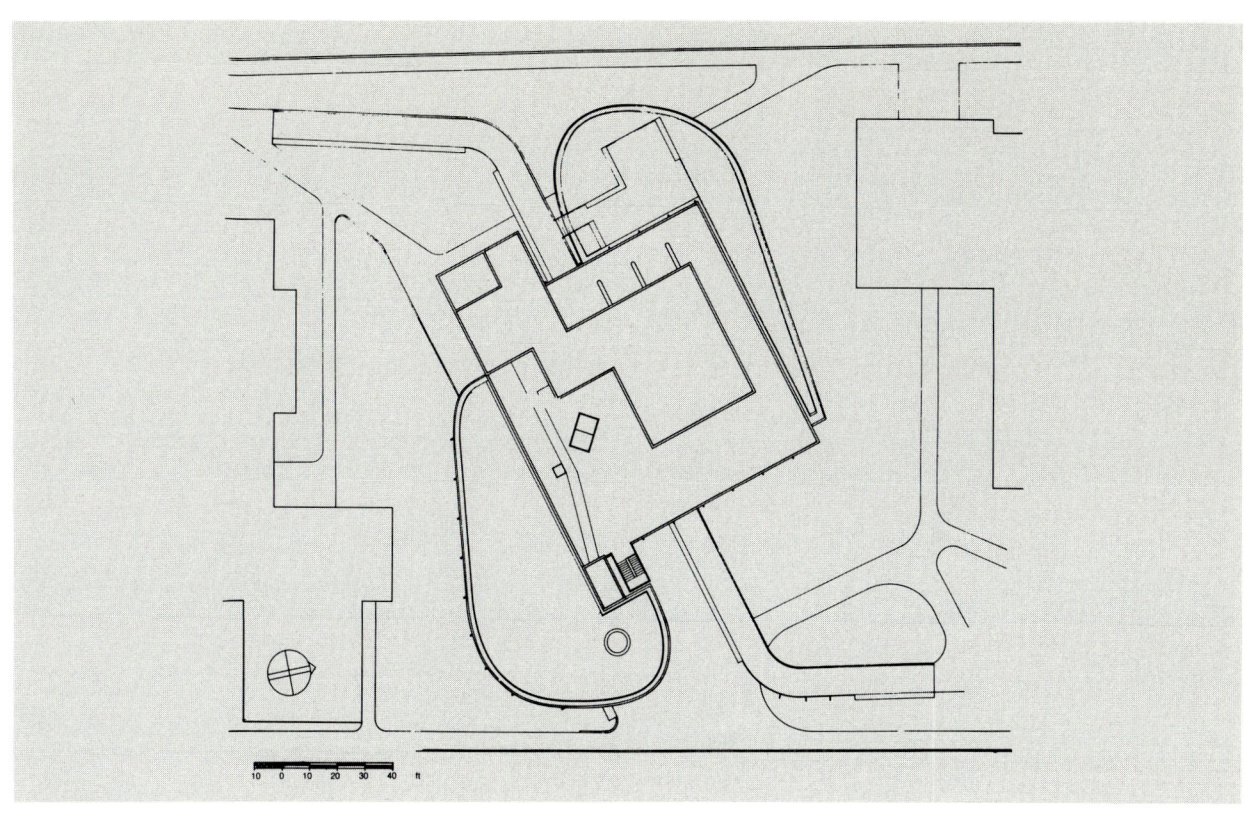

8. *Transversal section.*

9. *Longitudinal section.*

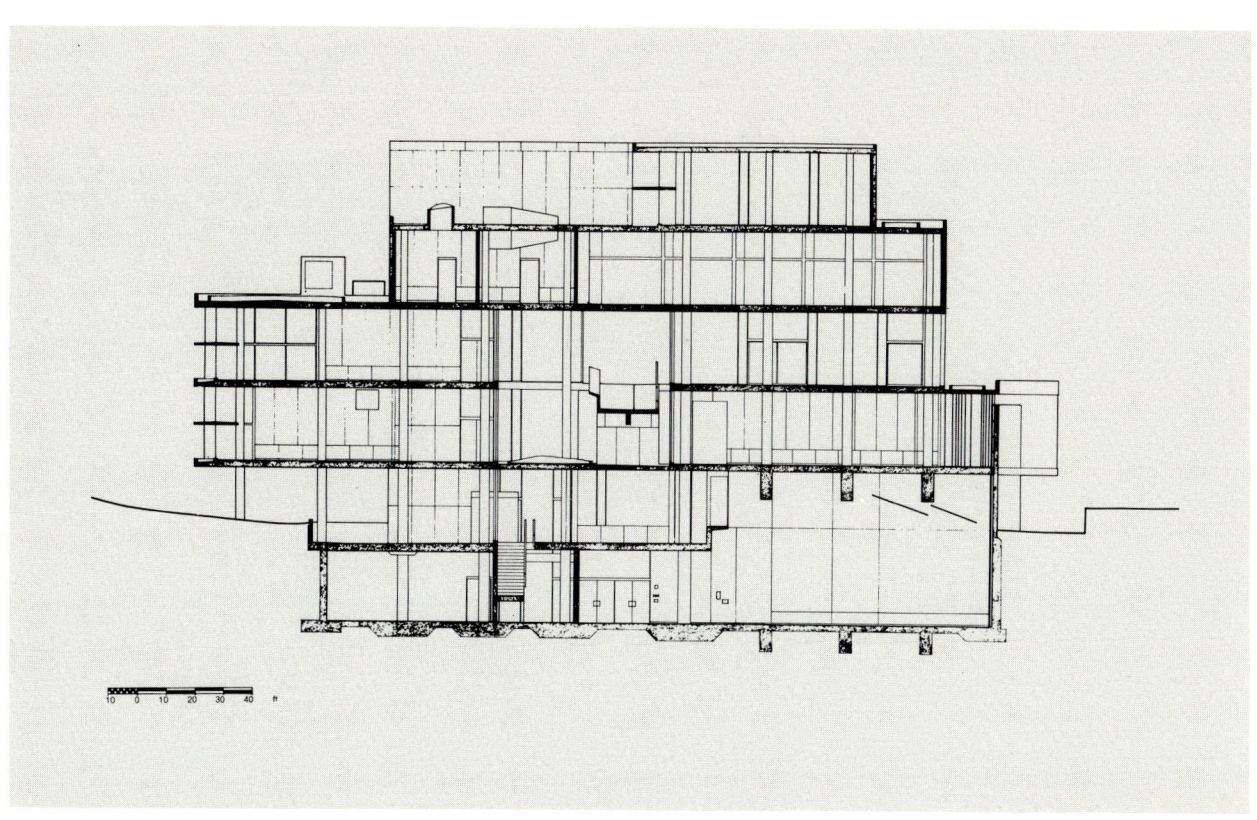

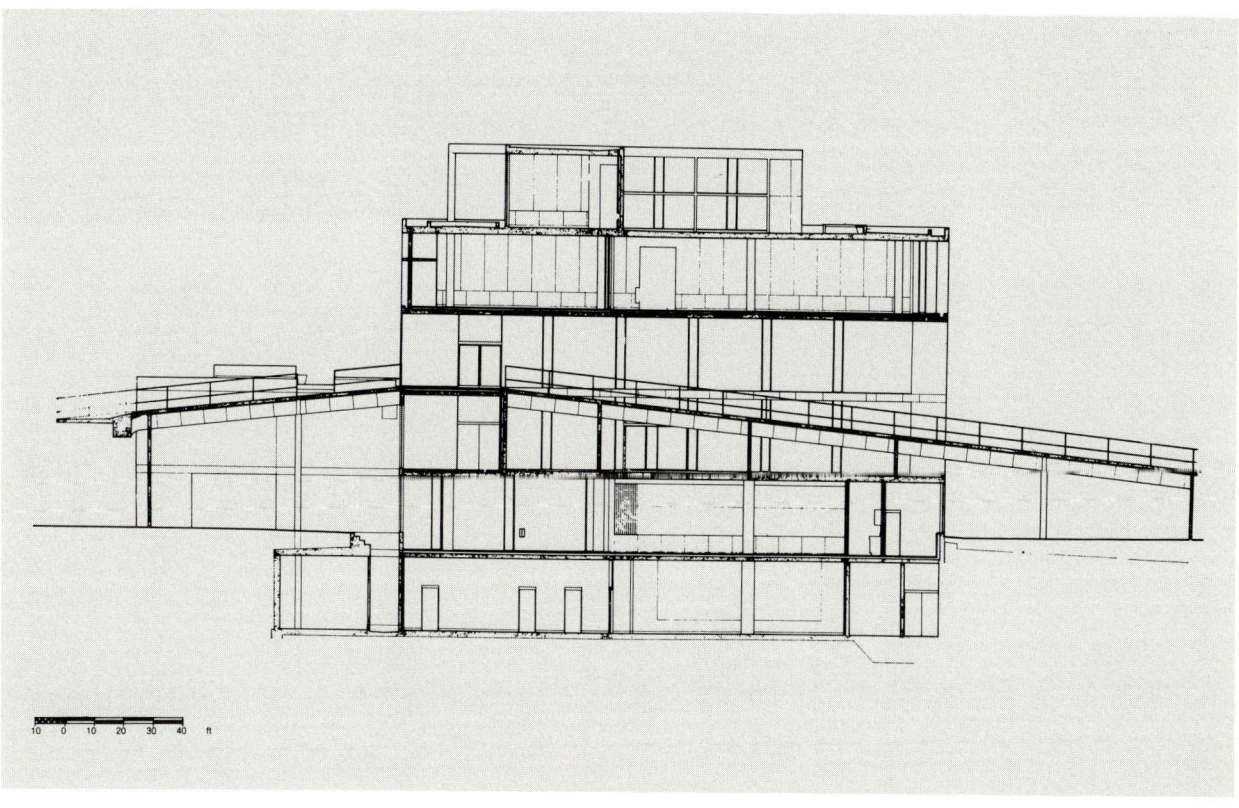

353

10. *West elevation, Quincy Street.*

11. *East elevation, Prescott Street.*

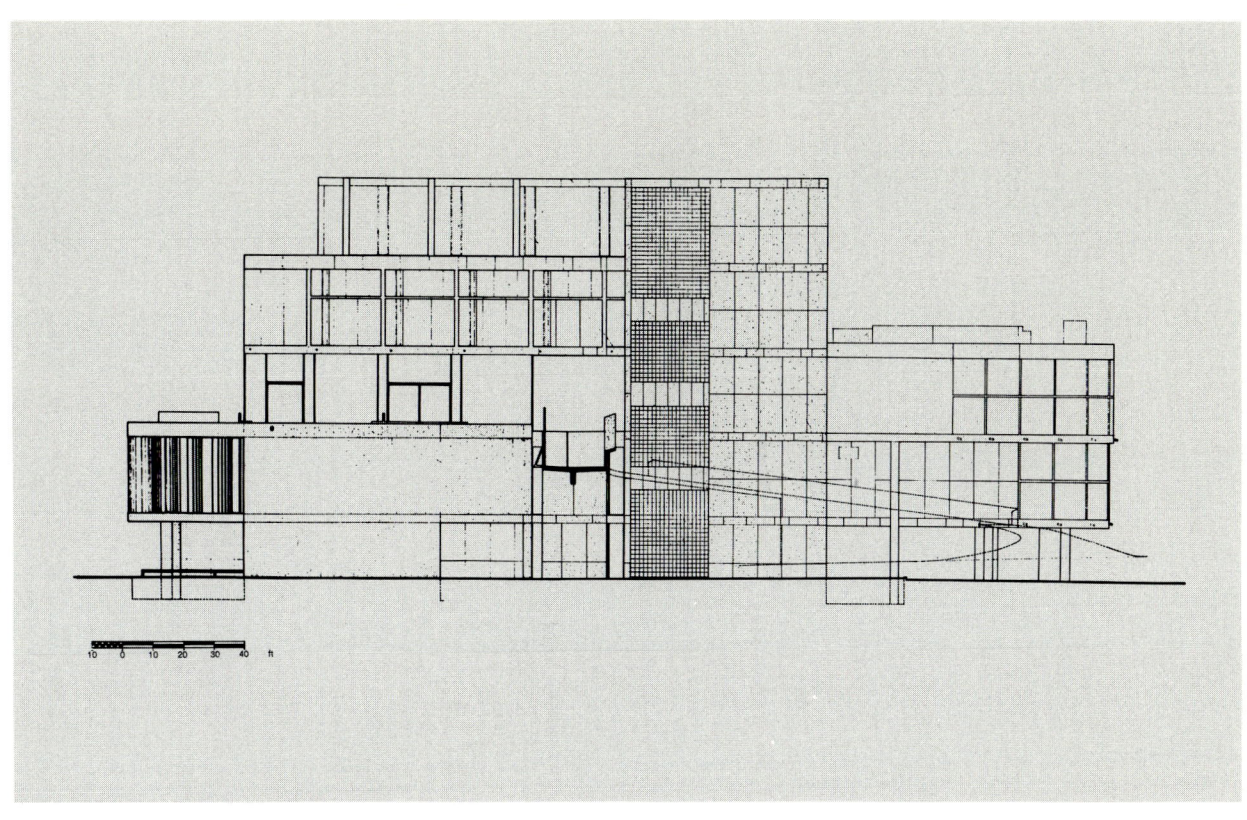

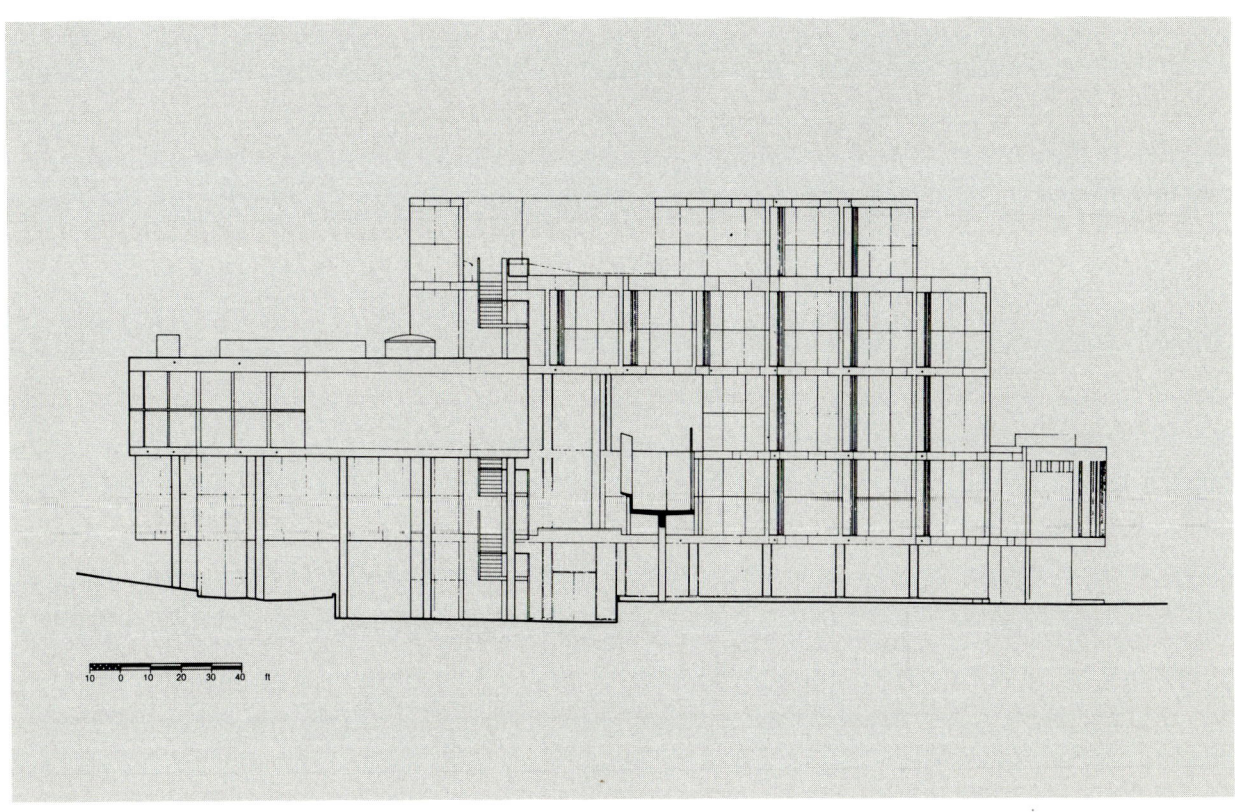

12. *North elevation, Fogg Museum side.*

13. *South elevation, Faculty Club side.*

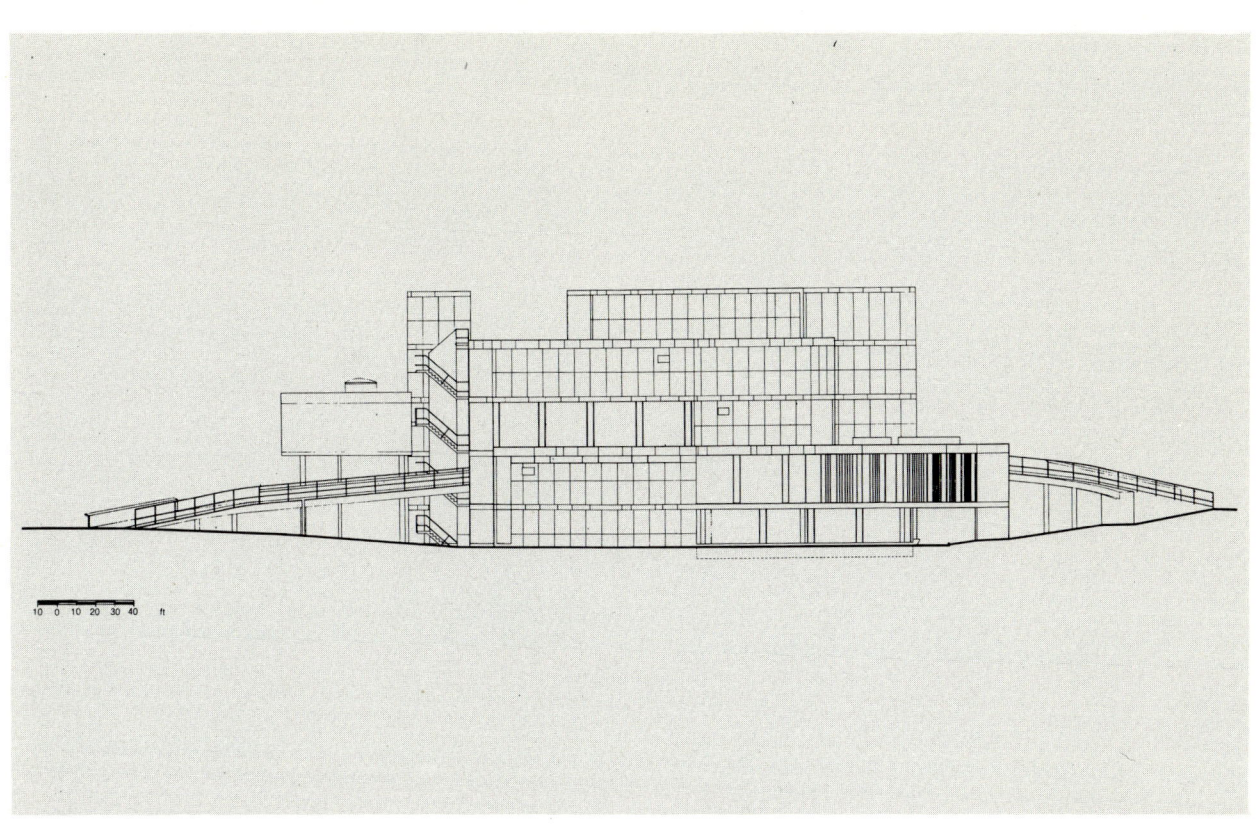

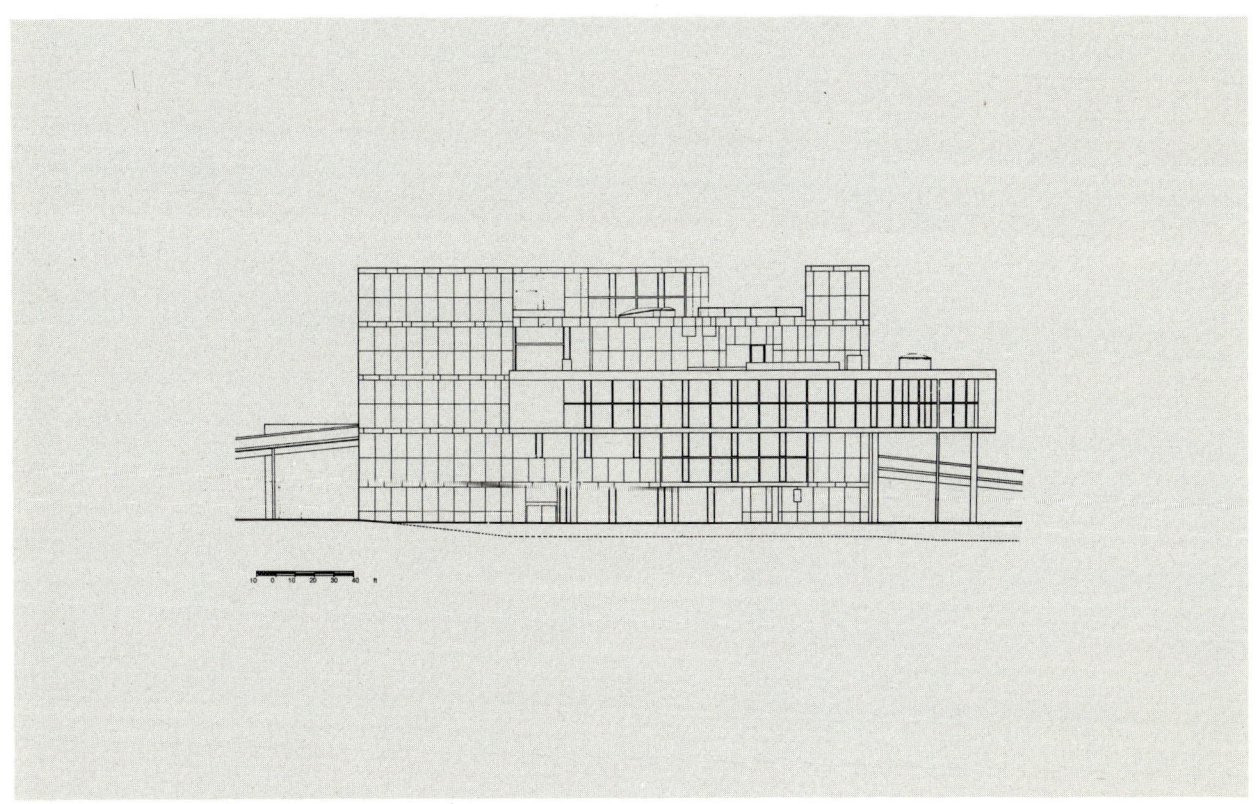

LIBRARY OF DAVIDSON COLLEGE